This is the first of a three-volume history of the oldest press in the world, a history that extends from the sixteenth century to the present day. Although there was, briefly, a press at Cambridge in the early 1520s, the origins of the modern University Press spring from a charter granted to the University by Henry VIII in 1534, empowering it to appoint printers who would be able to work outside London and serve the University. In the event, no book was printed until fifty years later, but from 1583 to the present the line of University Printers stretches in unbroken succession.

Covering the period from the Reformation to the end of the seventeenth century, and drawing on a wealth of unpublished or unfamiliar material, this volume explores the University's attitude to its Printers, the books they chose to print and the circumstances in which they worked. For the first time, the early history of the Press is set in its context – of authors, University authorities and readers – and its activities are fully related to the wider issues of the book trade in Britain and overseas.

A HISTORY OF

CAMBRIDGE UNIVERSITY PRESS

VOLUME 1

A HISTORY OF
CAMBRIDGE UNIVERSITY PRESS

VOLUME 1

PRINTING AND THE
BOOK TRADE
IN CAMBRIDGE
1534–1698

DAVID McKITTERICK

Fellow and Librarian
Trinity College, Cambridge

Published by the Press Syndicate of the University of Cambridge
The Pitt Building, Trumpington Street, Cambridge CB2 1RP
40 West 20th Street, New York, NY 10011-4211, USA
10 Stamford Road, Oakleigh, Victoria 3166, Australia

© Cambridge University Press 1992

Printed in Great Britain at the University Press, Cambridge

Library of Congress cataloguing in publication data

McKitterick, David.
A history of Cambridge University Press / David McKitterick.
p.   cm.
Includes bibliographical references and index.
Contents: v. 1. Printing and the book trade in Cambridge.
1534–1698.
ISBN 0 521 30801 1
1. Cambridge University Press – History. 2. Book industries and
trade – England – Cambridge – History. 3. Publishers and publishing –
England – Cambridge – History. 4. University presses – England –
Cambridge – History. 5. Printing – England – Cambridge – History.
I. Title.
Z232.C17M373 1992
070.5′94 – dc20   91-30372   CIP

ISBN 0 521 30801 1 hardback

CONTENTS

ILLUSTRATIONS

Sources

Illustrations are reproduced by permission of the following: the Syndics of Cambridge University Library (figs. 2, 4, 5, 6, 8, 9, 12, 13, 14, 15, 16, 19, 20, 22, 23, 25, 30, 31, 37); the Keeper of Cambridge University Archives (figs. 1, 10, 11); the Master and Fellows, Trinity College, Cambridge (figs. 17, 18, 26, 27, 28, 32, 33, 34, 35, 36); the President and Fellows, Queens' College, Cambridge (fig. 3); the Master and Fellows, St John's College, Cambridge (fig. 29); the Curators of the Bodleian Library (fig. 24); and the Provost and Fellows, Eton College (fig. 21). It is appropriate at this point also to add my particular thanks to the staff of the Photography Department in Cambridge University Library, who have once again met my requests with skill and imagination.

PREFACE

On 21 January 1697/8, by Grace of the Senate, the University of Cambridge appointed a group of thirty-seven men as the first *Curatores* of a University Press. This unwieldy body, made practical by a quorum of five, consisted of the Vice-Chancellor, the heads of the colleges, the various professors, and a number of others drawn from the more sympathetic senior members of the University.[1] *Curatores* rapidly gave place to Syndics as a term to describe those charged with responsibility for one of the University's most public activities; and as the eighteenth century wore on, syndicates, temporary or permanent, became a familiar feature of University government.[2]

The new foundation that was the subject of this legislation was inspired by, and in its initial stages the creation of, the classical scholar Richard Bentley, Keeper of the King's Library since 1694 and in 1700 to be installed, aged thirty-eight, as Master of Trinity College.[3] It existed, for a few years, alongside the last in the succession of presses embarked on 115 years previously by a former Fellow of King's eager to provide texts and other aids for University teaching. Only with the death of the last of the University Printers under the old dispensation, in 1705, could the new Cambridge University Press claim an exclusive position. By the 1690s the concept of such a press as that formulated by Bentley, at once institutional and, by virtue of its parent body, learned, was familiar thanks to the example set by John Fell and his associates at Oxford over the previous three decades.[4] Through the University, the Cambridge press could also count itself as the latest embodiment of an authority that went back ultimately to a charter granted by Henry VIII in 1534, on which the modern Press still relies.

Though much was later to be made of this charter, the events of the late 1690s owed little to the expediencies of privileges granted in the midst of the Reformation. These privileges had been critical to the establishment of a press at Cambridge in the sixteenth century and to its continuing survival. In the eighteenth century and subsequently, the charter was a legal and financial armour. Until the 1690s it defined the press's very being.

In 1534 the University was given the right to print *omnimodos libros*, a phrase that was gradually and painfully demonstrated to over-ride any other printing interests. Henry VIII's charter was intended primarily to protect the interests of local booksellers, not of printers. No reason was recorded for thus extending a printing privilege as well, though the king and his advisers may have seen potential advantage in the support of a University able to wield such a right at a time when Henry VIII was pursuing a vigorous propaganda campaign via sections of the London press.[5] Certainly, there does not appear to have been any suggestion that a university must necessarily require an associated University Printer and press: such a suggestion could, in the 1530s, have been demonstrated only inconclusively among other university towns on the continent.[6] A press at Cambridge, subject to the University's Chancellor (who was appointed by the Crown) might prove a valuable ally: if such was the thought, nothing was said. In fact, no printing took place until 1583. But even from 1583, with a hierarchy of authority that set the University Printers, Thomas Thomas and his successors, answerable to the Chancellor, Vice-Chancellor, heads of houses and professors, the concept of this earlier press was quite different from that eventually formulated by Bentley and his associates in the 1690s. The lapse of the last of the Licensing Acts in 1695, and with that the requirement for a licensing authority, brought an end to the need for the University authorities to be charged with the duties and responsibilities placed in London with ecclesiastical or other legally empowered bodies or individuals. Until the 1690s, the press at Cambridge was always a privately based business, whatever degree of responsibility the University officers of the day assumed for its legal (and therefore by implication financial) well-being. It was subject to, but was not part of, a University that as yet could boast only one department, the University Library. From 1698, under the hands of a Syndicate, the Press became another department of the University.

This distinction was a fundamental one, since it meant that Thomas Thomas and his successors until John Hayes at the end of the seventeenth century enjoyed an independence – commercial, economic, and in many respects legal – directly comparable with most of the London printing trade. However, in two exceptional, and crucial, respects, they were different. First, since Cambridge lies at some distance from London, the press could never pursue other than a severely circumscribed policy with respect to London stationers. Second, and even more importantly, the charter of 1534 offered a freedom to print, and publish, regardless of other, later, monopolies or interests. The frequency and vehemence with which London stationers challenged this privilege, and the frequent compromises that proved necessary, are measures of the power wielded by the press at Cambridge, and of its practical limitations. Poised between the corporate interest and institutional authority of the University, and the commitment of successive Printers, the press was defined finally by the interpretations and activities of a series of men more or less skilled or committed to a concern that some saw merely as a business, and others as a trust.

Whatever the perspective, the focus was the same: the production of editions of books for sale both locally and elsewhere. If printing is defined as the replication of ostensibly identical texts, in editions each of several hundred copies, then it is defined merely as a process of industrial manufacture. But while this process is indeed essential to its definition, it takes into account neither the materials required, such as paper, type and ink; nor the vagaries, preferences, skills and interests of those involved in setting type, preparing illustrations or printing off copies; nor the use to which the finished product, a printed image, was put. Furthermore, it does not address the initial encounters between author, bookseller and printer. The process broadly described as printing involves not merely those in the printing house; but rather, it is the culmination of a series of literary, technical and economic operations that in turn lead to a further series culminating in the reader. At each stage, individuality impinges on what is most readily defined by the central act of repetitive imitation, the act of printing. And even at the press, the text that in the sixteenth and seventeenth centuries passed under the platen was liable to change in a process that implied uniformity but that often provided variation.

It has been rightly stressed by others that while printing achieved a degree of uniformity impossible in a manuscript tradition, however highly organized, there remained, at least until the nineteenth century, an element of variation within editions as a consequence of press corrections, or of confusion within editions of printed sheets drawn from more than one stock. This emphasis on but one aspect of book production – the composition of type – is, while indeed crucial, also inadequate. First, it neglects the relationship between the reader and the printed word set before him that was, for most classes of books, generally assumed at least until the end of the seventeenth century. The exhortations accompanying so many lists of errata, that the reader should amend with his pen the various faults described, assumed that when printed sheets left the printing house they were not to be regarded as finished: they had merely reached the most textually advanced stage that was practical under a particular set of circumstances. The occasional examples of such manuscript correction carried out not by the reader, but in an organized way in the printing house, confirm the tentative, rather than final, status of the act of printing. Second, printing itself, defined as the activities of a printing house, is but one sequence of events in a much longer manufacturing process. It is therefore only one element in a reader's experience. The materials of a book or pamphlet, the quality and size of the paper, the format chosen, the quality, materials and design of the binding, and the context of a pamphlet or short work if bound up with others in a single volume, all contribute to the reader's critical response.

This volume is not the occasion to examine, in the detail they deserve, the varying reactions of readers to the books issued by the Cambridge University Printers. Its purpose is instead, partly at least, to make such study possible. Nevertheless, to a great extent, no account of a printing or publishing enterprise can ignore the powers which control its continuing existence: on the one hand the authors and on the other the readers in the market-place, these two of course being not infrequently synonymous. The demands and requirements of university teaching were put forward by Thomas Thomas in 1583 as the very reason for his establishing a press where none had been for sixty years. Booksellers, as publishers and customers, dictated the course which he and his successors took, and in the end brought about the demise of the University Printers in the form established in the sixteenth century. Although in the 1580s opposition to Thomas's press by the London trade focused on the addition of another press to a small and tightly restricted world, where (it was alleged) one more press would threaten the livelihood of London printers, the real danger was to the booksellers, who would, by virtue of the University's charter of 1534, lose control of what might be printed, and where.

In no sense was the University Printer only a functionary of the University with respect to printing or publishing.[7] He was licensed by the University authorities, and he was appointed by Grace of the Senate. But his livelihood came from the book trade, in competition with other printers, and in negotiation with booksellers. The books he printed were required to be licensed (in the words of the 1534 charter) by the Vice-Chancellor or his deputy and three doctors. As the only printer in Cambridge he was also frequently the most convenient. For its official printing, whether administrative or celebratory, the University expected to turn to him (and to pay him, like any other tradesman, for work done). In all this he was subservient to the University, most immediately in the person of the Vice-Chancellor. But that did not give the Vice-Chancellor the power to coerce, or to assume the responsibility for making what were, for all books, essentially commercial decisions.

For these reasons, this volume is concerned not only with the University Printers, but also with the manner whereby what they printed was a function of demands and limitations set by others, whether in Cambridge or in London, in Oxford or overseas. Like any other manufacturing process, the details of the physical creation of an object (in this case printed matter) are a poor explanation if its purpose and inspiration are not expounded also. For the Cambridge press, the functional context was in the first place (but, as will be seen, by no means overwhelmingly) the rest of the Cambridge book trade. Each book was an individual creation, the fruit of collaboration involving a sequence including at least author, bookseller, printer, retail bookseller, binder and eventually readers. But the impulse, at every stage, was a collective one — epitomized in the printing of an edition. This account of the Cambridge press focuses on some of those collective impulses, whether personal, institutional or bibliographical, balanced against the intentions, hopes, achievements and responses of individuals, whether authors, legislators, book trade personnel, readers or sometimes simply spectators.

The Cambridge press, like that at Oxford, was provincial only in an ambiguous sense. The nature of this ambiguity, the tension between on the one hand central authority personified in the Crown and in the legal and commercial powers of the Stationers' Company and on the other the authority vested in the University, forms a central theme of this book. It sets the context within which the Cambridge press had to operate. But other questions are no less important; and for some the Cambridge press has provided an opportunity to explore topics equally germane to the sixteenth- and seventeenth-century book trade generally. I have therefore also examined (when the surviving evidence has suggested that it is profitable to do so) such matters as book trade capitalization, the relationship of authors to printers and booksellers, the limitations of the Cambridge press compared with those in London, the manufacture and costing of some of the most popular books of all – including the Bible, almanacs and school-books. In the seventeenth century, as in the twentieth, the well-being of the Press came to depend on the assured income generated by a reliable stream of contractual regular orders. I have also given attention to the personnel at the Press. On the one hand, University Printers were drawn either from the Regent House, that is, the senior resident members of the University, or from the book trade: for much of this time, the academic had to complement the practical, but each might perceive the means to a profitable livelihood – or, sometimes, a comfortable sinecure. The University Printers naturally dominate the more personal aspects of this book: they are the figures most frequently alluded to in the archives, and they appear regularly in imprints. On their decisions or legal adventures depended the list of books printed at Cambridge. But their journeymen, apprentices and casual assistants, the men responsible for the manufacture of each book or pamphlet, have proved to be a less shadowy group than is sometimes assumed. Their backgrounds, their conditions of work, even, occasionally, their personalities, add a touch of humanity as well as factual evidence to the dry bones of bibliographical evidence and theory. Intermittently, the history of the Cambridge press provides details in this respect unparalleled in the London trade, and comparable even with those recorded in such exceptional detail in the Plantin archives at Antwerp. The implications for our understanding of the London trade, to which masters and men alike looked for comparison and guidance, scarcely needs to be stressed.

There were fundamental differences in the organization of the control of the Cambridge press compared with the much larger and more complicated presses in London. Similarly, there were differences in the daily organization of some aspects of the work of a London press, and one having no near neighbours with whom to share skills, equipment or tasks. But the extent of what was similar, or held in common experience, has suggested that the evidence *of* London, as well as *for* London, is sometimes more than comparative.

The retail book trade in Cambridge during this period deserves a study to itself. Even more than the University Printers, the local booksellers depended on London – not only for supplies, but also, as will be seen in their involvement with the printing house, as a market. For the first time, the production of books at Cambridge at the end of the sixteenth century created locally made goods that had a direct exchange value in the London book trade. The fortunes of the local stationers are inseparable from the history of the University Printers; and though I have referred to them frequently, much more remains to be rediscovered and analysed of their activities. Linked to them, the curriculum (or rather, curricula, for many different courses of reading, prescribed more by individual teachers in colleges than by statute, existed simultaneously even in the ordinary undergraduate career) pursued at Cambridge in the sixteenth and seventeenth centuries still calls for further attention, despite much recent work. It underwent a fundamental change in the first half of the seventeenth century, and University Printers responded with more or less zeal. I have referred to it only in order to illuminate aspects of Cambridge printing and bookselling, and the relationship of these activities to the London trade. Related also to this there remains the question of the circulation of books in manuscript – not only of sermons, political controversy or poems, but also of teaching materials. This essentially individual activity, in the private production of copies of educational works, has, like many aspects of the act of reading itself, had to be set aside for another occasion.

In other words, from the simple economic fact that printing depends on demand, and on a profitable return, it is inescapable that the history of a press must take into account not just what was printed and published. The changing reasons for its existence, its sources of raw materials, the degree of local enthusiasm and encouragement, local willingness to provide support in recessions, the requirements made of the press, its attractiveness or otherwise for authors without whom it could not flourish, and the reception its works were accorded in the trade, form but one group of considerations. In the arena created by them had to be made decisions as to what should be published, in what manner and in what appearance. For all the larger questions respecting book manufacture and trade, it was the customer, and reader, for whom books were printed, and to whom all of these questions were therefore ultimately addressed. The press at Cambridge had an institutional foundation; but in such circumstances only part of that foundation could be considered firm. As successive University Printers discovered to their pain, neither was their market guaranteed, nor did the privilege granted to the University by Henry VIII in 1534 provide a monopoly. In the period covered by this volume, the University Printers demonstrated that, as part of an institution, their business could survive. But like the University itself, it did so only by a continuous process of adaptation.

ACKNOWLEDGEMENTS

This is the first of three volumes conceived during the celebrations in 1984 that marked the four-hundredth anniversary of University printing and publishing in Cambridge. I intend in subsequent volumes to examine the periods from the end of the seventeenth century to the reform of the Press in the late nineteenth century, and from then until modern times.

In this first volume, I have sought to extend the scope, as well as the scale, of my investigation and comment beyond the University Press's two official histories, by S. C. Roberts (1921) and Michael Black (1984). It will nevertheless be clear how much I owe to these two previous studies by the Press's own officers. Michael Black has placed me further in his debt by reading most of this book in an early form, and making many suggestions towards its improvement, bringing his own experience as a publisher to bear on matters that must sometimes have seemed familiar despite the time when they occurred.

Of all those who have helped in the research for this book, whether by consultation, advice or practical assistance, I am first and foremost grateful to Elisabeth Leedham-Green, who has been a vital and generous guide to the papers relating to the Press and to Cambridge's book trade in the University Archives. I also owe particular thanks to Don McKenzie, most of whose two-volume study of the Press from 1696 to 1712 falls, strictly speaking, outside the period of this volume, but whose own work on the earlier printers has helped pave the way, and who has given of his time and knowledge with characteristic wisdom and generosity.

Most of the work for this book has been done in Cambridge University Library and in Trinity College Library, whose staffs, in all their various capacities, have accommodated my demands with continuing and much appreciated helpfulness. Apart from these two libraries, I am grateful also to staff in the libraries or archives of Christ's College, Corpus Christi College, Downing College, Emmanuel College, Gonville and Caius College, Jesus College, King's College, Magdalene College, Peterhouse, Queens' College, St John's College, Sidney Sussex College, Trinity Hall, and Cambridge Central Library; outside Cambridge in the British Library, Lambeth Palace Library, the Public Record Office, the Guildhall Library, the Corporation of London

Records Office, the Stationers' Company, the Bodleian Library, Balliol College, Eton College, the National Library of Scotland and Edinburgh University Library; and overseas in the Plantin-Moretus Museum in Antwerp, the Pierpont Morgan Library in New York, the Houghton Library at Harvard, and Yale University Library. Materials from the archives of the Stationers' Company are quoted by permission of the Master and Wardens; I am particularly obliged to the Honorary Archivist of the Company, Miss Robin Myers, for her ready interest.

It is a pleasure also to acknowledge in print the special assistance of Hugh Amory, Jean Archibald, Nicolas Barker, Terry Belanger, Alan Bell, Peter Blayney, Chris Coppens, Brooke Crutchley, Geoffrey Day, John Dreyfus, Mirjam Foot, Laurence and Helen Fowler, Brian Hillyard, Frans Korsten, Sheila Lambert, Ronald Mansbridge, Jeremy Maule, Paul Morgan, John Morrison, Paul Needham, Carolyn Nelson, Katharine Pantzer, Steve Parks, Mike Petty, Nicholas Pickwoad, Paul Quarrie, Julian Roberts, Roger Stoddard, Frank Stubbings and Christopher Wright. No less vitally, the shelves or catalogues of innumerable antiquarian booksellers have over the last few years yielded inspiration or evidence, with all the pleasure of serendipity.

The staff at the University Press have balanced their natural curiosity about their predecessors with tolerance and patience as I have completed the book. Both during the time they have awaited the manuscript, and in their care as it has made its way through the Press, they have once again earned my gratitude. But neither they nor any of the others named above have seen as much of the book as has my wife Rosamond. Her occasional wonder at the amount of evidence available for the history of the book in the sixteenth and seventeenth centuries, compared with the fragmentary nature of the evidence for her own much earlier period, has been a reminder for caution, while her constant encouragement has been inspiration far beyond any ordinary support.

ABBREVIATIONS

*In the following list of abbreviations and in the notes all books
are published in London unless otherwise stated.*

Acts P.C.   *Acts of the Privy Council of England*, ed. J. R. Dasent *et al.* (1890–)

Arber   *A transcript of the registers of the Company of Stationers of London;
1554–1640 A.D.*, ed. Edward Arber, 5 vols., 1875–94

Baillie, 'Privileged books'   William M. Baillie, 'The printing of privileged
books at Cambridge, 1631–1634', *TCBS*, 5 (1971), pp. 155–66

Baker–Mayor   Thomas Baker, *History of the College of St. John the Evangelist,
Cambridge*, ed. J. E. B. Mayor, 2 vols. (Cambridge 1869)

Bennet and Clements, *Notebooks*   Norma Hodgson and Cyprian Blagden, eds.,
*The notebooks of Thomas Bennet and Henry Clements (1686–1719); with some
aspects of book trade practice* (Oxford Bibliographical Society 1956)

Black, *Cambridge University Press*   M. H. Black, *Cambridge University Press,
1584–1984* (Cambridge 1984)

Blagden, *Stationers' Company*   Cyprian Blagden, *The Stationers' Company; a
history, 1403–1959* (1960)

Blayney, *Nicholas Okes*   P. W. M. Blayney, *The texts of King Lear and their
origins.* 1. *Nicholas Okes and the first quarto* (Cambridge 1982)

BNYPL   *Bulletin of New York Public Library*

Bowes, *Catalogue*   Robert Bowes, *A catalogue of books printed at or relating to
the University and town of Cambridge from 1521 to 1893* (Cambridge 1894)

Calendar of Patent Rolls   *Calendar of Patent Rolls preserved in the Public
Record Office* (1901–)

Carter, *Oxford University Press*   Harry Carter, *A history of the Oxford
University Press.* 1. *To the year 1780* (Oxford 1975)

Clark, *Endowments*   J. W. Clark, ed., *Endowments of the University of Cambridge*
(Cambridge 1904)

CLRO   Corporation of London Records Office

Cooper, *Annals*   C. H. Cooper, *Annals of Cambridge*, 5 vols. (Cambridge
1842–1908)

CSPD   *Calendar of state papers domestic*, ed. R. Lemon *et al.* (1856–)

Darlow and Moule   T. H. Darlow and H. F. Moule, *Historical catalogue of the
printed editions of holy scripture in the library of the British and Foreign Bible
Society*, 2 vols. (1903–11)

DNB   *Dictionary of national biography*

DSB   C. G. Gillispie, ed., *Dictionary of scientific biography*, 16 vols. (New York 1970–80)

Duff   E. Gordon Duff, *Fifteenth-century English books: a bibliography* (Bibliographical Society 1917)

Duff, *Century*   E. Gordon Duff, *A century of the English book trade* (Bibliographical Society 1905)

Dyer, *Privileges*   George Dyer, *The privileges of the University of Cambridge*, 2 vols. (1824)

EHR   *English Historical Review*

Emden, *BRUC*   A. B. Emden, *A biographical register of the University of Cambridge to 1500* (Cambridge 1963)

Emden, *BRUO 1500*   A. B. Emden, *A biographical register of the University of Oxford to A.D. 1500*, 3 vols. (Oxford 1957–9)

Emden, *BRUO 1501–1540* A. B. Emden, *A biographical register of the University of Oxford A.D. 1501–1540* (Oxford 1974)

Eyre and Rivington   G. E. B. Eyre and C. R. Rivington, eds., *A transcript of the registers of the Worshipful Company of Stationers from 1640–1708 A.D.*, 3 vols. (Roxburghe Club 1913–14)

Foster, *Great St Mary's*   J. E. Foster, ed., *Churchwardens' accounts of St Mary the Great, Cambridge, from 1504 to 1635* (Cambridge Antiquarian Society 1905)

Garrett, *Marian exiles*   C. H. Garrett, *The Marian exiles; a study in the origins of Elizabethan puritanism* (Cambridge 1938)

Gaskell, *New introduction*   Philip Gaskell, *A new introduction to bibliography* (Oxford 1972)

GJ   *Gutenberg Jahrbuch*

Grace Book A   *Grace Book A, 1454–1488*, ed. S. M. Leathes (Cambridge 1897)

Grace Book B, pt i, pt ii   *Grace Book B, 1488–1544*, ed. M. Bateson, 2 vols. (Cambridge 1903–5)

Grace Book Γ   *Grace Book Γ, 1501–42*, ed. W. G. Searle and J. W. Clark (Cambridge 1908)

Grace Book Δ   *Grace Book Δ, 1542–1589*, ed. John Venn (Cambridge 1910)

Gray, *Earlier Cambridge stationers*   G. J. Gray, *The earlier Cambridge stationers & bookbinders and the first Cambridge printer* (Bibliographical Society 1904)

Gray and Palmer   G. J. Gray and W. M. Palmer, *Abstracts from the wills and testamentary documents of printers, binders and stationers of Cambridge, from 1504 to 1699* (Bibliographical Society 1915)

Greg, *Companion*   W. W. Greg, *A companion to Arber* (Oxford 1967)

Greg and Boswell   W. W. Greg and E. Boswell, eds., *Records of the Court of the Stationers' Company 1576 to 1602, from Register B* (Bibliographical Society 1930)

Herbert, *Historical catalogue*   A. S. Herbert, *Historical catalogue of printed editions of the English Bible, 1525–1961, revised and expanded from the edition of T. H. Darlow and H. F. Moule* (1968)

Heywood and Wright   J. Heywood and T. Wright, eds., *Cambridge University transactions during the Puritan controversies*, 2 vols. (1854)

Hind, *Engraving in England*   A. M. Hind, Margery Corbett and Michael
  Norton, *Engraving in England in the sixteenth and seventeenth centuries*, 3 vols.
  (Cambridge 1952–64)

Historical MSS Commn   Historical Manuscripts Commission

Historical register   J. R. Tanner, *The historical register of the University of
  Cambridge...to the year 1910* (Cambridge 1917)

Jackson, *Records*   William A. Jackson, ed., *Records of the Court of the Stationers'
  Company 1602 to 1640* (Bibliographical Society 1957)

L. and P. Henry VIII   *Letters and papers, foreign and domestic, of the reign of
  Henry VIII*, ed. J. S. Brewer, J. Gairdner and R. H. Brodie, 36 vols.
  (1862–1932)

Leedham-Green, *Books in Cambridge inventories*   E. S. Leedham-Green, *Books in
  Cambridge inventories; book-lists from Vice-Chancellor's Court probate inventories
  in the Tudor and Stuart periods*, 2 vols. (Cambridge 1986)

McKenzie, *Apprentices 1605–40*   D. F. McKenzie, *Stationers' Company
  apprentices, 1605–1640* (Charlottesville, Va. 1961)

McKenzie, *Apprentices 1641–1700*   D. F. McKenzie, *Stationers' Company
  apprentices, 1641–1700* (Oxford Bibliographical Society 1974)

McKenzie, *Cambridge University Press*   D. F. McKenzie, *The Cambridge
  University Press, 1696–1712; a bibliographical study*, 2 vols. (Cambridge
  1966)

McKerrow, *Devices*   Ronald B. McKerrow, *Printers' & publishers' devices in
  England & Scotland, 1485–1640* (Bibliographical Society 1913)

McKerrow, *Dictionary*   Ronald B. McKerrow, ed., *A dictionary of printers and
  booksellers in England, Scotland and Ireland, and of foreign printers of English
  books, 1557–1640* (Bibliographical Society 1910)

McKitterick, *Cambridge University Library*   David McKitterick, *Cambridge
  University Library; a history. The eighteenth and nineteenth centuries*
  (Cambridge 1986)

Madan, *Early Oxford press*   F. Madan, *The early Oxford press* (Oxford 1895)

Madan, *Oxford books*   F. Madan, *Oxford books; a bibliography of printed works
  relating to...Oxford, or printed and published there*, 3 vols. (Oxford
  1895–1931)

Morris, 'Restrictive practices'   John Morris, 'Restrictive practices in the
  Elizabethan book trade: the Stationers' Company <u>v.</u> Thomas Thomas,
  1583–8', *TCBS*, 4 (1967), pp. 276–90

Morris, 'Thomas Thomas'   John Morris, 'Thomas Thomas, Printer to the
  University of Cambridge, 1583–8', *TCBS*, 4 (1968), pp. 339–62

Moxon, *Mechanick exercises*   Joseph Moxon, *Mechanick exercises on the whole art
  of printing (1683–4)*, ed. Herbert Davis and Harry Carter, 2nd edn (Oxford
  1962)

Mullinger 1   J. B. Mullinger, *The University of Cambridge from the earliest times
  to the Royal Injunctions of 1535* (Cambridge 1873)

Mullinger 2   J. B. Mullinger, *The University of Cambridge from the Royal
  Injunctions of 1535 to the accession of Charles the First* (Cambridge 1882)

Mullinger 3   J. B. Mullinger, *The University of Cambridge from the election of*

Buckingham to the Chancellorship in 1626 to the decline of the Platonist movement (Cambridge 1911)

Newton, *Correspondence*   Sir Isaac Newton, *Correspondence*, ed. H. W. Turnbull *et al.*, 7 vols. (Cambridge 1959–77)

Oates, *Cambridge University Library*   J. C. T. Oates, *Cambridge University Library; a history. From the beginnings to the Copyright Act of Queen Anne* (Cambridge 1986)

Oates, 'Congratulatory verses'   J. C. T. Oates, 'Cambridge books of congratulatory verses, 1603–1640, and their binders', *TCBS*, 1 (1953), pp. 395–421

PBSA   *Papers of the Bibliographical Society of America*

PCC, Wills   Public Record Office, wills proved in the Prerogative Court of Canterbury

Peile, *Christ's*   John Peile, *Biographical register of Christ's College, 1505–1905, and of the earlier foundation, God's House, 1448–1505*, 2 vols. (Cambridge 1910–13)

Plomer, *Dictionary*   Henry R. Plomer, *A dictionary of the booksellers and printers who were at work in England, Scotland and Ireland from 1641 to 1667* (Bibliographical Society 1907)

Plomer, *Dictionary 1668–1725*   Henry R. Plomer, *A dictionary of the printers and booksellers who were at work in England, Scotland and Ireland from 1668 to 1725*, ed. A. Esdaile (Bibliographical Society 1922)

Plomer, *Wills*   Henry R. Plomer, *Abstracts from the wills of English printers and stationers from 1492 to 1630* (Bibliographical Society 1903)

Pollard and Ehrman   Graham Pollard and Albert Ehrman, *The distribution of books by catalogue from the invention of printing to A.D. 1800* (Roxburghe Club 1964)

PRO   Public Record Office

Roberts, *History*   S. C. Roberts, *A history of the Cambridge University Press, 1521–1921* (Cambridge 1921)

SB   *Studies in Bibliography*

Shaaber, *Check-list*   M. A. Shaaber, *Check-list of works of British authors printed abroad, in languages other than English, to 1641* (New York 1975)

Simpson, *Proof-reading*   Percy Simpson, *Proof-reading in the sixteenth, seventeenth and eighteenth centuries* (Oxford 1935)

Starnes, *Renaissance dictionaries*   DeWitt T. Starnes, *Renaissance dictionaries* (Austin, Texas 1954)

STC   A. W. Pollard and G. R. Redgrave, *A short-title catalogue of books printed in England, Scotland & Ireland, and of English books printed abroad, 1475–1640*, 2nd edn, revised and enlarged by K. F. Pantzer *et al.* 3 vols. (Bibliographical Society 1976–91)

Stuart royal proclamations   James F. Larkin and Paul L. Hughes, eds., *Stuart royal proclamations*, vols. 1– (Oxford 1973–)

TCBS   *Transactions of the Cambridge Bibliographical Society*

Term Catalogues   Edward Arber, ed., *The Term Catalogues, 1668–1709*, 3 vols. (1903–6)

Tudor royal proclamations Paul L. Hughes and James F. Larkin, eds., *Tudor royal proclamations*, 3 vols. (New Haven 1964–9)

University Archives Cambridge University Archives, Cambridge University Library

VCH *Victoria history of the counties of England*

Venn J. and J. A. Venn, *Alumni Cantabrigienses*. Part 1. *From the earliest times to 1751*, 4 vols. (Cambridge 1922–7)

Venn, *Gonville and Caius* J. Venn *et al.*, *Biographical history of Gonville and Caius College*, 1– (Cambridge 1897–)

Voet, *Golden compasses* Leon Voet, *The golden compasses*, 2 vols. (Amsterdam 1969–72)

Wilkins, *Concilia* David Wilkins, *Concilia Magnae Britanniae et Hiberniae*, 4 vols. (1737)

Willis and Clark R. Willis and J. W. Clark, *The architectural history of the University of Cambridge and of the colleges of Cambridge and Eton*, 4 vols. (Cambridge 1886)

Wing Donald Wing, *Short-title catalogue of books printed in England, Scotland, Ireland...and of English books printed in other countries, 1641–1700*, 2nd edn, 3 vols. (New York 1972–88)

Worman, *Alien members* E. J. Worman *Alien members of the book-trade during the Tudor period* (Bibliographical Society 1906)

NOTE ON CURRENCY

The following may be useful to those unfamiliar with English currency before the Decimal Currency Act, 1971, when the pound was newly divided into 100 pence.

4 farthings = 1 penny (1d.)
2 halfpence = 1 penny (1d.)
12 pence = 1 shilling (1s.)
20 shillings = 1 pound (£1)
1 guinea = £1.1s.0d.

Sums of money are conventionally written, for example, as £5.13s.4d.

Perspectives

Between 1534 and the end of the seventeenth century, England lived through Reformation and Counter-Reformation, and two constitutional revolutions. Its population increased from *c.* 2·8 million in 1541 to *c.* 5·1 million in 1701.[1] In 1534 its foreign policy was dominated by Rome. By 1700 it had possessed itself of an empire, and had become a world power.

Thus stated, the nature and the circumstances of these experiences, two concerns fundamental to historical understanding, are obliterated by the beguiling summariness that usually characterizes chronology. Yet for all their periodization – a periodization determined by the critical dates in the history of printing in a small university town in East Anglia – they do hint at how great a change took place, one that affected every aspect of society. Changes in the manufacture, appearance and use of books and printing were no less profound; and with them the assumptions of authors and readers were modified also. Although it is conventional, and convenient, to divide the history of printing between the periods of the hand press and the machine press, the division falling in the early nineteenth century, it is important to realize that this distinction is defined by only one agent, the printing press, in a long series of processes involving production and consumption in all their several aspects.[2]

The recent rapprochement between historical, literary and textual studies has not only emphasized the integral structure of these disciplines, but also made plain the importance of recognizing and comprehending the nature of bibliographical change.[3] Textual criticism, and therefore the history of texts, is defined not only by its attention to verbal detail, authorized or otherwise, the creation of author, amanuensis, editor, compositor or proof-reader, but also by the unfolding interplay of social context, process of manufacture, assumptions as to physical appearance both on the page and in the surroundings of a volume or other form of publication, and the frame of reference, both preceding and contemporary, provided by other similar or related works. It thus draws on books both *en masse* and in particular: on editions and on individual copies. Such study, which is the essence of any historically motivated investigation of a literate or partially literate culture, requires understanding not only of the mechanics of textual manufacture and reproduction (including, in this instance, but by no means solely, the manner in which type is composed and printed off, within the small world of the printing house), but also of the circumstances governing choice of one alternative rather than another, whether in type design, format, printer, bookseller, binding or, finally, price. Insofar as religious, economic, political and (especially but by no means exclusively in the case of the presses at Oxford and Cambridge) educational requirements influenced these decisions, and even provide an environment in which a decision-making process is possible, they, too, influence the final form of the books and other printed matter eventually sent out for readers' consumption – and the continuation, therefore, of the cyclical interplay of writer and reader.

In other words, and to summarize the consequences of this, the following chapters have been conceived as more than the annals, recounted once again, of the history of printing in Cambridge. Their structure is chronological, beginning with the Letters Patent granted by Henry VIII in 1534 that enabled the University eventually to appoint a printer, and then to engage in direct competition in a trade otherwise dominated, in England, by London. The beginning falls before the incorporation of the Stationers' Company in 1557, an event whose consequences dominate much of this volume;[4] and the end coincides with the effects of the lapse of the Licensing Acts after 1695. But while the succession of University Printers has been allowed to dominate the book, their sequence is punctuated by more general considerations, some in separate chapters, of the press and its relations with authors, booksellers and the University. Their concern is with the printed word, rather than the manuscript, although for many purposes the manuscript remained an equal partner until after the close of this volume. This was true both of administration and of literary composition. 'Mens hearts may be poysoned, and seduced, as well by Manuscripts, and written Bookes and Pamphlets, as by those that be Printed, especially after they be once scattered and dispersed abroad into diverse mens hands', wrote Sir Christopher Sibthorp in 1625. His target was Roman Catholicism, but he was giving vent to what his contemporaries would have regarded as a truism: that for many purposes, circulation in manuscript was as acceptable as print.[5]

During the seventeenth century, the book trade underwent a revolution in the manufacture of books second only to the invention of printing itself, though it is one that has been less appreciated. The revolution was gradual rather than sudden; but it came to affect every aspect of book production, from printing house to retail customer, and was accompanied by changes in the sale, circulation and readership of books that were to prove equally enduring.

In changes in the outward presentation of books, in their binding materials, in their decoration and in the uniformity gradually applied to multiple copies of the same work, the trade responded to reader and market stimuli in ways whose origins can only in some respects be traced back to the fifteenth century. A larger reading public, with more money to spend on greater quantities of books, implied also a degree of uniformity. The trade was expected to produce more finished articles, while customers sought the social as well as the intellectual reassurance of conformity – a reassurance manifested both in the uniformity of print itself, and also in uniform pricing and uniform materials and finish.

The emphasis in the retail trade shifted from meeting the cost of printing and binding separately – the first as a fixed figure, the second as one that could be adjusted to individual circumstance – to an emphasis on the establishment of a range of prices scaled according to a clearly visible and easily compared range of economic, aesthetic and material values. That which was introduced as a trade convenience for large-scale sales of the more obvious works of education or devotion, or for the clearly focused requirements of legal publishing, became also an essential of large-scale consumer expectations. Formats of books, paper sizes and type sizes and designs, all of which affected and helped dictate the size of books on the shelf or in the hand, were combined with defined ranges of outward presentation, whether turkey leather, calf or sheep, or blind or gilt tooling of the leather. Thus, a much greater range of printed matter than ever hitherto available was presented in a clearly defined range of consumer choice, to meet both new lavishness in the increasing numbers of more wealthy households and the greater purchasing power of those with more middling incomes. It is conventional to speak of the emergence of a consumer society in the eighteenth century and later. In many manufactured goods the birth took place much earlier.[6] For the book trade at least, in its concentration on mass production at every stage (not simply in the act of printing), in its insistent attention to cost-cutting from type design to finished binding, and in its response to and manipulation of reader demand, many of the attributes of a consumer revolution are to be seen falling into order in the second half of the seventeenth century.

The sheer quantities of books published annually, to join the ever-growing accumulations from previous years, burgeoned during these years at a rate which every generation found difficult to comprehend or accept. 'The *Press* spawns *Books* and *Pamphlets*, in as great abundance as the River *Nile* doth Froggs', Edward Polhill commented in 1682, more tolerantly than many who had complained at the seemingly excessive numbers of printed books almost since the beginning of printing itself.[7] Though the inspiration for complaints was perhaps to be found both in the biblical 'Of making many books there is no end', and in Juvenal's 'scribendi cacoethes', their increase became a conventional *topos* in the late sixteenth century, one justified even more by 1700.[8]

Although the precise figures that might support such claims are now irrecoverable,[9] the evidence remains of catalogues, inventories, surviving libraries and, particularly, of books themselves – witnesses to their own history and thus, as witnesses, subject to examination. Many of those whose complaints were most vociferous had in mind a spawning pamphlet literature, much of it rapidly written and rapidly produced, whose speed of production added zest to theological argument and animosity to personal comment. Others, such as the Newcastle-upon-Tyne bookseller William London, spoke of the phenomenon in a context of learning and knowledge, and of 'our slippery memory' made good by books.[10] But quite apart from the increasing numbers of titles, numbers of books grew as well. The chapbook and ballad trade existed alongside that for the kind of books with which this volume is principally concerned, impinging on it insofar as both were involved in the Bible and almanac trade but otherwise having little contact. This trade dealt in the most popular of all literature, and it is here that some of the most noticeable quantities were to be found. The London chapbook publisher Charles Tyas left in 1664 a stock of perhaps as many as 90,000 books, almost all of them with a price of sixpence apiece or less, and over two-thirds of them priced at twopence to fourpence.[11] Much of the stock consisted of long-standing and traditional stories. Though a few publications, such as newspapers or topical pamphlets, might be expected to be printed in unusually large numbers, the larger editions were often of the most established books or other forms, whether the Bible, schoolbooks, almanacs, ballads or chapbooks.[12] For all the vast numbers of stock held by Tyas or others like him, there is little evidence that editions of many ordinary new books were much greater at the end of the seventeenth century compared with a century earlier.

In the 1580s, the decade that marked the beginning of University printing at Cambridge, there were perhaps as many as three hundred books or pamphlets published in most years. By the 1630s, this figure had more than doubled. The increase in new publications was by no means regular, whether measured in titles or in editions, and political crises in the 1640s, late 1670s and 1680s, for example, produced exceptional flurries of activity.[13] In 1680, there even appeared, 'very useful for Gent. that make collections', a *Compleat catalogue* of all the stitched books (or pamphlets) and single sheets printed since the discovery of the Popish Plot. Two continuations were published, to cover most of the rest of the year, but the first issue alone of this short-lived venture had listed almost seven hundred titles.[14] But amidst this vast increase in the amount of print in circulation, it is far from clear that a larger proportion of the population could be considered literate (in the sense of being able to read, write and understand) at the end of the seventeenth century compared with a century and more earlier.[15] The growth in population – again, not constant, though clear in its trend – coupled with the increasing stock of new and of old books or other printed matter, meant that each generation faced the world of books and reading anew. Fresh means had constantly to be found to enable more books to be produced for, and used by, more people. In the face of inexorable expansion, almost every aspect of the manufacture, marketing and storage of the printed word underwent radical change.

Libraries, both private and institutional, became larger and more plentiful, the most voluminous demanding in their turn increasingly detailed classification of knowledge,[16] while ownership of printed books spread to ever further levels of prosperity, education and achievement, even to some of the poorest, in an expanding population. Wren's new library at Trinity College, Cambridge (the largest such building to be erected in England in the seventeenth century), its great windows raised above the bookcases so as to provide extra space for books as well as light by which to read, provided for much-needed expansion, and turned its face against the tradition of centuries of design for such buildings, both in its fabric and in its fittings. It was completed in 1695, only months before Bentley (still Royal Librarian, and not yet Master of the College) took the initiative in establishing the new University Press at Cambridge. Where other libraries at both Oxford and Cambridge had been modified, or (as at Peterhouse at the end of the sixteenth century) rebuilt on traditional lines, Wren's design was constantly innovative. The sixteenth-century stall system, still visible in the Bodleian Library, Merton College and elsewhere, was itself a development designed to increase the amount of shelf-space provided by the lectern system.[17] But Wren introduced tables at which to read instead of shelves, and furnished the tables with revolving stands for books in use. Readers were not only faced with more books, stored in a different way; they were also expected to use them in a different manner.[18]

This increased acquisition of books, whether in private houses, modest or grand, or in institutional collections, affected authorship, printing, binding, bookselling and reading equally, as printing houses multiplied (and some increased in size) and booksellers strove to put before the public a variety and quantity unimagined by each generation's predecessors. Permanent changes were wrought in a more and more heavily stocked second-hand trade, and in book collecting, with the advent of auctions as a means of selling books, first developed in Holland in the sixteenth and early seventeenth centuries and introduced to England by 1676. Though clearly popular with private customers, such sales were viewed with suspicion and anxiety by some booksellers, of both old and new books, who felt their livelihood threatened.[19] For readers and booksellers alike, the need to find a path among so much, and to choose between it, was paramount. This demand was met on the one hand by trade lists, beginning in 1595 with Andrew Maunsell's *Catalogue of English printed bookes* – Maunsell 'thinking it as necessarie for the Booke-seller (considering the number and nature of them) to haue a Catalogue of our English Bookes: as the Apothecarie his *Dispensatorium*, or the Schoole-master his *Dictionarie*'.[20] In 1657 William London justified his catalogue of 'the most vendible books in England' with an analogy drawn from Sir Walter Raleigh: 'he knew there was a mine, but knew not how to find it and there seems to be no less, then as great need of a Register of Books, which else may be buried with their Authors'.[21] In the seventeenth century at least, such lists reached their apogee in the Term Catalogues, with their associated cumulations by Robert Clavell. On the other hand, the appearance of new reviewing journals (of which the *Philosophical Transactions* of the Royal Society offers an early example), some in London but most of the more successful in Holland or France, catered for a market, always international with respect to scholarly printing, whose size and complexity required increasing bibliographical sophistication. Both Clavell and the new reviewing (or often, more properly, abstracting) journals reiterated by example England's continuing dependence on imported titles.

Finally, the manners of publication and sale changed, and with them literary form. John Ogilby, having over-invested in engravings for a series of exceptionally heavily illustrated books, resorted idiosyncratically in the 1660s to lotteries as a means of selling stock and recouping investment.[22] Much more importantly, the advent of newspapers and other regularly issued periodicals, providing opportunities for advertisement and for review, wrought changes that eventually affected virtually every form of book and every subject. Although the first English newsbook is usually held to have been an account of the battle of Flodden in 1513, listing the principal dead, and printed soon after the event, and although newsbooks became common in the 1590s, the first English newspapers were not published until Pieter van den Keere's short-lived series of small folio broadsheets in Amsterdam in 1620–1.[23] But once created, the newspaper remained, for much of the century, in quarto, reverting to folio with the founding of the *London Gazette* in 1665. By the end of 1695, the last year of the *ancien régime* in printing at Cambridge before the first formal movements towards the foundation of the modern Press, London had several newspapers appearing twice or more a week.[24] A periodical press brought the opportunity to advertise in a regular and organized manner, and to widely distributed markets. Innovations in publishing itself, such as the development of the prospectus (and with it publication by subscription), the emergence in the latter part of the seventeenth century of a new breed of publishers, the commercial collaboration of congers, or the invention and successful application of part-publication, were all intended, at least partly, to spread costs, for stationer or for customer. Though serial, or part, publication affected the form of texts most obviously, the application of these other innovations also assumed texts requiring, or amenable to, such manipulation.[25]

These changes affected every subject, and in some subjects entirely new forms of publication or presentation made their appearance, such as coasting pilots, engraved sheet music, pocket engraved atlases, road books or commercial handbooks and summaries.[26] But even in those genres already established, the form and the appearance of books changed dramatically.[27] Reasons for this were complex, some social and others economic, and some a mixture of the two. Cheaper means of production were sought, imposed partly by the supplies of raw materials, while appearances grew more diverse even as paper-making, printing and binding imposed their own tendency to uniformity.

A few books can be kept on a shelf, lying on their sides. But as collections expanded, both public and private, so bookcases became necessary, their design modified according to the purpose or building for which they were intended.[28] And instead of being shelved with their fore-edges facing outwards (as they were in both chained libraries and in private collections), with their titles written on their fore-edges on those occasions when the number of volumes made it seem requisite, books were turned spine outwards, in a fashion introduced from France in the mid-seventeenth century but which can be traced back to Italy in the first part of the sixteenth. Like all such revolutions, the change was not brought about overnight. One of the first documented English examples of the very practical consequences of this, the introduction of spine-titles or title-labels, dates from 1660, though there are earlier isolated instances. In Cambridge the bookseller John Dennis owned 'a rose for the backe of a booke' in the 1570s, but this was merely for decoration; at Eton another bookseller, Williamson, was lettering the spines of some books as early as 1604.[29] By the time that Evelyn's translation and adaptation of Naudé's *Advis pour dresser une bibliothèque* (1627) appeared in 1661, the practice had become general in France, while in England old habits persisted. As usual, Naudé was unenthusiastic about gaudiness or show, preferring to spend money on the contents of volumes rather than their dress. But for England his remarks about the treatment of books' spines were opportunely timed:

As to the binding of Books, there is no need of extraordinary expence; it were better to reserve that mony for the purchasing of all the books of the fairest and best editions that are to be found; unless that to delight the eyes of Spectators, you will cause all the backs of such as shall be bound as well in Rough, as in *Calveskin*, or *Morroccin*, to be gilded with fillets, and some little flowers, with the name of the Authors...[30]

The nature of cover decoration changed also. The heavy blind-stamped decoration, extending over most of the covers and characterizing so much of late fifteenth- and early sixteenth-century calf binding in England, died out gradually during the sixteenth, and had become unusual by the early seventeenth century; panel stamps had fallen out of fashion first, by about the middle of the sixteenth.[31] The bindings from the shops of Nicholas Spierinck and Garrett Godfrey in Cambridge, and of their contemporaries in London and elsewhere, were essentially medieval in conception, both structurally and decoratively.[32] They were the last of their kind in Cambridge. In their place, there emerged a diversity of styles. Ordinary decoration was achieved by smaller centre-pieces, sometimes accompanied by corner-pieces – tools that in turn gave way to a general use of still smaller tools that could be used in combination to give yet greater variety. One of the seventeenth century's most distinctive decorative innovations, the rectangle impressed gilt or blind, with fillets or with rolls, and for the better or more showy work having ornaments at each of the rectangle's corners, lasted well into the eighteenth century. The earliest gold-tooled bindings made in western Europe were executed in Northern Italy in the first half of the fifteenth century; but the earliest so far discovered from England dates from 1519, and only a few survive from the 1520s.[33] Dennis, again, was equipped to provide gilt bindings in the 1570s in Cambridge, his shop including a 'gilding coushin with the kniffe to cut gold': numerous gilt bindings survive executed in late sixteenth-century Cambridge, and they were common in London. By the turn of the century gold was being used to decorate even relatively cheap bindings.

In a market with very diverse sums of money available to spend on books, the choice and nature of the materials of bindings changed as well. Though wooden boards can be found on seventeenth-century books, they had passed out of general use, even for substantial volumes, by the 1590s: in Cambridge, as elsewhere, wood was used in the second half of the sixteenth century principally for books destined for libraries rather than for personal ownership. By the end of the first half of the seventeenth century, wood boards were rare. So, too, boards composed of laminated sheets of waste paper, frequent in the early and mid-sixteenth century, were replaced by pulp boards of varying degrees of hardness and flexibility.[34] Rope-fibre millboard was introduced for better-quality work in the late seventeenth century. The choice, preparation and suppliers of leather changed equally markedly. The calf leathers used in the latter part of the seventeenth century were not only noticeably thinner than those used previously, but were also of a lighter colour: this was the result partly of the tanning and other preparatory processes, and partly of the use of much younger calves.[35] With the introduction of goatskin, or turkey leather (an allusion to the part of the Mediterranean whence the skins were first imported), much greater variety was possible in both colour and finishing, or tooling. These skins were first used in England in about 1550, and at first were a luxury.[36] They always remained superior to, and more expensive than, calf or sheep, but by the third quarter of the seventeenth century they were widespread. Sheepskin, so common in seventeenth-century schoolbooks and other cheap work, seems to have been used less even for cheap books in the sixteenth century, though Dennis left a dozen forels, or unsplit sheepskins, valued with a rabbit vellum at 3s.4d. Quarter-leather bindings whether of calf or sheep, and providing another means to cheapness, do not seem to have been employed in England until the mid-seventeenth century.[37]

This reshaping in fashion and design of books is illustrated in the deliberate archaism of the binding Pepys commissioned for his copy of Speght's edition of Chaucer (1602) – a binding so important to him that it is the only one mentioned in detail in his diary:

So to Pauls churchyard about my books – and to the binders and directed the doing of my Chaucer, though they were not full neat enough for me, but pretty well it is – and thence to the clasp-makers to have it clasped and bossed.

The result, one of the most instructive of all the bindings in his library, was a 1664 pastiche of a 'medieval' binding, complete with metal corner-pieces, central boss, brass clasps and blind-tooling arranged in an admixture of the sixteenth and seventeenth centuries.[38]

There were also modifications in the structure of bindings. Sewing structures, rarely properly visible, betray an overall trend towards cheapness and speed in execution. Among the more visible parts, vellum or parchment endleaves and pastedowns, a useful strengthening and protection to the text-block, remained plentiful until the supplies of medieval manuscripts regarded as waste became exhausted. These supplies, released by the declining value set on them and many of the texts they contained, or by the gradual accumulation of modern printed editions, increasingly depended also on the tolerance or uninterest of book-collectors or of other tradesmen: the extent to which monastic libraries contributed to the supply remains unclear, but is likely to have varied from one part of the country to another, depending on local interests.[39] Medieval manuscripts used in this way had become rare by the 1590s, and their heyday in Oxford and Cambridge is dateable between approximately 1520 and 1570, when they featured regularly. In London, they were little used for this purpose after about 1540, though both there and in the country they are to be found in use as a cheap form of wrapper well into the seventeenth century if supplies permitted it.[40] By the second quarter of the seventeenth century the use of second-hand vellum as a strengthening material was usually restricted to small slips employed as joints between text-block and cover: with the disappearance of supplies of medieval manuscripts, binders resorted to unwanted legal documents.

As the bulk of books diminished, and as they were assumed to be destined to be stored upright on shelves, tight against one another, rather than to lie flat with a few of their fellows, so the squares, or parts of the boards projecting beyond the text-block, were cut smaller, and clasps became unnecessary: by the late seventeenth century clasps were rarely found on new books other than Bibles, prayer books, almanacs and a few other titles designed similarly for table, rather than shelf, use. The materials used for sewing also affected appearance. Leather thongs, on which gatherings of leaves were sewn, were often displaced in the late sixteenth and early seventeenth centuries by the lighter cords. By the end of the sixteenth century the continental practice of sewing on recessed cords or thongs, a method which achieved a flat spine rather than one divided into compartments, had become widespread for smaller books especially, and was markedly so in Cambridge by the second quarter of the seventeenth century. By the later part of the century marbled edges were beginning to make their appearance, in place of the ordinary colouring or sprinkling: marbled endpapers were not common until about the same time.

But bindings, imposing their obvious uniformity of taste, and clothing both old and new books, not only emphasize changes in the appearance of new books. They also express changing evaluations – literary, historical, aesthetic or commercial – of earlier ones, and thus can to some extent mask the true relationship of new to old, earlier to current publications. Bookbinders' price-lists were, however, aimed principally at modern books requiring binding for the first time; and such documents as *A generall note of the prises for binding all sorts of bookes* (1619) assumed a congruity, if not conformity, represented by a search for a clearly distinguishing uniform price structure for such work.[41] For so long as booksellers were usually responsible for binding, or customers were expected to pay for binding separately, the degree of uniformity was obviously limited: not surprisingly in these circumstances, identical bindings on quantities of the same book made their appearance first among the cheaper educational or devotional works, which could be expected to be sold quickly or in quantity.[42] Booksellers' stock, divided between more or less simply bound volumes and unbound sheets, meant also that several copies of the same title might be bound up identically: examples are not difficult to find. Wholesalers' and, ultimately, publishers' bindings followed as a natural development; and though it is inaccurate to speak of edition bindings until later, there is some evidence to suggest that a few books in the mid-seventeenth century were provided with uniform bindings in quantities well beyond those required by individual booksellers. The volumes of verses issued at Cambridge to mark public occasions were one marked exception to this practice, since the University regularly paid not only for presentation copies of more or less splendour, but also for many dozens to be bound up in cheaper uniform styles – often, in the early seventeenth century, limp vellum.[43] In the ordinary trade, outside quasi-private publication of this kind, the two best known examples of uniform bindings, each of them decorated in the centre of their covers with a specially cut stamp bearing the title of the book, were Francis Roberts' *Clavis bibliorum. The key of the Bible* (1648) and James Howel's Δενδρολογία. *Dordona's grove* [1649]. Both were published in London.

By the late 1660s, many books were published ready bound, rather than in quires, both bound and unbound copies being advertised at a price named by the stationer. This trend became especially noticeable among the more popular or readily saleable books, though it was by no means confined to them.[44] Within a decade, it was affecting Cambridge-printed books as well: Lily's grammar and Tate and Brady's version of the Psalms were among those now offered not simply in sheets, or in quires, but put up in plain and uniform calf. The effect for the book trade was to impose uniformity on the external presentation of books just as typography had on the internal.

The controlling factor in the size and shape of books was, however, not binding, but paper. The increase in the range of available sizes of sheets came in response to manufacturing and marketing requirements. But the shapes, not simply the sizes, also changed. For so long as the rate at which sheets could be printed remained approximately the same (and it did not change significantly, despite many attempts at improvements in printing presses, until the advent of machine presses in the nineteenth century), the most effective way to increase output lay in typographical design and in the size of the page in relation to that. More text could be fitted onto larger sheets, and still more with careful thought and suitable type, while such sheets, whatever the format of the book, took approximately the same time to print as smaller ones. And as the proportional length of the sides of sheets changed, so also did the shape of books as a consequence. Folios became accordingly more narrow in proportion to their height, and quartos less so.[45] Whereas in the early sixteenth century an octavo was quite a small book, by the end of the seventeenth century, thanks to the manufacture of large quantities of larger-sized sheets of varying dimensions, it ranged in size from as little as about 15 cm. or less to 23 cm. or more. As increasing quantities of thinner paper became available, part of a necessary drive towards economy in materials and manufacture, so duodecimos became more common, part of a general trend towards books in smaller formats that accompanied the expansion of private ownership of moderate or even substantial libraries. Paper quality itself became cause for complaint by the end of the sixteenth century, as, first on the continent and then inevitably in Britain thanks to its continental suppliers, white paper was contaminated and resulted in stocks noticeably grey or brown in colour.[46]

All these factors affected the appearance and shape of the book and, therefore, reading as well. Within the book, illustration, page lay-out, and type design each witnessed fundamental changes, though in several respects they can be traced from the fifteenth century. Copper engraving, an intaglio rather than letterpress process whose execution had therefore a manufacturing as well as functional and visual effect on book design, was developed in Germany and the Low Countries in the mid-fifteenth century. Although a few isolated instances are to be found in English books before the 1540s, executed probably in the Low Countries, the earliest practitioner whose work seems also to have been printed in London was Thomas Geminus, author and illustrator of *Compendiosa totius anatomie delineatio* (1545).[47] The superior detail and tonal range offered by the medium outweighed its substantial cost in plate preparation, slowness in printing and limited life of plates before they required attention by retouching. In 1591, Sir John Harington, writing in the preface to his translation of Orlando Furioso, was loud in his praises of intaglio illustration, as he and his team of engravers were able to demonstrate the effect of his English translation by juxtaposing the text to a series of copies from the illustrations to the elaborate edition printed at Venice in 1584.

As for the pictures, they are all cut in brasse, and most of them by the best workemen in that kinde, that haue bene in this land this manie yeares: yet I will not praise them too much, because I gaue direction for their making, and in regard thereof, I may be thought partiall, but this I may truely say, that (for mine owne part) I haue not seene anie made in England better, nor (in deede) anie of this kinde, in any booke, except it were in a treatise, set foorth by that profound man, maister Broughton the last yeare, vpon the Reuelation, in which there are some 3. or 4. pretie figures … cut in brasse verie workemanly. As for other books that I haue seene in this realme, either in Latin or English, with picturs, as Liuy, Gesner, Alciats emblemes, a booke *de Spectris* in Latin, & (in our tong) the Chronicles, the booke of Martyrs, the book of hauking and hunting, and M. Whitneys excellent Emblems, yet all their figures are cut in wood, & none in metall, and in that respect inferior to these, at least (by the old prouerbe) the more cost, the more worship.[48]

Prompted by its supremely successful handling by Balthasar Moretus in Antwerp and by other Low Countries publishers, as well as by practitioners in France and Germany, the new technique came to dominate book illustration in even quite popular parts of the market.[49] The gradual impoverishment (save in very few hands by the end of the sixteenth century) of woodcut illustration and its replacement by copper engraving and other intaglio methods paved the way for many of the best features of baroque book design, whether engraved title-pages or more extended illustration.[50] In 1662 the publication within a twelvemonth of Evelyn's *Sculptura*, based on the work of Prince Rupert in mezzotint, and of William Faithorne's translation of part of Abraham Bosse's *Traicté des manières de graver* drew attention to the neglected possibilities of etching (Vasari's 'disegni stampati', or printed drawings) and to the new invention of mezzotint, as alternatives and complements to the more familiar engraving.[51] The structure of the trade, usually distinguishing between letterpress and rolling-press printing, helped however to ensure that comparatively few books, in Britain at least, carried both text and engraved illustration on the same page. This tendency increased in the seventeenth century, and affected the structure and appearance of books alike, as plates were printed on separate leaves for insertion by the binder, a procedure that also encouraged, in Bibles and prayer books especially, a strong market in illustrations varied to suit owners' tastes.[52]

Type design passed through two revolutions, one major and one more subtle, in the course of the two centuries. Black-letter remained normal for vernacular texts well into the seventeenth century, and was still used for some popular cheap literature, as well as for legal printing, even in the eighteenth. But it was gradually displaced by roman (first used in England by Richard Pynson in 1509) and italic.[53] The interplay of all three gave printers opportunities for textual orchestration unavailable to previous generations and neglected by most of those subsequently. Less ostentatiously, but no less importantly for the alterations in appearance that make it possible to distinguish between books of the late sixteenth and the late seventeenth centuries, the design of roman type itself changed, partly in the face of demands for more compact, and therefore more economical, faces, and partly in response to Baroque sensibilities. Sixteenth-century designs, modelled on the proportions of classical inscriptions, essentially calligraphic in their construction, and dominated in the late sixteenth century by the work of French punch-cutters such as Claude Garamond, Robert Granjon, Pierre Haultin and François Guyot, besides others whose names are now lost, were equally familiar to printers in England and on the continent.[54] In the seventeenth century the sources of design remained continental, England producing no distinct major contribution of its own until the advent of William Caslon in the 1720s.[55] But the emphasis moved from France to Holland and Germany. The punch-cutter Hendrik van den Keere's designs, fundamentally different in their concept from most others, and the herald of many subsequent developments in the seventeenth century, were bought by Plantin in substantial numbers, in time to be included in his type specimen of *c.* 1585. There they were exhibited alongside the work of Granjon, Garamond, Haultin and others.[56] Van den Keere's example was quickly followed, in the work of the punch-cutters Nicholas Kis, Christoffel van Dijck and Bartholomaeus and Dirk Voskens and typefounders such as Jacques Vallet in Amsterdam.[57] The new design produced types with thicker down-strokes, more contrast between thick and thin, greater x-height, and a noticeably more narrow set. Much of its character was caught in the felicitous phrase 'gros oeil'.[58] By the 1680s Moxon was able to write of 'the late made *Dutch-Letters*', 'so generally, and indeed most deservedly accounted the best, as for their Shape, consisting so exactly of Mathematical Regular Figures… And for the commodious Fatness they have beyond other *Letters*, which easing the Eyes in Reading, renders them more Legible; As also the true placing their Fats and their Leans, with the sweet driving them into one another.'[59] The new style was exemplified, however unsuccessfully as it transpired (since few of his designs were taken up by other printers), in Moxon's own specimen sheet of 1669.

Although several of these new designs were also offered by German type-founders (to the consequent bewilderment of later historians of typography), the earlier assumption that this was originally a Dutch innovation was correct. Fournier in 1766 used the term 'goût hollandois' to describe several of the roman text sizes in his *Manuel typographique*, commenting also

Ces différentes nuances *d'oeil* ou de grosseur de caractères, sont faites autant pour l'agréable que pour l'utile…L'oeil moyen est d'une nuance plus forte [than oeil ordinaire], qui rend le caractère plus lisible, avantage que le gros oeil rend encore plus sensible; mais les lignes étant plus rapprochées les unes des autres, les pages prennent un air trop matériel.[60]

The conventional term 'Dutch' remained, in an industry dominated for much of the seventeenth and eighteenth centuries by the Dutch.[61] But the impact of imported designs was not simply one of copying, as in the case of Moxon. Matrices and type made their way across the North Sea. Among the matrices purchased in Holland for the Oxford University Press in the 1670s were designs by Christoffel van Dijck as well as earlier faces by Haultin and Granjon, while the decision to employ such new designs was in great measure extended with the employment of a German letter-founder, Peter de Walpergen, at the Oxford press from 1676. At Cambridge, a similar path was followed at the end of the century under Richard Bentley's guidance, not only in the purchase of types from Holland by van Dijck, but even in the appointment of a Dutchman, Cornelius Crownfield, as first Inspector of the new Press and then, in 1705, as University Printer.[62]

The geographical position of Cambridge, on the edge of the fens and at the head of the navigable river, gave it many advantages in an agricultural economy, but offered few to the development of any manufacturing that would depend, for its raw materials as for its principal market, on London. The river brought most of its supplies, whether from the sea via King's Lynn or from the west via Huntingdon and the River Ouse.[63] The road from London ran through Ware, Puckeridge and Barkway, a much frequented course that from Puckeridge southwards was also part of the Great North Road and that could at times be heavy going. In 1680 Ralph Thoresby found the road between London and Ware 'most pleasant' in summer, 'and as bad in winter, because of the depth of the cart-ruts, though far off as bad as thence to Buntingford and Puckeridge'. Fifteen years later, on the same road, and even in May, unexpected rain caused drowning, and obliged him to ride through water lapping at his horse's saddle-skirts.[64] Though the fifty miles or so between Cambridge and London could be covered in a day, loads of any consequence, such as paper or books, took substantially more time. In general, the population of London depended on the countryside and its produce more than on what a small university town had to offer; but this helped encourage efforts in the 1570s to improve the River Lea, making trade between the capital and the corn-growing areas of Hertfordshire and south Cambridgeshire easier, and so incidentally improving trade connections with Cambridge itself. Further north, the Great North Road out of Wadesmill became the subject of the first Turnpike Act in 1663. The late sixteenth and seventeenth centuries witnessed numerous changes in internal communications of this kind, many of them prompted by the rapid growth of London, and Cambridge benefited greatly.[65] By 1681 there was a daily coach service to London, wagons left five times a week, and various carriers left six times a week. The London carrier became the usual means of transport for books to and from London from at least the late sixteenth century,[66] and had probably been so for years before then. Cross-country, there were regular connections with Norwich and Huntingdonshire, quite apart from the long-established network of river routes (now also supported by land as well) to Ely and King's Lynn in the north, and Huntingdon and St Ives in the west.[67]

Paper is heavy. A ream (480 sheets generally in the seventeenth century) of demy for printing weighed up to about 20 lbs., and royal about 28 lbs.[68] Thus an edition of 1,440 copies (three reams)[69] consisting of 200 pages in demy quarto, or twenty-five sheets in each copy, might weigh about 1,500 lbs. altogether in sheets only, unbound. The same edition size and format, but of 300 pages, required over a ton of paper. Since no printing paper was manufactured locally, all this had to be brought from London; and most copies of most books printed at Cambridge made the return journey as well.[70]

The road to London may have been for long periods inadequate and dangerous, and the voyage by sea awkward. But intellectually, socially, politically and (in the case of the book trades) economically, it was on these that Cambridge depended, whether for metropolitan or international interests. Until the construction of the Bedford Level and the Hundred Foot Drain in the mid-seventeenth century reduced the flow in the Cam and the Ouse, much to the dismay of both the town and the University, the rivers formed the essential commercial highway serving much of east central England. Able to take even sea-going craft, their importance gradually declined as smaller boats with shallower drafts became necessary, though they were not to be eclipsed until the building of the railways in the nineteenth century. Meanwhile the advantages of Cambridge's location, at the head of navigation and thus as a major inland port, were reflected in its fairs, the first at Midsummer and the second, much larger and more celebrated, for three weeks each September at Stourbridge, just after harvest time on the fields near Barnwell, about two miles out of the town towards Newmarket. Held since the thirteenth century, and by 1589 called by far the largest and most famous fair in all England ('in longe maximas ac celeberrimas tocius Anglie nundinas'),[71] Stourbridge Fair was of key importance in the Cambridge year. To Camden it was 'the greatest Faire of all England, whether you respect the multitude of buyers and sellers resorting thether, or the store of commodities there to be vented'.[72] Its location on fields lying between the Cam and the upland fields on the edge of the fens was a natural frontier.

Its importance, however, was both local and national – even, thanks to connections with northern Europe and the Baltic, international. A proclamation by the University in the 1540s not only charged students and others attending the fair neither to behave in an unruly manner, nor to wear any weapon, but also spoke of bakers, brewers, potters, vintners, fishmongers, butchers, chandlers, dealers in wool, linen, silk, worsteds, coal, salt, mustard, tar, groceries, charcoal and grain. Legislation in 1589 mentioned in addition goldsmiths, pewterers and tin-smiths.[73] In 1616 no fewer than 1,600 passes were printed for the fair for the University's use.[74]

On the whole, the fair depended less on road connections than on the river, and the drainage of the fens in the seventeenth century thus dealt it a blow from which it never recovered. In 1651 a petition signed jointly by the Mayor and the Vice-Chancellor, and delivered to the Commissioners for draining the fens, appealed against the diversion of river waters, which would interrupt traffic between Cambridge, St Ives and Huntingdon,

whereby not only the said, University and Town of Cambridge will be wholly undone, and all the adjacent Countries greatly damnified and impoverish'd, but also a great Prejudice will thereby befal to a great part of this whole Nation, by the Stoppage of the general Commerce at Sturbridge Fair.[75]

However, the effects of drainage were felt more slowly than had been claimed or anticipated, and the fair remained prosperous, if with different business, well into the eighteenth century, meanwhile celebrated by Bunyan as Vanity Fair. In 1700 Ned Ward, visiting Cambridge, found the town (as distinct from the University) but mean: 'the Buildings in many parts of the Town were so little and so low, that they look'd more like Hutts for Pigmies, than Houses for Men; and their very Shop-keepers seem'd to me to be so well-siz'd to their Habitations, that they appear'd like so many Monkeys in their Diminutive Shops mimicking the Trade of *London*'. But he found the fair thriving, well attended from London and with, not least, an active book trade.[76]

By the 1680s Edward Millington was holding auctions of books.[77] But even in the sixteenth century the University sought to control the sale of books at the fair as it did in the town. Control was exercised not only over the quality of goods, and the accuracy of measures, but even over attendance at the fair. 'None of us here in Cambridg do go to the fayer this year of our trade', wrote Legate in 1593, one of many years in which it was disrupted by plague, 'because the schollers are straytlie commanded upon payne of punishment not to stir abroad and some colledges do break up so that for us there wilbe smale takins.'[78] Besides those local stationers who wished to take advantage of a temporarily much increased market, others came up from London. Their names are not much recorded, but in 1602 Richard Bankworth, of St Paul's Churchyard, was complained against for dishonest dealing in Bibles.[79] In 1627 Bibles were being offered by Francis Williams, who usually dealt in popular literature, and by John Harrison, one of the leading London stationers.[80] These books were not necessarily cheap. Thomas Calvert, Fellow of Trinity, found a folio and quarto Bible on Bankworth's stall for 41s.; and Harrison's stock included at least forty Bibles, among them four in blue leather, gilt, while Williams also had over forty, many of them elaborately bound. The fair was the occasion for substantial business, and its wares were by no means restricted to those likely to have the widest common appeal. The strict control over the Bible trade and its patents brought commensurate court records (Harrison's offence was to have omitted Wither's Psalter);[81] and just as there were certainly more booksellers in attendance, who did not come to notice, so their stock comprised much more than Bibles. At the end of the century, Dunton spoke of William Shrewsbury, one of the more important London booksellers, as a 'constant frequenter' at the fair, adding however a word of warning that it required different skills from those of ordinary bookshops, Shrewsbury being 'perhaps the only *Bookseller* that understands *Fair-keeping* to any advantage'. In 1696 Shrewsbury took advantage of being in Cambridge to deal also with Hayes, on behalf of the English Stock.[82]

Many trades tended to congregate in particular parts of the fair, booksellers becoming associated with Cooks Row, an area (like Booksellers Row) nearer the main road than the river, its location suggesting not only an attempt at convenience for retail customers, coming out from Cambridge, but also that books were usually transported thither by land, rather than by water. 'This Learned part of the Fair is the Schollars chief Rendezvouz, where some that have Money come to buy Books, whilst others who want it, take 'em slily up, upon Condition to pay if they are catch'd, and think it a Pious piece of Generosity, to give St. Austin or St. Gregory Protection in a Gown Sleeve till they can better provide for 'em', wrote Ward at the turn of the century.[83] Not surprisingly, the fair was noticeable for the numbers of members of the University that attended at least some parts of it; but that never obscured the fact that it was an essential part of the economy's structure nation-wide.

By the end of the seventeenth century the population of England had grown by over one-third, to about five million, compared with the 1580s, when Thomas Thomas set up his press in the centre of Cambridge. But neither the national nor the local population grew steadily. In England as a whole it had peaked in the 1650s, reaching a total not to be matched again until after 1710.[84] London grew more steadily, from about four per cent of the population in 1550 to ten per cent or more in 1700, the most rapid period of expansion being, again, in the first half of the seventeenth century. This growth brought with it demands for foodstuffs and manufactured goods that quickly outpaced the traditional guild and company structures of the city, and led to inevitable tensions. Cambridge, like so many other parts of the country, looked increasingly to the metropolis; but no less importantly, for the purposes of this volume, many of the disputes concerning the book trades, ostensibly between the University and the Stationers' Company in London, were also about the manner in which an increasingly fractious London trade was to manage itself.[85] For generations, Cambridge had depended on London for the regular supply of books both from abroad and from the city's printers. From the 1580s it relied also on London to provide or enable a market for books produced in Cambridge itself. Though the net balance of trade in books between the capital and the university town could never be reversed, much of the following account of the press in Cambridge, down to the establishment of the first University Press Syndicate in 1698, is of the manner in which, haltingly, controversially and sometimes confidently, the emphasis was changed.

The University's fortunes were irregular, but for economic, social and political reasons did not follow the national trends in population. The attractions of the London Inns of Court as a fashionable alternative to university education (leading to their vigorous expansion in the late sixteenth century), the requirements for an educated clergy, the varying demands from the professions and from the gentry for entry of their sons into Cambridge rather than to other forms of training, all affected the fortunes of a University which, in the mid-seventeenth century, faced a crisis unparalleled since the Reformation and from which it recovered only painfully slowly in the face of subsequent national distrust of clericalism. Matriculations in the 1580s, averaging 344 per annum, peaked in the 1620s at 421, but then by the 1690s had collapsed to 191, the lowest since the mid-sixteenth century, though that figure was to slip lower still in the eighteenth century. In terms of numbers, though not necessarily of material wealth, the most populous and prosperous decades were the 1620s and the 1650s.[86] Overall numbers in the University are difficult to estimate, since colleges counted their members on the boards (including servants) in different ways. In 1573 John Caius calculated the total at 1,813, a figure which had, according to another calculation, risen by almost two hundred in three years. Another survey in 1581 discovered some 1,862 resident members. By 1618 it had risen to perhaps 2,998, and by 1622 to over 3,000. After the mid-century it ebbed, to 2,522 in 1672. But although such totals, based on different definitions, are unreliable as absolute figures, their drift is consistent with those for matriculations. In terms of resident members, the University was not again to enjoy such prosperity as it achieved in the first part of the seventeenth century until the nineteenth century's dramatic expansion.[87]

Many of these changes were reflected in a very practical and visible way. In 1574, by far the largest of the colleges, in terms both of resident members and of buildings, was Trinity, with 359 Fellows and students according to Caius' survey of that year. With St John's (271) it dominated the University, only two others – Christ's and Corpus – having more than half the number of St John's. Peterhouse, Trinity Hall, Gonville Hall and King's had fewer than a hundred, and Magdalene and St Catharine's less than fifty. But in the early 1580s the University was experiencing a growth of confidence, both in itself and in the country at large. The central government, ecclesiastical and secular, was dominated by Cambridge men. In Cambridge itself, Andrew Perne, Master of Peterhouse and Vice-Chancellor five times over, led a movement that in the 1570s saw the University Library newly supplied and catalogued, encouraged by gifts from the Archbishop of Canterbury, the Lord Keeper and the Bishops of Durham and Winchester. The University's international reputation as an established centre of Protestantism was acknowledged by Théodore de Bèze when in 1581 he presented the fifth-century copy of the Gospels and Acts of the Apostles that now bears his name. Matriculations had risen rapidly in the 1560s and 1570s, and were accompanied either by new building or by the conversion of old quarters. At Gonville and Caius College, Caius Court was occupied for the first time in 1569; at St John's, the old infirmary building to the north of the chapel, and further chambers on the other side of St John's Street, were converted; at Corpus the old tennis court and rectory house of St Bene't's were taken in; and at Pembroke, University Hostel was rebuilt. Sir Walter Mildmay's new foundation of Emmanuel College in 1584 provided for education of specifically puritan leaning.[88] Sidney Sussex College, founded in 1596 under the will of Frances Sidney, Countess of Sussex, was built like Emmanuel on the site of a former religious house, and like Emmanuel it was designed to train men for the parochial ministry.[89]

The turn of the century saw the second court at St John's under construction, and at Trinity the gradual creation under Thomas Nevile of Great Court, of which the new library range on the north side was completed in 1599–1600; work on Nevile's Court was concluded, temporarily at least, probably in 1614. When in 1602 Sir John Harington visited the town, a quarter of a century after he had entered King's, he found the colleges increased in number, beautified, and 'adorned in buildings'.[90] He saw with the eyes of an earlier generation. For most of the seventeenth century the mood in the University generally was more cautious. There were spectacular exceptions, particularly in the erection of the Fellows' Building at Christ's in 1640–3, and the wholesale rebuilding of Clare (begun in 1638, but not completed until 1669) and St Catharine's (1674–87).[91] But the provision for students established by the end of the first quarter of the century proved generally adequate. As Thomas Fuller, a member of Queens' (where a new range of rooms was built north of the chapel in 1616–19), explained, there was by mid-century much beautifying, but not so much new construction, 'every Colledge either casting its *skin* with the *Snake*, or renewing its *bill* with the *Eagle*, hauing their *Courts*, or at leastwise their *fronts*, and *Gate-houses* repaired and adorned'.[92] No new college was founded between Sidney Sussex in 1596 and Downing in 1800.

For libraries, similarly, it was a period of great contrast. John Williams' provision for a new building at St John's in 1623–4 (it was completed in 1628), and the two decades of effort at Trinity that led to the completion of the Wren Library in 1695, were exceptional.[93] In both colleges, substantial benefactions, rather than expenditure on new books, helped to enable the abandonment of earlier accommodation – in Trinity after less than a century. But such building was expensive, and in most colleges refurbishment was the order of the day. Plans for a new University Library were frustrated by the assassination of the Duke of Buckingham in 1628, though the temporary housing of the Lambeth Palace library in the 1640s and 1650s necessitated extensive new shelving.[94] Clare was provided with new library fittings in 1627. In Peterhouse, the Perne Library was re-equipped in the 1640s. In Jesus, new bookcases were installed at the expense of the Master, Edmund Boldero, in 1663–79. In King's, the side-chapels were pressed into service to receive a new suite of bookcases, beginning with those made with the bequest of Nicholas Hobart in 1659, and completed in 1677–80. The library at Caius was refitted in 1675. At Emmanuel, the erection of Wren's new chapel in 1668–77 enabled the College to fit up the old chapel as a library in 1679. Pembroke did the same in 1690.[95] For most colleges, it was a century in which to have survived was a matter for congratulation, where conspicuous expenditure bore no relation to the size or otherwise of the undergraduate population. It was also a period in which benefactors proved equally cautious with respect to founding new Chairs. Only three were founded in the whole of the century: in Arabic by Sir Thomas Adams in 1632 (the first such endowment since the foundation of the five Regius Professorships in 1540), in mathematics by Henry Lucas in 1663, and in moral philosophy by John Knightbridge in 1683.[96] Though the Restoration brought new confidence, it did not bring new wealth: the University did not become prosperous in this way until the eighteenth century.[97]

The fortunes of the town of Cambridge were inextricably linked with those of the University; but it is by no means clear what contribution the local printers and booksellers made beyond the markets provided by the colleges.[98] Outside the University's orbit, the population of the town, only modest in the mid-century, grew rapidly at the end of the century and in the first part of the next. From about 2,400 in 1563, by 1587 it had reached, according to one count, 6,490, of whom 1,500 were members of the University: this last figure was a serious under-estimate, even for members of the colleges, and many more relied on the University as servants, craftsmen or suppliers. With the population increase in the town came over-crowding, the number increasing to about 7,750 by the 1620s and to about 8,000 by 1674. Much of this increase was in the poorer parishes, away from the centre, and it seems that much of it was associated with agriculture. In other words, while the local non-University population grew, the number of those able and ready to take advantage of the presence of University Printers may not have grown very greatly.[99] As a town, rather than as a university town, Cambridge may have offered comparatively few opportunities to the ordinary book trade. But just as only the larger towns such as Cambridge could support shops whose sole or principal business was the supply of books, so these towns also, like smaller towns or villages, supported other outlets for books with which the University Printers had only a strictly limited concern – whether shops offering a side-line in the most popular literature, or the increasingly ubiquitous chapmen whose humble reading matter and other printed entertainment found its way into even the poorest of homes. One grocer's stock in the 1570s, for example, included battledores, ABCs and primers, besides other unspecified printed sheets with and without pictures, and a stock of writing paper.[100] And what was true of Cambridge was true also of other towns or villages. Specialist bookshops were few. At the end of the century, the Cumberland market town of Penrith depended on the local grocer for its supply of books,[101] and this lack of distinction between trades lasted for long after that; it was, for most places, the norm. For some books, and perhaps especially for two of the University Printers' seventeenth-century mainstays – Bibles and almanacs – many more copies were sold outside stationers' shops than were sold by the retail stationers themselves.

University Printers depended ultimately on all these outlets, whether in shops, fairs or pedlars' packs. But their disputes were not usually with those who worked at perhaps several removes from the printing shop, buying their stock through wholesalers. Instead, arguments about the division of some of the most popular, and therefore profitable, books and other publications were conducted with stationers: with the Stationers' Company and, occasionally, with the local trade.

2

The charter of 1534

Political, economic and educational demands cannot always be made to agree; but the charter granted to the University of Cambridge by Henry VIII in 1534 achieved a rare degree of harmony. It defined, and significantly extended, the University's authority in matters pertaining to the production and distribution of printed books. In the very year that the new Printing Act debarred foreigners from the book trades, it confirmed the University's need for such people. And yet, in the face of the government's commitment to centralization (a commitment that, in the book trades, was to last until the end of the seventeenth century), the charter can well be regarded as an anomaly.

It was no sudden gesture of royal generosity, or inspiration of the moment. It was, rather, the latest in a series of attempts to answer two difficulties at once: the definition of the University's authority, and the need on the part of the government to control the book trades, to establish answerable authority over stationers, booksellers and printers as well as to control the circulation of books.[1] Such needs were not altogether new. In 1409, Thomas Arundel's attack on the Wycliffite Bible, in his Constitutions of Oxford, had forbidden the circulation of English translations without their first being inspected. University studies at Oxford were constricted within the bounds set to theological discussion and the Constitutions' tight-reined insistence on licensed orthodoxy. Secular legislation, in similar vein, followed in Parliament in 1414, though the large number of surviving Wycliffite manuscripts written quite clearly at a later date, and emanating from all parts of the country, suggests that these prohibitions, both ecclesiastical and secular, were widely ignored.[2] Nonetheless, it was to Arundel's Constitutions (which remained in force until 1529)[3] that Cuthbert Tunstall, Bishop of London, turned when in October 1524 he summoned the London book trades to warn them against the importation of heretical (and therefore seditious) books.[4] Luther's books had been forbidden by Leo X in 1520. In Cambridge, the University accounts for 1520–1 include payment to Peter Cheke (father of John Cheke) of 20s. for a journey to Wolsey and the Chancellor of the University, John Fisher, 'cum literis pro operibus Lutheri'; and a little later payment of 2s. for refreshments and other expenses connected with the burning in Cambridge of Lutheran books.[5] At London, in May 1521, Fisher preached at the burning of Lutheran books in St Paul's Churchyard, a conflagration the more pointed as it took place at the very heart of the London book trade. Henry VIII's own *Assertio*, printed by Pynson, appeared in July. But while the King engaged Luther in argument, the responsibility for rooting out forbidden books lay, under the terms of the 1409 Constitutions, with the church and diocesan courts, who in turn were to be supported by the lay officers of the law: a proclamation issued by Henry VIII in October 1521 placed especial emphasis on the disciplinary difficulties faced by the Bishop of Lincoln, whose see included Oxford.[6]

Tunstall concentrated in 1524 on books printed abroad, not on those printed in England, warning the assembled stationers against the importation especially of English books printed in Germany or any other heretical Lutheran books; furthermore, they were not to import other books without reference to Wolsey, the Archbishop of Canterbury, Tunstall himself (as Bishop of London), or Fisher, Bishop of Rochester. Just over a year later, prompted by the appearance in court of Wynkyn de Worde charged with printing a translation by the stationer John Gough (who was to be in constant trouble for dealing in prohibited books) of John Ryches' *Ymage of love*, the Vicar-General extended his interest to domestic printing. In March 1525/6 Thomas Berthelet was obliged to confess that he had printed books by Fisher and Erasmus without having first shown them to any of the censors: the question was not of the books' being refused, but of failure to comply with the legally required procedures. In practice, some printers, particularly John Rastell and Richard Pynson, contrived to work under the protection of a general privilege – a protection in which they were joined in 1525/6 by Robert Redman and Berthelet himself – while others had to continue to seek their authority book by book. Tunstall again added his weight to the proceedings when in October 1526 he warned an assemblage of London booksellers, including Wynkyn de Worde, Pynson, Redman, Robert Copland, Robert Wyer, Thomas Berthelet, John Reynes and John Rastell 'that they neither themselves nor through others sell, hold, give or in any way part with any books containing Lutheran heresies or any other books conceived either in Latin or English, and that they neither print nor cause to be printed any other works whatever (except only works before approved by the Church) unless they first exhibit the same...' The booksellers were also warned against selling books printed abroad, whether in Latin or English, without, again, first exhibiting them to the appropriate authority.[7] Despite the few cases recorded in consistorial archives, the problem was a considerable one. Tunstall himself found it necessary to remind the booksellers in person yet again, in 1526, in response to a situation that threatened to get out of hand. The printing of Tyndale's New Testament had been undertaken at Cologne in 1525: no complete copy of this edition, which may indeed never have been finished, survives, but the full text was printed at Worms in the following year in an edition of three thousand copies: copies were available in England at between three and four shillings, with a wholesale price of as little as ninepence.[8] The cases brought by the Vicar-General all concerned booksellers; but the Hanse merchants and their servants proved a forum for the circulation of Lutheran books. A list of prohibited books drawn up by the Archbishop of Canterbury for the Bishop of Exeter in November 1526 included, besides Tyndale's New Testament and *Obedyence of a Christen man*, works by Luther, Hus, Zwingli, Brentius and John Frith's *Revelation of Antichrist* (of which however the earliest surviving edition dates from 1529).[9] In the diocese of Lincoln, a long-standing sympathy towards Lollards in Buckinghamshire and the Chilterns combined with the new threat of Lutheranism to cause yet further anxiety to the bishop, John Longland, who also looked with disquiet towards the North Sea ports.[10] When in 1533 Thomas More recalled the spread of heresy, and the numbers who had required punishment, the dioceses of London and Lincoln sprang first to mind:

& of those twayne fyrste to speke of Lyncoln, as great a dyocise as yt is, and as many shyres as he hath wyth in yt, yet haue I not herde of late many punyshed for heresy amonge theym all. But aboute a tenne yere ago to my remembraunce, there were in that dyocise about .xii. or fourteen abiured in one town, and at that tyme euery man that I herde speke therof, eyther in ye court or elles where, appered very glad that suche a bed of snakes was so found out and broken.[11]

The books posed a threat at the other end of the country as well. In February 1526/7 John Hackett reported from the Low Countries that forbidden books were being shipped to Edinburgh and St Andrews by Scottish merchants:[12] his investigations took him to Antwerp, Zeeland, Ghent, Bruges, Brussels, Louvain and elsewhere, and met with more success in unearthing hair-raising stories than in apprehending culprits or destroying copies.[13] By 1528 the threat was acute. While culprit after culprit was unearthed in Essex, where the ports and easy links with the underground trade in London made the circulation of Lutheran books and Tyndale's translation of the Bible relatively simple,[14] the two university towns faced difficulties little less severe. At Oxford, Thomas Garrett, one of the early Fellows of Wolsey's new foundation Cardinal College, brought two parcels of Lutheran books to sell in the University: over sixty volumes were acquired by the Prior of Reading alone.[15] Garrett made a dramatic escape from the authorities when arrested, but was recaptured, and abjured before the Bishop of London. Whilst at large, however, Garrett had managed to distribute books with considerable success, paying particular heed to those who knew Hebrew and Greek besides Latin, and approaching them under the guise of wishing to learn the scriptural languages. Garrett had been educated in Oxford, apparently initially at Corpus Christi College, and was later a Fellow of Magdalen; but suspicion also fell on John Clarke, who had been admitted at Cardinal College in 1525, had graduated at Cambridge, and who was now reading St Paul (aided by the commentary of Johann

Bugenhagen) with the young men of the College. John London, Warden of New College and an implacable conservative, was frank in his views to the Bishop of London, wishing that Wolsey had never brought either Clarke or any other Cambridge man to his 'most towardly college'. 'It was a gracious deed if they were tried and purged, and restored unto their mother from whence they came, if they be worthy to come thither again.'[16] By March, Tunstall had begun to discover the culprits among the members of the London book trade, and had approached John Gough of Fleet Street (whom he believed to be innocent), Thomas Forman, Rector of All Hallows in Honey Lane, and Forman's servant John Goodale, formerly another of Garrett's pupils. By now, Tunstall's own prisons were so full that Gough, despite his possible innocence (an impression he had made the more forcibly by providing details of the activities of one Theodoryke, an Antwerp bookseller secretly active in London) had to be accommodated, with others implicated in the trade, in the Fleet.[17]

Evidence for the importation of prohibited books pointed again and again to the Low Countries, and especially to Antwerp. But the culprits in England were, on an alarming number of occasions, either from, or influenced by, Cambridge, with its small but influential group in close contact with the German reformers. The University of which Fisher himself was Chancellor contained within it a group of men for whom the church seemed to invite criticism, and for whom criticism easily gave way to heresy. The celebrated sermon preached in St Edward's Church by Robert Barnes in 1525 was a calculated challenge to received opinions and beliefs. Barnes, friend of John Bale, was born in Norfolk, but after a period in the Augustinian priory at Cambridge had studied at the University of Louvain, before returning to Cambridge, becoming Prior, and making the house a centre for learning. Persuaded of the validity of Lutheran teaching by Thomas Bilney of Trinity Hall (likewise a Norfolk man), Barnes used his sermon on Christmas Eve 1525 to preach against both the special celebration of the great church festivals, and to attack prelatical pomp – and, it seems (the text of his sermon has not survived), that of Wolsey in particular. If he sought thereby to meet Wolsey face to face, he had his reward. Refusing to repudiate his statement when brought before the Vice-Chancellor, he was sent for trial in London, where he was aided by his fellow-Augustinian, Miles Coverdale.[18] His subsequent years were spent away from Cambridge: in the Fleet, in houses of his order in London and Northampton, in Germany, and back again in England before his immolation at Smithfield in 1540.

Barnes' self-centred, conceited and ostentatious activities were, however, at odds with those of most of the reformers actually in Cambridge. Latimer, who preached from Barnes' own usual pulpit in St Edward's Church on Christmas Eve 1525, and was likewise summoned before Wolsey, was adroit when faced with the Bishop of Ely, and abjured when the occasion demanded circumspection.[19] Bilney, for all his reforming opinions and influence as a teacher in Cambridge, was almost certainly no less cautious when he preached in the village churches of East Anglia. He, too, was charged with heresy, in 1527, at the same time as George Joye, Fellow of Peterhouse, and Thomas Arthur, Fellow of St John's and likewise from Norfolk. Bilney and Arthur both abjured, and Joye escaped to Strasburg.[20]

It is by no means clear when these, and others of like opinion, began to meet at the White Horse Inn; but they began probably in the early 1520s, while Segar Nicholson was a pensioner at Gonville Hall. Besides those mentioned in the last paragraph, there were others. Pembroke produced John Rogers, later to be martyred under Queen Mary, John Tixtill, a highly respected authority in the Divinity Schools, and Nicholas Ridley. Thomas Forman was President of Queens', and Simon Heynes was to become so in 1528. From Corpus there came William Sowode, Master from 1523, William Warner, friend of Bilney, and perhaps the young Matthew Parker.[21] 'This House [the White Horse] was chose', remarked Strype, 'because they of *King*'s College, *Queen*'s College, and St. *John*'s, might come in with the more Privacy at the Back-Door.'[22]

Forman was President of Queens' for only a few months, in 1526–8, and it may have been during this period that he secreted various Lutheran books when a search made it necessary.[23] Wolsey, meanwhile, sought to consolidate the authority of the University over selected local tradesmen, when drawn in to act as arbitrator (under the terms of the covenant of 1503)[24] between town and University. In 1523–4 the University paid 20d. 'to one that dyd emblase my lorde cardynalles armes vppon our lettres off lybertyes', and 3s.4d. 'to M. Kyng for wrytyng the sayd lettres twyse ynk velam and labowres'.[25] In 1503 it had been stated, among much more, that 'Stacioners, lymners, Schryveners, Parchment-makers, Boke-bynders … [etc.] shall be reputed & taken as common Ministers & Servants of the said Universitie … & shall have & enjoye lyke privilege as a Scholers Servant of the same Universitie shall have & enjoie.' As such they were, if they committed an offence, under the jurisdiction of the University. Wolsey's confirmation of the 1503 agreement added nothing new; but it was a reminder that in Cambridge at least the University was responsible for the control of the book trade.[26] It was also a reminder of his interest in the University. He had founded Cardinal College at Oxford in 1525, and had thought it appropriate – however misguided the exercise proved – to import much of the first Fellowship from Cambridge. His visit to Cambridge in 1520, so unwelcome to some, had been made memorable by the speech of Henry Bullock, President of Queens': 'Scarcely from the obsequious senators of Tiberius and Domitian did the incense of flattery rise in denser volume or coarser fumes', commented Mullinger from the security of late Victorian Cambridge.[27] Two years later, in 1523, he had refused to appoint a commission to seek out Lutheran sympathisers in the University.[28] For its part, the University was more than equal to the task of manufacturing the requisite flattery.[29] Like his handling of Barnes a few months later, and like his response to the demands of Richard Nykke, Bishop of Norwich, for sterner measures, Wolsey's treatment of the University was above all politic, to impose orthodoxy not by force, but by argument and, if possible, agreement. The University as an institution seemed a more powerful ally than those who met at the White Horse seemed a threat; yet to have broken up the latter would have been to risk losing the support of those who, like Barnes, were heretical but no enemies of the order of government. Wolsey was astute enough to license Latimer to preach, in the face of the Bishop of Ely, and his jealousy of the diocesan bishops was to bear further fruit for the University in 1528–9. A dispute between the University and Robert Clyffe, Chancellor to Nicholas West, Bishop of Ely, over Clyffe's excommunication of a member of St Bernard's Hostel led not only to the University in turn excommunicating Clyffe, but also to Wolsey's ordering him to submit to the University's authority, even to receive absolution from the Vice-Chancellor.[30] Episcopal authority could not be held to apply within the University. The Clyffe affair was among the last challenges in a battle that had lasted for three hundred years, and of a kind that was by no means restricted to Cambridge.[31] In itself, it had nothing directly to do with the book trade; but in that much of the argument during the 1520s (as, indeed, for decades to come) stemmed from the need to define the boundaries of secular and ecclesiastical authority, its timing was not without significance. As so often, while the book trade and its principal activities, printing, binding and bookselling, seemed to follow their own sequence of self-reliant processes, they also reflected and depended in their own way on considerations of wider note: in this instance religious and political, but in others economic or social. Set within the context of the struggle for authority between ecclesiastical and university power, the charter granted to Cambridge in 1534 was confirmation of the University's prerogative.

Most of the conflict over Lutheran books and Tyndale's New Testament (linked together in the minds of many as but two aspects of the same danger) took place in ecclesiastical courts. As if to emphasize this, a synod of the diocese of Ely held at Barnwell, just outside Cambridge, in June 1528, forbade incumbents and curates (but, noticeably, not all clergy) to use the English translations of the scriptures.[32] Moreover, by 1529 both Wolsey and the king were anxious to secure the Pope's agreement to free both the universities, besides their respective towns, from episcopal authority.[33] For the University, however, the question was increasingly one of jurisdiction. The privileges of members of the University, and the degree to which they were answerable to the municipal authorities, were subjects of lively debate, requiring constant appeal to higher opinion. In this, the various classes of local tradesmen, and particularly those on whose services the University most depended, presented an especially complicated series of questions. Hard on the heels of victory in the affair over Clyffe, the University presented its case for bringing within its own control the bookselling and stationers' trades in Cambridge, but on its own terms. By the same letter in which it expressed to Wolsey its appreciation for his handling of Clyffe, the University pointed out the current inclinations towards heresy, and asked that there should be but three booksellers in Cambridge, under its own control: 'homines probos atque graves', who should neither adventure nor sell books without permission from the University authorities, or 'censores'.[34]

The petition went further. In a university that no doubt realized all too clearly the dangers of seeming to harbour heretics (it is noticeable that, with very few exceptions, attacks were on individuals rather than identified corporate groups), the need to be seen to be attacking heresy was paramount. And despite local inclinations the Chancellor of the University, John Fisher, was a conservative. This apart, however, the University also needed to plead a special case if it was to preserve the well-being of just those local foreign booksellers who were best able to supply from the continent the texts which teaching, learning and the curriculum required. The University's appeal to Wolsey is undated, but it was presented either in March 1528 or the first few weeks of 1529. Its timing was critical. By a statute of 1523, the trading activities of foreigners had been severely restricted throughout the country save in Oxford and Cambridge: the legislation was not entirely new, and had its origins in an act passed in 1484.[35] It was moreover part of a general policy, not one restricted to the printing, book-binding and bookselling trades, to encourage home-based production and thus to cut imports and provide work for the English poor.[36] In February 1528/9 the Star Chamber, faced with a case brought against some Flemings, confirmed the broad outlines of the law as it stood, and, again, effectively exempted the two universities.[37] There was thus a very practical advantage for foreigners in Cambridge trades to shelter under the University's wing, while for its part the University was anxious that its servants should be able to continue to deal as before. 'Quos tum bibliopolas, quoniam e re nostra magis erit, Alienigenas esse, sic enim consuletur librorum pretiis, summe credimus necessarium, illâ uti libertate et immunitate gaudere, quibus indigenae tui fruuntur, ita provinciali jure donati, ut Londini aliisque regni huius emporiis, ab exteris negotiatoribus libros emere possint.'[38]

It is unlikely that those who drew up the appeal did not have three specific candidates in mind. It is not so clear who all these candidates were; but it is reasonable to suppose that they included Nicholas Spierinck and Garrett Godfrey, as the most prominent of the local stationers.

Of these two, the better connected (at least in professional terms) was probably Spierinck, member of a numerous family with a disconcertingly limited choice of Christian names. The family came originally from Zwijndrecht, a village on the Scheldt near Antwerp, and by the end of the fifteenth century it had built up extensive and important links in the book trade: members were to be found as far apart as Lille, Bruges, Audenarde,

Antwerp and Lyons.[39] Some, such as the artist who signed a number of manuscripts between 1486 and 1519, and who came perhaps from Haarlem, were illuminators.[40] One, Jan Spierinc, from the diocese of Cambrai, was Professor in the Faculty of Medicine at the University of Louvain at the end of the century. Nicholas Spierinck's father Claes came from the diocese of Tournai, but it is not known when Nicholas, whose relatives included the powerful Cologne bookseller Arnold Birckman, moved to England. On 2 September 1505 he imported through the port of London printed books to the value of ten pounds;[41] and he made his first appearance in the Cambridge records in the University's Grace Book for 1505–6: 'recepti pro appellacione Nicholai stationarii pro uxore sua … xij*d*.'[42]

By then, Garrett Godfrey had been in the town for at least three or four years. Much less is known of Godfrey's kinsmen: the name may, as Gray suggests, have been an anglicization; in the surviving records he is more frequently cited as Garrard(e), Gerrard, Garret, or Garreit. Like Spierinck, he was described as a 'Ducheman', and it seems likely that he came from Gratem, a village in the province of Limburg a little to the west of Roermond.[43] The earliest record of his presence at Cambridge dates from 11 July 1502, when he and sixty-five others were named in a covenant designed to preserve peace between the University and the town by assigning to various tradesmen the same University privileges enjoyed by scholars: the fact that Godfrey's name appeared last may suggest that he was only recently arrived.[44] Between then and ten years later nothing more is known of him. But by the mid-1520s the two men, Spierinck and Godfrey, had become the principal stationers in Cambridge and prominent among the townsfolk. Godfrey served as churchwarden of Great St Mary's, the University Church, in 1516–17 and again in 1521–2. On each occasion he was succeeded by Spierinck. No one gave more than Godfrey (though three equalled him) when in 1518 a fund was organized for 'the Stoles in the Body of the Chirche';[45] and both men became friends of Erasmus, who seems to have lodged with Godfrey for a while.

Of the other known stationers in Cambridge in the late 1520s, the most substantial was Peter Bright, who had been in the town since at least 1515/16, when he had crossed with John Lenton of Queens':[46] since he left in his will the sum of 6s.8d. to the church at Holwell, on the boundary of Hertfordshire and Bedfordshire, and 20d. to the poor of the same parish, he may have come from there, but he lived, at least in his later years, in St Sepulchre's parish in Cambridge. By the time of his death in January 1545/6 he was a widower, and apart from various personal bequests left instructions that his house was to be sold and his moveable property to be distributed amongst his kinsfolk. By 1545 his trade had clearly prospered, for he lived in a substantial house with six bedrooms, comfortably furnished and equipped with a considerable assortment of plate. In view of the quantity of wines in his cellar, it has been suggested that he had become a vintner.[47] By then, however, he had clearly retired from his living as stationer, his occupation in 1527 when he took a lease from St John's College for a garden abutting on the King's Ditch.[48] Nothing whatever is known of the details of his trade, though it is worth remark that, unlike Garrett Godfrey or Spierinck, he was a native Englishman. So, too, was Richard Lychefylde, of the parish of Great St Mary's, who died in 1544, a little over a year before Bright, but who left a considerably smaller estate,[49] while virtually nothing is known of one 'Leonard of Christ's College', who was paid the substantial sum of twenty shillings by the churchwardens of Holy Trinity in 1527–8 for repairing an antiphoner and organ book.[50] The only other stationers whose names are known are Nicholas Pilgrim, also a 'ducheman', who worked with Godfrey until he succeeded to his business in 1539, and Segar Nicholson, a man who achieved some notoriety outside his ordinary livelihood and who became the third of the first three University Printers.

Nicholson was described in Godfrey's will as his 'cousin', a term that may have meant no more than reasonably close relative. He was born in Maastricht, and was younger than either Godfrey or Spierinck. Like Godfrey, he anglicized his name: in 1530 the Queens' College bursars' accounts still refer to him as Cegart;[51] a little later the Proctors' accounts refer to 'Sygar'; and when in 1565 his son came to be apprenticed to the London printer William Seres he in turn was noted in the records of the Stationers' Company as 'Benjamin Nycholas alias Seger'. Segar was the only one of the three stationers eventually appointed under the charter of 1534 who is known to have been registered as a student at a Cambridge college. In 1520 he entered Gonville Hall as a pensioner, where he remained for three years.[52] It is not clear whether or not this marked his arrival in Cambridge. The College had no regular connections with the Low Countries, but of all the Cambridge houses it was closest to the geographical centre of the University – and closest also to the University's book trades. Johann Lair, or Siberch, established his press in Cambridge probably at the end of 1520, within a few months of Segar's entering Gonville Hall and in a house only just outside its gateway, while both Spierinck and Godfrey lived in the parish of Great St Mary's. It is not impossible that Godfrey, Segar's relative, encouraged his 'cousin' to come to Cambridge for part of his education, and saw him enrolled in the college closest at hand.

At Gonville Hall, of which the conservative Richard Nykke, Bishop of Norwich, was in 1530 to write to Archbishop William Warham, 'I here no clerk that hath commen ought lately of that College but saverith of the frying panne tho he speke never so holely';[53] Segar found himself in a community with distinctly – and, as it transpired, dangerously – reforming opinions. Many of the college's junior members came from the Cluniac priory of Lewes or its dependencies, but the Fellows included Edward Crome, friend of Hugh Latimer and Thomas Bilney, Nicholas Shaxton, who narrowly escaped the stake in the last months of the reign of Henry VIII, John Skipp, an accomplished preacher, reviser of the Epistle to the Hebrews for the Bible of

1540, chaplain to Anne Boleyn and part author of the *Institution of a Christian man* (1537), and Simon Smith, likewise a friend of Latimer and an early exponent of marriage for the clergy. A few years later, Skipp was to decline the invitation to a fellowship at Cardinal College, Oxford; but Godfrey Harman, who came as a scholar to the college in the year before Nicholson arrived as a pensioner, did move to Oxford, whence his violent Lutheran views made his departure inevitable.[54]

Amongst so many dissidents, Nicholson found kindred spirits. There is no record of his graduating, and it is not impossible that his matriculation was an act of convenience for a newly arrived foreigner who in fact quickly found a niche in the local book trade. It is not clear when he was finally imprisoned, and in the absence of all but circumstantial evidence it can only be presumed that it was for circulating forbidden books. In 1530–1 the University spent a modest sum on burning such books ('Item pro facibus libros comburendos iiij^d'), and rather more on proceedings for heresy against Segar himself. The eight shillings paid to Edward Haynes suggests that the case involved considerable paper work,[55] while the university servant charged with Segar's custody 'in carcere tempore examinationis' received 2s.4d.[56] For at least a part of his imprisonment (perhaps as little as four or five days), Segar was in the hands of Sir Thomas More, though More afterwards denied the tales circulated by Tyndale that Segar had been bound to a tree in More's garden, beaten, and also 'bounden about the hed wyth a corde & wrengen, that he fell downe dede in a swowne', and that More stole his purse to boot.[57] For a time he was held also by one Hubberdine, to whom Latymer complained in a now incomplete and undated letter, 'Do ye not hold Nicolson, Smyth, Patmore, and Philips, with many other, in prison, yet at this howre.'[58] Like Tyndale, Foxe too was ready to broadcast accounts of the ill treatment Segar received;[59] but none of these details provides any evidence of the period for which he was incarcerated: perhaps his freedom came with More's resignation as Lord Chancellor in May 1532.

Nicholson is an elusive figure in the events of 1529–34. If he was one of three stationers anxious to promote their interests in 1529, he was a dangerous – or perhaps simply unlucky – partner. And if he was one of the three, he must have been arrested subsequently. In any case, his business and reputation as a reliable bookseller must have recovered very quickly, for he was included in the fresh negotiations leading up to the charter of 1534. Meanwhile, however, in 1529, nothing came of the appeal to Wolsey, and it was five years before the University was to gain its point, in very different circumstances. With More's accession to power, the suppression of heresy became sometimes synonymous with press censorship. Of two proclamations framed in 1529–30, that issued in June 1530 railed specifically against 'blasphemous and pestiferous English books' printed abroad, concentrated on the work of Tyndale, Simon Fish and John Frith, and, while holding out the hope of a new translation of the Bible by 'great, learned and Catholic persons', also ordered copies of existing translations to be surrendered.[60] Among those who were caught trading in forbidden books, George Constantine (who had taken his degree as Bachelor of Civil Law at Cambridge in 1523/4) was arrested late in 1531; on Constantine's information Richard Bayfield, a monk from Bury St Edmunds much influenced by Barnes and who had successfully landed books in Colchester, Norfolk and London, was finally taken.[61] Both were examined by More. In the burning of Thomas Bilney at Norwich in 1531, the University lost one of its most talented theologians, as well as a leader of the White Horse circle.[62] Nicholas Shaxton, of Gonville Hall, had played a careful game, as one of the commissioners appointed by the Vice-Chancellor to join with a similar group from Oxford and whose deliberations helped form the proclamation of June 1530. He was, moreover, one of the University commissioners whose report on the King's marriage to Catherine of Aragon had, after some pressure, so met with the royal hopes.[63] But with pastoral duties in the diocese of Norwich, he, like Bilney, came under the jurisdiction of Nykke, who forced him to renounce Lutheran heresies. Shaxton narrowly escaped the flames.

The political events of these years – first Wolsey's and then More's downfall, the rise of Cromwell, the death of William Warham in 1532 and the consecration in 1533 of Thomas Cranmer as Archbishop of Canterbury, the annulment of Henry VIII's marriage to Catherine of Aragon and his marriage to Anne Boleyn – shaped the scene in which the limits, dangers and opportunities of the book trade were brought sharply into focus. During the 1520s, the authorities, both lay and ecclesiastical, ultimately found it impossible to contain the spread of English Testaments or of Lutheran and other heretical literature. The proclamations issued during More's chancellorship, in 1530, heralded a new approach to censorship, and introduced measures of a kind already familiar on the continent. 'It was as if More despaired of the bishops' stamina against literate heretics… He had erected an *Index librorum prohibitorum*, and had empowered himself to enforce it in Star Chamber by virtue of the Council's interest… powers to punish breaches of proclamation. It was, in fact, the beginning of Star Chamber's censorship jurisdiction.'[64] More's instincts were repressive.[65] Those of his successor demonstrated a more imaginative understanding of the implications of the printing press, though considerable energy had in fact already been given to printed propaganda from 1530 onwards. Led by Thomas Cromwell, the government was to turn the printing press to its advantage, and conduct an energetic and successful propaganda campaign to promote the new order.[66]

The events of the 1520s had made it plain that control of illicitly circulated books was only possible to a very limited extent; but whereas the emphasis then had been on those aspects of the trade concerned with circulation and sale, in the early 1530s far more attention was paid to the production – and therefore printing – of books. In the list of books printed by the King's Printer, Thomas

Berthelet, who succeeded Richard Pynson in 1530, a clear political thread is to be found, just as a lesser, and more conservative, one can be seen among the plays and other works printed by William Rastell, nephew of Thomas More. The fundamental differences between bookselling and book production could not have been more plain, and they were made clearer still by the June 1530 proclamation ordering that no theological book in English was to be printed until it had been approved by the bishop of the diocese:[67] so far as possible, censorship was to be imposed before production and publication, not after.

Officially, Henry VIII's position in the early 1530s was put forward in a series of documents printed by Thomas Berthelet the royal printer,[68] while his case was given further support by the aged Christopher St Germain, whose most popular work proved to be the two *Dialogues* between a doctor of divinity and a student of the laws of England, which appeared for the first time in English (the first had already been published anonymously in Latin in 1528) from the presses of Robert Wyer and Peter Treveris in 1530–1: further editions of the *Dialogues* appeared regularly throughout the sixteenth and early seventeenth centuries.[69] These official and semi-official publications, presenting arguments concerning the break with Rome in English as well as in Latin, appeared during the same period that produced a series of Erasmian books and translations – a phenomenon not discouraged, if not actually sponsored, by Cromwell.[70] None of Tyndale's books had been hitherto printed in England, but he was probably responsible for the first published translation of Erasmus' *Enchiridion militis christiani*, printed by Wynkyn de Worde in 1533, and frequently republished thereafter.[71] But while publications of this kind thrived, the appearance of books antagonistic to Henry VIII's policies was a reminder that the voice of conservatism had not died. More resigned in May 1532, following the clergy's submission to the King, yet in the same year Rastell printed More's *Confutacyon of Tyndale's answere*,[72] as well as sermons by John Fisher. In 1533 further of More's works were printed by Rastell, including his *Apologye*, and his *Dialoge of comfort against tribulacion* was published by Tottel in the same year.

In this context, the *Act for printers and binders of books*, of 1533/4 (25 Henry VIII c. 15) was intended primarily for the protection of the English book trades, so much swelled since the admission of aliens to these activities under 1 Richard III c. 9, 'by force of which provisyon there hath comen into this Realme sithen the makyn of the same a marveylous nombre of prynted bokes and dayly doth'. In the years after the passing of the 1533/4 act, few aliens found it profitable to continue.[73] The trade was not only concentrated to the advantage of Englishmen; its members, who could no longer be aliens, were thus subject to English law. What was ostensibly a protective measure for booksellers was also a means of controlling the press. It was an arrangement that had an obvious attractiveness for the established native trade, and one which was to be epitomized in the charter granted to the Stationers' Company

Fig. 1 Letters Patent granted to the University by Henry VIII in 1534, giving permission to appoint three stationers or printers, and to print 'omnimodos libros', or all manner of books.

in 1557, whereby no one might print books unless he was a member of that Company.

This somewhat lengthy excursus into the early sixteenth-century English book trade provides the context of the charter granted to the University by Henry VIII in 1534 (see fig. 1). The government and conduct of the book trades in Britain were assuming a radically different appearance, while on the other hand the University's pronouncements on the royal divorce, and its determination against papal supremacy, were not only proofs of its political acumen. They also lent credibility to its political reliability.

The Letters Patent, on 20 July that year, came in a summer during which the country accustomed itself to a new queen, Anne Boleyn, to the Oath required under the Succession Act, to the Oath of Supremacy denying papal authority, and to the imprisonment in the Tower of London of More and Fisher. The

Treason Act, making the denial of royal supremacy high treason, was passed the following November. A fresh translation of the New Testament, commissioned by Cranmer, was under way by the end of the year.[74] Amidst this concatenation of reform, the implications of the powers, part new and part confirmatory (in the allusion to *alienigeni*) of the status quo, was a delegation of trust and a mark of reward, no less remarkable for being granted when the University's own Chancellor, Fisher, to whom these powers were delegated, was in prison.

In one respect, the charter was simply one further clarification of the University's privileges, awarded as it was in the same month that John Edmunds, Master of Peterhouse, and William Buckmaster, Lady Margaret's Professor of Divinity and Fellow of the same college, successfully appealed at Lambeth before the Lord Chancellor, the Archbishop of Canterbury and others for the right to hold a civil court at Stourbridge Fair.[75] In another respect, it was an extension to the control of the book trade: a development of the censorship arrangements contained in the proclamations of the previous years. In bestowing upon the University authorities the power to approve books for printing or for sale (whether printed at home or abroad), it both enshrined provision for the specific needs of the University and designated the powers hitherto exercised more by the ecclesiastical and metropolitical authorities. Only that spring, the Mayor of Cambridge had courted the stranger community in the town, exhorting them to become freemen.[76] If Spierinck and the other *alienigeni* were tempted, they chose in the end to pursue the legislation that was to grant them independence not under a corporation, but under the University. Specifically, the three 'Stacionarii sive impressores librorum' were now to be governed by the Chancellor or by his vice-gerent and three doctors. The consequences of this can hardly have been foreseen; and certainly there is no hint in the charter that any thought was given to the possible effect on the London trade. Moreover, the charter specifically authorized the stationers or printers to exhibit their books for sale both within the University and in the country at large. For the stationers of Cambridge, it was of more immediate importance that the University could elect either foreigners or natives with equal propriety, so long as those elected paid all taxes and other dues.

The charter, granted on 20 July 1534, read as follows:[77]

Henricus Dei Gratiâ Angliae et Franciae Rex, Fidei Defensor et Dominus Hiberniae, Omnibus ad quos praesentes Litterae pervenerint Salutem. Sciatis quod nos de Gratiâ nostra speciali, ac ex certa Scientia et mero Motu nostris concessimus et Licentiam damus pro nobis et Heredibus nostris dilectis nobis in Christo Cancellario Magistris et Scholaribus Universitatis nostrae Cantebrigiae, Quod ipsi et Successores sui in perpetuum per eorum Scripta sub Sigillo Cancellarii dictae Universitatis sigillata, de tempore in tempus, assignent, eligant, et pro perpetuo habeant inter se et infra Universitatem nostram praedictam perpetuo manentes et inhabitantes tres Stationarios et Librorum Impressores seu Venditores tam alienigenos et natos extra Obedientiam nostram, quam Indigenos nostros et natos infra Obedientiam nostram, tam conductitias quam proprias Domus habentes et tenentes. Qui quidem Stationarii sive Impressores Librorum in Forma praedictâ assignati, et eorum quilibet, omnimodos Libros, per dictum Cancellarium vel eius Vices gerentem, et tres Doctores ibidem approbatos seu in posterum approbandos, ibidem imprimere, et tam Libros illos, quam alios Libros ubicunque, tam extra quam infra Regnum nostrum impressos sic, ut praedicitur, per praedictum Cancellarium seu eius Vicem gerentem et tres Doctores ibidem approbatos seu approbandos tam in eadem Universitate quam alibi infra Regnum nostrum ubicunque placuerint, Venditioni exponere licitè valeant seu valeat et impunè. Et quod iidem Stationarii sive Impressores etiam extra Obedientiam nostram oriundi, ut praedicitur, et eorum quilibet, quamdiu infra Universitatem praedictam Moram traxerint, et Negotio praedicto intendant, in omnibus et per omnia tanquam fideles Subditi et Legei nostri reputentur habeantur et pertractentur, et quilibet eorum reputetur, habeatur, et pertracetur; ac omnibus et singulis Libertatibus, Consuetudinibus, Legibus et Privilegiis gaudere, et uti valeant, et quilibet eorum valeat liberè et quietè prout aliquis fidelis Subditus et Legeus noster quoquo Modo uti et gaudere possit, ac Lottum, Scottum, Taxam, Tallagium, et alias Consuetudines et Impositiones quascunque non alitèr nec alio Modo quam ceteri fideles Subditi et Legei nostri solvunt et contribuunt, solvant et contribuant: aliquo Statuto, Actu, Ordinatione sive Provisione inde in contrarium facto, edito, sive proviso in aliquo non obstante. Proviso sempèr quòd dicti Stationarii sive Impressores extra Obedientiam nostram sic, ut praemittitur, oriundi, omnia et omnimoda Custumias, Subsidia, et alios Denarios pro Rebus et Merchandizis suis extra vel infra Regnum nostrum educendis vel inducendis, nobis debita, de tempore in tempus solvent, prout Alienigenae nobis solvunt et non alitèr. In Cuius Rei testimonium has Literas nostras fieri fecimus patentes. Teste meipso apud Westm. 20° Die Iulii, An. Reg. 26°.

Henry VIII, by the grace of God King of England and France, Defender of the Faith, and Lord of Ireland, To all to whom these present letters may come, greeting. Know ye that we of our special grace, and by our certain knowledge and mere motion, have granted and given licence, and by these presents grant and give licence, for ourselves and our heirs, to our beloved in Christ the Chancellor, Masters, and Scholars of our University of Cambridge, That they and their successors for ever may, by their writings under the seal of the Chancellor of the said University, from time to time assign, appoint and in perpetuity have among them, and perpetually remaining and dwelling within our aforesaid University, Three Stationers and Printers or Sellers of Books, both aliens born outside our obedience and natives born within our obedience, having and holding houses both leased [?] and owned. These Stationers or Bookprinters, assigned in the aforesaid manner, and any of them, shall have lawful and incontestable power to print there all manner of books approved, or hereafter to be approved, by the aforesaid Chancellor or his deputy and three doctors there; and also to exhibit for sale, as well in the same University as elsewhere in our realm, wherever they please, all such books and all other books wherever printed, both within and outside our realm, approved or to be approved (as aforesaid) by the said Chancellor or his deputy and three doctors there. And that the same Stationers or Printers born (as is aforesaid) outside our obedience, and every of them, for as long as they dwell in the aforesaid University and occupy themselves in the aforesaid business, shall in all things and by everyone be reputed, taken and treated as our faithful subjects and lieges, and each of them shall be so reputed, taken and treated. And they shall be entitled to enjoy and use all and singular liberties, customs, laws and privileges, and each of them shall be so entitled, freely and quietly, such as any faithful subject and liege in any manner can use and enjoy. And they shall pay and render Lot and Scot, taxes, tallages, and all other customs and impositions none otherwise and in no other manner than our own faithful subjects and lieges pay and render to us; any statute, act, ordinance or provision made, published or provided to the contrary notwithstanding. Provided always, that the said Stationers or Printers so born (as is premised) outside our obedience shall pay to us all and all manner of customs, subsidies and other monies owing to us from time to time for their goods and merchandise to be exported from or imported into our realm, in such wise as aliens pay us and not otherwise. In testimony of which matter we have caused these our letters to be made patent. Witness myself, at Westminster, the 20th day of July, in the 26th year of our reign [1534].

So, in the summer of 1534, the University promoted a Grace that at once took advantage of the King's recent grant, and made clear that this had been obtained 'at the procuratyon and costes' of Spierinck, Godfrey and Nicholson.[78] It was one of several Graces that year and in the adjoining years that had to do with University reform and, particularly, the defence of University privilege and jurisdiction. But it made no mention of printing, and two generations were to pass before the University turned its attention seriously to what it had acquired almost incidentally.

3

University stationers, 1534–1583

The Letters Patent of 1534 were thus prompted partly by policy, partly by expediency and partly by the needs of booksellers and their customers; but not by the needs of printers. A decade and more previously, the first press at Cambridge had proved abortive: a private venture to which the University was persuaded to advance a loan, but not one in any way to be accounted official or institutional.[1] Johannes Lair, born near Siegburg, to the south-east of Cologne, had spent several years in the lower Rhine valley, in the southern Low Countries, and in travel to Leipzig, before he was persuaded to settle at Cambridge as a printer. His acquaintances made as a bookseller, moving among an international circle of humanists, had been beguiling, while his wife's family connections with the Cologne printers and publishing family of Birckman lent further encouragement and inducement.[2]

But Siberch's authors had perhaps more faith in the viability of his enterprise than had Siberch himself. He came to Cambridge in 1520 or 1521 already provided with an edition of Richard Croke's *Introductio in rudimenta graeca* printed for him at Cologne by Eucharius Cervicornus; and in the following months he continued to print largely for the group of Cambridge humanists among whom Croke was a prominent and influential member. Henry Bullock's *pièce d'occasion*, the *Oratio* for Wolsey's visit to the University in 1520, was followed by a curious amalgam of astrology and St Augustine, a brief translation by Bullock from Lucian, and a sermon by the twelfth-century Archbishop of Canterbury, Baldwin. The very diversity of subject matter suggests the work of a man who was easily swayed by others' enthusiasm, at least as much as by commercial awareness. But with the unauthorized edition of Erasmus' *De conscribendis epistolis*, which would normally have been published by Froben, Erasmus' usual printer in Basel, Siberch took a desperate risk in attempting to increase his income with the work of a well known and respected writer, and a popular subject. Not surprisingly, the edition drew a stinging rebuke from Erasmus himself, who countered Siberch in the most practical way possible: with a revised (indeed, rewritten) text printed by Froben.[3] The Erasmus marks a break in Siberch's output. It was followed by two major works: the first edition of Linacre's new translation of Galen's *De temperamentis*, and Sir Thomas Elyot's *Hermathena*, characterized by Gold-schmidt as 'the most explicit manifesto of the humanist movement issued in England'.[4] But these were accompanied by other books, in which Siberch surely hoped for a yet wider market: a Latin grammar prepared by William Lily and Erasmus originally for St Paul's School and much reprinted both in England and on the continent from its first appearance, and a prognostication (in English this time) of disasters to be expected in 1524. Among the last books to be printed by Siberch in Cambridge was a yet further departure, in the Scottish poet Alexander Barclay's *First ecloge*, originally printed by Wynkyn de Worde in about 1515.

It is unlikely that all of Siberch's output is known. Only fragments survive of Barclay, just as they do for an indulgence for a nunnery at Stamford in Lincolnshire and of a letter of confraternity for another unidentified religious house. Work of this everyday kind, as for many another printer, offered a necessary path to money with little expenditure and little risk: the market was assured, and the commitment small.

It also seems doubtful that Siberch was still in Cambridge at the end of 1524. His wife dead, he returned to the continent, possibly to Antwerp, probably to Cologne, and certainly to his home town of Siegburg, where he was to die in 1554. His press at Cambridge had not been a wholehearted success, and it certainly had not demonstrated that a living could be made in this way in a small university town, even within the context of international humanism. In the case of all but the books by Galen, Erasmus, Lily and Barclay, Siberch's editions were the only ones to be published in the sixteenth century. The Galen, a standard text, was printed again, this time in a folio edition, by Simon de Colines in Paris in 1523; but no other English printer thought it necessary to reprint the work by itself.

In 1534 there had apparently been no press outside London since John Scolar's brief link with Abingdon Abbey in 1528.[5] Despite the extreme rarity of the surviving books and fragments, it seems all but certain that more printing was done in provincial centres than is now known – perhaps even substantially more. A press is known from documentary evidence to have been working in Canterbury in 1536, though little is clear about its output.[6] It is improbable that between 1525 and 1534 Thomas Rychard printed nothing at his press in Tavistock, though nothing dated between these two years is now known. In 1534 there was also a more local press towards which the newly appointed university stationers at Cambridge could look if they wished. John Lydgate's translation of the life of St Alban, produced by John Hereford at St Albans in that year, marked the beginning of a brief renaissance of printing at the abbey, in which the most remarkable book to be published was a breviary after the local use, and which ended, amidst suggestions of heresy, with the dissolution of the abbey in 1539. Unlike the first St Albans press, which had had some links with Cambridge, Hereford's books show no signs of any connection with the University. His work was prompted and supported by the abbey, and remained an isolated phenomenon, possible only because of the abbey's great wealth. These sporadic and isolated presses, the fruit of local enthusiasms and individual enterprise, did not amount to a movement. A successful press depends on an adequate market, and in the 1530s there was no sign of the requisite conditions. Several reasons may be advanced for the Cambridge charter of 1534 speaking specifically of printing, as well as of stationers. Widely scattered or not, local presses – elsewhere as well as in Cambridge – were becoming familiar. It is not impossible that the king himself regarded Cambridge as a possible ally in the propaganda war. Other university towns on the continent had long had presses (though there had been none at Oxford since 1519–20). More importantly, however, as it was to prove, the Cambridge authorities were given independence from other legislation respecting examination or licence for printing, and hence of much which ensued. The immediate effect of the 1534 charter was to protect the University from the effects of legislation against non-native stationers, and thus to preserve its vital links with the continental trade. But the wording of the charter, as generous in its inclusiveness ('omnimodos libros') as it was scrupulous in determining precisely where responsibility lay (in the Chancellor of the University or his deputy and three doctors) suggests that printing was included after careful deliberation.

Such were not circumstances designed to encourage printing in Cambridge after 1534. The University's Chancellor, John Fisher, was dead. But even under Thomas Cromwell, his successor, the principal local booksellers, Spierinck, Godfrey and Nicholson, were in no position to break into the now well-established London trade with controversial or propagandist literature. The attacks on the religious houses in the 1530s, and the break with Rome, heralded the collapse of a lucrative market for indulgences. But most important of all, only London had either the wealth, population or trade connections to support the necessarily continuous and repetitive output of the press. And London itself did not compete with the products of the learned press overseas, from which Cambridge (like other institutions of learning, whether schools or Oxford) had for years drawn its supply of essential texts in Latin or, gradually, Greek. The right of the University to print was one to be treasured, but it was of no apparent commercial value whatever.[7]

It is difficult to compute the size of the University in the mid-1530s, and with it the size of the largest part of the local book-buying population. Between 1525 and 1544 the average number of those taking degrees, at all levels, remained at just over seventy-eight per annum, the annual numbers varying between 101 in 1533 and seventy-four in 1541, with a minimum of fifty-seven in 1536, the first year after the injunctions of Henry VIII and thanks largely to the absence in that year of any candidates as Bachelor of either Canon or Civil Law.[8] Of the fifteen colleges, including the Benedictine house of Buckingham College, by far the richest was King's, with an annual income of over £751 in 1535 and consisting in 1545/6 of a Warden and thirty-two Fellows. King's Hall, which was to be suppressed in 1546 on the foundation of Trinity College, had a larger fellowship still, but an income of only about two-sevenths that of King's. The most recent foundation, St John's, had an income in 1535 of over £507, and in 1545/6 supported a Master and thirty-seven Fellows: in 1547 Roger Ascham claimed that the college had over 170 resident members in all.[9] Trinity Hall and St Catharine's, with but three Fellows each in 1545/6, were both tiny and extremely poor.[10] This potential market for books, by the 1540s so small with respect to the colleges, had once been swelled by the religious houses. The Augustinian Friars, near the east end of St Bene't's church, the Dominicans (on the site of Emmanuel College), and the Franciscans (on the site of Sidney Sussex College) formed the largest groups within the town, far outnumbering the tiny houses of the Gilbertines and the Carmelites, while the house of the Augustinian Canons at Barnwell, a little to the east, was both in the country and yet close enough to be considered a part of the local population. Beyond Cambridge, the local booksellers could look to Ely, the port of King's Lynn, Huntingdon, Peterborough and Norwich. Apart from these permanent centres of population, they could also look to the fairs, particularly to the annual Midsummer Fair and the much greater September fair at Stourbridge Common.[11] The direct impact of the Stourbridge Fair on the book trade within Cambridge itself in the early sixteenth century is obscure, and by the end of the century it was at least as important for some parts of the London trade; but as the occasion in the year which more than any other set Cambridge in the centre of a web of national and international trading it took an increasingly influential hold on local booksellers, no less so for being seasonal and for emphasizing the more popular books and the second-hand market.

At least for its teaching and other academic needs, the University in the early sixteenth century had little need even of London printers. The standard texts of the unreformed arts curriculum, by Duns Scotus, Peter Lombard, Thomas Aquinas, the legal texts of Justinian and the Decretals, and the medical texts of Galen, Philaretus and Theophilus were all printed regularly at Paris, Basel and Venice. Donatus and Terence were printed in Cologne and the southern Low Countries as well as in London. Of the surviving books known to have been bound in Cambridge by Garrett Godfrey and Nicholas Spierinck after about 1520 (to go no further) the overwhelming majority are from abroad, particularly from Paris, Basel and the lower Rhine valley. The exceptions, books printed in London, are so few as to be worth recording: two schoolbooks, printed by Wynkyn de Worde and Pynson in 1521,[12] a copy of Cuthbert Tunstall's *De arte supputandi* (1522),[13] Thomas Linacre's *De emendata structura Latini sermonis* (1524),[14] a copy of the conclusions of the French and Italian universities on Henry VIII's marriage to Catherine of

Aragon, printed by Berthelet,[15] and the first edition (1531) of Thomas Elyot's *Governour*.[16]

Of these surviving books in Cambridge bindings, scarcely any came from Venice: among the few examples known to me in the period between about 1520 and the deaths of Godfrey and Spierinck are a copy of the Hebrew concordance printed by Bomberg in 1524, bound by Godfrey, and the 1525 Aldine edition of Galen in Greek. The University Library, possessing no funds of its own with which to buy books, relied on benefactors for all its acquisitions. It acquired its first Greek books only with Tunstall's considerable gift in 1529, in which, besides his own *De arte supputandi*, there were the 1488 Homer, Apollonius Rhodius (1496), the Aldine Aristotle (1495), Theodorus Gaza (1495), the *Thesaurus* of 1496 and the Callierges Etymologicum (1499), Simplicius (1499) and Ammonius (1500), the last six all from Venice. The copy of the Complutensian polyglot Bible, probably acquired in Spain in 1525–6, was perhaps the most modern of these books to have entered England: for all the standing of the editions, the group is notably lacking in even relatively recent books of this kind.[17]

The surviving books known to have been in College libraries in the early 1530s tell the same story. Apart from the most elementary textbooks, by Whittinton, Donatus and Stanbridge, the English educational, learned and scholarly world depended on the continent for its books at all levels. So habituated to this had the market become that scholars published abroad rather than in London. Among many books of more general import, two prepared specifically for the English universities may be cited. In about 1512, John Barker's *Scutum inexpugnabile*, a textbook on logic written for undergraduates at Cambridge, was printed not in London but at a press either in Antwerp or Louvain: the sole fragments now known, once no doubt part of an edition commissioned by a Cambridge bookseller, have been preserved in a binding executed in or after 1512 by the shop of Garrett Godfrey.[18] The much used *Libellus sophistarum*, first printed *ad usum Cantabrigiensis* by Pynson in 1497 and also adapted *ad usum Oxoniensis*, was printed at Cologne in 1525, still ostensibly for Oxford.[19] A small local population, weak communications, an entrenched and inward-looking printing trade in London, established and efficient channels for imports from overseas, and fundamental changes in the 1530s in the kinds of materials being published, were all discouragements to the heavy capital investment essential to the establishment of a new press.

The injunctions of 1535 brought changes to the curriculum, but not to these considerations. In that year Thomas Cromwell succeeded Fisher as Chancellor, and under him the University formally embraced things with which it had previously dallied: humanism and protestantism. 'That students in arts should be instructed in the elements of logic, rhetoric, arithmetic, geography, music, and philosophy, and should read Aristotle, Rudolphus Agricola, Philip Melanchthon, Trapezuntius, etc., and not the frivolous questions and obscure glosses of Scotus, Burleus, Anthony Trombet, Bricot, Bruliferius, etc.'[20] 'I never saw yet any Commentarie upon Aristotles Logicke, either in *Greek* or *Latin*, that ever I lyked, bicause they be rather spent in declaryng scholepoynt rules, than in gathering fit examples for use and utterance', wrote Ascham some years later.[21] At Oxford, one of the 1535 commissioners was prompted to record dramatic scenes as Duns Scotus was sent on his way.[22] No such vivid witness described the events at Cambridge. The medieval authorities were still to be found in college libraries and in bookshops for years afterwards: the process of change must have been a gradual one. For the stationers, it meant demand for new textbooks, but not demand for a press wherewith to print them. All too little is known of the books actually possessed (rather than studied) at this time, but they were certainly modest in number. In 1540/1 Leonard Metcalfe, scholar of St John's, was executed for the murder of a burgess, and as a consequence his goods were listed by the 'common prizers of the Universitie' [a group of officials whom we will meet repeatedly in the following pages]. They discovered amongst his effects eight volumes, including Calepinus' Greek lexicon, 'of the worst', value 1s.8d., a plain copy of Horace, the *vocabularius iuris* with the *Gesta Romanorum*, elementary textbooks by Jacobus Faber, by Petrus Tartaretus on Petrus Hispanus, a *Compendium quattuor librorum institutionum*, Erasmus' *Moriae encomium* and a copy of *The shepheard's calendar*. The total value was 3s.8d.[23] It was a meagre haul, and there is no overwhelming reason to think it typical save in its poverty. Yet within a few months, in 1542, Ascham felt able to write to John Brandesby of St John's that

Aristotle and Plato are now read in their own language by the boys – as indeed we have done for five years in our own college. Sophocles and Euripides are more familiar than Plautus was when you were here. Herodotus, Thucydides, Xenophon are more on the lips and in the hands than Titus Livius was then. Now you would hear of Demosthenes what once you did of Cicero. More copies of Isocrates are in the boys' hands than there were formerly of Terence.[24]

Cheke, claimed Ascham, was furthering this enthusiasm for Greek by reading through the whole of Homer at public lectures, along with Sophocles and Euripides, as well as most of Herodotus. He would have done the same for all the Greek poets, historians, orators and philosophers, but for the stultifying effect of the Bishop of Winchester's attack on Cheke's pronunciation.[25]

Ascham's account sounds an ideal, exaggerated and even perhaps with a satiric edge. John Dee was scarcely a typical pupil, but some evidence of his book-buying in his early years survives. He entered St John's College in 1542, graduated BA in 1545–6, and was nominated by Henry VIII as one of the first Fellows of Trinity College in December 1546. In these years at Cambridge (he went abroad in 1547), already showing the signs of a serious book collector, he acquired Gaza's Greek grammar in the Basel edition of 1529 and his Tacitus in that of Lyon, 1542 – both from Spierinck. His Ptolemy was Froben's edition of 1533, his Cicero was Stephanus' folio edition of 1539 and his Ovid that of de Colines, 1529. If he owned Isocrates, so common in boys' hands at St John's according to Cheke, he had lost it by the time that his library was catalogued in later life: the only edition listed then was the folio Oporinus edition of 1570.[26] Yet the 1545 statutes of St John's, written probably at least in part by Cheke, confirmed much of what Ascham had claimed.[27] Like those of John Fisher before them, granted in 1530, they alluded to the past neglect of Hebrew and Greek. Plato, Demosthenes, Isocrates and Xenophon were all named explicitly, the authors to be studied in relation to Latin idioms as well as for their content and their vocabulary, 'tam rerum quam verborum proprietatem et naturam'. The Linacre lecturer in medicine (who was to be well read in Aristotle and Galen) was to follow the College's, rather than any university, or schools, curriculum: in his teaching of Galen he was to use texts translated by Linacre himself.[28]

Not one of the Greek texts mentioned was printed in England until John Day's edition of the *Troades* in 1575. No Greek edition of any part of Aristotle appeared in England until the *Rhetorica* in 1619, none of Demosthenes, Herodotus or Homer until 1591, none of Plato until Thomas Thomas printed the *Menexenus* at Cambridge in 1587, and none of Xenophon until Sir Henry Savile printed the *Cyropaedia* at his Eton press in 1613. The Greek revival in early sixteenth-century Cambridge may have seemed to many a golden age; but after Siberch's departure it relied (at least for texts such as these) wholly on what could be imported from the continental presses. Not until the 1570s did the London trade feel confident enough of its market to print even Latin classical texts in very great quantities. No edition of Terence's plays was apparently published in England between Wynkyn de Worde's quarto edition of about 1510 and Thomas Marsh's of 1575 in the by then more popular schoolboy format of octavo. Plautus, of which Ascham made such play, was first printed in England in the original Latin in 1595. In the case of many of the Latin authors, the changes, when they came, were dramatic: these school texts proved to be a valuable monopoly eventually, but for several generations the trade was content simply to import what was needed.

The political and religious turmoil in the years following the death of Henry VIII in 1547 had little effect on these fundamentals of the book trade. Changes in the syllabus, the decline of Greek studies, the conservative reaction under Mary and the detailed provisions made in the Elizabethan statutes of 1570 all had their effect on the University, but not on printers. Of all the authors, Latin or Greek, specified in the 1570 statutes, in philosophy, medicine, cosmography, arithmetic, geometry, astronomy, logic or oratory, only Hippocrates had been published recently in England, in Latin. Dee's edition of Euclid broke a long absence in 1570; no edition of Galen other than an English translation had been printed in England since the 1520s. Tunstall's arithmetic had not been printed in England since its first appearance in 1522; and there had been no edition of any work by Aristotle, even in Latin, since Theodoric Rood's edition of the *Ethica Nicomachea* at Oxford in 1479.[29] The new statutes repeated much of the old, and there could not be a more graphic illustration of the University's continuing dependence on continental presses.[30]

Of the books bought by Whitgift for his pupils at Trinity in the 1570s,[31] John Seton's *Dialectica*, the work of an Englishman, was one of the few texts that had a history of having been printed regularly in London, and not at all on the continent. In 1578 the local stationer John Dennis had several copies of Peter Carter's annotated edition in stock, valued at a shilling apiece bound, and no less than twenty-two copies still in paste boards, valued in total at 16s.6d.[32] It was one of the most ubiquitous of all Cambridge textbooks, the work of a member of St John's (albeit one who was never reconciled to the Reformation), and after its initial publication by Thomas Berthelet in 1545 it was republished repeatedly – but not, so far as is known, at Cambridge until 1631. The two most influential books by Thomas Wilson, translator of Demosthenes, who had graduated from King's in 1545–6, were likewise printed constantly in London and not at all on the continent: *The rule of reason*, printed by Grafton in 1551 and 1553 and thereafter by John Kingston, was the first book on Aristotelian logic to have been published in English, and *The art of rhetorique* was also taken over by Kingston, after its first appearance from Grafton's press in 1553. The publication and successful marketing of such textbooks suggests that the London trade was sufficiently equipped and organized to cater for this highly specialized (and indeed lucrative) market; but the old domination of educational publishing by imports disappeared only slowly, as the inventory of Dennis's stock attests repeatedly. The list contains many works by Ramus, reflecting the overwhelming influence he had come to have on Cambridge teaching since the late 1560s;[33] but even in 1578 few London-printed editions of the *Dialectica* were available. Roland MacIlmaine's annotated edition was first printed by Thomas Vautrollier in 1574, and Vautrollier rapidly established himself at the centre of the new fashion, able as both printer and, probably, importer, to dominate the market. In the same years he also published MacIlmaine's English translation; yet though he had a ten-year patent to print the work[34] (and alert to the import trade), he printed the Latin text only once again, in 1576, before Thomas Thomas printed a newly annotated text at Cambridge in 1584 as one of the first books from his new press.[35] Other editions appeared meanwhile from the press of Andreas Wechel at Frankfurt in 1579 and 1580. Dennis stocked copies of both MacIlmaine's edition and of that annotated by Omer Talon, or Talaeus, published in Paris, Basel and Cologne.[36] On this point at least, Vautrollier's penetration, as a printer, of the Cambridge trade was not exclusive: the preference in the University, if preference there was, for Talon is perhaps confirmed by the University Printer John Legate's decision in 1592 to issue the *Dialectica* in the same volume as Talon's own *Rhetorica*.[37]

The evidence of the publication history of Ramus, and of the stock kept by Dennis, is borne out if the question is examined from yet another point. Among 150 inventories of books surviving from the period 1535 to 1590,[38] the most popular authors and books included Aristotle's *Ethica*, not published in England between 1479 and Bynneman's edition of 1581. Cicero's *De officiis*, *Epistolae* and *Orationes*, were not printed in England until the 1570s, Quintilian did not appear until 1629, Ovid until 1570 and Laurenzo Valla's *Elegantiae* until a Cambridge edition in 1688. Ceporinus' Greek grammar, available in editions from both Zurich and Cologne, was finally printed at London by John Windet in 1585; and no edition of Calepinus' standard and widely used Greek lexicon was published in England until well into the seventeenth century. If the surviving copies are to be believed, no edition of Lucian's Dialogues, in either Latin or Greek, was printed in England between Erasmus' edition of 1531 and a new one in 1634. In the 1570s, Henry Bynneman and Thomas Vautrollier wrought considerable changes in their systematic attack on the market for Latin educational texts, encouraged no doubt by Arnold Birckman's death in 1574.[39] But with relatively few exceptions the market remained dependent on imports.[40]

Of the three original University Printers and Stationers, Spierinck, Godfrey and Nicholson, the first to die was Godfrey, whose will was proved on 11 October 1539.[41] In his stead, on 16 October the University appointed his partner Nicholas Pilgrim,[42] who also inherited some of Godfrey's binding equipment but who remained in office less than five years before himself dying early in 1544/5.[43] Pilgrim's death fell, moreover, within a year of that of Spierinck, whose own will was proved on 27 January 1545/6.[44] The University acted promptly to fill the vacancy left by Pilgrim's death, appointing Peter Sheres in his place.[45] Nothing is known of Sheres before his appearance in the Grace Book, save that like Pilgrim he was described as 'alienigena' as well as 'stationarius'. The Graces by which the two men were appointed were couched in very similar terms, with due reference to the Letters Patent of 1534; but Sheres was the last man to be thus appointed until the London bookseller John Kingston was elected on 8 February 1576/7.[46] Between appointing Pilgrim in 1539 and Sheres in 1544/5, the University also appointed Richard Noke as 'unus ex stacionariis apud vos' in 1539–40, an appointment that raises some difficulties.[47] Since Nicholson, Pilgrim and Spierinck were all alive, Noke was a fourth where only three were permitted – an anomaly which the Grace itself tacitly admitted by making no reference to the 1534 Letters. It is by no means clear how his appointment came about, or why it was deemed necessary: it may possibly have been one of the University's ways of meeting legislation (most recently the Act of 1540) restricting to two the number of aliens who could be employed by aliens in the two universities.[48] Noke lived on at least until January 1564/5, when he appeared in the Vice-Chancellor's Court in connection with the lease of a house in Walls Lane, the modern King Street;

but no formal measures were taken to fill the place left vacant by Spierinck, and from January 1545/6 the University was thus apparently left with only two official stationers: Nicholson and Sheres.

The reasons for this can only be surmised. As an alien, his position gave Sheres a measure of protection in the same way as it had to the three original holders. Though nothing is known of his activities in Cambridge before 1544/5, Sheres came almost certainly from the Low Countries: another member of the family occurs in the returns of aliens in London, where James Sheres, bookbinder from Antwerp, who was already a brother in the Stationers' Company in 1556, was said in 1571 to have lived in England for thirty-eight years.[49] In Cambridge, Peter lived on until August 1569, when he was succeeded by his son John, the last member of the family to make his living as an independent stationer. For much of his career, Peter was the only officially appointed University Stationer. In 1564 Nicholson, now an old man of sixty-four, was ordained by the Bishop of London, having long since ceased to work as a stationer. The lease of a tenement in St Michael's parish that he held from St John's from 1544 passed to Richard Modye, or Moody, in 1562, but even in 1551–2 Nicholson had already become 'olim bibliopola huius achademie nunc vero publicus zithi confector'.[50]

The provisions of the 1534 Letters were thus allowed to lapse, not to be revived explicitly until 1583 with the appointment of Thomas Thomas. The reasons for this are nowhere apparent, but some suggestions may be made. By the end of the 1540s, after a decade of mixed fortunes, the University had lost much of the impetus and popularity it had enjoyed in the heyday of humanists such as Cheke, Ascham and Latimer. The decade had opened with the founding of five Regius Professorships, in Divinity, Hebrew, Greek, Physic and Civil Law, only a few months after the closing of the monastic houses in the town. It had endured the serious prospect of the University itself being closed in 1545. It had witnessed the foundation by Henry VIII in 1546 of Trinity College, created out of two older ones; but three years later it also witnessed Clare Hall and Trinity Hall facing merger. The times were not propitious. St John's College, once so well endowed, now stared inflation and poverty in the face. 'Where once twelve pence would do, now one cannot live for twenty', complained Ascham on the college's behalf in a plea to the Duke of Somerset in November 1547.[51]

The seemingly trivial argument over the pronunciation of Greek was both disheartening and enervating, as well as damaging to Greek studies. Moreover, the population of the University had declined in the late 1530s; in 1544 Cheke himself left to become tutor to the young Prince Edward; Sir Thomas Smith left in 1547, first to join the household of Somerset and then to become Provost of Eton. In 1550 Ascham left for Germany, and though this did not prevent his continuing as University Orator his departure helped to mark the end of an era. Ascham, Richard Latimer, Thomas Lever of St John's, John Caius and others, all complained of the changes to be seen in the undergraduates: a lack of the old leavening of mature men to influence mere 'pueri', sons of wealthy parents more anxious for social than educational advantage; the consequent crowding out of poor students; an over-preoccupation with theological disputes. So far the University had failed to attract endowments from those who had grown wealthy with the destruction of the monasteries.[52] The controversies among Protestant sects and surrounding the introduction of the new prayer book were succeeded by the accession of Queen Mary, when, according to Ascham, 'mo perfite scholers were dispersed from [Cambridge] in one moneth, than many years can reare vp againe'.

Verely, iudgement in doctrine was wholy altered: order in discipline very sore changed: the loue of good learning, began sodenly to wax cold: the knowledge of the tonges...was manifestly contemned: and so, ye way of right studie purposely peruerted: the choice of good authors of mallice confownded. Olde sophistrie (I say not well) not olde, but that new rotten sophistrie began to beard and sholder logicke in her owne tong: yea, I know, that heades were cast together, and counsell deuised, that *Duns*, with all the rable of barbarous questionistes, should haue dispossessed of their places and rowmes, Aristotle, Plato, Tullie, and Demosthenes...[53]

Ascham was not a dispassionate observer; but he was not a dishonest one either. In the mid-sixteenth century the University had lost its initiative, as the centuries-old tradition of training for the Church became less important than preparation for political or administrative careers in secular surroundings.[54] Educationally, theologically, politically and financially, the University and colleges were the subjects of repeated suspicion and examination. The Cromwellian commissioners in the 1530s, the Edwardian visitation of 1549, the Marian commissioners in 1557 and the Elizabethan commissioners in 1559, all reflected the government's anxiety to suppress dissent, and its reluctance to trust the officers elected by the University and colleges themselves. If the establishment of a press depended partly on economic, educational or ideological confidence, the times were scarcely propitious. Among a multiplicity of causes, it was perhaps for this reason that the practice of invoking and appointing under the 1534 Letters fell incidentally into desuetude. Outside Cambridge as well, the University's privilege was forgotten or ignored. None of the proclamations by which the monarchy sought to control the national book trade in the mid-sixteenth century mentioned the peculiar place of the University, even when there was a natural opportunity to do so. The proclamation of 1546 prohibiting heretical books, and requiring printers to print their own name as well as that of the author and the date of publication on each book, said merely that the printer 'shall present the first copy to the mayor of the town where he dwelleth'.[55] The proclamation assumed the existence of provincial printing, but all trace of the University's special authority had disappeared. It was, under these circumstances, scarcely surprising that when the Stationers' Company reached an accommodation with the government in its charter of 1557, the implications of existing regulations for Cambridge were not mentioned at all. The 1534 Act against aliens, and the University's Letters Patent of the same year, had been complementary in that on the one hand the Act protected the interests of the London stationers against foreign competition, and on the other the Letters Patent answered the University's claim to special consideration of its reliance on the foreign trade. No such considerations were reflected in the Stationers' Company charter, and no evidence survives to suggest that the University made any attempt to offer counter-arguments when the Stationers were canvassing their proposals in the 1540s.[56] The Elizabethan injunctions of 1559 referring to the book trade addressed the Stationers' Company specifically, not the universities. At a time when there was no thought of a press at either Oxford or Cambridge it would have been superfluous to have done so, and instead the Chancellors of the two universities were simply allotted a part in the licensing of books.[57]

The disappearance of stationers' elections from the Grace Books did not mean an hiatus in the Cambridge book trade, or even herald a decline. The records for the mid-century are scanty, but in a period when the demand for books was diversifying and expanding, sufficient can be discovered at least to present the principal features. Just as in 1534 the charter had been obtained at the instigation of three leading stationers in the town, to the consequent exclusion of others, so between then and the 1580s the town and University continued to support considerably more than were dignified in the Grace Books. Many of these booksellers and stationers were foreigners, of either the first or second generation, and they virtually all depended on foreigners, or strangers, who controlled the import of books through London.[58]

Of the few dynasties to be founded in the mid-century, by far the largest was to be that beginning with John Scarlet, whose will was proved on 1 August 1551.[59] Scarlet came originally from Leominster in Herefordshire. In Cambridge, he rented the small shop hard against the west wall of Great St Mary's, and was quickly drawn into the tiny world of booksellers and stationers who clustered round the University. With William Spierinck, son of Nicholas and churchwarden of the University church in the mid-1540s, he became involved in a grandiose scheme to print the English Bible, discussed more fully below, but the two men died within a few months of each other. Scarlet left his wife Elizabeth, his brother Philip, and his parents, still in Leominster. Elizabeth soon remarried, this time to Simon Waterson, or Watson,[60] who in 1555 supplied Great St Mary's with 'a fayer messe boke & a legent' to answer the needs of the new religious conservatism.[61] John's brother Philip, born in Leominster in about 1533, had come to Cambridge also in about 1551, probably at the same time as his brother,[62] and he rose to enjoy some prominence in the University. He was principally a bookbinder, receiving three shillings from St John's in 1563–4 for a stout chained binding to a copy of Vesalius,[63] and in 1570 his appointment as one of the four official University vintners made him yet another example of a tradesman who found it convenient to deal in both wine and books:[64] Spierinck had left the inn known as the Cross Keys to his grandson in 1545, and both Watson and Nicholson divided their interests thus. Peter Bright had likewise turned to a similar business by the time of his death in the same year. Scarlet's appointment as wine merchant savours of unease, however. It came only six months before he was sued for debt by creditors both in Cambridge and in London, who claimed to be owed several hundred pounds;[65] by the end of the year, the owner of his shop, Simon Watson, was trying to persuade him to leave Cambridge altogether.[66] For two years, in 1568–70, he had been churchwarden at Great St Mary's, but the collapse of his credit was disastrous. On his death in 1582 his goods were valued officially at a mere £3.18s.5d., and his estate recorded a deficit of over £370.[67]

Philip Scarlet had had at least one partner or employee, a French bookbinder named Gilbert Vremtoete;[68] but the remains of the business seem now to have been closed. Of the other members of his family, Peter, who served three terms as churchwarden at Great St Mary's in 1583–4 and subsequently, appears as an apothecary in December 1589;[69] Philip, born in about 1571, was still too young to inherit; and William, the first bookseller known to have inhabited the site on the corner at 1 Trinity Street, is not recorded as a stationer before about 1592–3.

For nearly all his career in Cambridge, Philip Scarlet had known members of the Sheres family, immigrants first to London and then to Cambridge. His assistant Gilbert Vremtoete was likewise a foreigner, born in Rouen in 1528 and resident in Cambridge from at least 1565. For the first seven decades of the century, the local book trade was permeated with such men. By no means all their names have survived, but an unusual amount is known about John Dennis (Denys), a Frenchman, who was in Cambridge by August 1565 when he was prosecuted by John Caius for the recovery of a printed Latin service book sent to him for binding.[70] He lived not near Great St Mary's, like most of the trade, but in the parish of All Saints, where in 1573 he was threatened with imprisonment after failing to make his Easter communion.[71] By the time of his death in 1578, when he and most of his household succumbed to plague, he owned a thriving business, with a well-equipped bindery including 'an alphabet of Roman letters' (to be used for the boards of books rather than the spines) and a substantial bookshop valued at £42.10s.1d. It is not clear what happened either to his books or to his binding equipment. His estate did not cover the cost of his debts; his children were dead; and by the time that his effects had been sold and a division arranged amongst his creditors, his wife had remarried.[72] Dennis may have been one of the most successful of his generation, but he was not the last alien to trade as a Cambridge stationer. In 1588/9, John Bartholomew, a bookbinder who had trained in Germany but was not a free denizen in England, was convicted of illegal trading in the town;[73] and from about 1590 to 1604 the town was also the home of Manasses Vautrollier, a Huguenot from Edinburgh and the son of a successful London printer whose work was familiar to the University in the Ramist texts from his press.[74]

But more and more, the Cambridge trade passed into the hands of native Englishmen. Family connections, so crucial to the book trade in the earlier years of the century, counted for less in the international trade as London consolidated its position as an *entrepôt*, with an increasingly tightly organized wholesale trade dominated by the Birckmans. Richard Noke, who was appointed University Stationer in 1540, has already been mentioned. He was still active in 1564/5, when he lost a case in the Vice-Chancellor's Court over a lease in Walls Lane, though nothing is known of the size of his business.[75] Rather more is known of the man variously recorded as John Seth, Sothe and Sowght, who supplied various service books to Great St Mary's in 1550–1, and whose stock of books when he died in 1552/3 was valued altogether at £56 – considerably more than that of Dennis fifteen or so years later.[76] It is unfortunate that no detailed inventory of Sowght's books has survived, for they were easily the most substantial part of his estate, the binding equipment being considerably more modest than Dennis's sophisticated collection. Other stationers in the 1550s included John Baxter, who with Peter Sheres and Simon Watson was required to answer the Visitors of the University in 1557/8,[77] and who by 1559 had married Sowght's widow Katherine. Like most booksellers, Baxter was obliged to sail with the theological wind, supplying a processional to Great St Mary's in 1557 and Geneva Psalters to St John's in 1563.[78] He lived until at least 1589, when he and his son John crossed swords in the Vice-Chancellor's Court with a London draper over various chattels, and he is perhaps to be identified with the Esquire Bedell who served the University from 1556 to 1596.[79] In January 1563/4 he also became one of the University's four official wine merchants, just as another Simon Watson had been licensed as a vintner in November 1553.[80] Watson's career by 1564 was, on the other hand, all but ended, if his disappearance from the records of Great St Mary's is a reliable guide. He may have been related to Thomas Watson, servant to Nicholas Spierinck's son William: if so, he was one of the last who could claim a link with the three original stationers under the 1534 Letters.[81]

Two decades later, the trade had changed yet again. Besides the long-established family firms of Sheres and Scarlet, and the only slightly more recently established John Baxter, there appeared a new generation of stationers, some of whom were to live long into the seventeenth century. The Stationers' Company received its charter in 1557, the better part of a century after many of the other livery companies.[82] Its incorporation, a masterpiece of political and economic strategy that gave assurance both to the London book trade and to the government, was the principal force that determined the shape of the book trade in the country as a whole until the end of the seventeenth century. For

Cambridge, as for Oxford, the effects were to prove in turn difficult, expensive and, occasionally, stimulating.

Though the number of 'country' members always remained small (in 1571 it was eleven),[83] John Cuthbert lived most of his life in Cambridge between being made free of the Company in 1566 and his death in 1597. Like so many others, he, too, seems to have supplemented his income as a stationer by trading also as a vintner or innkeeper.[84] For a few months, Cuthbert occupied the shop at the west end of Great St Mary's. Nothing is known of the manner in which his business was established, but among his apprentices were two men whose names were to be familiar in the Cambridge book trade for two generations. Reginald Boyse, from Dallington in Northamptonshire, and John Porter, from Haslingfield, were both apprenticed to Cuthbert in 1568.[85] The various members of the Porter family named John have given rise to some confusion. On 7 October 1589 another John Porter testified in the University Commissary's Court that he had been born at Winchester in about 1549, and had been in Cambridge for eleven years, i.e. since 1578.[86] In 1581 he took an apprentice, Samuel Beck, the son of a London draper, who must have been virtually at the end of his apprenticeship when he appeared with Porter in the Commissary's Court in 1589.[87] But already in 1580 Porter was employing John Almond, whose temporary departure to the household of another bookseller, Thomas Bradshaw, in 1581 may have been the occasion of Porter's engaging Beck.[88] Neither Porter nor Bradshaw found Almond a satisfactory employee: both sued him for debt, and in 1581 he was imprisoned for failing to serve Bradshaw 'truly and honestly'.[89] Thereafter Almond seems to have worked independently, still relying on other people's money: in 1584 he failed to repay another small loan from a local blacksmith.[90] At his death in 1588 he was poverty-stricken, his collection of the most basic of binding tools valued at a mere six shillings, his books in the shop (three Bibles, and copies of Peter Martyr) at 10s.6d. The oddity, in an inventory where the contents of the shop made such a poor showing, was a collection of no fewer than 234 'almanackes with pronostications', valued at 23s.8d. They almost certainly betokened a particular connection with the country trade of chapmen. The total came to £19, against which had to be set claims of £12 from Bradshaw and of £36 from Thomas Thomas's widow Anne.[91]

Thomas Bradshaw, for a brief time Almond's employer, had been apprenticed to the London bookseller (and member of Queens' College) Humphrey Toye between 1562 and 1570, and was in Cambridge by 1578, when he helped Peter Sheres to appraise the stock and equipment of John Dennis.[92] He, too, lived in the parish of Great St Mary's, and for a short time rented the two west-end shops: in 1587 he was in trouble with the churchwardens for alterations that damaged the wall and blocked the light through the windows.[93] But though he was able in 1610 to make generous dispositions in his will, bequeathing his four sons £60 apiece quite apart from legacies to other members of his family, the poor and the prisoners in Cambridge castle, nothing is known of his stock at the time of his death.

Nor is anything known of Walter Anderson, a bookseller who appears briefly in 1575 in the legal records when threatened by Richard Woodhouse, a surgeon:[94] if indeed he lived in Cambridge, he was more probably an employee than a bookseller in his own right. Another bookseller, Nicholas West, was not even fully literate.[95] Of the remaining stationers in the 1570s and early 1580s, the most important was Bennet Walker. He, too, was probably apprenticed in London, to George Bishop in 1566: in his turn, Bishop had been apprenticed to Robert Toye, father of Humphrey, to whom Thomas Bradshaw was apprenticed in 1562–70. The date of Walker's removal to Cambridge is unknown. His will is dated 23 November 1588, and among his possessions were not only plate to the value of £10.5s., but also a stock in which the books necessary for the University curriculum were leavened with theology and popular devotion.[96] Soon after his death, his widow Joan married Reginald Bridges, whose estate became a matter for dispute and will be discussed further below.[97]

The community of stationers, bookbinders and others having to do with the book trade in Cambridge was close-knit, if rather more extensive than might at first be expected. It was composed of a considerable number of small businesses, dominated by two or three large ones. The varied array that has just been described may have arisen partly out of competition and the belief that the University offered exceptional opportunities. More importantly, it allowed capital investment to be spread: the largest surviving post-mortem inventories of booksellers' stocks in sixteenth-century Cambridge are those of Nicholas Pilgrim (1545) and John Dennis (c. 1578), which contain about seven hundred books apiece, valued in all at £26.11s.6d. and £42.10s.1d. respectively.[98] Of the stationers mentioned in the last pages, John Sheres in 1581 and John Porter in 1608 both left estates valued at over £700. Sheres left an active business, with stock worth £150, while Porter's stock in 1608 had already passed into the hands of his son-in-law Leonard Greene. But both men died with considerable sums of money owed to them: Sheres 'in reddye monye & dett bye obligationes' £260, and Porter 'good dettes' totalling £480 besides. These two men were among the most prosperous tradesmen in Cambridge. Thomas Thomas, building on Sheres' estate, was equally wealthy, though his work as a printer rather than simply as a stationer and bookbinder places him in a slightly different category. Apart from these men, only John Sowght among the stationers established before 1584 (of whom the appropriate details survive), left an estate valued at more than £100, and over half of Sowght's was in the form of debts owed to him.[99]

This tiny community, following a specialist trade and relying not only on each other but also on the same supply routes and the same customers, and offering much the same wares and services, came from very different backgrounds. By no means all had served apprenticeship to a member of the Stationers' Company; but some had, and in some respects the bonds between the London and Cambridge trade were much closer than those made necessary by ordinary trade. Thomas Bradshaw, Bennet Walker, John Porter and probably John Cuthbert were all apprenticed to London stationers; in 1583 Bradshaw accepted the London bookseller Thomas Chard's apprentice William Knoseley (or Knowsley) for the remainder of his time; and John Sheres was perhaps related to James Sheres, bookseller in St Paul's Churchyard. Both Cuthbert and Bradshaw, as well as Peter Waters, who traded in Cambridge in the early 1580s, were made free of the Stationers' Company.[100]

The everyday business of the book trade was however quite another matter. With relatively little coin in circulation, much depended on credit. This is reflected not only in the large sums of money owing to some tradesmen at their deaths, but also in the cases for debt brought in the University courts, where London stationers were familiar figures. In 1570 Philip Scarlet's creditors, alluded to above, included the London stationers Peter du Puys, Augustine Laughton, William Seres and members of the Birckman family, to whom he owed no less than £196.12s.1d., compared with less than £75 owed to all the others together.[101] In the case of Seres at least, who was owed £35.14s., the debt was not for unbound sheets, but for bound books. Scarlet also owed £50 to Thomas Burdock, a London draper; it may be that here, too, the debt was for books, and that Burdock, like several other members of the Drapers' Company at the time, was principally involved in the book trade.[102] Scarlet's case dragged on for some months, in March 1570/1 the creditors being joined by two further London booksellers, Gerard (or Garret) Dewes and Cornelius Clipius, who claimed to be owed £25.11s.7d.[103] It is noticeable how many of these creditors were members of either French or lower Rhineland families. They were not printers, and some of them were among the principal London stationers: their trade was in the sale of books, and it is likely that a large proportion of Scarlet's debts was for books imported by these men. Much the same was true of John Dennis, who on his death in 1578 left debts which his property proved insufficient to meet: the creditors had to be content with about half what was owed them.[104] Peter du Puys, one of a dynasty of Parisian booksellers, and one of Scarlet's creditors, was owed £16.10s.8d., slightly more than twice another member of his family, Baptiste du Puys, and a little less than the sum of £16.13s. owed to the widow Birckman. These debts may all have been for imports, while the money owed to George Bishop, Under-Warden of the Stationers' Company in 1578–9 and 1579–80, and to Thomas Marsh, may have represented, at least partly, books in which the two men had a share.

Among the London booksellers whose names have occurred in the last few pages, several are known to have been at least partly, and some heavily, engaged in international trade. Arnold Birckman, George Bishop, Baptiste du

Puy (or Puys) and his partner Hercules François, who had once traded in Paris, and Humphrey Toye (to whom Bradshaw was apprenticed) all had dealings with Christopher Plantin, who in turn not only sold his own publications, but also acted as agent at the Frankfurt book fair, where he kept a warehouse.[105] There is however no evidence that Plantin himself ever dealt directly with the Cambridge stationers: the route from continental booksellers and printers involved middlemen both on the continent and in London.

Of the other London stationers who had dealings with those in Cambridge, one of the most heavily involved was John Harrison senior, Master of the Stationers' Company in 1583–4 and twice again later.[106] While Master for the first time, he sued Nicholas West for £11.2s.7d. in payment for 'certeyne bookes & wares'.[107] It was a small enough sum, and the case was perhaps brought because Harrison heard of the differences between West and Thomas Warren – differences originally concerning a property in University Street sublet to Warren, but revealing themselves most recently in Warren's claim to be owed £300 after West had failed to keep an agreement with him not to play 'cardes bowles tables or dyse' on pain of paying 20s. for each lapse.[108] Harrison's anxiety not to lose money by default exhibited itself similarly in the case of Reginald Boyse, but on a rather larger scale. In 1583 Cornelius Clipius had some difficulty in regaining the sum of £5.10s. from Boyse: the debt was acknowledged in May, but was still unpaid four months later.[109] By a bond dated 2 January 1583/4, Boyse became bound to Harrison for payment of £108.15s., and on Boyse's failure to pay Harrison prosecuted him in the Commissary's Court. The outcome is less important than the sum involved. Dennis's entire stock of books had been valued in 1578 at only £42.10s.1d, and John Sheres' stock (in the shop, rather than in his house, where he kept what was presumably his private collection) was to be valued in 1588 at £120. Nothing is known of Boyse's stock in 1584, but the debt to Harrison suggests that it was not inconsiderable. In the next few years, the London stationer Thomas Chard was to clash with Thomas Bradshaw, and Hercules François was to clash with the estate of Bennet Walker, but the sums involved were modest by comparison.[110]

Modest or not, the evidence that was produced in connection with the dispute between Chard and Bradshaw is of the greatest interest. By 1589 the two men had been trading for a considerable period. In 1583 Bradshaw had taken over one of Chard's apprentices.[111] Besides the ordinary wholesale trade in books, Bradshaw also obtained from Chard pasteboard and thread for binding, while Chard in turn used him as an agent to supervise books destined for Stourbridge Fair, and even in 1584 to see to the delivery of books to Chard's retail customers,[112] then at Queens' College. Chard supplied books both bound and unbound, and on a considerable scale. One bill in October 1583 listed over two hundred volumes besides five dozen almanacs; another, dated May 1584, listed over a hundred; and a third, undated, 335 titles – again often in multiple copies. Only a few of the books listed in the bills were published by Chard: they included two by Gervase Babington, Fellow of Trinity, four copies of Simon de Voyon's *Testimonie of the true church of God*, seven of *A true discourse of the assault committed upon the Prince of Orange*, ten of an attack on Edmund Campion by William Whitaker, Fellow of St John's and Regius Professor of Divinity, and eleven of the first book by Richard Mulcaster, Headmaster of Merchant Taylors' School, on the education and rearing of children. In the absence of any organized trade list of recent publications, it is impossible to tell how Bradshaw or Chard managed to ascertain what was needed.

The books supplied in October 1583 fell into two broad categories: those that were bound or stitched, and those that were still in sheets. Among the former were assured sellers such as the *Short catechisme for householders*, as well as almanacs, essentials of church government ('12 Queens Iniunctions; 6 Articles of Religion') and books of Psalms – the last supplied in a variety of vellum and cheap leather bindings. The remainder of the list, comprising books in quires, was largely of Greek and Latin books, many of them standard textbooks but also including a copy of Saxton's atlas priced at 3s.6d. The most expensive were the Geneva edition of the *Corpus iuris civilis* at 25s., a folio volume of Beza's *opuscula* at 20s., and a Hebrew concordance (perhaps that published at Basel by Froben in 1581) at 15s. Chard's third surviving invoice was likewise divided into sections that presumably reflect, however obscurely, the management of his business. The first was devoted to theology, mostly in Latin but including some Hebrew; the second covered classical literature, and textbooks of rhetoric, with a smattering of history and law; the third column, now much damaged, listed books in the mathematical sciences, geography, astrology, etc., with a few French books; and the last listed books in English, arranged in approximately alphabetical order where in the other sections there had been none, and covering all subjects. Among these English books were popular literary texts such as *Sir Bevis of Hampton*, *Euphues*, *Guy of Warwick* and *Piers Plowman*. Two copies of Elyot's *Governour*, presumably the edition printed by Thomas East in 1580, cost 1s.4d. for the pair, and the recent edition of Seneca in English cost 1s.8d.

By no means all of Bradshaw's purchases were new or recent books. A folio *Destruction of Troy*, last published in 1555, cost 1s.8d., while copies of *The ship of fools* priced at 3s.4d. and *The shepherds' calendar*, at 10d., are also likely to have been second-hand. In most cases Bradshaw received (and presumably had asked for) only one or two copies; but in a few cases his orders were substantial: twenty-five copies of (again) Dering's *Short catechism*, twelve copies of *A declaration of the recantation of John Nichols (for the space almost of two yeeres the popes scholar at Rome)*, published in 1581, twenty-five of Richard Edwards' *Paradyse of daintie devises*, first printed in 1576 and republished several times since. Bradshaw's stock was not restricted to the University curriculum. He had an eye on the leisure and popular market, and was alert to other local needs as well: of Robert Payne's *Vale mans table*, a broadside on which was 'taught … how to draine moores', printed only a few weeks before, he took nineteen copies.[113]

Bradshaw did not enjoy any official position other than his ordinary licence from the University as a tradesman. He had never been appointed one of the three officially designated officers of the University in the book trades, and he was certainly not the wealthiest stationer or binder in the town. The contents of three bills, and those moreover imperfect, may not have been properly representative of his stock. But despite these disadvantages, the papers are of considerable value to the study of the late sixteenth-century book trade. They shed light on the wholesaling activities of a London stationer; in their allusion to Thomas Hobson, the carrier, they confirm that even heavy loads of books were transported from London by road rather than by the long water route via King's Lynn; and in their overwhelming emphasis on recent publications they present a perhaps more accurate overall impression of the preoccupations of the Cambridge trade than the ostensibly more representative inventories of deceased booksellers. They offer, in other words, the best available picture of the conditions in which the Cambridge book trade conducted its purchasing.

4

Prejudice and the printing privilege

The last few pages have been concerned with stationers, booksellers and bookbinders. The 1534 Letters Patent, however, permitted printing as well, and it remains to be seen how much thought was ever given to their implementation on this point. While nothing was printed at Cambridge between Siberch's departure in perhaps 1524 and Thomas Thomas's new press in 1583, the University, with its printers and stationers, was not always heedless of the possibilities thus offered. The evidence for such aspirations as there were is, hardly surprisingly, fragmentary. Neither William Spierinck (son of Nicholas) nor John Scarlet operated a press; but after Spierinck's death it was alleged that in 1551 the London stationer John Birckman had asked Scarlet to persuade Spierinck to provide £100 'towarde the printynge of his great englishe bible'.[1] Birckman did not apparently plan to print such a Bible in England, but instead intended to send the money abroad, perhaps to his relations in Antwerp: the scheme was thwarted partly at least by a royal proclamation that summer against the unlicensed export of gold or silver.[2] No such edition appeared, despite Spierinck's having paid Birckman either £70 or £100 (witnesses differed as to the exact amount). Spierinck may have regarded the book as no more than an investment; but with the loss of his money there went also the nearest place that any Cambridge stationer came to appearing in an imprint during the middle of the century.

In 1553, the bookseller and binder John Sowght was said to have owned a printing press, valued at 3s.6d.,[3] though no type or other accompanying essentials were mentioned. It was not until the mid-1570s that the University as a whole again addressed itself to the question of establishing a printer, and this time appointed not a member of any of the established book trade families, but an outsider from London, John Kingston.

Whether the stimulus was from London or from Cambridge is not clear. But certainly the effect seemed, for a time, to be promising. Nicholas Carr, Regius Professor of Greek from 1547, and who in the later years of his life had supplemented his stipend by a medical practice in Cambridge, died in 1568. In 1571 his Latin translation of Demosthenes was printed in London, and five years later there appeared his polemical *De scriptorum Britannicorum paucitate oratio*, a work made to seem more bulky by an unusually large gathering of other contributors to the volume. The editor was Thomas Hatcher of King's, son of a Regius Professor of Physic, friend of John Caius and of John Stow, and by 1576 living apparently independently on the family estate near Stamford.[4] He dedicated Carr's book to another Kingsman (and one, like Carr, an enthusiast for Demosthenes), Thomas Wilson, whose academic career had been ousted by a distinguished diplomatic one that was to lead in 1577 to his appointment as Secretary of State. The occasion of this volume, inspired by Carr's papers and so much the product of Cambridge minds, also provided the opportunity for comment with some asperity on the British book trade. The lack of any learned press in England (unlike Germany) meant that *bonae literae* could not flourish. Moreover, English printing was expensive, English printers were ignorant, and they were so greedy that scholarly authors were put to publish their work at their own expense. To Hatcher, it seemed that while English-language books must for ever remain isolated and hidden away in their native country, much could be done by merchants more willing to exploit an export business in books as there was already in other goods.[5]

Hatcher's view took perhaps too little notice of the complex interests of the Latin trade, whose profits depended on maintaining a balance between London printers and the potential thereby offered for importers. But Wilson, to whom this suggestion was dedicated, may perhaps have proved to be the critical link that made printing at Cambridge seem to be both possible and attractive. Certainly Hatcher framed his indictment of the English book trade with a directness (not least on behalf of the late Carr) that demanded attention. For Wilson, one member of that trade in particular was at hand. The several recent editions of his two early publications, *The rule of reason, conteinyng the art of logic* (1551) and *The arte of rhetorique* (1553) had been printed by John Kingston, who had in them two books in constant demand.

Kingston was a member not of the Stationers' Company, but of the Grocers'. His connection with Cambridge was in one respect of long-standing, for the first book on which his name had ever appeared as a bookseller was *A meditation upon the Lordes Prayer*, published in 1551, the year in which its author, Thomas Lever, was admitted Master of St John's College.[6] Twenty-one years later, in 1572, he printed a revised collection of Lever's sermons originally preached in 1550: by this time Lever had returned from exile under Mary, and had become established as a leading puritan whose nonconformity was unwelcome to the establishment. For his part, Kingston had become established mainly as a printer, responsible in 1568 and 1574 for two editions of an instruction manual for the lute, in 1574 also for the second edition of Robert Record's geometry textbook *The pathway to knowledge*, and in 1571 for a work by another puritan Fellow of St John's, William Fulke's *Confutation of a popishe libelle*. In an effort to exploit a profitable market, he clashed with Thomas Marsh in 1573 over the printing of Aesop's fables, the *Epitome* of

Erasmus' *Colloquies* and Castalio's *Dialogorum sacrorum libri quatuor* – all three steady sellers that were to be the subject of contention in 1579. The 'divers debate and controversy' alluded to in 1579 between the two men does not suggest that Kingston was either pacific or unambitious.[7] The main focus of his attention in the 1570s was on the printing of Latin educational texts, including the Latin poems of Baptista Spagnuoli and Joannes Sulpitius, a grammar by Joannes Susenbrotus, the first edition in England of Paolo Manuzio's *Epistolae* and a handful of books by Cicero. This combination of interests, in theological debate and in educational texts, would have made his name not unfamiliar at Cambridge; but no evidence survives of the mode of his approach to the University in the first weeks of 1576/7. Some members of the University may have felt that the presence of a printer in Cambridge would be beneficial to teaching. But although the phrasing of the subsequent letters from the Chancellor of the University, Burghley, suggest that the University was the principal instigator, this probably reflects no more than the technical position, in that Kingston needed the University's approbation in order to print. The absence of surviving documents makes it impossible to be certain of his reasons for either wanting or agreeing to set up a press in Cambridge. Under the provisions of the 1534 Letters, which had left the University free to print all manner of books, he could, however, expect to gain considerably. In London, the Stationers' Company had become divided between those who enjoyed lucrative patents, and those who suffered as a result. In 1576, concern at the number of presses and employees in the trade had led the Company to organize searches for infringements of its regulations. In August 1577 the dissatisfaction of many printers and booksellers was to come to a head with their complaint (those affected included Kingston) that the privileges 'hath and will be the overthrowe of the Printers and Stacioners within this Cittie being in number .175. Besides their wyves Children Apprentizes and families'.[8] The University might offer prestige; but it also offered the means to a more lucrative business as a printer. In 1569–70 another London printer, Henry Bynneman, had established his right to print a variety of schoolbooks,[9] basing his appeal partly on a claim to be able to do better than the editions of classical authors then being imported; in 1572 Thomas Marsh acquired a licence to print and sell another wide-ranging selection of schoolbooks;[10] and in June 1574, only weeks after Arnold Birckman's death, Thomas Vautrollier acquired a monopoly to print, among others, the works of Ovid and Cicero in Latin, as well as of Ramus with the notes of Roland MacIlmaine.[11] These interests all clashed with what may be deduced to have been Kingston's hopes of specializing, at least partly, in educational textbooks, and thus building on the overseas interests which he sought in autumn 1576 when his folio edition of Peter Martyr Vermigli's *Loci communes* was exported to the Frankfurt fair.[12] Both activities, in educational publishing and international trade, made his platform the stronger with respect to the University.

Kingston was appointed University Printer by Grace on 8 February 1576/7.[13] Objections from the London trade were inevitable; but none came until the following July, when Burghley wrote to the Vice-Chancellor Roger Goad, at the instance of one of the patentees. Francis Flower was not a member of the Stationers' Company, and was not actively involved in the book trade at all. A few years later he was to be described by a group of disgruntled booksellers and printers simply as a 'gentleman'.[14] However, since 1573 he had held a patent as royal printer and bookseller in Latin, Greek and Hebrew,[15] a privilege capacious enough in its wording to satisfy all but the greediest monopolist and to ensure the jealousy of those who were excluded: Flower farmed it out the same year to six others including Christopher Barker, John Wyghte, William Norton, John Harrison, Garrat Dewes and Richard Watson, who paid him £100 per annum as his assigns.[16] Flower was especially anxious that his monopoly to print grammars should not be infringed, as Burghley explained:

I vnderstand by him that having some notice of his intention yow haue to bring the art of printing to be practised in that vniuersitie by interteyning one of y^t facultie to be resident and inhabiting among yow, he doubteth lest by coulo^r of some of y^r privileges, there maie somewhat be attempted and put in ure y^t would be to his p̄iudice in that behalf, so wth cause he hath desired my l̄re vnto yow to require yow to forebeare the admitting of any person to print any kind of grammers of what sort or Language soever. The wch if yow haue good warranty to do by any yor privileges, I praie yow advertise me thereof, forbearing neverthelesse to put any thing in execucōn that maie be to his preiudice as tuching his said priviledge vntill I maie haue considered of such matter as yow shall pretend to haue by force of any graunt made to this vniuersitie in any former tymes.[17]

The implication of that last part of this letter can only be that Burghley was aware, however dimly, of the University's privileged position in the book trade. Goad's reply has not survived; but only a week later Burghley had to write again, this time at the instigation of three other London printers.

when I vnderstand yow haue an intention to bring the exercise of printing to that vniuersitie, and for that purpose haue interteyned one Kingston of London to come and inhabite there, and meane to protect him wth yor priviledges to print certein psalters bookes of comon prayer and other bookes in English for the wch Hir ma^{ie} hath alredie graunted speciall priviledges to divers psons and namely to Will̄m Seres Richard Jugge, and John Daye I do not think good as I haue heretofore written to yow in this matter at the sollicitacon of Mr Flower that any thing should be attempted to the preiudice of any that hath such graunte from hir ma^{tie} but that yow should rather employ such an artificer for the printing of matter pteining to y^{or} scholes, or such the travayles of the studentes there as maie be thought fitt to be published for the com̄endacon of the authors and ornament of that vniuersitie.[18]

Of the three new printers named, Seres' privilege to print some of the more popular and service books, originally granted by Queen Mary, had been renewed by Queen Elizabeth in 1559;[19] Richard Jugge was the Queen's Printer, and had the printing of the Bible in quarto and 16°;[20] and John Day, who had taken especial pains to protect himself by patents, was (among other privileges) licensed to print two of the most popular books of all, the ABC with the little catechism, and Sternhold and Hopkins' Psalms in metre.[21] It was holders of patents such as these who had most to fear from a printer becoming established beyond the control of the most powerful members of the London trade. In fact, Kingston is not known to have set up a press, or to have printed anything, at Cambridge. If the University remembered its own Letters Patent, it did not see fit to champion Kingston either as challenger to these more recent patents, or as a printer of the kind of books Burghley suggested would cause less political embarrassment. Moreover, it is unlikely that the Vice-Chancellor, Roger Goad, Provost of King's, failed to realize that in offending Jugge and Day the University was offending two men who had close connections with the same college. Jugge had entered it in 1531, and John Day was the father of Richard Day, Fellow since 1574. On his death in August 1577 Jugge was to leave £10-worth of books; Richard Day had already given in 1575–6 two medieval manuscripts (one supplied with elaborately printed title-pages) and five books printed by his father; and John Day himself had presented his editions of Asser, Thomas Walsingham, William Alley's *Poore man's librarie*, the collected works of William Tindall, John Frith and Robert Barnes and Foxe's *Book of martyrs*.[22] Whichever of the threats offered – by the displeasure of the Chancellor, the élite of the London trade, or by college benefactors – was strongest, the cumulative effect was the same. No more was heard of Kingston, who remained in London until 1584, when the last books bearing his name in imprints appeared. If his principal interest in obtaining a post at Cambridge was independence, and especially the opportunity to print books offering certain sales but which were protected by royally granted monopolies, then his withdrawal was the result of Burghley's more astute political manipulation. Certainly, when the question was again raised, in connection with Thomas Thomas's aspirations, there was no suggestion of an interest in any other than the ordinary requirements of the daily teaching and theology of the University.

Kingston's position in the London trade was not unique. It was one both subservient, in economic terms, to many of his fellows and one which members of the Stationers' Company sought to make seem invidious as held by a member of another company. For Kingston, his appointment at Cambridge was a response to the Elizabethan monopolies system as operated within the book trade; but in this respect his personal interests had much in common with those of the University. Monopolies in Bibles, law books, the ABC, catechisms, almanacs, Latin books for grammar schools, other Latin texts, music, Psalters, primers and grammars both circumscribed the unprivileged, and denied to them a share in some of the most lucrative parts of the market.[23] In a system that depended on privilege for survival, Henry Bynneman left the ranks of the hindered, to join the élite, on obtaining in 1580 the exclusive right to print dictionaries and histories, though in the opinion of Barker, one of the most experienced in the London trade, it was one fraught with risk.[24]

Protest in 1577 gave way in the early 1580s to revolt.[25] Between 1581 and 1583 a series of infringements against these patents amounted virtually to a campaign, carried on most notably amongst the printers by Roger Ward, John Wolfe and John Charlewood, and amongst booksellers by Abraham Kitson, Thomas Butter and William Wright. By December 1582 Wolfe was imprisoned in the Clink; Ward was committed to Ludgate prison following a raid on his premises by agents of the Stationers' Company.[26] From these disputes, presented as affecting the well-being of the 'poorer sort' of the London trade, there eventually emerged the English Stock of the Stationers' Company, a trade-sponsored monopoly protected by royal privileges adapted to the needs of a cartel, and organized by the mid-1590s under a treasurer and stock-keepers.[27]

Kingston's ambitions were prompted by a crisis in the printing trade. In bookselling, too, the established oligarchy in London sought to defend its position by a renewed attack on the long-standing tolerance of alien members of the trade. As earlier in the century, Cambridge continued to rely on these men, who offered a knowledgeable and efficient link with the continental markets. The tensions in the London trade between native and foreign workmen, resurgent after a wave of sympathy following the St Bartholomew's Day massacre in 1572, had further exercised the Court of the Stationers' Company in 1578, and the Court of Aldermen had found itself obliged to follow Burghley's instructions not to permit wholesale prosecution of stationers for employing foreign labour.[28] By far the most powerful of the aliens in the book trade in these years was the long-established Birckman family, who acted as middlemen between the overseas and the Cambridge (and other) stationers.[29] But their position offended the London stationers; and thus the University was caught up in the argument between the Privy Council and the City over the extent to which strangers should be either encouraged or permitted. When in May 1579 several consignments of books from the Birckmans and other stranger stationers were seized en route to Cambridge, matters seemed set to come to a head.[30] It was an act of desperation by what the Lord Mayor was pleased to call 'certaine meane Cittisens' in the Stationers' Company – a company much weakened by the dominance of Birckman and, now, 'divers Frenche men' in the import trade.[31]

It was perhaps for these wider reasons that in 1580 complaint came to the University not direct from the Stationers' Company, but from the Lord Mayor of London, Nicholas Woodroffe. His choice of Thomas Norton as moderator, both legal adviser to the Company and 'one of your vniuersitie, and that greatly fauoreth yow', brought also the threat of proceedings before the Privy Council.[32] Had such a threat materialized, the University might well have won its cause, for the Council had already shown itself displeased at the events of the previous year. Woodroffe's clear distinction between townsmen's and University interests had little relevance to the matter in Cambridge. Certainly the University's dealings could be construed as offending against the legislation prohibiting employment of foreigners or strangers in the London book trades, from which waivers had been necessary for both James Sheres and for the staff of Thomas Vautrollier. But by 1583 the Privy Council committee on privileges, which included Norton, was recommending that the laws respecting the employment of strangers should be applied to the book trades just as to others. Complaint had come originally from the 'poorer sort' of binders; but it survived the vacillations of public policy to be used as another means of advancing the interest of the more powerful.

Not surprisingly, Norton's visit to Cambridge in the wake of Woodroffe's letter, in August or September 1580, proved to be inconclusive. The University stalled, mindful not only of its need for books but also of the City's various endowments for the well-being of teaching and students; but it also adopted an air of injured misunderstanding that was not entirely naive. Norton and Woodroffe spoke of books being supplied by 'forrainers' – 'of wch grefe we haue some mervaile, consideringe the longe continuance of o^r vsage heretofore', remarked the Heads in reply.[33] Pleading the briefness of Norton's visit, the need to consult properly amongst the booksellers, and a press of other business, they found it impossible to return an immediate answer. For the present, the University asked Woodroffe to ensure that 'our old servante Jhon Sheres Stacioner, no Townesmane but one of our bodie', should be suffered to continue to operate as hitherto.[34]

Thus, by masterly inaction, the University delayed the impending crisis between London and Cambridge trades, native and foreign tradesmen, and ensured a continuing supply of books. Sheres was by far the most important bookseller in Cambridge in 1580; but his University connection, beyond the ordinary licence and his service as churchwarden of Great St Mary's, is not clear. The distinction between townsmen and members of the University, whilst strengthening the latters' hand in his particular instance, might not have borne scrutiny. Sheres' family connections with the London trade and with the Low Countries placed him in a position at once favourable and exposed. In choosing to defend the livelihood of only one of the Cambridge booksellers, the University in fact elected to protect the person most likely to be affected by any embargo.

The matter was, however, cut short in the following July, with Sheres' death. His business, including a book-stock valued at £120, debts due to him recorded in his debt book of £300, and cash and other debts amounting to a further £260, was left to be managed by his wife, all his children being under age. The University's material interest in his business, as its principal supplier, coupled with the unresolved differences with the London authorities (by now the Lord Mayor, the Stationers' Company and the Privy Council were all, or were about to be, implicated) did not permit a detached or disinterested view of the fate of Sheres' estate.

The protests of 1577–83 eventually strengthened the hands of the monopolists. The report commissioned by the Privy Council in 1582 to enquire into these nascent privileges, and in particular into their operation, was of but limited help to the 'poorer sort'. It was accepted only after the findings of the original Commissioners, John Hammond and Thomas Norton, had been confirmed by three further Commissioners, including John Aylmer, Bishop of London. In one respect, the report proffered comfort in confirming the unrestricted right to print ballads, and so to partake of a large part of the most popular market. But no less importantly, the commissioners had negotiated with each of the patentees save two, Marsh and Vautrollier, an agreement to release a selection of titles controlled by the patents: the importance lay not in their release (few in fact were returned to open competition), but in the patentees' ostensible willingness to negotiate at all, even if some of the titles under discussion had little current commercial value.[35] The commissioners had assessed the position judiciously, preserving the interests of printers and stationers throughout the economic spectrum: their object was made clearer in their arguing for stringent control of London's press capacity overall, by means of annual surveys supported by a licensing system for typefounders and for blacksmiths or joiners engaged in building new presses. As a further check, the commissioners suggested that each printer should deliver a printed specimen of his type and ornament stock to Stationers' Hall. The number of apprentices in any workshop was not to exceed the number of journeymen.

Not all these recommendations were practicable, and there were organizational as well as manufacturing difficulties in the way of the suggestion of deposited specimens for a central file. But some of the principles in the report became embedded, more or less, in Stationers' Company administration. It was an argument for stasis, not for expansion or for response to a market economy. It would have ensured work enough for every press, but only at the expense of imposing a stultifying control on expansion even in the face of a widening and growing market. The abortive attempt of the Stationers' Company to tighten its hold on the trade by Act of Parliament in 1584–5 had perhaps a similar end in view.[36] The tensions in London arose not from fear of a collapse in the market for printed matter, but from jealousies over who was to share it. Those who entered the market for the first time, and established their own presses, as did Thomas Thomas in Cambridge in 1583, did so because they did not share the prevailing view in some influential London circles that it was better to reap assured profits by limiting production (and therefore the number of employees) than to risk reward by expansion and competition.

The only patentees whom the 1582–3 Privy Council Commissioners had been unable to interview were Thomas Marsh and Thomas Vautrollier, who held in their hands the control not only of schoolbooks, but of most Latin texts.[37] Their failure to appear earned a recommendation that their privileges should be curtailed: no other patentees were named in the Commissioners' final report, which thus bore the hallmark of circumspect negotiation in the course of investigations.[38] For the University, Marsh's and Vautrollier's position in, and contributions to, the book trade were uniquely crucial. The Commissioners, including Norton, were unconvinced by arguments for patents when interpreted to the exclusion of other printers' livelihoods, and when based on false allegations or premises. Such restrictions encouraged neither individual printers nor the interests of the Stationers' Company. In the light of the 1583 report, Norton's undated memorandum 'Concerning privileges of printing', with its adverse comments on patentees, is less removed from London interests than it might appear.[39] But to establish a new press would be to challenge the Company directly, and it is probably for this reason that Norton, as the Company's legal adviser, sought a compromise that was intended to meet the aspirations of the University, the limited encouragement given the University by its Chancellor, Burghley, and the interests of the Company for the overall supervision of the London book trade.

After rehearsing the same arguments as appeared in the 1583 report in favour of the first authorized printer or publisher of a work retaining rights in it 'so allway that such printer doe not suffer such boke to be out of print that it be not to be had', Norton continued with two examples that were especially pertinent to Cambridge interests, and incidentally, in their reference both to Latin textbooks and to dictionaries, to Thomas in particular:

Priuiledges generall, as of all schole bokes, or of such bokes as were in vse before & were the liuinges of other men either in printing or bringing them as merchandise, as the priuiledge graunted to Thomas Marsh of a greater multitude of schole bokes than he doth or can serue the Realme, also the priuiledge to Byneman wherby the Realme, & specially the vniuersities, canot be serued neither of histories nor Dictionaries in any language, and priuileges for musike bokes in generall and other of like sorte, are verie inconuenient and hurtfull to learning.

These sortes of priuiledges are commonly graunted vpon vntrue suggestions, and so repeallable in lawe, & equitie.

Marshes priuiledge is fonded vpon these suggestiones, that schole bokes were not to be had by reason of the restraint of trafike wth the lowe contreys: And that he had for that purpose prouided more store of better than any other printer, w^{che} suggestions be bothe vntrue.

Bynemans priuiledge is founded vpon suggestions and preamble concerning onely my Lord bishop of Lincolnes Dictionarie and Chronicle, and in the ende concludeth with graunte of priuilege of all Dictionaries and histories without aleginge any consideracon.

Bothe those priuiledges doe not onely carrie the sole autoritie of printing, but allso a prohibition of bringing in or selling those sortes of bokes wch before were lawfull merchandise vsually brought, yea and such as there were plentie of them in the Quenes subiectes handes to be sold.

These maters opened to the Chancellers of bothe the vniuersities by the certificates of the sayd vniuersities, there may be order obteyned to examine the vntruthe of the suggestions, and so to repelle them if ther be cause.

Petition also is to be made that her Matie will not graunt any such priuiledges whereby the vniuersities, & scholes are to be vnserued or ill serued of bokes.[40]

Norton's opinion, addressed presumably to the Stationers' Company (by whom he was paid), was made available to Cambridge, and is of considerable importance. It reveals some of the London background to the eventual seizure of Thomas's equipment, but makes clear that the London trade was by no means united. Indeed, it left open the question of whether or not Cambridge had any right to print. Not least significantly, it also treated both universities as one, and in doing so interpreted Thomas's challenge as a symptom of wider questions, concerning the adequacy, structure and competence of the British book trades at large, rather than as simply the eccentric aspirations of one man motivated by educational or religious beliefs.

All this necessarily influenced considerations of a new press in a university context. The argument over Thomas's right to print became ostensibly a legal and constitutional one, over the relative authority of Letters Patent granted in 1534 and of others, granted subsequently, for individual monopolies whose specifics trespassed on earlier more general provisions. In fact, the argument was an economic one, in which a new press (and especially one seemingly beyond the control of an increasingly powerful Stationers' Company) was a threat to a barely achieved equilibrium. In such a situation, the choice of books to be printed became of critical importance, as Burghley implied in his opinion that the University should restrict itself to its own needs, and so avoid infringing the patents granted to Seres, Jugge, Day and others.

Such needs were, however, difficult to identify beyond the most basic. Unaccustomed to providing its own texts, but relying on imported or London-printed matter provided through the local retail booksellers, the University was thus faced with economic as well as educational challenges. It had never hitherto been expected to absorb a complete edition of a book, amounting to perhaps 1,000–1,250 copies, in a market where the continuing sale would be only moderate once a generation had been supplied. The annual undergraduate intake, though more than doubled since the 1550s, amounted at most to about 340 per annum;[41] by no means all of these would come up expecting to read the standard texts, but would be looking for a more flexible approach to preparation for gentlemanly life. In any case, within a twelvemonth, the second-hand trade could be expected seriously to affect trade in new copies of any textbook. Not surprisingly, neither the University nor the local booksellers seem to have been eager to finance such editions as Burghley hinted at.

No doubt with these considerations in view, Norton put forward a 'devise' intended simultaneously to answer the University's everyday needs for teaching texts from London, rather than from a new press, to keep prices moderate by setting up a special stock, to avoid a charge for Cambridge stationers, and ensure work for London printers; although he did not say so, his proposal would also have made the import of these texts from the continent unnecessary. Norton proposed:

That a competent stock be obteyned for printing of bookes for poore schollers, as for example, x^{li}.

That the reders intending to reade any smale parcell of any author, as a tragedie or oration etc in greke or latine, (in which case it is costly for poore schollers to bye the greate bookes), shall signifie to some persone at London to whome the order of that stock shalbe comitted, what booke he intendeth to reade.

The reader is also to make such aduertisment ij or iij moneths afore he reade it.

Also what nomber will serue his auditorie, wherein he is not to certefie a greter nomber than nedeth, for so much runneth to losse, and consequently to the decaye of the stock for the poore schollers.

Also with his said aduertisment he is to procure and send a letter from the vniuersitie directed to some learned man resident in London, to take peyne in the correction.

The bokes are vpon such aduertisement to be putt to printing, at charge of the stock and sent downe to the reader wth a note of the price of euerie boke.

The reader is to giue to eury poore scholar of his auditorie a boke and of those that be able, he shall take the price: and shall certefie to the stocke keper the names of euery one that haue a boke, bothe such as payed, and such as haue bokes in respect of pouertie.

He shall allso send vp the money so receued and the bokes remaining that the stock may extend the further, and continue longer to this good vse.[42]

No such stock was ever established. Indeed, given the limited market each year, the requirement to give books to the poorest, and the number of texts required, it is doubtful that Norton's suggested initial investment of £10 would have been sufficient. His proposals for detailed stock-keeping, imposing considerable administrative burdens on lecturers, were hardly such as to win ready favour. It was a device for co-operation, ingenious and far ahead of its time, but one that offered advantages neither to printer, nor to lecturer, and it found little support. If this was the best that the Stationers' own adviser could devise, then the University's options were limited indeed, and its resolve to support the effort of a single entrepreneur can be readily seen as corporate self-protection not simply for privilege, but for the very means with which to teach.

Legislatively at least, the curriculum in the 1570s and 1580s was governed by the University statutes of 1570. They prescribed a course, divided between the trivium and quadrivium, requiring four years leading to the BA and three to the MA, that had changed little in principle since the Middle Ages. Rhetoric in the first year led to dialectic in the second and third, and to philosophy in the fourth. The authors specified covered much beyond this, however, providing for study that continued in the higher faculties, of medicine, law and theology, after the completion of the BA. Aristotle, Pliny, Quintilian, Hermogenes, Cicero, the Greek orators, Homer and Euripides were joined within a single chapter of the statutes by provision for the more specialist post-graduate studies in law and medicine described further in those ensuing. Cuthbert Tunstall and Girolamo Cardano were to be followed in arithmetic; Pomponius Mela, Pliny, Strabo and Plato in mathematics; Euclid in geometry; and Ptolemy in astronomy. Much of this, and especially the emphasis on Aristotle, had a long university tradition behind it. The list of prescribed reading in 1570 was repeated almost verbatim from the statutes of Edward VI.[43] But the statutes enshrined a conservatism that was not followed in practice, and that left considerable opportunity for manoeuvre in individual courses. Trinity College's statutes of 1560, following the University's of 1535 at many points, specified also Rodolphus Agricola's *De inventione dialectica*, and for Greek grammars prescribed either Clenardus, Ceporinus or Theodorus Gaza.[44] In other words, they provided for a curriculum that was to some degree modified by college custom; and what was true here of Trinity was true also of other colleges. The principal authors were agreed; but textbooks and expository works were subject to changes not necessarily envisaged by University statute.

University booksellers, and to varying degrees University Printers, were concerned with a wider, and different range of texts that displayed broader emphases than the central attention to Aristotle and, increasingly, Cicero. In many respects, the Press's output was to depend on, and be dictated by, London interests. But in others it was generated in response to the ordinary teaching needs of the University expressed sometimes through particularly influential teachers, such as Andrew Downes or (later) Isaac Barrow, and sometimes through more commonly held requirements for what were, for many, standard textbooks.[45]

Accounts of tutors for books for their pupils, post-mortem inventories of members of the University, surviving copies of books with owners' names, and lists of booksellers' stock are but some of the sources that offer a supplement and corrective to the provisions of the statutes in determining what was most in demand. At Trinity, between 1570 and 1577, John Whitgift bought books for two dozen of his pupils, including the young Francis Bacon (admitted Fellow-Commoner in 1573).[46] Ramist influences were well established, at Trinity as elsewhere in the University, and were reflected in repeated needs for copies of Peter Carter's annotated edition of John Seton's *Dialectica*, first published in at least 1563.[47] For Whitgift's pupils, a diet of Aristotle and Cicero was varied by purchases of Erasmus' *Apophthegmata* and *Colloquia*, of Julius Caesar and Justinus, as well as of the authors specified by statute: there seems, in Whitgift's case at least, to have been no discrimination between Fellow-Commoners, pensioners and sizars, or between those reading for a degree and those who were not. In 1577 another member of Trinity, Robert Devereux, Earl of Essex, ran up, during his first year, a bill for books including Ramus on logic, his commentary on Cicero's orations, Sturmius' *De universa ratione elocutionis rhetoricae*, Beza's *Quaestiones et responsiones Christianae*, Grimalius' *De optimo senatore* and Isocrates.[48] Such lists did not of course represent all the books that a student might hope to have to hand. Cooper's Latin dictionary was essential, its price of about 14s.–16s. placing it in a category well apart from the more ordinary textbooks. The equivalents for Greek were Calepinus, Crespin, Scapula or Phavorinus' old *Lexicon*, while the elements of the language were taught, elsewhere as at Trinity, from Ceporinus' *Compendium grammaticae graecae* or Clenardus' *Institutiones*, the universal introductions for the later sixteenth century.[49] In literature, the stock of John Dennis in 1578 included Plutarch, Demosthenes, Aristotle, Isocrates, Sophocles, Herodian, Lucian and Euripides.[50] In Hebrew, Cevallerius' *Rudimenta* and Petrus Martinius' *Grammatica* were the texts used.[51] But none, except Aristotle and the various commentaries on him, compared in Dennis's stock with the numbers of books by Ramus (about seventeen copies of his *Dialectica* in its various forms alone), or with the twenty-seven copies of Seton's *Dialectica*.[52] If the University were to follow Burghley's suggestion, and print what was needed for its teaching, it was in authors such as these that the choice would have had to be made initially. Apart from the dictionaries and one or two of the collected editions of classical authors, they were all commonplace quartos or octavos, designed for economy and for student use,[53] and available from a plentitude of overseas sources as well as, in some instances such as Seton or Ramus, in London. Gabriel Harvey, who came up to Christ's as a pensioner in 1566, owned a folio Livy whilst still an undergraduate, the gift of his kinsman Henry Harvey, Master of Trinity Hall: but such volumes were unusual on student shelves.[54]

The prices of these basic books left little room for profit, if binding was left aside. John Sheres and Thomas Bradshaw, two experienced Cambridge stationers, valued six copies in pasteboard (only) of *Sententiae* from Aristotle at just over fourpence each, and copies in similar condition of Seton at ninepence apiece. Unbound copies of Ramus's *Dialectica* were valued at about 2¼d. each, and of Euripides' *Alcestis* at a penny. No such inventory, based on written-down prices, was likely to produce high valuations, and retail prices were certainly more: the equivalent books charged for by Chard to the same Cambridge bookseller Thomas Bradshaw in 1583–4 included Ramus's *Dialectica* at fivepence each.[55] But the wholesale, and more important still in this context, the manufacturing, price was not so far removed. For trade at this level, there was little profit in printing far distant from the principal markets, as the wide-flung geographical scatter of editions of Ramus and Clenardus, for example, testify.[56] Furthermore, to sell into a tightly organized market, with a large regular turnover of second-hand copies that often never even saw a bookseller's shop after they were bought new, was a prospect offering little appeal to London entrepreneurs. It was one which Burghley could therefore safely proffer as a course for the University to follow.

Furthermore, the assured stance and vigour in controversy of William Whitaker, Regius Professor of Divinity from 1580, were to provide the requisite (if not always uncontroversial) local devolution of London authority in his own field. In education, the London printers had not so far proved their case. And the Letters Patent granted by Henry VIII in 1534 remained quite explicit.

It was against this background of unrest within the London trade, jealousy between London and country booksellers, and imminent changes to this precarious balance as a consequence of Thomas's preparations for his new press, that on 31 October 1583 the Vice-Chancellor and Heads promulgated a series of regulations, fuller than ever before, for the ordering of the Cambridge book trade. The preamble spoke of the threat posed by 'abuses and dysorders' in the trade both to the University and to its students. But then the regulations moved from the familiar terms of an exordium to confirm the long-standing requirement that local tradesmen should be licensed by the University, and to restrict future booksellers and other merchants to those who had served their apprenticeship in Cambridge, unless given special leave. Bookbinders, booksellers and stationers were to stand bound (for £40) to 'provyde suffycyent store of all manner of bookes fit and requysyte for the furnyshinge of all students contynewinge or abydinge within this Vniuersytie, and the same bookes to be well bounde and to be solde at all and euery tyme and tymes vpon reasonable pryces'.[57] Similar insistence on acceptable quality was to be a feature of regulations and graces governing successive printers; but despite Thomas's by now well formulated plans there was no mention of printer or printers in these 1583 rules.

The University's orders were designed, in large measure, as a retort to the London stationers; but they also reflected many of the same concerns at an over-populated trade. As employer, Thomas Thomas, like the other Cambridge stationers, was thus defended by just that kind of protectionism against which the University had argued in its dealings over Sheres and the stranger booksellers. As so often, local interest proved stronger than a consistent and nationally agreed policy.

The last few pages have dealt in some detail with events in the late 1570s and early 1580s, before there was a new press established at Cambridge. In examining the London trade more generally, and the opinions expressed both of its operation and of suggestions that a new press should be established in a town remote from the Stationers' Company's immediate control, I have sought to suggest what circumstances gave rise to the conclusion, on some people's part, that such a press was either necessary or feasible. What was it that distinguished Thomas's motives from those of Siberch sixty years previously?

How was it that the University found itself obliged, and willing, to support his initiative? The 1583 press succeeded, and became permanent, whereas Siberch left Cambridge after only a few months. Both Thomas and Siberch found personal support amongst senior members of the University; but the 1583 press grew out of very different circumstances: a disappointed, disjointed and inadequate London trade suspicious of foreign goods if not within its immediate sphere of influence and control. Such a trade left the way open for the application of a neglected University privilege, on behalf of a person willing to exploit a vacancy in the local trade, to challenge received ideas in London and so to create for himself the means of pursuing a programme of printing and publication that rapidly assumed qualities of its own. The manner in which Thomas Thomas established his press, and the course of publication he chose, or was obliged, to pursue, form the subject of the following chapter.

5

Thomas Thomas, 'that puritan printer'

The decision of a former Fellow of King's to marry the widow of a wealthy local bookbinder and stationer, take advantage of a University privilege that had never been exercised and open a modest printing shop as near to the centre of the University as it was possible to be (see fig. 2), did not catch the world by the ears. In 1583, as for most of its history, much of Cambridge University's strength lay in the ability at once to appear remote even from the majority of the literate population, and yet be involved at the very hub of political, theological and other debate.

If it felt inclined, few places could be more introspective, as was demonstrated all too clearly in the parochialisms of the popular college plays – themselves acted in Latin or Greek rather than in English – and in the continued witticisms of Gabriel Harvey, Edmund Spenser, Christopher Marlowe or Thomas Nashe. Yet no place had been more responsible for the form of late Elizabethan secular and religious government. Lord Burghley, Chancellor of the University since 1559, had been educated for six years at St John's; Sir Francis Walsingham, a Kingsman, had succeeded Sir Thomas Smith, a Queensman and a former Vice-Chancellor, as Secretary of State in 1576. All three Elizabethan Archbishops of Canterbury – Parker, Grindal and Whitgift – were at one time or another Fellows of Cambridge colleges, and every Bishop of London during the reign had attended the same university. The well-being of the University repeatedly depended on the connections forged in this manner, while in Cambridge itself William Whitaker led the way at the end of the century in support of the Protestant cause. Religion in the University was distinctly cosmopolitan, not least because of Calvinism's international frame of reference: its tenets were encouraged by Whitaker and demonstrated abundantly not only in the books printed at Cambridge by Thomas Thomas and his successor John Legate, but also in the personal libraries to be found amongst ordinary Fellows of colleges. Among the other professors in 1584, the Lady Margaret's Professor of Divinity (Peter Baro) came from France; and the Regius Professor of Hebrew (Edward Lively) had been taught by Johannes Drusius in the Low Countries. For generations, the work of members of the University had been published not only in London,

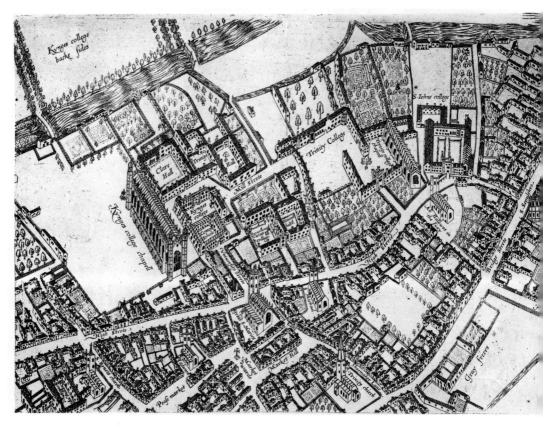

Fig. 2 Cambridge in 1592, after the plan by John Hammond. Thomas's premises were in University Street, or Regent Walk, at the west end of Great St Mary's church. The street is now beneath the Vice-Chancellor's lawn, outside the Senate House.

but also – and often for the first time – abroad. In the last decades of the sixteenth century, and first of the seventeenth, English authors became increasingly attractive to foreign printers and booksellers, thanks partly, at least, to the international intellectual movements associated with Calvin and Ramus, partly to the necessarily international arguments between protestantism and catholicism and partly to new trading arrangements. However, all of these factors were enhanced by the great expansion in the printing and bookselling industries during the period both in England and on the continent. This market was fuelled most dramatically by exiled recusants, but it was much more diverse than this implies. Among Cambridge figures alone, the Ramists George Downame and William Temple, and the physician Timothy Bright, all appealed to booksellers at Frankfurt in particular, where the Wechel firm of printers, busy about its largely successful attempt to dominate much of the central and north European market for Ramus and his followers, was particularly hospitable to English authors in Latin guise.[1] The puritan William Perkins found a much more widely distributed market in translation, not only into Latin but also into French, Dutch and Spanish, with the continental publication of his works concentrated principally at Basel, Hanau, Amsterdam and Haarlem, and with collected editions of his works published at Geneva in 1611–18 and again in 1624. Geneva, too, saw in 1610 a collected edition of Whitaker, though in his case the firm of Christopher Corvinus at Herborn, north-west of Frankfurt, was of much greater significance and, as will be seen, can be shown to have been more directly connected with the Cambridge book trade than can most of the continental international booksellers.[2]

There is, therefore, something more than a simple contrast in the context of the events of 1583–4 that surrounded the establishment of Thomas's press. In the annals of printing, these months coincided with the introduction of printing into places as remote as the Azores in 1583 and Lima in 1584. Nearer home, and certainly of more importance to Cambridge, Christopher Plantin removed briefly from Antwerp to Leiden, where he thus avoided the siege of Antwerp. Here, encouraged by the presence of Justus Lipsius, he was able to print over thirty works under the auspices of the University,[3] including Simon Stevin's pamphlet *De thiende* advocating a decimal system. At Paris, in 1583, the inheritor of the Estienne press, Mamert Patisson, produced Scaliger's *De emendatione temporum*, both a typographical masterpiece and a revolution in historical comprehension. At Bordeaux, the first two books of Montaigne's *Essais* had been published in 1580. In Italy, Tasso's *Gerusalemme liberata* came out in 1581; Caesalpinus' pioneering work on plant classification *De plantis* was published at Florence in 1583; Lomazzo's mannerist *Trattato dell'arte della pittura, scoltura, et architettura* came out in Milan in 1584 (and was to be translated into English in 1598); and the election of Felice Peretti as Pope Sixtus V in 1585 was to set a seal in Rome on a period of lavish creativity in building as well as to usher in the revision of the Vulgate: the Vatican Press itself was to be founded in 1587. European expansion overseas was reflected in the publishing industries by the appearance in the mid 1580s of two major works: Waghenaer's *Spieghel der zeevaerdt*, printed by Plantin at Leiden in 1583, and Gerard Mercator's *Atlas*, of which the maps describing France, Germany and the Netherlands were published at Duisburg a little later. Hakluyt's first work, *Divers voyages, touching the discoverie of America* was printed at London in 1582, the year before Sir Humphrey Gilbert's unsuccessful attempt to colonize Newfoundland and three years before Sir Walter Raleigh's expedition to Roanoke in Virginia.

For England, relations with the continent were dominated by fears of Catholic expansionism. The threat to Geneva by Charles Emmanuel, Duke of Savoy, was met in 1582–3 by a highly successful public collection sponsored by the Privy Council and organized through the church as well as the City of London.[4] Protestant La Rochelle looked to England for financial support after the St Bartholomew's Day massacre in 1572, and by 1582 was estimated to be £40,000 in debt to the City of London.[5]

The wars in the Low Countries were to engage an English expeditionary force in 1585 – but only after Antwerp had been attacked by the French in January 1582/3 and the Duke of Parma had taken first Ypres and then Bruges early in 1584, before Ghent surrendered to him in the following September. The capitulation of Antwerp to Spanish troops in 1585 set a seal on its decline from its premier position as an international port. Domestic politics in England were thrown into a crisis with the discovery of the Throckmorton plot in December 1583, the consequent expulsion of the Spanish ambassador for his part in it, and Throckmorton's own execution in July. In the Church of England, Whitgift was enthroned as Archbishop of Canterbury following Grindal's death in July 1583; and in Lincolnshire Burghley was in the midst of a long building programme at his house near Stamford, to be completed only by 1587. Whitgift, former Master of Trinity College, and Burghley, Chancellor of the University, were each to affect the development of the Cambridge press, though from very different viewpoints. Meanwhile, the government sought to impose its own will on the book trade as a whole in 1583, by a proclamation against the circulation of Brownist propaganda,[6] and in 1584 by first the seizure of various 'trayterous and popish bookes' imported probably from Antwerp,[7] and secondly a further proclamation directed (with a contrasting lack of specificity) against 'books defacing true religion, slandering administration of justice, endangering Queen's title, etc.'[8]

In London, where in May 1583 it was calculated that there were some fifty-three presses in all, at twenty-three establishments, the principal development in the disposition of the book trade was the establishment of the Eliot's Court Press, a partnership of four men who, having acquired the equipment of Henry Bynneman (d. 1583), established themselves as printers with an especial penchant for Latin texts.[9] For the London printers, the year 1584 was no *annus mirabilis*.[10] The previous year had become memorable for the first, and posthumous, appearance of Sir Thomas Smith's *De republica Anglorum*, which had circulated in manuscript since its composition in 1565, which John Day had thought to publish in 1581, and which was now issued by Gregory Seton, brother-in-law of Day's widow.[11] The book proved an instant success and, dressed up with extra material and convenient summary, quickly achieved classic status. Yet while the year 1584 saw no achievement of this kind, the variety and scope of the year's publications serve as a reminder of the multitudes among which Thomas's first books had to find their way. As usual, by far the greater number were of new editions of established titles; but the year was also marked by several notable débuts.

In literature, four new books by Robert Greene included his *Arbasto*, *Gwydonius*, *Morando the tritameron of love* and *The myrrour of modesty*; Lyly's *Campaspe* appeared for the first time, and was printed in three editions during this year alone; and George Peele's *Araygnement of Paris*, based on an Italian original, added further to the plays printed during the year. Thanks to the activities of John Wolfe, Machiavelli's *Discorsi* (not translated in print into English until 1636) and *Il prencipe* (translated 1640) were made available for the first time from the London press. They were accompanied by Aretino's *Ragionamenti* and (in Latin, and more openly) Tasso's *Solymeidos*, while from John Charlewood's press there was surreptitiously issued a group of books by Giordano Bruno, an offshoot of his stay at Oxford during these years.[12] Thomas Lodge's *Alarum against userers* took up a popular theme, represented also by a new edition of Thomas Wilson's *Discourse uppon usurye*, originally published in 1572 and in which the rights had by January 1583/4 passed from the first publisher, Richard Tottel, to the Stationers' Company.[13] Moving away from literature and politics, a fresh edition of John Shute's *First and chief groundes of architecture* made available again an introduction to classical architecture first published in England in 1563.[14] Sir Thomas Chaloner's *Shorte discourse of the most rare vertue of nitre* was the precocious work of a young man fresh home from Italy, who was later to establish the first alum mines in England and to take a prominent part in the education of Prince Henry. Chaloner's pamphlet was never reprinted; but a medical book by the Manchester physician and schoolmaster Thomas Cogan, *The hauen of health*, printed for the first time in 1584, found a following for whom it was to be repeatedly reprinted. Such practical books, subject to heavy use, have survived in lesser numbers than some larger and heavier volumes on less everyday subjects, and A. W.'s *Booke of cookry*, 'newly enlarged with the seruing in of meats to the table' is represented now only by fragments – themselves part of only the earliest surviving, not the first, edition of a book now of extreme rarity. By contrast, John Astley's *Art of riding* appeared in but one edition, and was never reprinted. Yet among all these, and among the religious discussion, sermons, lawbooks, school textbooks and government propaganda, one book published during the year was to have an influence that is belied by its subsequent publishing history. Reginald Scot's *Discouerie of witchcraft*, published in 1584 by William Brome, was not to be published again until 1651. It is a sharp antidote to the temptation to judge a book's influence or success solely by its edition numbers.[15]

In Cambridge itself, the University had to absorb not simply books. The foundation of Emmanuel College in 1584, by the Queen's firmly puritan Chancellor of the Exchequer Sir Walter Mildmay, brought a new and distinct *frisson* to University affairs. It was the first college to be founded since Henry VIII had created Trinity in 1546, and its statutes departed from those of Christ's (on which they were modelled) by placing particular emphasis on the new college's responsibility for the training of the parochial ministry: the requirement was in marked contrast to the existing habits and assumptions preoccupied with ecclesiastical or political preferment and with the collegiate status quo. In its first Master, Laurence Chaderton, Mildmay ensured that his new college would conform with his own religious viewpoint. The new foundation was to prove a difficult and sometimes outrageous sibling for the other colleges, until the success of its new breed of preachers, and its influence in the North American colonies, both commanded and demanded respect.[16]

From 1583 to the present, University Printers have held office in all but unbroken succession. In 1583–4 there were published the first books to have been printed at Cambridge since the time of John Siberch. Much of the rest of this volume will be concerned with those who held office, and with their publications. But the final establishment of a press (rather than simply the right to do so) entailed both accommodation with the Stationers' Company – and that, as will be seen, at a particularly tense stage in its history – and an implicit belief in the necessity for a printer in the University.

Kingston and the University, not perhaps very enthusiastic partners, had failed in their attempt in 1577. In 1583 the London trade was no less jealous; but the University was to prove more determined, perhaps partly because one of its own number, rather than a tradesman from elsewhere, was the principal most involved. The difficulties facing the printing trade in London in the early 1580s, arising partly from an apparently excessive number of printers, and partly from the difficulty of controlling unauthorized printing, were summarized by Christopher Barker in December 1582. In a report to Burghley that also surveyed the monopolies then operating, Barker explained that these monopolies had become necessary because of the inescapable capital investment and charges for 'learned Correctors'. His conclusion, that the number of printing houses should be reduced from twenty-two to eight or ten for the whole of England, and even for Scotland as well, offered the advantage that such a restriction would discourage 'frivolous and vnfruitfull Copies ... which are dayly thrust oute in prynt, greatly corrupting the youth, and preiudiciall to the Comon wealth manye wayes'.[17] Such a course, had it been taken, would presumably have benefited principally the richer or more powerful of the Company; but an undated appeal to Burghley from the whole of its members, submitted probably at about the same time, laid emphasis on the poverty of the Company – 'consistinge of manye poore housholders relieued by printinge of bookes' – and on the onerous nature of the Company's responsibilities in rooting out seditious and popish books.[18] The following months witnessed repeated complaints and arguments over patents, which had been a bone of contention between the privileged and the poorer London stationers since at least 1577,[19] while the unauthorized activities of John Wolfe, a member of the Fishmongers' Company, in printing books that were the properties of established patentees, focused complaints more particularly. Moreover, as a further petition submitted in February or March 1582/3 made clear, Wolf was by no means the only offender.[20]

Had he reflected, a politically astute man would not, perhaps, have chosen this moment to engender still more jealousy. Or perhaps Thomas Thomas – if indeed he considered the matter – found succour in the activities of so many blatant offenders. In any case, determination dictated its own timetable, and in the middle of March Thomas presented a letter to the Chancellor of the University, Burghley, from the Vice-Chancellor, Roger Goad, and requested his approval:

After my very hartie Commendacions I haue receved your letters of the xiith of this moneth by this bearer Mr Thomas written in his favor being one of that uniuersitie and desirous to putt in vre the art of printing there under the priviledg of the uniuersitie graunted by Charter. Wherein besydes myne own opinion, I thought good also to vse the advice of the Mr of the Rolles, Who hath considered lykewise of your charter whereof I sent him the Copie. And fynding it in his opinion concurring with myne a graunt of good validitie, I do assent to that which yow shall think fitt for the apointing of Mr Thomas to print by vertue thereof, having regard that he be sene to be furnished with all thinges fitt and requisit for that purpose, and that his letters and paper be answerable with any the foreyn printes & the prices lykewise agreable. Of which thinges or any others to be thought of and considered in this matter if yow shall conceve some instrument by waie of articles or decre, I will be redie to geve myne assent and furtheraunce as shall be requisite. And so I bidd yow hartely farewell. From my Howse in the Strand this xviiith of March 1582.

[Postscript in Burghley's own hand] I thynk it good that the partyes that shall be licensed or authorised to print, may have their authorite with Condition, or otherwise bound to stand to the order of the Chancellor and the heades, in case of any cause of mislykyng of the use of the sayd authoritie.

Your assured loving frend,
W. Burghley.[21]

All too little is known of the man who was eventually to be the first practising University Printer. He had been born in London in 1553, the son of Thomas Thomas, 'gentleman', and though entered at Eton there is no evidence that he was educated there: his association with the school may simply have been to gain entry to King's College, where he arrived in 1571 and became a Fellow in 1574, three years later to the day. He took his MA in 1579. During the whole of his time in Cambridge, from 1571 until his death in 1588, the Provost of his college was Roger Goad, whose reforming approach to the college affected the library and chapel alike, and whose firm wielding of authority engendered complaints, revolts and allegations of malpractice. 'But', remarked a more recent historian of the College, 'his energy and zeal, and the efficiency of his government of the College, cannot be questioned.'[22] Of Thomas's relations with the Provost no details survive, but it may be pertinent to recall that when the University had elected John Kingston printer, the Vice-Chancellor of the day had also been Goad.

In 1582, Thomas had published no book. Both his textbook edition of Ovid, and his Latin dictionary, were still to come. He was not an established author:

at an age less than thirty that would have been surprising. The reasons for his decision to resign from his fellowship, and to launch himself on a new career can only be surmised. If he was waiting for an opportunity, it came in May 1581, with the death of John Sheres, the leading local bookbinder and a man of considerable property.

Sheres left an estate valued at £893.16s.10d., including (besides a flock of sheep valued at £7) a stock of books valued at £120, and a quantity of binding equipment: a press (13s.4d.), '30 duss of lether' (£10), 500 pasteboards (15s.) and '2 cottyng presses w^t plowes, bordes, pryntes & other worken tooles' (£3.10s.). He was survived by his wife Anne, who inherited most of his estate; and he appointed as overseers of his will, Michael Wolf, a member of his wife's family, and Thomas Thomas.[23]

With his marriage to Sheres' widow, probably by March 1582/3,[24] Thomas embarked on a new career, one in which he was able to develop Sheres' bookselling and binding business into one of printing and publishing. It is noticeable that in all the subsequent debate about Thomas's press, no allusion was made to his continuing in business as stationer and bookbinder, the trades he inherited through Sheres' widow and to which his testamentary documents bear at best residuary witness. The University provided for the well-being of the Cambridge retail and binding trade generally when in October 1583 regulations were agreed, following complaints by local stationers, restricting (save by special permission) such trade to those whose sole business was in Cambridge and to those who had been apprenticed in the town. Such protectionist measures, which had very similar counterparts in London, seem to have caused little dissent at the time. There was no mention in this document of printing, for which the articles eventually drawn up in 1585/6 served as equivalents. In other words, the University made the same distinction between bookselling and binding on the one hand, and printing on the other, as that which obtained in London.[25]

There is no evidence that Burghley consulted with the London stationers, though their interest had not waned. Now, with Thomas duly appointed on 3 May,[26] they moved smartly onto the attack, in a memorandum addressed to John Aylmer, Bishop of London, but clearly intended for Burghley's eyes as well. Christopher Barker and Francis Coldock, who drew up this document, alluded to the abundance of printers in London (itself, as will be recalled, a matter for distress), and particularly to the difficulty already experienced in controlling printers – a difficulty that could only be increased by the existence of a press so far away in the country: 'Yet is yt an endles toile to withstande the lewde attemptes of manie of our profession beinge even within our citie and at our elbowes and daielie looked vnto, howe muche more troublesome and daungerous bothe for matters of the state and religion and other inconvenyences yt wilbe to haue a printing house erected soe farre of.' Thomas was spoken of as 'vnskilfull', 'a Scholer, altogether vnacquainted' with printing, while his workmen and apprentices would be beyond the control of the London stationers. The same criticisms were to persist for long after Thomas's death. But skilful or no, his business posed a threat to economic and political stability, and to the London trade. In return, Barker and Coldock uttered a threat of their own. Thomas would not be able to claim what he printed as his own copy, as London printers could with their privileges and their link with the Stationers' Company and its Register, to which they were legally obliged. Thomas, having no such link, would be open to abuse. 'Moreouer, whatsoeuer were graunted to him there [i.e. in Cambridge, by the Cambridge authorities] we mighte printe heere without perill for soe doinge, to his vndoinge; And though he might preiudice vs by some shewe of his generall graunte yet shoulde he vtterlie vndoe himself althoughe he had .1000. li stock to begynne.'[27]

By then the Stationers had already gone further than threats. On Aylmer's warrant to search out illegal presses, various equipment had been discovered and seized, amongst it a press and the associated 'furniture' (the sources are not more specific) alleged to belong to Thomas Thomas. The Vice-Chancellor, John Bell, Master of Jesus College, supported his demand for its return with a copy of the 1534 privilege, and thereby put Aylmer under the necessity of explaining his action to Burghley. Like the Stationers, he emphasized Thomas's inexperience – 'a man (as I heare) vtterlie ignoraunte in printinge'. Alluding to Burghley's letter of 18 March he was also quick to point out that whatever agreement was made about the quality of Thomas's work, it would be difficult to put into practice without skilled help. Aylmer (no friend of religious radicalism, and therefore perhaps doubly fearful of Thomas) and the Stationers had no legal claim on Thomas's equipment, and it is a measure of the alarm felt by Barker and Coldock that they offered to buy Thomas off, an outrageous suggestion that does not seem to have been seriously considered: 'We will', wrote the two men, 'recompence the said Scholler for all his charges that he hath beene at in the suite aforesaide, and also paie him to the full for all suche instrumentes as he hath alreadye prouided, and withall be moste readye to doe to the said vniuersytie or annye there such acceptable seruice in printinge as anye waie he or his might be able.'[28] It was scarcely surprising that Burghley's attempt to steer a course towards conciliation, admitting the interests of at once the University and the Stationers, and suggesting a conference of the warring factions,[29] was met with renewed firmness. Supported by eight other heads of houses, Bell complained to Burghley again, on 14 June, only three days after Burghley himself had written from the Strand:[30]

Our humble duties to your ho. remembred. whereas we vnderstande by your ho. lettres that certaine of the company of the Stationers in London haue sought to hinder therectinge of a print within this vniuersity of Cambridge and to impugne the auntient privilege graunted and confirmed by divers Princes for that purpose to the greate benefitt of the vniuersitie & advauncement of Learning. Theise are in most humble manner to desire your ho. not somuch in respect of Mr Thomas (who hath alredy receaved greate iniury and damage at theire handes) as in the behalf of the vniuersity (which findeth yt self very much agreved with the wrongfull detayninge of those goodes wherewithall as we are persuaded in right and equity they ought not to meddle) to continue our honorable patron, and to direct your favorable warrant to the wardeynes of the Stationers that he may haue his presse delivered with speede, least that by theire meanes as he hath bene dissapoynted of Master Whittakers his booke, so by theire delayes he be prevented of other bookes made within the vniversity, and now redy for the presse. As for the dowbtes which they cast (rather in respect of their private gaine and commodity, and to bringe the uniuersitys more auncient priuiledges in this behalf then theirs vnder theire jurisdicion at London, then for any other good consideracon, the decidinge or perill whereof also pertaineth not to them,) we dare vndertake in the behalf of Master Thomas whome we know to be a very godly and honest man that the presse shall not be abused eyther in publishinge thinges prohibited, or otherwise inconvenient for the Churche and state of this realme. And this we promise the rather for that his grace (whereof we haue sent a coppy to your honour by him self) was graunted vnto him vpon condicion that he shoulde stande bounde from tyme to tyme to such articles as your honour and the greatest part of the heades of Colledges shoulde tye him vnto. And for the conference wherevnto your honour moveth vs. yf yt shalbe your honour's pleasure we as desirous of peace and concorde (the premisses considered) shalbe ready to shewe our willingnes therevnto, yf yt shall please the company of the Stationers in London to sende hither some certain menne from them with sufficient aucthority for that purpose. Thus most humbly desiring that his presse may no longer be stayde, and hopinge that your honour will furder our desire hearein, we do in our dayly prayers commend your lordshippe to the blessed tuicon of the almighty. From Cambridge this 14. of June.

your Lordshippes most bounde

	Jhon Bell vicechancellor
Robert Norgate	Andrew Pern
Edmund Hownds	William Fulke
Thomas Neuile	John Still
	Tho Legge
	Edmund Barwell

No further correspondence concerning Thomas's equipment survives, and it must be assumed that the Stationers released it later in the year: the accounts of the Company for 1583–4 record merely payment of ten shillings to their legal adviser Thomas Norton (who had already helped in 1580–1) 'for his counsell for Cambridge matters'.[31] Of the press about which Aylmer and Bell had written, and the other vaguely described 'furniture', nothing detailed is known before Thomas used them to print his first books. It is not even known whether his press was new or second-hand.

Of the twenty-three printers in London in 1583 eight had only one press each; John Charlwood, Robert Waldegrave, John Kingston, Thomas Vautrollier, Thomas Purfoot and Richard Jugge had two apiece, while John Day and Henry Denham had four each, and Christopher Barker, the royal printer, no less than five. John Wolfe also owned five, but admitted to only three until two more were discovered in a secret vault.[32] The number of presses at work in London was subject to some degree of control, but at this stage Thomas does not appear to have envisaged a very substantial business. Perhaps his press was old, or perhaps it was misused or poorly maintained; but by the time of his death only five years later it was valued at but £3.6s.8d., a figure that his successor John Legate considered too much to pay, especially when he faced a repair bill for forty marks.[33]

Apart from a press, Thomas needed type: the fact that this is nowhere mentioned in the correspondence of 1582–3 may suggest that he eventually acquired his first, with some of his other decorative materials, late in 1583. Much – perhaps all – of it came from one or more of the French typefounders then working in London, the smaller text types in Pierre Haultin's roman and in Granjon's italic. There was nothing out of the ordinary in either, and Thomas obtained, in all, six sizes of roman type, in various cuttings, from the tiny bourgeois (used in side-notes and other restricted spaces) up to great primer, and including also a set of canon capitals for titling. Haultin, designer of several of the roman founts, typefounder and printer in the Protestant town of La Rochelle, had connections with the Protestant wholesale trade in books as well. His nephew Jérome had been settled in London since at least 1568, when he had been working for the typefounder Hubert Danvillier;[34] the matrices sold by Pierre Haultin to his nephew in 1575 were presumably for the London market, and may have signified Jérome's establishment as type-founder on his own account.[35] Haultin's types were to become common in London. In 1583 they were used also by, among others, Thomas Vautrollier, John Kingston, Henry Middleton, Henry Denham and Thomas Purfoot, with some of whose books some of Thomas's have as a consequence visually much in common.[36] Besides the accompanying italic, for most of the founts, there were also two sizes of Greek, long primer and pica. Thomas had no black letter. It would have been inappropriate for Latin anyway; but by the 1580s roman type, long associated with humanism, was also linked with the distinctive typography of the Geneva Bible, first published in 1560 and now the most widely circulated of all versions in England.[37] Besides his text founts, Thomas also obtained a cast alphabet of decorated capitals in a design common among the London trade, a pair of almost equally common factotums, a decorative headpiece and a small group of tailpieces, some of which he also used to ornament his title-pages. Gradually over the next few years this collection was expanded. A further factotum depicted John the Baptist, and an isolated initial I depicted St Andrew; in 1587 Thomas added two further decorative alphabets, following them in 1588 with another, narrower, headpiece. All were designs to be found in other printing houses as well, the result either of casting or of close copying. His large-cast alphabet of decorative capitals was one of the most widely used in the London trade.[38] His factotum initials could also be seen in various London printing houses, including those of Edmund Bollifant,

Thomas Este, John Jackson and Robert Waldegrave. His most regularly used headpieces offered little but their ordinariness, and the same was true of his tailpieces. Versions of several ornaments could be found overseas as well: a tailpiece featuring a human face at Frankfurt, and two arabesque ornaments in Haultin's press at La Rochelle.[39] Much in Thomas's inventory of type and ornament could thus be paralleled elsewhere, whether in London presses, the Wechel press at Frankfurt, or the Haultin press at La Rochelle. The result for readers was as important as the routes of supply and choice taken by Thomas for his press. In his typography, just as much as in the books he chose to print, he was making constant reference to particular interests among his contemporaries, and establishing a frame of visual reference, whether Protestant or Ramist, for his readership, whose books were drawn indifferently from London and overseas printing.[40]

But in addition to these standard designs, cast or copied, Thomas came into possession of one or two more individual decorations. On the title-pages of two books published in 1584, one a book by Timothy Bright and the other William Temple's new edition of Ramus's *Dialectica*, he used an oval depicting the shield of the University. In its printed form, it appears on only these two books, and never thereafter. Instead, it either reverted to, or was adapted for, use as a binder's tool, where it became familiar.[41] This ornament may have been specially made for Thomas, though there is no direct evidence that he did not inherit it from Sheres. He also obtained casts of ornaments from some London printers, one of them of an unusual design that he never managed to reconcile with the rest of his equipment. John Day died in July 1584, leaving his estate to his wife. Because his son Richard disputed the will, it was some months before matters were finally settled. Of all John Day's books, the most ambitiously illustrated had been Richard Day's *Book of Christian prayers*, first published in 1578 and printed again in 1581: a further edition, printed by Richard Day's assigns, was to appear in 1590. Much of the book's appeal lay in the woodcuts surrounding each page, and there was every reason to keep the set together. The appearance of a cast of the figure of Humility, used sideways-on as an incongruous headpiece in two of Thomas's last books (Carmichael's Latin grammar, 1587, and Whitaker's *Disputatio*, 1588), does not explain why it was that only one of the set was copied for Cambridge.[42]

Like any other printer, Thomas thus assembled his materials gradually. At his death, an expert inventory was taken not only of his personal goods and chattels, as was customary, but also of his stock, and – a novelty for the Cambridge appraisers – his printing equipment and materials. Not all of his decorative material appears to be accounted for here, but it seems to have been a careful enough survey nonetheless.[43]

It 39 Reames of pott paper in the garret	-	-	viij^{li}
It 3 reames of hand paper " " "	-	-	viij^s
It 5 reames & a half of small Rochill paper	-	-	xvj^s

It 5 realmes of demy paper - - - xxx[s]
Itm waste paper - - - - xl[s]
It old parchement books - - - v[s]
Itm 8 skynnes of parchement ruled with read ynck - ij[s] viij[d]
It a bourde & a short planck - - - ij[s]
Itm past bourds 4 doz & 9 - - - ij[s] iiij[d]
It certayne paper ruled with read yncke - - vj[d]
It certayne loose endes founde about the house - lx[s]—16 9 6

Lr̃es in pages
  Imprimis the longe primer Roman & Italique 130 lib
    It ye pica Roman & Italique - 288 lib } 658 lib
    It ye brevier Roman & Italique - 240 lib

Lr̃es in cases
    Itm ye pica Roman & Italique - 190 lib
    It ye brevier   "   " - 216 lib } 674 lib
    It ye longe primer "   " - 268 lib
        Rebate for cases - 360[lib]

                                      xxj[li] xxij[d] ob

Lr̃es in basketts
  Itm the greeke letter - - 232 lib
  Itm ye longe primer Italiq - - 108 lib
  Itm ye longe primer Roman - - 52 lib } 503 lib
  It ye brevier letter - - 21 lib
  It ye pica letter - - 90 lib

        Rebate for basketts - 30[lib]
      Sm̃a 1445[lib] at iij[d] ob ye lib

Metall to be melted
  Imprimis of M[r] Thomas hath - - 214[lib]
  Itm the wast of ye brevier - - 326[lib]
    the longe primer - - 126[lib]
    ye great primer - - 250[lib]
    ye cutt letters - - 114[lib] } x[li] ix[s]
    ye Quadrat - - 110[lib]
    ye old letter in cases - - 164[lib]
                    1304
      Rebate for baskets & paper - 50[lib]
  Sm̃a 1254[lib] at ij[d] the pound

                      31—10—5½

Necessaries for pryntinge
  Itm iiij[or] payer of chases - - xiij[s] iiij[d]
  Itm iij alphabets of cast letters - - xij[s]
  Itm iij marks xij[d] - - *It* vj factotumes xij
  It xvij payer of cases xlij[s] vj[d] - *It* vj frames ix[s]
  Itm ij great stooles xij[d] - *Itm* vj paper bourds xij[s]
  Itm one presse with the furneture - lxvj[s] viij[d]
  Itm iiij[or] gallies xvj[d] - *Itm* ij payer of cards xij[d]
  It the wasshing troufhe xij[d] - *Itm* a tankard iij[s] iiij[d]

                      12.6.2

In the almost complete absence of any direct personal comment, the motives of Thomas in establishing his press must be sought in the books that he chose to print. Some of his authors came to him out of convenience or friendship, no doubt; some perhaps as an alternative to the London trade. But overall his list reveals him as a man of Calvinist sympathies in religion, a conservative (on the whole) in his choice of authors, and an educationist in the options he proffered within the accepted curriculum. Throughout the seventeenth century, the Cambridge press was to produce a substantial number of the copies of the Aristotelian texts required at the two universities. But none of Thomas's successors was to prove so enthusiastic in this as Thomas himself, who counted among his colleagues some of those most deeply engaged in the debate over protestant Aristotelianism, and particularly over Ramus, in the 1580s.[44] Apart from the dictionary which was to ensure his fame long into the seventeenth century – and which in any case he did not publish until three years after the first books had appeared from his press – his publications included five works each of continental and English theology, a short Greek text, two Latin grammars and one Latin poet, his own edition of Ovid. It was a scholarly list; it was also one that in its authors, editors and subject matter usually adhered faithfully to the interests of the University; and inevitably it was one that, for all Thomas's efforts to avoid direct conflict, posed a direct challenge to the London trade.

It was thus an essentially domestic trade, at most one with London – and hence, via an established network of connections, other parts of the country. It was certainly not one that looked overseas, a market to which few English printers or their books contributed in the late sixteenth century. England was not just a net importer of books; the disparity was overwhelming. International trade centred on the biannual Frankfurt book fairs; and although the seasonal catalogues may not necessarily record everything offered there, the overall paucity of books printed in England underlines how little London stationers had to offer in return for heavy buying. Thomas Vautrollier, John Wolfe, François Bouvier and, from 1585, the Oxford printer Joseph Barnes were exceptional among English stationers in offering new books in the catalogues of the 1570s and 1580s as a part of international exchange. Their wares were noticeable, perhaps predictably, for protestant apology such as Jewel, though they also included in 1578 (three years after its publication) Tallis's *Cantiones sacrae* – a rare excursion of its kind.[45] Much of the history of learned publishing in late sixteenth and early seventeenth-century England is the history of the country's entry into the European market. But Thomas's eyes were focused more closely, their field of vision bounded by the North Sea and the English Channel.[46]

For a printer seeking to meet local needs, as seems to have been Thomas's initial intention (his first book being the only guidance on this point), it was a straightforward matter to gauge demand. Teaching was structured round the possession of only a few books. Although conservatism in the selection and allocation of these texts meant that the second-hand market, from one generation of students to another, was widespread, it also ensured that predictability which was an essential feature of the successful prosecution of printing and marketing in the field. The numbers of those attending each course were known, or could be ascertained. In 1589, 305 students were recorded as studying rhetoric, 317 dialectic, and 584 the more advanced courses in philosophy. Whitaker taught 263 students and Peter Baro, Lady Margaret's Professor of Divinity, 122. From the point of view of a local printer, these central subjects offered the most fruitful potential market. Thomas Lorkyn's sixteen students in medicine, and Thomas Legge's sixty-four in civil law, were in subjects that neither depended on the same kinds of books nor offered the numbers that might support publication.[47]

Until now, it has generally been thought that Thomas began to print in 1584, the year in which he established himself with editions of Ovid, Timothy Bright, Ramus, Rouspeau and Chandieu, or Sadeelius. Only one small item, a gift-plate for the library of King's College dated 1583,[48] suggested otherwise, though as the record of an event it might well have been printed subsequently. It now however seems certain that Thomas not only regained his equipment, but also began to print in the last months of 1583. His first project, of which no complete copy survives, was a plain text of part of Pliny's *Historia naturalis* (see fig. 3).[49] The choice of such a book, in the context of the furore of the previous several months, is instructive. The letter to Aylmer by Christopher Barker and Francis Coldock had emphasized the threat that Thomas posed to printing interests in London. Though Barker was a printer and Coldock a bookseller, there was no conflict (as there was to be subsequently) on this occasion; since both were concerned for the sale or production of domestically produced books. Neither had an interest in the Latin trade. Thomas was to challenge the assumptions of the majority of London printers and booksellers, and publish both in English and for a non-university, or non-educational, audience; but his choice of Pliny as his first book may well have been partially intended as an olive branch. Book II of the *Historia naturalis*, with its account of the creation of the world, had been printed separately most recently at Leipzig ten years previously, and ten years before that at Frankfurt – on each occasion on a more lavish scale than that now planned by Thomas. No edition of any part of the *Historia naturalis* seems to have been printed in London. Thus Thomas, perceiving in it a vehicle for teaching, both served his own purposes and avoided an unnecessary and unprofitable challenge to the most immediate London interests. Having seen his hopes of printing Whitaker disappointed, he turned from religious controversy to the more specialist Latin educational market, in which fewer London stationers were directly involved.

Thomas's edition of Pliny was a text with a minimum of notes and cast in the octavo format familiar in other Latin texts, printed both on the continent and in England, intended for schoolboys or undergraduates. The title-page, with its phrase *in usum philosophicae lecturae auditorum*, was explicit. It was also precise in its reference to a specifically university audience and the University statutes of 1570, which had ordained 'Philosophicus lector Aristotelis problemata, moralia, politica, Plinium vel Platonem publice doceat.'[50] The

C. PLINII SE-
CVNDI NATVRA-
LIS HISTORIAE
LIBER II.

IN *VSVM PHILOSO-*
phicæ Lecturæ Auditorum.

CANTABRIGIAE,
Excudebat Thomas Thomas
Typographus,
1583.

PHILOSOPHICAE
Lecturæ Auditoribus.

FEci quod est ere vestra, & vti spero, quod-
que in primis cupio, Academiæ (cui omnia
debeo) vtile & iucundum. Priuatis rationibus
quàm iniquè consuluerim, ipse mihi sum testis,
& illi optimè norunt, qui mihi authores erant,
vt hunc laborem Academiæ concederem. Sita-
men intellexero, vestram & publicas lecturas
propter defectum librorum pene iacentes, posse
hac ratione excitari, & Auditores alacres &
frequentes ad easdem confluere, fatebor me am-
plissimum fructum suscepti operis esse cõsequu-
tum. & pollicebor, publicis & priuatis Acade-
miæ & Collegiorum rationibus, quantũ
est, velle deinceps inseruire.

C. PLINII SE-
CVNDI NATVRA-
LIS HISTORIAE LIBER
SECVNDVS.

CAP. I.
An finitus sit Mundus, & an vnus.

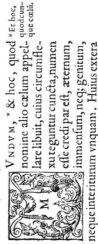

Vndvm, *, & hoc, quod *Et hoc,
nonine alio cælum appel- quodcun-
lare libuit, cuius circumfle- que cæli.
xuteguntur cuncta, numen
esse credi par est, æternum,
immensum, neq; genitum,
neque interiturum vnquam. Huius extera
indagare, nec interest hominum, nec capit
humanæ coniectura mentis. Sacer est, æter-
nus, immensus, totus in toto, imò verò ipse
totum:* finitus, & infinito similis: omnium *T.inf-
rerum certus, & similis incerto: extrà, intrà, nitus, &
cuncta complexus in se, idemque rerum finito si-
A ij
millis.

Fig. 3 C. Plinius Secundus, *Naturalis historiae liber II,* 8°, 1583. Thomas Thomas's first work, of which only the first pages survive: there is no evidence that printing was ever completed.

address to 'Philosophicae lecturae auditoribus' gave Thomas the opportunity to be even more precise; and since they represent Thomas's earliest surviving utterances on his new venture, his words are of especial import:

Feci quod est e re vestra, & vti spero, quodque in primis cupio, Academiae (cui omnia debeo) vtile & iucundum. Priuatis rationibus quam inique consuluerim, ipse mihi sum testis, & illi optime norunt, qui mihi authores erant, vt hunc laborem Academiae concederem. St tamen intellexero, vestram & publicas lecturas propter defectum librorum pene iacentes, posse hac ratione excitari, & Auditores alacres & frequentes ad easdem confluere, fatebor me amplissimum fructum suscepti operis esse consequutum: & pollicebor, publicis & priuatis Academiae & Collegiorum rationibus, quantum est, velle deinceps inseruire.

His apologia, expressing gratitude to his *alma mater*, and hope for improvement in teaching by his issuing of texts otherwise unavailable or inferior, and with its allusion also to the venture as therefore a public service, was in many ways what might have been expected. But while in the context of events earlier in 1583 it was more than convention, it nevertheless ignored – publicly at least – what the London stationers well realized: that Thomas's press could neither survive on the Cambridge trade alone, nor, sooner or later, fail to affect that in the capital.

It is not now known whether Thomas ever finished printing his edition of Pliny. Only a single copy of the first sheet survives, the same text printed twice over, once on each side in conventional half-sheet imposition. It is an eccentric way in which to begin such a book. If it was ever finished, the volume would have consisted of about 120 pages. No copy is listed among Thomas's effects, and it is not mentioned in early lists of his books. If, as seems probable, no more of the book was printed than the first few pages, then Thomas rapidly realized that there were shorter texts of which the University had even greater need. Despite the statutes, Pliny was, from his point of view, a personal enthusiasm. Religious controversy, and the standard Ramist texts required by most undergraduates, both offered better advantages and a means to finance his own edition of Ovid's *Metamorphoses*. No more was heard of Pliny, nor did any London printer or bookseller take up the challenge to print a rival edition, as was to be the case with Ovid.

His first modern author was William Whitaker, Regius Professor of Divinity since 1580, Fellow of Trinity since 1569, a Calvinist defender of the Church of England, and an antagonist respected even by his enemies for his learning (see fig. 4). Whitaker's most recent works, including a translation into Latin of John Jewel's attack on the recusant Thomas Harding,[51] and his own attack on Edmund Campion, had been printed by Thomas Vautrollier at the expense of Thomas Chard, the London bookseller. Both Vautrollier and Chard had links with Cambridge, that were to develop further with Thomas.[52] But the Stationers' seizure of his equipment successfully prevented Thomas from printing Whitaker's new book, as John Bell explained in his letter to Burghley

GVILHELMVS WHITAKERVS THEOL.
WHITAKER validis oppugnans ictubus hostes
pro CHRISTO victor sæpe triumphat hero Æ

Fig. 4 William Whitaker (1548–95), Regius Professor of Divinity. Thomas hoped in 1583 that Whitaker would be his first modern author. From Henry Holland, *Herωologia Anglica* [1620]. Original plate-mark, 163 mm. high.

on 14 June 1583.[53] It is not clear to which of Whitaker's two new books that year Bell referred: both were dedicated to Burghley. The first, published in the autumn, was a refutation of Campion's *Rationes decem* printed two years previously and now answered at the request of Aylmer; and the second, published probably the following February, attacked Nicholas Sanders (Professor of Theology at Louvain) and Gregory Martin, the principal translator of the Rheims New Testament. Both books were parts of extended controversies, and both would have appealed to Thomas.[54] It seems most probable, however, that in the summer of 1583 his eye had been on the first, which was entered in the Stationers' Register to Chard on 10 June,[55] just four days before Bell's final letter to Burghley: on this occasion, and on this occasion alone among Whitaker's books, it was Henry Middleton whose name appeared with Chard on the title-page, rather than Vautrollier.

Of the six books published by Thomas in 1584, five were octavo in format, and one was a quarto. He was to remain with these sizes for the whole of his printing career, producing neither smaller duodecimos nor larger folios. His chosen formats were those most suited to theological controversy on the one hand and to educational textbooks on the other. They were of a kind familiar in the London trade from the presses of Vautrollier, East, Waldegrave, Bynneman and others, and in imports from the presses of Plantin in Antwerp and the Wechel press in Frankfurt.[56] The books from Thomas's press shared characteristics in typography as well as in subject matter with those from all of these. Unlike John Day, who died in July 1584 and whose all but estranged son Richard, once a Fellow of King's, Thomas can hardly have failed to know, Thomas made no attempt to print in any way that was out of the ordinary.

His choice of books, on the other hand, for all its ostensible conservatism, showed independence and even, on occasion, bravado. Among those published in 1584 (probably early that summer: the dedication is dated 16 March), there was little that was dangerously controversial in the *Animadversiones* by Timothy Bright on the work of a Ramist MD from Marburg, Wilhelm Adolph Scribonius, whose book on natural philosophy, first published at the Wechel press at Frankfurt in 1577, had been published in London the year previously.[57] Bright shared Thomas's puritan sympathies in some measure, for his name is to be found among the signatories to Mildmay's statutes for Emmanuel College, in October 1585.[58] His earlier books, including his lectures on medicine delivered at Cambridge, had been published by Thomas Man in London, and on his move to St Bartholomew's Hospital in the spring of 1585 he had no need to keep any professional connection with his birthplace or with his university: his *Treatise of melancholie*, chiefly remembered today for its influence on *Hamlet*, was printed in London by Thomas Vautrollier. The Cambridge University Library copy of Bright's *Animadversiones* is bound up with a new edition, by William Temple, of Ramus's established *Dialectica* (fig. 5): the two books share an almost identical lay-out in their title-pages, an impression enhanced by the appearance in both of Thomas's device displaying the University shield. But whereas Bright quickly moved on, Temple became a contributor of some importance to Thomas's programme, notwithstanding his departure from King's in 1583, the year Thomas established his press.

Since his exile at Basel in the 1550s,[59] Temple had become established as one of the most influential of the English Ramists,[60] the author of three books published between 1580 and 1582 addressed to Everard Digby and Johann Piscator. In 1576, two years after Thomas, he was elected Fellow of King's, where he became responsible in different ways for two of Thomas's earliest books. In June 1584, Vautrollier's ten-year patent in MacIlmaine's standard edition of Ramus's works came to an end:[61] in fact Vautrollier had never had a complete monopoly of Ramus, for other editions were easily available from the Wechel press, and perhaps as a consequence only two editions of the *Dialectica* bear Vautrollier's name in the imprint. Temple's edition engaged with the continental commentator Johann Piscator, no more than a few months established. He dedicated it, as Bright had his book a little before, to Sir Philip Sidney, and the book was published in early summer: Sidney's letter of acknowledgement is dated 23 May.[62] Thomas could expect assured sales for Ramus, supported and promoted by Temple's reputation. But it was Temple, too, who introduced a less obvious text by James Martin, a native of Dunkeld in Perthshire who spent the later part of his life teaching in Turin. Martin's exposition of Aristotelian and Galenic theories of generation, now introduced by Temple, had been published originally at Turin in 1577. No book by Martin had hitherto been published in England; but in the case of Temple, as with Whitaker, Thomas was taking away an author already established in London, whose books had all formerly been printed by Henry Middleton for one or another London bookseller. The London stationers could not raise any legal objections; but they could not fail to notice the manner in which Thomas's list was developing.

Even his own literary work could arouse similar jealousies. His edition of Ovid, accompanied by the commentary of George Sabinus (as the Wittenberg scholar and minor *littérateur* Georg Schuler was known, after Ovid's own friend) was fresh, but only in some respects. On the one hand, Schuler's commentary was already established in England;[63] on the other, Vautrollier, again, had been granted a ten-year patent to print Ovid's works in Latin. The patent expired in June 1584. Thomas's was the first separate edition of the *Metamorphoses* to be published in England, but it could offer more than simply chronological distinction. Its freshness lay rather in Thomas's editorial treatment. He did not trouble to add another dedication of his own to that by Schuler; but instead of printing Schuler's Greek quotations in their original language (as, in fact, he was equipped to do), he translated them into Latin. Other recent editions of the *Metamorphoses* from continental publishers had tended to be 16mos, a size too small to be annotated with reasonable convenience by a reader. Thomas chose an octavo format, with adequate margins, and the overall result was an edition ideally suited to school or undergraduate use.[64]

Hitherto, the Stationers had found an ally in Aylmer, Bishop of London. But with the election of John Whitgift as Archbishop of Canterbury in September 1583, and his subsequent campaign to root out the ringleaders of presbyterianism, there was an ally of potentially more power still, and Thomas played into their hands. Of all the puritan activists, few were more energetic, or more capable in controversy, or, therefore, posed more of a threat, than Walter Travers, once of Trinity College, subsequently of Geneva and Antwerp, who with Thomas Cartwright had expounded the puritan position ten years before in a book entitled *A full and plaine declaration of ecclesiastical discipline*, printed secretly at Heidelberg.[65] By the early 1580s, Cambridge had become identified as the intellectual centre of presbyterianism. There was hope of a meeting of those sympathetic to the idea in 1582; St John's and Trinity (Whitgift's own college) housed many of its supporters; and by the end of the decade not only had the annual Stourbridge Fair provided the occasion for a synod, but a meeting at St John's in 1589 had also been the occasion on which the puritan *Book of discipline* was 'made perfect'.[66] In such a context, given Thomas's own opinions, and given that it would have been difficult to obtain permission from the Bishop of London to publish a book arguing the presbyterian position, the notion of issuing such a work in Cambridge had many attractions. The letter in which Burghley alerted Whitgift to the printing of a new book by Travers in Cambridge has not survived; but Whitgift's reply of 30 June 1584 makes it clear that the two men were in sympathy – despite Travers having once been Burghley's chaplain.

Ever sens I hard that they had a printer in Cambridge I dyd greatlie fear that this and such like inconveniences wold followe, nether do I thingk that yt wyll so stay, for allthowgh Mr Vicechancellor that now ys, be a verie careful man and in all respects greatlie to be commended, yet yf yt may fawle owt hereafter, that some such as shal succeade hym wyll not be so well affected, nor have such care for the publike peace of the Church, and of the state, but what so ever your L[ordship] shal thingk good to be done in this matter, or wyll have me to signifie to Mr Vicechauncellor ether in your name or in my owne, yf yt shal please you to signifye the same to Mr Dene of Westm[inster] or otherwise, I wyll performe yt accordinglie. I thingk yt verie convenient that the bokes shold be burned, being veri factius and full of untruthes: and that (yf printing do styll there continew) sufficient bonds with suerties shold be taken of the printer not to print anie bokes, unless they be first allowed by lawfull authoritie, for yf restrante be made here, and libertie graunted there, what good can be done. The boke ys the same which Travers ys supposed to have sett forth in Laten, without anie addition or retraction.[67]

Thus condemned, probably before printing had even finished, Travers' book was never published at Cambridge, and seems indeed to have been

Fig. 5 Petrus Ramus (1515–72), *Dialecticae libri duo*, 8°, 1584. This was one of the first books to be completed at Thomas's press. Height of original, 142 mm.

destroyed. Under the circumstances, Thomas and the University were wise to enter into a bond of five hundred marks on 24 July, whereby Thomas was to print nothing further without the consent of Burghley, the Vice-Chancellor and the University generally.[68]

Besides English theologians, Thomas turned also to the continent, proving a willing cosmopolitan in this subject as with topics closer to the immediate University curriculum. The *Two treatises of the Lord his holie supper*, by Yves Rouspeau and Jean de L'Espine were by authors well familiar to the London booksellers: Vautrollier had printed John Field's translation of L'Espine's *Excellent treatise of Christian righteousnes* frequently since 1577, and three editions of another translation of Rouspeau's tract had appeared since about 1570.[69] The two tracts together did not make a long book. By the summer of 1584, however, Thomas was absorbed in a much more ambitious project, a collection in Latin of the works of the French theologian and martyrologist Antoine de la Roche Chandieu, known more briefly as Antonius Sadeelius.[70] Since the St Bartholomew's Day massacre Chandieu had lived in Switzerland, publishing his works at either Lausanne or Geneva. In England, his meditations on the twenty-third Psalm and his *Treatise touching the word of God* had both been published in translation. No collection of his works was to appear at Geneva until 1592, but Thomas now conceived a quarto edition, a format that broke with Chandieu's normal smaller ones. More importantly for Thomas, it was the first quarto volume he had attempted, and was by far the most substantial.[71] By late July it was in the midst of production, and it was specifically exempted from the moratorium then imposed on Thomas. But its completion appears to have been a hurried job. Apart from the title-leaf and contents list, the book contains no preliminaries by way of preface or dedication.

After the hasty reappraisal of his work brought about by the attempt to print Travers, Thomas's output betrayed a certain caution. The books dated 1585 were unexceptionable sometimes to the point of slavishness. On the one hand he contrived to supply the demand for Ramus's works with a new translation (the first ever to be published in English: see fig. 6) of the Latin grammar which had first been published at Paris in 1559: instead of including the *Rudiments*, as was customary, and as was familiar in the Latin texts,[72] Thomas's edition concluded with an anonymous 'Example of a grammatical analysis' of an epistle by Cicero – a substitution which did not, however, prove popular. In printing Andrew Willet's new textbook *De animae natura et viribus quaestiones quaedam*, drawn from Aristotle and elsewhere, Thomas laid the foundation of what was to prove a considerable association between successive university printers and an active and popular author. It was Willet's first book, published in the year he took orders and three years before he married the daughter of the Provost of King's.[73] On another hand, Thomas resorted to established theology, in *A godlie exposition upon certaine chapters of Nehemiah*, by James

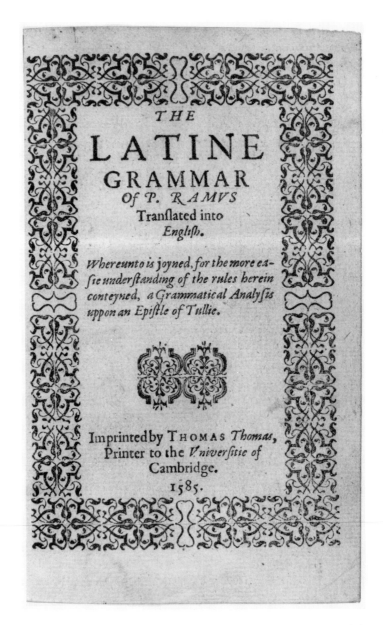

THE
LATINE
GRAMMAR
Of P. RAMVS
Translated into
English.

Whereunto is joyned, for the more ea-
sie understanding of the rules herein
conteyned, a Grammatical Analysis
uppon an Epistle of Tullie.

Imprinted by THOMAS *Thomas,*
Printer to the *Universitie* of
Cambridge.
1585.

Fig. 6 Petrus Ramus (1515–72), *The Latine grammar translated into English,*
8°, 1585. Height of original, 150 mm.

Pilkington, Bishop of Durham and former Fellow of St John's, who had been dead since 1575. The characteristically vigorous anti-papist preface was the work of Pilkington's friend John Foxe, who may have been responsible for suggesting Pilkington's unfinished manuscript to Thomas.[74] But the book concluded with a tract by Robert Some, of Queens', that had originally been appended to a book published by George Bishop in London in 1583.[75] Once again, Thomas was stepping close to the interests of a London stationer, but he printed Some's tract and part of Pilkington's *Exposition* twice over, in quarto and octavo, saving labour by re-imposing the same type for a second appearance.

In his edition of Zacharias Ursinus' *Doctrinae Christianae compendium*, a collection of Protestant declarations of faith centred on the Heidelberg catechism, Thomas turned to an already established text: the collection, edited by Simon Goulart of Senlis, had been published at Geneva only in 1584, a little after Ursinus' death.[76] In England, it proved a perhaps predictable success, and after its publication (at Joseph Barnes' new press at Oxford) in a translation by Henry Parry was to be reprinted continually until it was finally published in folio in 1633. But while Thomas exploited established authors in one way, printing the works of those who were now dead, he also maintained his distinctive list with the work of one whose presence would ensure a sympathetic hearing in London, even if the printing of his books in Cambridge would seem aggressive. William Whitaker's previous work, as has been seen, had been printed in London, by Vautrollier and by Middleton, for the London bookseller Thomas Chard. Both had been dedicated to Burghley as, now, was his *Aunswere to a certaine booke* by William Reynolds, in which he advanced a wealth of textual reasons for disagreeing with Reynolds' defence of the Latin sources for the Rheims New Testament, and for a proper consideration of the Hebrew and Greek texts as well. His book was not least noticeable for being in English (as had been Reynolds' attack on him in 1583), rather than in Latin, like his previous works. For Thomas, however, the book broke fresh ground in other ways. For the first time, his name was associated on a title-page with a London address, albeit one unattached to a person's name: 'to be sold at the signe of the white Horse in Canon-Lane, ouer against the North Doore of Paules'. The address, so close to that of Thomas Chard, has been associated only tentatively with Robert Waldegrave, whose relations with Thomas are still not entirely clear.[77] Waldegrave's customary address was outside the city altogether, near Somerset House in the Strand, but he spent much of 1585 in prison,[78] and the address in Canon Lane smacks of convenience. Whitaker, as Regius Professor, could hardly allow his name to be associated in too dubious an enterprise, even if it was the best London foothold that Thomas could secure at this stage.

In fact, Thomas had printed only part of the book. The preliminary sheets had been printed by Waldegrave, whose ornaments appeared on the title-page and whose typography belied the claim of the title-page that the book had been printed by Thomas. Shared printing was common within the London trade; either for convenience or from necessity, Thomas's work was completed by another, perhaps for no other reason than commercial or organizational economy.[79] Unlike Thomas's own books, the title-page was set not in capitals, but in a mixture of capitals and lower-case, as Middleton had done when he printed Whitaker's attack on Campion in 1583: the illusion of continuity by these typographical means was furthered by his choice of ornaments within the book, echoing those used by Vautrollier for his printing of Whitaker's attack on Sanders in 1583.

The title-page of Whitaker's book suggests some accommodation between Thomas and at least one member of the Stationers' Company. Further copies, supplied with a cancel title-leaf (but still showing Thomas's name in the colophon) were issued by Thomas Chard, and another, quite separate, edition was printed at the Eliot's Court Press. But not all copies had been sent to London. As part of what seems to have been a marketing arrangement, Thomas retained some in Cambridge, and at his death there still remained 122 copies unsold, which his successor John Legate reissued in 1590, provided with yet another title-page.

The details of Thomas's relations with Waldegrave (with whom he was linked by the author of the Marprelate tracts) and with Chard are by no means always apparent. Neither was an easy bedfellow for the Stationers' Company, and their inclination to independence may have made it easier to work with Thomas. In Cambridge, Chard was well known to the trade. He had regular dealings with Thomas Bradshaw, the only Cambridge stationer who was also a member of the Company in London. No evidence has survived of Thomas and Chard dealing in the same way; but in a trade which depended on credit rather than on cash transactions, the relations between three different parties, University Printer, Cambridge bookseller and London bookseller, were essential to the financing of most of the books printed at Cambridge in the sixteenth and throughout the seventeenth centuries. Thomas's and Bradshaw's premises were only across the street from each other, Thomas at the Great St Mary's end of Regent Walk and Bradshaw's hard against the west wall of the church itself, where in the mid-1580s he was engaged in building two shops, one each side of the door.[80] These connections were thus based on the one hand on a wholesale trade to Cambridge booksellers and, on the other, on Thomas's supplying Chard with Whitaker's new book. But these were not the bonds of friendship. It is at least possible that Thomas supplied Chard in exchange for other books that could be offered for sale. In any case, relations between the two men had by 1587 seemingly deteriorated so much that Thomas referred on his new edition of Ursinus' collection to the 'vitiotissima' edition meanwhile published by Chard.[81]

Relations with Waldegrave were slightly different. Waldegrave was a printer, not a bookseller. In 1583 he owned two presses, but he was not among the most privileged of the Stationers' Company; and after a series of confrontations in the next few years he was to remove his press into hiding and print several of the Marprelate tracts. In London, he seems not to have been over-particular of other people's property, and in 1582–3 the Stationers' Company even imposed a bond for the unusually large sum of £40 whereby he agreed not to print anything that would infringe William Seres' patent.[82] Thomas, too, fell victim to Waldegrave's swashbuckling irregularities, in a way that makes the circumstances of Whitaker's book the more obscure. The Cambridge edition of Ramus's Latin grammar, mentioned above, was much like other of Thomas's work. It was set, as usual, in roman and italic, Thomas possessing no black letter. As will be recalled, the customary *rudimenta* were not included, Thomas instead printing a 'grammatical analysis' conducted according to Ramist principles, of part of Cicero. The translation does not appear to have been a great commercial success, in that no fresh editions appeared either in Cambridge or London after 1585, and Thomas himself still owned 178 unsold copies in 1588.[83] But in 1585 Waldegrave reprinted most of Thomas's edition, setting it in black letter rather than roman type, disguising the translation slightly by introducing one or two extra words – unjustified by the original Latin – at the beginning, and printing the *rudimenta* at the end as usual, in place of the analysis of Cicero. Waldegrave's was the more conventional edition, and in his decision to use black letter he was appealing to a market where the standard grammars and textbooks still conformed to vernacular habits. As so often in the case of schoolbooks, which were used and read to pieces, the absence of further surviving editions, in this case after 1585, is somewhat negative evidence: but on this showing at least his own enterprise was not a success either.[84]

In the two years that Thomas had been printing, the difficulties of running a press in a provincial university town had become clear. On the one hand, the University needed to be seen exercising control over what was printed; and on the other, the objections of the London trade had been expressed in deeds as well as words – by the exploitation of Thomas's unprotected copies as well as by vilification. Seven months after he had been obliged to enter into a bond not to print anything more until further orders, Thomas's case was once again the subject of a formal university decision. He was reappointed by Grace on 11 February 1585/6,[85] and on the same day was made subject to a series of seven articles. The first four of these articles simply rehearsed, with slightly different phrasing, what was already established; but the last ones were quite fresh. In view of recent events, the University was wise to disclaim responsibility for costs arising from Thomas's disputes; the sixth placed on a formal footing what was already implied by the need for Thomas to be reappointed by Grace; and the seventh, concerning deposit of his books in either the University Library or *in Archivis Academie* betokened both common sense and a somewhat tardy realization that the Library's importance had risen dramatically in the last decade or so:[86] the arrangements for deposit were the first such ever to be introduced at Cambridge.

Articles of Mr Thomas Thomas Towchinge his Printinge

1 That his paper Incke and Letters shalbe as good so neere as maie be as any other that are occupied for Printinge.

2 That suche bookes as shall be by the said Thomas Prynted shalbe solde at a resonable Price rated from tyme to tyme by the iudgement of the vice chauncelor then beinge with the doctor of the Chaire in that facultie with Consent of the auctor of the booke and advise of suche Stationers, as they shall thincke good to associat vnto them for the prisinge of the same before they be put to sale.

3 That he shall not Print any seditious booke, or eny pamplet or such as shall not be agreable to the lawes or orders receyved in this realme.

4 That he shall not Print any booke Pamplet or P[aper?] but suche as shalbe first allowed by the Chauncelor or the Vicechauncelor with other appointed by the Cha[uncelor].

5. That he the said Thomas shall Paie and discharge[e a]ll expences if any sute or Controversie shall rise aboute eny Cause towchinge his Printinge, thuniversitie [on]lie impartinge unto him their Privileges and other their good favour.

6 That the said Thomas shall leave of his said Printinge and Render up again his licence of Printinge graunted unto him when and as sone as thuniversitie shall revoke the same.

7 That the said Thomas shall give unto thuniversitie librarie one perfect copie or booke well and sufficientlie bounde of everie impression that he shall prynt within Sixtene Daies after he hathe fynished the said bookes. And also One copie of all verses or other matters by him to be prynted, to be receeved in Archivis Academie within Fower Daies after he hathe Prynted the same.[87]

But while the University thus sought to control Thomas, and at the same time to distance itself financially ('thuniversitie onlie impartinge unto him their Privileges and other their good favour'), it had also an eye on the threat from the London stationers. In 1584, Convocation at Oxford had lent Joseph Barnes, a local bookseller, £100 with which to establish a press – the first at Oxford since 1520.[88] The first books appeared from Barnes' press in the following year; and Cambridge now moved to safeguard both University Printers in a Grace which sought to exclude the London trade so far (it was not very far) as was practicable. In future, Cambridge booksellers were not to buy, bind or offer for sale any book printed in London or elsewhere in England that had been, or would be in the future, printed at either of the two universities.

Cum Londinenses librorum impressores inciviliter abvtuntur et nostra et Oxoniensi academia et libros in vtraque academia impressos in pernitiem nostrorum impressorum omni cum festinacione imprimunt Placet vobis exemplo Oxoniensis academie statuere ne quisquam bibliopolarum nostrorum ab isto die in futurum aut emat liget aut venditioni exponat aliquem librum Londini aut alibi infra regnum Anglie impressum qui aut hic vel Oxonii fuit impressus aut deinceps imprimetur sub pena exilii perpetui et confiscatione librorum huiusmodi Et insuper ne vllus huius academie alumnus et hic literis deditus dum moram trahat in nostra vniuersitate emat aliquem librum huiusmodi Londini aut alibi sic impressum cuius copia vel hic aut Oxonii prelo commissa fuit aut erit sub pena inobedientie et amissione dictorum librorum quousque aliter per academiam decernetur Proviso semper quod impressores nostri non pluris vendant aliquem librum per ipsos impressum quam estimabitur per dominum procancellarium pro tempore existentem et reliquos nominatos in articulis magistri Thome Thomas[89]

Despite his difficulties, in both 1584 and 1585 Thomas had printed half a dozen books besides various broadsides of more or less complexity. He was never to print so many titles in such spaces of time again; and though the editing and production of his Latin dictionary, published in 1587, was more time-consuming than any other of his projects, this still does not account fully for the apparent decline in his energy. The Star Chamber decree of June 1586 concerning printing acknowledged the legality of both the Cambridge and Oxford presses, at the same time imposing restrictions on the number of apprentices that might be at each, and permitting the employment (with no restriction as to numbers) of any journeymen freemen of the City of London.[90] It brought, apparently, no complaint from Thomas, who completed two books during the year, both of them substantial. In one, Thomas combined three anti-catholic tracts, one a defence of William Charke, Fellow of Peterhouse until his expulsion in 1572, against the attacks of Robert Parsons, and the others by one of the most prominent (and prudent) of the Cambridge puritans, William Fulke, against attacks by William Allen and Peter Frarin.[91] The volume, written largely if not wholly by the Master of Pembroke, was unexceptionable in London and Cambridge alike. With his other book, however, Thomas once again provoked episcopal displeasure. On 8 August Whitgift wrote in some annoyance to the Vice-Chancellor:

Salutem in Christo. I doo understand that there is nowe in printinge by the Printer of that Universitie a certen book called Harmonia Confessionum fidei in English, translated out of Latin: which book for some speciall causes was here reiected, and not allowed to bee printed. Theis are therefore to requyre you, that presently upon receipt hereof you cause the sayd book, to be stayed from printing any furder, and that nothing bee done more therein, untill you shall receaue furder direction from mee. And whereas there is order taken of late by the Lordes of the Councile that from hensefourth no book shall bee imprinted either in London, or in any of the Vniversitees, unlesse the same shall bee allowed and authorized by the Bishopp of London or myself, I doo lykewise requyre you to take speciall care that hereafter nothing bee imprinted in that Vniversitee of Cambridge, but what shall bee authorized accordingly. And so not doubting of your diligent circumspection herein, I committ you to the tuition of almighty god. From my House at Croyden, the viiith of August, 1586.

Your Loving Frende in Christe
Jo: Cantuar[92]

With the Privy Council and the University thus now at loggerheads, Thomas was nevertheless permitted to continue to print *An harmony of the confessions of faith of the Christian and reformed churches*, to which he now added the Scottish general confession of faith agreed at Edinburgh in January 1581/2, a little after the Geneva edition of the collection had appeared in 1581.[93] Defiantly, Thomas added the phrase 'Alowed by publique authoritie' above his imprint on the title-page, but this did not prevent the seizing in London of part of the edition on Whitgift's authority: the volumes were still in the hands of the Stationers' Company in 1590.[94]

This proved, in fact, to be the last time that the University and the public authorities were to clash over the appropriateness or otherwise of Thomas's books. The year 1587, dominated by Thomas's dictionary, saw also the publication of three other books. A second edition of Ursinus' *Compendium*, with a somewhat expanded text and a rather more crowded page than in 1585 (both editions were set in long primer) appeared within a few months of the first English translation, printed at Oxford that year. No obvious reason has been given, on the other hand, for Thomas's printing a Latin grammar designed apparently for Scotland, dedicated by its author James Carmichael to James VI from Thomas's house on 13 September 1587.[95]

Carmichael, already a distinguished educationist, had been among the presbyterians forced to flee to England in spring 1584 in the wake of the reaffirmation of episcopal authority by the 'Black acts', and had taken a leading part in advocating the exiles' cause to Walsingham and others. It is possible that he visited Cambridge that first summer, and that he made Thomas's acquaintance at that time. The funeral the following October in London of one of the ministers' number, James Lawson, provided the opportunity for a demonstration, on a grand scale, of mutual support between English puritans, exiled Scottish presbyterians, and French stranger churches.[96] All three interests are represented in the output from Thomas's press. No bookseller is named on the title-page of Carmichael's book, and though his subsequent career is obscure it is not impossible that he took the entire edition back to Scotland. The volume may, perhaps, have been linked with Robert Waldegrave, who was to flee to Edinburgh in 1589. If, as may otherwise perhaps have been the case, the book was intended for or commissioned by Thomas Vautrollier, who had fled north in 1584, Thomas would have been embarrassed: Vautrollier died in July 1587, two months before Carmichael put the final date to his dedication. The absence of any bookseller's name from the title page would thus have been either politic or inescapable. In any case, Thomas appears to have cleared copies immediately, for none is recorded amongst his property at his death.

Besides these two, Thomas also ventured, perhaps for the first and only time, into printing a Greek text. The choice of Plato's *Menexenus* is unlikely to have been his alone. The book was set as a teaching text, plain and with space for annotation by pupils. It was almost certainly printed as a part of the curriculum established by Andrew Downes, Regius Professor of Greek. As copy, Thomas used the text provided in the Stephanus edition of the collected works published at Cologne in 1578: even the brief preface, a summary explanation of the text, was adapted with only the most modest alteration. The volume had no pretensions other than as an elementary text, and like many such books it has all but disappeared: only one copy is now known. But on current evidence it seems to have been the first book in Greek ever to have been printed at Cambridge, and the first of any work by Plato in the original to appear from an English press. If Thomas was proud of either achievement, he did not allude to it.

But neither Carmichael's book nor the Plato was Thomas's main preoccupation. On 3 September, only ten days before Carmichael, Thomas set the date at the foot of his preface to his most influential work, a Latin–English dictionary (see fig. 7). Like most such compilations, it was modelled on previous work, and in this case part of the working copy has survived: pages from the edition of Guillaume Morel's Latin dictionary printed by Henry Bynneman for the assigns of Richard Hutton in 1583, much annotated with contributions culled from Thomas Cooper's established and popular *Thesaurus linguae Romanae et Britannicae*, first published in 1565.[97] Not surprisingly (and perhaps with his eye to a pun), Thomas dedicated his dictionary to Burghley, 'summo Angliae Thesaurario' and the University's Chancellor. It had been prepared, he explained, in the intervals of other work; and it was an immediate success. Cooper's own *Thesaurus*, printed again as recently as 1584, appeared then for the last time. Until his death in April 1583, Bynneman had held the privilege to print Cooper's dictionary as well as those of others; but though this privilege passed thereafter to Ralph Newbery and Henry Denham,[98] Thomas showed no compunction about ignoring it – indeed, the timing of Bynneman's death may have hastened Thomas's decision to produce a successor to Cooper.[99] Though he had both printed and published many of the books bearing his name, Thomas had also, as we have seen, entered into arrangements – openly or *sub rosa* – with booksellers elsewhere. To turn now to Newbery and Denham was obviously impossible; and instead he arranged for his dictionary to be sold in London by a bookseller of puritan sympathies, relatively fresh to the trade. Richard Boyle had been made free of the Company only three years previously, but this opportunity seems to have brought difficulties as well as commercial success.

The Stationers' Company, believing that it had the sole right to print dictionaries, quickly complained of Thomas's work, and once again the University was obliged to appeal to Burghley. 'We finde yt a verie hard matter', explained the Heads, 'for oure Printer to doe anie good by his trade' by reason of the Companie of Stationers and Prynters in London: who as they have heretofore taken divers of his Copies and printed them againe, to his great losse and

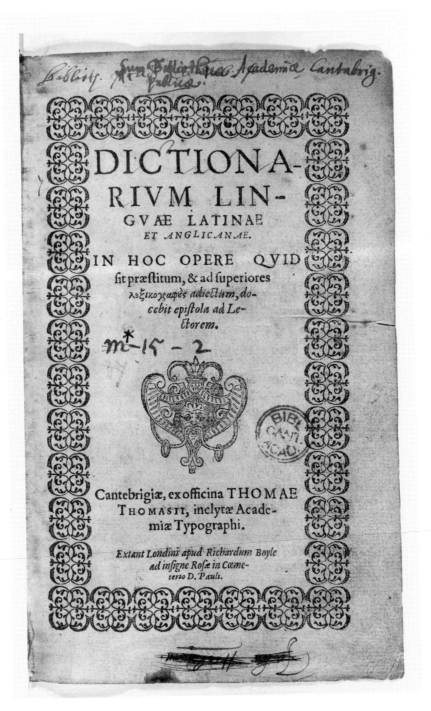

Fig. 7 Thomas Thomas (1553–88), *Dictionarium linguae Latinae et Anglicanae*,
8° [1587]. Height of original, 170 mm.

hinderence, so doe they still threaten to attempt the lyke hereafter: namely and specially, with a Dictionarie of his owne compiling, and lately set oute by him: and this they challenge as their owne right and proper Copie, by vertue of a general Clawse, graunted to them from her Maiestie *To prynte all Dictionaries whatsoever*: which generall Clawse, eyther for Dictionaries or anie other bookes, if vnder your Honours correction we may interprete, in our judgment extendeth to suche bookes and Dictionaries only, as were then extant, when this graunt was made, & not to any that should afterward come forthe. For elles might yt be verie preiudiciall, and hinder the setting forth of manie good & profitable bookes, if learned men might not make choyse of their printer, eyther to reape the frute of their laboures themselves, or otherwise bestowe them on whome they thought good: but must all come to the printers in London only, and have their workes publisht by them. Whiche practyse of their supposed privilege, hath already greatly discouraged and almost vtterly disabled our Printer to goe forward in his trade: in so muche as we perceave, yf it be not looked vnto in tyme, yt will tourne to the vtter overthrowe of printing in our Vniuersitie for ever.[100]

The answer, it seemed to the writers, was for the Queen to grant a special licence to Thomas for his dictionary, and to do the same from time to time for other books as well. 'So as both we may mainteyne a print in our Vnuersitie with credyt, according to her Maiesties intent and the tenore of our Charter, and also oure Printer may followe his trade with some profyt, and not be molested, as heretofore, to his great hinderance and impayring of his pore stock.'

It was a letter if not of despair at least of desperation. In appealing for such licences, the signatories were in fact resigning the position that the University had adopted from the first: that the 1534 charter was in no way affected by the charter granted to the Stationers' Company in 1557. Perhaps fortunately, the suggestion was taken no further, and was allowed to be forgotten. On 2 May Thomas completed his final book, an attack by Whitaker on Bellarmine and Robert Stapleton which once again took catholic scholars to task for their reliance on the Vulgate text of the Bible. The dedication was dated only two days before, but the volume's production seems to have been fraught with difficulty and indecision: much of the work had to be set twice, so that the requisite number of copies could be made up in an operation that may even have been organized by Thomas's successor.[101]

Not all the works that Thomas printed have survived. The 1588 inventory records the stock of each of his books, and among them are several titles that can no longer be traced. Only one copy is now known of Plato's *Menexenus*, and none at all have survived of Thomas's printing of Terence or, apparently, of the '1100 catechisms in a sheete in ye garret', valued at 13s.4d., about one-seventh of a penny apiece.[102] Besides books, Thomas had also printed for the colleges and for the University. For his own college he printed bookplates to record gifts by Sir Francis Walsingham in 1583, and William Wickham in 1586.[103] He was also called on regularly for University purposes. The broadsheet *Catalogus rectorum et cancellariorum* became an annual event. In the 1570s it had become the custom for the so-called Tripos, or Act, verses, Latin verses distributed at the formal disputations in the Regent House, to be printed at London: previously they had been circulated simply in manuscript.[104] Thomas quickly took over the task (his last known work was in fact the series required for the summer of 1588), and eventually – long after his death – the University itself was to pay for their printing. How much other, less regular work also passed through his press it is now impossible to say. Like most other printers, and like every University Printer since, Thomas found a proportion of his income in jobbing printing, the kind of work for which the University was quickest to thank him and which also put the running of a printing shop slightly less at risk.

While a survey such as that of the last few pages reveals much of Thomas's preferences, of his circle of acquaintances and of those whom he offended, it does not necessarily show the extent to which his business was either profitable or successful. In its letters to Burghley, the University repeatedly complained of the economic effects of the Stationers' Company opposition to Thomas: in May 1588 Thomas Legge's letter even spoke of his being 'almost utterly disabled...to goe forwarde in his trade'. Not all of this was hyperbole. Although at his death his estate was valued in all at over £920, over £220 of this was in debts (£60 'debts desperat'), and the remaining stock of the books he had printed was valued at £80.19s.6d., plus £66.13s.4d. for 'the Copies of the Dictionary with the rest of such copies whatsoever that were graunted unto Mr Thomas to prynte'. His printing equipment (listed above on p. 85) amounted to another £43.16s.7½d, and there were another £13 or so allotted to his paper stocks.[105] Altogether, the inventory records how deeply Thomas was committed to printing as his principal means of livelihood. The binding tools which he had inherited from Sheres had, very largely, been either passed on or allowed to decay, though he still owned modest stocks of pasteboard and sheep (a mere six skins of the latter), and the 'iij marks', one of which he had used on his early title-pages. In the shop, apart from the stocks of his own books, the appraisers found a stock which they valued at only £12.6s.2d. – compared with £120 under the same head for Sheres in 1581.

He had been printing for only five years, and not surprisingly he still owned stocks of most of what he had printed. Very little is known of his edition sizes; and though in 1587 the Stationers' Company limited editions normally to 1,250 or 1,500 copies,[106] Thomas was not obliged to observe such a rule: he was limited by what was practical, and, like all other printers, could equally well print smaller quantities if that seemed to reflect the potential market more accurately. In October 1588, however, only five months after its publication, Thomas still had 1,381 copies of Whitaker's attack on Bellarmine, a stock that may well have represented virtually all the impression.[107] Of Whitaker's earlier answer to Reynolds, for which Thomas had a London bookseller, only 122 copies remained, while on the other hand there were still 429 copies of Pilkington on Nehemiah, published the same year. There also still remained 377 copies of James Martin's *De prima simplicium*, but on the whole the books published in 1584, Thomas's first full year as a printer, had sold reasonably well. To be sure, there were 233 copies of Temple's edition of Ramus's *Dialectica*; but only 125 remained of Timothy Bright, twenty-nine of Thomas's own Ovid, and the *Two treatises* on the Lord's Supper was almost out of print: the appraisers noted but sixteen copies, all of them in the shop. The classical texts had sold well: apart from the Ovid there were only ninety-nine copies of Terence and 147 of Plato, the last a book printed only the year before Thomas's death. No subsequent Cambridge editions of either the Ovid or the Plato are known; but in 1589 John Legate was to issue another of Terence – perhaps only two years after Thomas's, if Thomas himself did not print his (no longer extant) edition until after Thomas Marsh's death in 1587. In all, while he had confounded the predictions of the Stationers' Company in 1583 that he would 'utterlie undoe' himself, Thomas had not made a fortune either. And as we shall see, there were those who were ready to claim that even his stock and equipment had been over-valued.

Like many another printer, he did not find wealth. But in other respects he had little in common with the majority of the trade, quite apart from being 'utterlie ignoraunte in printinge'. The University gave not only protection. It also supplied editors, authors and a ready market. As versions of Thomas's dictionary continued to be printed after his death, so his reputation grew. Despite threats, no edition was ever printed in London, until Legate himself did so in 1615, though it was to be extensively raided (much to Legate's annoyance) by Francis Holyoke for his revised edition of Rider's Latin dictionary in 1617.[108] By 1619, Legate was comparing Thomas to the Estienne dynasty, so recalling not only Robert Estienne's own dictionary but also a tradition of scholarly publishing.[109] Yet to his contemporaries, Thomas cut a different figure. In one of the Martin Marprelate tracts printed secretly by Waldegrave, for example, he was referred to as 'that puritan Cambridge printer'.[110] He had set out, partly at least, as a scholarly printer, and he left his Ovid and dictionary as witnesses to that. But, so far as is known, no one in Cambridge in the early 1580s shared the ambitions of the author of a memorandum written at Oxford for the benefit of the University's Chancellor, the Earl of Leicester. Besides pointing out the lack of any press outside London, the lack of a Latin press in particular, and the expense of staying in the capital to see books through the press, the document also drew attention to the important manuscripts lurking in the libraries of the University which could be rescued and disseminated in print.[111] Neither Thomas nor Legate ever seems to have envisaged printing manuscripts from the Cambridge counterparts.

Thomas had dated his final book 2 May 1588. With that summer's Act verses printed, on 28 July he made his will. As a printer, his exact position was still the subject of dispute.[112]

Of other books that he might have printed, had he lived, only a clue remains. Amongst the stock of his own editions were listed two copies of Hieronymus Zanchius, the Neustadt theologian and yet another of the Heidelberg protestant circle. Zanchius' links with England were of long standing, and he was an obvious candidate for Thomas's press. But it was left to Legate, in 1592, to publish the first of his books to appear from an English press, *An excellent and learned treatise of the spirituall mariage betweene Christ and the Church*, and in 1599 to publish his *Confession*.[113]

No allusion was made in Thomas's estate to any work in hand, and it therefore seems likely that for some weeks that summer of 1588 he was too unwell to supervise his press. He died in the first week of August: one of his last acts was to give a copy of his recent edition of Whitaker's *Disputatio* to Richard Gerrard, former Fellow of Caius and now Rector of Stockport, who had suffered particularly ill at the hands of the allegedly papist Master of his college, Thomas Legge.[114] On 9 August, Thomas was buried in Great St Mary's. By his will,[115] he left most of his property to his widow and daughter, apart from a few personal gifts including one to his niece, with the proviso that she should only receive it if she did not marry a catholic.[116] Even from beyond the grave, Thomas continued to struggle for a cause that had been much of the justification for his press's foundation and existence.

❧ 6 ❧

John Legate, printer by profession

The office of University Printer was no place for grey hairs. Thomas had not yet passed thirty-five when he died, and his successor, John Legate, had been free of his apprenticeship for only three and a half years when he was appointed. Thomas left no children save for his infant daughter Joan: his son John, christened on 1 August 1585, had died soon afterwards. In his will, he also remembered his niece. But by her previous marriage his wife Anne had already borne five children between 1570 and 1579, only one of whom is known to have died young. It was by this means that the dynasty was eventually to be continued, when on 6 February 1588/9 Anne's daughter Alice married the next University Printer.[1]

Thus the succession was to be doubly effected: by election and by marriage. In fact, however, the transition was neither smooth, comfortable, rapid nor amicable. It was dominated by disputes between Anne Thomas and the man who became her son-in-law: disputes that were finally settled only in court amidst much personal animosity. Anne and the infant Joan Thomas inherited virtually all of Thomas's estate, valued at £920.12s.9d., of which nearly a half was in the business, either in debts, stocks of books and paper, or equipment. Apart from the books he had printed himself, and the equipment in the printing shop, special note was taken in the inventory of 'the Copies of the Dictionary with the rest of such copies whatsoever that were graunted vnto Mr Thomas to prynte'. These 'copies' were thus immediately marked out as being of especial interest, and the entry must refer both to unsold copies of the dictionary (not mentioned elsewhere in the inventory) and to its 'copyright' value. Along with the appropriate valuations, again mentioned nowhere else, of Thomas's other properties, it was, at £66.13s.4d., easily the most substantial figure in the entire account apart from the debts owed to him.[2] Apart from Thomas's debtors, of whom very little evidence survives, virtually every part of the printing inheritance was to be the subject of dispute.

Though the valuation of Thomas's property was done ostensibly by the usual officers, the 'publique [ap]praisers' of the University on this occasion, faced with unfamiliar machinery and equipment as well as the more usual stocks of books, turned to specialist help from London. Their adviser was John

Legate, who later claimed to have been utterly unfamiliar with Cambridge at the time, and who, having only recently come out of his apprenticeship, may have been recommended by his old master Christopher Barker. In 1588 he was seeking to establish himself in London. On 31 May he had paid the customary sixpence, and had entered to him in the Stationers' Register an attack on the sectarian Robert Brown and his followers. The book was described as 'A defence of the admonition to the followers of Browne', but no book of this title appeared: instead it was included in *The rasing of the foundations of Brownisme*, a book printed not by Legate but by John Windet, and sold by the aged John Wight.[3] The reason for Legate's withdrawal from this enterprise is nowhere recorded, and this was his only appearance in the Register that year. There is no evidence that he was involved in an attempt, instigated by John Whitgift and forwarded by a group of London printers,[4] to buy Thomas's equipment, and thus silence the troublesome and threatening Cambridge press. But he did gain Anne Thomas's confidence, and managed to persuade her to help him forward as her late husband's successor. Though it was not hers to give, Anne was later said to have promised that she would procure for him a patent as University Printer, a post that would give him independence of the regulations and exigencies of the London trade.[5]

Unlike Thomas, Legate was a printer by training. His connections with the book trade were commensurately closer; and his priorities in what he printed were consequently different. Thomas had taken advantage of the tensions in the 1580s, whether in the curriculum or in religion, to print a list of books that was noticeably well defined within the bounds set by the University. Legate regarded the press as an instrument offering wider possibilities. So, while on the one hand Thomas's initiative in printing Ramist and Aristotelian texts (a course which drew him to a small group of London stationers, Henry Bynneman, Henry Middleton and Thomas Vautrollier) suggested a worthwhile future for the Cambridge press, on the other Legate allowed his initiative to slip.[6] Quite apart from Thomas's dictionary, Legate instead turned his attention especially to the potential of the Bible trade, and to an increasing number of popular religious books.

In the months immediately following Thomas's death, Legate also seems to have come to an informal agreement to lease the printing equipment and to take over the stock and copies, in return for a quarterly payment of £30.[7] Anne further agreed to part with the shop on the corner of Regent Walk, just opposite Great St Mary's, and half her house, keeping the other half for herself. Thomas's stock of his books was to be passed on (at more or less their appraised value), to Legate for £140 – a figure which he later much regretted, having found them 'very dead ware'. These were to be paid for gradually, and he had handed over half the money by 1590/1. By that date however the two had fallen out so seriously that the case was heard in the Vice-Chancellor's court, where as a result it is possible to learn a great deal about Legate's establishing of his business.

For his family, the University's appointment died with Thomas. His widow could not inherit it, and Anne's course of action as she saw to the winding up of her husband's estate is not clear. Her brother subsequently claimed that the Heads of the University permitted her to continue to print.[8] Some at least of Thomas's staff remained if not actually employed by her then at least close enough to be taken on when Legate set up his own press over a year later. Of these, Benjamin Pryme, apprenticed in December 1584, was released by Thomas's widow shortly after her husband's death, though he returned to work for Legate.[9] In January 1588/9 Anne entered a claim against the estate of a recently deceased binder, John Almond,[10] but the marriage of her eldest daughter (by her first marriage) to Legate early in the following month was to presage little relief. For all the promises that she was said to have made, Anne Thomas was unable to engineer Legate's appointment as Printer without much delay. He was finally elected by Grace only on 2 November 1589, fifteen months after Thomas's death.[11]

Legate found much to complain about in a bargain for which there never seems to have been any written record. Thomas's property had been greatly over-valued, he believed, alleging (not very helpfully, since they were presumably seeking the best possible saving) that the London printers had bid but twenty nobles for the equipment and copies.[12] The type was for the most part 'worne to the stumps', and fit only to be melted down for re-casting. 'By using the letter he found', claimed Legate, 'he should both much have hindered him self and discredited the ... universitye which he serveth.' By 1590/1 he claimed to have spent £200 on new type from London,[13] more than six times the value set on the whole of Thomas's type. The printing press was in such bad condition that it had cost him forty marks,[14] or more than the value of two new ones, to have it put right: again, if he spoke candidly, the sum was not trivial, since in 1588 the press (there was only one) had been valued at £3.6s.8d.: he now thought it was worth no more than three pounds. Not all of Legate's complaints are very clear. His claim that his mother-in-law had not supplied specimens of her husband's books (so that he had copy-texts for future editions) was straightforward enough. But he claimed also that she had supplied a very imperfect copy of the dictionary, and that it 'cost him £20 legalis &c. to procure it to be made perfitt': he was almost certainly exaggerating. More convincingly, he could claim to have been misled into believing that she could procure the printing patent for him, and that in the end, after over a year, he had obtained it only through his own efforts. Amidst a flurry of accusations and counter-accusations, Legate forcibly expressed his dislike for an agreement which obliged him to lease, at £30 per annum, equipment that he reckoned to be worth no more than £100 in all. The court also heard Legate's voluble complaints concerning his annual rent of £4. Though the house was supposed to be divided in two, Anne Thomas claimed use of the kitchen, so that Legate (and, presumably, his wife) had no privacy in which to dress or eat, while Mrs Thomas also persisted in using their bedroom as a common passage to and from her own rooms: 'So that by this her usadge...[he] hath bene both continually disquieted, & lost divers thinges owte of his howse.'

Perhaps not surprisingly, Legate's claims were generally supported (at least in so far as they concerned his equipment rather than his domestic arrangements) by his employees whom he called as witnesses: Edward Smith, Simon Stafford and Benjamin Pryme.[15] Smith confirmed the poor condition of the type, adding that he had melted some of it down on Legate's instructions. Pryme referred specifically to the type used for the dictionary ('worn verre bare and...allmost unfitt for any further worke'), and said that the press had been seriously out of repair in 1588. And Stafford, who had worked at the press for two years, spoke of it being 'soe bad and insufficient that it hath greatlie hindered mr Legate, but this deponent [continued the court summary] cannot directlie depose to what value or summe of monie'.[16]

The outcome of this case, which took the Vice-Chancellor's court into unaccustomed areas of technical evidence, has not survived. Amidst all the arguments about the condition of the type, no one seems to have recalled, in court at any rate, that when Thomas's effects had been valued, the appraisers had set aside over 86 per cent of his type as 'metall to be melted'.[17] Much of this was of the brevier, the size used in the dictionary and which caused particular opprobrium. More seriously, few people seemed to be clear as to the value of the 'copy' of Thomas's dictionary. Apart from Legate's claim that it was considered so miserable that the London printers, even when offered it, had suggested little or nothing,[18] the lack of any legal protection against others printing either the dictionary or any other book made Thomas's copies all but worthless. Both Smith and Stafford knew the London trade, and were unequivocal in saying that in effect Legate was without any commercial protection.[19]

Arguments between the Stationers' Company and the University were not to be settled finally until several generations later. The position for Legate in his first few years was very different, as he challenged some of the London booksellers' most profitable monopolies. In 1586 the Star Chamber decree concerning printing had been clear about the two university presses in several respects: there was to be only one press in each town, and the printers there were to keep only one apprentice at a time, though they might employ whatever journeymen they pleased provided such men were freemen of the City of London.[20] The decree was less clear about the authorities under whom these presses operated, in that it did not mention either the Chancellors or any other university figure or body. The same section dealt also with infringements of patents belonging to the Stationers' Company without making its meaning clear as to the interests of the university presses. The issues raised by the 1534 charter granted to Cambridge were ducked, in that no confirmation was made of the University's historic position, while on the other hand the restriction in the number of presses was no doubt considered sufficient gag against any threat to the richer parts of the London trade.

Now and for decades to come, the Stationers' Company assiduously sought not only to preserve its interests and the interests of its London members, but also to appear to do so as a united corporation, and as the only body invested with the prosecution of the printing and bookselling trades. To achieve these ends, it sought out legislation, whether by decree or by Act of Parliament, that both limited the number of presses in London, and vested in the Company specific powers of execution. These powers both appeared to protect national interests and, no less vitally, permitted the most powerful members of the Company to continue to exercise a stranglehold over the book trade, and over printing in particular.[21] The Company's continuing success depended partly on the preservation of what was always in some respects a fiction, and partly on the domination within the Company at any one period of a small group of like-interested individuals, united either by economic interest or by opposition. In fact, the Company never controlled the trade absolutely, either in London or in Cambridge. The contract between licence by those appointed under central government or ecclesiastical authority, and entry in the Register books of the Company, depended more on acceptance than on punitive legislation. Though recusant presses, for example, were troublesome to the authorities in Whitehall and in Lambeth, the gradual sapping away of the rights and privileges expressed in the Stationers' Company charter of 1557 was a much greater danger to its interests. Within the Company, increasing dissent between printers and booksellers, and between the richer and poorer members, brought strains that led sometimes to breaks. In the book trade, as in other trades and manufactures, the monopoly power of a single livery company did not hold in the 1570s, and by the end of the century it was in many respects in disarray.[22] By the middle of the seventeenth century, it may be said to have disappeared. Despite the apparent transfusion of new authority under the Licensing Acts from 1662 onwards, the Company was in decline for more than half the period between the 1580s and the end of the seventeenth century. In itself, despite all that was said, the privilege to print at Cambridge was never a great threat to the interest of the Company as a whole. In this, Cecil was right. But it did threaten the interest of individuals, a minority within the Company, but in practice its most powerful members. From this, the Company forged a usually united front. The confrontation between Cambridge and the Stationers was ostensibly between two conflicting corporate interests. But such compromises as were contrived were essentially financial, based on specific interests (such as the English Stock), and on individuals (most notoriously George Sawbridge and John Field) rather than on principle. By the 1620s, though it still dealt in name with the Company, the University was, in effect, dealing only with the English and the Latin Stocks.[23]

Some of the most dramatic parts of the battle between Legate and the London monopolists were fought out quickly, between the end of 1589 and the end of 1591: they may be said to have been concluded with an agreement that allowed Legate to make free choice of what to print among the books listed in the Frankfurt catalogues, unhindered by rival London editions. Of the books which in 1589 provoked particular animosity, Legate's edition of Terence – one of the first books that he printed – infringed Thomas Marsh's patent for schoolbooks; the English Bible had for years been confined to the Queen's Printer or (in the case of Christopher Barker) his deputies; and Thomas's dictionary seemed to infringe the patent enjoyed by Henry Bynneman to print all dictionaries.[24]

It was with a tone more of apology than of expostulation that the University wrote to Burghley on 2 January 1589/90 to say that after trouble over the dictionary, the London stationers had now seized Legate's edition of Terence, a duodecimo described as 'contractiore volumine & minutioribus, sed scitissimis litteris'.[25] Legate's edition was unadorned, without commentary, whereas Marsh and, indeed, continental printers had preferred to publish editions with an apparatus – usually that of Muret. But Legate's challenge to the established market, with a slightly different product whose form may have been influenced by teaching requirements at Cambridge, met with scant sympathy. If surviving copies are a sufficient guide, neither Legate nor his successor Legge printed such an edition again, and when editions of the text were again printed at Cambridge, in the 1630s and this time at the instance of the Stationers, they appeared once again with commentaries. Meanwhile, however, Legate devised a method of circumventing the London trade by a device which nevertheless required that trade's connivance. On Thomas Marsh's death, his rights in various schoolbooks (including Terence) died also. A single surviving copy bears witness to the enterprise of Robert Dexter, a London bookseller who issued an edition in even smaller format (24°) in 1597; but in the following year Legate published the first extended selection from Terence translated into English. It was the work of Richard Bernard, a puritan-inclined minister at Epworth in Lincolnshire and a recent graduate of Christ's College. Bernard's version, accompanied by the Latin text, proved successful: in 1607 Legate published a second edition, and by 1629 it had passed through five editions in all. It also escaped the wrath of the Stationers' Company, perhaps because it was thought, with its translation, not to conflict with the lucrative educational market.

The dispute over the printing of the English Bible was much less amicable, and much more prolonged. By the 1580s, the English market for Bibles was dominated by two versions, the Geneva, first published in its entirety in 1560, the work of a group of refugees in which the influence of Calvin is clearly to be seen in the explanatory notes, and the Bishops', undertaken under the auspices of Matthew Parker by the Anglican establishment and first published in 1568. The Bishops' version was hallowed by an order in 1571 to place a copy in every cathedral and church.[26] But the Geneva proved to be the more popular, its roman type (as distinct from other versions' black letter) becoming so familiar that the phrase 'Geneva print' passed into everyday language.[27] In 1576 the New Testament of this version was further revised by Laurence Tomson, secretary to Sir Francis Walsingham, and from 1587 it was generally this version that was published with the Geneva. Demand persisted long after the publication of the King James, or Authorized, version in 1611.

The English Bible, in both the Bishops' and the Geneva–Tomson versions, was the property of the Queen's Printer, Christopher Barker, who from 1583 assigned it to deputies.[28] The pattern of publication did not change significantly with the appointment of Barker's deputies. Among their first achievements was a fine edition of the Bishops' version, intended to supplement the dwindled supplies of the previous such edition, in 1584. By this time, moreover, the Geneva version had come to dominate the market for the more domestically suited quarto edition: it was supported by the still more handy octavo, while the market for the Geneva New Testament was further supplied with duodecimos and, apparently, with yet smaller 24°s – though little evidence survives of this last. Not surprisingly, the appearance of these books became ever more uniform, partly in answer to the needs of printing house convenience.[29] Familiarity and economy, besides a clear text, were required by printer and customer alike.

Legate printed the scriptures at least twice. Copies survive of an octavo Bible, dated on the title-page 29 May 1591, and a minute 32° New Testament, undated but also apparently printed by June that year, when the University wrote to Burghley in support of Legate's right to print these books.[30] In his Bible, Legate followed closely most of the typographical conventions established in the London editions. His title-page, however, was startlingly different, in its bold use of a woodcut border, the first such to be used at Cambridge since Siberch's day. It was derived from a design used originally for an English translation of Beza on the Book of Job, published in Latin by George Bishop in 1589 and printed by Legate in another edition probably in the same year. Though there was never any suggestion of a house style, its introduction, like the much more familiar and enduring *Alma mater* device of 1600 (see fig. 9), suggests that Legate had some sense of the importance of distinctive decoration in the successful promotion of books.

Several fragments of evidence suggest a close commercial link between Legate and Bishop. Legate's new border echoed that used by Bishop, in the placing of its masks and cornucopia, as well as in the royal shield at the head, though it was an altogether more flamboyant rendering of these elements. Bishop's, in turn, had been cut originally for Christopher Barker, and it displayed beside the royal badge the arms of Walsingham and of the Drapers' and Stationers' Companies. Legate's became a celebration of the Chancellor of the University, in its display of various elements drawn from the Burghley arms. Within the Bible, Michael Black has drawn attention to Legate's use of spaced capitals for the page heads, where London printers had preferred upper and lower case;[31] but generally the orchestration of the nonpareil type used for the main text of the London and Cambridge editions alike was remarkable more for its similarities than for its differences. From the first, Legate insisted on an edition (printed on Rochelle paper) that should require no more sheets than the octavo printed at London in 1590: his principal journeyman and compositor, Edward Smith, later claimed that in return Legate was to give him fifty copies of the book, which were valued (whether wholesale or retail is not clear) at four shillings apiece.[32]

The challenge to the Queen's Printer was not ignored. Initially it was alleged that Barker's deputies alone had been wronged; but in 1590 Legate had also printed a 32° edition of Sternhold and Hopkins' metrical Psalms, and thus, seemingly, infringed the monopoly enjoyed by Richard Day and his assigns.[33] Accusations naturally developed so as to include this as well. The Stationers, or a group of them, alluded to in a second letter from the University to Burghley simply as 'our Adversaries',[34] thus sought to make Legate's misdemeanour appear all the greater, by emphasizing the offence given to Barker and to Day. More immediately, they had also applied to Burghley to stay the sale of Legate's Bible until the next legal term, and so make him forego selling it at the Stourbridge Fair in September, when he would have been able to recoup many of his costs with little difficulty or expense.

These were matters of immediate concern; but once again the University rehearsed more general arguments, founded on the 1534 charter and on a point already made within the London trade only a few years earlier, when complaints had been lodged against monopolists. The Charter provided a peroration:

Suerlie yf this charter, so equable in it selfe, so commodious to the studentes of the Universitie, so beneficiall to manie other subjectes of the realme, graunted by her majesties most noble father, ratyfied by the gratious bountie of her selfe, established by acte of parlament so manie yeres past, may not be thoughte suffycient againste there grauntes, so latelie obteined, wee know not upon what privilege wee may hereafter repose ouer trust.

But the previous sentences contained the University's grievances against which the charter had come to be perceived as a defence. London monopolies, it was claimed, had forced up the price of students' 'needfull bookes', while the printer was in effect excluded from a reliable living. 'We shall accompt ouer selves well apaied, yf ouer poore printer may, with there good patience, now and then deale with some fewe of the most salable copies for his necessary maintenaunce in honest sort.'[35] The economic argument was an obvious one, and, consciously or not, related to a point already made by some of these very patentees to the Privy Council in 1588.[36] Despite these petitions the case was still not settled the following October, when the Stationers' Company authorized John Wolfe (a notorious poacher turned gamekeeper) to assist Day in seeking remedy against Legate.[37]

This proved, however, to be the temporary end of Legate's struggle with the Company. An entry in the Company's court book the following April records that Bibles, Testaments and Psalters recently seized were to be restored to their owners: though Legate is not mentioned by name in this connection, no other offensive editions of these texts survive from this period printed by anyone else.[38] More importantly, on 6 December 1591, 'for quietnes to be established betwene the Vniu'sitie of Cambridge and theire Printers and this Companie for matters of pryntinge', it was agreed by the Court that for a period of one month after the Frankfurt fairs, the Cambridge printer was to have free choice of any foreign book, provided that the book was thereupon entered in the Register.[39] It seems, indeed, a 'handsome arrangement'.[40] But Legate paid a high price. He had escaped the Stationers' wrath before Burghley, and now he was to be given preferential treatment. But with the single exception of an Apocalypse printed, with an extended commentary by François Du Jon, in 1596 (a book that can have provoked few jealousies or fears among the London stationers), no further Bible, Testament or metrical Psalter was to be completed at Cambridge until 1628.

The agreement over the Frankfurt catalogues was not in fact especially generous. For most of the books listed there the market in England was inadequate to support a separate English edition. The original Latin editions of books likely to have an interest for an international market presented no linguistic barrier to their potential English-speaking audience. Only among the more popular books of protestant theology could it be expected that regular candidates for English editions would appear. Legate took scant advantage of his new liberty, but the London trade showed (at least in the years 1591–3) little interest either. In 1592, only two of Legate's books showed him to be exploiting his position: editions of works by Jean de L'Espine and Hieronymus Zanchius. L'Espine was proven in English translation and regularly published in London since 1577. In 1584 he had been one of Thomas's earliest authors, and in 1588 the London bookseller George Bishop had had entered in the Stationers' Register the French edition of a new work published at Geneva in 1587.[41] Bishop seems, however, to have taken this matter no further, and Legate now used his prerogative to print *A very excellent discourse, touching the tranquilitie of the mind*, a translation after the new French edition listed in the Frankfurt catalogue of spring 1591.[42] Zanchius' *Excellent and learned treatise* on Christ's spiritual marriage to the Church had been published in Latin at Herborn in 1591, and was listed in the same Frankfurt catalogue.[43] He was a timely addition to Legate's list, an appropriate accompaniment to Beza and Perkins, and for the last several years had been a common presence in the private libraries of Oxford and Cambridge alike.

Both books were of course advertised much longer than a month previous to Legate's and the Stationers' agreement. Only the Zanchius was entered (on 9 August 1592) as that agreement required and, in fact, the pact between the two parties was never properly either executed or exploited. For his part, Legate was to gain more by being perceived to be a member of the stationers' establishment, though this did not preclude other arguments. Prompted presumably by demand in Cambridge, and in an effort to become yet more associated with the international market, in 1592 he issued an unauthorized collection of short pieces by Justus Lipsius, *Tractatus ad historiam romanam cognoscendam*. It was yet another occasion when Legate's interests moved alongside those of the London bookseller George Bishop, the man most responsible for bringing London-printed editions of Lipsius to the English market. But for reasons that are not clear, not only did Legate publish (to Lipsius' great irritation) without the author's approval; he also printed two issues, one bearing his own name and one bearing that of Raphelengius in Leiden, the latter even sporting a faked printer's device of the celebrated golden compasses.[44]

More importantly, between 1592 and 1606 he printed five further enlarged editions of Thomas's dictionary, offering it in quarto (rather than octavo) for the first time in 1592. At Oxford, John Rider's *Bibliotheca scholastica*, printed by Joseph Barnes in 1589, had presented a potential challenge to Thomas's work, if not at first a serious one. 'I pray signifie to the stationers in Oxford that my dictionarij is printed', requested Legate of a London stationer in 1593, 'for I do knowe their want of them and yf they will have any let them send to you and I will send you as many as you shall writ for.'[45] Though no subsequent edition of Rider is known until seventeen years later, Barnes' son John saw it entered in the Register in 1602, when the unusual provision was included that it should be printed only in London: the metropolitan trade aquired the prize properly with its assignment to the London stationer Cuthbert Burby a few months later, and by him to his assigns in November 1604.[46] It was against this background that in 1606 a new version of Rider was finally published, much expanded by Francis Holyoke, a schoolmaster and now minister in Warwickshire. Holyoke borrowed freely from Thomas, so following lexicographical tradition, though Thomas Fuller (a Cambridge man) thought such borrowing '*Plageary-ship*', which 'ill becometh *Authors* or *Printers*': 'the *Dove* being the Crest of the *Stationers Armes*, should mind them, not like *Rooks*, to filch copies one from an other'.[47] Once again, Legate found himself at loggerheads with the London trade, this time in the form of a group of partners including some of the most senior members of the Stationers' Company: Thomas Man, Master in 1604, John Norton and William Leake. He had printed no edition of Thomas since 1600, when in March 1605/6 he was constrained to agree that if he should print any within the next three years he should deliver the impression to the Rider-Holyoke partners at 2s.6d. a copy if his edition was a quarto, or 8d. if an octavo. Only if these copies were sold successfully by the partners could Legate print a further edition. On the other hand, the partners had to give Legate notice of any fresh edition of Holyoke that they intended.[48] Editions of both Holyoke and of Thomas appeared dated 1606, and both must have been at least envisaged, if not virtually completed, when this reprehensible agreement was reached. Whatever the exact timing, the result of this double appearance was that no further edition of Thomas was required until 1610, and none of Holyoke until 1612. Despite Legate's son obtaining a patent for Thomas's dictionary (and thereby hoping to stop publication of Holyoke's plagiary) in 1621, the Court of the Stationers' Company was obliged to record even in 1625 that 'the Controversye remayneth vndecyded'.[49] It was decided only when both dictionaries had passed out of fashion.

Thus, while Legate was, unlike Thomas, a member of the Stationers' Company, the attitude of the London printers and booksellers was often scarcely less intransigent towards him than it had been to his predecessor. Two of his principal achievements as a stationer in Cambridge, the successful printing and publishing first of the New Testament and then of the complete Bible, were accomplished in the teeth of opposition from London and challenged trade privileges at one of their most lucrative points. Though in 1593/4 the officers of the Company came to his support, in providing evidence in the Cambridge courts, he did not always enjoy, and could not always command, such confidence.

Matters flared up yet again in the spring of 1596–7, this time not over Bibles or Psalms, but over school grammars and accidences – a market no less profitable, and no less protected. As usual, complaint came from London, orchestrated by the stationers and expressed by those willing to take up their cause – led, on this occasion, by John Whitgift. But it was a charge that John Jegon, as Vice-Chancellor, turned easily aside, claiming simply that he could find no evidence that Legate had printed such books, and proceeding briskly instead to distract Whitgift with difficulties over a preacher in Great St Mary's.[50]

Much of the danger lay less in open hostility than in inertia. With no regular trade openings in London through which to sell his books, Thomas had been noticeably more successful as a printer than as a bookseller. To be sure, his dictionary had been available from Richard Boyle, and in selling Whitaker's *Aunswere* to Reynolds he had had a somewhat obscure arrangement with Thomas Chard and perhaps Robert Waldegrave; but generally speaking he had suffered simply by exclusion from the country's most profitable market, and the one that gave access to most others. Legate quickly remedied this, by an arrangement with Abraham Kitson, who had inherited the shop at the sign of the Sun in St Paul's Churchyard in London in 1578.[51] Kitson was not one of the most important booksellers, but his proven opposition to the major monopolists may have helped to make him sympathetic to Legate: in 1582/3 he had been included among a group of stationers (chief among them John Wolfe) accused by the Company of printing privileged copies 'at their pleasure', and selling them in fairs and markets up and down the country.[52] Until the mid-1590s all Legate's books that bore a London stationer's imprint carried that of Kitson – usually printing his address rather than his name. Among the first were Beza's exposition of Job and Ecclesiastes, and Bastingius on the Heidelberg catechism; and by 1591 he was appearing on books by the increasingly popular puritan master of the pulpit, William Perkins. By no means all of Legate's books were graced in this manner, but it is noticeable that of those that were, the most obvious was Thomas's dictionary – the very book for which Legate most needed protection in London. The considerations that governed whether or not Kitson was openly involved in a book are nowhere recorded, and it is therefore unclear how frequently one sought the other's collaboration. However, with the exceptions of the dictionary and of Paul Greaves' *Grammatica anglicana* (1594), a textbook organized on Ramist principles, Kitson's address appeared on none of the more strictly educational books printed by Legate. Cicero (1589), Terence (1589), Demosthenes (1595?), Lysias (1593), Lycophron (1595) and Plutarch (1595) were all issued apparently without Kitson's support.

The threat of competition for the sale of books such as these came more from abroad than from London. Though Bynneman had issued the Greek text of Plutarch, *De educatione puerorum*, in 1581, and it proved to be a substantial success, the related text of Plutarch which Legate chose (again in Greek), *De recta audiendi ratione*, seems to have been printed by no other English press during this period. Bishop had printed texts of Demosthenes in 1591 and 1592; but again, when Legate printed his edition in about 1595 he chose two orations that had not been printed already in London. Lycophron (in Greek) had already been printed *in usum Academiae Oxoniensis* by Barnes at Oxford in 1592, when Legate produced a companion edition to the Plutarch in 1595; and though, again, there was no London rival, the text (with Scaliger's translation) was readily available from continental presses. In the case of Lysias' *Eratosthenes*, where a short text was accompanied by a full commentary by Andrew Downes, he had no English rivals whatsoever. Terence and Cicero were on the other hand both familiar among London printers, though even here, as has been said, Legate seems to have shown independence by printing unannotated editions in duodecimo. Their market was a university one, not metropolitan. Even the copies of Lycophron and of Plutarch deposited in the University Library were interleaved ready for students' use.[53] In Oxford, Joseph Barnes was printing for a similar clientèle when he produced short texts

of Herodotus (1591), Lycophron (1592), Aristophanes (1593) and Demosthenes (1597), only the last of which bears any London address on its title-page.

In Cambridge, first Thomas (with Plato's *Menexenus*) and then Legate aided
the revival of Greek studies led by Andrew Downes, Regius Professor of
Greek since 1585. Not for the last time, the number of a man's known or
acknowledged publications bore little relation to the extent of his influence.
Apart from his share in the preparation of the Authorized Version of the Bible,
and his contributions to Sir Henry Savile's great edition of John Chrysostom,
Downes was ostensibly responsible for two books only: the textbook Lysias
printed by Legate and, in 1621, a similar Demosthenes – the latter printed not
in Cambridge, but in London. In his edition of Lysias (1593), he took
advantage of a dedication to a fellow member of Trinity, Robert, Earl of Essex
(who was not to become Chancellor of the University for several more years)
to set out his opinions of Cambridge students and education more generally,
though typographically it is more remarkable for the introduction of a few
words of Hebrew, apparently the first to be printed in Cambridge.[54]

It remains unlikely that either Thomas (with his plain-text Plato) or Legate
(with Demosthenes, Lycophron and Plutarch, besides the Lysias) ventured
into printing such texts without at least seeking some assurance for a market.
But these classical investments, seemingly produced without the support either
of Kitson or any other London bookseller, do not appear to have been great
commercial successes, if the record of surviving editions is used as the criteria.
Sales were limited to within the universities, and were therefore necessarily
slow. In another sphere, William Whitaker's attack on Stapleton, published in
1594 and bearing no name in its imprint other than Legate's, might be
considered a book of sufficient weight on its own to need no such aid. But with
Kitson's death, Legate cast round for another regular associate. In 1595
Richard Bankworth, Kitson's successor at the sign of the Sun, was responsible
for William Perkins' *Two treatises*; and in the same year it was left to Legate
to complete for Bankworth the printing of William Covell's *Polimanteia*, of
which all but one sheet had been executed in London. More importantly, from
1601 Simon Waterson (also in St Paul's Churchyard, and who eventually
became one of Legate's executors[55]) finally took Kitson's place after an interval
of six years in which Legate had apparently acted without any regular London
outlet. For the next nine years, until he removed to London, Waterson was
responsible for, or took at least a few copies of (among others) works by Sir
Christopher Heydon, King James I, Andrew Willet and John Cowell, besides
(in 1606) the seventh edition of Thomas's dictionary and several works by the
prolific Perkins, culminating in two of the three volumes containing his
collected works, published in 1609.

Legate came from London, and by about 1609 was to return there. His links
with the London trade were always a part of his business. In Cambridge, he
drew his support, so far as the book trade was concerned, from John Porter,

one of the most powerful local booksellers. The two men acted in concord in 1593 when they prosecuted one John Tidder for the unauthorized sale of books in Cambridge market,[56] but they were also business partners in the publishing of books and in the beginnings of publication by Cambridge stationers of books printed in London. As I have already suggested, on the whole Legate does not seem either to have expected or relied on the formal support of the London booksellers in his publications. The books with either Kitson's or Waterson's imprint formed less than a quarter of his output, though the proportion was nearer a half in 1602–5. In some respects Legate remained isolated, like Thomas.

But also like Thomas, his position as supplier to the Cambridge and the London trade, and the constant need for working capital, meant that isolation in some matters went hand in hand with enterprises that were not of the establishment. Although he was for a time under suspicion of having printed part of the pirate edition of Sidney's *Arcadia*, issued from Robert Waldegrave's shop in Edinburgh in 1599, the charge was denied by William Scarlet. Indeed, Legate's interest (which could not be denied, as Scarlet, a bookbinder and bookseller, admitted having sold copies for the use of and on behalf of Legate) was not as a printer, but as one dependent on London booksellers. His twenty copies, part of a much larger consignment that had been brought from Edinburgh to Cambridge, had been sold to Richard Bankworth and to Cuthbert Burby. Of all the English defendants who faced the accusations and suspicions of William Ponsonby, the owner of the London edition, only Legate was a printer; the others were booksellers.[57] Like Thomas, he seems to have sought to keep an interest in Scotland as well as in London – an interest that makes his edition of James I's *Princes looking glasse* (1603) less eccentric than it might otherwise appear.

The *Arcadia* episode was a yet further example of Legate's willingness, even eagerness, to engage with and manipulate other parts of the book trade to his own advantage. Thomas, too, had occasionally shared the printing of books with printers in London. But Legate not only collaborated in this manner, as in the case of *Polimanteia*. He was willing also to face the certain displeasure of an influential foreign author, Lipsius, by an unauthorized edition; to put a misleading imprint on his title-page; and, in the case of *Anti-Sanderus* (an attack on Nicholas Sanders) in 1593, set his own name to sheets printed elsewhere. Thomas had been an amateur. Legate, with training in a London apprenticeship behind him, was not only a professional, he was something of a buccaneer.

His apparent affinity with outsiders, rather than with the established local dynasties, may have made him more sympathetic to the case of Manasses Vautrollier, whose brief term as bookseller and bookbinder was, however, brought to an end by Legate himself.[58] Here, again, there was opportunity for exchange of goods with London. In buying the foreign books on which it so much depended, Cambridge was by the 1580s at the end of a chain of middlemen, importers and agents all of whom added their charges to the price structure. In some measure Thomas Thomas's work acted as a counterbalance; but it could only be for a few titles, and he was not in any case solely concerned to offer alternatives to overseas rather than London printing. Moreover, the Cambridge stationers shared many of the anxieties of their London counterparts that unbridled expansion would lead to distress and ruin: the University's licensing system was designed for the control not only of quality, but also of numbers, and was thus, like that of the Stationers' Company, actively conservative. So it welcomed newcomers only cautiously. The 1583 regulations for Cambridge bookselling[59] had specifically excluded, as a general practice, those already established in bookselling elsewhere, and had restricted those setting up shop in the town to those who had served their apprenticeship in Cambridge. When therefore, in 1590, three years after his father's death, Manasses Vautrollier sought to establish himself as a bookseller in Cambridge, his sponsor, Whitgift, was suitably circumspect:

He is an honest youngman, his skill in forrein bookes verie sufficient, & whereas you are now served at the third hand & at the highest price, hee shall be able to furnished you wth outlandishe bookes at the first hande, and afford them also better cheape. w[ch] woould be a greate pleasure to the students of that Vniversitie.[60]

The University admitted him, but imposed regulations so circumscribing that he could never be much more than a middleman. The requirements that he was to stock none but books printed overseas, and none other than in quires, and that he was not to charge above what was charged in London, each protected the established local interests, and made him but a tolerated convenience whose family connections would at least not hinder the University's interests.[61]

But convenience or not, Vautrollier became established as a bookseller, one of ten licensed booksellers in the town, obtaining his books from, among others, the London bookseller François Bouvier, member of another Stranger family.[62] He also developed close links with Legate. His son Thomas was apprenticed to Legate, and in 1600 Manasses borrowed money from him which he was eventually unable to pay. In 1604, when his goods were distrained for debt, Manasses Vautrollier owned an extensive binding shop (explicitly forbidden fourteen years before), well stocked with finishing tools.[63] Not for the last time, regulations promulgated by the University and designed to preserve a status quo proved to be impractical, and were overtaken by events. In this respect, Vautrollier was more fortunate than John Tidder, agent of the London stationer William Barley, whom Legate and Porter combined to prosecute in 1593/4 for selling books in Cambridge without licence. Unlike Vautrollier, Barley, offering no advantageous connections with the continent, could plead no special case save that of need and hope.[64]

It was scarcely to be expected that a London stationer need have an interest in such essentially local productions as Downes' Greek texts, the University verses of 1603 on the death of Queen Elizabeth (the first such collection to be published for Cambridge),[65] or many sermons from Cambridge pulpits. In 1598 Legate printed the visitation articles for William Chaderton, former Regius Professor of Divinity and President of Queens', and now Bishop of Lincoln. Chaderton was to call on his services three more times by 1607,[66] Legate thus becoming the first Cambridge printer to help supply the administrative needs of the established church. Otherwise he adhered to the path marked out by Thomas, in that the theology that he printed included further examples of continental protestantism, notably Hieronymus Zanchius, Jean de L'Espine, François Du Jon and Jeremias Bastingius; but only L'Espine and (perhaps) Zanchius were of immediate interest to the London book-sellers.[67] Of the eight works that he printed by Francis Dillingham (Fellow of Christ's and, in the new century, one of the Cambridge team of translators for the Authorized Version) between 1599 and 1606, only one, an attack on the Catholic Edmund Thomas Hill, bore Waterson's name.

In the case of the 'learned and laborious' theologian Andrew Willet, the position was to become more diffused. Like Dillingham, Willet was a member of Christ's; but he relinquished his fellowship in 1588 on his marriage to the daughter of Roger Goad, Provost of King's. He spent the remainder of his life in his livings, first at Childerley, a now lost village to the west of Cambridge, then at Little Gransden, on the borders of Cambridgeshire and Huntingdon-shire, and finally at his father's parish of Barley, in Hertfordshire, where the memorial brass erected after his death in 1621 survived the virtual rebuilding of the church in 1872.[68] All were villages within reasonably easy reach of Cambridge, and Legate and his successor Cantrell Legge played a central part in the printing and marketing of one of the more prolific theological authors of a generation not noticeable for its reticence. Willet composed rapidly and became almost a best seller. 'He had no sooner once suffered the Presse', wrote his son-in-law, 'but everie yeare after during his whole life, the Printer heard some thing or other of him, either some new booke, or some renewed edition of an old was prepared for him.'[69] In 1605 Legate introduced a long list of errata in one of his books by explaining that not only was Willet absent from Cambridge, 'and could not recognize what was printed,' but also that the printer 'might easily be deceaued in the copie, beeing but once written in all, and that with a running hand, & in some places not very legible'.[70]

Willet's first book had been printed by Thomas in 1585. Five years later, Legate printed his tract on the conversion of the Jews,[71] and a few months after that he was responsible for Willet's collection of Latin emblem verses *Sacrorum emblematum centuria una*:[72] the verses were accompanied by translations that were an inauspicious beginning to the printing of English poetry in Cambridge. The collection, hailed as an original contribution to the genre, marked the end of Willet's confinement to the Cambridge trade, and for the next several years the publication of his books was marked by an increasingly complicated series of arrangements involving printers and booksellers in both London and Cambridge. In 1592, a London bookseller, Thomas Man, was responsible for Willet's *Synopsis papismi, that is, a generall viewe of papistry*, a book which remained popular still in the 1630s and in which, by then, a whole clutch of booksellers shared interests.[73] Man too (this time in partnership with John Norton) acquired Willet's monumental *Hexapla in Genesin* in 1605, the year in which Legate first printed it;[74] and by then he had become established as Willet's principal – but by no means his only – London bookseller. Legate's place was meanwhile further complicated by Waterson, who handled three of Willet's books printed at Cambridge in 1602–4. In 1604 Willet's *Thesaurus ecclesiae*, which bore both Legate's and Waterson's names on the title-page, was in fact printed mostly in London by Richard Field, an instance of shared printing of a kind common enough within the tight circle of the London printing shops, but uncommon between London and a provincial press. Legate, and his successor Cantrell Legge, remained essential to the publication of Willet's work, their position perhaps strengthened by Willet's own proximity to the University: Legge had some success in regaining the Cambridge hold over his work in 1611, when he printed Willet's commentary on Romans, sharing the impression with the Cambridge bookseller Leonard Greene. Fresh to his post, Legge had demonstrated his determination only the year before, in 1610, when he had sought to give new life to old sheets, and dressed up Thomas Man's London-printed edition of the *Synopsis papismi* dated 1610, describing it as Willet's 'larger workes';[75] if the unique example of this exercise that has survived is a trustworthy guide, the experiment did not involve many copies, while Man himself responded with an enlarged edition two years later. By then, however, Legate had established himself in London, where he put out his own selection of Willet's works in 1614;[76] he did not repeat the experiment.

Even Willet, however, fell far short of being the Cambridge press's best known author. For years afterwards, no one challenged the success achieved by the puritan preacher William Perkins (see fig. 8), four years Willet's senior and elected a Fellow of Christ's in 1584, a year after him.[77] Perkins' tenure as Fellow lasted until his marriage in 1594, but his appointment as preacher at Great St Andrew's church, just opposite the college, ensured that his sermons were not lost to Cambridge. He died in 1602, aged but forty-four, in the midst of a singularly successful career that owed much to his ability to present his arguments (always staunchly, even vehemently, puritan) from the pulpit both in a manner comprehensible to his hearers and in a form familiar to members of the University from their other studies.

Perkins' earliest works, in 1585–7, and including an attack on almanac makers for their arrogance and deceit in their prognostications, were printed in London by John Wolfe and Robert Waldegrave; but he rapidly became established as an essentially Cambridge author. Even in 1587, his *Foure Godly*

GVILIELMVS PERKINSVS S.THEO. D.

PERKINSVS Christi defendens dogmata talis
Vultu erat, ingenium scripta facunda probant. ÆB

Fig. 8 William Perkins (1558–1602), Fellow of Christ's College, and successful alike as a preacher and author of popular religious works. From Henry Holland, *Herωologia Anglica* [1620]. Original plate-mark, 150 mm. high.

treatises were entered in the Stationers' Register jointly to Richard Watkins, a long established printer in St Paul's Churchyard, and the Cambridge bookseller John Porter. Occasionally in conjunction with Legate, but more frequently using London printers, and in partnership with London booksellers, Porter was to have a share in more than a dozen editions of works by Perkins. Only one other Cambridge stationer, Hugh Burwell, seems at first to have had a share in Perkins' phenomenal popularity, and that in the appropriately titled *Graine of musterd-seed*, printed in London by Thomas Creed for Ralph Jackson and for Burwell. The portion was small indeed.[78] Legate alone, however, was responsible for Perkins' first notable success, *Armilla aurea*, translated and published quickly as *A golden chaine … conteining the order of the causes of saluation and damnation according to Gods word*. The original Latin first appeared in 1590, and Legate had printed three editions of it by 1592, marketing the later ones in London through Kitson. Further editions of the Latin were printed at Basel, and in 1606 the Cloppenburch press at Amsterdam issued a translation into Dutch.[79] By 1600 there had been seven editions of the English version, including one printed by Waldegrave in Edinburgh. The first of these was published in 1591 by a London bookseller, Edward White, who issued a second edition in the following year. Had this happened five years earlier, the translation would have been put forth without demur. But by 1592 Legate was confident enough to put the matter to the Court of the Stationers' Company, who found in his favour: he won the right to print the translation 'as his owne prop*er* copie', while White was obliged to buy such copies as Legate had already printed at the rate of £4.16s. per hundred.[80] It was this confirmation of his position that no doubt enabled Legate in effect to remove part of his business back to London, where a much larger market offered itself than that to be found in Cambridge alone. So in 1595 Legate was having books printed in London, and selling them there without any need to transport them to Cambridge.

A golden chaine was printed by Adam Islip and then in 1597 by Joan Orwin. Other books were treated similarly, as Legate and Porter acted together within the London trade. Links with Kitson and with Bankworth were not broken, as Legate continued to print in Cambridge; but his business now acquired, albeit briefly, another dimension. Perkins' commentary on the Lord's Prayer, pirated in 1592 by Edward White, passed into the hands of an obscure (and at least formerly disreputable) London stationer, Robert Bourn, who shared it with John Porter, and in 1595 it was printed by Islip for Legate. In 1590 (the same year as the first, Latin, edition of *Armilla aurea*), there also appeared the first surviving edition of *The foundation of Christian religion*. It was printed by Thomas Orwin for Porter, who retained an interest in the book until his death. Orwin's widow Joan printed the 1595 edition for Porter and Legate together, just as she did in the same year a treatise by Perkins on grace that had likewise on its first publication been the property of Porter alone.[81]

The position was all the more complicated when, inexorably, Legate considered a collected edition of Perkins' principal works. It was not a task to be faced lightly. The first formal collection, graced by a preliminary general title-page, appeared in 1603. But Legate had already made other, less formal, collections previously, within Perkins' lifetime. The first seems to have been in 1597, and involved several London printers as well as other booksellers.[82] In 1600, however, Legate was able to print an entire collection, and in 1603 he produced the first in a series of collections in folio format that were still being published in the 1630s. By 1609 they had reached a third volume, and required the co-operation of nine members of the trade, including Legate's successor Legge. Perkins' works, including those he left in manuscript at his death, were quickly recognized as valuable properties, so much so that his executors claimed to have obtained a 'generall Inhibition out of his maiesties court of high Commission, prohibiting the publishing of any of his works without their consent'.[83] The precaution was a necessary one. The Stationers' Company had no jurisdiction over editions printed in Edinburgh, where Robert Waldegrave printed Perkins' work in 1592–3, while in London in 1606 the bookseller Thomas Pavier was fined forty shillings for buying 800 copies of *A graine of musterd-seed* from Legate after the title had been assigned to another bookseller, Cuthbert Burby.[84]

These authors inclined to Legate, rather than to London, not simply because of their university connections. As the dominant printer of Perkins' prolific output, Legate was *ipso facto* a leading puritan printer as well as being in tune with the University's inclinations. His authors, like those of his successor Cantrell Legge, showed their hearts on their title-pages, in the styles by which they were presented. Robert Hill, Fellow of St John's, was also 'preacher of Gods word in S. Andrewes in Norwich';[85] James Manning, of Jesus, was 'minister of the word';[86] Samuel Hieron, of King's, was 'minister of the word at Modburie in Devon';[87] Miles Mosse, of Caius, was 'pastor of the church of God at Combes in Suffolke';[88] Roger Gostwike, of King's, was 'minister of Sampford Courtnie in the countie of Deuonsh.';[89] Richard Betts, of Peterhouse, was 'pastor to the church at Ashele [Ashill] in the countie of Norfolke'.[90] Thomas Pickering, of Emmanuel, the editor of Perkins, chose not surprisingly to be called minister rather than vicar of his parish at Finchingfield in Essex.

The Cambridge press was by no means unique, either in attracting a significant number of puritans or in printing the works of so geographically widespread a body of authors. By no means all these men were prolific. But it is noticeable, among those that were, how few showed a consistent loyalty to a single press, or bookseller. Perkins and Willet were exceptional – prolific and inclined towards Legate or (in the latter's case) his successor Cantrell Legge. Thomas Taylor was not. A graduate of Christ's, where he matriculated probably in 1592, Taylor remained in Cambridge after ceasing to be a Fellow of his college in 1604, and in 1608 made himself notorious by an outspoken attack on Bancroft in the University Church.[91] So far he had published no book; but in the following year, 1609, he dedicated a sermon preached in the tiny Cambridge church of St Peter's to the Mayor of the town and to the rest of the corporation. His outburst in the University Church had earned a rebuke from the Vice-Chancellor, and it is therefore the less surprising that his St Peter's sermon should have been printed in London.[92] Thereafter his career took him to Watford, Reading and London, until his death in 1632/3. Despite the events of 1608, and despite the difficulties placed in his path to a DD from the University in 1628, many of his books were in fact printed by Legge. But these, in turn, might bear the names of London booksellers on their title-pages: of Thomas Man or Ralph Mab, or, in Cambridge, of Leonard Greene. His later books, after about 1620, were usually published in London by John Bartlet, and printed there as well. It was a more convenient arrangement than any involving Cambridge, where Legge's own business fell into rapid decline in the early twenties. Yet despite his very considerable following in puritan circles, witnessed for example on the bookshelves of North American colonists,[93] Taylor never achieved the same popular commercial success as Perkins. No posthumous edition of his works appeared until 1658. However, his books do raise again the question of Legge's relations with the London trade, to which we shall return.

Unlike his contemporary at Oxford Joseph Barnes, Legate seems to have made no serious effort or appeal to exploit the publication possibilities of the manuscripts lying to hand in the University and college libraries.[94] Yet the list of his books demonstrates a variety both in subject matter and in presentation that Thomas never achieved in his much shorter career. His output was dominated by the work of local theologians – notably Whitaker, Willet and Francis Dillingham, and, above all, Perkins. Yet he broke new ground even here. Whitaker's attack on Thomas Stapleton, published in 1594,[95] was the first book in a folio format to be printed at Cambridge, and the surviving fragments of Whitaker's manuscript, intended as part of the setting copy to be integrated with passages from Stapleton's original text, do not suggest that its setting was straightforward.[96] Legate employed the same format in Cambridge for only two other authors: for Perkins, in 1598, 1603 and 1605, 1608 and 1609, and for Willet in 1605.[97] Generally speaking, the subject matter and nature of his books did not lend themselves to so large a format, and in any case the physical constraints involved in transporting such bulky and heavy volumes to London, where most of the sales could be expected, encouraged a more portable product.

Apart from these local names, Legate continued to pursue Thomas's interest in continental Calvinism, so reflecting many University members' preoccupations, though reformers' names appear noticeably less frequently among his books after the turn of the century. His title-pages reveal the homes of his

English authors, though in nearly all cases he was dealing with Cambridge men. Samuel Bird, once of Queens' and Fellow of Corpus, whose *Lectures* on the Epistle to the Hebrews Legate printed in 1598, was by then of Ipswich; Henry Holland, author of *A treatise against witchcraft* (1590), had been incumbent of Orwell, a village about seven miles south-west of Cambridge, before his departure in 1594 to London; John More, whose chronological *Table* (1593) was slightly different in that this celebrated puritan preacher in Norwich (and member of Christ's) had died in January 1591/2, leaving the work to be seen through the press by his widow's new husband, Nicholas Bound of Peterhouse. Robert Hill, the creator of a compilation on *Life everlasting* (1601), was both a minister at St Andrew's, Norwich, and also Fellow of St John's. In 1606 Samuel Hieron, a member of King's who was to become one of the best known preachers of his generation in London, was still at Modbury in Devon when Legate printed one of his earliest books, two sermons on a verse from Proverbs.[98] The celebrated religious turncoat Thomas Bell, whose *Motives concerning Romish faith and religion* Legate printed in 1593, had once been a member of St John's, though he spent much of his career as a recusant in the north.[99] For both Bell's work and for Giles Fletcher the Elder's *Licia, or poems of love*, Legate used casts of the blocks originally employed by Day in *A booke of Christian prayers*: one had been used previously by Thomas, but they seem rarely to have been otherwise employed at Cambridge. The circumstances of the production and publication of this volume, the first of English poetry to be printed at Cambridge, are, however, unclear: in the absence from the book of the name of any member of the book trades, including Legate, it has been suggested that it was privately printed, a suggestion perhaps supported by the unusual appearance of casts of Day's old blocks. Though Fletcher, former Fellow of King's and deputy University Orator, had contributed to the volume of verses (printed in London) on the death of Sir Philip Sidney in 1587, he had been long absent from the University by 1593, and he gave no reason for turning now to Legate.[100]

Some of Legate's schoolbooks have already been mentioned. A Latin *Syntaxis* was the work of John Greenwood, once Fellow of St Catharine's and now master at Brentwood in Essex. In 1602 there appeared a selection from Cicero's *Epistolae familiares*, made by Thomas Cogan, retired High Master of Manchester Grammar School and former undergraduate both at Cambridge and at Oriel College, Oxford. Two years later, in 1604, a physician at Bury St Edmunds, and former pensioner at Christ's, Thomas Oliver, saw printed his idiosyncratic collection of tracts on medicine and geometry. Together with a small work on urine by I. Fletcher, printed in 1598, these were virtually the sum total of Legate's medical output. East Anglia provided other authors as well. These were by no means all. Sir Christopher Heydon's *Defence of judiciall astrologie* (1603) was the work of a prominent member of Norfolk society, and Charles Gibbon's *Watch-worde for warre* (1596), 'published by reason of ... the suspected comming of the Spanyard against us', was dedicated to the Mayor and Aldermen of King's Lynn. Gibbon, too, was responsible for a proposal for a more equitable taxation system, *The order of equalitie*, printed by Legate in 1604.

In many ways, however, one of the legal books printed in these years was to have the most lasting effect on the course of Cambridge printing. Until his death in 1593, the London stationer Richard Tottel held licence 'to imprint all manner of books concerning the common laws of this realm', and on his death this right was awarded to a clerk of the signet, Charles Yetsweirt.[101] Since Legate had already insisted on his right to print all books regardless of such arrangements, the appearance of a slim volume explaining the laws of usury in 1594 may be no more than a coincidence.[102] The anonymous summary of the poor laws, *An ease for overseers of the poore* (1601) was a more important contribution to the literature. But with the work of John Cowell, Legate finally saw himself established as a legal publisher, though in circumstances that were neither agreeable nor promising. Cowell, educated at Eton and King's, was appointed Regius Professor of Civil Law in 1594, became Master of Trinity Hall in 1598, and in 1603–4 served as Vice-Chancellor. In the following year Legate printed his *Institutiones iuris anglicanae*, a small handbook modelled on Justinian and designed, in its attempt to reconcile English and Scots law, as much for politicians as for lawyers. In 1607 there appeared, again from Legate's press, a book characterized by Holdsworth as 'much more useful': Cowell's *The interpreter … wherein is set foorth the true meaning of all*, *or the most part of such words and terms*, *as are mentioned in the lawe writers*, *or statutes …* In the early eighteenth century, the book was to prove itself an invaluable aid. But for Cowell, it fell victim to constitutional wrangling and jealousies between parliamentary and monarchical interests. He wrote at the instance of Archbishop Bancroft, to whom he dedicated his book, and he was rewarded with appointment as Vicar-General following the death of Sir Edward Stanhope in 1608. What Cowell had offered in good faith, the Commons saw, or were persuaded to see, as an instrument with which to embarrass the King; and the outcome of a complicated campaign was that on 25 March 1610 James I issued a proclamation against *The interpreter*, in which he not only pointed to Cowell's limited qualifications as a civilian lawyer ('medling in matters above his reach, he hath fallen in many things to mistake and deceive himself'), and indicated the joint interests of Crown and Parliament, but also, equally astutely, avoided criticism of the University authorities. The proclamation, said to have been penned by James himself, spoke only of his resolve to appoint commissioners whose task it would be to oversee legal or constitutional books in the future. It is doubtful if the order to deliver up copies was taken seriously: the book remains common, and nine copies survive in Cambridge alone.[103] King James himself was unwilling to prosecute Cowell, and indeed made the occasion a reason for a two-hour address to the Lords and Commons at the Banqueting House in Whitehall, not only to demonstrate his public dislike of

Cowell's work, and emphasize the monarch's constitutional obligation to the laws of the realm, but also to take the opportunity to plead for better treatment of recusants and for changes to woodland and corn laws. His speech was well received, and thus Cowell became an instrument of policy, obliged to appear before the King and Council, and kept under surveillance in London until he did so.[104] He was finally to resign, and he died in 1611 as a result of being cut for the stone. Henceforth, until the mid-eighteenth century, there was no serious legal publishing at Cambridge.

By the time of the furore over Cowell, however, Legate had abandoned Cambridge for London, in a translation that seems to have been made only gradually. For three years, between 1606 and 1609, and until Legate's final departure, there were for the first time two practising University Printers, Legate and his former apprentice Cantrell Legge. Legge had been admitted a freeman of the Stationers' Company on 11 December 1599,[105] and was appointed University Printer by Grace of 5 June 1606. His appointment, at a time when there was already a printer at work in the city where it had been ordained by the Star Chamber in 1586 that there should be but one press,[106] raises two questions immediately: why was it considered necessary, and what, if any, was the business relationship between the two men?

Legge printed no book over his own name until 1607, when two came out, both by Willet and both financed, at least partly, by other stationers – Leonard Greene in Cambridge and Richard Bankworth in London.[107] For no very clear reason, his name did not appear on the issue of Willet's commentary on Samuel that bore Greene's name. With one exception in 1608, when the names of both Legge and Thomas Brooke (both describing themselves as University Printers, though no record of Brooke's election has been found) appeared on a book by Perkins,[108] Legge's name never appeared with that of any other Cambridge printer. His business, and that of Legate, were separate. An examination of their typographical equipment confirms this. One of the more curious features of Legge's need to equip his press was the reappearance of two parts of an old title-page border cut originally for the London printer Richard Grafton in 1539: Legge used them as ornaments in 1607 and 1613, but the effect was hardly distinguished.[109]

As for Brooke, his place seems to have been as sentinel: perhaps at first as reassurance to the University while Legge, the apprentice, found his footing, and surely as a balance to the merely practical. The intention may have been for an arrangement such as the later and more celebrated joint appointment of Thomas Buck, of St Catharine's, and Roger Daniel, the practical printer from London. Both Brooke, a Fellow of Clare College, and Buck were Esquire Bedells, and thus held an office already in many respects a supervisory and administrative one for the University as a whole. It is unfortunate that, although he had been a Bedell since 1591 (and was to remain so until his death in 1629), no record survives of Brooke's election as Printer save for the anomalous Grace for the replacement of his lost Patent in July 1614.[110] But apart from the one instance in 1608, and an obscure dealing with the University over grammars in 1613–14, Brooke paid as little everyday part in the press's affairs as he did apparently in his other offices, whether as Bedell, or, from 1623, as University Librarian.

Meanwhile the device *Alma mater Cantabrigia* which Legate had first used on the title-page of Perkins' *Golden chaine* in 1600 (see fig. 9), and which helped more than any other innovation to establish a distinctive livery for Cambridge-printed books, remained Legate's property, as did the various smaller versions of the same device cut over the next few years.[111] When he removed to London in 1609, Legate took them with him, and as late as 1644 his son was still using one of the 1603 blocks on the title-page of the fourteenth edition of Thomas Thomas's Latin dictionary.[112] Similarly, the same woodcut used by Legate for Perkins' works at the beginning of the century was brought out (although eventually cracking across) for successive editions of the collected works printed by him in London in the 1630s.

Legate's association with the London bookseller Simon Waterson continued long after 1609. The two men dominated the lucrative trade in the works of Perkins, into which Legge successfully insinuated himself in 1609 with a third volume of collected works. Until 1615, Waterson's name was hardly ever absent from Legate's title-pages: the arrangement had all the seeming regularity of a partnership, though it had begun probably as an agency agreement of a kind similar to that between Waterson and the Oxford printer Joseph Barnes.[113] The partnership was dominated by the works of Perkins, though Waterson also turned to Legate to print the second revised edition of Camden's *Remaines, concerning Britaine* in 1614; it may be said to have come to an end with the publication in 1615 of a group of Perkins' most popular books not, as hitherto, with the imprint of both Legate and Waterson, but of Legate alone.[114] There had already been signs of independence in the previous year. In 1614 Legate alone was responsible for the fifth edition of Bastingius' *Exposition … upon the catechisme taught in the Low Countries* (a revival on his own account of a book he had first printed for Abraham Kitson in 1589 but which had not been printed in England since 1595); a new enlarged edition of Willet's *Ecclesia triumphans*, first printed by Legate in Cambridge in 1603, to be sold by Waterson, now appeared bearing Legate's name alone; and he produced a fourth edition of Richard Bernard's successful *Terence in English*, of which he alone had always enjoyed command since its first publication in 1598.[115] Larger and more complicated than any of these (since it involved several existing owners of copy, including Cantrell Legge) was the first attempt at a collection of the writings of Samuel Hieron, a much esteemed member of King's. Work on it had begun in 1613, and though in later editions Legate was to share the printing with others, he alone seems to have been responsible for this beginning.[116]

A golden Chaine:
OR,
THE DESCRIPTION OF
Theologie,
containing the order of the causes of Saluation and Damnation, according to Gods word. A view
whereof is to be seene in the Table
annexed.

Hereunto is adioyned the order which
M. Theodore Beza vsed in comforting afflicted
consciences.

Printed by IOHN LEGAT, Printer to
the Vniuersitie of Cambridge. 1600.

Fig. 9 William Perkins (1558–1602), *A golden chaine: or, the description of theologie*, 4°,
1600. This was the first book on which the *Hinc lucem* device was employed. When Legate
subsequently left Cambridge for London, he took with him the right to print most of
Perkins' works, a loss from which his successor did not recover.
Height of original, 230 mm.

All this betokened increasing independence and business. But though they concerned a man who still styled himself as Printer to the University, in Cambridge responsibility for printing had passed on Legate's departure into the hands of Cantrell Legge, formerly Legate's apprentice and, as it was to prove, a man never entirely able to disentangle his affairs from those of his erstwhile master.

☙ 7 ❧

Cantrell Legge and the University's common cause

Although we have a fairly clear idea of what the early University Printers printed, other aspects of their work – aspects intimately allied to their work as printers – are much less well understood. The varying degrees to which each acted also as a bookseller, the ways in which their printing and bookselling activities were financed by local or London capital, the extent to which printing for the London trade enabled the successful prosecution of a bookselling trade by others in Cambridge, are all topics on which it is possible to offer little documentary evidence, but on which, equally, the requirement for explanation makes some speculation obligatory. To these major questions may be added those concerning the marketing of both the Cambridge press's products and the retail stocks of a bookselling business, the extent of credit in the trade and to customers, and the position of each man in the printing and bookselling hierarchy locally in Cambridge, nationally (principally in London, but also in Oxford), and (intermittently at least) internationally. Legge's career as University Printer has been memorialized not least as the occasion for a revival of the tediously prolonged row between the University and the Stationers' Company. The outcome of the dispute was of critical importance to the subsequent development of Cambridge printing; but an understanding of its significance requires an appreciation of many of the problems raised in this paragraph. For that reason, we must look first at Legge's career in rather a wider context than has been customarily presented.

Legge was, it will be recalled, Legate's apprentice, admitted a freeman of the Stationers' Company on 11 December 1599. Although he may be presumed to have passed the whole of his apprenticeship in Cambridge (in 1595 accused of fathering the illegitimate child of one of his master's servants),[1] like Legate he looked to the Company as the qualifying authority; and, like Legate, he continued as long as possible to acknowledge the Company's authority, especially in matters affecting copyright. But unlike Legate he remained in Cambridge for the whole of his time as University Printer; and, unlike Legate, he was eventually forced to seek independence from the ties of the London market, and thus to provoke unprecedented bitterness between the University and the Company.

For the first years of his term, however, the pattern of co-existence between the Cambridge printers and those in London, established by Legate, remained little changed. Legge's financial position could scarcely allow otherwise. Nothing is known of his career between his being freed in 1599 and his election as University Printer on 5 June 1606. In the absence of other evidence, he must be presumed to have continued as journeyman at Legate's establishment in Regent Walk, moving away to set up a new business in 1606, on Market Hill. There is no trace of him as a bookseller during these years, and there is, indeed, no evidence that he ever acted as a general bookseller later. Like Legate's, his business centred on his own printed stock. Legate's name had appeared as bookseller on a few books by William Perkins printed by Orwin, Adam Islip and Richard Field in the 1590s; and even in 1606 Humphrey Lownes printed for him the anonymous pamphlet *A supplication of the Family of Love. Examined, and found to be derogative*. This was not Legge's practice.[2] Unlike Legate, he had, moreover, inherited no stock.

Legge's financial position may be presumed to have been precarious in 1606. It remained so, and he died heavily in debt. The attempt in the last years of his life, in the midst of a trade depression,[3] to wrest from the Stationers' Company some of its most lucrative business was a last desperate act in a long search for financial success, a success which consistently eluded him.

His success depended, first, on the willingness of booksellers to co-operate. By far the most substantial of those locally was John Porter, who had shared the copy in some of Perkins' works with Legate, and for whom, indeed, Legate had printed Perkins' *Foundation of Christian religion* in 1601 and again in 1604: most of Porter's publishing interests were in Perkins, though by 1605–6 his works had been displaced by those of a former Fellow of Emmanuel and future Bishop of Exeter, Joseph Hall. On 13 May 1606 the third Century of Hall's *Meditations and vows* was entered to Porter and another Cambridge bookseller, Leonard Greene, jointly:[4] it was just eight days before Greene married Porter's daughter Joan at Great St Mary's. Father and son-in-law appeared together on only one other book, a sermon by Samuel Walsall printed, again in London, by George Eld, which was entered to Greene alone on 14 November 1606 and of which two editions appeared within a twelvemonth.[5] Though born in Haslingfield, just outside Cambridge, Porter had pursued his career in both London and Cambridge, making comparatively little use of the Cambridge press. Under his son-in-law the emphasis changed. Having succeeded to the largest bookselling business in Cambridge, Greene concentrated on that, turning to Legge for Willet's major commentaries on 1 Samuel (1607), Daniel (1610) and Romans (1611). A rather smaller volume, one of Perkins' most popular works, he had printed at London in 1608, as earlier editions of the same book had been printed for Porter and Legate since 1595.[6]

Greene was eventually appointed one of the University Printers, on 31 October 1622, and this appointment was confirmed again on 16 December

1625, following Legge's death.[7] But he possessed no press during these years. For much of the early part of his career he traded from shops hard against Great St Mary's, in 1612 and again in 1614–18 sharing the rent with William Williams, another stationer: the two men kept separate businesses, one at each side of the tower, in 1613.[8]

Moreover, a glance at the pattern of imprints reveals Greene as a bookseller unable, even with his father-in-law's bounty, to finance by himself the publication of large scale volumes, even of so notable an author as Willet. Each of the commentaries was shared with Legge, the two men dividing the edition between them. The Perkins may well (too few copies survive to be certain) have been shared with Legate. Entries in the Stationers' Register tell a similar story: of no less than eleven copies entered to Greene on 4 August 1608, eight were of half shares only, and two (of works by Joseph Hall) were in turn reassigned on the 2 December following.[9] Once Porter's estate had been disposed of, with the block entry in August, Greene's name occurred only at irregular intervals, the last being in January 1629/30 for a collection of sermons by one of the most successful of a new generation of pulpit orators, John Preston.[10] This final volume, printed in London at two separate addresses and shared with a London bookseller, James Boler, was characteristic of Greene's career in that financial responsibility was once again not his exclusively.

In other words, while Greene was never in a position to finance the whole of the cost of a publication by himself, he could offer two crucially important benefits to Legge. In the first few months of Legge's career as an independent printer, in 1606–8, he brought the stability of an established bookselling business, thanks to Porter; and by agreeing to share the costs of printing Willet's substantial folio commentary on 1 Samuel he enabled Legge to embark almost immediately on a major investment. With the single exception of Thomas Brooke, whose name appears with that of Legge on the title-page of Perkins' exposition of the Sermon on the Mount, no name of any other Cambridge stationer appeared on the output from Legge's press. In Greene he had effectively his sole local business of this kind.

Legge never experienced the regular publishing arrangements with individual London stationers that Legate had with Waterson. He was noticeably independent – whether at first by design, foolhardiness or accident, is uncertain – and the consequences might perhaps have been foreseen. Of the ninety or so books (as distinct from broadsides of various kinds) he printed between 1607 and 1625, less than a quarter acknowledged on their title-pages any link with London booksellers. Richard Bankworth shared with Greene the publication of works by Willet in 1607; between 1613 and 1618 Matthew Law appeared in the imprint of works by a former member of Emmanuel, Richard Kilby, notably his popular *Burthen of a loaded conscience*, first published and printed by Legge alone in 1608 and of which Kilby only later acknowledged authorship. Both Ralph Mabbe and Thomas Man had an interest in the works of the puritan Thomas Taylor; in 1612 Matthew Lownes shared Giles Fletcher's edition of a work by a recently deceased student of Christ Church, Nathaniel Pownoll, *The young divines apologie for his continuance in the universitie*; and in 1616 Arthur Johnson took over the sheets of a defence of Perkins by John Yates, Fellow of Emmanuel and appointed that year to St Andrew's, Norwich: the book had been printed by Legge the previous year. After 1618, all but one of Legge's books appeared with his name alone in the imprint. A yet further suggestion of his idiosyncratic position may also be found in the regularity with which two separate title-pages were printed for the same book, one bearing his name and one the name of the collaborating stationer. The practice was by no means unusual, but it is not impossible in Legge's case that it signified a wish to distance himself from the London trade. Legge's name usually appeared on the London title-pages, however, since he could not very well avoid it.

Unlike Thomas and Legate, who had each in their different ways established an identifiable tone to their lists, Legge failed to do so. His involvement in the printing of Perkins, Taylor and Willet (he last printed Willet's commentary on Romans in 1620) was for years the principal support of his business. Much of it was carried over from Legate, or grew from Legate's earlier nourishing; but this essential business gradually slipped away. Between 1607 and 1614, about half the books printed by Legge were by these three alone. However much they reflected tastes in Cambridge, they afforded a precipitately narrow base for the well-being of a business.[11] Perkins's influence was to be found in other of Legge's books as well, such as Richard Kilby's *Hallelu-iah* (1618, to be sold by Matthew Law, in London), which provided an opportunity, rare outside Sternhold and Hopkins, to use the music type: among Kilby's compositions was 'My noone Psalme to a tune which in *Cambridge* is called Mr. Perkins tune.' Other books offered more innovation; but they were not innovations that brought with them the steady expectation of capital-generating profit. The printing in 1610 of Giles Fletcher's *Christ's victorie* marked a firm commitment to English poetry, which had established a toe-hold with *Licia*. In Henry Farley's *The complaint of Paules*, published six years later, was a reminder that doggerel (in this case a plea for money towards the repair of the cathedral) was no less a part of a printer's business. In law, Legate had in 1601 printed a guide to the poor law and in 1605 John Cowell's *Institutiones iuris anglicani*; but the experience of Cowell's *Interpreter* (1607), banned by proclamation in 1610, may have discouraged Legge from pursuing further work of this kind.[12] In medicine, Legate and Legge were instrumental in aiding the career of Francis Anthonie, a member of Pembroke, whose clashes with the College of Physicians in London were provoked not least by the success of his nostrum, which he had the acumen to call *aurum potabile*. Anthonie was also to publicize his remedy in a pamphlet printed at Hamburg in 1618, but in England he turned first to Legge, who in 1610 printed his pamphlet *Medicinae chymicae, et veri*

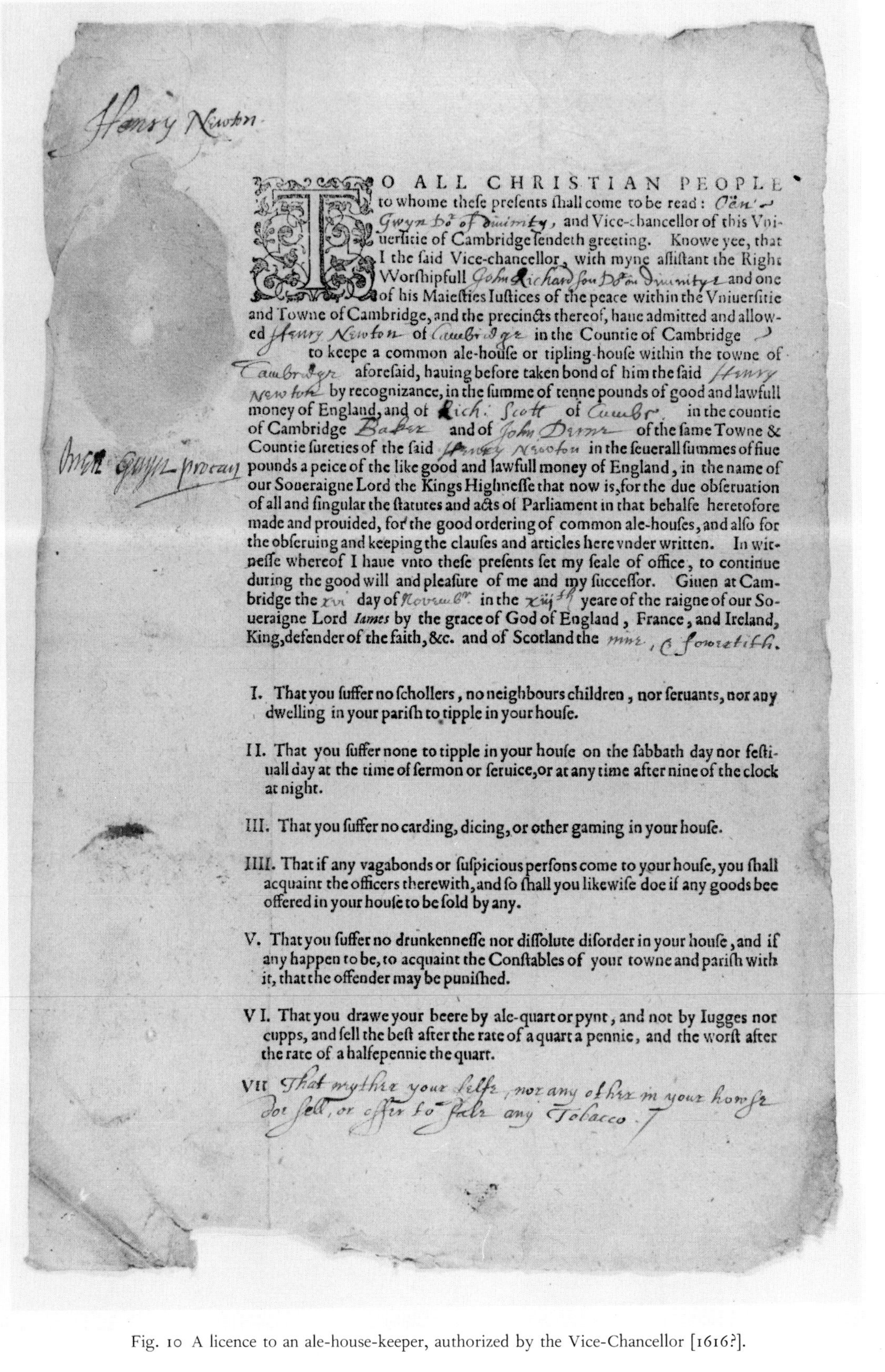

Henry Newton

O ALL CHRISTIAN PEOPLE
to whome thefe prefents fhall come to be read: *Oēn Gwyn dō of diuinity*, and Vice-chancellor of this Vniuerſitie of Cambridge ſendeth greeting. Knowe yee, that
I the ſaid Vice-chancellor, with myne aſſiſtant the Right
Worſhipfull *John Richardfon Dr̄ in diuinitye* and one
of his Maieſties Iuſtices of the peace within the Vniuerſitie
and Towne of Cambridge, and the precincts thereof, haue admitted and allowed *Henry Newton* of *Cambridge* in the Countie of Cambridge
to keepe a common ale-houſe or tipling-houſe within the towne of
Cambridge aforeſaid, hauing before taken bond of him the ſaid *Henry
Newton* by recognizance, in the ſumme of tenne pounds of good and lawfull
money of England, and of *Rich: Scott* of *Cambr* in the countie
of Cambridge *Baker* and of *John Dunn* of the ſame Towne &
Countie ſureties of the ſaid *Henry Newton* in the ſeuerall ſummes of fiue
pounds a peice of the like good and lawfull money of England, in the name of
our Soueraigne Lord the Kings Highneſſe that now is, for the due obſeruation
of all and ſingular the ſtatutes and acts of Parliament in that behalſe heretofore
made and prouided, for the good ordering of common ale-houſes, and alſo for
the obſeruing and keeping the clauſes and articles here vnder written. In wit-
neſſe whereof I haue vnto theſe prefents ſet my ſeale of office, to continue
during the good will and pleaſure of me and my ſucceſſor. Giuen at Cambridge the *xvi* day of *Nouēbr* in the *xiijth* yeare of the raigne of our Soueraigne Lord *Iames* by the grace of God of England, France, and Ireland,
King, defender of the faith, &c. and of Scotland the *mne, & fouretibh.*

Oēn Gwyn procan

I. That you ſuffer no ſchollers, no neighbours children, nor ſeruants, nor any
dwelling in your pariſh to tipple in your houſe.

II. That you ſuffer none to tipple in your houſe on the ſabbath day nor feſti-
uall day at the time of ſermon or ſeruice, or at any time after nine of the clock
at night.

III. That you ſuffer no carding, dicing, or other gaming in your houſe.

IIII. That if any vagabonds or ſuſpicious perſons come to your houſe, you ſhall
acquaint the officers therewith, and ſo ſhall you likewiſe doe if any goods bee
offered in your houſe to be ſold by any.

V. That you ſuffer no drunkenneſſe nor diſſolute diſorder in your houſe, and if
any happen to be, to acquaint the Conſtables of your towne and pariſh with
it, that the offender may be puniſhed.

VI. That you drawe your beere by ale-quart or pynt, and not by Iugges nor
cupps, and ſell the beſt after the rate of a quart a pennie, and the worſt after
the rate of a halfepennie the quart.

VII *That mythir your felfe, nor any of hir in your howfe
doe fell, or offer to fell any Tobacco.*

Fig. 10 A licence to an ale-house-keeper, authorized by the Vice-Chancellor [1616?].

potabilis auri assertio, and then in 1616 to Legate, now in London. His MD from Cambridge, awarded in 1608, may have encouraged him to turn to Legge, but it could not protect him from the jealousies of the establishment, or from seemingly justifiable suspicion of chicanery. Anthonie's work was hardly a reliable foundation on which Legge might build further.

The much less challenging requirements of ordinary administration were another matter. Legge provided visitation articles for the bishops of Ely (Lancelot Andrewes), Peterborough (Thomas Dove) and Norwich (John Jegon and John Overall). For the University he continued to print Act verses, as had Thomas and Legate before him, as well as such essentials of an increasingly print-dependent administration as ale-house licences, or orders for vagrants (see figs. 10 and 11). For the colleges he printed bookplates.[13] The fashion for printing books of congratulatory or consolatory verses, introduced at Cambridge in 1587, brought a further assured, if irregular business: Legate had printed for the death of Queen Elizabeth, and Legge continued, commemorating the deaths of Henry Prince of Wales in 1612 and of Queen Anne in 1619, the return of Prince Charles from Spain in 1623, the death of James I in 1625, and the marriage of the new King Charles later that summer.[14] No printed edition was deemed essential when in 1613 Frederick, the Prince Palatine, visited the University in the company of Prince Charles: the verses written for the occasion were instead collected into a manuscript book, suitably bound with the University arms.[15]

With the exception of the last category, which was produced in a form (a quarto pamphlet) and in circumstances that virtually ensured its survival in generally reasonable quantities, few of these necessities required to be kept. Their consequent apparent irregularity in survival, quite apart from their absolute present-day rarity,[16] makes it difficult to determine the extent to which Legge came to depend on such work, or, indeed, how far he was an innovator in these matters. Other publications, hardly less rare, related to the University's administration, but were not directly a part of it. In 1585 Thomas Thomas had printed a list of University officers, and in 1622 Legge printed for an enterprising antiquary, John Scot, a broadside sold also in London by George Humble, *The foundation of the Universitie of Cambridge*: only single copies survive of the Latin and English versions printed that year, of a survey that, with various changes, survives even today in the official publications of the University.[17]

Even if other evidence (to which we shall soon turn) were not available, it is clear that in the last few years of his life Legge had lost virtually all other business as a printer of the kind on which his predecessors had depended. Both Thomas and Legate, as well as Legge himself, had proved that, despite the formidable transport difficulties, it was possible to print for the London trade. But Legge's business became isolated from it, and in 1620 he printed only one substantial book, a new edition of Willet's *Hexapla* on Romans, a book that

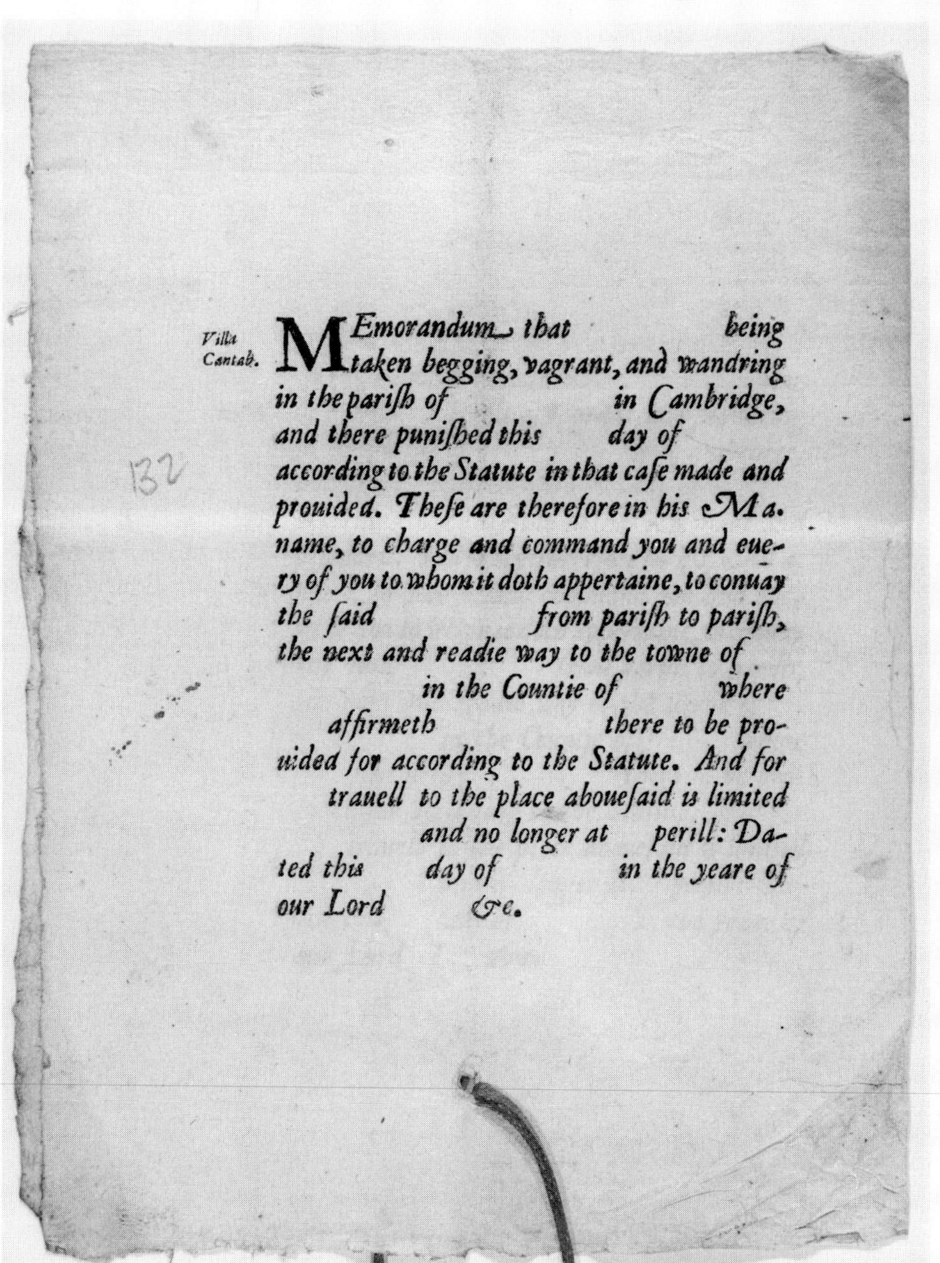

Villa
Cantab.
MEmorandum that   being
taken begging, vagrant, and wandring
in the parish of   in Cambridge,
and there punished this   day of
according to the Statute in that case made and
prouided. These are therefore in his *Ma.*
name, to charge and command you and euery of you to whom it doth appertaine, to conuay
the said   from parish to parish,
the next and readie way to the towne of
                    in the Countie of   where
    affirmeth   there to be pro-
uided for according to the Statute. And for
    trauell to the place abouesaid is limited
                    and no longer at   perill: Da-
ted this   day of   in the yeare of
our Lord   &c.

Fig. 11 An order to deal with a beggar [1617?].

he had first printed in 1611 and which now, again, he shared with Leonard Greene. Despite talk of printing editions of the Church Fathers, and with the crucial exception of Lily's grammar, to which we shall return,[18] the year 1621 was still less active; an octavo volume of sermons by Thomas Playfere was virtually all that could be shown by the end of the year. This book, likewise, was a return to an earlier success; but on this occasion Legge's sheets had by 1623 been absorbed into a more ambitious collection of Playfere's sermons issued by the London bookseller Matthew Law.

Legge did not possess a general bookselling business. Though he himself financed many of the books that he printed, he ran no shop. His livelihood depended on his printing; and as the volume of printing declined, so did his financial well-being. At the outset of his career he embarked with none of Thomas's wealth or Legate's trade connections. As, over the following few years, he borrowed from others, repayment became increasingly difficult. A bond by Legge to pay Edward Goodwin, his brother-in-law, £110 in November 1610 was still unpaid in 1625.[19] For the repayment of a loan of £200 from the University, Legge could only discover his 1618 edition of the third volume of Perkins' works, of which he agreed to sell two hundred copies for £225 to the local bookseller William Williams. Unfortunately, Williams paid only a small part of the debt.[20] In 1619, in conjunction with Anthony Harrison, Legge borrowed a further £105 of Robert Newcome, LlD; and with Edward Goodwin and Robert Twells he borrowed a further £100 from Thomas Goad. His death was the signal for the demands to rattle in: from Goodwin, from his neighbours Talbot Pepys and John Wolfe, from Goad, from John Swetson, and, not least, from the University itself. In total, his estate was found to owe £435.[21]

In such circumstances, it is not surprising that Legge was tempted, like Legate before him, into what by convention if not in law had been seen as the preserve of the London stationers. Legate had printed the Bible (once) and the New Testament (again, once), even though both books were held by the London trade to be the prerogative of the Royal Printer. He had ventured into the schoolbook trade only extremely cautiously, challenging here the lucrative markets of the English Stock of the Stationers' Company.[22] In 1614 Legge tried again to force his way into the Bible market, and actually printed part of an edition; but on discovery, and on complaint from Barker, he was obliged to sell both the printed sheets and the unused paper to Barker.[23]

For Legge, the rivalries between printing interests in London and in Cambridge were complicated by new and more organized interests in the overseas trade. The Stationers' Company Latin Stock was not formally floated until January 1616,[24] its purpose being the domination of the import trade, to the exclusion of other parties. But its floatation came after several years of dissent among the London stationers, as a small group manoeuvred for influence and position.[25] Among the casualties of this struggle was Henry

Fetherstone, former apprentice to Bonham Norton, the man best positioned to gain from a new monopoly of this kind.[26] For generations, the overseas trade had been in the hands of foreigners, or strangers (at the end of the sixteenth century principally Arnold Birckman, Hercules François and Ascanius de Renialme, until they were replaced in turn by native Englishmen, John Bill, Bonham Norton and their successors), but also, crucially, of several interests rather than one. Though Norton dominated the trade, and thus found himself possessed of a lucrative, because essential and much demanded, business, he possessed no patent for it. Instead, it was usual for several English stationers to attend the Frankfurt fairs. Such rivalry as was thereby engineered was allayed by the failure of any single stationer to dominate overwhelmingly, and by the practical constraints set by the fairs, which included too many books to be discovered by a single stationer or agent in the brief time available.[27] As Fetherstone explained,

By reason of the Freedome of trade, each one hath diuerse sortes, that the other haue not, by reason of the multitude of booksellers at Franckfort, and the short time there allotted to buy bookes, besides they taking their jornies diuerse waies one through France, an other through Antwerp, & the 3ᵈ through Holland, buying many bookes by the way, that neuer come to Franckford; all striuing to giue content to schollers, both in Choyce of bookes, & prices, euery man willing to putt of his wares, though for small profitt to make there retornes, whereby if one haue the former sale, the other haue the latter, so that there is little want betweene martes, wᶜʰ possibly can neuer bee, if it be in on hand...

A monopoly, on the other hand, would be particularly injurious — and not least to the universities:

It is vnpossible, that one merchante cann be furnished of all sortes so well not stored with quantities of sortes as sufficient whatsoeuer they pretend, but must & wholly want of some sortes vnlesse there supplies could be made in euerie month which is not, but from 6 months to 6 months and so thereby there other sortes more vendible that were out will not only grow scarse but rise in the handes of those that haue them and make a greater gaine of the buyer and a dearth before neede, whereby men cannot haue that Contentment as formerly and bookesellers that come from the vniuersities and else where if they come not by the first cannot haue ther notes furnished, besides many more discomodities and I think not one of a 100 but will make my Complaint theres.[28]

Fetherstone's early chopoetters and petitions against the impending monopoly of this trade are all undated, and the exact sequence of documents is unclear. But the events of the next few years, as a small group within the Stationers' Company sought not only to create a new Stock, but also to obtain a patent granting a formal monopoly, took a clear course. A 1616 16° edition of Virgil, published by the Stationers' Company, was one manifestation of this campaign: the title-page was printed in London, probably by Richard Field, but the rest of the edition consisted of imported sheets. By July 1617 there were six Latin stock-keepers: Thomas Dawson, Henry Cooke, Nathaniel Butter, John Budge, John White and Thomas Norton.[29] Fetherstone was given no part in the arrangement. The rewards did not lie only in the ability to control the price and movement of imports. Such a monopoly, if achieved, would also permit the manipulation of domestic production, and confident investment in overseas printing. In 1619 Norton and Bill held considerable stocks of books overseas, in partnership with stationers at Frankfurt and elsewhere.[30]

By investing in the printing of foreign editions, these stationers could reap profits twice over – in manufacture and as middlemen. Those most forward in claiming a monopoly were, according to Henry Fetherstone, writing from an inferior position in the London trade:

some of them Cheefe sharers and of good note … the only Causes, of the printing of all the Fathers, Councells, & others at Colon: of the corrupt edicons, bearing a 4th pte in those bookes, w[ch] cost many thousand pounds,[31] The halfe of w[ch] mony, if it had bin bestowed wth the Geneuians, to haue printed them according to the Ancienst, & truest Edicons, there the bookes hadd neuer bin printed, there or else of little worth by reason, that the Cheefest sale of those bookes be hither, whereby men are Constrained to haue of that edicon or none.[32]

Fetherstone's subsequent international standing was to be reflected in the dedication to him of an octavo Quintilian printed at Frankfurt for the London trade in 1629,[33] and he eventually dominated the import trade himself as his former master, Bonham Norton, had previously. Before long, but not yet, he was to join in with the other London importers, in a business that could expect to see a regular profit of $33\frac{1}{3}$ per cent.[34] Meanwhile he went on to explain that he had recently come to an arrangement with a Geneva bookseller visiting London to share in the printing of the works of St Augustine, 'of the truest, ancienst Coppie'. The threat Fetherstone now faced, of exclusion from a lucrative trade, was arguably also against the University's interests, since prices would inevitably go up, and scholarship and learning be thereby impeded. He claimed that prices might rise by as much as twenty or thirty per cent, a claim unsupported by any evidence save a general remark about other book trade monopolies affecting, he estimated or alleged, over two hundred different titles.[35]

Not surprisingly, the issues of overseas printing and of imports became muddled in some minds with the University's own position and interests as expressed in the 1534 charter and as gradually defined in the course of the prolonged conflict with the Stationers' Company. In 1534 the charter had protected the University's interest in the book trade, both by permitting the employment of strangers notwithstanding other legislation that would have excluded them, and also by allowing the University to print *omnimodos libros*. So, too, in a similar vein, the Grace of 25 June 1622[36] tackled both questions within a single legislative act, seeking amongst various provisions to control the routes by which Cambridge booksellers obtained their wares, to vest copies in the office of University Printer rather than individuals, to commit members of the University to the University Printer rather than to others elsewhere and to ensure that any graduate who became a schoolmaster used textbooks printed at Cambridge in preference to any other.

Such provisions, for all their idealism and impracticality, in other words offered a view of the national, and international, book trade that was at odds with much of what was already established. They paved the way for the decision, taken within a decade, to collaborate with the Stationers' Company in the printing of school texts, and thus, for the first time, achieve a noticeable impact in this ever attractive sector of the market. But meanwhile they offered yet again the belief that the University might control its own well-being by excluding other possible interests.

The roots of the problem lay not only in the differences concerning printing privileges in London and Cambridge. Both markets also depended on imports, a portion of the book trade that was defined by what was, and what was not, printed in England. Of the four London stationers named in the Grace of June 1622, John Bill and Bonham Norton, linked by their common Shropshire background, by apprenticeship, and by partnership, were printers. All four were booksellers, with a shared interest in the Latin Stock of the Stationers' Company.[37] But unlike the English Stock, which proved a prosperous business for many decades, the Latin Stock enjoyed little success, even for short periods: in the end the overseas trade proved too heterogeneous, in both its personnel and its goods, especially at a period of commercial depression. In an attempt to bring this trade under tighter control, arrangements were made in the winter of 1620–1 for several unspecified members of the Company (almost certainly the partners in the Latin Stock) to buy up John Bill's share in foreign trading. The consequence would have been all but to create a monopoly in the importation of books – controlling not merely, in the words of Thomas Goad, writing from Lambeth Palace, 'such pamphlettes as invey against oʳ Church & Estate', but all other books as well. The effect, in Goad's view, would be to raise the price of all such books, as had already happened with monopolies in, among others, the singing Psalms, grammars, almanacs and primers.[38] In this his fears were identical with those of Fetherstone, though his interest was different. Goad found his correspondent in Cambridge, Samuel Ward, a discouraging ally, apparently unable to grasp the implications of such a step, and unwilling to bestir himself to attend in London so as to present the case which seemed to Goad so obviously the right one for the University. While he expected attendance from Oxford daily, and intended that the two universities should argue *pari passu*, Ward seemed to misunderstand the situation. (Bill's own recent part in supplying to the Bodleian Library from the Frankfurt fairs[39] may have made others appreciate his position better.) The 1534 charter might serve as a bulwark for Cambridge's printing rights, and also as one for the stationers licensed by the University. But, as Goad pointed out, lapsing as he was wont to do in the heat of the moment,

to defend a Charter is to fight wth but one hand. there is another head of the monster to be cutt of … and that is the engrossing of all bookes into one hand at London. What is y^r Charter to this? This is duely and deeply relished at Oxford, and shalbe so in ye Convocacion (if I can help it) being like to lay a proportionall subsidy vpon the Clergy & all Schollers … No mortall man can perswaded mee but that a monopoly of bookes in London will suck the blood deeply of the Clergyes and Schollers purses, Lett the Vniuersities imploy or gett what priuileges they can. and sett vp as many as they list for immediate Stationers. Scio quid Loquor. this great oake, if it grow alone will ouerdropp and quash all those shrubbs …[40]

Notwithstanding Goad's energy in the attack (he drew in at least two former Vice-Chancellors, Valentine Carey, Dean of St Paul's, and Barnabas Gooch, MP and University Commissary), the Stationers' Company agreed a few days later to the redistribution of Bill's interest. That the plan proved a forlorn hope scarcely mattered: the Bodleian Library turned from Bill to Fetherstone as principal supplier of mart books from Frankfurt, and continued unhindered by the efforts of the Latin Stock. But so long as the threat of a monopoly of imports remained, so too did the threat to retail book prices, and to a structure of the English book trade that permitted, however imperfectly and inconsistently, competitive pricing and competitive editions.

It is not to be supposed that the Cambridge trade's dismay at such events – which the University Registrary, James Tabor, does not appear at first to have fully understood – necessarily betokened anxiety for its customers. Much more importantly, these imported editions demanded extra investment, and were a reminder of how limited a freedom from the Stationers' Company the University in fact enjoyed.

Those Stationer printers, and all other that by Patent or theire owne orders haue appropriated any bookes soly to themselues, print in what paper, & wth what lre & incke they list, & sell as they list, knowing that no man dareth adventure to better them or pull downe their price. So that the Subiect is forced to pay two partes in 3, or at least half in half more for every such priviledged appropriated booke.[41]

The University was persistent in its belief, or allegation, that one of the principal *raisons d'être* of its press lay in its being able to print books more cheaply than it could obtain them otherwise. The point had been made in Legate's time, when it had been estimated that Bibles might be produced at two-thirds of the London price; and a few years later the Cambridge booksellers claimed that they might cost even less. But the intrusion of overseas-printed books into the market challenged this assumption, and the gradual extension of the foothold gained in the early years of the century was both to make the University's traditional assumption sound hollow, and to influence the very course of the press itself.

Although arrangements were thus made, on a scale now difficult to establish since little was recorded in title-page imprints of these international co-operative editions, with German and Genevan printers (the latter having a natural affinity with a largely Protestant English trade), the centre for overseas trade remained Frankfurt, whose twice-yearly fair was regularly attended by three or four London stationers. In the 1620s this long-established routine faced two quite different threats. On the one hand, the economic disorder brought about by the Thirty Years War affected Germany, the Low Countries and France alike, the three principal sources of Britain's imports. Not only could stationers no longer pass easily from place to place on their way to and from Frankfurt; but even their money was liable to variable rates of exchange, and their goods were liable to tariffs.[42] On the other hand, the Stationers' Company proposals to restrict those able to trade overseas suggested that the regular trawl through the book trades of northern Europe on the way to and from Frankfurt would no longer occur. Naturally Fetherstone made the best of his case to the University in drawing attention to poorly edited texts and to the threat of a more restricted choice of books available from overseas. In fact, these proved, with one major exception, to impinge on the University Printers in ways he did not perhaps envisage, and which are discussed further below.[43]

By 1620 Legge's business was in desperate straits. The death of Legate in the summer of that year might, from one point of view, have released a valuable series of copies into Legge's hands. But unlike the office of Royal Printer, there was no right of succession for the University Printers. On 2 January 1620/1 Legate's copies passed formally into the hands of his son John, who thus inherited part or all of twenty-six titles by Perkins, and sixteen other titles.[44] Six weeks later the younger Legate consolidated his hold by obtaining a special licence for the sole printing of Thomas Thomas's dictionary.[45] The University was in no position to offer an objection, but it did express its opinion in June 1622, eighteen months later, in the Grace ordaining that henceforth any title printed by a University Printer should remain the property of that office, rather than of a particular printer, his heirs or assigns. The list of books in which Legge had an interest was insufficient, and there was little hope of retrieving his business in the face of the London trade. During the next few years many of the reasons for this failing were to become the concern of the University's officials, to be rehearsed in arguments against the Stationers' Company in what developed into a prolonged struggle, ending only (and then by no means finally) with a declaration by Charles I in favour of the University in 1628. Between 1620 and then, however, the University's position rarely seemed strong in practice, however powerful its arguments in theory. The Stationers' Company's control of the printing trade was, so far as the University was concerned, all but absolute – not so much by the legal position which it claimed, as by the hold its principal members had over the wholesale and retail price structure. At one level the dispute was fought out in the Privy Council and before the King; at another it was in the success or failure of Cambridge or

London to control the movements of stocks of books. The Stationers acknowledged this by confiscating copies and by fixing prices. Legge did so by resorting to false imprints and seeking out the least ostentatious London tradesmen that he could. And the University did so in the Grace of 25 June 1622, that, in an attack on the ambitions of the Latin Stock, expressly forbade any Cambridge stationer to have dealings with John Bill, Bonham Norton, William Barrett or Clement Knight (the men perceived to be the principals in London), and also introduced its own form of protectionism for trade between London and Cambridge stationers generally. It may be doubted how effective this was in practice.[46]

In itself, Cambridge was an insufficient market. Despite the evidence of the few surviving examples of administrative and other ephemeral printing, it did not generate the volume of demand for printed material that would have helped to sustain Legge's press. As consumers, the University could not absorb what Legge needed to print in order to be reasonably profitable.

Legge's difficulty lay, in fact, not so much in the London monopolies' seeming to challenge the Cambridge charter of 1534, as in the price structure which resulted from the received system. The possessors of patents 'print in what paper, & wth what lettere & incke they list, & sell as they list, knowing that no man dareth adventure to better them or pull downe their price'. As an example, Legge opined that the octavo Bible, sold currently at 4s. in quires, might be printed and sold at 2s.; that Sternhold and Hopkins' singing Psalms, sold at 37s. or more a ream in quires, could be sold at 15s.; Lily's grammar, sold at 20s. the ream, could be sold, again, at half that price. And these prices were for books of which there were easy and rapid sales.

Convinced that he could print more cheaply, and desperate for a secure foundation to his business, Legge turned first to Lily's grammar (see fig. 12). The departure was not entirely new. Brooke had received ten pounds from the University to meet the costs of his attempt to print Lily's grammar in 1613 or 1614,[47] and in February 1614/15 Robert Barker, the King's Printer, had been sufficiently alarmed to urge on the Vice-Chancellor a decree that Legge and Brooke should not print the Bible, New Testaments, the communion book, Acts of Parliament, injunctions or proclamations.[48] Nothing is known to have survived of these ventures, and there is certainly no evidence that Brooke himself ever owned a press: he was to play little part in the events of the next years.

Working within a small market, the Cambridge press required unhindered access to that controlled by London, or the sound economic base of a steady selling list centred on books for which a guaranteed provincial market could be assumed as well. Yet those books were of the very kind that had been already appropriated by the London trade. Legge, it was argued, had no access to the profits of the English Stock, since he was excluded from printing for it.[49] He alleged that even if he did procure copy in a book in English, and print it, the

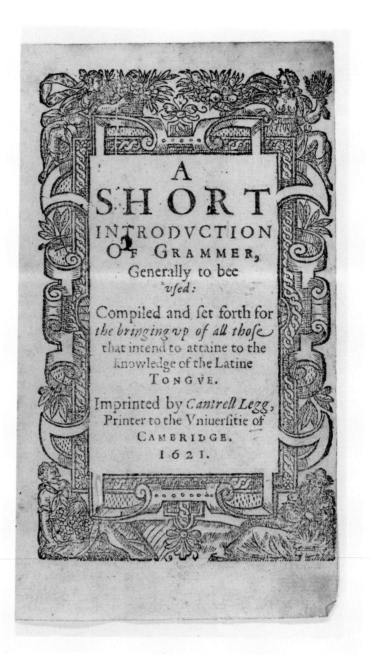

A
SHORT
INTRODVCTION
Of GRAMMER,
Generally to bee
vsed:

Compiled and set forth for
the bringing vp of all those
that intend to attaine to the
knowledge of the Latine
TONGVE.

Imprinted by *Cantrell Legg*,
Printer to the Vniuerſitie of
CAMBRIDGE.
1621.

Fig. 12 William Lily (d. 1522), *A short introduction of grammer*,
8°, 1621. Height of original, 152 mm.

Fig. 12 continued.

concerted action of the London booksellers forced him to sell sheets at so low a price that they reaped a profit of sixty per cent or more. When he printed books in Latin, and did sell them at a reasonable rate, the University claimed that the Stationers had the same book published again overseas, to be imported and so undersell the Cambridge edition: in this manner, Legate's editions of works by Whitaker and Perkins, and the Oxford editions of books by John Case, had been spoiled by overseas pirating.

The patent for Lily's grammar belonged partly to Bonham Norton, as a portion of the patent to print Greek and Latin grammars. It was a highly profitable, and therefore much disputed, privilege, shared in 1615 (when at least £60 had been spent on its defence) between Norton, William Leake, Thomas Adams, John Dawson, George Swinhowe and George Bishop. By 1619, Norton's eighth part was valued at £200, though the annual income was considerably more.[50] Before permitting Legge to attack such a target, the University felt itself sufficiently uncertain to take legal opinion. In July 1621, Norton petitioned the King, citing his own Letters Patent and complaining

that nowe of late one Cantrell Legg Printer to the vniuersitie of Cambridge by Colour of some license from the vice Chancellor and others of that vniuersitie, hath imprinted a great number of the said Grammers and doth intend to disperse and sell the same at his pleasure in Contempt and derogacion of his Majesties prerogatiue Royall.[51]

In London, however, the matter was to pass backwards and forwards between the King, the Privy Council and the Stationers' Company, the Privy Council referring the matter on 24 July 1621 to the Attorney General and the Solicitor General. Norton had timed his petition unfortunately, in that the University quickly pointed out that 'in this time of vacacion' they could hardly defend their rights; and so the matter was adjourned, leaving Norton to take it up again in September – by which time, of course, Legge had finished printing, and was selling the offending books.[52] By then, Legge alleged that he had parted with all the 1,500 perfect copies printed. Furthermore, he had another 1,500 copies not yet completed;[53] but he was constrained by the Vice-Chancellor to sell no more of these until the outcome of the case was known. On 25 November the legal officers offered their opinion:

Wee are of opinion that the Vice Chancellor and doctors cannot Authorise their Printer to Imprint such bookes which his Matie. hath by his Patent of priviledge appropriated to any others. Neuerthelesse in respect there was some colourable groundes for the said Legg to Imprint and as it is Credibly informed vs the not venting of the bookes already printed might be the vtter ouer throwe of the poore man, Wee wish that the peticoner should take of him the Bookes already printed at some reasonable rate that may make the poore man a sauer, which wee are alsoe informed may be done and the peticoners haue some moderate gaine, and for the future the printing against his Maties priviledg granted to his own printer to be forborne.[54]

It was an opinion likely to please neither Legge, the University, nor Norton, whose own relations with his fellow stock-holders had suffered strain.[55] While admitting Legge's considerable investment, whose loss 'might be the vtter ouer throwe of the poore man', it left the rate of payment undecided, and denied utterly the right that the University claimed so vociferously, to print all kinds of books.

The size of Legge's edition is not clear. Although he claimed to have disposed of 1,500 copies, and to have another 1,500 incomplete, it is not recorded by how much the latter were unfinished. In any case, the matter had still not been concluded by March 1622, when Norton again petitioned against Legge, this time to John Williams, Bishop of Lincoln and Keeper of the Great Seal: Legge, it seems, had continued to deal in the grammars, despite the judgement of the previous November.[56] Two separate editions survive, both dated 1621: it was the completion of the second of these that caused the Stationers' Company to complain once again, in October 1623, to the Privy Council. Legge had now gone further. Not only, they complained, had he

agaíne imprinted greater nombers of the said grammrs & Accedences but also of late hath printed the psalmes in Octavo to Ioyne wth the Bybles & dyuerse other psalme bookes in smaller volumes, readie to be shewed to yor lo[ps]. wherew[th] if he be suffered to goe on in this sorte he will not onlie vndoe the poorer sorte, but in short time ruyn the whole Companie, and make his Ma[ties]. prerogatiue in this kinde of no validitie.[57]

While for their part Legge and with him, more or less enthusiastically, the University officers, thus systematically tested each of the London trade's most lucrative monopolies, the London stationers were forced to meet each different attack anew. Too few copies survive of either Lily's grammar or Sternhold and Hopkins' Psalms for it to be certain that all the editions of these texts which Legge printed in his last years are still recorded. Of the 1621 Lily only three copies survive. In 1623 the Stationers' Company complained not only of an octavo edition of the metrical Psalms, but also 'other psalme bookes in smaller volumes'.[58] Of these the octavo edition is relatively common, but a tiny 32° printed by Legge in the same year exists in one copy only.[59] With such evidence, it is not easy to gauge the impact that Legge had on the retail trade. Some at least of these Psalters were sold by him to William Lee, a young bookseller in Fleet Street, from whom the two Wardens of the Stationers' Company, Anthony Gilman and Thomas Pavier, confiscated stock in 1622.[60] By November 1623, with Legge hauled before the Privy Council, the University (this time in the person of the Vice-Chancellor, Owen Gwyn, of St John's) spoke also of Bibles, a hitherto neglected topic whose sudden introduction at this juncture adds further to the impression of a deliberately contrived sequence of attacks on the London privileges; and by December, when the Privy Council sought to impose a further agreement, their document spoke of almanacs as well, to which Legge had by now probably also turned his attention.[61]

The Privy Council's decision on 10 December 1623 was arrived at after the

King had given it a clear hint that he found the University's case one that had been reasoned considerately and with moderation; 'hee found the Vice Chancello^r soe reasnable, as in stead of printing the Bible in 8°, wch is soe much insisted vpon, the Vniuersitie wilbe content to haue the printinge of it in 4°. or 12°'.[62] The Stationers, on the other hand, made themselves appear more reluctant. The effect was a compromise. The first of the clauses was straightforward: that all books should be sold 'at reasonable and fitt prizes', if prices were not to be imposed by statute. The second was less so. It gave the University the right to comprint with the Stationers in all books, including privileged titles except for Bibles, the Book of Common Prayer, Psalters, grammars, primers and books on common law. In any such privileged printing, however, Legge was to employ only one press. The copyright in any new books falling within a privileged class (this would affect, for example, new editions of school texts, and new Greek or Latin grammars) was to go to whichever press was first approached. Thirdly, the University was to print no almanac of which the copyright already belonged to a London stationer. Fourthly, the Stationers' Company was not to hinder the sale of Cambridge-printed books. And finally, Legge was to be free to sell such copies of Lily's grammar and the metrical Psalms as he had already printed, the Stationers' Company and the London printers returning to him the sheets that they had seized.[63]

There remains one further major complaint by the Stationers against Legge, in an undated appeal concerning his printing of the ABC and of Pond's almanac, in both of which they claimed a monopoly.[64] In view of the explicit treatment of almanacs in the decree of December 1623, it is not impossible that this complaint preceded it. The extreme scarcity of early almanacs, and the complete disappearance of many editions, again makes it impossible to comment usefully on Legge's assault on this extremely profitable market. The earliest surviving edition of Pond is that for 1601, and Legge was therefore again attacking a well-established corner when in 1624 he printed a new edition for the coming year. For the Stationers, it was a yet further challenge, to be complained of in the same breath as his printing the singing Psalms, and to be met by confiscation.[65] Unfortunately, the nearest preceding edition is that of 1612. It is therefore impossible to establish how much, if at all, Legge's version differed from the received one in London, or even whether he did indeed print an edition late in 1623 for the coming year. The surviving evidence suggests, however, that once seized, Pond's almanac was allowed to remain with the Cambridge press: no subsequent London ones are recorded.[66]

Legge had made his own general position clear to the Vice-Chancellor in 1623,[67] pointing out that the Stationers had confiscated six hundred of his books, and threatened to remove more, and alleging that even though he offered them trade prices fifty per cent or more below the retail he still found the London stationers combined against him. By this time, Legge's estate was almost entirely in printed books, which had been rendered effectively all but worthless. Not surprisingly, his solution was one offered *in extremis*: that the Vice-Chancellor should commend to members of the University Richard Betts' translation of James I's attack on Cardinal Du Perron, so that any money received by the sale of this might be devoted to defraying the costs arising from the battle with the Stationers. The King's book, printed in French by John Bill in 1615 and in Latin by Bill in 1616, had first appeared in English from Legge's press in the latter year. Two separate editions printed in Cambridge are dated 1619; and though no London edition in English appeared during Legge's lifetime, it was perhaps Bill's reissue of James I's collected works in 1620[68] which Legge had in mind when he accused the Stationers of printing his copy.[69]

The settlement of December 1623 could only be a temporary one. For Legge, the position was at last clear, even if the work of his press in his final years is less so now. After his death, Bonham Norton was to complain again of his activities, claiming this time that Legge had continued to print Lily's grammar, providing it with a false date in an attempt to deceive the trade that copies had been printed back in 1621. Further, he alleged, others overseas had seen in the Cambridge edition an opportunity to introduce illegal imports, again bearing false Cambridge imprints.[70] Of the latter at least no examples have so far been discovered: similar difficulties over Bibles were to become much more acute in the 1630s.[71] Legge himself continued to be hounded. Notwithstanding the arrangements of December 1623, the Stationers, having seized some books printed at Cambridge, threatened to seize more, 'intending', as the University's petition explained, 'by these continuall vexations to vndoe our printer, & wearie vs with extreame charge of suite & travaile'.[72] In the end, Legge's business became obscured by claims of false imprints, and it is therefore difficult to decide whether one clue to his market relates to books printed openly or clandestinely. In the spring of 1625 he agreed with the London grocer Humphrey Atkins to deliver six hundred reams of grammars at 11s.6d. a ream, spread in instalments to be completed by Christmas Day following.[73] The price was better than Legge could hope from the Stationers' Company.

A royal proclamation on 1 April 1625 seemed further vindication of the University's case, and was an early sign of the new King's inclinations. It applied to both Oxford and Cambridge, and was cast in conventional terms, speaking of preventing 'common errors of the presse', and sending forth works 'in their owne originall purity, without corruptions and blemishes of misprinting' before proceeding to allude to corrupt editions of Oxford- or Cambridge-printed books having been printed overseas at lower rates and on inferior paper —

whereby the Authors haue been enforced to disclaime their owne workes so reprinted, the first Printers much impouerished, and Our owne people much abused in laying out their Moneys vpon falsified or erroneous Copies: The ill consequence whereof hath not only discouraged many of Our louing Subiects, (good Schollers of both Uniuersities) from publishing in Print, diuers good and vsefull Bookes of Latine, by them prepared for aduancement of good Letters, and the trueth of Religion.

How real this danger was at Cambridge, and how far it became a rhetorical pawn, is not clear. The consequence of the argument was, however, logical: that no one should offer for sale imported editions of Latin texts already printed at either of the two universities, so long as the editions printed in England remained in print.[74]

Though Legge was dead before the expiry of his agreement with Atkins, the case between the University and the London trade was not to be resolved for another four years. His successors brought new vigour to the argument. Meanwhile one can only sympathize with the poetaster who wrote on one of the papers relating to Legge's case:

> Three thinges make me fly y[e] Courte and greate menns places
> ill feedinge, ill spendinge, longe waytinge on L[ds] & their graces.

The wait was a long one for all concerned, and the inevitable repetitiveness of the surviving documents does nothing to dispel the tedium of parts of the argument today. Yet it had concentrated the University's mind on aspects of its printer's business that were quite different from those raised two decades earlier by Legate. Ostensibly the questions were about copyright, the already familiar clash over London and Cambridge as enabling authorities. In fact they were about production costs, about profits, and about the very survival of a Cambridge press. The urgency of the cause needed some pressing on the University which, it will be remembered, had once sought to dissociate itself from the printer's office in all matters save appointments and jurisdiction over it. A letter from James Tabor, the University Registrary, to the Vice-Chancellor of the day summed up the matter: the letter is undated, but may have been written as early as 1613.

> To doe nothinge is to yeld & betraye that cause, to seeme to be doeinge & not to bringe what you intende to preserve, is to leave the case worse then you finde it, & to hope of an ende by ymaginacion, as many of your predecessors have done; who like ill Archers thought to shott home, but were loath to drawe their arrow to the head.[75]

By no means the least important outcome of the renewed disputes between the Cambridge press and the London trade was that the University's own position changed. In 1603 it was made explicit in the rules governing Legate. Apart from a general observation about materials to be used, a clause governing the price of books, and a proviso that anything Legate printed was to be deposited either in the University Library or in the Archives, the University restricted itself to the right to dismiss a printer and to its duties in governing what was printed. It refused any financial responsibilities, such as might accrue in any legal suit.[76] Under the pressure of legal proceedings no such policy was sustainable. Brooke was reimbursed for legal fees in 1613–14. In the 1620s both the Vice-Chancellor and the Registrary incurred costs in attending proceedings and in meeting legal fees. The University accounts record in 1621–2 expenses incurred in London, Royston and Newmarket as the court moved round the country; in 1622–3 the matter shifted between Huntingdon, Royston and London. The charges could be heavy. One hearing, involving the Vice-Chancellor, Tabor and Legge, lasted eighteen days, and quite apart from the presents it was thought appropriate to give to the King, the way had also to be smoothed past intervening officials. Among the bonds noted to be passed on to the next Vice-Chancellor in 1624 was one from Legge himself to bear the charges in the case; but there cannot have been much hope of its redemption, in view of Legge's own inability to contribute to the cost of the defence of the University's printing privileges.[77]

Tabor, more astutely, saw the question as a rather more complex one, and explained it from Legge's point of view. If Legge were to win the argument, then there would be other printers apart from him to share in the benefit. But if he lost, no one would contribute to his costs. The University would have no press, and it would not even have the comfort of knowing that it had fought to preserve one.[78] Tabor's analysis was by this time perhaps sharpened by the knowledge that the Grace of 22 June 1622, imposing sanctions against particular London booksellers, had little or no deterrent effect.[79]

By the time of Legge's death the point had been made. The University had accepted responsibility for the legal position of its printer beyond simply licensing him; it had met costs where previously it had specifically refused to do so; and it was presenting an ever more varied range of demands. In many respects, Legge had already become the official mouthpiece of the University by 1622. The link was made closer with his publication that year of David Owen's *Anti-Paraeus*, a book which, at the least, the University (having officially licensed it) could be further expected to receive charitably, and which could also hope for some wider interest. On 31 May that year the Privy Council wrote to the University ordering that Paraeus' works should be searched out and destroyed, following a sermon he had preached at Oxford tending, in the Privy Council's view, 'to no less than sedition, treason and rebellion against princes'.[80] The Vice-Chancellor, Leonard Mawe, went to work quickly, demanding copies of colleges, enquiring after them in the local bookshops, asking who had bought copies of Paraeus' one offending book, a commentary on the Epistle to the Romans published at Frankfurt in 1609, and finally, on 21 June, completing his task with a bonfire in Regent Walk.[81] At the same time, Mawe took the opportunity of asking after Hubert Languet's much older *Vindiciae contra tyrannos* (of which there were only continental editions available) and Gulielmus Bucanus' *Institutions of Christian religion*, printed in English at London in 1606 but also available in Latin from abroad. This was less successful, in that very few copies of Languet's book were in circulation, and that in the following November all the seized copies of Bucanus were returned to their owners.[82]

Anti-Paraeus was Legge's sole new book in 1622, an attack delivered by Owen in the Schools three years before, on 19 April 1619. Owen had already revealed himself as a ready combatant, assaulting the extreme positions of Roman Catholics and puritans alike in *Herod and Pilate reconciled*, printed by Legge twice over in 1610. His diatribe of 1619, dedicated now to the King, must have been a welcome aid.[83] In the circumstances, it carried with it the implied authority of the University itself.

Corporately, the press was in a much stronger position. But in achieving this it had lost the interest of its greatest potential benefactors. In 1620 Legate's death, and the inheritance by his son of his copyrights, had been an uncomfortable reminder of how little Legge, the other University Printer, owned himself.[84] In June 1622 the University had sought to rescue Legge by Grace, ordaining that any member who wrote a book should offer it first to the University Printers.[85] The measure produced, for Legge at least, apparently only two books: a Latin tract by Richard Crakanthorp on the providence of God, and the translation by a member of Peterhouse of a book on duelling.[86] Crakanthorp's book came out without Legge's name on it, but with that of Leonard Greene, who was appointed University Printer on 31 October 1622.[87] Instead, members of the University turned once again to London, where their books could be printed and published unhindered by trade difficulties. It was, in the circumstances, scarcely surprising that Tabor found it difficult to persuade a new Vice-Chancellor of the urgency of the case.

Legge's widow, presented with an estate heavily encumbered with debt, divided a little of his stock among the local stationers. In this way, Leonard Greene, Philip Scarlet and Richard Ireland, among others, acquired a few unsold copies of the Psalms and other books still in quires. Legge's own library seems to have been meagre. Elizabeth Legge claimed that it was worth no more than ten pounds in all, and at his death it was in the hands of her brother, Edward Goodwin: it certainly included copies of Hakluyt, *Purchas his pilgrimage*, and Mayerne Turquet's *Generall historie of Spaine*.[88] It is not clear what happened to the principal part of the unsold stock of new books; but the unhappy relationship between Legge and the Stationers' Company came formally to an end on 1 June 1629 with the transfer of Legge's remaining copies to James Boler, the London bookseller already mentioned, amongst whose apprentices was the son of the Cambridge bookseller William Williams.[89] Immediately after the entry in the Stationers' Register a valedictory note was added: 'Saluis Juribus cuiuscunque presertim. Academiae Cantabrigiensis.'

Under Legge, the office of University Printer may be said to have become institutionalized. The Grace of June 1622, enunciating the view that copies should pass from office holder to office holder, rather than from an individual to his heirs or assigns, and the manner in which the University (largely at Tabor's instigation) met the legal obstructions erected by the Stationers' Company and individual London printers, made it clear that the office had become more than a privilege to be conferred. Temporarily at least, there was reconciliation between the Printers' private enterprise and the public expectation that the University would promote its own interests even through the actions of an individual.

8

A new beginning: Thomas Buck and Roger Daniel

Death deprived Legge of the chance to benefit from the compromise between the University and the Stationers' Company. In the light of his much diminished output during the last few years, it must be doubted whether he would have found the energy to do so. However, two things were clear from the events of the early 1620s: first, that the printing privilege was a valuable, but under-exploited, asset; and second, that there was insufficient liaison between the University and the Printer who worked under its protection. All this was to change rapidly. Within twelve months of Legge's death, the Vice-Chancellor and heads had agreed measures that reiterated, and strengthened, the administrative link.[1] The 1534 charter offered an even more effective route. Neither Legate nor Legge had been a member of the University. Each had come out of the London trade, seeking University protection to pursue printing and bookselling free from the restrictions of the Stationers' Company. They owed no loyalty to the University beyond that of office. Each had, however, worked singly, as the sole practising University Printer at any one time, whereas the charter allowed for three persons to hold office simultaneously. The appointments made in 1625 brought such monopolisation, temporarily at least, to an end, by introducing three men who were clearly intended to complement each other: Leonard Greene, and the brothers Thomas and John Buck.

In itself, there was nothing unexpected in the election as University Printer of a person who already held other University office. Thomas Brooke, of Clare College, had been one of the three Esquire Bedells since 1591 when he became a University Printer in about 1608.[2] But Brooke had shown little interest in the post, and seems to have held it simply to ensure the University's presence. In 1624 another of the Bedells, John Wiseman, resigned and in his place was elected a young man who, aged little more than thirty, was to prove a vigorous, frequently controversial and often generous figure in the University until his death in 1670. Thomas Buck, who was also appointed University Printer in 1625 on the death of Cantrell Legge, was born in Essex, and graduated from Jesus College in 1612–13. He then moved to St Catharine's, where he was elected Fellow in 1616 and subsequently demonstrated in the College an aggressive benevolence that swept criticism aside by means of a long purse. As Steward and Bursar he was also responsible for initiating reforms in the College's accounting. Wealth, based on extensive holdings of land in villages in the countryside north of Bishop's Stortford, gave him the means to power, and encouraged him to expect it. Though often cautious to follow where he led, the College in the end benefited greatly, particularly as the result of a series of property transactions in Cambridge in 1622–4.[3] For the press, his election in July 1625[4] marked the beginning of a long period embittered by personal jealousies and ambitions, but one that proved to be by far the most distinguished in the period covered by this volume.

In 1625 he was aged about thirty-two, his brother John, also of St Catharine's, about twenty-eight. For much of their long lives (they were to die in 1670 and 1680 respectively)[5] they held office as University Printers together, joined briefly by their younger brother Francis. But it was Thomas, the eldest, who took the lead.

The circumstances of Brooke's and Buck's elections as Printers differed in one critical respect. In 1608 there was already a skilled practising University Printer, in charge of a successful printing house. When Thomas Buck was elected on 13 July 1625, the printing house had become conspicuously unsuccessful. Its future depended not least on the outcome of disputes with the London trade that were by no means settled. Moreover, Buck was to take the place of Legge himself. He could offer no experience as printer or stationer, and had no influence in the London trade. But by courage, fortitude and guile he was to see the press established on a stronger footing than ever hitherto. He played no direct part in the negotiations between the University, the Stationers' Company, the Privy Council and the King. His contribution was a more local one, but it was scarcely less jealously challenged.

Greene was the only man with any skill or experience in the book trade. He had served his apprenticeship with John Porter, the principal local bookseller;[6] and having married his master's daughter then went on to administer the business. On Porter's death in 1608 he inherited a profitable trade, for the use of which he had been paying Porter £30 per annum. As if to confirm that the end of his apprenticeship did not mark the end of association, an edition of Joseph Hall's *Meditations divine and moral* was entered to Porter and Greene in the Stationers' Register, less than a month after Greene had been admitted a freeman of the Company in April 1606.[7]

Between 1612 and at least 1617 he had kept a shop at the west end of Great St Mary's, before moving to Porter's old house opposite the south door. His stock of books was valued in 1630 at no less than £600, though the scale of his business is reflected equally clearly in the slightly larger amounts of money then owed to him. Greene was no printer; but he was a businessman of substance and, to judge by these figures, proven acumen. In Legge's lifetime he and Legge had been closely associated, in joint ownership of books by Andrew

Willet, Thomas Taylor and John Yates, a group entered in the Stationers' Register to the two men in November 1622 and marking Legge's last appearance in its pages. Though Greene had had a previous interest in parts of earlier editions of the two commentaries by Willet in question, it is not impossible that this entry, in 1622 and when Legge's embarrassments began to crowd about him, was a regularizing of financial support. By then, the Register recorded Greene's interest in Joseph Hall, Perkins, Willet, and Taylor in particular, as well as in Thomas Whitgre's broadside *Necessary instruction to cast account by*, a simple introduction to arithmetic whose survival in a single copy of a 1615 edition having no apparent connection with Greene may perhaps inadequately represent a once popular text.[8] Although for a space of six years after 1622 Greene made no entries in the Register, he had begun again two years before his death, concentrating once more on Perkins and, in January 1629/30, taking a share in John Preston's sermons.[9] All were books of widespread appeal to the Cambridge market; for though Greene pursued a successful course in London (where many of his post-mortem creditors must have lived), his business was founded firmly in Cambridge. By astute trading of stock of, and interests in, a well defined market, paying for books for his bookshop with either Cambridge-printed books or from his shares in London publications, he achieved that balance which eluded most of his contemporaries. If, as seems probable, the University wished in 1625 for a Printer equally attuned to London and to Cambridge, as well as a figure of some financial substance, Greene was the obvious and appropriate candidate. His membership of the Stationers offered added reassurance at a difficult period.

The description of the three new men as 'Celeberrimae Academiae Typographi' on the title-page of William Bedell's Latin translation of Paolo Sarpi's history of the quarrels of Pope Paul V with the State of Venice (1626) reflected the trio's responsibilities more than its manual skills. The mixture of book trade experience with the aggressiveness of an incoming academic possessed of a keen eye for personal, as well as corporate, improvement, was uncomfortable from the beginning however. The arguments that rapidly developed, and the near estrangement of the Bucks from their partner, may be reflected in the disappearance from Cambridge-printed title-pages of the names of the printers. Greene's name appeared only once, early in the partnership. Meanwhile he continued also to trade independently, both as a bookseller in Cambridge and in copies in the Stationers' Register.[10] Later, he declared that he had encouraged Thomas Buck to apply for the office left vacant on Legge's death in 1625, and had supported him when the Vice-Chancellor seemed hesitant. But he also made it clear that it was Buck who had first suggested himself.[11] To Greene, a bookseller of nearly thirty years' standing, the opportunity to buy Legge's press was an irresistible temptation, to which Buck's wealth would bring the means. Buck was duly licensed on 13 July 1625, and on 16 December following both he and his brother John were confirmed, with Greene, as the three University Printers. John Buck again followed in his brother's footsteps in becoming an Esquire Bedell in 1626.[12]

Though distinguished in modern memory, Thomas Buck did not hesitate to court unpopularity amongst his contemporaries. His work for his college made him a respected member of the society; but for many of the University's officers with whom he had daily contact, either as Esquire Bedell or as Printer, his self-regard seemed a hindrance and a threat to the institution of which he was a member. His activities as Printer earned him the enmity of James Tabor, University Registrary since 1600 and one of those most responsible for the University's successful prosecution of its case against the London monopolists.[13] The position of Printer offered opportunities that Buck may only dimly have appreciated in 1625. Legge left a business under threat, one unable to make a course for itself despite the freedom apparently granted by the 1534 charter, and one to which the most lucrative markets, in schoolbooks and in Bibles (with their accompanying texts) were still denied. Within a few years much of this was to change, and that it did so was due not least to Buck's own energy. But in 1625 few would have cared to predict it. Buck was soon to be criticized for manipulating his position so as to extort the maximum financial return for the least possible responsibility or risk, but there was little in 1625 to suggest that he would ever be rewarded very substantially by the methods he was later to employ.

Much more attractively, the University's constant rearguard view, to the history of its privileges, and in particular to the history of its Printers, offered the example of Thomas Thomas. Like Buck, Thomas had been a Fellow of a college before turning to printing. His reputation as a scholar-printer, comparable in some eyes to the Estiennes or Plantin, was a reminder of what might be achieved. In the event, though he encouraged others, Buck was never to put his name to a book as either author or editor. Instead, his long career as University Printer was punctuated by University and family dissent, as he exploited each for his own gain. By the time of his death, he had seen seven colleagues as other University Printers, and even in the 1660s he was still the cause of controversy.

Buck's own relations with his younger brothers John and Francis were patronizing. He inherited most of his wealth from his father, also called Thomas; and for a period family arguments interfered with the printer's office as the two older brothers tussled over a portion of their father's estate alleged to have been promised to John. However, for long periods their names were linked, whether on title-pages or as Esquire Bedells. Francis, the youngest, played only a passing role in his brothers' ambitions.

Much of the unusually detailed record of the Bucks' activities is the result of lawsuits. The allegations of Thomas's enemies may not always be reliable, and they were often in the form of unsubstantiated recollections; but the atmosphere of mistrust in which they were made, epitomized in the legal long-windedness of many of the more formal business agreements of Thomas Buck's career, lend credence to many of their contents. In his treatment of Greene, and the introduction of his brother John, he revealed himself as neither accommodating, generous nor unselfish. Greene claimed that though he had offered various alternatives to Buck so that the two might collaborate, no such collaboration proved possible. As only one-third in a partnership, Greene believed himself to be denied the profits of books that he might, as a member of the Stationers' Company, have printed for himself alone. Having bought Legge's printing equipment from his widow, who faced considerable debts, the partnership was then unable to agree on the prosecution of the press. Just how little real expertise was available is reflected in one of Greene's many proposals at this period: that a printer should be engaged from London, while Buck should act as press corrector and Greene himself as warehouse manager. Even the location of the printing house became a matter for dispute. The premises in Regent Walk, used successively by Thomas and by Legate, were central and convenient, and alternative accommodation, in John Crane's old house near Great St Mary's, hardly less so. But in the event the press was moved no further than to the Angel, on the north side of the market place, barely a hundred yards away from Greene's own shop opposite the south door of the University Church but still, in Greene's words, 'so farre as he could not possiblie be there and followe his trade'. The distance was in fact less important than what quickly emerged as Buck's real motive in moving the press. Having taken advantage of Greene's absence in London to remove the partnership's stock — consisting principally of Legge's old schoolbooks and Psalters not already sold to other Cambridge stationers[14] — Buck then took the lease for the Angel in his own name alone, and demanded a fee as corrector of the press, a fee said by Greene to be four times that customarily paid in London. After eighteen months, Greene thought resignation the least possible evil.[15] No record exists of his taking such a course; but the reappearance of his name in the Stationers' Register, after an absence of six years, may, in the light of his earlier remarks about being obliged to share his copies, be evidence of his withdrawal from the Cambridge press. He may perhaps have left the partnership during the period that John Davenant's exposition on Colossians was going through the press: the title-page, dated 1627, bears only Thomas and John Buck's names, though Greene claimed (apparently unsuccessfully) one-third of the copy.[16] When in 1630 Greene went on to publish a collection of sermons by John Preston of which he shared the copy, the book was printed in London and there was no suggestion that Greene was a part of the Cambridge press.[17]

The confirmation of the University's printing privileges, given under sign manual on 6 February 1627/8, alluded to the disputes of the previous years and was a clear direction to the book trade at large: that subject only to the authority of the Chancellor or Vice-Chancellor and three doctors of the

University, it should be legal for the Cambridge printer to print even books which were the subject of other patents.[18]

The University's reluctant election of the Duke of Buckingham as its Chancellor in 1626 no doubt aided its cause;[19] but this fresh authority, on which the University was to base its right to print the Bible and the prayer book (and thereby eventually to establish the Press on a reliable financial footing), is best regarded in the context of other events in the London trade. The Cambridge press presented a general threat; but other particular challenges to the entrenched powers of the stationers added no less to the confusion surrounding an increasingly besieged trade hierarchy. On the one hand it was threatened by clandestine imports of schoolbooks printed overseas;[20] on the other it was threatened by unauthorized presses, operated by those who were not master printers.

Thus far, the quarrel over the printing patent, nominally with the Stationers' Company generally, had become defined round particular interests. Although the Cambridge press might theoretically affect any part of the London trade, its existence offended three principal parts in particular: the printers, the Latin (or import) trade, and the English Stock. Each of these caused tensions within the London trade quite independent of any Cambridge interest, and to some extent the arguments with the University (whether in printing or, as we shall see, in bookselling) were simply further aspects of these metropolitan struggles. The manner in which the Stationers' Company controlled the London printers illustrates the point aptly.

By Star Chamber decree of 1586, not only were Oxford and Cambridge allowed one press each. Much more importantly, since it affected a much greater part of the trade, the Stationers' Company was given supervision of the number of presses in London: no presses were to be set up until the excessive number of London printers had been reduced. Unauthorized presses were to be broken by the Wardens of the Company or their deputies, and the number of apprentices was also to be limited.[21] In July that year, some twenty-five master printers were recorded, possessing a total of fifty-three presses.[22] By limiting the number of presses, it was in principle easier to control the output of the trade. Equally importantly, controlled limits could guarantee adequate business to a relatively small number of people on whom the booksellers, or publishers, were forced to depend. No practical steps were taken, however, to reduce the number of presses; and in 1603–4 the Company prepared a Bill which would have limited the number of printers by statute to fourteen, plus those at the two universities.[23] Evidence of alleged occasions when London booksellers looked abroad for their printing is, so far, somewhat piecemeal;[24] but the fact that they did so is testimony to the strain placed on the persistent application of regulations devised for the benefit of a minority smaller than a generation previously. Parliament considered the matter in May 1614,[25] but in the end it was left to the Stationers to legislate – and to do so, notably, at the explicit complaint of the master printers.[26]

The number of printers was again set out. Of nineteen printers listed in May 1615, fourteen were permitted two presses each, and the remainder only one each: the total was still larger by five than that suggested twelve years earlier, and it is therefore the less surprising to discover the same matter eight years later, in 1623. Again, although the decision was reached by the Court of the Company, the relevant minute makes clear that it was the business of the self-governing master printers, not of the Company at large. Although there had been some changes in personnel due to illness or death, the list of interested parties is chiefly remarkable for containing the same number of presses (thirty-three) as in 1615.[27] One London printer, Augustine Matthews, had already offended that summer in keeping more than one press, but efforts were now renewed to enforce the 1586 decree, and with it to ensure adequate work for all the master printers: as so often, the Company's efforts were spurred by commercial motives as much as by political. In May 1622 the Court of the Stationers' Company ordered that newly cast type was not to be supplied without the Master and Wardens being acquainted of it.[28] Between the summers of 1623 and 1628, presses were destroyed or dismantled belonging to Matthews at Bunhill, in the Ward of Bishopsgate Without, near Holborn Bridge, in Southwark, at Barley in Essex, at Old Ford (Middlesex), and on Lambeth Hill.[29] Most were isolated instances, and the press at Bunhill was a recusant one found to be printing the Rheims New Testament. The Company had already acted in the case of George Wood, a journeyman printer who after acquiring a patent in 1619 to print linen cloth turned quietly to book printing, paying especial attention to primers and almanacs: it was ordered that his press 'shalbe sawed in peeces, melted & defaced & made vnseruiceable for printing'.[30] So far as possible, equal care was given to controlling the number of people employed in the trade. In the same period, Augustine Matthews and William Jones, both printers, were ordered to put off members of their staff.[31] In similar vein, Kingston was chosen printer for the parish clerks in London in 1626 only on entering into a bond of £500 not to use that press for anything other than the weekly bills.[32]

In this context, the London anxiety to minimize the effect of the Cambridge press may be seen as one part of a much more general campaign in defence not of the Stationers' Company as a whole, but of the master printers. The difference was that, unlike in London, in Cambridge the Stationers had already been proved to have no authority to destroy presses. The authority of the University to print was no longer disputed. What it might print was another matter entirely.

The death of Legge was by no means the end of the matter. As we have seen, arguments about his printing English Stock titles echoed for several months after his death, and they were further prolonged by another petition from the

Stationers' Company. But when, on 6 February 1627/8, the University obtained the explicit confirmation of most of its privileges, the Company's protest had perforce to be couched in different terms. To complain that 'the printers of Cambridge are schollers not skillful in printinge', as the Company now did, was not original (the same had been said of Thomas Thomas); but it was especially pertinent in the case of the new University Printers, Thomas and John Buck. It was also pertinent, in the context of the London trade, to complain that, once the University's charter had been confirmed, the University Printers had installed new presses and engaged fresh labour – 'prentizes and workemen with out number limitacn or order'.[33] By so doing they had created a larger printing shop than any establishment in London apart from that of the King's Printing House.

Neither side can have expected to be vindicated completely. Legally, the University had the upper hand; but commercially the Stationers were in the stronger position. A long-winded report by the Lords Chief Justice, Sir Nicholas Hyde and Sir Thomas Richardson, in March 1628/9 paved the way for a more realistic decision, finally reached in the Privy Council on 16 April 1629. By this conclusive measure the University saw its rights confirmed to print the Bible (but only in folio and quarto), and to print the prayer book and metrical Psalms, and three thousand copies (only) each year of Lily's grammar. Those grammars, accidences and primers already in train could be sold. The King's Printers and the Stationers' Company were to restore all books seized from the Cambridge printers since 1623, and were to refrain from interfering with the sale of Cambridge books in the future.[34] It was a conclusion which the University had cause to expect, after putting forward a combination of political, educational and financial arguments in its defence. But it was also one in which the press, as distinct from university politicians, had an important part. Davenant's folio commentary on Colossians, published in 1627, was an unusually lavish achievement for the Cambridge press (copies were printed on large and ordinary-sized paper), and may have been partly designed from an early stage – as it certainly was subsequently – as a demonstration of ability. 'Suppose,' wrote Samuel Ward in May 1628,

your Lordship hath seen my Lord of *Sarum*'s Readings upon the Colossians, which should have been exhibited, *nomine Academiae*, to his Majesty, when he was here about the beginning of *Lent*. But my Lord of *Winchester* hindred that intention, though herein he prejudiced the University. For we having received a Favour from his Majesty, to enjoy the priviledg of our Charter for printing all kind of Books, against the *London* Printers, thought to shew to his Majesty a *Specimen* of our Printing, both for good Letter, and good Paper, of both which his Majesty had complained in printing the Bibles at *London*.[35]

Whatever the profits – real or imaginary – in schoolbooks, Ward also made clear that the University's long struggle was for many motivated by the hope of printing one book only, the Bible. The eventual compromise of 1629 was a strictly commercial one, in which the University had been awarded only limited rights. And like the Privy Council orders of 1623, to which allusion was now made,[36] the 1629 decision helped to establish a legal constituency for copyright that was independent of the Registers of the Stationers' Company. Neither the Bucks, nor Roger Daniel, the University Printers who succeeded Legge and Greene, entered a single book in the Registers.

For the University, the London printers had been an obstruction, which it sought to render contemptible by applying to them, in private at least, a variety of depreciatory remarks. To Tabor, writing a little earlier, they were 'illiterate baboons'.[37] In January 1628/9, just after the final compromise, they were *Lychnopolae*, or lamp-sellers, an allusion to Aristophanes' *Knights*. 'Lychnopolas prostravimus, multarum fraudū peritissimos artifices'; they were not merely small traders, but perpetrators of fraud as well.[38]

For seven years, with the single exception of Bedell's translation of Sarpi, the only names of University Printers to appear on Cambridge-printed books were those of Thomas and John Buck, sometimes Thomas alone, and sometimes in effect obscuring the true position with such terms as 'Printers to the Universitie', or 'Ex Academiae Typographeo'. The agreement which admitted the Bucks' most celebrated partner, whose arrival brought to an end a period of uncertainty, was reached only in August 1632,[39] after Greene had been dead two years and Francis Buck had helped his brothers to a yet stronger position, in what seems to have been envisaged as a family monopoly. Against their own incapacity to run a press, the Bucks could weigh an express desire to see it reflect to the credit of the University; but in the negotiations of the following years, as each in turn received his portion for what was in effect largely a sinecure, it is difficult not to suspect that their primary concern had become financial profit.

They turned for the man who was intended as in effect their manager to London. Roger Daniel was intruded into the University, and was from the beginning a protegé of the Bucks: the subsequent differences between the brothers and Daniel were all the more acerbic because of this initial arrangement. Born in about 1593,[40] Daniel was not a native of Cambridge, and he seems originally to have been trained for some other career than printing. Of the little that is known of him before the Bucks introduced him to the University for their own ends, it is clear only that he possessed a business in London where prints were at least as important as books. Between approximately 1623 and 1625 he had been the publisher of various suites of engraved illustrations: of military training, of fauna, of the seven champions of Christendom, of Sybilline prophecies, of the exercise of arms, as well as of John Davies' *Writing schoolmaster* and of separate portraits.[41] These early experiences as a printseller were to influence the choice and appearance of some of the books which were to appear from the Cambridge press in the 1630s, when Daniel's connections with the engraving trade enabled him to introduce books whose publication would otherwise seem extraordinary when set against what had previously been produced.[42] Daniel's shop, in Pope's Head Alley just off Lombard Street near the Royal Exchange, was close to two other printsellers, George Fairbeard and George Humble; in 1626 he was joined, if not succeeded, by William Sheffard, who, unlike Daniel, was a member of the Stationers' Company.[43]

Apart from these engravings, Daniel's name appears on no publication before 1628. One of the very few authors in Cambridge to observe the instructions of 1622, that members of the University were to offer their new books first to the University Printer,[44] was William Bedell, who in 1628 (two years after his translation of Sarpi on the Council of Trent) saw into print an attack on those who would be Roman Catholics. For this, Daniel acted as London bookseller to the Cambridge press.[45]

Similarly, in 1628, the aged John Carter of Clare College, now Rector of Belstead in Suffolk, saw into print his *Winter-evenings communication with young novices in religion*, printed at Cambridge and bearing Daniel's name as the London stationer. The series of editions printed at Cambridge in 1628 of Sternhold and Hopkins and naming Daniel as the London bookseller created a predictable furore on which the Stationers were obliged to compromise. It would on the other hand have been unwise to have played any named part in the publication of the Bible by the Cambridge press in 1629, and Daniel's name is not known to have appeared on any Cambridge edition of Lily's grammars at this period.[46] How much his part was a silent one in some of these enterprises may only be guessed, but the engraved title-page of the 1629 Bible was quite probably his doing. It was unlike anything published before by the University Printers, and required special equipment, a rolling press, unavailable to the Bucks. But Daniel's part in this, as in other books, was a silent one. The absence of his name from a title-page may have signified very little, if the example of Ralph Winterton's translation of Gerhard's *Meditations* (1631, with an engraved title-page) was ever repeated: the entire impression, printed in Cambridge, was sold by Daniel to Michael Sparke, though neither Daniel's nor Sparke's name appears on the book.[47]

In other words, Daniel was introduced only gradually. Apart from his involvement in the metrical Psalms, which by including his name in the imprint so blatantly offended the London trade, his position was no different from that of other booksellers who had become in effect long-term London agents. But Daniel was no part of the establishment. Both the metrical Psalms and an edition of the ABC, printed in 1630, were challenges to the authority of established London monopolies, and in 1628/9 Daniel became the subject of formal complaint to the Privy Council.[48] For such a person, the opportunity of partnership in a press beyond the confines of the London trade must have seemed irresistible.

Yet Daniel was not the Bucks' immediate choice. Leonard Greene's death from plague in October 1630[49] found Thomas Buck in London, to be recalled in some haste by his brother:

I pray return w[th] all speed to the Vniue*r*sitie, Leonard Greene is dead theres a patent void, and w[th] in 14. dayes a third man must be chosen. I pray be not dishartened att it. for I haue the Vicechancellor & ten heads and p[r]sidents sure to vs, and they haue all (I humbly thank them) promised me faithfully to prick whomesoeuer yow & I shall desire; I think my brother Francis would be a fitt man to comend vnto them; but if you know y[t] to bring in M[r]. Barker would proue more advantageous to vs I desire yo[w] to intreat him to come down wth yo[w]. or any other in London whome yow best like of.[50]

Barker's name in this context sufficiently reveals the Bucks' preoccupations. In October 1629 Robert Barker had regained possession from Bonham Norton of his share in the King's Printing House, so bringing to an end over a decade's rivalry with the man who had also taken a lead in the London struggle against the Cambridge privileges. An accommodation with such a man, involving comprinting the texts over which the King's Printing House already exercised rights, would have offered even greater advantages to the Cambridge press than those which might accrue to it on the Bucks' concluding a few months after Greene's death with another member of the London trade, Edmund Weaver.[51]

The necessity for speed, imposed by the University's regulations, made Francis Buck the obvious man to be put forward to the Vice-Chancellor and Heads' obedient will. Meanwhile Roger Daniel, apparently more compliant and certainly less powerful than Barker, was brought gradually into the business in a manner that makes no sense unless it is remembered that Thomas and John Buck's primary purpose was not to run a press, but to gain from it. If the suggestion was ever made that Daniel should be simply their servant, it was never pursued publicly. Instead, a sequence of elaborate agreements passed as much executive and responsible authority to Daniel, eventually as University Printer, in return for regular income to the two elder brothers.

The first to reach a formal arrangement was Thomas Buck, who from soon after Greene's death received a proportion of £150 per annum for one-third of the printing business executed by Daniel. In January following, this was altered to two hundred marks for the whole business, Daniel also now paying a further one hundred marks to John. But by January 1631/2 Thomas was anxious also to obtain his brother John's portion; and after a theatrical display to his brother of illness and suffering ('Meere deuises & plotts to bring downe the price of his brothers patent for his owne endes'), he finally succeeded in so doing.[52] Thus, by the beginning of June 1632, Thomas was able to negotiate with Daniel unhindered by others' interests, and moreover, he did so having arranged to pay for the other parts of the privilege less than he would expect to receive from Daniel. Thanks to his opportune display of suffering, Thomas Buck had managed to argue that the value of a third part of the business was worth only £50, instead of a hundred marks.[53]

So, in the summer of 1632, Thomas Buck consolidated his position. His brother Francis, who had been University Printer only since 27 October 1630, resigned on 21 July 1632,[54] to be replaced immediately by Daniel. By this time, however, relations between Buck and Daniel had already soured, Daniel now suspecting that his only hope of peace was to remain in London. In return for his printing privilege he had paid out seasonal sums to Thomas and John Buck (John claimed that Francis never received anything, but held his office only 'for the good & benefitt' of his brothers) since October 1630; and within a few months he was to petition the Vice-Chancellor, accusing Thomas Buck's servants of attacking him, so that he and his own staff were, as he put it, 'Weary of their lives'.[55] It was the more remarkable that in July 1632, the same month in which Francis Buck resigned his post as Printer, Thomas Buck was able to entice Daniel back from London, and to do so even as he arranged to let out the printing patents at the new sum of two hundred marks per annum.[56] Daniel was elected Printer on 24 July,[57] and on 22 August that year the two men concluded an agreement which finally established Daniel in Cambridge. In return for a rent to Buck of £190 per annum he now acquired the use of most of Buck's house in the old Austin Friars, behind St Bene't's Church (see fig. 25), the exclusive use of the presses and other printing equipment, and the services of each of the Bucks' several apprentices.[58] In addition, he assumed responsibility with Buck for comprinting with the London stationer Edmund Weaver.[59] In a further agreement, signed on 2 February 1633/4, the two men held themselves to be partners for five years, Buck having twice the interest of Daniel.[60] Each of these agreements was of critical importance to Daniel, since they governed virtually all of his activities as printer.

Thomas Buck was subsequently to be much criticized for his pact with Edmund Weaver, Treasurer of the Stationers' Company (and therefore principally responsible for the English Stock).[61] But he presided over the course of the University's dispute with the Company after Legge's death, culminating in the further, confirmatory, charter from Charles I and the triumphant appearance in 1629 of a folio edition of the Authorized Version of the Bible. Less satisfactorily, the new order severely limited schoolbook printing, and explicitly forbade the University to print the Bible in sizes other than folio or quarto, or any other books already governed by patents belonging to the King's Printers or the Stationers' Company.[62]

So the University Printers remained excluded from some of the most lucrative parts of the market, notably small format Bibles, Testaments and Psalters, most schoolbooks and the almanac trade. But this public pact with the Stationers was complemented by another, secret, one, whose existence emerged only four or five years subsequently,[63] and which, once its existence was known, caused offence simultaneously to the University and to the stationers of Cambridge. Its mutual advantage to Weaver and to Thomas Buck lay in the fact that it provided Buck with a regular, predictable income; and it allowed the Stationers' Company not only to control the number of books printed by Buck, but also to treat the Cambridge press merely as another printer to help feed the English Stock's ever greater appetite for books. Thus both sides could profit; but the agreement implicitly denied the freedom always hitherto claimed by the University, to print whatever books it chose. In sum, the University Printer could now print what had until now been controversial commercially. But he did so within strictly defined limits: 2,240 reams of almanacs, 500 reams of Psalms, the quantities controlled by the Londoners' assuming responsibility for providing the paper. Buck's agreement with Weaver was known to Daniel from the beginning, in September 1631, and it lasted until its full course had run, in September 1634.[64] But as Daniel pointed out, it was an agreement whereby the 'University Presse is servant to the said Stationers and the University and commonwealth deprived of that benefit which is intended by our Privelege.'[65]

9

An uneasy partnership

Buck and Daniel remained the joint dominant figures in the Cambridge book trade until 1650, not always in partnership and not always in amity. But while Buck's reputation as a scholar-printer was restricted to the University, and was never remotely comparable with the Estiennes', or even Thomas's, the period did produce a series of books of lasting importance. Much of the credit for the revival of the press's fortunes in the 1630s and 1640s has in the past been given to Buck.[1] But it was Daniel who for most of this time was the effective printer; and it was Daniel who was responsible for the preliminary notes to be found in several Cambridge books during these years.[2] Buck, a graduate of the University, secured his reputation; Daniel, a London craftsman, was expected to support it.

Posterity was quick to take up Buck's praise, led by Isaac Barrow, who was bound in private duty and gratitude to remember him as one of the executors of Henry Lucas, founder of the Lucasian chair in mathematics. Buck, he wrote, had pursued the University's printing interests even at the expense of his own welfare and that of his family: there could be no doubt that his fame, printed in clear type (*nitidis impressa characteribus*) would last for ever into posterity, just as the Bibles whose value and esteem he had done so much to advance.[3] But Barrow, who believed that Buck had been the person principally responsible for obtaining Lucas's benefaction, wrote nearly twenty years after Daniel's death, and over fifty after the disputes of the early 1630s. The press was in a condition that made the time of Buck's heyday seem almost a golden age. The University had forgotten the disputes that lay behind it, and saw only in retrospect, its evidence on the title-pages bearing Buck's name.

In unravelling the respective contributions of Buck and Daniel, it is important to distinguish between the different parts of their list: those books printed at the behest of the Stationers' Company and those originating in Cambridge. The distinction was not always clear even to contemporaries. Tabor, the University Registrary, made his own notes on these privileged books, for example, and others supplemented them.[4] With the agreement on Bible printing in 1629, the limited confirmation of the University's right to print Latin schoolbooks (soon to be extended in practice by secret agreement between Buck and the Stationers' Company), and the arrangements with the Stationers' Company over almanac printing, the Press was able at last to exploit its position. Pocket editions of Cicero, Ovid and Virgil, of Lily's grammar, Aldus Manutius' *Phrases linguae latinae*, Baptista Spagnuoli's verses and Talaeus' *Rhetorica* were produced for an established, protected educational market. Much of Buck's energy had been concentrated on achieving this, and together with Bibles and almanacs they guaranteed business to the press and income to himself.

Daniel, however, wished, or professed to wish, otherwise; and in the selection of new textbooks produced at Cambridge after his appointment there are to be found the results of a compromise between Buck's commitment and Daniel's desire that the Press should demonstrate some independence and initiative. In Greek, a new collection of the minor poets by Ralph Winterton, Fellow of King's and Regius Professor of Physic, became immediately popular from its first appearance in 1635, as a convenient amalgam of earlier editorial work (see fig. 21). But it was supplemented by other texts as well: Winterton's own edition of Hippocrates had appeared in 1633,[5] and in 1640 Posselius' Σύνταξις was printed at the behest of Francis Eglesfield, the London bookseller – the first English edition of a book familiar enough, but only in continental printings. Richard Busby's new Greek grammar came out later, in 1647.

According to Daniel, such books, and others he claimed as part of his attempt to bring honour to the University rather than merely cash to its servants and officers, were not welcome to Buck. Their diversity is described below; but despite the conjunction of the two men's names on the title-pages, there was, in their own minds, a clear distinction of interest:

Perceiving that I was able to goe on wth ye printing busines wth out his helpe' [wrote Daniel] 'and that I was Forward and willing to print other bookes w^{ch}: would more honour the Universitie presse then those schoole books wch he had agreed to print for ye Londoners. He many wayes as well by letters as complaints sought to disgrace yor petitioner to the Universitie & at London and hath done his best to thrust yor petitioner out of his printership.[6]

And yet Buck retained his position as University Printer, 'glorying that what book soever is printed, is by his care and industry, though he took no paines about it'.[7] To Daniel, the solution seemed at one point to lie only in the separation of the joint posts into two, or even three, presses: such a division would not only make it easier for authors to have their works printed; it would also (so Daniel claimed) bring advantages already proved at Oxford, where John Lichfield and William Turner ran independent establishments:

Whereas at Oxford, more things are printed, wher they have not so Large a Charter, I conceive the reason is because they have two printing houses; And were there two or more in Cambridge, no doubt but more bookes & such as would bring more honour to the Vniversitie would here be printed.[8]

No one quarrelled with Daniel's complaints of his difficulties; but his suggested solution offered no real advantages. Wedded on the title-pages of their books, Buck and Daniel were forced to live together. The pattern of production, and the relationship of innovation to conservatism, of the popular to the scholarly, were born out of a combination of tension and forebearance.

In one unexpected sphere, the Cambridge press was pre-eminent. Hitherto, the major poets who had graduated from the University had been printed, if at all, usually in London. The work of Giles Fletcher, an exception, had been printed at Cambridge in 1610, but made a reappearance in 1632, five years after the publication there of his elder brother Phineas's *Locustae*: Phineas Fletcher's *Purple island* appeared in 1633, a production made lavish by the patronage of Edward Benlowes.[9] Herbert's *Temple* (see fig. 13), first printed in 1633, was exceptional for the Cambridge press at least in being posthumous; in that it established the printed appearance of a group of poems whose visual form was essential to the sense, it was arguably one of the most typographically influential of all Cambridge books during this period. Its duodecimo format became the established one, into the eighteenth century.[10] Milton's 'Lycidas' (1638) was composed for a volume of poems (including also contributions by Henry More, Joseph Beaumont and John Cleveland) to the memory of a member of Christ's, drowned in the Irish Sea in August 1637; and volumes by Henry More appeared in 1642 and 1647. Other poets were printed in Cambridge for London booksellers: the 'second' edition of Quarles' *Emblemes* in 1643 for Francis Eglesfield, John Hall's *Poems* in 1646 for John Rothwell, and the rather less distinguished *Ovids festivalls*, 'translated into English verse equinumerally' by John Gower, sometime of Jesus College, whose volume of 1640 was available in London from the younger Michael Sparke.

All appeared from the Cambridge press in the same years as a vigorous appetite for contemporary poetry was satisfied also – in Cambridge as elsewhere – by anthologies in manuscript: print and manuscript were complementary. Of the Cambridge poets, Phineas Fletcher, seeking patronage, had first circulated versions of his *Locustae* in manuscript fifteen and more years before it was eventually printed in 1627. Richard Crashaw of Pembroke, Robert Herrick of St John's and Thomas Randolph of Trinity were more familiar to their readers in manuscript than in print, gathered into anthologies and accompanied there by contemporaries from Oxford or elsewhere.[11]

To this notable series of poets, there were added college plays by Thomas Randolph of Trinity and Peter Hausted of Oxford. But lest such a list should suggest that Buck and Daniel had persuaded members of the University of their exclusive appeal as printers and publishers, it is salutary to recall that volumes by other Cambridge poets were printed elsewhere. John Cleveland's poems written while he was in the University reached print only several years after he had left for Oxford in 1642. Cowley's precocious *Poetical blossomes* was published at London in 1633, before he even came up to Trinity; but with the

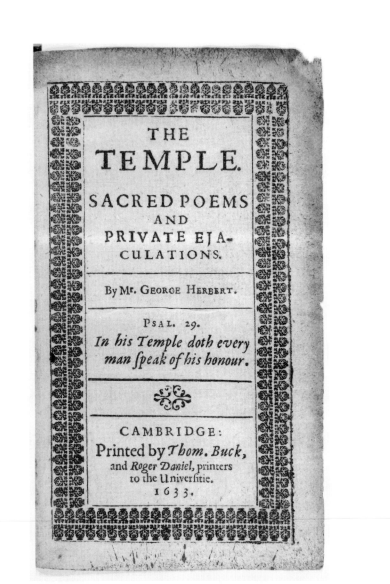

Fig. 13 George Herbert (1593–1633), *The temple*,
12°, 1633. Height of original, 140 mm.

exception of his contributions to the University's occasional anthologies none of his work was printed at Cambridge. Thomas Philipott, though the title-page of his *Poems* (1646) proclaimed him a member of Clare Hall, saw his work published and printed in London. University plays, widely circulated in manuscript, were more normally printed in London than in Cambridge. The most celebrated of all, George Ruggle's *Ignoramus*, was printed in 1630, fifteen years after its entry in the Stationers' Register a few weeks after its earliest recorded performance; and John Hacket's *Loiola*, acted at Trinity for the first time in February 1622/3, appeared only in 1648.[12]

The demand for tuition in modern languages was met by two unusual books, the first of which was to prove the beginning of a long series of similar works by emigrés who had found a temporary home at Cambridge teaching their native tongues. Gabriel Dugrès, a protestant from Saumur, produced a French grammar, written in Latin, in 1636, and published it himself with the help of his pupils (see fig. 14): three years later he followed it at Oxford with a series of tri-lingual dialogues. In the following decade, Giovanni Torriano, teacher of Italian, continued his English career begun in London with two books from Daniel's press, a collection of Italian proverbs in 1642, and a new edition of his Italian grammar in about 1645.[13]

Political upheaval, and the consequent wanderings of scholars, brought some of these books to the Cambridge press, and not only from abroad. It was the rebellion, almost certainly, that indirectly caused Daniel to receive for printing William Harvey's rejoinder to Jean Riolan on the circulation of the blood, *Exercitatio anatomica de circulatione sanguinis*, published twenty-one years after he had first made public his conclusions in print at Frankfurt. Barred from London, Harvey turned to his own University's press to produce a book whose small format suggests that there was some desire that it should be easily portable: further editions appeared at Rotterdam and Paris within the next few months.[14]

The press's medical list was otherwise modest. But apart from the books described above there were others on law, on the wonders of the Nile (principally crocodiles), and on the virtues of drinking warm beer. Political and military upheaval may have helped latterly in driving authors and London booksellers to seek out help in the country; but most aspects of the unexpectedly various output were the result of Buck and Daniel's own energy. The press was criticized for failing to meet the needs of Cambridge authors, and for giving preference to the more reliably lucrative London work. In fact, the University's increasingly dispersed interests were met with a more flexible policy than had been evident hitherto.

Daniel's early connections with the engraving trade helped to shape the way in which the press responded more directly to the military interest first of overseas campaigns and then of civil war. John Cruso's *Militarie instructions for the cavallrie*, accompanied by Cornelis van Dalen's series of full-page

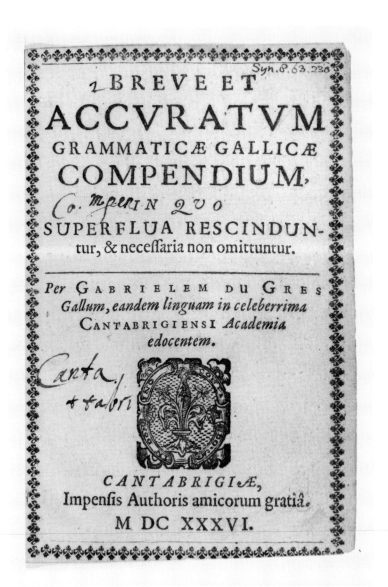

Fig. 14 Gabriel Dugrès, *Breve et accuratum grammaticae Gallicae compendium*,
8°, 1636. An early example of a modern languages textbook, using different
type-faces to distinguish between the languages in the manner commonly
found in books printed elsewhere. Height of original, 35 mm.

utimur particulâ *que*; ut, *Il est plus grand que moy d'un pied*, Ipse est altior me pede uno. Utimur comparativo cum articulis, *le, la, les*, secundum casum, genus, & numerum, quando res includit aliquem respectum ad alia, ut cùm Latini dicunt, Ille est totius Academiæ doctissimus; Angli, **He is the learnedst man of all the Universitie**; nos sic reddimus, *C'est le plus docte de toute l'Université* : *C'est la plus honneste Dame d'Angleterre*, Honestissima est totius Angliæ Domina; Anglicè sic reddendum esset secundum phrasim nostram, **She is the more honest Ladie of England.**

DE PRONOMINIBUS.

Quinque sunt veluti pronominum genera, *Personalia* videlicet, *Possessiva, Relativa, Demonstrativa, Indefinita*; omnia ferè & singula ipsorum in duas dividuntur species, nimirum in conjunctiva & absoluta.

Personalia conjunctiva, utpote quæ cum verbo junguntur, sunt hæc.

Singul. Nominat. *Je* ego, *tu* tu, *il* ille, *elle* illa.

D   Genitivo,

Fig. 14 continued.

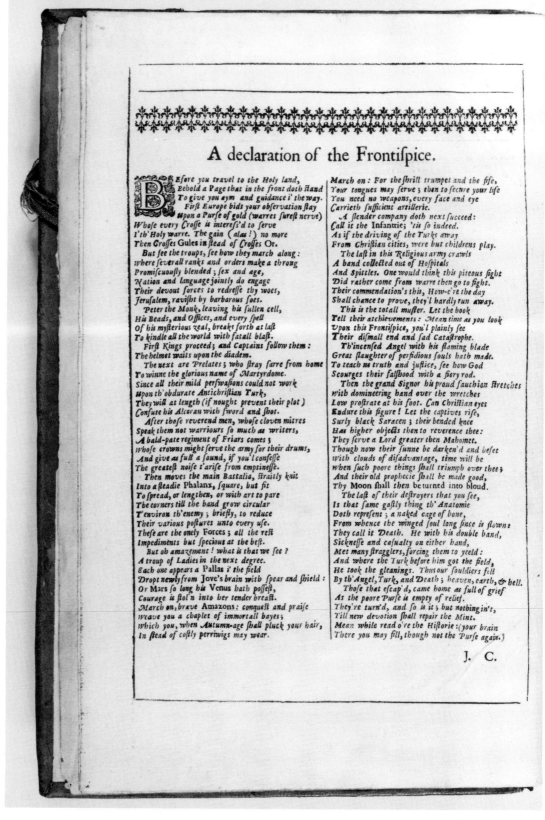

Fig. 15 Thomas Fuller (1608–61), *The historie of the holy warre*, f°, 1639. The engraved title-page, by William Marshall, depicts an interpretation of the Crusades: Peter the Hermit can be seen leading the armies of Christendom in the bottom left-hand corner, while the verses on the opposite page offer a more detailed interpretation. Height of original, 283 mm.

Fig. 15 continued.

engravings (1632), was modelled on similar foreign publications, and was brought up to date with the help of men who had served in the current campaigns in the Low Countries.[15] Cruso acknowledged in his preface that his work had been prompted by the lack of any English book on cavalry practice, and he cited as a foreign example the work of J.-J. van Wallhausen, some of whose illustrations were pillaged in van Dalen's engravings. The wars in the Low Countries created a demand for such books, whose folio format, however, made them more suited to the library than the field: copies of similar treatises on military practice were brought back, for example, by Henry Newton from a tour in Italy; and even James Duport, dedicated to his career as a Cambridge Hellenist, owned treatises on the subject by Giorgio Basta, Diego Ufano and van Wallhausen, besides Cruso himself.[16] In the English book trade, Cruso's book was the more noticeable in that the London bookseller Edward Blount died before he was able to publish translations of the military treatises of Lodovico Melzo and Giorgio Basta, after entering them in the Stationers' Register in 1631.[17] For Daniel, the genre fell easily within the tradition in which he had worked in London nearly a decade earlier; and though it bears no printer's name specifically in the imprint, Cruso's work may be presumed to have been principally his, rather than Buck's, responsibility. The London stationer named on the engraved title-page, Nicholas Alsop, was to become a familiar figure on Cambridge books. Cruso, meanwhile, had discovered a useful métier. By the time that the *Militarie instructions* was republished in 1644, he had also produced two further works, both translations: first of an established French treatise by Du Praissac on *The art of warre* (1639), and then in 1640 of a selection from Julius Caesar supported by a commentary on modern warfare by the Duc de Rohan.

The theological list, no longer headed by Perkins, centred from the late 1620s (bibliographically if not doctrinally) on John Davenant, Bishop of Salisbury, whose relations with the Cambridge press are discussed below.[18] Like Davenant, Thomas Fuller also turned to his old university for the publication of his books, beginning in 1639 with *The historie of the holy warre* (see fig. 15). It is, so far, rather less clear how the University Printers came to print Donne's *Six sermons* (1634), the first such collection to appear in print after his death the previous year. By 1650, Daniel had also been responsible for works by Lancelot Andrewes, Quarles, Henry More, Joseph Glanvill and Ralph Cudworth, as well as of continental figures such as Nicolas Caussin and Juan de Valdes. In 1627 there appeared the first of many editions of the *Meditations* of Johann Gerhard, its translation the work of Ralph Winterton, whose handy edition of the Greek poets has already been mentioned. These apart, Winterton was also responsible for translations or editions of Hieremias Drexelius, Hippocrates and Terence, an assortment of professional and other interests that identifies him as an early example of the kind of figure who was later to become familiar, a press work-horse. Of all his books, Winterton had perhaps highest hopes for his *Hippocrates* (1633), to which he prefaced no less than thirty-three pages of Greek and Latin epigrams by colleagues in Oxford and Cambridge: within two years he was rewarded with the Regius Chair of Physic. But it was the Greek poets, of 1635, that established his reputation most permanently in the minds of several generations of classics pupils, and that offered an improvement even to the text of Henri Estienne's edition of 1566.[19]

The revived attention to Greek, represented in Winterton's work, was most prominent, perhaps, in an edition of the Greek New Testament published in 1632, the first to have been printed in England for a decade. Duport's Φρηνοθρίαμβος (1637), and subsequent similar exercises, had about them much of the same academic bravura as the contributions to the various collections of university verses, where printed Hebrew (and Anglo-Saxon) appeared for the first time in 1641.[20] In Hebrew studies proper, an edition of Maimonides' *Canones poenitentiae* (1631), and the publication the following year of Mede's *Clavis apocalyptica*, marked a considerable departure.[21] The arrival in Cambridge as an exile from Oxford of the Polish Hebraist Victorinus Bythner created a further stir fifteen or so years later, first with a new edition of his own *Lingua eruditorum*, and then with Johann Buxtorf's well-established *Epitome grammaticae Hebraeae*.

The University's interest in exotic types, another manifestation of a new concern for the oriental languages, was largely frustrated, however. The published output of Buck and Daniel's press in its first years did not reveal the whole of their ambitions. In several respects these were years of frustration, the result of over-optimism mingled with commercial innocence and a disabling tardiness on the part of the University. In no episode was this more apparent than in the attempt to establish an oriental press. Cambridge had possessed a professorship of Hebrew since the foundation of the Regius chair in 1540: from about 1622 to 1645 this was held by Robert Metcalfe, Fellow of St John's before he moved next door and became Vice-Master of Trinity. Metcalfe was, however, not a man to expose himself to the world by urging change, and the contrast must have been striking between him and Abraham Whelock, the first to hold the new lectureship in Arabic founded by Sir Thomas Adams in 1632.[22] For all his unassured manner, Whelock was much the more active. His edition of the Gospels in Persian appeared only after his death, and in London; but his chair had been created in response to international stimuli. The continuing missionary attack by the Roman Catholic Church, the pre-eminence of Dutch scholarship in oriental languages (abetted by colonial expansion), and the realization, exemplified eventually in Walton's polyglot Bible, that middle-eastern languages other than Hebrew offered their own authority to the text of the Bible, all combined to make oriental languages seem obligatory.[23]

For Cambridge, as for others, the death of the Leiden orientalist Thomas Erpenius in 1624 offered an opportunity that was not to be missed. Both his library and the press which he had equipped to produce oriental texts promised to whoever would acquire them a place unrivalled in their field. Leiden, naturally, hoped for the manuscripts and printed books, which would have joined those of J. J. Scaliger bequeathed in 1609, and there were also rumours of Jesuit interest.[24] Thanks to an alert agent, however, the manuscripts were bought by the Chancellor of Cambridge, the Duke of Buckingham, and they eventually passed, after much anguished negotiation with Buckingham's widow, to the University – nearly eight years after Erpenius' death.[25] With the manuscripts already in Buckingham's hands, Samuel Ward felt it useful to pursue the matter further, and to try to obtain not only Erpenius' printed books, but the matrices for his Syriac, Arabic, Ethiopic and Samaritan types as well. He learned, too late, that Isaac Elzevir had bought them, to be kept therefore at Leiden. It may, perhaps, have been some consolation to Usher, Ward and others that they had not fallen into the hands of the Antwerp Jesuits. But the opportunity for Cambridge, as well as for other English printers, had been let slip.[26] It is doubtful whether any English printer would have been willing to employ a specialist staff of the size at the Elzevir house, where for the oriental press alone there were eight special journeymen and five correctors.[27]

The University's failure to obtain Erpenius' oriental matrices did not destroy expectations for a learned press, but it did restrict them. In 1627 the orientalist John Greaves assumed that matrices for Samaritan type could be procured 'without any great charge'.[28] Buck and Daniel, perhaps more knowledgeable and certainly more cautious, declined to pursue the matter further, and restricted their work in exotic types to Greek and Hebrew: the University's hopes of persuading Adams, founder of the new Arabic lectureship, also to support an Arabic press, came to nothing.[29]

The ambitious hopes that Erpenius' oriental types and matrices might come to Cambridge were proved to be dead when they had barely taken root; but this was not the only chance offered to the University. The second came from William Bedwell, a member of Trinity College and for the last years of his life incumbent of Tottenham, then a village on the outskirts of London. On his death in May 1632 he left to the University the manuscript of his Arabic lexicon, to which he had devoted much of his later years, as well as type with which to print it. By the time he died, the manuscript consisted of nine volumes, besides bundles of loose notes.[30] Its existence was well known; but opinion on its value was divided, his family and immediate circle rating it rather more highly than did others who perceived it to be out-dated and incomplete. Erpenius himself had been among the critics. Among those who wished to see it in print, none seems to have been more forward than Bedwell's son-in-law William Clerke, or Clarke, who was however fearful lest so fragile a treasure should be misplaced, 'tossed & torne in the Librarye'. Such dangers made the need to put Bedwell's manuscript into print seem all the more urgent, and at the same time he was writing to Whelock about its keeping he was also writing to Barnabas Oley of Clare College in an attempt to move the Heads to action:

Why surely he hath giuen a rare & great gift namelye his Arabicke Dictionarye with all the types to print itt withall…My request therfore to you is yt you would bee pleased to moue the heddes of the Uni*u*ersitye yt if they themselves will not bee att the charge to print itt yt they would bee pleased to accept a copye I meane a booke when itt is printed…My mother might haue made a great benefitt of itt if itt had beene left to her to make the best of. Sir Kenelm Digbye would haue giuen five hundred pounds for the booke & types.[31]

Apart from Kenelm Digby, Edward Pococke also was said to have commended it. Clarke, however, proving more anxious to boost his father-in-law's reputation than to execute his wishes, had still not delivered either lexicon or type when Daniel visited Sir Thomas Adams, founder of the Arabic lectureship held by Whelock, in the following November.[32] Bedwell's manuscripts and type reached Cambridge a little later, and it then became the University's turn to prove dilatory. Nothing seems to have been seriously thought of for the type until in October 1646 a Grace was passed voting up to £40 to support the printing of Arabic texts.[33] It was a project of which no more was heard, and from which Sir Thomas Adams was distracted: he might have been expected to pursue so obvious an accompaniment to his lectureship, save for his own troubles as a result of his royalist sympathies, which took him from the mayoralty of London to the Tower.[34]

Although the Greek New Testament had formed part of the Stationers' Company Latin Stock between 1618 and the time of the Stock's winding up in 1627, and it was entered to the English Stock in June 1631,[35] few editions were printed in London: only one, from the press of John Bill, appeared between 1592 and 1652. Instead, the market was supplied with editions from the continent, printed for the most part in Geneva or Holland until the publication in 1642 of a sumptuous folio edition by the new Imprimerie Royale at Paris. Even this last, however, an assertion alike of the new press's presence and of Mazarin's pre-eminence, was based on the edition published by Elzevir at Leiden in 1624. In 1633 the London bookseller Richard Whitaker simply imported sheets of another printing from Leiden for his edition, rather than have it printed in London. The established recognition of the 1624 edition, based principally on Beza's text, avoided the need for serious revision in the eyes of most customers, and save for a handful of alterations the octavo edition printed at Cambridge in 1632 repeated the 1624 text: no record survives of who was responsible for its editing.[36]

For the Greek type, of which Buck possessed none of a size suitable for a largish octavo, and of which the London trade had none either, Cambridge turned to Oxford. In 1619 Henry Savile had presented to the University the matrices of the type he had used to print his edition of Chrysostom at Eton in 1610–13, one of the few publishing enterprises in England able to stand comparison with those on the continent in the early seventeenth century.[37] Type cast from these matrices had been used for some books printed at Oxford.

No record survives of who prompted the events that, on 16 June 1629, led the Heads at Cambridge to write to the Earl of Pembroke, Chancellor of the University of Oxford, requesting the loan of the matrices from their sister university. The instigator was almost certainly Buck himself, still at this stage anxious that his new press should be a learned one: 'So it is that having devoted our endeavors to the setting vp of a Presse for the edition of Authors in the Greek Language (wherein our adversaries beyond the seas so much boast them selves), that our successe therein may be the better and our speede the greater we humbly desire to borrowe those matrices for greeke Letters which were Sr Henry Sauiles.'

Oxford agreed, encouraged no doubt by Pembroke's unwillingness to see Cambridge put in a position where it might have an 'advantage of vs as we should denye them those thinges which lye Idly by vs'. Buck received the matrices on 28 August 1629, and kept them until 24 June 1631. The type cast from them, and used to print the octavo Greek Testament published the following year, must have been cast in London, since Cambridge possessed no facilities for this.[38]

Buck's edition (there was no mention of Daniel or of any other printer on the title-page) met with lasting success. Like the other major biblical texts from the Cambridge press during this time — the 1629 and 1638 English Bibles, and the 1642 Greek–Latin New Testament — it was issued on different sizes of paper to suit customers' different requirements. Copies were often bound in two volumes rather than the one suggested by the single title-page, and it became a regular feature in the wealthier private libraries. One copy, now in the University Library,[39] belonged first to William Sancroft, to whom it was given by the printer, before passing in turn to, among others, John Worthington, the Duke of Lauderdale, the London bookseller Christopher Bateman, and then, as Bateman's gift, to John Moore in 1690: on Moore's death in 1714 as Bishop of Ely it returned to Cambridge with the rest of his library, given to the University by George I. Daniel himself was the first to reprint the text, in 1652, two years after returning to London from Cambridge.

Despite all this activity, Daniel and Buck's achievement had usually fallen short of the kind of achievement which might have been expected of a learned press. Indeed, most of their energies were directed at the almanac and schoolbook market, where long subsidized print-runs and assured markets offered better chance of profits. In London, by contrast, Thomas Bayly's edition of the theologically fashionable Theophylact (F°, 1636), and Patrick Young's of Nicetas on Job (F°, 1637), followed by Young's edition of Gilbert Foliot in 1638, suggested a new seriousness in the King's Printing House. At Oxford, Laud's hopes for a learned press to exploit the Barocci manuscripts were to be thwarted, but Patrick Young's ingenious edition of Clement I's first letter to the Corinthians, rescued from the Codex Alexandrinus, showed what might be done.[40] There was, however, one exception, in which, for the first time, the Cambridge press produced a book of unquestionable international distinction on a subject other than current theological controversy.

The reputation of Abraham Whelock now rightly dominates Anglo-Saxon studies in seventeenth-century Cambridge. But he was not unique in his interest, and among those who were also attracted to the subject none was more active than William Lisle. Lisle had entered King's College in 1584, and took his MA in 1592. In 1623 he published in London his edition of Ælfric, *A Saxon treatise concerning the Old and New Testament*, in which he spoke also of following John Foxe's edition of the Gospels in Anglo-Saxon, printed by John Day in 1571, with further biblical texts: 'and (by the Grace of God) I meane ere long to let the world know what is more remaining; as more I haue seene both in our Vniuersitie Libraries, and that of Sir *Robert Cotton*'.[41] From his house at Wilbraham, only six miles from Cambridge, Lisle went on to pursue an edition of the Psalter, using manuscripts from, amongst others, Spelman, the University Library, Trinity College and Corpus Christi College, and providing a translation 'taken & fytted wth the phrase of our tyme' – 'not as a new English translation, but as the ouldest of all'. His work received its imprimatur from the University on 3 December 1630 (see fig. 24. on p. 262 below).[42] Had it been printed, the Cambridge press would have been obliged to obtain Anglo-Saxon type a decade before it eventually did; and thus provided, events might have taken a different turn. But the investment was not made, and Lisle's edition, for commercial or editorial reasons, was never published.[43]

Whelock's edition of the Latin and Anglo-Saxon text of Bede's *Historia ecclesiastica*, completed in 1643 (see fig. 16), was to be superseded as regards the Latin in 1722 only because of the discovery of a much earlier manuscript than any of those which he had used, and as regards the Anglo-Saxon only in 1896.[44] Whelock (1593–1653) matriculated as a sizar from Trinity in 1611, and from 1619 until his marriage in 1632 was a Fellow of Clare. Having failed to obtain the Greek chair in the scramble to succeed the aged Andrew Downes in 1625 (the post fell to Robert Creighton of Trinity), Whelock was appointed University Librarian in 1629. It was a position to which his methodical mind, linguistic prowess, and apparently invariably courteous mien made him almost ideally suited, though his becoming modesty made him sometimes un-necessarily timorous. In 1632 he was appointed the University's first lecturer in Arabic, thanks to Sir Thomas Adams, and in 1638 the first in Anglo-Saxon. He held all these posts until his death in 1653 after a career in which the fear of financial ruin never wholly deserted him. In his scholarly work, which he saw as both a natural extension of his library duties and as the essence of his teaching appointments, his edition of the Persian Gospels remained un-completed at his death, and was published posthumously. His Anglo-Saxon studies were considerably more rewarding. Although neither his grammar nor his dictionary of the language was to be published in the form he had once envisaged, his work on Bede was brought to the press with his own hands.[45]

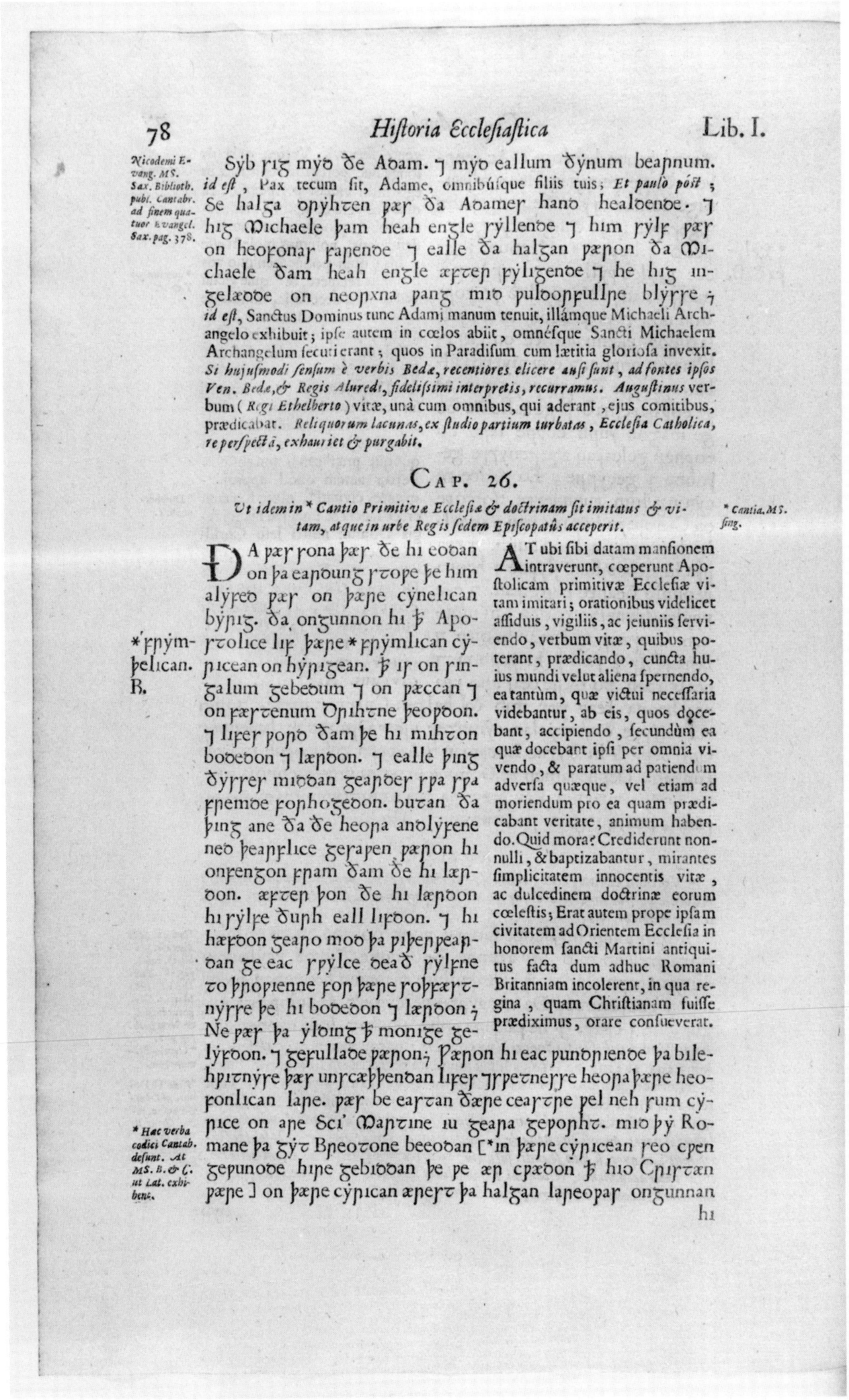

Nicodemi E-vang. MS. Sax. Biblioth. publ. Cantabr. ad finem qua-tuor Evangel. Sax. pag. 378.

Syþ rig myð ðe Adam. 7 myð eallum ðynum beaþnum.

id est, Pax tecum sit, Adame, omnibúsque filiis tuis; *Et paulo post;* Se halga onyhten pær ða Adames hand healdende. 7 hig Michaele þam heah engle ryllende 7 him rylf pær on heoronas rapende 7 ealle ða halgan pæþon ða Mi-chaele ðam heah engle æften pyligende 7 he hig in-gelædde on neorxna pang mið puldorrullne blyrre;

id est, Sanctus Dominus tunc Adami manum tenuit, illámque Michaeli Arch-angelo exhibuit; ipse autem in cœlos abiit, omnésque Sancti Michaelem Archangelum secuti erant; quos in Paradisum cum lætitia gloriosa invexit. *Si hujusmodi sensum è verbis Bedæ, recentiores elicere ausi sunt, ad fontes ipsos Ven. Bedæ, & Regis Aluredi, fidelissimi interpretis, recurramus. Augustinus ver-bum (Regi Ethelberto) vitæ, unà cum omnibus, qui aderant, ejus comitibus, prædicabat. Reliquorum lacunas, ex studio partium turbatas, Ecclesia Catholica, reperspectâ, exhauriet & purgabit.*

Cap. 26.

Vt idem in * *Cantio Primitivæ Ecclesiæ & doctrinam sit imitatus & vi-tam, atque in urbe Regis sedem Episcopatûs acceperit.*   ** Cantia. MS. sing.*

* Fnym-belican. R.

Da þær rona þær ðe hi eoðan on þa eanðung rtope þe him alyred pær on þære cynelican byrig. ða ongunnon hi þ Apo-rtolice lif þære * fnymlican cy-rrcean on hyrigean. þ ir on rin-galum gebeðum 7 on pæccan 7 on rærtenum Drihtne þeopdon. 7 lifer pord ðam þe hi mihton boðeðon 7 lærdon. 7 ealle þing ðyrrer middan geardes rpa rpa fnemðe forhogedon. butan ða þing ane ða ðe heopa andlyrene neð þeanrlice gerapen pæþon hi onrengon fnam ðam ðe hi lær-don. æften þon ðe hi lærdon hi rylfe ðurh eall lifdon. 7 hi hæpdon geano moð þa piþerpeap-dan ge eac rpylce deað rylfne to þnopienne fon þære roþfært-nyrre þe hi boðedon 7 lærdon; Ne pær þa yldoing þ monige ge-lyfdon. 7 gefullade pæþon; pæþon hi eac punðriende þa bile-hpitnyre þær unrcæþþendan lifer rrpetnerre heopa þære heo-ronlican lape. þær be eartan ðære ceartre pel neh rum cy-rpice on ane Sci Maþtine iu geapa gepophr. mið þy Ro-mane þa gyt Bneotone beeoðan [*in þære cyrpicean reo cpen gepunoðe hine gebiodan þe pe æp cpædon þ hio Cpirtan þæþe] on þære cyrpican æpert þa halgan laþeopar ongunnan hi

AT ubi sibi datam mansionem intraverunt, cœperunt Apo-stolicam primitivæ Ecclesiæ vi-tam imitari; orationibus videlicet assiduis, vigiliis, ac jejuniis servi-endo, verbum vitæ, quibus po-terant, prædicando, cuncta hu-ius mundi velut aliena spernendo, ea tantùm, quæ victui necessaria videbantur, ab eis, quos docebant, accipiendo, secundùm ea quæ docebant ipsi per omnia vi-vendo, & paratum ad patiendum adversa quæque, vel etiam ad moriendum pro ea quam prædi-cabant veritate, animum haben-do. Quid mora? Crediderunt non-nulli, & baptizabantur, mirantes simplicitatem innocentis vitæ, ac dulcedinem doctrinæ eorum cœlestis; Erat autem prope ipsam civitatem ad Orientem Ecclesia in honorem sancti Martini antiqui-tus facta dum adhuc Romani Britanniam incolerent, in qua re-gina, quam Christianam fuisse prædiximus, orare consueverat.

* Hac verba codici Cantab. desunt. At MS. B. & C. ut Lat. exhi-bent.

Fig. 16 Bede, *Historiae ecclesiasticae gentis Anglorum libri V*, edited by Abraham Whelock (1593–1653), f°, 1643. Height of original, 350 mm.

He had been appointed to a lectureship made possible thanks to Sir Henry Spelman, whose visits to the University Library and to Corpus Christi College had persuaded him of the need for an assistant in research who would be permanently settled at Cambridge: the results of the two men's collaboration are to be seen in Spelman's own edition of the British *Concilia*, published in 1639 and printed in London. Spelman had been cautious at first to admit Whelock as an equal,[46] but in June 1638 his protégé's course was becoming shaped, influenced at least partly by theological considerations. Whelock wrote to Spelman:

I am now reading of Bede with King Alured his translation wch I see will correct many thinges, wch time hath corrupted in the Latin copie. wch we may reduce to the ould Latin, but the maine busines wch possessth my thoughtes, is, the discouery (out of Bede, & others, especiallie in Manuscripts) of the Apostolicall doctrine, by comparinge our præsent church with the auncient church here in England: wch work will most properlie suite wth yor Reader, because he is to be a searcher of truthes out of the fountaines themselues.[47]

A year or so later, by now appointed formally to his new post as lecturer in Anglo-Saxon, antiquarian, linguistic, palaeographical and theological interests had combined to determine Whelock on an edition of Bede that would present both the original Latin and – for the first time in print – the Anglo-Saxon. His admission of his proposed task brought from Simonds D'Ewes (no great friend of Spelman's, though in his puritanism and in his shared interest in Old English one likely to encourage such a project) cautions that were by now probably unnecessary:

Your printing of Bede alone without some other additions will hardlie bee undertaken. I wish you had advized with mee before it been begunne. Besides it must bee compared with some other Saxon copies & the various readings added in the margent: Iff the copie you transcribe bee not above seven hundred yeares old it is faultie in the main passage of it.[48]

At the University Library, the Anglo-Saxon text found in the eleventh-century Worcester manuscript Kk.3.18, given by Matthew Parker in 1574, served as Whelock's principal authority; and for the Latin he had recourse principally either to the 1601 or the 1612 Cologne edition. Both were in turn supported by other manuscripts, not only from Corpus (where MS 173 formed, with others in the Cotton library, the basis of Whelock's text of the Anglo-Saxon Chronicle printed at the end, and with his own translation), but from other libraries as well.[49] In a letter written two days after Christmas 1639, in which he sought also to soothe relations between Spelman and Trinity following a misunderstanding over the Eadwine Psalter,[50] Whelock explained a little of the scale of his work on Bede: he was using six manuscripts in all, equally divided between Latin and Anglo-Saxon, and had received help from Samuel Ward in borrowing the crucial Cotton text.

There was already in existence a serviceable Anglo-Saxon type in the London trade, used by Badger in 1639 to print Spelman's *Concilia*. Its design bore traces of that used by John Day in the 1560s, but in the recutting it had lost much of its life. Whelock's ordinary handwriting shows him to have been a man acutely aware of the potential beauty of letter forms: his own Anglo-Saxon used many of the elements of Day's, but brought fresh spriteliness, and even some new ideas. His type was also much better cut and it is unfortunate that the name of the punchcutter responsible is no longer known.[51] The finished type seems to have been on the verge of delivery at the end of March 1640, which thus sets a terminus to the production of Whelock's edition.[52] It made its first appearance in a printed book eighteen months or so later, in contributions to *Irenodia Cantabrigiensis* by Whelock and another member of Clare, William Retchford. The great primer, in which these verses were set, was supplemented by a single smaller-size pica, which, however, apparently arrived only in time to be used for the later parts of Lambard's Ἀρχαιονομια, included with Bede in the London reissue of 1644.

The last sheets of the Bede were printed off during the later part of 1643, and by 22 March 1643/4 Whelock was able to present a copy to Joshua Hoyle, Professor of Divinity at Trinity College, Dublin. In the course of five years or so he had prepared and seen through the press the central texts which he had perceived as essential to his lectureship. Within a single volume there were contained not only a parallel text of Bede's history, with the first edition of the Anglo-Saxon Chronicle and a translation of it, but also a life of Bede (drawn from a Corpus manuscript), a brief genealogy of the West Saxon kings, and a substantial apparatus and index. In his dedications to the Cambridge authorities and to Thomas Adams ('Mecœnatem meum semper colendissimum' – Spelman died without seeing the book in print) Whelock repeated his theological motives.[53]

The 1643 volume was not faultless, and Whelock's translation of the Anglo-Saxon Chronicle has since drawn especial criticism. But Spelman's *Concilia* of 1639, and Whelock's volume of four years later, were almost all that were to appear of a grandiose scheme for the organized publication of the essential Old English texts. In March 1640 Whelock himself had indicated that Roger Daniel was prepared to countenance an edition of Simeon of Durham, based on the thirteenth-century manuscript in Corpus.[54] Nothing came of this. The text was published for the first time, partly through the agency of another Cambridge scholar Ralph Jennings, in Sir Roger Twysden's *Decem scriptores* in 1652. The London bookseller, and publisher of the *Decem scriptores*, Cornelius Bee, took up Daniel's work. Already able in 1637 to take a leading part in the importing of no less than 350 copies of Mercator's *Atlas maior* from Amsterdam,[55] Bee was later, in 1660, to undertake publication of the nine folio volumes of Pearson's *Critici sacri*, and in 1659 he drew the praise of the antiquary William Somner as 'viro sanè, ob plures melioris notae libros ipsius curâ & impensis in vulgus emissos, de re literariâ bene merito, adeoque apis instar industrio ut nomen ei optimè conveniat'.[56] In 1640 he was one of the two booksellers to publish William Watts' new edition of Matthew Paris, an edition superseded only in the 1870s.[57] The next year, Bee was importuning Twysden to supply editions of the early English historians for the press: Twysden in turn called on Ussher and John Selden, 'by whose industry and good affection to learning, ten writers of the *English* history were transcrib'd from originals in the *Bennet* and *Cottonian* Libraries, and faithfully collated with all different copies, by an expert Amanuensis Mr. Ralph Jennings...To adorn the work, Sir *Roger Twisden* was to acquaint the Reader with the occasion of the book, and the conveyance of those MSS. from which it was compil'd. Mr. *Selden* was in a longer preface to give account of the ten Historians, and their writings.'[58]

Although Daniel's name alone appeared at the foot of the title-page of the 1643 Bede, the intervention of Bee at this point was therefore entirely appropriate. In 1644 he reissued the sheets of Whelock's work, prefixed now by the first edition to have appeared since its first publication in 1568 of William Lambard's 'Ἀρχαιονομια.[59] Whelock's name had not figured on the title-page of 1643, and it was still absent from the new general one to the volume now issued by Bee: the prominence given, by contrast, to the words 'E Bibliotheca Publica Cantabrigiensi' may well be further silent evidence of Whelock's character and of his conviction of his position as a scholar, or amanuensis, in the Library.[60] Lambard's text was printed, as Whelock explained, at the instigation of none other than Twysden, who added further early legal material of his own, while Whelock himself used the opportunity to add materials he had earlier supplied to Spelman. The authorship of the accompanying glossary was not divulged.[61] It may be presumed that Bee himself was responsible for inserting the map of Britain originally engraved by William Hole for Camden's *Britannia* (1607, and later editions). Most copies of the 1644 volume were issued of a piece, with that of 1643; but Bee also published the new compilation separately: Simonds D'Ewes bought a copy for seven shillings in December 1646.[62]

Whelock's own publishing career was to prove to have ended, the victim partly of the Spelmans' deaths (Henry in October 1641, and John in July 1643), partly of civil war and partly of demands in the University Library dominated in the last years of the 1640s by the arrival of the so-called Pragi collection of oriental books and the entire library from Lambeth Palace. The collapse of Spelman's arrangements on Whelock's death for a permanent post in Anglo-Saxon studies at Cambridge, and the consequent all too brief tenure of his successor William Somner, further discouraged the development for the time being of what had once promised so well.

The preparation of the Bede left its mark on the pattern of Daniel's other work: the number of books to appear from his press was noticeably smaller in 1643 and 1644 than in the previous few years, and their bulk was less. I have been unable to discover how the Bede was financed: its Saxon type alone was a considerable investment, for which Daniel was never to find further use. Bee's intervention in 1644, however, meant not only that Daniel gained access to a metropolitan (and international) market hitherto difficult to approach, but also that by selling a large part of the edition he could recoup his costs conveniently and rapidly. In the face of the commercial and political crisis brought on by civil war, it was essential that he should do so.

In this revived attention to the learned side of his press, Daniel's achievement was in one respect to be quickly overshadowed. His edition of the New Testament in Greek and Latin, published in 1642, was presented with especial care, even commanding a new etching by Hollar of the press's emblem for the title-page. Conceived quite differently from the Mazarin folio New Testament of the same year, though each had about it an air of ostentation, Daniel's edition offered not one, but three texts – one Greek and two Latin. Beza's Greek and Latin were presented in parallel with the Vulgate, and the whole was accompanied by the commentary of Joachim Camerarius. However, the outbreak of civil war, and the concentration of scholarly attention on other versions in preparation for Brian Walton's polyglot edition of the whole Bible, published in 1655–7, distracted attention away from Daniel's achievement. It remains the largest, but least remembered, of the series of major editions for which he was responsible in the last few years before his press was disrupted. Once again, copies were printed on both large and ordinary paper. The various states of the title-page reveal the probable course of subsequent events. In 1642 copies were printed both for Daniel's own use in Cambridge and for sale in London at his old shop 'sub signo Angeli, in vico Lumbardensi (vulgo Lumbardstreet) Londini', each version of the title-page bearing Hollar's device. Other copies, printed only with a woodcut device and with the name of the London bookseller Benjamin Allin, or Allen, added, clearly represent a sale or other agreement not envisaged at the time of printing the edition, but which must have occurred before Allen's death in May 1646.[63]

This increasingly varied list, in which the established strands of theology and elementary classical textbook were supplemented by English poets, and engraved title-pages added grace to books as well as cost to their production, set a pace which it was difficult to maintain. The Bible and almanac trades were established, to provide a reliable if not always very steady income, while *The temple* and Winterton's translation of Gerhard's *Meditations* each reached their fifth edition in 1638. The reissue of Daniel's old military plates after de Gheyn, as *Directions for musters*, in 1638,[64] was another example of his readiness to turn to proven successes, in the year in which 'Lycidas' slipped out concealed in the traditional mould of Cambridge verse obsequies. New editions of Davenant in 1639 were another manifestation of an established list. But the same year heralded hope of new vigour. Both Fuller's *Holy warre* (1639, 2nd edn 1640) and *Holy state* (1642) were printed by Buck and Daniel for John Williams, of

St Paul's Churchyard, whose name is also to be found during this period on copies of Daniel's editions of Cruso's Du Praissac (1639) and of Gerhard's *Meditations* (1640). Fuller's books were, in the context of the previous few years, unexpectedly ambitious. With its gallery of twenty engraved portraits by William Marshall, *The holy state* was a book utterly unlike any previous production of the Cambridge press. In some ways it canonized Cambridge protestantism, with its representations of William Whitaker, William Perkins and William Cecil, though the company they kept, from St Augustine to Gustavus Adolphus, helped to point Fuller's wider purposes.[65] In 1639 Fuller was no longer resident in Cambridge, as a curate at St Benet's, but was incumbent of a small Dorset living, where he wrote *The holy warre*. His single earlier book, verses on *Davids hainous sinne* (1631), had been both printed and published in London, but a combination of loyalty, familiarity and friends drew him back to Cambridge for his first major works: his uncle, the Bishop of Salisbury John Davenant, was well acquainted with the press (and was also, instructively, the only other contemporary author to be printed in folio format at Cambridge during this period). Among those whose poetical addresses were prefixed to *The holy warre* was James Duport, a figure hardly less influential in the press's circles. Daniel was to retain the printing of *The holy state* even after he had retired to London, but in the London bookseller John Williams, Fuller had found a regular publisher who was generally to prefer a London printer. Davenant, who might have continued to influence matters, died in 1641.

Despite several major achievements, and despite attempts to obtain the specialist types that would have provided the technical wherewithal – if not the skills or financial investment – to create an oriental press, there is nothing in Buck and Daniel's output between 1625 and 1650 to suggest a Laudian concept of a learned press, of the kind pursued, briefly, at Oxford. Such editions of early texts as appeared, whether of Greek poets or of Bede, did not constitute a programme. Laud's vision proved a chimera; but Cambridge apparently lacked anyone even with the vision. More prosaically, the Cambridge printers pursued a path between meeting the everyday demands of the University and making the most of the opportunities offered by the 1628 charter to share in the most profitable parts of the London trade. The initial folio Bible of 1629 was followed by further editions; the Book of Common Prayer and Sternhold and Hopkins' Psalms were essential adjuncts, hardly less profitable. Besides these there were almanacs, and above all schoolbooks, which for a few years dominated the press's output. However, each was subject to various restrictions, imposed either (in the case of the Bible) by the Privy Council,[66] or (in the case of almanacs and schoolbooks) by private agreement between the University Printers and the Stationers' Company.

❦ 10 ❦

Privileged books

In the eyes of Laud, busy about a new learned press at Oxford, the Cambridge charter of 1628 seemed to offer a model – 'very large, and of great honour and benefit to that University'. His letter, to the Vice-Chancellor at Oxford, made the most of ancient rivalries; but, as he also implied, the two universities' common interests made it easier to plead precedents once Cambridge had successfully argued its case:

They of Cambridge have been far more vigilant both to get and keep their Privileges, than you at Oxford have been, for they have gotten this and other of their Privileges confirmed by succeeding Princes, and I think some of them by Act of Parliament, which for Oxford hath not been done. Upon consideration of this I thought it very just and equal, that the two Universities should enjoy the same Privileges, especially for printing. And when I had weighed all Circumstances, I adventured to move his Majesty on your behalf, who, according to his great and princely favour to the University, did most graciously grant it: The motives, which I used were principally two, the one that you might enjoy this privilege for Learning equally with Cambridge; and the other, that having many excellent Manuscripts in your Library, you might in time hereby be encouraged to publish some of them in Print, to the great honour of that Place, this Church and Kingdom.[1]

Laud put a learned press first, able, again, to profit from Cambridge's experience: 'Though your *Patents* be large, yet coming over the Heads of the King's Printers and other Stationers here in *London*, I shall advise you not to suffer any of your Printers as yet to print *Bibles*, *Service-Books*, *Grammars*, *Primers*, &c. (which caused the late and chargable Controversy betwixt Cambridge and them;) but let your Privilege settle a while, and gather strength quietly.'[2] It was advice no less astute for being obvious; but it also reflected the difference between two apparently irreconcilable ways of proceeding. Laud chose to encourage (however unsuccessfully) a learned press. By 1632/3, when he wrote this letter, Buck and Daniel had already chosen to pursue the mass market. By 1636/7, having watched their fortunes, Laud saw no reason to change his mind about his own University. 'Certainly', he concluded, 'it will be more beneficial to the University for the advance of a Learned Press to receive 200*l.* a Year, than to print Grammars and Almanacks, &c. And more Honour, too … to what extraordinary good use you turn this Money.'[3]

The 1628 charter, intended to ensure the interests of both the London and the Cambridge printers, under-estimated the determination of both. The Bible trade was, in one respect, regulated by the division of the market between larger and smaller formats. But for schoolbooks and almanacs, where the potential profits seem to have been at least comparable, and the market was larger if measured by annual sales, there remained ample opportunity for manoeuvre. The measures taken ensured that each side secured the maximum possible profit and transformed the Cambridge press without damaging the cartel controlling the English Stock. The charter provided the University with a firm legal base, but it was one whose design was dictated by commercial interests.

The Bible trade after 1628 was to remain in a measure straightforward until the collapse of royal authority (and with it the London monopoly of the King's Printers) in the 1640s. The difficulties came not from London, but from abroad, as cheap imports were introduced to meet requirements that domestic production could not meet.

Between 1591 and 1629 no complete Bible was published at Cambridge.[4] By the mid-seventeenth century it had become one of the Press's mainstays, and it has remained the most important single economic component of the Press's list for most of the three and a half centuries since. Its importance as the generator of profits that could in turn be used to subsidize less widely popular books can hardly be over-estimated.

Reasons have already been advanced for the gap in production between the printing of the Geneva Bible in 1591 and the first Cambridge edition of the Authorized Version – eighteen years after its first publication – in 1629. During this period, no complete Bible was printed in England outside London: none was to be printed at Oxford until 1675. Instead, the Bible remained the monopoly of the King's Printers, first of Christopher Barker, later of Robert Barker, Bonham Norton and John Bill. These men, and after 1649 a small caucus of the London trade, retained their dominant position long after 1629, able to do so not only by virtue of being well-established and controlling from London most of the country's book distribution network, but also because of the size of their printing houses.

Cambridge was still formally entitled to one press only, while the King's Printing House was unaffected by any limitation. In London eyes, one of Buck's offences was that in 1628/9 he possessed four presses, and thus gained an advantage both illegal and unfair over a trade that only in 1628 had concluded that London master printers should each possess not more than two presses each.[5] Thus Buck offended both the King's Printing House and the Stationers' Company more generally.

An insatiable public demand for Bibles was met by the King's Printers with a profusion of presentation, in formats ranging from folio to duodecimo (but most popularly in quarto and octavo), in black letter and in roman type. As identical editions were sometimes called for twice within a single year, the printers regularized production to the point where traditional discrete editions became obscured in a process of continuous reprinting, as fresh sheets were composed and printed to meet shortfalls of sheet, rather than edition, stock.[6] Despite the precautions of the London trade, Bible printing had become international by the beginning of the century: Robert Barker complained of Bibles in English being printed at Dort in 1601.[7] In 1630, the Privy Council, acting on information from Robert Barker that English Bibles and other church books belonging to him as King's Printer had been printed overseas and imported, authorized him to search out suspects and to seize any such books that he found. Barker quickly demonstrated the legitimacy of his complaint, by seizure of stock of the offending books and by, eventually, the arrest of Michael Sparke.[8] Another large stock of imported Geneva Bibles was seized in 1632, and its custodian, Richard Blagrave, imprisoned.[9] In 1633 Laud prohibited the import of Geneva Bibles altogether, in legislation that can only have referred to Dutch printers.[10] In 1635 one of the searchers of the London customs house was convicted of dishonestly handling illegally imported Bibles.[11] So general had the trade become that, it was alleged, English Bibles were even used as cover for other prohibited books.[12] The part of the monopoly holders in the London Bible trade is neither clear nor unambiguous, but London was by no means the only port faced with such difficulties. Bristol and York were both specified in the papers relating to the case of Michael Sparke, whose enterprise brought him also, in another context, into contact with the stationers at Cambridge.[13] With the dislocation of the business of the King's Printers in the early 1640s, imported Bibles became even more a necessity: their great numbers can only mean that the existing English means of production were hopelessly inadequate. By 1646, it was claimed, Amsterdam alone was responsible for over 150,000 copies.[14] There, the printer Jan Frederickz. Stam mingled, with editions of works by Prynne, Henry Burton and others, a series of misleadingly dated and signed editions of the Geneva Bible, many purporting to be the work of the King's Printer himself.[15] In March 1644 Stam and Thomas Craffort agreed to sell to Hugo Fitzer six thousand duodecimo English Bibles, to be delivered in August;[16] within a twelvemonth Daniel's name, too, was making unauthorized appearances on the title-pages of Bibles printed overseas.[17]

The Dutch trade's readiness to use the names of those in England authorized to print the Bible obscures the Cambridge press's real contribution. Under the Privy Council orders of 1629, the University Printers were restricted to quarto and folio:[18] no octavo edition of the Authorized Version was completed in Cambridge until 1658. Thus some of the most lucrative parts of the market remained to be exploited by the London trade, at a time when that trade itself faced a series of crises. Jealousies were rife. Within the King's Printing House, the so-called 'wicked' Bible of 1631 was almost certainly the result of sabotage carried out on behalf of one part of the syndicate who controlled it following John Bill's death in 1630.[19] On the other hand, foreign editions were a threat to English printers: 'They in Amsterdam, had gott up an English presse, and had printed the Bible in better paper, and with a better letter, and can undersell us 18d. in a bible', explained Laud after the 1631 fracas, in arguments supported by George Abbot:

I knewe the tyme when greater care was had about printeing, the Bibles especiallie, good compositors and the best correctors were gotten being grave and learned men, and the paper and letter rare and faire every way of the best; but now the paper is naught, the composers boyes, and the correctors unlearned: There is a farmer and he makes the benefitt, and careth for nothing about it. They heertofore spent their whole time in printeing, but these looke to gaine, gaine, gaine, nothing els.[20]

Both of the major editions of the Bible printed in Cambridge during this period, in 1629 and 1638, differed markedly from those printed in London. In 1591 Legate challenged London by imitation. But while the same was true in the early 1630s of the quarto editions, those in folio were remarkable for their independence. Both in 1629 and 1638 efforts were made by the Cambridge printers to correct errors made in earlier editions of the Authorized Version: among those responsible for correction in 1638 were Samuel Ward, Thomas Goad, John Bois and Joseph Mede.[21] Within a few years, special merit was being claimed in both Holland and England for Bibles set from the 1638 edition (see figs. 17 and 18)[22] and no further serious textual revision was thought necessary until 1762 for this Bible, 'of which', in Thomas Fuller's admittedly partisan words, there was 'none exacter or truer Edition in England'.[23]

Both the 1629 and the 1638 Bibles were issued on different-sized papers, of varying quality. In the range offered to customers in 1629 there is to be seen both a sense of experiment with the first such production from the Cambridge press, and an alertness to the commercial necessity of reaching all possible markets. No less than seven different grades of paper have been identified, in sheets of various sizes.[24] Equivalent numbers were printed of the Book of Common Prayer and of the metrical Psalms (see fig. 19), and are generally found within the same covers.[25] Copies could be bound up as a customer wished. 'I have chosen your Bible of Dutch paper which with the Service & Psalmes is in quires 12s.6d. It is stronger & better for your project then Venice (as they tell me) & will be very white & faire being beaten', wrote Joseph Mede to Sir Martin Stuteville on 27 February 1629/30, just before embarking on a discussion of an appropriate binding.[26] Mede had chosen expensively. Other issues of the new Bible, on inferior paper, cost ten shillings. The 1638 edition was printed in three sizes, royal, medium and demy, at prices ranging from 16s. to 30s. in quires.[27]

THE HOLY
BIBLE
CONTAINING THE
OLD TESTAMENT
AND THE NEW:

Newly translated out of the originall Tongues, and with the former translations diligently compared and revised, by his Majesties speciall command.

Appointed to be read in
CHURCHES.

Printed by Tho. Buck, and Roger Daniel, Printers to the University of Cambridge.

This variety, still reflected in modern Bible publishing, and also to be seen, to a lesser extent, in the large and ordinary paper issues of the Cambridge Greek Testament of 1632, was not only for the benefit of the customer. It also enabled the Cambridge press to undercut London prices, in a struggle that lasted for more than a decade and which affected such other popular texts as almanacs and textbooks as well. Michael Sparke, *provocateur* and London bookseller excluded by his peers from the most profitable lines, summed up his own view succinctly – twelve years after the first Cambridge folio had appeared – to challenge what he thought politic to present as his colleagues' disproportionate profits:

In the yeare 1629, the want of these sorts of Folio Bibles caused *Cambridge* Printers to print it, and they sold it at 10ˢ in quires: upon which the then Kings Printers set six Printing-houses at worke, and on an instant printed one Folio Bible in the same manner, and sold with it 500. Quarto Roman Bibles, and 500. Quarto English, at 5s. a Book to overthrow the *Cambridge* Printing, and so to keep all in their own hands. It were well if they would alwayes sell at this price.[28]

On this occasion, London tactics were successful. The claim that stationers had failed to win by legal argument in the 1620s was won by a combination of commercial verve and the connivance of the University Printers in the 1630s. No edition of a folio English Bible was printed at Cambridge between 1629 and 1638,[29] though three are recorded from London. 'The Monopolists have compounded with them that they shall print no more Bibles, but for the Monopolists', alleged Sparke in 1641 – a plausible and probably deliberate misrepresentation of the Privy Council permission to comprint of 1629.[30]

The Cambridge booksellers who eventually allied themselves with Tabor against Buck did not do so entirely to protect the reputation of the University. Of much more concern to them were, as always, the prices of books, whether printed in England or overseas. Since many locally printed, or London printed, books could be set in the often specialist Cambridge trade against similar titles from abroad, it is as well to consider imports first.

Despite transport costs, printing in the 1620s, like other manufactured goods, was cheaper overseas than in London.[31] In the 1630s, Buck's contract with Weaver depended on it being cheaper in Cambridge than in London. Both the Cambridge and the Oxford presses suffered as a result of the difference in manufacturing costs in England and on the continent, as the University pointed out, drawing once again on its long memory to support arguments for which more recent evidence was not easily explained. Thus Legate had seen his editions of Whitaker rapidly reissued in new guises closely imitating his own by Christoph Corvinus at Herborn, and Oxford had seen the works of John Case taken up enthusiastically by printers at Frankfurt. If the arguments put

Fig. 17 (opposite). William Marshall's engraved title-page for the Bible of 1638: the emblems of Thomas Buck and Roger Daniel, a deer and a palm tree (see p. 296), appear in the centre at the foot. Original plate-mark, 302 mm high.

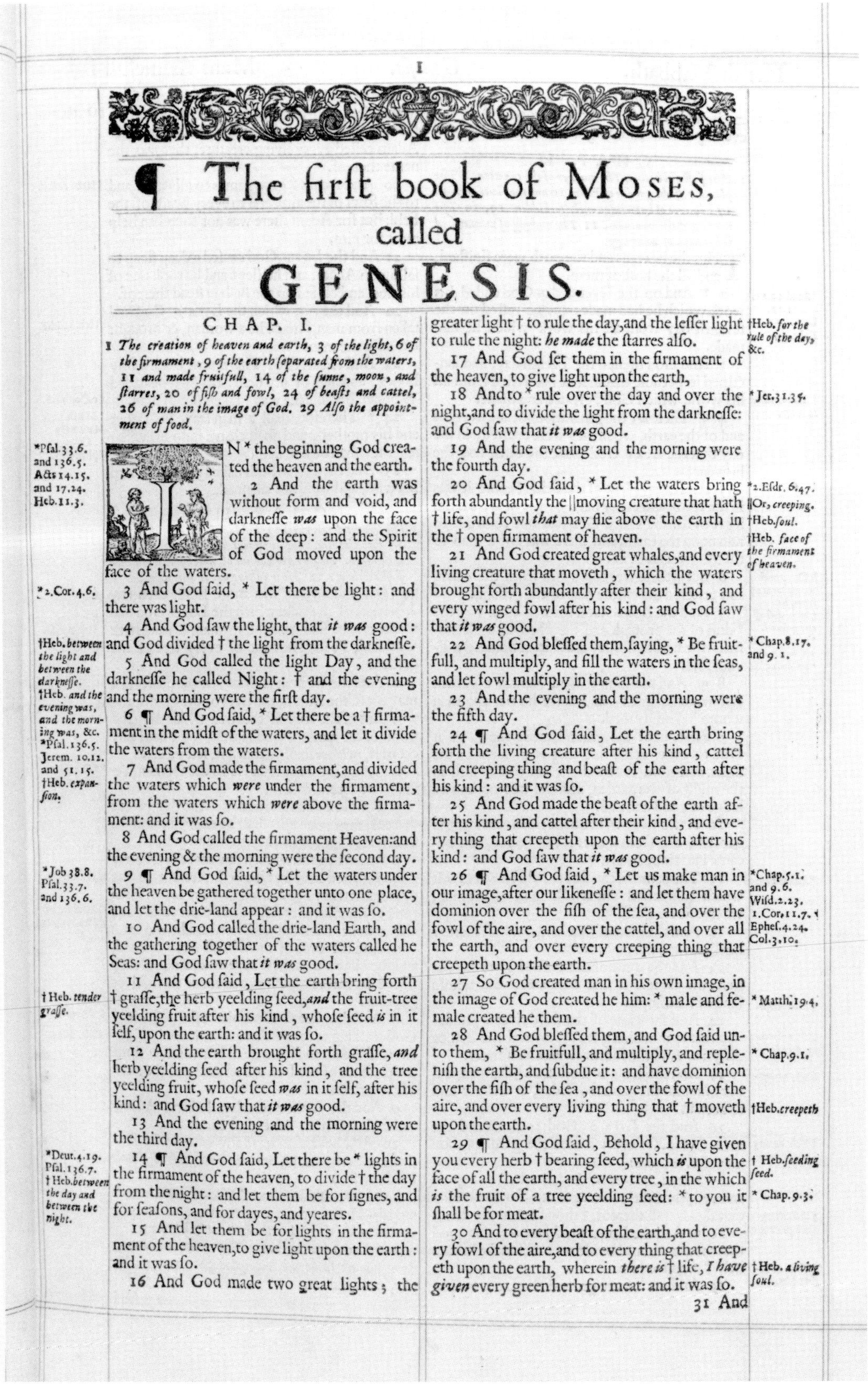

¶ The first book of MOSES,

called

GENESIS.

CHAP. I.

1 *The creation of heaven and earth, 3 of the light, 6 of the firmament, 9 of the earth separated from the waters, 11 and made fruitfull, 14 of the sunne, moon, and starres, 20 of fish and fowl, 24 of beasts and cattel, 26 of man in the image of God. 29 Also the appointment of food.*

*Pfal.33.6. and 136.5. Acts 14.15. and 17.24. Heb.11.3.

N * the beginning God created the heaven and the earth.

2 And the earth was without form and void, and darkneſſe *was* upon the face of the deep: and the Spirit of God moved upon the face of the waters.

* 2.Cor.4.6.

3 And God ſaid, * Let there be light: and there was light.

4 And God ſaw the light, that *it was* good: and God divided † the light from the darkneſſe.

†Heb. between the light and between the darkneſſe.

5 And God called the light Day, and the darkneſſe he called Night: † and the evening and the morning were the firſt day.

†Heb. and the evening was, and the morning was, &c.
*Pfal.136.5. Jerem. 10.12. and 51.15.

6 ¶ And God ſaid, * Let there be a † firmament in the midſt of the waters, and let it divide the waters from the waters.

†Heb. expanſion.

7 And God made the firmament, and divided the waters which *were* under the firmament, from the waters which *were* above the firmament: and it was ſo.

8 And God called the firmament Heaven: and the evening & the morning were the ſecond day.

* Job 38.8. Pfal.33.7. and 136.6.

9 ¶ And God ſaid, * Let the waters under the heaven be gathered together unto one place, and let the drie-land appear: and it was ſo.

10 And God called the drie-land Earth, and the gathering together of the waters called he Seas: and God ſaw that *it was* good.

11 And God ſaid, Let the earth bring forth † graſſe, the herb yeelding ſeed, *and* the fruit-tree yeelding fruit after his kind, whoſe ſeed *is* in it ſelf, upon the earth: and it was ſo.

†Heb. tender graſſe.

12 And the earth brought forth graſſe, *and* herb yeelding ſeed after his kind, and the tree yeelding fruit, whoſe ſeed *was* in it ſelf, after his kind: and God ſaw that *it was* good.

13 And the evening and the morning were the third day.

*Deut.4.19. Pfal.136.7. †Heb.between the day and between the night.

14 ¶ And God ſaid, Let there be * lights in the firmament of the heaven, to divide † the day from the night: and let them be for ſignes, and for ſeaſons, and for dayes, and yeares.

15 And let them be for lights in the firmament of the heaven, to give light upon the earth: and it was ſo.

16 And God made two great lights; the greater light † to rule the day, and the leſſer light to rule the night: *he made* the ſtarres alſo.

†Heb. for the rule of the day, &c.

17 And God ſet them in the firmament of the heaven, to give light upon the earth,

18 And to * rule over the day and over the night, and to divide the light from the darkneſſe: and God ſaw that *it was* good.

* Jer.31.35.

19 And the evening and the morning were the fourth day.

20 And God ſaid, * Let the waters bring forth abundantly the ‖moving creature that hath † life, and fowl *that* may flie above the earth in the † open firmament of heaven.

*2.Eſdr. 6.47. ‖Or, creeping. †Heb.ſoul. †Heb. face of the firmament of heaven.

21 And God created great whales, and every living creature that moveth, which the waters brought forth abundantly after their kind, and every winged fowl after his kind: and God ſaw that *it was* good.

22 And God bleſſed them, ſaying, * Be fruitfull, and multiply, and fill the waters in the ſeas, and let fowl multiply in the earth.

* Chap.8.17. and 9.1.

23 And the evening and the morning were the fifth day.

24 ¶ And God ſaid, Let the earth bring forth the living creature after his kind, cattel and creeping thing and beaſt of the earth after his kind: and it was ſo.

25 And God made the beaſt of the earth after his kind, and cattel after their kind, and every thing that creepeth upon the earth after his kind: and God ſaw that *it was* good.

26 ¶ And God ſaid, * Let us make man in our image, after our likeneſſe: and let them have dominion over the fiſh of the ſea, and over the fowl of the aire, and over the cattel, and over all the earth, and over every creeping thing that creepeth upon the earth.

*Chap.5.1. and 9.6. Wiſd.2.23. 1.Cor.11.7. Epheſ.4.24. Col.3.10.

27 So God created man in his own image, in the image of God created he him: * male and female created he them.

* Matth.19.4.

28 And God bleſſed them, and God ſaid unto them, * Be fruitfull, and multiply, and repleniſh the earth, and ſubdue it: and have dominion over the fiſh of the ſea, and over the fowl of the aire, and over every living thing that † moveth upon the earth.

* Chap.9.1.
†Heb.creepeth

29 ¶ And God ſaid, Behold, I have given you every herb † bearing ſeed, which *is* upon the face of all the earth, and every tree, in the which *is* the fruit of a tree yeelding ſeed: * to you it ſhall be for meat.

† Heb.ſeeding ſeed.
* Chap.9.3.

30 And to every beaſt of the earth, and to every fowl of the aire, and to every thing that creepeth upon the earth, wherein *there is* † life, *I have given* every green herb for meat: and it was ſo.

†Heb. a living ſoul.

31 And

Fig. 18 Adam and Eve, from the beginning of Genesis in the Bible of 1638.

56

Pſalme XCix. C. Ci.

4 'His grace and truth to Iſrael
in minde he doth record:
That all the earth hath ſeen right well
the goodneſſe of the Lord.

5 Be glad in him with joyfull voice,
all people of the earth :
Give thanks to God, ſing and rejoyce
to him with joy and mirth.

6 Upon the harp unto him ſing,
give thanks to him with pſalmes:
Rejoyce before the Lord our king
with trumpets and with ſhalmes.

7 Yea let the ſea with all therein
for joy both roar and ſwell:
The earth likewiſe let it begin,
with all that therein dwell.

8 And let the flouds rejoyce their fils,
and clap their hands apace:
And eke the mountains and the hils,
before the Lord his face.

9 For he ſhall come to judge and trie
the world and every wight:
And rule the people mightily
with juſtice and with right.

Dominus regnavit. Pſal. XCix. J.H.

*He commendeth the power, equity, and excellency of
the kingdome of God, by Chriſt, over the Jews and Gen-
tiles, provoking them to magnifie the ſame, and to ſerve
the Lord, as the ancient fathers, Moſes, Aaron, and Samuel, who calling upon God, were heard in their prayers.*

Sing this as the 77 pſalme.

THe Lord doth reigne, although at it

Jubilate Deo. Pſal. C. J.H.

*He exhorteth all men to ſerve the Lord, who hath made
us to enter into his courts and aſſemblies, to praiſe his
name.*

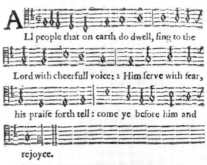

ALl people that on earth do dwell, ſing to the

Lord with cheerfull voice: 2 Him ſerve with fear,

his praiſe forth tell: come ye before him and

rejoyce.

3 The Lord ye know is God indeed,
without our aid he did us make:
We are his flock, he doth us feed;
and for his ſheep he doth us take.

4 O enter then his gates with praiſe,
approach with joy his courts unto:
Praiſe, laud, and bleſſe his name alwaies,
for it is ſeemly ſo to do.

5 For why? the Lord our God is good,
his mercy is for ever ſure:
His truth at all times firmly ſtood,
and ſhall from age to age endure.

Another of the ſame, by J.H.

Sing this as the 68 pſalme.

Fig. 19 The 'Old hundredth', from Thomas Sternhold and John Hopkins, *The whole book of psalmes
collected into English meeter*, f°, 1629. Music printing in seventeenth-century Cambridge was
rudimentary, and generally restricted to the few lines required for copies of the metrical Psalms
to be bound up with the Bible and Book of Common Prayer.

forward at this time are to be believed, foreign-printed editions of English
authors were not necessarily evidence of overseas popularity, but, partly at
least, a reflection of the need for London booksellers to have their books
printed as cheaply as possible. Cologne and Paris were said to be favourite
bases, whence cheaply printed books could be imported and charged at forty
or fifty shillings a ream, that is, four or five times the cost of manufacture.[32]
The response to this officially was, as we have seen, a proclamation in
1625 forbidding the importation of editions of books already printed at the
university presses.[33]

This was some protection to the printers, but very little to the booksellers,
who were still victims, potential or actual, of a system that concentrated book

imports in the hands of a London cartel less concerned (despite protestations to the contrary) to control the import of popish or seditious books than to share in the profits of other imported books.

Fetherstone's emphasis a few years earlier on editions of the Fathers and of the councils of the Church, while flattering to a press which liked to be thought learned, was of little relevance to the more mundane concerns of the Cambridge printers. Roger Daniel's edition of Heinsius' *Sacrarum exercitationes ad Novum Testamentum libri XX* (1640) was the most substantial work to come from his press in response to unsatisfied demand for an overseas edition.[34] But popular textbooks, formerly printed abroad, became a mainstay, lasting (if on a lesser scale) long after Buck's contract with the Stationers had come to an end. And when Fetherstone wrote originally to the University he could not have foretold the speed with which overseas presses were to take advantage of an inadequate domestic supply of Bibles.

The University consistently claimed that privileged books printed in London were excessively priced. Under Legge it had been said that Bibles costing 4s. each in quires could be printed and sold for 2s., and metrical Psalms at 37s. a ream need cost no more than 15s.[35] Of the English Stock it was said that prices were two to three times what they could be were they printed by others.[36] The Cambridge press was intended here; but it was well known that prices also varied in London, those in the shops of Field, John Bill, Adam Islip and Felix Kingston being higher than other less privileged ones.[37] In calculation after calculation, Tabor and his advisers set out the comparative costs of printing those publications that had become the prerogative of London cartels: almanacs, Bibles, metrical Psalms, grammars, basic classical texts. The principal source of the disagreement with Buck lay in his insistence on selling a textbook to the Cambridge trade at the same rate which he was demanding in London. This unwelcome inflation affected almanacs as well.[38] Lily's grammar, once fourpence, was now sevenpence; almanacs were two shillings a hundred more than previously. Even, it was alleged, Bibles cost less in London than in Cambridge.[39] These were charges that Buck found impossible to refute; but because so large a proportion of the London equivalents lay not in production, but in profit, such comparisons bore little relation either in London or in Cambridge to true costs. In fact, the Cambridge printers could only succeed in this fiercely competitive national market if the raw material, paper, was supplied to them.

Buck's arrangements to print almanacs and schoolbooks for the London trade caused offence not only to Tabor and others who saw in this an abrogation of University responsibility. In London, the almanac and school-book monopolies belonged to the English Stock, with whom, on 22 July 1631, Buck reached agreement in the person of Edmund Weaver, its treasurer. The agreement, made at a time when the Stationers' Company itself thought it prudent to ensure that its own almanacs were of a reasonable standard, formalized two years' practice, and restricted Buck to 590 reams of paper for various kinds of almanac, of which seventy could be reserved for sale in the Cambridge district. In guaranteeing sales of 520 reams for a total of almost £400, the agreement provided just the kind of security that Buck preferred in his office.[40] Similar restrictions, and guarantees, were agreed on the printing of the metrical Psalms, whereby Buck was to print five hundred reams annually on paper supplied by Weaver.[41]

The rarity of surviving almanacs, and the complete disappearance of many editions, obscure the extent of Buck and Daniel's contribution to the genre.[42] Of the fourteen surviving titles known to have been printed at Cambridge between 1625 and 1640, none survives in a complete annual series. Moreover, only a single imperfect example survives (from 1636) of a broadside,[43] rather than an octavo, almanac; yet it is recorded that the Cambridge press printed sixty reams of broadside almanacs alone between 1631 and 1633, almost thirty thousand copies in all, with a wholesale price of less than a penny each.[44]

In 1624 the Stationers' Company had seized copies of Pond's almanac, printed by Legge.[45] But despite complaint the incident does not appear to have affected the attitude of Legge's successors, from whom editions survive for all the ensuing years with only one exception, until the agreement with Weaver. Pond's almanac was still appearing in the early eighteenth century. By 1631, indeed, Pond was also accompanied by other, almost certainly pseudonymously written, Cambridge-printed almanacs, by Peregrine Rivers, Jonathan Dove, Thomas Swallow, Eustace Clarke and, possibly, Fr. Waters.[46] In other words, Buck's agreement with the Stationers' Company should be seen as the formalizing, for both parties' benefit, of an existing situation. Further titles appeared from the Cambridge press from that date; but with very little effort the Stationers had contained, for the present, any threat from the provinces. In the context of the national trade, of a genre where in 1640 one title alone was printed in an edition of 12,000, and in 1648 another sold 15,000 copies, Buck's permitted maximum of nearly 590 reams was an important, but not a majority, ingredient.[47]

For over eighty years, almanacs formed a regular, and assured, part of the press's output. Their production was brought to an end only in 1706 when, in return for an annual payment of £210 in compensation, the University agreed to forego its right to print them.[48] From the 1620s to the opening of the eighteenth century, however, the Cambridge press was of crucial importance in the supply of the most popular single form of printed matter, a form challenged only (albeit in a much greater variety of titles) by the trade in ballads and chapbooks. Here, even more than in Bible or in schoolbook printing, a measure of agreement between London and the two university presses was essential. Buck's crude, and surreptitious, contract with the Stationers' Company was gradually refined, as cash compensation took the place of licence, and the number of almanacs printed at Cambridge was thereby reduced. Figures are available only intermittently, but they summarize clearly enough the gradual decline of Cambridge influence under Buck and Daniel as it was bought out by London interests.

Of the three different kinds of almanac in circulation – broadside, 'sort' and 'blank' (the latter two in octavo)[49] – Buck and Daniel printed 520 reams in 1631–2. Of these, twenty reams were used for 9,600 copies of the broadsides. The rest of the available paper, five hundred reams or 240,000 sheets, provided for many more in octavo. Figures for the next two years were the same,[50] and there is no reason to doubt that any significant change was made for several years thereafter. The 1639 agreement, however, brought a drastic remodelling. Its purpose was to limit the influence of the press on the most lucrative parts of the book trade. Of the three principal genres affected, schoolbooks, the Bible, and almanacs, only in the case of the last was any specific figure mentioned. In future, the London stationers were to deliver a mere five hundred reams. With this paper, no more than four different titles were to be printed, this too requiring a drastic contraction of what had once augured so well. Of the series produced in Cambridge earlier in the 1630s, only those by Jonathan Dove, Pond, Swallow and Rivers survived into the next decade. So violent a contraction, and so modest a residue, reveals the anxiety felt by the English Stock, which in the case of these titles continued to print parallel editions to meet national demand. As with the other restricted categories, Daniel was left to pursue a course that could take little advantage of this market, the scale of which is reflected in figures of a few years later, for 1664. In that year, at least 363,800 copies, covering over thirty titles, were printed in all.[51] The manner in which the Cambridge press came to be responsible for over a quarter of these, and, at the same time, the Stationers' Company consolidated its hold on the press, is explained in chapter 18 below.

Schoolbooks posed quite different questions. The expansion of formal education in early seventeenth-century England had a natural consequence for printers and stationers, as pressure was placed on the monopolies to produce an ever-increasing supply of books, to an extent well beyond anything envisaged when they had been established. Endowments for grammar schools blossomed, particularly in the second and third decades of the century. In Cambridgeshire, where there had been grammar schools at Wisbech and Ely since the 1540s, and a new grammar school was founded at Cheveley in 1568, the Perse was the first to be successfully founded in Cambridge itself – almost forty years after the Corporation had contemplated the matter – in 1615, though there had been less formal facilities available previously.[52] By 1660 there was, nationally, a grammar school for every six thousand members of the population; and by 1678 it seemed necessary to enquire 'whether the English Free Grammar Schools be over-proportion'd to the occasions of the Church and State of England'. Christopher Wase, who framed the question in order to refute it, was aware that not all parts of the country were equally well served; but he was still able to remind his readers that by this time there were free schools to be found in every market town.[53]

Though the small proportion of ordinary grammar schoolbooks to have survived makes detailed discussion impossible, it is clear that the book trade was called on for ever more copies; that the monopolies, mostly established in the sixteenth century, became commensurately more valued; and that it became generally assumed that books would be produced domestically rather than from overseas. Thomas himself had launched his career as a printer partly through his edition of Ovid, one of the staples of classical secondary education;[54] but he made no serious attempt to challenge the much more valuable properties in the most popular or elementary texts. Notwithstanding the seeming licence of the 1534 charter, Legge failed to make his way into what was by the 1620s a still more lucrative market. It was left to Buck and Daniel to achieve, albeit for only a few years, what Legge had striven for, and to do so not by antagonism (since in a schoolbook context those who already control the market will always be in a commanding position), but by negotiation and eventually licence.

In 1624 the Stationers' Company had complained of infringement of their patent for the ABC.[55] In 1629 the Privy Council specified that the University Printers might print three thousand copies of Lily's grammar each year. This was a considerable reduction, if Buck's declared stock figures of seven thousand unfinished grammars, eleven thousand unfinished primers, 304 completed grammars and nine hundred accidences are to be believed:[56] it is of course possible that he exaggerated the 'unfinished' figures so as to benefit more than was intended. As in 1629, so in 1631 he again ensured that his existing investment was not spoilt: the agreement with Weaver specified that Buck was to be permitted to complete the otherwise only doubtfully legal edition of Seton's *Dialectica*. Again, if the record of surviving copies is to be believed, this had not been printed in England since Felix Kingston's edition for the Stationers' Company of 1617, though it seems unlikely that for more than a decade the University had therefore been dependent on imported editions of this, as it was for other allegedly inaccurate foreign printings of classical texts.[57] Further, and more serious, embarrassment was avoided in the much more extensive agreement reached secretly in 1631 on Buck's printing of textbooks. In the future, he was to keep off most of the elementary ones, and concentrate, by agreement, on those most useful to the University. Of one of the most lucrative of all, Lily's grammar, no Cambridge edition survives between 1630 and 1634, when Buck's agreement with Weaver expired. But with the blessing, or at least the licence, of the Stationers' Company, the Cambridge press embarked on an ambitious programme for the publication of Latin grammars and texts. Ovid, Cicero, Virgil and Aesop (in Latin) were supported by the manuals or exercises of Vives, Ravisius Textor, Corderius, Mantuanus, Castalio, Aphthonius, Erasmus and Aldus Manutius. Most, though not all, were the subject of agreement between London and Cambridge, an agreement which, as for the almanacs, restricted Buck's edition sizes but also helped to ensure sales. For three years running, the Cambridge press printed an octavo Aesop, in editions of four thousand copies, and editions of the other texts were customarily of three thousand. All, however, were dwarfed by the *Sententiae pueriles*, a Latin conversation book by Leonhard Culmann intended for those at the very outset of their studies.[58] Fewer than three copies survive of all the editions published between the time that the Stationers' Company acquired the copyright from Henry Bynneman's estate in 1584 and 1640, and only one survives of any Cambridge edition. Yet in 1631–4 Buck and Daniel alone printed three editions, a total of eighteen thousand copies. Only one other book was printed in a comparable edition size, and that was for a similar market: but no copy survives at all of the version of Evaldus Gallus' *Pueriles confabulatiunculae* of which six thousand copies were printed at Cambridge in 1632–3.[59] Because these books were printed under licence from the Stationers' Company, and given that so few copies of any edition, whether from London or Cambridge, have survived, and many editions have vanished completely, it is not easy to tell whether or not the Cambridge output was sufficient for national needs in these years. Such is, however, at least possible. Buck's, and through him Daniel's, purpose was not in doubt. It was to share in a profitable trade by printing the most established texts. Though on the one hand they printed no edition of Lily, the most established of all – if already widely thought to be obsolete – on the other they did not challenge newcomers such as John Brinsley, whose explanation of Lily's grammar remained the preserve of individual London stationers, not of a cartel within the Company. Like the English and Latin Stocks themselves, most of Buck and Daniel's schoolbook publishing and printing was characterized by the innate conservatism of the market.[60] As if to emphasize the portrait of national demand depicted by the Press's production figures, a pupil made a note of *Librorum meorum Catalogus* on the flyleaf of his copy of John Withals' Latin dictionary (1634: 'devised for the capacitie of children, and young beginners'). First he noted Cato, Spagnuoli's *Adolescentia*, Ovid's *Epistolae* and *Metamorphoses*, Virgil, Horace, Juvenal and Persius. Then, under *libri veteri*, he listed the *Sententiae pueriles*, Corderius' *Colloquia scholastica*, Erasmus' *Colloquia*, Justinus, Sallust, Ravisius Textor's *Epistolae*, Smetius' *Prosodia*, a Thesaurus, Ravisius Textor's *Epithetorum epitome* and a *Phrases latinae*.[61] It was a list offering not the slightest hint of originality. Of all the books listed, no less than six were printed in large editions at Cambridge between 1631 and 1634 (see fig. 20).

It can have surprised no one that Buck's arrangements with the Stationers' Company proved unpopular at Cambridge. Although the quota of almanacs allowed by Buck's agreements of 1631 with Weaver, Treasurer of the Engish Stock, seems not to have been challenged, the exclusive nature of his contract to print standard textbooks was provocation in itself. Daniel's own

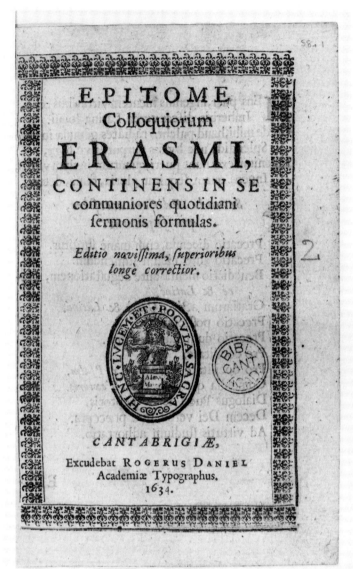

EPITOME
Colloquiorum
ERASMI,
CONTINENS IN SE
communiores quotidiani
fermonis formulas.

Editio naviſſima, ſuperioribus
longè correctior.

CANTABRIGIÆ,
Excudebat ROGERUS DANIEL
Academiæ Typographus.
1634.

Fig. 20 Textbook publishing in the 1630s.
(a) Erasmus, *Epitome colloquiorum*, 8°, 1634. Height of
original, 143 mm.

PUB.
OVIDII NASO-
NIS HEROIDUM
EPISTOLÆ,

Unà cum *A. Sabini* Epiftolis
tribus, ad totidem *Ovidi-*
anas refponforiis:

Amorum,
De arte amandi, } Libri { III.
De remedio amoris, III.
Aliáq; quæ fequens pagella
indicabit. II.

Acceſſerunt in Nafonis *Epiſtolas annotati-*
unculæ quædam è variis autoribus
hinc indè excerptæ operâ
& impenſis
CANTABRIGIENSIS ACADEMIÆ
Typographorum.

Ex Academiæ celeberrimæ
typographeo. 1635.

Fig. 20(b) Ovid, *Heroidum epistolae*, 8°, 1635. Height of original,
149 mm.

Fr. Burgersdicii
INSTITUTIONUM
LOGICARUM
Libri duo.

Ad juventutem Cantabrigiensem.

Quod vetus est, juvenes, in Relligione sequamur:
Quod placet in Logica, nil vetat esse novum.

CANTABRIGIÆ,

Ex Academiæ celeberrimæ typographeo. MDCXXXVII.

Fig. 20(c) Fr. Burgersdijck, *Institutionum logicarum libri duo*, 8°, 1637.
Height of original, 148 mm.

embarrassment in the matter, as a consequence of his covenant with Buck, is reflected in the fact that Buck was forced to promise before the Vice-Chancellor that he would give 'satisfaction' for any 'preiudice' suffered by his associate.[62] Meanwhile, however, Buck and Daniel were one and the same, in the eyes of the three principal Cambridge stationers who, in the spring of 1635, brought the matter before the Vice-Chancellor. William Williams, Francis Greene and Richard Ireland turned up more than, perhaps, they expected, and forced Buck and Daniel in another direction from the sure profits of the English and Latin Stocks.

Their arguments in the final paragraph of their deposition were not original: that the University press had become a servant to the Stationers' Company, with whom the University had argued for so long at such expense. It is not unreasonable to suspect Tabor's hand here, and it may indeed have been Tabor who saw in the booksellers' quarrel a means to attack Buck for his own ends. The other points were much more to the booksellers' own interests, and related to more particular complaints. Buck's affront was felt the more keenly in that the booksellers were expecting to deal not only with slow selling titles, of which they had taken stocks in the past, but also with titles for which rapid sales were assured.

Buck himself travelled the stock of schoolbooks to the Cambridge trade in February 1634/5. This in itself was unusual; but the offer was none the less welcome – until it emerged that although his edition of Ovid (fig. 20b) was printed, Buck was unwilling to fulfill his earlier promise. Only five hundred copies, or one-sixth of the edition, were available for the Cambridge trade, which had sought to buy not less than a third, or even the whole. The rest were for London, from whom the Cambridge booksellers could of course buy at whatever price was set by the English Stock. This unsatisfactory arrangement met with little sympathy from the Vice-Chancellor, William Beale of St John's, who used his powers to set the wholesale price in Cambridge at sevenpence a copy, or sixpence if the local trade chose to take the whole edition.[63] His decision drove each party to plot against the other. Buck countered the local booksellers' demand for the whole impression first by claiming that the sheets of the Ovid were still drying, though in fact they had been printed for several days and were awaiting the London carrier. The Cambridge booksellers, having bought the impression at sixpence a copy, quickly found themselves faced by an alliance of Buck and the Stationers' Company, who rapidly organized a new edition of two thousand copies, with a price set at fivepence – threepence less than what was customary. Buck had boasted to Williams that the Cambridge trade would not benefit, and for the present his prediction proved to be correct.

The position was complicated by others. There were plenty of people in London willing to join in a cause against the monopolists and their allies.[64] The establishment of the Latin Stock caused offence through its policy of importing texts, rather than printing them at home, a measure that helped further to restrict artificially the size of the London trade where, as a result, most journeymen had little hope of ever becoming masters. Both the English and the Latin Stocks were perceived as profiteering, setting unnecessarily high prices on books and yet answerable in practice to none but themselves.[65] In his anxiety to force for himself a share in the trade that was denied to him by his more established London colleagues, and from which he was excluded by the limitations governing the number of printers at Oxford and Cambridge, Michael Sparke had already fallen foul of the Commissioners for Causes Ecclesiastical. His collaboration with the Oxford printer, William Turner, the suspicions aroused by his dealings in Bibles and his readiness to deal in unlicensed books or other men's copies, were aspects of a business that also helped to ease Buck and Daniel's way in the London trade.[66] Sparke's first loyalties were to neither Oxford nor Cambridge, but to himself. It is therefore unfortunate that no record survives of the beginning of his correspondence with the Cambridge booksellers in the first weeks of 1634/5. Was Sparke, in fact, the instigator of the case between Buck and the booksellers; or did the booksellers appeal for help to Sparke as one who could be expected to help their case in a practical way? The brevity of the earliest surviving letter, addressed to the 'Gentellmen Bookesellers of Cambridge', makes it clear that he had received at least one letter already:

Lett me Intreet you all to Ioyne in one vnanimous Consent not to buy vp trash or the worst sorte of bookes but to buy the best I pray Lett not that privyledg go from your vniversity; that you shall be like Tantalus, but if yow would be Ruled by me I would help to put some Crownes in your purses for yow myght make a Littell myne at Cambridg and keep a settled marte do not our Bookesellers here Eate Rost meat drink wyne and you pay for it as for Exampell in Cottons Concordance they take the Cotton from yow to Lyne theyr Cotes then be advised Buy the Bybell 4to I will that yow please cary a share or be one of the 4 for it with [?] yow and steare a Corse for yow to the hauen of profitt...[67]

Sparke's allusion to the booksellers' considering buying an entire impression of a quarto Bible suggests that efforts were being made to circumvent Buck well before matters came to a head with Ovid. The rapidly developing complexity of the argument is clear from Sparke's next surviving letter, where, again, he sought to strengthen his argument by metaphor. This time he wrote to Richard Ireland:

You^r Generall Letter I Receaued wth gladnes and did apprehend a great Trade in folyo with some Comfort & Content, but it Proues to be likely to be in 32, I must Confess it did glad me and I Thought good to take John Willyames to Ioyne with me, hopeing of Rost mett, to my Crownes, but it proued a Red heringe, and Oynions, for to leave Complementts on Munday I Resolued to haue all your bookes, but I herd by Chance m^r Bucke was wth the Company, that day and on Tuesday morning the wynd Rose and then I Expected a Storme, for before night the Report was y^t the Stationers would ouerthrow Cambridg priviledge, I stird not but desyred to see the Euent and on wensdaye morning I had one of the Cheeff assistants as I may say because a Storkeeper, and a honest man, Cam to me desyred I would sett my hand to a wryting for my good wch if I would not he would not shew it me so I ryled [?] vnto it and by that menes, saw it in wch I saw at lest vnder men hands 2000 Ouids Epist, to be deliuered vnto them at 5^d a booke: so now you see what a losse it would be if I should giue such a Rate to yow, and this man tould me thay were now Resolued to do so in all bookes, I will not say Mr Buck was an Acitophell, in this but it I am perswaded it was a great part of his plott yett I would not haue yow dismayd, but doubell your Corages, and fight out a while for this may be but one shott, & the Rest false fire, I doubt not but if yow print with notes, the very Cry of Cambridge will do good, Mr Danyell I think goes to Cambridge he will tell yow all...[68]

Goaded always by the hope of profit, and therefore incapable of resistance to whichever party so much as hinted at it, Sparke was an untrustworthy ally. This letter was found by the Cambridge booksellers to be pusillanimous – 'fraught', in Richard Ireland's words, 'with needelesse feares'.[69]

What; Courage man! fear not, I & your friendes heare tooke you, till now, to be a trew Bilbo blade, & a noble Sparke: one that neither fort nor fizell could scare. lett vs be cannon proofe menn, a whole volly of that shott (you wright of) cannot daunt vs, nor would I have this littell buzinge you heard, dismaye you, you shall see all will turne to smoke, or a false fyre, or else will vanish, & proue an ignis fatuus.

The survival of a draft of Ireland's letter in the University Archives is eloquent witness of the caution with which the Cambridge booksellers felt it necessary to proceed. The exchange was not one simply of allies encouraging each other; it had become one in which the Cambridge trade had to show itself determined – possibly to an enemy. Ireland continued:

I & my fellow stationers heere, have acquaynted an ould freinde of the Stationers & ours, wth the contentes of yor letters, he sayeth he moore feareth (wch we question not) your honest, & playne dealinge wth vs, than these cunninge plottes, & devises of the partyes you wright of; he telleth vs, he well knoweth what malignant humors domineere in that Company & hath heretofore felt their pulses, & cast theire waters, yea purged & made them bleed well...

You wright they will new print that booke we have sent vpp, & sell it for 5^d a booke. oh terrible bugbeare, cann you here it wthout laughinge? Achitophell never thought wee would be gulled wth such an idle proiect. doe you beleive those (you wright of) are such dull ignorants, that they will... bringe downe the pryse of this one booke, & soe sett open a gapp for all the rest? what privileaged bookes have they that may not then be printed here; & soe wilbe vndersould to those vsuall pryses they have sett them att these many yeeres; this course will cry all downe, downe, & make even Achitophell hang himselfe, & those that thus plott agaynst vs hazard so.

The draft reveals the extent to which Sparke had become associated with the Stationers' Company – the very body from whom he seemed to wish to distance himself. 'Your Company' in draft became 'those (you wright of)';

but within a few lines these words were allowed to stay, as Ireland grew confident of the strength of the booksellers' position following the University's discovery of Buck's secret agreement.

This stirringe you wright of, will make vs, & you thus, & inable vs to eate Rost meate, & drink sack & sugar, as yor Company doe after there meetinges; therefore rest contented, let nature worke a whyle, & you shall see the desease breake out in some terrible botch, that cannot be cured, w^{h}out such an incision, that it will hazard some of the best members whereby they subsist.

Our Printers are now discovered to have bene of late your Companyes iourney men, & our presses their harbages; & that is the reason, you & we have beene iaded, & fedd wth that coarse meat you wright of, be you trew, & honest to vs, & with speed helpe of this booke, wee know the pryse is easey, & the booke vendible & you shall finde we will be trew to you, & accomplish your desyer accordinge to your former requestes. only in this small matter deceive vs not, & you shall see we will double our files, & courages for the hon^r of our vniversitye, & good of those that wish well to it; we are sure to have stout & skillfull leaders, & such as neither feare the shott nor fyre you dreame of...

The Cambridge booksellers had come as close as they dared to accusing Sparke of conniving with the London trade. From the first, the partnership had promised to be a risky one; the dangers could now no longer be avoided, and when on 12 May they wrote again they cannot have expected to be accommodated. The conciliatory appearance of the opening of their earlier letter, 'Good Mr Sparke', became plain 'Mr Sparke':

We are troubled heere & some of our friendes wth vs, that demurrs & delayes are made in takeinge of our Ovides Epistles at 7^d, wch the stationers now sell for 8^d & 10^d, there cann be noe direct dealinge in this, & therefore we praye your direct answer, whether you will take them or not, that soe we maye returne & vent them an other way, wch nowe is offered, we feare not, but rather desyre that the Company will sell theirs at 5^d a peece, to bringe downe our pryse, & spoyle our sale. you & we will gayne by this course. we praye your answer this weeke w^{t}hout fayle...[70]

Tabor, the University Registrary, had meanwhile not been idle either, first in gathering information about the detailed financial affairs of the partners in the English and Latin Stocks, and second in pursuing a separate correspondence with another London bookseller, Henry Fetherstone, whose independent, yet informed, attitude to the Stationers' Company promised a route to compromise. Fetherstone was a familiar figure to Cambridge, his catalogues, printed by John Legate's son, even bearing the University Printers' device on their title-pages. He had been a member of the Court of the Stationers' Company since 1630, and in July 1635 was to be elected Warden. Although by then he had retired as one of the trade's principal importers, he was a figure of some significance both in London and to the University.[71] Tabor may well also have been aware of his unwillingness to let a status quo be taken for granted. Certainly Fetherstone was a man more cautious, more influential, more imaginative, and (not entirely irrelevantly) more wealthy, than Sparke. When Ireland wrote his last letter to Sparke, Fetherstone and Tabor were already in correspondence – originally about other matters, including the affairs of another Cambridge bookbinder, Henry Moody, but eventually about the way best to deal with Buck.[72] Fetherstone had his own anxieties in London about the future of the Latin trade,[73] and favoured conciliation rather than confrontation. Astutely, he recognized Tabor's fears, and thus Tabor found much in his letter to approve: 'The only ende of my wrighting is to offer to you such propositions as should accordinglie redowne to the benifitt of your vniuersitie, in a liberall & anuall way.' 'Rest assured that wherin I maye doe your vniuersitie seruis without preiudising our corporation, I shalbe most readie to expresse my vtmost endeuors.'[74] Fetherstone's hints, supported with a friendly postscript promising to attend to Tabor's need for spectacles, led in turn to a meeting between the two men at the George at Ware, roughly half-way between London and Cambridge, Fetherstone and his party 'to be there soe tymelie to bespeake your dinner but if you chance to be thare first be pleased to doe ye licke for vs that soe we maye haue the benifitt of the after none to confer of our busines, & y^t if any difference or difficultie arises, by taking the counsell of our fellowes, the next morning we may ye more easilie reconsile it'.[75] Even seven years previously, such a meeting would have been thought compromising; and even now Fetherstone showed considerable anxiety that the meeting should be kept confidential.

The row that had University officers against each other, and forced into the open the Cambridge booksellers' dislike of Thomas Buck, was brought formally to an end on 27 October 1635. Buck and Daniel agreed in future not to commit any edition to the Stationers' Company or to the King's Printer without first offering such an edition to the local trade at a rate to be determined by the Vice-Chancellor. Editions of the Bible and of Lily's grammar were the last books allowed through under an arrangement that had infringed the University's own regulations, and threatened to destroy its independence in respect of printing.[76]

Four years later, in 1639, Buck and Daniel claimed to have been printing Bibles, service books, singing Psalms, grammars and other schoolbooks for many years past.[77] It was no intention of the Vice-Chancellor to bring such work to an abrupt halt, but only to bring it back under Cambridge, rather than London, control. Tabor's and Fetherstone's mutual political acumen proved in the end irrelevant, and from the first it must have been doubtful how much Fetherstone himself could sway his fellow stationers. But despite Buck and Daniel's bold claims in 1639, in fact the standard texts they had printed in the earlier part of the decade became of progressively less importance proportionate to the output of their press as a whole. Their list instead became considerably more general, as Daniel pursued a course that he had already begun, one that was no longer either dominated by the easy profits of schoolbooks, nor restricted by University myopia. Buck had tried the first course, taking Daniel with him as an unresisting partner. Legge had failed with the second. Though by no means entirely independent, Daniel could now follow the third, comparatively unhindered by his discredited, if not absolutely disgraced, co-printer.

The compact between the Stationers' Company and the Cambridge press reached in 1631 had had much in it of compromise, just as had the decision in 1629 to allow Cambridge to print only folio and quarto Bibles. As so often with compromise, the results were not as the parties had assumed. Schoolbook texts became a staple part of the Cambridge output, while the almanac contract helped to bring further profit. But the market became overstocked, especially with Cambridge editions of schoolbooks, in a situation that could benefit neither party. In the case of Bibles (a trade which included the associated prayer book and the metrical Psalms), first the 1629 folio had proved Cambridge's ability, and then that of 1638 introduced into the market a text of demonstrable superiority.

The next agreement reached with the English Stock, on 5 September 1639, made no allusion to any specific contract to print school or religious books for the London trade, and was a more amicable document designed to safeguard the interests of both parties simultaneously. Once again, it limited the extent to which the Press could print in these categories, in that the numbers were effectively set by the members of the English Stock; but there was no suggestion of a guaranteed contract for a specific number. Prices to Cambridge booksellers were, moreover, to be set by the Vice-Chancellor, as had always been required by the University.

Apart from this welcome attention to the University's own regulations, the 1639 contract, which was designed to last for ten years, affected the press in two crucial respects. First, it restricted Buck and Daniel's freedom to print the Bible, at just the time when their reputation as Bible printers was at its peak following the publication of the new revision of 1638. After the agreement, no quarto Bible appeared from the Cambridge press until 1663 apart from a reissue of the most recent edition (1638) in 1640. No octavo appeared until 1657, and no folio until 1660. Daniel next printed a quarto edition in London, in 1653, after he had left Cambridge. Most of the editions in smaller formats attributed to the University Printers in the 1640s are suspect. The 1638 text, so generally respected, was of no commercial benefit to those who had printed and published it, once the first edition was sold. Second, almanac printing was to continue, but to be limited to just fifty reams (the paper to be supplied by the English Stock, as a control), and four titles only. In return, Thomas Buck was to receive £75 per annum, and Daniel £125, the proportions once again reflecting Buck's position as an inactive partner.

For the Company, the purpose of the 1639 agreement with Cambridge was the same as that reached with Oxford two years previously: not to disable the press entirely (a course which had already proved impractical), but to limit its impact on the wealthiest of the London stationers by restricting manufacture of those books considered to be the property of the King's Printer, or of the English Stock. Although individuals in both universities alluded to their common cause, and legislation such as that governing the number of presses, or restricting the import of books, had spoken of both jointly, the most important decisions as to each university's freedom were taken with regard to each separately. Thus the order by the Privy Council of April 1629, and before it the order of December 1623, permitting a limited amount of comprinting with the King's Printers and the Stationers' Company, and otherwise giving the Cambridge press considerable freedom (albeit more limited than was claimed under the 1534 charter), had referred to Cambridge alone. Similar rights and restrictions were granted to Oxford only in 1636;[78] and in the following year Oxford and the Company came to an agreement about the printing of Bibles, in a move that sought by its prophylactic nature to avoid complications such as those at Cambridge.[79] In return for £200 per annum, it was agreed that the Oxford press should refrain from printing either Bibles, other books belonging to the King's Printers, or Lily's grammar.[80] These documents made much of Cambridge precedent, but the turn of Cambridge came again with the similar agreement in 1639 – though unlike their opposite numbers at Oxford, Buck and Daniel were also left with a modicum of the almanac trade and the expectation of further work for the English Stock. 'At a cost of £200 a year, competition from Cambridge had been bought off', wrote Blagden, with Company eyes.[81] The benefits were not wholly one-sided. Apart from the financial *douceur*, the Cambridge printers were relieved of embarrassing overstock, which was now to be sold on their behalf in a wider market; and they could concentrate on the learned press. Whelock's Bede, for which the investment was considerable, was to be one of the first results.

Once again, the 1639 agreement explicitly distinguished between the prices current in London and in Cambridge. As we have seen, this was at the seat of the difficulties between Buck and his fellow townsmen. The price structure of some of the most relevant parts of the book trade, involving paper supply, printing and wholesale costs, form the subject of a later chapter.

~~~ 11 ~~~

Books for university teaching

As has been emphasised in the foregoing pages, the more successful Cambridge printers always relied on there being sufficient demand for standard works, be they Bibles, schoolbooks, university textbooks or almanacs. Without that economic base, the press rapidly became commercially impractical. In the 1630s, Buck and Daniel became the country's principal suppliers of the ordinary elementary Latin texts, producing a list that was remarkably akin to the books listed in the schoolbook privilege granted to the London printer Thomas Marsh in 1572.[1] Of the twelve there specified, Buck and Daniel printed at least seven, some in several editions. Such national markets in textbooks were of much more value than any the University might provide. Nonetheless, the relationship between successive University Printers and the University curriculum is of central importance in the relationship between two activities of the University: teaching and printing.[2] In 1534 the charter had been not only a licence to print, but also, and at the time more importantly, a protection for the University's own teaching and other scholarly interests. In 1583, Thomas Thomas embarked on his new venture with an over-riding purpose: to print texts for teaching in Cambridge, whether Pliny, Ramus or Ovid. His dictionary maintained its hold on the Cambridge curriculum until at least the 1630s, outstripping its immediate, and slightly later, rival by John Rider.[3] Within a few years of Thomas's embarking on this course, however, this central concern for the University's curriculum had been displaced. Although there were many books designed principally for the local trade, the pattern promised by Thomas never became established. There were, of course, notable and successful exceptions, such as Winterton's *Poetae minores Graeci* (see fig. 21). It is noticeable also that one of the most frequently printed books other than the ordinary monopolies was Winterton's translation of Drexelius' tiny *Considerations upon eternitie*, of which at least five editions were printed at Cambridge between 1636 and 1650. But in practice, despite the existence of a press at Cambridge, most of the books needed for teaching in the University were still imported from abroad, or brought from London or Oxford.

The principal exception was Franciscus Burgersdijck's *Institutionum logicarum libri II*, first published at Leiden in 1626 and nowhere more popular

Fig. 21 *Poetae minores Graeci*, edited by Ralph Winterton (1600–36), 8°,
1635. The inscription is by Daniel himself, but the leaf has been inlaid and the
Greek inscription has been added later. Original plate-mark, 137 mm. high.

than at Cambridge (see fig. 20).[4] Editions were printed seven times by the University Printers between 1637 and 1680, as well as by the recently disgraced Daniel in 1651. No other Cambridge textbook surpassed, or even challenged it, as it eclipsed even Ramus. Burgersdijck's *Idea philosophiae*, first published in England at Oxford in 1631, was on the other hand never printed at Cambridge, which therefore depended on one of the several Oxford editions, or on those printed in the Low Countries. Of the other central texts, Eustachius' *Summa philosophiae* had already reached its seventh edition at Paris in 1623, and other editions appeared in the Low Countries. It soon became clear, however, that one part of this fairly long text, printed twice in rapid succession by Daniel at Cambridge in 1648–9, was of more interest than others in the University. The *Ethica* ('very good, & may be read in a short time', according to Holdsworth) was printed on its own twice at Cambridge between 1640 and 1654, before it was taken over by London printers including, in 1658, by Daniel. Like Burgersdijck, it remained in use in Cambridge until the early eighteenth century.

So too, for Greek grammar, Clenardus was displaced by Possel, whose Σύνταξις *graeca* was printed by Daniel (for Francis Eglesfield, in London) in 1640. Possel's various manuals were widely used in Cambridge, though no edition was printed there of his steady-selling colloquies, which remained a product of the London press alone, and the privilege of the Stationers' Company. But in addition many other copies of the Σύνταξις, of his *Apophthegmata* and of his *Calligraphia oratoria*, as well as of his colloquies, also found their way in from overseas presses. A similar pattern emerged in Hebrew, for which the favoured teaching authority by the mid-seventeenth century was Johann Buxtorf. His convenient *Epitome grammaticae*, 'breviter & methodice ad publicum scholarum usum proposita', was printed twice by Daniel, once at Cambridge in 1646, and then again at London in 1653. By 1669 it had reached what was described as the tenth edition, printed however in London. But the *Epitome* was also available in editions printed elsewhere, at Basel, Utrecht or Amsterdam, and all found their way to Cambridge. Of his other works, his octavo *Lexicon Hebraicum*, printed once only in London, in 1646, was never printed at Cambridge. Instead, copies were also imported from Basel or Amsterdam, while others again preferred his *Thesaurus grammaticus*, printed regularly at Basel. So also, his *Grammatica Chaldaica et Syriaca* was used, for years after publication, in the Basel edition of 1615.

Again, in other words, it seems that Daniel was most adventurous, most willing to print an edition in the face of existing imports from overseas, and persisting, even after he had returned to London, in printing for the university market, the one he had come to understand. Buxtorf's *Epitome* had been entered to two London booksellers in 1644,[5] who never however produced their edition: Daniel's came out two years later, without reference to the Stationers' Register. Though successive entries in the Register reveal considerable concern about ownership of Buxtorf's *Lexicon*, from 1644 onwards, no edition was printed in England except for that of 1646. Nor did anything come in London of a translation of the *Epitome*, or of a London edition of the *Thesaurus*.[6] In the end, as so often, self-interest outweighed intellectual interest. Yet with Daniel's departure the University's needs were put on a different footing once again, requiring more books printed in London, and more from abroad, to meet a situation where only the commonest texts were normally printed close at hand. The position was made all the more complicated as the list of books recommended for study became ever more diverse, in the face of debate in mathematics, philosophy, and natural philosophy.

The curriculum, so carefully controlled in sixteenth-century statutes, was much less restrictive than the legislation made it appear. In a university which sought to educate boys from very different social backgrounds, with a correspondingly diverse future before them, where there was always a broad division between those intended for a life in the church and those expected to pursue a secular career, this was inevitable. There was, naturally, much uniformity. At Magdalene College in 1610 the books amongst the possessions of an undergraduate seized by a tutor as recompense for debt offered little out of the ordinary: various octavo copies of Cicero, Nizolius' *Thesaurus Ciceronianus*, a 32° volume of Horace, Juvenal and Persius, an octavo Virgil, Seton's *Logic*, Ramus and Talaeus' *Rhetorica*, another work by Talaeus and a Lycosthenes. Together with a hint of more personal tastes, *De moribus Turcarum*, this minimal collection was valued at but four shillings in all.[7] But the shift in emphasis from University to college as the centre of education, and with it the increasing influence of individual tutors, encouraged individuality still more.[8] The accounts kept by Joseph Mede at Christ's between 1614 and 1637 reveal a pattern of recommendation, purchase and (by implication) study remarkable primarily for its flexibility, and for its interweaving of curriculum and education.[9]

Mede's biographer John Worthington was later to confirm the evidence of these accounts:

he preserv'd his knowledge in Academick Learning by the private lectures which he read to his Pupils, to whom he was an able and faithful Guide. For, being a Fellow of a Colledge, he esteem'd it a part of his Duty to further the Education of young Scholars; which made him undertake the careful charge of a *Tutor*: and this he managed with great Prudence and equal Diligence. After he had by daily Lectures well grounded his Pupils in Humanity, Logick and Philosophy, and by frequent converse understood to what particular Studies their Parts might most profitably applied, he gave them his Advice accordingly: And when they were able to go alone, he chose rather to set every one his daily Task, than constantly to confine himself and them to precise hours for Lectures. In the Evening they all came to his Chamber to satisfie him that they had perform'd the Task he had set them. The first question which he us'd then to propound to every one in his order was, *Quid dubitas? What Doubts have you met in your studies to day?* (For he supposed that *To doubt nothing* and *To understand nothing* were verifiable alike.)[10]

The small part played by the University Printers, even thirty years after Thomas's death, is clearly to be seen in Mede's accounts. The standard introduction to the Cambridge curriculum was Keckerman on logic – never printed at Cambridge and apparently only once printed in England, in 1606:[11] all copies had to come from abroad. In 1617, for example, one Edward Dudley entered Christ's as a Fellow-Commoner. Although others in his position followed a more relaxed course of reading, Dudley seems to have kept to one notable for its ordinariness: logic, Greek (Camden's grammar and the *Iliad*) and the Heidelberg catechism in his first months were followed by Keckerman on ethics, physics, and (again) rhetoric, Hebrew (Buxtorf's grammar) and Cornelius Schonaeus' *Terentius Christianus* in 1618, and yet more Keckerman (theology), Erasmus, Martial, Socrates, Ovid, Cicero, the *Odyssey*, Seneca, Sleidan's *De quatuor monarchis*, Ortelius' *Theatrum epitome* and the Greek New Testament in 1619. The occasional modicum of relief, such as Persius in English, and Giovanni Botero's *Relations of the most famous kingdoms* in 1618, or the less textbook-bound course in 1619, merely serves as a reminder of how far the major part of an undergraduate's reading depended on imported books. In 1619, Dudley would certainly have used an edition of John Rainolds' *Orations* from the Oxford press; but it must be less likely that he would have used the Cambridge Ovid of 1584.[12]

Mede was perhaps exceptional in the range of his accomplishments, listed by Worthington as encompassing logic, mathematics, philosophy, anatomy, botany, philology, history and chronology, quite apart from theology;[13] but others shared some of his interests. At Emmanuel, the young John Wallis, future Savilian Professor of Mathematics at Oxford, came up from Ashford School in December 1632 already determined (according to his own account) to pursue mathematics 'not as a formal Study, but as a pleasing Diversion, at spare hours'. Emmanuel produced hardly anyone as competent as he, and the University as a whole (so Wallis claimed) did not look upon it as 'academical learning'.[14] Like most undergraduates, he began with logic, proceeding thence to ethics, physics and metaphysics. From there he moved on to medicine and anatomy (in which he was the first to defend Harvey's theory of the circulation of the blood in a public disputation at Cambridge), to astronomy and geography ('as parts of Natural Philosophy') and other parts of mathematics. 'For', as he later recalled, 'I made no Scruple of diverting (from the common road of Studies then in fashion) to any part of Learning'.[15] There is some danger in attributing too much to the generality, and concluding too much from such individual instances of exceptional pupils, and from recollections years later, by which time the studies of some of the subjects remembered had changed very considerably. But such examples do not suggest a University devoted wholly to preserving an outmoded curriculum.

Indeed, Milton's sneering dismissal of the 'scragged and thorny lectures of monkish and miserable sophistry' was scarcely relevant by the time he wrote, in 1641.[16] The celebrated story of Seth Ward's failure to find anyone capable of teaching him mathematics at Sidney Sussex College in the early 1630s cannot perhaps be accounted as typical. Just along the road, at Christ's, Mede was encouraging his pupils to read Gemma Frisius for arithmetic and Peter Ryff for geometry, as well as Keckerman and Blundeville, quite apart from historical, theological and geographical texts. However, modern editions of such authors were not available from the Cambridge press, nor, apart from Blundeville, even from those in London.[17]

Though Ramist thought continued to permeate the official curriculum, no edition of the *Dialectica* was printed at Cambridge between 1592 and 1640. Instead, the textbooks in logic adopted for college and university teaching became ever more diverse. Mede alone recommended, or had recourse to, about thirty different texts between 1620 and 1630.[18] Seton, the text generally favoured in Cambridge, and even on occasion written into college statutes in an irregular bid to formalize arrangements,[19] was controlled by the Stationers' Company, and printed at London in 1617. But then (or so it seems from surviving copies) there was a gap, and no further edition apparently appeared until that at Cambridge in 1631, the one occasion on which any Cambridge printer was associated with this, one of the most demanded of all texts. No edition was printed in England in the seventeenth century after the next, published at London in 1639. Instead, the cheap logic texts by Samuel Smith and Robert Sanderson (both Oxford men) and Pierre Du Moulin costing threepence or fourpence apiece, jostled with the slightly more expensive equivalents by Edward Brerewood and Richard Crackanthorp. All in the end were displaced by Burgersdijck's *Institutiones logicae*. It alone attained general approbation at Cambridge.[20]

In a curriculum whose most obvious feature had become diversity, the position of University Printer as supplier (such as Thomas had envisaged, and Legate at first assumed) was untenable except for the most commonly used texts. As the proportion of members of the University who took no degree increased, and tutors such as Mede or Holdsworth met the needs of gentlemen's sons for a general education rather than a specifically clerical or professional career, so University Printers could expect less. They became, perforce, general printers tied to the London trade. Simplicius' song in Thomas Randolph's play *Aristippus, or, the ioviall philosopher* (1630) spoke of familiar names, but they were more familiar to some than to others:

> Hang Brirewood and Carter, in Crakenthorps Garter,
> Let Keckerman too bemoane us,
> Ile be no more beaten, for greasie Iacke Seaton,
> Or conning of Sandersonus.[21]

Against such a background, Holdsworth's alternative suggestions to the traditional curriculum, made in the late 1640s but based on experiences of a decade and more previously, are of considerable interest. Because each tutor was in a measure free to recommend alternative reading towards a general gentlemanly education, as well as choose amongst a much increased range of textbooks in logic, rhetoric and philosophy, this part of his *Directions* is less easily demonstrable to have been of general application. But while the individuality of Holdsworth's scheme can only be gauged approximately, the generality of the student was familiar:

Such as come to the University not with intention to make Scholarship their profession, but only to gett such learning as may serve for delight and ornament and such as the want wherof would speake a defect in breeding rather then Scholarship, may instead of the harsher studies prescribed Callendar read some of these or the like.

Of the following forty-odd suggestions, Thomas Fuller's *Holy state* and *Holy warre*, George Herbert and Richard Crashaw had all been printed recently at Cambridge, to mix in Holdsworth's list with *The anatomy of melancholy*, *Utopia*, *Mercurius Britannicus*, Sandys' Ovid, Thomas Browne, Francis Bacon, Overbury's and Earle's *Characters*, Sir Henry Blount on the Levant, and Thomas Godwin on Jewish antiquities.[22]

Little has so far been assembled on the usually tiny collections of books actually owned by undergraduates, rather than those recommended to them. Mede's accounts, though serving his own pupils in many of their daily needs, naturally took little notice of the informal or formal trading of textbooks from generation to generation. Nor could they reach beyond his own college. Holdsworth's *Directions*, for all their appearance of comprehensiveness, were likewise personal, a theory for his own pupils that may even never have been put into practice. One fortunate survival, from Holdsworth's own college, offers what must be a general caveat. When in January 1639/40 the possessions of Samuel Dike, an undergraduate at Emmanuel, were distrained for debt, his two dozen or so books were seized as well. Apart from the obligatory copies of Scapula's Greek lexicon and Thomas's Latin dictionary (a late survival: it had not been printed since 1631), the modest collection of essentials included Lycosthenes' *Apophthegmata*, Nicholas Ling's *Wits commonwealth*, Thomas Draxe's *Calliepeia: or a rich store-house of Latine words and phrases*, poetry by Thomas Heywood and William Ames' *Medulla S.S. theologiae*, none listed or recommended by either Holdsworth a few years later, or by Mede in the previous few years at Christ's. Nor did Holdsworth suggest Smetius on prosody, Richard Rogers' *Practice of Christianitie*, Nicolaus Reusner's

Symbolorum imperatorium classes, Valerius Maximus, or even Seton or Ramus. All were found amongst Dike's possessions, a collection that was noticeably conservative in its thrust.[23] No details were provided of editions, though it is probable his copy of Cicero's *De officiis* was from one of the many Cambridge editions of the 1630s. Seton's *Dialectica* had not been printed at Cambridge since 1631, Ramus's *Logic* not since 1592, and Sabin's Ovid not since 1584.[24]

Mede at Christ's, Holdsworth at Emmanuel, and (later in the century) Samuel Blythe at Clare have been widely quoted for the evidence their accounts or instructions provide of undergraduate education. Their evidence is partial, both carrying an unknown weight of individuality, and representing but a small portion of a university composed of colleges whose diversity was readily apparent. Other evidence is however available. First, though incomplete because so many books have been discarded, the surviving copies of books once belonging to undergraduates confirm not only many of Mede's and Holdsworth's preoccupations, but also make it clear that editions of the same title printed in Britain and overseas existed side by side in Cambridge. The same is equally clear of booksellers' stocklists, though few of the surviving inventories of Cambridge booksellers indicate which exact editions were to hand, and much must therefore be inferred. Roger Suckerman, for example, by no means the most important of the booksellers in Cambridge, had in 1638 an appreciable stock of duodecimos and other small formats from Amsterdam, of Latin texts as well as (amongst much more) Cluverius, Owen's Latin epigrams, Justus Lipsius, Erasmus and Ausonius, besides Ames' *Medulla S.S. theologiae* and *Coronis* – both also published in London.[25] His copies of Epictetus and of Theophrastus in Greek were both from Leiden, Scaliger's Caesar and Heinsius' Virgil both from the Elzevir printing house.[26]

The pattern of publishing of what may be termed core texts (though they were not compulsory), the interval between one edition and the next, and the various editorial changes in each, coupled also with the records of local bookselling, provide a context of interests and preoccupations more generally applicable to the University as a whole. Thus in the early 1630s another Cambridge bookseller, Peter Scarlet, resident since at least 1590 and by now a senior figure in the local trade, supplied various books to his more junior colleague Francis Greene. Apart from odd copies of *Hamlet*, of *Bevis of Hampton*, a popular account of Samson and quantities of almanacs, Greene took multiple copies of Phineas Fletcher's *Locustae* (printed at Cambridge in 1627, and clearly still in print, some at least of the stock owned by Scarlet), of Perkins' so-called catechism, *The foundation of Christian religion*, of Robert Sanderson's *Logicae artis compendium* (printed most recently at Oxford in 1631), of Ovid *De tristibus*, and of Nicholas Byfield's best-selling *Marrows of the oracles of God*, of which in the 1630s the printing was by John Legate. The brief excitement generated by John Russell, of Magdalene, whose verse account of *The two famous pitcht battels of Lypsich and Lutzen* was published by Philip

Scarlet in 1634, was represented by Greene's order for twenty-three copies. Ryf on geometry, Richard Crakanthorp on metaphysics, Keckerman on logic and on mathematics, Du Moulin and Downame on logic, all also featured, if less prominently.[27]

At about the same time, another Cambridge bookseller, Troylus Atkinson, was supplied by the London bookseller Robert Allot, who seems to have operated as a wholesaler as well as a publisher. If Atkinson stocked undergraduate books in quantity, as he almost certainly did in his shop in Great St Mary's parish, he was not supplied by Allot.[28] The two men's dealings seem barely to have touched on most of the usual texts in logic, rhetoric or philosophy. Even Rider's dictionary, the handbook for those who did not wish to use Thomas's, figured only twice in their accounts for the whole of 1634. Instead of the originals, Atkinson bought from Allot English translations – of Aristotle's *Problems*, of Virgil, of Persius, of Lucan, of Phalaris, of Homer, even, once, of Thucydides, in Hobbes' unsuccessful version. In June 1634, exceptionally, he bought copies of Farnaby's octavo Seneca and Virgil. The same month he also ventured into French, buying Maupas' new *French grammar and syntaxe* and La Primaudaye's *French academie* in the 1618 edition, following these in October with, again, cheaper textbooks, Robert Sherwood's *French tutor* and Claude Holyband's longer established *French schoolmaster*. Though, as for most of his new books, Atkinson did not restock these books – at least from Allot – his interest in these French aids was probably no sudden enthusiasm. Only two years later, in 1636, Daniel was to print Gabriel Dugrès' *Breve et accuratum grammaticae Gallicae compendium* 'impensis authoris amicorum gratiâ' (see fig. 14 on pp. 178–9 above), a book that marked the peak of its author's career teaching the language at Cambridge from 1631.

Atkinson stocked most books in up to three or four copies at most, and often in a single copy only – even if it meant reordering unexpectedly soon. Whether or not this was a result of customers' requests, rather than his prudence, capital or willingness or otherwise to venture a new work on his shelves is of course irrecoverable. Even Bibles were supplied two or three at a time, coming ready bound, like the majority of the books, and occasionally gilt tooled as well. Of more ordinary books, by far the most popular were Bayly's *Practice of piety*, published by Allot since 1626, Quarles' poems, and Perkins' catechism (published by 1633 also by Allot, and of which Atkinson took twenty-five for 2s.6d., or about $1\frac{1}{4}$d. apiece, in February 1633/4). In June he took no less than twenty-five copies of the new edition of William Fulke's *Most pleasant prospect into the garden of natural contemplation, to behold the naturall causes of all kinde of meteors*, a popular guide (not printed since 1602) also to such matters as weather forecasting, the movements of tides, and elementary metallurgy. Like much of Atkinson's stock, it was intended for a market well beyond the confines of the University.

Cambridge academic plays recurred often, most notably *Ignoramus* but also

Pedantius, Edmund Stubbe's *Fraus honesta*, and Thomas Tomkis' *Albumaȝar*, all but the last published as recently as 1630–2. Atkinson had much less demand, apparently, for English plays, his purchase of two copies of Heywood's *English traveller* in October 1633, and an unspecified '3 masques' in the following February being rare exceptions. In poetry, the order for two copies of Donne's 1633 *Poems* in October 1633 was not repeated, until a volume of his juvenilia and poems came in June the following year. Herbert and Quarles were, as usual, more popular, though the appearance in January 1633/4 of the collected poems of Robert Gomersall of Christ Church, Oxford, caused a brief flurry of interest. Similarly, in May 1634 Atkinson bought three copies of William Habington's undistinguished, if well regarded, collection in praise of his wife, *Castara*, repeating the dose eighteen months later. By contrast, Atkinson's choice of Latin verse was remarkable only for its consistent poverty. The repeated invoices for Alexander Ross's latest book *Virgilius evangelisans*, published also in the winter of 1633–4, were perhaps to be expected in the wake of his established reputation as an ingenious Latinist. Three copies of his fellow Scot Andrew Ramsay's *Poemata sacra*, printed at Edinburgh in 1633 and in Atkinson's hands in September that year were, perhaps, more to test the market. The following summer Atkinson went on to buy three copies of a book printed at Cambridge but published in London by Robert Milbourn, and that had a special local interest: William Hawkins' *Corolla varia*, an ostentatiously annotated series of quasi-Virgilian verses by the Master of Hadleigh School, sought among other exercises to suggest in its author's native Cambridgeshire, and especially the country round Oakington, a landscape comparable with that to be found in the *Eclogues* themselves. Such were the books, in a university which taught the writing of Latin verse as a part of the ordinary curriculum, where aids to prosody and composition were to be found by the dozen and where national events were habitually celebrated in Latin verse, that rubbed shoulders in the bookshops with Phineas Fletcher's *Sylva poetica* and Crashaw's *Epigrammatum sacrorum liber*, printed at Cambridge in 1633 and 1634 respectively.

In theology and popular piety, apart from Bayly's bestseller, there were repeated demands for Owen Feltham's *Resolves*, for Richard Field's *Of the church*, for John Prideaux and for Peter Heylyn on the Sabbath, and for Thomas Taylor on Titus, the last not printed since 1619. The appearance at Oxford in the winter of 1633–4 of an edition of the Polish Jesuit Marcin Smiglecki's *Logica*, the first to be printed in England, elicited an immediate demand for copies, Allot supplying ten within three weeks. Characteristically, however, no more were listed in the accounts even though the book found favour at Cambridge. Other orders for multiple copies included a treatise on gout (*Gutta podagrica*, 1633), Fletcher on urine, Philip Barrough's equally long established *Method of physick*, Peter Lowe and the more recent Alexander Read on surgery, Rastell's *Termes de la ley*, George Sandys' travels, Charles Butler's *Feminine monarchie, or the history of bees*, and Thomas Moffet on insects. Atkinson took repeated consignments of Heylyn's Μικρόκοσμος ('a little description of the great world'), Burton's *Anatomy of melancholy*, and Thomas Gale's *Horologiographia, the art of dialling* and, not least, *Hocus pocus junior; the anatomie of legerdemain*, published in 1634 and rapidly republished, much enlarged, the following year. But in more than two years he bought only one copy of Gervase Markham on archery (in 1634, the year of publication), only one of Thomas Johnson's *Mercurius botanicus*, the account of a botanical excursion in the summer of that year through the south of England, and only one of Edmund Wingate's Λογαριθμοτεχνία, *or the construction and use of the logarithmeticall tables*.

There are many discrepancies about Atkinson's account, which suggest that Allot was but one of several suppliers. The practice which permitted London stationers to dump unordered books on Cambridge (and presumably other provincial) booksellers, in return for a five per cent discount, adds further possible distortion.[29] Orders for single copies, unexplained gaps in the expected reordering of popular books, and equally unexplained intrusions such as the sudden appearance of two copies of the sixth part of a newsbook, *The Swedish intelligencer*, and of its supplement, in the summer of 1634, all suggest that these records, while they may be representative of Atkinson's stock, are not an easily defined portion. Many of the books listed were, naturally, Allot's own publications, or books in which he had a more than passing interest. Of these, apart from *The practice of piety*, Heylyn's Μικρόκοσμος, Perkins' catechism, and Farnaby's Virgil, all mentioned above, Atkinson also took copies of Matthew Griffith's *Bethel*, Luis de Granada's *Meditations*, sermons by Walter Balcanquhall, Edward Boughen and George Wall, Willet's *Synopsis papismi*, and George Hakewill's *Apology of the power and providence of God*. Above all, however, Atkinson paid close attention to what was new. Cautious not to over-order, he was also alert to supply, for university and town alike, a range of new titles, and fresh editions, representative of the English trade in general. The years covered by the surviving records of his transactions with Allot, 1633–5, coincided with some of the most productive in the University printing house's history. Atkinson traded in those books, in return for credit from Allot. He sent, for example, no less than six hundred copies of George Herbert's translation of Lessius' *Hygiasticon, or the right course of preserving health* at various times between 1633 and 1634,[30] and a hundred copies of Robert Shelford's *Five pious and learned discourses* in the summer of 1635, as part payment for books from London. On occasion, he even bought Cambridge-printed books back from Allot: four copies of Donne's *Six sermons*, bought in September 1634, had been printed that year for the London booksellers Nicholas Fussell and Humphrey Moseley; and the twenty-five copies of Herbert's *Temple* bought in quires for £1.0s.10d. (10d. apiece: a wholesale price) in January 1633/4 had been in London only briefly before they returned to meet Cambridge demand. At a time when the Cambridge press was making such an effort to meet local demand, from authors and from readers or other users of print, the context that Atkinson's daybook supplies, of a wider reading public, is an essential counterweight.

He was not of course the only Cambridge stationer. In 1639/40 there were at least fifteen in the town, a number further swollen by the arrival of unauthorized immigrants from London. They relied not only on bookselling, but also on binding, a trade recently thrown into a crisis by the practice of buying books ready-bound from London – as, for example, had Atkinson.[31] These men's stocks naturally varied greatly in size, as well as in composition. But though the surviving evidence of their holdings and turnover is piecemeal, it is noticeable how few copies they owned at any one time of even the most frequently recommended books. Like Atkinson, Roger Suckerman in the late 1630s stocked quantities of *The practice of piety*. His seventeen copies, gilt-edged, were exceeded by only two other titles, both schoolbooks: Lily's grammar and the *Pueriles confabulatiunculae*. Behind it in popularity came a dozen copies of the sermons of Humphrey Sydenham, of Wadham College, Oxford, and six copies of a timely sermon by Robert Abbot, Vicar of Cranbrook in Kent, *The young man's warning-peece: or a sermon preached at the buriall of William Rogers, apothecary*.

The healthy sales that could always be assumed for Lily's grammar were reflected in the twenty-five copies, valued at 14s., in Suckerman's inventory: they were not impossibly from one of the several recent Cambridge editions. Likewise, the eighteen copies of Gallus' *Pueriles confabulatiunculae*, the half-dozen of Aesop, and the five of Corderius' *Colloquia* were also probably Cambridge imprints. The seventeen copies of *Catonis disticha*, a Stationers' Company monopoly printed in London rather than Cambridge, were for a similar market. Among other books of which Suckerman might reasonably hope for regular and appreciable sales amongst undergraduates – of Burgersdijck, of Samuel Smith, John Sanderson and Edward Brerewood on logic, the several works recently printed at Oxford of Christoph Scheibler, of Pasor's *Lexicon* of New Testament Greek, of Joannes Magirus' *Physiologia peripatetica*, he seldom had more than four copies.[32] Though the inventory was taken in October, just after the beginning of the academic year, it is difficult to argue that these consistently low figures, among five hundred-odd stocklines, the vast majority of which were of single copies, seriously misrepresent the general level of Suckerman's investment.

Most of both Atkinson's and Suckerman's trade was with members of the University. Much of it was, clearly, for junior members pursuing the various courses of reading enjoined by their tutors. But all of it was pursued only a short walk from Daniel's printing house, scarcely two hundred yards from Great St Mary's church, in whose parish the Cambridge stationers concentrated. The relationship between printer and stationer was complicated. Local booksellers not only published on their own account, with their names on title-pages (Herbert's *Temple*, bearing Francis Greene's imprint, was but one example), but also bought heavily into other books so as to be able to trade Cambridge-printed stock with London. Though Buck and Daniel were more adventurous and imaginative than other seventeenth-century Cambridge printers, and, indeed, than many in London, they could not hope to meet all the developments and variations prescribed by tutors on the themes prescribed to the University by the 1570 statutes. Their choice of books was, in the end, the result of a combination of external and university-based forces of unexpected complexity, in which the trade in particular books, like the printing of particular editions, was made to serve a purpose not necessarily obvious in the ordinary rehearsal of editions and imprints. It is this inter-relationship, based not on the demands of members of the University but on the demands of London as printer, wholesale supplier, retailer and publisher, that partly explains much of the irregularity of the Cambridge press, and the dramatic modification forced on it, away from the course set by Thomas Thomas.

What was true of local interests was true in some crucial respects of the Massachusetts colonies, which became, in effect, the University Printers' first organized overseas market. By the end of the century, with the Cambridge press identified with such standard works as Newman's Concordance to the Bible, and Gouldman's and Littleton's dictionaries, trade seemed assured. But the development of this market was slow, initiated not by printers or booksellers but in the carefully selected luggage of colonists with little space spare. Organized trade came principally, so far as the printers in Cambridge were concerned, with organized secondary and university education. And because the curriculum at the new college founded in 1636 and named after its first benefactor, John Harvard, was so closely modelled on that of Harvard's own university, the relationship between University Printers and the curriculum in Cambridge was not dissimilar from that in the new Cambridge. So, in a chapter concerned with the curriculum, it is appropriate also to consider one aspect of export, in which textbooks rubbed shoulders with theology and other interests. The market was varied, its customers those who looked backwards – and forwards – to traditions, be they educational, theological or social, each with different expectations. In some respects, the Cambridge tradition was a strong one, and nowhere more so than in secondary and higher education. But it represented only a small portion of an ever more diverse, widespread and populous country, where each succeeding generation found increasing independence.

In Cambridge, the tenuous connection between teaching needs and the local press assumed a constant, if varying, supply also of books from London, Oxford or abroad: there was never any question of being self-sufficient, even, save for the shortest periods, with respect to the most basic or standard books. For emigrants in some of the North American colonies, and particularly for those in Massachusetts Bay, the memory of Cambridge, and the experience of university life and teaching, enshrined (at least in some respects) a model from which to recreate a shared experience in a new town, even one bearing the same name. Most obvious, and most celebrated, the puritan tradition of Emmanuel College, founded specifically for the training of ministers to be sent out for the propagation of the faith and the well-being of the faithful, was translated into the founding of Harvard College. But the links with the old Cambridge were more diverse, as well as more numerous, than this single, though influential, instance of one college. Apart from the prosopographical evidence of the early settlers, there remains, again, much work to be undertaken on the import and circulation of books in mid-seventeenth-century North America. As in England, the local printed output, from Steven Daye's first sheets in 1639 onwards, offers an entirely inadequate account of what was sold, read and discussed. As in Cambridge, Ramist influence was strong. And as in Cambridge, much information on private book ownership, and on the balance between local and imported books, remains fragmentary so far.[33] But it is nonetheless worth drawing out, however imperfectly, those books of known provenance known also to have been printed in Cambridge: parts, but essential parts, of the trans-Atlantic links between two communities sharing many interests and traditions in common. As in England, the admixture of Cambridge-printed books in private hands was never more than a tiny minority; but their identity offers evidence of what was most valued, whether for educational or for other purposes – remembering always that what was true in Cambridge of dependence on other sources was no less so in Massachusetts.

The book trade with Germany and the Rhine valley was established and organized, one involving imports as well as exports. For North America, where many of the early Massachusetts settlers had a natural affinity with Cambridge, the earliest evidence is on the other hand of casual imports by individuals – sometimes brought with them on the voyage out, sometimes acquired subsequently either in the colonies or on a return visit to England. So far as is known, bookselling in Boston developed only in the 1640s;[34] and although later in the century a few books to be printed in North America were systematically exported, for long after the first press was set up in 1639 it was more usual for important books by native American authors to be sent to London for printing and publication.[35]

The Plymouth colony, founded in 1620, could boast only one graduate, William Brewster of Peterhouse; but the early settlers of Boston and its vicinity included a noticeably high proportion of men educated at Oxford or

Cambridge.[36] Among the most prominent from Cambridge, John Cotton had matriculated at Trinity in 1598, moved to a Fellowship at Emmanuel before taking the vicarage of Boston in Lincolnshire, and finally moved in 1635 to Boston in New England, where he remained as minister until his death in 1652. Nathaniel Ward, who shared with Cotton responsibility for the first code of laws to be framed in New England, had entered Emmanuel in 1596, and arrived in New England in 1634, one season ahead of Cotton. John Winthrop, the central figure in the great migration to Massachusetts Bay in 1630 that led to the founding of Boston, and the first Governor of Massachusetts, had entered Trinity in 1603. In the young Harvard College, Nathaniel Eaton (Master of the school out of which the college was cast) entered Trinity in 1629–30; Henry Dunster, first President, had entered Magdalene in 1627; and Charles Chauncy, his successor, had entered Trinity in 1610, becoming a Fellow in 1614. These men had their several particular reasons for leaving England, but they shared an education that, in its essentials, was transported to Massachusetts.[37]

Many of the colonists, and particularly their ministers, brought out at least part of their libraries with them – not simply a Bible or two, but occasionally collections of several hundred volumes. Educated, in many cases, in a puritan-dominated university, these men chose to keep beside them books by those who had influenced them, directly or indirectly, whilst they had been students. Some of these books, though by Cambridge authors, had of course been published in London, or (as in the case of William Ames) in separatist exile in Amsterdam. Others were from the Cambridge press itself. William Brewster, who entered Peterhouse in 1580, emigrated to the Plymouth colony in 1620 on the Mayflower, after several difficult years in Amsterdam and Leiden. On his death in 1644 he left an estate valued at £150, of which his library represented about thirty per cent. Among his books were works by Andrew Willet, William Perkins and Thomas Taylor, all from the presses of Legate or Legge. His Latin dictionary was Thomas Thomas's.[38]

The most celebrated early colonial library of all, that of John Harvard, is less completely documented. Harvard had entered Emmanuel College in 1627, aged twenty and therefore rather older than usual. Ten years later he sailed for Massachusetts, having spent much of the intervening time after graduation in 1631–2 in manning the family's London business. He died in 1638, and in the absence of any surviving post-mortem inventory of his estate, knowledge of his library depends essentially on his benefaction to the new college that was to bear his name – a collection that itself was never listed reliably and most of which was burned in 1764. The surviving evidence suggests that almost three-quarters of his library was published by 1630, midway through his Emmanuel career. Amongst it were copies of the second edition (1630) of Davenant's commentary on Colossians, first published by the Bucks in 1627. Otherwise there was little else to show from the press of his old university, though the standard textbooks, as well as Alabaster's college play *Roxana* (London 1632) were reminders of his time there.[39] The absence from the list of earlier figures such as Whitaker has been remarked on;[40] but by the late 1620s Whitaker had lost his central position. William Perkins, of whom the younger John Legate republished yet again a three-volume collected edition in 1626–31, is a more noticeable omission.

In its catholicity of taste, Harvard's library was scarcely typical. He was not a minister who had kept abreast of that theology which seemed most sympathetic, but a businessman with literary tastes, for whom the Cambridge press could offer comparatively little. The library of Thomas Jenner owed more to its owner's origins. Jenner entered Christ's in February 1623/4, aged eighteen, the son of an Essex farmer. He emigrated to Roxbury in 1635, and became minister successively at Weymouth, a little to the south of Boston, and at Saco, in Maine, before returning to England in 1650. Among his two hundred or so books were the three volumes of Perkins, Willet on Genesis, Thomas Taylor on Titus, Samuel Hieron on *Davids penitentiall psalme opened* (1617), and John Yates' *Gods arraignement of hypocrites* (1615), all by Cambridge men and all printed at Cambridge.[41] More Cambridge books were recorded in the library of Jonathan Mitchell, a congregationalist who graduated from Harvard in 1647. He, too, possessed the three volumes of Perkins, as well as Thomas's Latin dictionary, Herbert's *Temple* and, probably, Winterton's edition of the *Poetae minores Graeci*. His copy of Samuel Newman's *Concordance*, one of the most generally successful of all the books printed at Cambridge in the latter part of the seventeenth century, had been published only in 1662, six years before Mitchell's death.[42]

Though the puritan secessionist William Ames (1576–1633) died before he was able to reach America, his library displayed a similar selection from the output of the Cambridge press, by William Whitaker, Davenant, Thomas Taylor, and Thomas's edition of the *Harmony of confessions* (1586): the principal absentee in a list which cannot in any case be assumed to have been complete was, again, Perkins, of Ames' own college.[43] The taste for many of these authors persisted. When, in 1698, Thomas Bray instigated the gift of a library to the King's Chapel in Boston, the selection of books included editions of Perkins printed by Legate as well as more recent products of the Cambridge press, the Hebrew Psalms of 1685 and Robert Sanderson's *Casus conscientiae* (1688).[44] Four years later, the inventory of Thomas Weld of Roxbury recorded further copies of Willet and of Thomas's dictionary, as well as Samuel Newman's *Concordance*.[45]

The Mather family library, in John Dunton's eyes the glory of New England, was larger than any of these, and not surprisingly echoes the pattern of interests that was apparent elsewhere, with copies of Perkins, Davenant, Thomas's dictionary, and Winterton's Greek poets, as well as Joseph Mede,

Lightfoot's *Horae Hebraicae*, Herbert's *Temple*, and an assortment of textbooks dating back to the late sixteenth century.[46] Even after the end of the seventeenth century, these and other Cambridge publications still held their appeal in Massachusetts, in the copies bought by Thomas Prince (1687–1758), whose father had emigrated in 1633 and who, after graduating from Harvard in 1707, spent some years back in Suffolk in England. Among the books he eventually bequeathed to the Old South Church in Boston were many he had bought during his English sojourn – not only by Davenant and by Taylor, but also Duport's *Job* (1637) and the 1643 Marcus Minucius Felix' *Octavius*.[47]

Some books, such as Davenant's commentary on Colossians (in a third edition by 1639) and Thomas Taylor on the Epistle to Titus (first published in 1612), recurred constantly in New England. Both Harvard (as has been mentioned) and John Winthrop made sure that the new college had Davenant's books.[48] Such were books to be kept, and for the mid-century it can only be guessed how many lesser books, such as schoolbooks, found their way in luggage over the Atlantic. Burgersdijck's *Institutiones logicae*, printed repeatedly at Cambridge, was still in use at Harvard at the end of the century, often with its accompaniment, Adrian Heereboord's Ἑρμενεια *logica*. Winterton's *Poetae minores Graeci*, originally published at Cambridge in 1635, remained in use in New England even in the early nineteenth century. Golius' epitome of Aristotle's *Ethica* (Cambridge 1634) had found its way to Harvard by the 1640s; and the earliest surviving copy of the Iliad known to have been in the hands of a Harvard student was the Cambridge edition of 1672. William Morden's editions of Gassendi's *Institutio astronomica* (1653) and Henry More's *Enchiridion ethicum* (1668), both printed in London but principally for a Cambridge market, also found repeated use at Harvard. As in the English learned market, these books rubbed shoulders with continental equivalents. Links, personal and educational, with Harvard's Cambridge origins were a help, and were sustained by courses of reading in the respective universities that remained in some respects remarkably resilient against change. But even for a colony whose personal and intellectual origins owed so much to Cambridge, it could scarcely be claimed, on the evidence so far available, that the presses of any of the Cambridge printers in the early or mid-seventeenth century contributed systematically to regular or organized export.[49]

For Buck and Daniel, the distant North American market, despite all its similarities to that more local, could never be accounted regular or predictable in the same way. It seems never to have been mentioned in the almost continual flurry of correspondence and dispute over the usually opposing interests of printing in London and in Cambridge. The interests of local booksellers, and the maintenance of a difficult balance between continental, London and Cambridge printing, enabled as much by compromise as by publishing innovations, were of much more direct concern.

By the end of the century it was possible to point to a few exceptions, books intended by their authors or by others involved in their publication as much for an overseas market as for a national one.[50] But the beginning of the trade with North America was accidental, fruit not of policy but of the accidents or plans in the careers of private individuals, many of whose habits and interests and attitudes had been shaped amongst a commingling of subjects that together constituted the often loose form of the undergraduate curriculum in seventeenth-century Cambridge.

Authors and printers

The Cambridge printing house was larger than most in London, and it was endured as such by the Stationers' Company, if sometimes with bad grace, for so long as it printed books under licence. Such an arrangement had the advantage of enabling members of the English Stock to profit while the total press capacity of London remained within such bounds as guaranteed inferiority to those not admitted to the central caucus.[1] Overall, the effect was to limit the press capacity in the country at large, at a time when retail demand and authors' aspirations required more. The failure of domestic production to meet the demand for Bibles was met by illegal or clandestine imports, and by the more public exploitation of the Latin trade. Even the King's Printers shared in the import Bible trade. Among secular books, Farnaby's pocket editions of classical texts, printed in the Low Countries, Germany and France, as well as other similar editions from Leiden and elsewhere, were but part of a publishing policy oriented as much towards the continental as British markets.[2] For authors of new books, the restricted capacity of the London presses, and the disabilities inherent in an insular trade, led sometimes to foreign publication: Frankfurt, with its fair and its trade links with Britain, made a natural centre.[3] Other authors simply financed their own works, thus buying for themselves a place in what was perceived by Daniel as a printers', rather than booksellers' or publishers', domain: 'It is a common complaint [he wrote] that whereas schollars have taken great paines in writing usefull bookes, they cannot get them printed but at their own great charges.'[4] Daniel's purpose was to create two printing houses in Cambridge, and so to gain independence of the Bucks. He was unable to name those in Cambridge who had been so affected, though he might have done so. But the fact that he saw in such scholars' plights an argument for increasing press capacity (and hence competition) suggests that booksellers, too, found themselves under constraint, their operations limited not so much by capital, as by the availability of presses.

The tensions between authors and their hopes for publication, between the domestic printing trade and that overseas, between local interests and those elsewhere, were not new. As we have seen, in 1576 Thomas Hatcher had been sharply critical of the effect of book trade restrictions and practices on the interests of authors and readers. He had made it clear that he was not a lone voice.[5] Many of the same criticisms remained pertinent in the 1620s. Richard Montague wrote in 1622 of printers' σκαιότης and μικρολογία, their stupidity and meanness – resorting to Greek no doubt lest his remarks were correctly interpreted by his printer.[6] Much was made of printers' ignorance of Latin, quite apart from other learned languages; and much, of course, was made of stationers' eagerness to take advantage of authors whose desire for publication was greater than their power to command more than a minimal reward.[7] In such contexts – geographical, commercial, educational and linguistic, as well as personal – the perennial questions affecting authors have their own particular nuances in the seventeenth century.

Why did an author in the seventeenth century choose one bookseller rather than another? Did he have any choice in the matter? Can printers be said to have had reputations that affected the kind of work they were asked to print? How much were authors paid? Was there such a thing as a 'list' – a stable of authors encouraged by a particular publisher? Did booksellers, as publishers, expect to specialize?[8] How far were authors' decisions about their books affected by their distance from London?

For authors in Cambridge, many of these questions were irrelevant if they looked only to the University Printers. But in other ways, these questions, and others like them, were fundamental to publication in a way that was not so vital amidst the *mêlée* of the London trade. In Cambridge there was but one press: conveniently close for proof-reading, but having only limited capacity, and able to draw on only severely limited capital. The press, and the local booksellers, with their modest trading links with London, were entirely adequate for sermons or the minor effluvia of academic life. But for more ambitious works (or more ambitious authors), the London trade was essential. There were few books of obvious contemporary scholarly or religious consequence printed in seventeenth-century Cambridge for which there were no major London outlets – either named explicitly on the title-page or organized as a part of the normal credit arrangements between London suppliers and the stockholding booksellers of the University.

The repeated notes of apology at the heads of errata lists in sixteenth- and seventeenth-century books, explaining that faults were attributable partly at least to authors' distance from the press, were no bombast. Printing-house schedules, dictated by limited equipment and minimal staff, meant that there was little time for authors' proof-reading. In most houses, any systematic proof-reading was subservient to the timetable of production, and continued (however haphazardly) throughout a print-run. To authors anxious for their text, yet unable to attend in person, the pitfalls were all too obvious. In 1624, for example, John Downe, former Fellow of Emmanuel College but now Rector of Instow in Devon, thought to have published his recent visitation sermon, and to send it to Edward Blount in London for this purpose. But 'having not acquaintance ... to have a little care of the comming forth of it', he successfully entreated his neighbour Oliver Naylor (former Fellow of Caius) to write to John Cosin – who might, it was hoped, be prevailed on to look after the manuscript in London.[9] Without local supervision, an author could only expect to make his text good once an edition sheet had been printed off, when errata lists and (to some extent) pen correction could rectify the more obvious faults.

So in January 1624/5 Richard Montagu complained of Thomas Snodham's work on his forthcoming *Gagg for the new Gospell*?:

I received a sheet of the printer, *caetera probo*, but in 4 page, *monstrum horrendum*, a *niggling* trick for a *juggling* tricke. This must in *spongiam incumbere*, and be mended with a pen or we are shamed for ever ... I praye by the next returne of our boate to morowe, lett me have what is printed, *et sic deinceps* to collect the *errata*.[10]

The text remained unaltered, and the list of errata in some copies did not mention the faults. But what was true of John Downe and of Montagu was true of anyone living in the country whose work was printed at a distance, whether in London, Cambridge or Oxford.

From London to Cambridge is about fifty miles. This distance both helped independence from the London trade, and yet was not so great as to prevent co-operation when it was thought advantageous. The extent to which, at the end of the seventeenth century, practices in the printing house of the newly founded University Press reflected those in London has been a matter for lively – though not always life-giving – debate.[11] But since throughout the century, and indeed from the time of Thomas Thomas onwards, the running of the Cambridge press depended on there being a constant supply of London-trained journeymen who could take a responsible part in composition and presswork, there is no reason to suppose that production practices were seriously different in the two centres. The disposition of the labour force, concurrent production, the rate of printing, charges for printing and composition, were all expected to agree. Much the same remained true for the treatment of authors, editors and their texts, in that parallels between London and Cambridge are more noticeable than differences. Although the following pages relate almost solely to the Cambridge press, they are, therefore, also pertinent to the much more complicated situation in London.[12]

The printer and the stationer were made familiar stage figures by Ben Jonson, as essential parts of the literary world.[13] So too, at Cambridge, the play audience was expected to recognize figures, if not individuals, from the book trades. The anonymous *Second part of the return from Parnassus*, acted at St John's in 1601–2, included the figure of Ingenioso, a Cambridge author recently arrived in London, who meets first with Iudicio, a printer's reader, and then with Danter, a printer.[14] The figure of Ingenioso owed a good deal to Thomas Nashe; but Iudicio, the proof-corrector, was also a figure familiar enough to the Cambridge academic audience to require little introduction:

Iudicio: ... What ere befall thee keepe thee from the trade of the corrector of the presse.
Ingenioso: Mary so I will, I warrant thee, if pouerty presse not too much; Ile correct no presse but the presse of the people.
Iudicio: Would it not grieue any good spirritt to sit a whole moneth nitting ouer a lousy beggarly Pamphlet, and like a needy Phisitian to stand whole yeares tooting and tumbling the filth that falleth from so many draughty inuentions as daily swarme in our printing house?[15]

A few minutes later Danter, the printer, enters, and faces Ingenioso, whose address reveals him as a practical author in such circumstances – just as Danter can readily counter his suggestion that his new pamphlet *A catalogue of Cambridge cuckolds* would meet a ready (and, it was suggested, necessarily clandestine) market.

Danter: It's true; but good fayth M. *Ingenioso*, I lost by your last booke, and you knowe there is many a one that payes me largely for the printing of their inuentions; but for all this you shall haue 40 shillings and an odd pottle of wine.
Ingenioso: 40 Shillings? a fit reward for one of your reumatick poets, that beslauers all the paper he comes by, and furnishes the Chaundlers with wast papers to wrap candles in: but as for me, Ile be paid deare euen for the dreggs of my wit.[16]

Danter is forced to accept: 'Ile haue it whatsoeuer it cost.' Ingenioso's book was very different from those emanating from Legate's press at the other end of Trinity Street from St John's, but the exchanges in these two scenes dealt with a world different only in kind from that surrounding academic publication. In Cambridge, too, authors were known to fund publication of their own books, while to many a reward of even 40s. would have been better than nothing or a few free copies of their own work.

This shared experience of the press, the same in its essentials in London and in Cambridge, in high seriousness and in Grub Street, means that much of what has been gathered on the conduct of individual authors and printers (as distinct from governing bodies such as the Stationers' Company) in London, holds true also for a provincial university.

'Gentle Reader many faults escaped the Author being absent, and the coppie somewhat darke.'[17] John Legate, who sought with these words to explain the imperfections in the text of Thomas Rogers' attack on puritanism, *The faith, doctrine, and religion ... expressed in 39 articles* (1607), was in a very far from unusual plight. The 'darkness' of authors' or amanuenses' handwriting remained a challenge in printing houses until the advent of the typewriter, while the minimal equipment possessed by nearly every Elizabethan and early seventeenth-century printing house made it rarely possible for authors to read proof unless they attended themselves every day. Rogers' difficulty was that he lived at Horringer, near Bury St Edmunds. Legate, and then Legge, made similar excuses at the head of much longer lists of errata in Andrew Willet's *Hexapla in Genesin* (1605) and his commentary on Romans (1611), freely confessing that the copy he had sent to the printers was no fair one, but as first composed:

Whereas diuers faults are escaped in this painefull and profitable worke, more then vsuall: I would desire the Reader to haue both the author excused, who was absent, and could not recognize what was printed, and the Printer, who might easily be deceaued in the copie, beeing but once written in all, and that with a running hand, & in some places not very legible.[18]

The plea was much the same six years later, from Legge:

Whereas the copie was in many places darke and obscure, as beeing but once written, as it was first framed by the Author, neither could he be present himselfe to ouersee the worke, I praye thee, Courteous Reader, with patience to amend the faults, which fell out to be more, then either we had thought, or could by our diligence (which was not wanting) preuent.[19]

For most books, even those by authors close to the press, accuracy was striven for only intermittently. Devices such as cancel leaves, paste-on cancels, and manuscript emendations could not make all well, and there were usually more faults than appeared in lists of errata. Faults were, moreover, corrected at press as they were discovered; and so within an edition sheets can be found varying one from another, each forme in different stages of amendment and different volumes made up of different permutations of the sheets. All this, which was quite acceptable in sixteenth- and seventeenth-century books, not only implied (so far as the author was concerned) the expectation that his text could never be absolutely stable, but also assumed that the reader would, likewise, respond according to the varied and shifting quality of the text before him. It was variety and irregularity such as this (quite apart from what was clearly, or agreed to be, inaccuracy) that the corrector of the press was expected to combat, and remove. But there was no talk of such a figure at Cambridge until the late 1620s. Though much has been claimed for the uniformity of print from the fifteenth century onwards, in practice texts retained a fluid quality, varying, if ever so slightly, from one copy to another,[20] this fluidity being increased, not stabilized, by frequent re-setting for new editions. Though the Bible itself was presumed to be accurate, and much was made, especially in the mid-seventeenth century, of the need for a responsible, authoritative and stable text, mistakes were commonplace even here, and some of the more serious became notorious.[21] Claims were likewise made for the accuracy or otherwise of elementary classical texts. For most books, however, a general level of accuracy had, of necessity, to be deemed sufficient. As one writer explained to the 'courteous and friendly reader' in 1598, in a book printed at London:

Many faults have escaped heerein, some by my owne ouersight, some through the Printers negligence, which I would desire the skilfull, courteously to correct with their penne, or friendly to pardon through their courtesie. For such as are vsed to the

Presse, are priuie to this, that few bookes goes cleare without an *Erata*: yet this much
I dare presume, that to my knowledge, no fault heerein committed, hath either spoyled
the sence, or mangled the Storie.[22]

In 1601 Robert Hill of St John's, Preacher at St Andrew's, Norwich,
described more ornately than most what was – as he was the first to lament –
not so much commonplace, as seemingly inevitable. He wrote in this instance
of Legate, but he might have written equally had his book been printed in
London:

As the best man cannot euer speake in printe, without fayling: so the best composer
cannot euer set in print without missing. And as the painter may erre from the liuely
fauour, so the Printer may from the copie of a writer. If therefore thou finde a point
dispointed, a word mistaken, or happily in some place a little sentence left out: pardon
I pray thee both the Author, and the Printer. The author, who hath enough to doe to
look to the liues of his people, not the lines of his booke: and the printer, because it
cannot be but in large impressions there must needs be some errours. The fairest fruit
will haue a worme, the finest cambricke may haue a fret, the best cloath is not without
a knot, and beautiful Venus hath her mole. In a word, the best booke that is printed,
I except not (which would I might) the sacred Bible, hath his typographicall both frets
and knots, and moles in the face.[23]

Such apologies were among the very last parts of books to be printed. They
came, therefore, only at the end of a sequence that included the author's drafts
and redrafts, transcription (sometimes) by an amanuensis, editing, composition,
proofing and printing. These activities could be, and often were, confined to a
fairly short period of concentrated activity; but they could also be spread over
several years: as the press's work became more complex, manuscripts had to
take their turn in production programmes that allowed other books to go
through simultaneously. Sometimes the author was close at hand, but often he
was not. During the first fifty years of the seventeenth century the Cambridge
press grew unrecognizably, while the status of printers vacillated according to
their backgrounds until Daniel could no longer be treated with academic
patronizing. But for authors the principal considerations remained the same.

Thomas Fuller, John Davenant and William Bedell were among many that
still, after they had left Cambridge, turned to the press with which they were
familiar. Others, such as Christopher Heydon of Baconsthorpe in Norfolk,
were attracted to the press because they were able to find agents in Cambridge
willing to act as intermediaries. Heydon's own college was Peterhouse, but his
younger brother was, while an undergraduate at Caius, a contemporary of John
Fletcher, a devotee of astrology and later a Fellow of that college. When,
therefore, Heydon's own son entered Caius in February 1597/8, and was
placed under Fletcher, there was a natural channel through whom Heydon
could conduct the publication of his reply to John Chambers' attack on their
shared enthusiasm. Heydon's *Defence of judiciall astrologie* was printed by
Legate in 1602–3.[24] The consequent correspondence between Fletcher and

Heydon, and similar exchanges between other distant authors and their local agents, such as Bedell's or Samuel Ward's, record the anxieties, hopes and demands familiar to most authors: those living in Cambridge, from whom no such correspondence survives, had no need to write at such length or in such pained detail to a printer living only a few hundred yards away from their college rooms. 'I am not a little glad y^t y^{or} printer is willinge to vndertake ye matter, for by that meanes I am sure to have y^{or} ouersight in ye press, wch I pray y^{ow} assure y^{or} self I will liberally consider', wrote Heydon in August 1602, taking care to broach the question of a fee before possible embarrassment.[25]

Such agencies brought other responsibilities. Fletcher not only brought expert knowledge, but also acted as research assistant, editor and indexer, though this did not prevent what seemed to Heydon catastrophic mistakes. 'Only', he wrote, shortly before the final sheets were printed, 'my comfort is y^t I am already excedingly beholding...for ye paynes y^{ow} haue taken in collecting ye places off scripture, ye authors and ther tymes, besyd ye making of a very artificiall index, and y^{or} helpe and correction in other passages of ye book it self; so if my aduersary replye y^{ow} will not se me stick fast for want of y^{or} syde.'[26] Davenant, in 1634, expected similar co-operation from Ward in ensuring that his scribbled notes had been accurately transcribed and read:

My hand and mine eyes are so badd, as I much doubt you will be troubled in reading ye determination: but I had much adoe to gett it finished thus soon, & no possibility of getting it fairlie transcribed. For divers of the Quotations I took them out of mine own Notebooks, and wanted time to search all ye particular authors; what errors in that kinde or any other, you must withall, I pray reforme, before ye Printer goe in hand wth it.[27]

In 1640 Davenant sent to Ward part of the manuscript copy for his next book *Ad fraternam communionem inter evangelicas ecclesias restaurandam adhortatio* with the words, 'The supervision of my written Copie I comitt to your selfe, & Dr Bromrick, intreating you to look it over before it goe to ye Presse; & to mend what you find faulty or defective.'[28]

When the manuscript copy reached the printer, it had thus already sometimes passed through several hands. Davenant claimed poor eyesight for several years, and employed an amanuensis for his readings on Colossians, printed by Thomas and John Buck in 1627; even the transcription, however, required to be checked by a third hand:

I cannot revise them as were fitt; mine eyes not serving mee to read mine own hand. Yet...I have caused my scholler Vincent to transcribe those my readings vppon ye Epistle to ye Coloss: wch hee has now finished. Yf you shall iudg them fitt for ye presse, I will committ them to your disposition. I have appoynted my Chaplain to peruse them and yf hee meet wth any wants or faults to be supplied or corrected to give mee notice thereof. As for my selfe I have nether eyes nor leysure to runn them over again.[29]

'It is penance to mee, to read what my selfe has written', wrote Davenant on another occasion.[30] His impatience (feigned or genuine) at Ward's expectation that what he had written he would publish, and his dislike of the labour necessary in preparing work for the press, each helped to ensure that his work would be properly appreciated by the time it reached the printers. In 1631 Ward required a dedicatory epistle to Davenant's *Praelectiones*, but it was supplied only with bad grace, even after he had travelled to Wiltshire in person to see the author:

I have donne according as you wished mee to doe at your beeing heer, & drawen an Epistle Dedicatory to his Maiesty, & another to ye Reader. I have sent them as they were scribled & blurred by mine own hand, because I was vnwilling to have them transcribed by another. Revise them, & doe wth them as you please. This Dedication will draw vppon me a necessity of beeing at London.[31]

To a very great extent, convention dictated format and typographical form, but there were modest opportunities for authors to manoeuvre. The minute duodecimo format of William Perkins' *Graine of musterd-seed* (1603) alluded more to the book's title (and the phrasing of the Gospel) than to convention. William Bedell, in 1628, wished the type and the format of his Latin translation of Paolo Sarpi's *Quaestio quodlibetica* to be the same as his version of the *Interdicti Veneti historia* printed two years previously.[32] Davenant's commentary on Colossians, published in 1627, was a folio at Davenant's own request, though its bulk could hardly have permitted otherwise.[33]

Not every book went to press immediately. Circulation in manuscript often seemed more useful to authors than outright publication in print, and this was to remain the case until the eighteenth century.[34] 'I confesse I have alwaies been, and am very backward to putt any thing of mine in print', wrote Davenant in 1625,[35] two and a half years after he had written of this same work: 'For my readings [on Colossians] I could willingly vndergo ye paynes of perusing them; but when I come to review them, they seem vnto me so rough and tedious...that I fear they will not abide the impartiall censure of others.'[36] Donne's sermons were not published until 1634 – after his death – and then not from his own papers, but from another manuscript collection.[37] The best known of all books printed at Cambridge in the early seventeenth century, Herbert's *Temple*, was likewise printed only after its author's death. Of those still living when their work was published, apart from Davenant, Andrew Willet found cause in 1614 to complain of the time Legge had taken to put to press his *Harmonie upon the First Booke of Samuel*.[38] Fuller's *Holy state* (1642) was a year in the press.[39] Richard Perrot, Fellow of Sidney Sussex College before he took a Lincolnshire living, seems to have suffered particularly as a result of Legge's declining powers. *Jacobs vowe, or the true historie of tithes*, was dated 1621, and had been delivered in York Minster the previous year. The book appeared only in 1627, however, with Thomas and John Buck's names on the title-page and a plaintive note from the author:

sixe yeares agone this discourse was finished, since which time it hath laine at the Presse like the lame man at the Poole of *Bethesda*, not for want of friends to put it in, but for want of Angells to moove the Printers waters. Had it beene some idle Pamphlet, or foysted Curranto of false or ill newes, it would have found Midwives to hasten it into the world; and though it had suffered abortion, and come maymed forth as most of them doe, yet should it not have wanted welcomers & entertainers. But such is the miserie of these times, such the evill will that men beare generally to Gods Sion that even those men who can sucke gaine out of the most idle and scurrilous subjects, dare not attempt to print any thing of this nature, for feare of losse and dammage. The consideration whereof made me oftentimes resolve to relinquish all further prosecution of the Presse, as expecting but poore entertainment at their hands who must pay for my labours, when those that were likely to gaine by them, for some sinister respects seemed to sleight them.

Perrot was a victim of circumstance, and was in no position to complain until too late. Others, however, felt more able at least to speak freely about their intentions or aspirations for their books, and to expect a sympathetic ear from the printer. Whether or not the printer heeded the advice given on such occasions no doubt depended partly on financial arrangements with the author or publisher: Perrot, lacking 'Angells', also lacked influence.

Once their books were in the press, authors had only limited opportunities to correct them, particularly if they were not resident in Cambridge.[40] Here, clearly, there was no difference between metropolitan and university printing shops. For Heydon, despite all his anxieties that Fletcher should oversee his book, the results were disastrous:

Y^e printer hath so blemished eury page almost wth grosse and intollerable errors, y^t except ye bookes be corrected befor they are deliuered or sould it will not be possible for the reder to vnderstand me, ye errata ar so thik and gross; For not lettres or sillables wch eury common person may supply by his owne vnderstanding, but euen whole wordes omitted and changed often tymes to ye contrary sence.[41]

Heydon's book was an unusually complicated object by the time copies reached their readers. Thanks to changes in his text while it was in the press, cancel leaves had to be introduced; even the unusually long list of errata, compiled as production drew towards its end in January 1602/3, produced further mistakes — and more anguish on Heydon's part.[42] Legate agreed to correct the press's misprints, but even so Heydon was especially anxious lest presentation copies should be sent out before John Blackbourne, a young graduate and former pupil of Fletcher's, had emended by hand everything that required it.[43]

For all Heydon's confidence in him, Fletcher seems to have been a negligent proof-reader. Practice necessarily varied, depending on the easy availability or otherwise of the author. 'The Printer hath faulted a little: it may be the author ouersighted more', quipped the note at the head of a brief list of errata to Foulke Robartes' *The reuenue of the Gospel is tythes*, printed by Legge in 1613: the implication, that Robartes had read proof, was an important one.[44] Francis

Dillingham, Fellow of Christ's, was unable to be present in Cambridge when his *Tractatus brevis*, an attack on Bellarmine, was printed in 1603. He blamed all the typographical mistakes on the printer, and the book was published with his name mis-spelled on the title-page. Willet's habitual absence from the press has already been alluded to: others included Samuel Collins of King's, who seems to have arrived only when his book was all but finished, and to have taken Legge's word that mistakes had been attended to.[45] Even a conscientious author could not however guard against printers' haste or their ignorance of Latin, which William Perkins was compelled to offer as excuse for Legate's work in 1598.[46] Until Buck and Daniel made provision for regular, and informed, proof-reading, responsibility for the accuracy of texts fell between two parties each of whom preferred to make assumptions of the other. There was only one regular exception to this general rule, in the volumes of verses issued periodically by the University to mark major national occasions and for which an official *Preli corrector* was appointed on each occasion. In 1619 this conventionally anonymous figure ended the collection commemorating the death of Queen Anne with the words

> Hic operis Finis, sed non moeroris & idem,
> Iste doloris abest, ille laboris adest.

In 1625 and 1632–3 the corrector for these verses was Ralph Winterton, the editor of Hippocrates.

Surviving proofs are often as puzzling as they are revealing, and can be confused with corrections added by hand after, rather than before (or during) the press-run. Since proof might be read either in the printing house before printing, by the author (or his agent) inside or outside the premises, or by either the author or the press crew during the day on which a particular sheet was being machined, there is room for this kind of doubt.[47]

In all save the largest printing houses, where there was sufficient type and the number of presses allowed it, proofing was difficult to fit into regular daily patterns. Although in 1683 Moxon wrote as if all printing houses employed correctors of the press, housed in 'some little Closet adjoyning to the Composing-Room',[48] such was in fact very far from the case. As we have seen, they were employed especially at learned presses (in about 1638 the King's Printing House employed four);[49] but it seems doubtful that they were a normal feature of the Cambridge press before the end of the 1620s. Daniel even suggested that one of the Bucks should perform this office.

Partly as a consequence of this, it is not always clear, among the surviving fragments of proofs from the late sixteenth and early seventeenth centuries, who was responsible for the marks they now bear. The earliest marked proof from the Cambridge printing house is also by far the most extensive, some eight sheets from a quarto completed by Legate in 1594, Lambert Daneau's *Fruitfull commentarie upon the twelve small prophets* (see fig. 22). The translator of the

One, the singular praise of the true God (whome Ionas witnesseth that he called vpon, and by whome he was deliuered) by comparing him with idols, it containeth, I say, the praise of God as the fountaine of all mercie, of al good things, of all saluation, and that the onely fountaine, of the which they doe depriue or bereaue themselues, whosoeuer call vpon & worship other gods. Therefore Ionas being now deliuered, & rauished as it were besides himselfe, doth triumph vpon the earnest consideration of so great a benefit, and as a conquerour ouer the idolatours, auoucheth the glorie of the true God, crieth out that al men may heare him, that this God alone is the father of all clemencie and mercie, that is, of all good thinges, the which benefits they through their owne fault forsake, which flee vnto idols. Wherefore in this place I take the word *mercie*, for the effects of mercie, the which God being merciful, bestoweth vpon men. The second part of this verse hath a very excellent and most true description of idols, the which by the way of contrarieties is opposed or set against that most bounteous nature of the true God. For he is true: the idols are lyes: He is bounteous in deede: the idols are vaine, that is, without any effect. Those therfore which call vpon them, and in their necessities pray vnto them, and not vnto the true God, doe willingly depriue themselues of true and certaine helpe of all good things: of saluation it selfe: because they forsake the true God the fountaine of all good things, as Ieremie, or rather God by Ieremie complaineth, *Ierem.2.13. My people (saith God) haue committed two euils: they haue forsaken me the fountaine of liuing waters, to digge them pittes, euen broken pittes, that can hold no water.*

A notable description of idols by way of contrarieties set against God.

Vers. 19. *But I will sacrifice vnto thee with the voyce of thanksgiuing, and will pay that I haue vowed: saluation is of the Lorde.*

A thanksgiuing containing 1. praising of God by voice. 2. Offering of sacrifice.

A Full thanksgiuing for the benefit receiued. This containeth three things. First, Ionas with voice praiseth the true God, with voyce confessing and acknowledging him to be the true and onely author of his deliuerance. Secondly, it containeth a sacrifice offered vnto God according vnto the worship at that time commanded. For Ionas sacrificeth a sacrifice *eucharisticall*, or of thanksgiuing, in steade of which sacrifice we nowe haue almes towards the poore, and giuing of thanks, as we are taught, Hebr. cap.

fully nor darkely, those things the whic[h] unto them: he doth not first go and put[e] will of some towards him, but committ[eth] out of things, and as much as in him ly[eth] worke commanded. And whereas God granted vnto the Niniuites for repentance not forthwith be destroyed, this declareth patience and bearing of God euen tow[ard] Roman.cap.2.ver.4. blameth those whi[ch] rance of God as an incouragement boldly to sinne, when he saith, *Despisest tho[u] the riches of his bountifulnesse and patience, & long sufferance, n[ot]* knowing that the *bountifulnesse of God leadeth thee vnto repentance.* 40. dayes respite sheweth that in these thr[eat] was included a condition of repentance ning was conditional not simple or pure a notwithstanding doe think, wherein against the wordes of the prophet.

Vers.5. *So the people of Niniue beleeued Go[d] and put on sackecloth, from the greatest of* of them.

THE fruite or effect of the former pre[aching] the vnbeleeuing Niniuites, being vnto sinne, namely their repentance. Wh[at] the ministerie of Ionas through the grace o[f] or of force euen among the Niniuites, as Ch[rist] teach Mat.12. *The men of Niniue shall arise i[n] generation, and condemne it: for they repented nas: and behold a greater then Ionas is here.* W[e] ceiue good hope of happy successe, who go[eth] vnto any worke, or ministery to be execu[ted] faithfull, or among the vnfaithfull. But the Ni niuites is briefly here described first by two afterwards the whole matter is more at lar[ge] of explanation or laying out of the same me two signes are namely the faith of the Niui[tes] saide to haue beleeued God) and the out[ward] or behauiour touching their body, to e[x]p[resse] feeling of the sorrowe for their sinnes mitted, to wit, fasting and sackecloath. Touching the fai[th] of the Niniuites they

God is long suffering euen towards infidels.

The threatning of God toward the Niniuites, conditionall.

The effect or fruit of Ionas preaching.

Two signes of the repentance of the Niniuites.

Fig. 22 Proofs of Lambert Daneau, *A fruitfull commentarie upon the twelve small prophets*, 4°, 1594. Apart from the marks of the proof-correctors, the sheet has also picked up ink from the side-sticks in the forme: these parts were usually masked off by a frisket during final printing. Height of original, 348 mm.

work, John Stockwood, lived not in Cambridge but in Kent, and was thus unable to see the volume through the press. The proof corrections, if not by Stockwood, are the work either of his local agent or, perhaps, of a corrector in the printing house itself, who was alert to textual mistakes and was able to insert words for which the compositor (perhaps unable to decipher his copy) had left only spaces.[50]

There is no hint here of the kind of attention to typographical, as distinct from textual, detail to be seen in two related fragments of forty-odd years later, one well known and one unfamiliar. Milton's 'Lycidas' (see fig. 23) has left an unusually full textual and bibliographical trail behind its first publication in 1638 among the verses in memory of Edward King. Apart from the holograph in Trinity College Library, there survives a fragment of proof, with corrections marked in before the final printing.[51] This proof is emphatically not Milton's, but of the printing house. This is clear if it is compared with another fragment from a much less absorbing work printed two years later, Eustachius' *Summa philosophiae quadripartita*. The same hand is at work in both, marking faults which in many cases would be only the printers' concern, such as battered letters, misalignments and loose setting. Here is not an author, or even his agent, at work, but a printer's reader – and a reader, moreover, who was anxious that the merely adequate was shunned. The proofs show, in their attention to details of presentation as well as to textual error, typographical standards that by the next decade were becoming unusual in London.[52]

Even after they had been formally proof-read, and the necessary corrections made, as was the case with each of these examples, texts had not necessarily assumed their final form. Further, less organized, reading could continue throughout the press-run, resulting in different states of the same page in different copies. For anything other than the briefest pamphlet, few editions consisted of a number of identical copies. Variation was the norm, though obviously each individual forme of type from which the book was printed assumed a final state by the end of each run. *The temple* (1633) was quite normal in this respect, but its principal variants have been better documented than most seventeenth-century books printed at Cambridge.[53] Even the title-page was corrected for Perkins' *Exposition of the Creed of the Apostles* (1596),[54] while the errata list attached to Samuel Collins' *Epphata* (1617) spoke of faults that had been 'alreadie mended in some copies'. Failing this, errors could be scraped out or pasted over, amended in ink or by stamping in new words or characters by hand. Every one of these techniques was employed in Whelock's Bede in 1643. Heydon's exhortation to Fletcher that presentation copies of his book should be so corrected has already been mentioned.[55] Some copies of William Sympson's *Full and profitable interpretation of the genealogie of Iesus Christ* (1619) have manuscript corrections that may emanate from the printing house,[56] while in some surviving copies of 'Lycidas' are manuscript corrections of incorrect readings and of the compositor's omissions.[57]

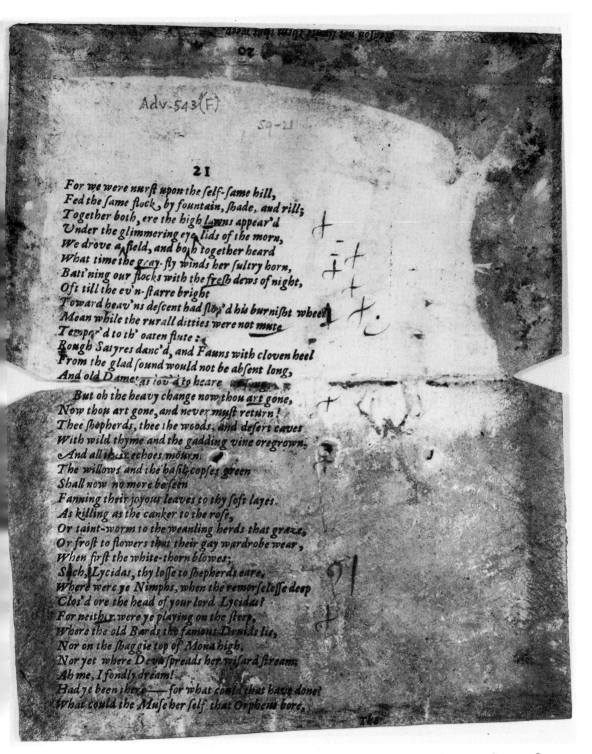

21

For we were nurſt upon the ſelf-ſame hill,
Fed the ſame flock, by fountain, ſhade, and rill;
Together both, ere the high lawns appear'd
Under the glimmering eye-lids of the morn,
We drove a field, and both together heard
What time the gray-fly winds her ſultry horn,
Bati'ning our flocks with the freſh dews of night,
Oft till the ev'n-ſtarre bright
Toward heav'ns deſcent had ſlop'd his burniſht wheel.
Mean while the rurall ditties were not muſe,
Temp'r'd to th' oaten flute :
Rough Satyres danc'd, and Fauns with cloven heel
From the glad ſound would not be abſent long,
And old Dametas lov'd to heare our ſong.

But oh the heavy change now thou art gone,
Now thou art gone, and never muſt return!
Thee ſhepherds, thee the woods, and deſert caves
With wild thyme and the gadding vine oregrown,
And all their echoes mourn.
The willows and the hazil copſes green
Shall now no more be ſeen
Fanning their joyous leaves to thy ſoft layes.
As killing as the canker to the roſe,
Or taint-worm to the weanling herds that graze,
Or froſt to flowers that their gay wardrobe wear,
When firſt the white-thorn blowes;
Such, Lycidas, thy loſſe to ſhepherds eare.
Where were ye Nimphs, when the remorſeleſſe deep
Cloſ'd ore the head of your lord Lycidas?
For neither were ye playing on the ſteep,
Where the old Bards the famous Druids lie,
Nor on the ſhaggie top of Mona high,
Nor yet where Deva ſpreads her wiſard ſtream:
Ah me, I fondly dream!
Had ye been there——for what could that have done?
What could the Muſe her ſelf that Orpheus bore,

The

Fig. 23 John Milton (1608–74), 'Lycidas'. Printer's proof from *Justa Edouardo King naufrago…*, 4°, 1638. Height of original, 200 mm.

All these methods had a common aim: to ensure that most, or the most important, copies of an edition were as textually correct as possible. Their execution assumed a conception of the printed word of less uniform authority than is usually assumed today. The same was equally true of the London and Oxford presses, and further confirm the shared tradition in authors' and printers' practices.

But among so much that was common, authors did sometimes turn to Cambridge not out of familiarity or convenience, or as a result of University decree. For a few, and perhaps for rather more who have left no memorial of their hopes, the Cambridge press offered other advantages. The *Articles of enquiry* issued by Richard Montagu, Bishop of Norwich, in 1638, were printed first in London, and then in Cambridge with an explanatory statement on the title-page: 'This Book of Articles, being extremely negligently printed at London, (which Impression I disavow) I was forced to review, and have it printed again at Cambridge.'[58] Ralph Winterton, in a new Cambridge edition of his translation of Gerhard's prayers in 1631, used his irritation at a London stationer to excuse himself from social embarrassment as he penned a new dedication:

But the Stationer (whom I would not name, because he is dead; and yet I must name, for feare lest by my silence I may seem to wrong others) *Richard Jackson* of Fleetstreet, to whose trust I committed the book to be printed, usurped the dedication, and obtruded it upon a Religious Countesse; whose name for honour I conceal: Hereupon I committed it unto the presse at Cambridge, being first purged from innumerable errates. Since *Jacksons* death, the copie it seems came to one *Williams* his hands Stationer in Popes-head-alley...[59]

Much of such animosity was directed at the London printers and stationers in little more than a negative way: Cambridge was second resort, and second choice. But for some, the Cambridge press and the Cambridge authorities seemed to present overwhelming advantages, that rendered the London system a poor second. The reasoning of John Downame, Rector of All Hallows, Thames Street, in the City of London, as he sought to get his brother's work into print without interference from the licensing authorities in London, is described in the next chapter.[60] On such occasions, friendship and a benevolent eye were worth more than convenience.

Authors, at the hands of Cambridge printers as usually elsewhere in the scholarly and quasi-scholarly market, could expect few direct financial rewards for their work. This was established practice. 'Authors seldom receive money for their books', Abraham Ortelius had written in 1586, 'for they are usually given to the printers, the authors receiving some copies if they are printed.' Ortelius went on to remind his correspondent of the hopes and implications of dedications, and to point out that on occasion Christopher Plantin (with whose business he was most familiar) had required money from an author to pay for engraved plates.[61] There was a distinction between those who wrote for honour, fame, patronage or 'the indulgence of their minds', and those who wrote on commission, as Ortelius observed and as authors, whether in the Low Countries or England, were quick to point out. But equally, the assumption that a learned press need not pay its authors save exceptionally had the effect of dividing the trade. While large payments may indeed have been unusual, in any part of the trade, in the early seventeenth century, the implication of the comments by George Wither in the early 1620s is that some were made, and made unequally:

What need the Stationer be at the charge of printing the labors of him that is Maister of his Art, & will require that respect which his paine deserveth? Seeing he cann hyre for a matter of 40 shillings, some needy IGNORAMUS to scrible upon the same subject, and by a large promising title, make it as vendible for an impression or two, as though it had the quintessence of all Art?[62]

Wither distinguished not only between different payments to different classes of author – the scholar and the hack – but also between the different overall investment. A scholar, he suggested, would write at more length, and expect some care to be given to printing what he submitted. It was a bookseller's view, of a question that would have been expressed in Cambridge rather differently.

Daniel, accustomed to London and to Cambridge, used the argument that scholars were often obliged even to pay for their work to be published, as a support for his campaign for a learned press at Cambridge.[63] Secure in the knowledge that such books would always be brought forward in a sufficiency to support the available printing capacity, stationers could afford to treat the question with what, even in the seventeenth century, seemed bland effrontery. As one anonymous commentator put it in about 1625,

If any Author himselfe would for the generall good, or for his owne proffitt, haue the printing of his owne labours, and procure his Freindes to disburse the charge, they [i.e. the stationers] were euer ready to further them in it.

In any case, he went on,

And most of the best Authors are not soe penurious that they looke soe much to their gaine, as to the good they intend to Religion or State. They are too Mercenary that write bookes for Money, and theire couetuousnes makes theire labours fruitles, and disesteemed.[64]

The climate for authors gradually changed through the middle years of the seventeenth century. Former assumptions – that the majority wrote more for renown, or at least for indirect reward, or hope of patronage, than for immediate cash – became weaker in the face of repeated challenge and of a book trade obliged to an increasing number of suppliers of copy who were unable to rely either on ecclesiastical or educational support or on the patronage of wealthy households. Although the evidence for payments to authors is only piecemeal in the late seventeenth century in England, such as survives suggests the beginning of a change in attitude that by the early eighteenth century was to grant authorship the respectability of a profession in its own right.[65]

By 1643, as the Stationers' Company found it expedient to insist that no book be printed without the author's name and consent, it was claimed by a group of divines that

> Considerable sums of money had been paid by stationers and printers to many authors for the 'copies' of such useful books as had been imprinted, in regard whereof we conceive it to be both just and necessary that they should enjoy a property for the sole imprinting of their copies; and we further declare that unless they do so enjoy a property, all scholars will be utterly deprived of any recompense from the stationers and printers for their studies or labour in writing and preparing books for the press; and that if books were imported to the prejudice of those who bore the charge of impressions, the authors and buyers would be abused by vicious impressions, to the great discouragement of learned men, and extreme danger of all kinds of good learning.[66]

Payment and recompense was not necessarily in cash. Patents offered one means of control and hence reward; but it was not one followed at Cambridge, where authors were most commonly rewarded with copies of their work, to sell or give away as they chose.

Even for publications that might be expected to make a commercial profit there is little evidence that fees or royalties changed hands. 'As for Leonard Green, I perceavd hee supposeth ye printing of my book will be beneficial vnto him', wrote Davenant to Ward in December 1625 of his work on Colossians, 'and in y^t regard he is not vnwilling to show some kinde of thankfulness. But for that matter, I leav it wholy vnto you; when you shall see whether ye sale of ye book will answer his expectation or no.'[67] For Davenant, a prominent and profitable author, there was at least the chance of payment – but only once sales had been proved, not necessarily as a payment for publication in the first place. His correspondence with Ward is filled with instructions for the disposition of presentation copies, the common form of payment to an author, sometimes in considerable numbers. Yet no author's entitlement ever seems to have been fixed at the outset: it was, rather, a matter for subsequent negotiation. His *Praelectiones* (1631), dedicated to the King, required a specially bound copy, done up under Buck's instructions; but there were others, too, who had to be remembered. 'I have some other freinds both at London, & here [i.e. in Wiltshire], who also will take it vnkindely yf I forget them: and therefore you must intreat Mr Buck to furnish mee with some reasonable number of copies for my special freinds. It is all ye gain I desire to make of my Books, that I may have some to distribute amongst my freinds.'[68] Normally the author paid for the binding, and Davenant was especially anxious that superior copies of his works should be presented to his own college, Queens'. So in 1640 he wrote of Daniel, as he contemplated the completion of his *Ad fraternam communionem adhortatio,*

I hope ye Printer will not think much to bestow vppon mee a competent number of Bookes, for ye Distribution wherof in Cambridge, I leav it wholy to your self; desiring that none of my freinds there, vnto whome you gaue any of my former Bookes bee now forgotten. As for those wch my self am to bestow amongest my other freinds, I would have six (at ye least) verie handsomlie bound, for persons of extraordinary quality. The rest may be bound or stitched vp after ye ordinary fashion.[69]

His *Adhortatio*, published in 1640, was a duodecimo, a contrast to the folios of a few years earlier, and he may therefore have felt able to be even more generous than usual when considering who should receive a copy, though the status of the potential recipients suggests more than natural generosity:

My purpose is to tender one of them to my Lord Grace, another to my Lord of London, and to such other of my Brethren ye Bishops as are about ye City: I shall likewise have occasion to tender some others, vnto frinds of Quality heer in ye Country. For this vse I would have a doozen at ye least sent bound; some fairly for ye Bishops, all handsomely. Besides these, I desire to have sent onlie stitched vp, or in quires, about 20 or thirty.[70]

But although no sum might be fixed until publication, there was clearly an expectation that, in ordinary circumstances, the copy would be paid for. Of his *Determinationes quaestionum quorumdam theologicarum* he received from Daniel at least twenty copies.[71] But by the early 1630s Davenant's success had become established, his commentary on Colossians printed in 1627 and again in 1630. Back in 1625, as contact was first made with Buck respecting the commentary on Colossians, and thought was given to the book's format (it was printed in folio at Davenant's specific request), the question of payment – in cash or in copies – had, as we have seen, to be approached more circumspectly.[72] Though the Bucks were in partnership with Greene, and Davenant seems to have understood some distinction between them, by the time the book was published in 1627 there was no sign of Greene in the imprint.

Davenant's experience is a reminder that authors' copies need not be limited to half a dozen or so. In the Netherlands, Ortelius had received twenty-five from Plantin of his *Synonymia geographica* in 1578, and others received even as many as two hundred, all of which might be sold if the author so wished. Such payments were, however, only for books that Plantin had himself initiated, and in this he seems generally to have been less generous than practices at Cambridge.[73] Nothing is known of any agreement between Abraham Whelock and the University Printers for his edition of Bede (1643); but the number of presentation copies suggests that he took payment in kind. Sir Chrisopher Heydon received a dozen copies of *A defence of judiciall astrologie* in 1603.[74] In

July 1628 Bedell requested that Buck should send copies of his *Examination of certaine motives to recusansie*, 'so many as he will allow me for the Copy, and some 50 more'.

If he had rather let me haue some copies of the *History of the Interdict* it shalbe at his election. If he haue printed the Quodlibeticall question I desire to haue some 30 or 40 or more of them...Some I hope to receiue for that copy also without paying for them.[75]

Payment might be in kind: in copies of the work in question, or perhaps as credit for other books; but it was implicit that there would be payment of some nature.[76]

If an author chose to meet the costs of printing, then there were many more opportunities to reap a reward. At Oxford, Nathanael Carpenter's *Geography delineated* (1625) was undertaken at Carpenter's own expense. The impression of 1,250 copies cost £92.10s., of which paper represented £45. On completion it was divided between the printer and the local bookseller Henry Cripps in a proportion 1:3, Carpenter selling copies to Cripps at a little over twice the manufacturing cost. Thus, though Cripps did not have to pay the whole immediately, Carpenter gained a handsome return on his investment. Yet the imprint on *Geography delineated* mentions only the printers and Cripps, and does not allude to Carpenter's part at all.[77] The agreement, which is unlikely to have been unique of its kind in the English trade, suggests that some authors, in Cambridge as well, may have played a larger role in financing their works than the imprints suggest, and that they thereby were able, if the book in question was successful, to receive some financial reward for their pains. The advantage to stationers and printers at the expense of authors (most of whom were in no position to pay for their books to be printed) is obvious. But since few books allude in their imprints to authors' parts in their production, it is impossible to discover the extent to which the trade drew on investment in this respect.

The imprints of Cambridge books do not always make publication arrangements clear, as we have already seen in the case of booksellers. Among private individuals and patrons, Edward Benlowes had a considerable interest in the publication of Phineas Fletcher's *Purple island* in 1633, as well as in his own *Sphinx theologica* of 1636: both seem to have been treated almost as private publications, and both offer typography of an individual kind. There was no obligation for Benlowes' name to appear in the imprint, and it did not. The imprints of Joseph Mede's *Clavis apocalyptica* (1627), 'Impensis authoris, in gratiam amicorum', and of Bythner's *Linguae eruditorum* (1645), 'Impensis authoris', were unusual in that they appeared at all: other instances where similar imprints would have been appropriate can often only be surmised. Likewise, the imprints on Thomas Mace's *Musick's monument* (1676) and on Joshua Barnes' *History of Edward III* (1688) were rare exceptions for the

Cambridge press. In 1647, John Hall, whose *Poems* had been recently printed by Daniel, proposed to pay for the entire impression of his *Modell of a Christian society*, yet only Daniel's name appears in the imprint.[78] There is no reason to suppose that some other books were not paid for by their authors as well.

Sometimes of course only a subsidy was required – as, again, Plantin had done regularly. Roger Daniel's background in the engraving trade brought to the Cambridge printing house not only the means to print engravings, but also encouragement to investment in more decorative books. Engraved title-pages became commonplace, and though it is by no means clear what part authors such as John Cruso or Thomas Fuller played in their commissioning and cost, it is probable that Edward Benlowes met the cost of others, notably those for Phineas Fletcher's *Purple island* (1633) and Quarles' *Emblemes* (1634). In the absence of such patronage, an author had to meet the cost of engraving himself, as Quarles claimed to have done originally for his *Emblemes*.[79]

Much later, in the 1680s, Joseph Moxon, writing about printers rather than booksellers, directed his remarks on authors to the need for clean copy, clearly marked for the press with respect to capitalization, punctuation and consistent spelling.[80] He voiced the needs of printers, but not all authors heeded them. Within a decade of his request, the cramped and untidy copy submitted by Joshua Barnes to Hayes for his edition of Euripides was still in spectacularly unreadable form – far beyond the inevitable awkwardnesses of an ambitiously annotated edition of this kind.[81] But the relationship between author, printer and bookseller depended on much more than an untidy manuscript, and more than Moxon was on this occasion prepared to recognize. The last few pages have glanced also at authors' attitudes to printers and booksellers, at payments to authors, at subsidies by authors, at arrangements for communication between author and press and, albeit briefly, at the author's very decision to allow a manuscript to be printed at all. How often this last, but fundamental, decision was always the author's is unclear, in the preliminary rhetoric to the published volume, and the conventions of the *captatio benevolentiae*. In 1614, Andrew Willet wrote of Legge's having held his book for some time before printing it, and finally putting it to press 'without my priuitie' – adding nonetheless, 'yet upon the perusing thereof, I find nothing which I acknowledge not to be mine'.[82] But between submission to the press, and final publication, lay not only the bookseller and the printer. For most of the seventeenth century all books were also required to be licensed. The following chapter examines some of the ways in which this too affected the Cambridge press, and its authors.

❧ 13 ❧

By due authority: licence and the title to print

For virtually the whole of the period discussed in this volume, until the lapse of the Licensing Acts in 1695, the University authorities had an obligation to license, or approve, every book issued from the Cambridge press. The Elizabethan injunctions of 1559 had provided for the Chancellors of the two universities to be amongst those permitted to examine, and license, books before they were printed.[1] On this, and particularly on the 1534 charter (providing for licence by the Vice-Chancellor and three doctors), the University relied for its independence: independence confirmed in 1621, 1623 and 1627. Through all the vicissitudes of ecclesiastical, royal and parliamentary provision for licensing, the University was able to retain its original authority in this respect.[2]

The act of licensing was quite separate from that of entry in the Stationers' Register, for which there seems for much of the seventeenth century to have existed no direct equivalent at Cambridge. The first was a necessity; the second was at the discretion of the stationer concerned. In the opinion of the Stationers' Company, copyright was conferred normally by entry in the Register. But there was a considerable weight of opinion even among the London stationers against the need for entry, in that up to one-third of all books published in the period 1576–1640 were not entered. Failure to enter a book was an offence; but it was an offence easily and cheerfully embraced, and one that seems to have been only very rarely pursued or punished by the Company authorities. In virtually all instances, failure to have a book entered seems to have caused no difficulty for the stationer, save that it made redress against piracy a more difficult matter than it might have been. In other words, licence (granted in London, Oxford or Cambridge, usually according to where a book was printed) and the right or title to a copy, might be – and were – two separate matters in which some overlap between London and the universities was always in theory possible. In practice, the overlap, and thus the possibility of real or imagined conflict of interest, seems to have been very little once the special concerns of the English Stock and of Bible printing are set aside.[3]

Usually, the University's authority was confined to its own press: these pages are concerned principally with the operation of licensing in Cambridge.

But occasionally academic authority impinged on London, as London authority impinged more often on Cambridge. Sometimes it was for the trade's convenience, sometimes for the author's. In 1597, William Perkins' *Reformed catholike* was entered in the Stationers' Register at Legate's behest, Legate claiming that it had been duly authorized by the University. Thus he was able to establish his right to the copy.[4] As University Printer he made a convenience of the Cambridge licence. But there were a few occasions on which the Vice-Chancellor's licence was granted to other than the University's own printers. In 1598, for example, John Jegon, Vice-Chancellor, was one of two who allowed William Smyth's Latin verses to the local bookseller John Porter: the book was printed by Felix Kingston in London, where Porter also traded.[5] Quarles' *Emblemes*, entered in May 1634, was licensed by Richard Love, the Vice-Chancellor, though the book was printed and published in London.[6] Such cases were rare, however, whether on behalf of University Printers or of other members of the book trade. But in this respect at least, Cambridge jurisdiction was acceptable in London. The explicit exclusion by the 1637 Star Chamber decree of the universities' authority in London sought therefore to put an end to a practice that might otherwise have become sanctioned by custom.[7] Although examples of this kind are few, they do not seem to have been challenged even after 1637: twice in 1641 the Cambridge licence was quoted as adequate in transfers from Daniel to London stationers.[8]

Essentially, however, the Vice-Chancellor's authority was normally confined to the University. The effect was to relieve the London licensers of some of the burden, though law books had still to be printed in the capital, and so be licensed there. Just as the University's Elizabethan statutes had seen power devolved in a hierarchy of responsibility on the Chancellor, Vice-Chancellor and Heads, so licensing legislation in the seventeenth century granted a controlled independence. The government, in fact, was consistently reluctant to interfere in the affairs of Oxford or Cambridge in this respect. While provision for licensing changed repeatedly in London, and authority for different subjects was vested in individuals or bodies whose brief turns of office suggest more of experiment and suspicion than of conviction, the respective Chancellors or their deputies were left with their powers intact in successive legislation.

But University authority, delegated in a way similar to that in which other powers were delegated in the 1570 statutes, in practice affected London as well, in that many Cambridge-printed books also bore a London imprint, and most in any case found their way into the London retail trade. In the first half of the seventeenth century, this occasionally allowed the boundaries between trade in the two towns to be blurred. In 1618, Richard Kilby, minister at All Hallows, Derby, and a member of Emmanuel College, dedicated his book *Hallelu-iah* to Jesus Christ, and addressed it 'to those learned men which in Cambridge haue authoritie to iudge of books before they be there imprinted': the book was printed by Legge, sold in London by Matthew Law, and was not entered in the Stationers' Register.[9] On the other hand, permission at Cambridge seemed sometimes superfluous. Hamon L'Estrange's *Gods Sabbath briefly vindicated*, printed by Daniel in 1641, was ordered, not merely licensed, by the House of Commons to be printed, 'unlesse the Vice-Chancellor do shew just cause to the contrary, within convenient time'. Holdsworth's acquiescence, printed on the same page, was almost craven:

I have read over this Treatise, and am so farre from pretending any thing against the printing of it, that I must needs professe it to be a work both Learned and Orthodox, and highly meriting both the best care of the Printer now, and the best attendance of any Reader afterwards.

Similarly, Ralph Brownrigg, Vice-Chancellor in 1639, added a second imprimatur to the Earl of Arundel's for Du Praissac's *Art of warre*, in what can only have been determination to affirm the University's authority. Such occasions may have been few, but such jealousies helped to suggest a sense of danger. The Civil War brought its own needs for accommodation with the powers of the day, rather than the powers ordained originally by royal authority. In 1647 Roger Daniel printed the *Solemne ingagement of the Armie, under the command of Sr. Thomas Fairfax: with a declaration of their resolutions as to disbanding*. The 'ingagement' was read and subscribed to by the several regiments at Newmarket on 5 June; and on 8 June Fairfax inscribed the copy as, in practice, the licenser: 'It is my desire, That the humble Representation of the dissatisfactions of the Army, together with their Ingagement, be forthwith printed and published.' The Vice-Chancellor, Thomas Hill, Master of Trinity College, had been one of the original members of the Westminster Assembly, and owed his present position to Parliament: he presumably saw no reason to jeopardize it. In 1651, William Ball urged that the universities' jurisdiction should be restricted: 'not in London or elsewhere, not medling with Books of Common Law, matters of State, Military Discipline and Heraldry'. Finally, in 1662 the Licensing Act echoed the old Star Chamber legislation, in specifically restricting the universities' powers for licensing books to those printed or reprinted within their own confines.[10] Cambridge and Oxford were to remain independent, and also at arm's length.

In practice, such restrictions made little difference in a trade where books were printed in both London and Cambridge for sale in the other town. Much more seriously, at least in the eyes of some, the question was one less of corporate authority than of personal sympathies. Licensing was carried out by individuals, not by committees, whether in London or Cambridge, as the accusations and defence in the trial of Archbishop Laud made abundantly clear but as had been apparent for many years before then. In 1593, theological and state opinion had differed over Cowell's *Anti-Sanderus*, printed by Legate at Cambridge that year and thus presumably licensed by the Vice-Chancellor. 'The staying of the boke bredith a great scandall, and discoragith men willing to imploy there labors in such matters', complained Whitgift to Cecil, before continuing with a further plea for a unified policy in the face of Catholicism: 'Nether hath anie, as yet, signifyed unto me, what or how the boke shold be mended. I had sett on work this way, divers as sufficient men as are in this Land, but partlie, this accident and especiallie lack of instructions hath caused them to surcease.'[11]

Authors, or their agents, were likewise aware of the manner in which a different opinion might ease the way to publication. In 1636, as Laud pursued a vigorous policy of censorship in London, it seemed to John Downame, preparing to get into print his late brother's *Godly and learned treatise of prayer*, that Cambridge offered certain advantages; his view was shared by the expectant publisher, Nicholas Bourn.

George Downame had been a Fellow of Christ's from 1587 to 1596, and a leading Ramist. For the last eighteen years of his life he was Bishop of Derry, where he died in 1634. Both brothers were prolific authors, with experience between them of most of the reputable London trade, as well as of having books licensed for publication. John Downame's approbation of the University Printer, and his reasons for wishing his brother's work to be printed at Cambridge rather than at London, are therefore of unusual interest. He addressed the problem, and his proposed strategy, to Samuel Ward:

I wrote vnto you longe since desiring y^t you would be pleased to peruse a worke of my brothers of the doctrine and practise of prayer, wch though he only intended for his owne vse, yet seeing it may now y^t he resteth wth God be profitable for the benifitt of many others I desire y^t it be made publique. The stationer as allso myselfe desire to haue it licensed by the vniuersitie y^t it may come out wth as little alteration as may be, lest he may be forced to speake otherwise dead than he did livinge, as allso because we haue a greate opinion of the sufficiencie & faithful diligence of Mr Bucke your printer, vnto whom when it is licensed we intend to committ it. We desire y^t it may be dispatched with all conuenient speed that it may come out (if it may be) in the time of your worthy orthodox and vigilant vicechancellor, lest vpon the change it may retayne some rub or disturbance.[12]

And so Brownrigg's licence was recorded in the Stationers' Register. The Vice-Chancellor had changed several times over by the appearance of Downame's *Godly and learned treatise of prayer* in 1640, and Daniel's, rather than Buck's, name appeared on the title-page as printer. Copies were shared between Daniel himself and the London stationer Nicholas Bourn. But the tribute to the advantages of Cambridge was no idle one, even from one of her sons. If it had about it an air of special pleading, it also made plain an assumption that may sometimes have been implicit: that the succession of opinion and authority in Cambridge made regulations for licence in London seem all the more rigid in both their structure and their application.

William Jones' commentary on Philemon and Hebrews was printed in 1635 not in Cambridge, but in London, and a lesson was quickly drawn from it.

Jones, sometime Fellow of Emmanuel and now Rector of East Bergholt in Suffolk, dedicated his book to the Chancellor of the University, also of Emmanuel. But his treatment at the hands of the licenser became evidence against Laud. His text (it was alleged) was so purged by the licenser, Samuel Baker, chaplain to the Bishop of London, and then printed from the 'expunged, altered copy' that he 'disclaimed it to be his work, saying, it was the Licenser's only, not his, who had made him a favourite of those Popish opinions, by his corrupting and changing his words'. While of course it is possible that in some cases (not necessarily Jones') it suits authors to be able to claim this of their texts (and Prynne was to provide minute details of several more similar instances), Prynne's care in his account of Laud's career to name individual licensers is sufficient emphasis of the fact that since licensing depended on individuals, so it was inevitably applied unequally.[13]

Having seen Downame's hopes achieved, Daniel may have perhaps encouraged a similar course for John Ball's *Friendly triall of the grounds tending to separation* a few months later.[14] Despite the restrictions of the Star Chamber and of the 1662 Licensing Act, many books were in fact licensed in Cambridge for publication elsewhere. Such was inevitable in legislation that placed the primary responsibility on the printer. North's Plutarch in 1676 (printed by Hayes, but sold by Sawbridge and by Thomas Lee, in London), almanacs and elementary Latin texts were all tolerated in this way. So long as the University authorities did not countenance scandalous or seditious texts, they were left unhindered by regulations aimed primarily at an increasingly amorphous and loosely disciplined London trade, and designed to restrict printing to the established centres. In 1642 Daniel had repeatedly printed books and pamphlets that were politically controversial: the consequences, both for himself and the Vice-Chancellor, are described in chapter 16. But despite their previous records, neither Field nor Hayes printed controversial matter of this kind once they were established under the University. And most noticeably of all, the outbursts from the London press that accompanied the exclusion crisis, the popish plot and the glorious revolution and its aftermath found no echo from the Cambridge press.

Notwithstanding the ostensible strictness of the legislation, licensing was applied, in Cambridge as in London, only intermittently and (it seems) irregularly. Before printed imprimaturs were included in finished books, there is no evidence of what proportion of books printed in Cambridge was formally licensed. As in London, not all were, while the successive Vice-Chancellors took their responsibilities in this respect with varying degrees of seriousness. Too little survives for confident generalization, respecting either the nature of what was, and what was not, licensed, or the attitudes of successive Vice-Chancellors – or, indeed, of authors. Henry Butts, who in 1630 headed the list of those who licensed William Lisle's abortive edition of the Psalms in Anglo-Saxon, was Master of Corpus, and hence had a particular interest in this volume that drew directly on his own college's library.[15] But it is not impossible that Lisle himself was especially anxious for due licence: he was a man who habitually took an unusually close personal interest in the publication of his works. The theological overtones of such a volume made licence wise in any case. So, too, John Layer's *Reformed justice*, a legal textbook and as such rare for the University Printers to attempt, was licensed by Holdsworth and others, who would have been foolish to neglect to license such a work.[16] In the event the book was not published, but that was for different reasons.

When in 1635 Robert Shelford's *Five pious and learned discourses* was published, eight years after its author's death, the Vice-Chancellor was William Beale, the high church Master of St John's, a man who was however no Laudian lackey.[17] It is reasonable, in view of the book's campaigning tone, made plain in the prefatory verses by Crashaw and others, to speculate on how far the timing of publication was influenced by Beale's position as licenser. The University was certainly divided over the issue, as Usher, writing from Drogheda, made clear his opinion to Samuel Ward:

While we strive here to maintain the Purity of our ancient Truth, how cometh it to pass that you in *Cambridge* do cast such stumbling-blocks in our way? by publishing unto the World such rotten Stuff as *Shelford* hath vented in his five Discourses; wherein he hath so carried himself, *ut Famosi Perni amanuensem possis agnoscere*. The Jesuits of *England* sent over the Book hither to confirm our Papists in their obstinacy, and to assure them that we are now coming home unto them as fast as we can; I pray God this Sin be not deeply laid to their charge, who give an occasion to our Blind thus to stumble.[18]

There was, however, no printed licence, nor was it usual for books printed in Cambridge to include them until a few years later. The names of those heads willing to support Beale in what became one of the more notorious documents in ecclesiological debate are therefore unrecorded.[19]

Printed imprimaturs were obligatory in London from 1631/2, though few printers in fact included them. They were introduced in Oxford books only in 1638; and at Cambridge, too, nothing seems to have been done with any consistency, at least in print, until about the same time.[20] One of the first at Cambridge to include such a feature was James Duport's translation of Job, Θρηνοθρίαμβος (1637), licensed by the Vice-Chancellor (Thomas Comber) and three heads: Samuel Ward of Sidney Sussex College, Thomas Bainbrigg of Christ's and Richard Sterne of Jesus. Under Comber's successor, Ralph Brownrigg, who seems to have taken an exceptional interest in the formal supervision of the press (he was Master of Buck's own college), printed imprimaturs became commonplace: his name, with three others, appeared on, for example, Davenant's *Declamationes*, Fuller's *Holy war* (both 1639), and alone – in breach of legislation – in John Ball's *Friendly triall of the grounds tending to separation* (1640).[21] The struggle between Buck and Daniel was reflected in the imprimatur, dated 18 June 1639, to Edmund Gurnay's *Toward the vindication of the second commandment*, licensed to Buck alone and specifically. Brownrigg seems to have been exceptional in expecting a printed imprimatur as well as the ordinary manuscript licence. As in London, the imprimatur never appeared on more than a minority of books printed at Cambridge.[22]

Before the late 1630s, allusion to licensing was made only rarely in the finished books. John Legate was unusual in 1607 in printing on the title-page to Thomas Rogers' *Faith, doctrine, and religion…expressed in 39 articles*, 'Perused, and by the lawfull authoritie of the Church of England, allowed to be publique.' Less formally, but hardly less seriously, the 1634 edition of Quarles' *Emblems* was commended, and licensed, in verse:

> By Fathers, backt; by Holy Writ, led on,
> Thou shew'st a way to Heav'n, by Helicon…
> When Poets prove Divines, why should not I
> Approve, in Verse, this Divine Poetry?
>   Let this suffice to licence thee the Presse;
>   I must no more; nor could the Truth say lesse
>   *Sic approbavit* RICH. LOVE
>   *Procan.* Cantabrigiensis.

This upstaged even Ralph Winterton, who for his edition of Hippocrates' *Aphorismi* had the previous year obtained a paragraph of commendation – not simply the formal words of licence – from the Vice-Chancellor, Thomas Comber, as well as recommendations, or *censurae*, from five others.

If the 1637 Star Chamber decree was observed to the letter, then not only did licence have to be obtained before printing (as also ordained in 1586) but, in addition, two copies had to be produced for signature, one of which remained in the Vice-Chancellor's hands. It seems that the 1637 provision repeated a practice already established, at least in Cambridge. The few licensed manuscripts or other copy-texts that survive (even those dating from a few years earlier) owe their existence to this last requirement, rather than to printers', booksellers' or authors' care. The Tanner manuscript of Herbert's *Temple*, bearing the licence of Benjamin Lany, Thomas Bainbrigg, Matthew Wren, William Beale and Thomas Freeman, was the licensers', not the printers', copy.[23] In a different genre, the licensed manuscript of Matthew Wren's sermon at Whitehall, printed by the Bucks in 1627, and approved by the King, was not that eventually used as printers' copy.[24] A copy of the Augsburg 1605 edition of Origen's *Contra Celsum* in Trinity College Library bears Theophilus Dillingham's signature supported by Benjamin Whichcote and Ralph Cudworth, the inscription dated 14 August 1657: Morden's edition, printed by Field, appeared in late summer the following year, based partly on the 1605 edition, but not, for printing, on this copy.[25] William Lisle's edition of the Anglo-Saxon Psalter was never published; but though the licensed copy, dated 3 December 1630, survives amongst Laud's manuscripts (see fig. 24), it was not there for any political reason. Lisle had based his edition of Ælfric (1623) on a Cotton manuscript that likewise came to Laud, and it is probable that both these and several others passed to Laud after Lisle's death in 1637.[26]

In 1642/3 the warrant, or licence, was spoken of as a separate piece of paper.[27] In practice, however, the fact of licence seems to have been recorded haphazardly. Not until 1650 was any real attempt made in Cambridge to parallel the Stationers' Register. The printing orders of that year spoke, for the first time, of a book to be kept by the Registrary for the purpose, where there were to be entered not only the names of the licensers, but also the owner of the copy. The fee set for this, one shilling, was just double that charged for the equivalent by the Stationers' Company.[28] A single register survives, one whose irregularity and time-span suggest that it was the only central attempt by the University authorities to monitor licences.[29] Begun in September 1656, and continued until April 1691, it bears only a haphazard relationship to the books actually printed in Cambridge, or even to those in which the University's imprimatur was printed.[30] For most, if not all, of its life the register was compiled, correctly, in advance of printing, with the inevitable result that some projects were subsequently lost to sight.[31] In this way the register could, like that of the Stationers, be made to serve as one of intent, in which copyright could be reserved. Nothing was heard, for example, after the entry of an ambitious plan for a new edition of the Greek New Testament accompanied by the notes of Robert Estienne, Scaliger and Casaubon. Such a book would have provided an opportunity to bring into use the Codex Bezae, and it was perhaps intended to complement (if on a rather different scale) John Pearson's Septuagint of 1665. Nothing came either of projected editions of Genesis in Greek, entered to Field and licensed on 15 February 1663/4, or an annotated Latin Bible entered the following June. Since the name of no contemporary scholar was recorded, it is at least open to question how serious were these plans. Duport and Pearson, for example, may both have been involved; but these entries may have been intended primarily to lend credence to Field as Bible printer in the struggle with London. In 1656, and again in 1662, he had entered small format English Bibles as his copy, in an attempt to strengthen his position. But Bibles apart, nothing came either of projected editions of Simon Episcopius in the 1670s (instead one was printed by Moses Pitt, in London, in 1678), or of Longinus in the 1680s.

Such registrations, combined with the irregularity of entry even when licence had been correctly obtained, pose questions about the University's attitude to licensing in many ways as complex as those in London. In the end, entry in the University's register had more to do with copyright than with licence, despite the obligatory names of the Vice-Chancellor and his fellows. This muddled view of the matter is implicit in the manner chosen to protect Duport's Greek verse rendering of the Psalms, printed in 1666/7 by Field. It

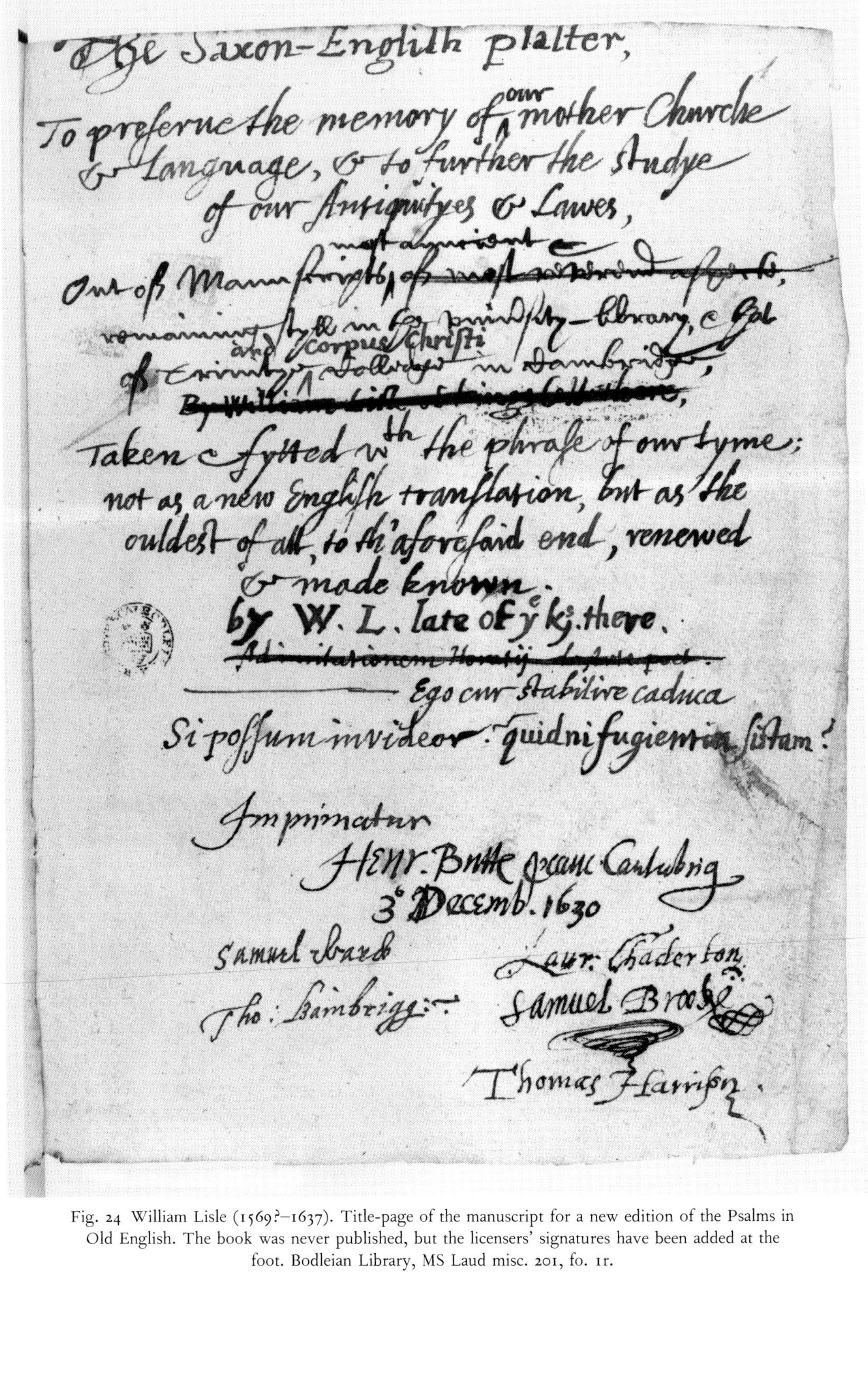

The Saxon-English Psalter,

To preserue the memory of our mother Churche
& Language, & to further the studye
of our Antiquityes & Lawes,

Out off Manuscripts ...
remaining ... in the ... Library, ...
and Corpus Christi
of Trinity College in Cambridge,
By William ...

Taken & fytted with the phrase of our tyme;
not as a new English translation, but as the
ouldest of all, to th'aforesaid end, renewed
& made knowen.
by W. L. late of ye kj. there.

—————— Ego cur stabilire caduca
Si possum invideor. quidni fugientia sistam?

Imprimatur
HENR. Butts Vicecanc Cantubrig
3° Decemb. 1630
Samuel Ibard   Laur. Chaderton
Tho: Bambrigg   Samuel Brooke

                  Thomas Harrison

Fig. 24 William Lisle (1569?–1637). Title-page of the manuscript for a new edition of the Psalms in Old English. The book was never published, but the licensers' signatures have been added at the foot. Bodleian Library, MS Laud misc. 201, fo. 1r.

was not included in the list of licensed books at Cambridge, nor was it entered in the Stationers' Register. Instead, and most unusually for a seventeenth-century provincially printed book, it was the subject of a royal privilege, an expensive and comparatively complicated protection that was to be much more widely resorted to in the eighteenth century.

The 1662 Licensing Act seemed hardly to affect the issue. For all the strictness with which its provisions were often enforced among London printers, in Cambridge licence seems to have been applied for only irregularly. In the hands of both John Field and his successor John Hayes, the Cambridge press followed a reliably unadventurous policy, to the profound irritation of some members of the University. It may be doubted how far such caution, or from another point of view idleness or failure of inspiration, was the consequence of a failure by the University itself (as Dillingham seems to have held); how far it was the result of lessons hard learnt in the market of rival tensions between printers and booksellers, London and Cambridge; and how much it reflected a response, in common prudence or necessity, by the licensing authorities in Cambridge in the face of the 1662 Act.[32] In 1663 Sir Roger L'Estrange's proposals for Surveyors of the Press, agents, in his words, 'authoris'd and appointed for the care of the press', made each Surveyor responsible for a particular province: one for law, three for divinity, physic, philosophy and other arts or sciences, one for heraldry, and one for history, politics and state affairs.[33] Thus not only was the licensing system to be more closely supervised; but the way was also open for a daily independent examination of every aspect of the book trade. L'Estrange noted that the Act assigned the licensing of 'All Books of Divinity, Physique, Philosophy, or whatsoever other Science, or Art' to the Archbishop of Canterbury, the Bishop of London, one of their deputies, or the Chancellor or Vice-Chancellor of either university. In other words, notwithstanding the provisions of the charter granted by Henry VIII in 1534, the Licensing Act, by restricting specified groups of books to particular licensers, barred the University from printing books of law, heraldry, state affairs, politics or history.

In fact, the Act had been self-contradictory, on the one hand restricting what might be licensed by the University authorities, and specifically forbidding 'medling either with Bookes of the Common Lawes or matters of State or Government', and on the other including a proviso that nothing in the Act should be construed as prejudicial to the 'just Rights and Privileges' of the two universities touching their licensing or printing.

L'Estrange's appointment as Surveyor of the Press, and his subsequent activities in that capacity, were little encouragement.[34] Whether accidentally or no, Cambridge showed no sign of wishing to challenge the licensing arrangements set in place by the 1662 Act, which in essence remained in force until 1695 save for the six years between 1679 and 1685. Politically as well as commercially, the University Printers tended to steer a course of unimpeachable conservatism. It was a course that neither attracted L'Estrange's or his agents' vigour, nor responded readily to the stimulus of those who desired more than Field, an astute survivor of political upheaval, was prepared to venture. In fact, rather than appearing the means to control in the sense envisaged by L'Estrange, licence became in the hands of the Cambridge authorities first a means to titular security, and second a mark of academic (not only legal) approbation. It became confused with commendation, notoriously in the anonymous *Tables for renewing and purchasing leases* (1685; 2nd edition 1700), where Newton's commendation was set out in just such a way as the normal Vice-Cancellarial imprimatur. But this was not the only example of academic approval being mingled with legal requirements. In 1679, the University authorities made a rare sortie among the London printers in this way, adding their imprimatur to Joshua Barnes' Αὐλικοκατοπτρον *sive Estherae historia*, an annotated translation of the Book of Esther into Greek and Latin verse, printed at Barnes' own expense in London. The imprimatur was dated 3 July 1676, perhaps a relic of an unsuccessful attempt on Barnes' part to have his work printed at Cambridge. But Isaac Barrow, as Vice-Chancellor, was not only out of place in London. He also appeared both as first signatory to the imprimatur opposite the title-page and then as author of the first in a series of laudatory verses gathered up by Barnes to promote his book.

The sometimes seemingly disorganized application of printed imprimaturs may be seen in another aspect in Barrow's own books. Second thoughts, and rearrangements in publication, however practical a means of keeping a momentum in the circulation of his works, meant that the various printed licence leaves in his books, when neglected by an inattentive binder, made it seem that their disorder implied how little value was set by the legal requirements. The imprimatur facing the title-page of Barrow's *Lectiones XVIII*, signed by Edmund Boldero, Peter Gunning and John Pearson, and dated March 1668/9, appeared also on his edition of Archimedes and others, printed at London in 1675. Not only was this another instance of a Cambridge licence being applied to a London-printed book (both were printed there by William Godbid); the imprimatur was applied even to the wrong book. By 1675, moreover, Barrow had succeeded Pearson as Master of his College, so that his book appeared to bear a double disablement.[35]

If in respect of licensing there was about Barrow's book an air of misunderstanding, and about the *Tables* one of deception, on the other hand the University register's periodic entries for school texts (of which not all can now be attached to surviving editions) were the means of legal reassurance. It was no accident that entries for almanacs form by far the largest proportion of entries until 1671, and that thereafter none was entered at all: Hayes had come to his agreement with the Stationers' Company the year before, and his position was secure as it had not been hitherto.[36] Both for Hayes and for Field, copy was more important than licence.

🐏 14 🐏

Running the printing house

The protagonists in the arguments over privileged books were all agreed on one point. For the University Printers, for University officers, for the local booksellers and for the Stationers' Company alike, the central issue was the cost of printing. Part of Buck's offence was that in agreeing on a sum with the Londoners, he had violated the Vice-Chancellor's prerogative of setting the price of books. The booksellers resented having to pay London, rather than Cambridge, prices; and each agreement reached between Cambridge and the Company specified which rate, country or metropolitan, was to apply.

Since the Cambridge printing trade depended in three crucial respects on goods or skills only readily available via London, the potential for price difference was limited. Paper and type were both governed by London; and the London trade supplied personnel – both University Printers such as Legate and Daniel, and a leavening of skilled journeymen. Once carriage was added to the cost of raw materials, costs had inevitably to be added on. Little information survives of the cost of bulk transport by wagon or carrier between Cambridge and London, a journey that took up to two days even for unimpeded travellers and which for a part of the way ran over noticeably poor roads. The only alternative was by water, via King's Lynn, though there is no evidence that for books this was seriously considered.[1]

By the early 1640s, the University's printing business had become considerable. No longer consisting of a single press with a few cases of type, no longer restricted in its output to the extent that a dictionary and half a dozen other slimmer books could be accounted a year's work, no longer staffed by only a couple of men, it was no longer amongst the least significant manufacturers of books in the country. Fuller's *Holy state*, and the elaborate edition of Beza's Greek and Latin New Testament, both published in 1642 were followed by Whelock's Bede in 1643. Each marked a departure, calling for typographic innovation and on a scale that made contemporary books from the Cambridge press seem almost pigmy-like. As folios, they stood literally taller than their fellows. *The Holy state* consisted of 112 sheets, with portrait engravings to be organized into the text as well, while the even larger Bede (of 149 sheets) was set in a new and unfamiliar type. The last chapters have examined, from political, educational and literary viewpoints, the manner in which this change came about. It remains to consider the means that were employed.

The post-mortem inventory of Thomas Thomas's workshop described his equipment in full. Besides one press, he had possessed text types (long primer, pica and brevier) in roman and italic, a quantity of Greek, 'cutt letters' (presumably decorative drop-initials), three alphabets of cast letters for chapter openings, and a few factotums.[2] Compared with other printers, Thomas was comfortably overstocked with type, having almost 2,000 lbs. weight of his three principal text sizes: it has been estimated that in 1607–8 the London printer Nicholas Okes could have printed his entire output with about 120 lbs. each of his most frequently used types.[3] Thomas's stock included type waiting to be melted down; but though his successors added fresh type as well, by the time of Cantrell Legge's death in 1625 – a low point in the fortunes of the press – it was estimated that there was no more than about a thousand lbs. in all, besides the single press.[4]

Thomas's business, like those of his successors, was limited not only by economic constraints, but also by legislation designed originally to preserve a balance of power in the London trade. The Star Chamber decree of 1586, intended to reduce an 'excessive multytude of presses', limited the two university presses to a single press each, and one apprentice each, but permitted an unlimited number of journeymen provided they were freemen of the City of London. The apparent liberality of the last provision was of course rendered ineffectual because of the limited capacity imposed by the restriction to a single press. If the university presses could not be prevented, they could at least be contained in such a manner. But they would not pose a threat to the interests of the London printers by whose influence the decree was obtained.[5] In 1583, twenty-three master printers in London possessed fifty-three presses between them: the largest house was that of Christopher Barker, the Queen's Printer, with five presses in all.[6] Three years later, Barker had six; but nine of the twenty-five printers then entered in the official list possessed only one apiece, and eight had two each.[7] In 1615, when Legge was University Printer, the controlling power wielded by the master printers in the Stationers' Company enabled them to win formal recognition for a reduction in these numbers. Apart from the King's Printers, nineteen printers were to share thirty-three presses altogether, five businesses possessing only a single press each.[8] Neither the Cambridge nor the Oxford press was listed in any of these surveys, whose purpose was not only political: they were also engineered to ensure full production for master printers by limiting the number of presses overall. The closed shop of the London printing trade, an élite within the Stationers' Company, made the opportunity to print in one or other of the university towns all the more attractive: at Oxford, Joseph Barnes (not a member of the Company) ensured his fortune by means of his son, who was a London stationer.[9] At Cambridge, Legate avoided the delays of the London trade by succeeding to Thomas's business two years after completing his apprenticeship in London under Barker. Once he could do so, he moved back into London, where, now with two presses rather than one at his disposal, he was in a better position than he was in the country. Legge, also, avoided the London restrictions; and Daniel avoided impasse, transforming himself by giving up most of his London book- and print-selling business to become a printer.

The provinces, in short, made it possible for these men to become master printers, and to have a share in the then most lucrative part of the book trade. The provinces also provided protection of another kind. Despite the efforts of the London master printers, their trade was over-supplied with journeymen by 1635, and apprentices had come to take a disproportionate part of the available labour market.[10] For the Cambridge press, this was of little consequence; it is likely that Buck and Daniel ignored even the second Star Chamber decree on printing, of 12 July 1637, which once more explicitly regulated the number of presses permitted not only in London houses, but in the university presses as well – this time to two. In the twelve years since Legge had died, leaving a paltry inheritance of a single press and a much reduced stock-in-trade, Thomas Buck and Daniel had transformed the business, sometimes, as we have seen, at the expense of the Londoners, and frequently (in Buck's case) at the cost of amity. Their expansion required that the legislation of 1586 and subsequently should be ignored; and they were able to do so on a scale which would have been prevented had they been in London.

When Legate finally set up his own press in Cambridge in November 1589, with equipment leased from Anne Thomas and with a stock of Thomas's books to dispose of, he had perhaps three assistants. Within a year or so he had five. Benjamin Pryme had served Thomas as apprentice since December 1584, and Cantrell Legge, a native of Norfolk, had become apprenticed to Legate only in June 1589.[11] Pryme was released from his remaining years of apprenticeship by Anne Thomas in January 1589/90, and does not seem to have worked regularly for Legate thereafter.[12] Besides these two apprentices, there was one journeyman whom Legate had brought up from London, Simon Stafford. Like his master, Stafford had served his apprenticeship with Christopher Barker, though he was subsequently made free of the Drapers' Company, and was not admitted a freeman of the Stationers' until May 1599.[13] He did not remain long in Cambridge. In the summer of 1592 he caused a major row in the printing office when he was called away to London and arranged to pay Pryme (who by that time had himself found other casual employment in the town) as pressman in his place.[14] He had probably left Legate's employ entirely, and returned to London, by February 1595/6, when a pamphlet by an erstwhile member of Trinity and now convicted criminal, Luke Hutton, described as *The black dog of Newgates lamentation for all his knavery*, was entered to him at Stationers' Hall.[15] Stafford, Pryme and Legge were quickly joined in about 1590 by another journeyman from London, Edward Smith, then aged about thirty, who seems to have worked as a compositor, whereas Stafford worked the press with the help of one of the apprentices. Smith, too, had entered the trade by way of the Drapers rather than the Stationers,[16] and he was already a figure of some notoriety in London as a result of his involvement in an infringement of Francis Flower's right to print grammars.[17] He was outspoken in his uncomplimentary opinion of both the equipment and his colleagues in the country – 'binders which knowe not what the worcke means'. Smith's particular disdain for Thomas's worn type, some unusable because it was the wrong height, supports his claim in 1592/3 that he was 'noe presse man'. His skill as a compositor was, indeed, essential for Legate, whose books had to challenge London formats and London prices. When the Bible was printed at Cambridge in 1590–1, Legate was subsequently alleged by Smith to have agreed to give him fifty copies if he could contrive to set it so that it took no more sheets than the equivalent London edition: Smith did so, and claimed by Legate's not having fulfilled his part of the bargain to have lost as much as £10 in bonus payment.[18] Finally, there was another compositor, making three in all to work beside the two pressmen; but it is not clear whether this shadowy figure stayed long: he may have been employed only whilst the Bible and dictionaries were going through the press, for he does not seem to have been available when Pryme's case came to court in the first months of 1593/4.[19]

Between them, Legate, Stafford and Smith all displayed a spirit of independence, sometimes aggressive and even buccaneering, in their dealings with the rest of the trade. All three showed themselves at various times in their careers to be impatient of the monopolistic restraints encouraged by the Stationers' Company. In this they had much in common with Thomas Thomas, despite the differences in their backgrounds and training. Thomas had only gradually found means to invade the preserves of the London stationers; Legate and his workmen were already familiar with, and practised in, them.

Not all of the staff whom Legate recruited were entirely new to Cambridge. By February 1593/4 he had another apprentice, Thomas Parker, born and bred in the town and presumably taken on to replace Pryme;[20] in 1599, another of his assistants, Thomas Vautrollier (perhaps the brother of Manasses) was convicted for causing a disturbance by taking part in a rowdy musical parade through the streets at night.[21] There were no doubt others, also engaged locally, for more or less casual labour.

Apart from the irregular Pryme, these men were expected to work at least a twelve-hour day, beginning at six a.m.[22] During this time, the two pressmen were expected ordinarily to print 2,500 impressions (i.e. 1,250 perfected sheets), though the differing sizes of edition quantities meant that the day could not always be organized exactly to this figure.[23] Not surprisingly, this figure was comparable with the output (generally 2,500 or 3,000) expected in London, while it also echoed precisely that agreed at Plantin's press in Antwerp.[24] So far as the Stationers' Company was concerned, the daily rate effectively set an upper limit to edition sizes for ordinary books, limited in 1587 to 1,250 or 1,500 copies.[25] The size of the type made no difference, the 2,500 daily impressions (for 1,250 copies) of Thomas's dictionary, an octavo in nonpareil type, being no more difficult – so far as the pressmen were concerned – than the daily 2,500 printed by Pryme and his partner Thomas Parker of Ramus: 'suche a dayes worke as everie man is able to do both vpon a small letter & vpon a great letter'.[26] In Cambridge, as elsewhere, the workmen, both pressmen and compositors, were paid by the day or week, on the understanding that they would produce an agreed amount of work: otherwise their wages were to be docked, and others in the shop who had been delayed as a result compensated accordingly.[27] They received 1s.8d. a day, or ten shillings a week: the rate seems to have been increased to this from nine shillings or less in about 1591, though Pryme claimed that Thomas had paid the larger sum several years before then.[28] The amount of work done in return for these rates is not specified, but the interdependence of press and composition was apparently so close at that time that when one pressman, Pryme, slacked, 'all the rest of the sayd Legates woorkemen and especially three Compositors and the said Primes Fellowe Presseman' were obliged also to slacken their usual pace: Pryme's offence was considered serious enough to have justified his dismissal.[29] Pryme was not a reliable witness, but in general the claims made by Legate himself and by his employees were supported by a document signed on 2 February 1593/4 by George Bishop (Master of the Stationers' Company), with two Wardens and two Assistants, and produced in Legate's defence:

To all to whome these presentes shall comme, we whose names are hereunder written beinge the M[r], wardens, and of the assistauntes of the companie of Stacioners of the Citie of London, doe sende greetinge: Forasmuche as it is the dutie of everie Christiane manne to certifie and declare the truth in all matters of Difficultie and controversie; Therefore beinge in this behaulf requested by John Legatt of the vniuersitie of Cambridge Printer; we doe certifie and for a truthe infaileable declare, That the Dictionarie called Thomas Thomas his Dictionarie late printed by the saide John Legatt, in the volume called large octavo, is of the printe of the sorte of lettres, called Nompareil letters: And that the workinge of drawinge off of Twentie and Five Hundred leaves or sheetes of the saide Booke and lettre or of the like, and not lesse nomber of sheetes or leaves, ever hath beene and nowe is ⟨accustomed⟩ accompted of Printers an ordinarie Daies worke, for a presse man in the arte of printinge: And that the wages of a Presseman for the saide worke of xxv[c] per diem is nowe, at the moste ⟨is⟩ after the Rate of x[s] the weeke, and noe more, and ordinarilie heretofore hath beene ix[s] and under. And that if anie Presseman hired for the like worke and wages as aforesaide, shall not accomplish his full worke of xxv[c] per diem as aforesaide; That then the Presseman not accomplishinge his saide worke of xxv[c] per diem shall, and ever heretofore did, and ⟨stoode⟩ shoulde by the aunciente order, custome, and usage, of and amonges Printers; recompence and allowe to the M[r] printer, by whome he is, or hath beene, retained in service; the Damage losse and hindraunce by the saide M[r] susteined, or to him to growe by Reason of the defaulte made by suche presseman in not accomplishinge his saide worke of xxv^e per diem And also satisfie the losse and charge of all his other Fellowes that worke uppon the same worke with him. In witnes whereof herevnto we have subscribed our names the Seconde daie of Februarie, stilo Anglie 1593.

Geor. Bysshop. M^r
Ga: Cawood
Tho: Woodcocke
Richard Watkyns
francis coldocke[30]

This emphasis on a rigorously controlled timetable, a fixed working day in which a pre-ordained amount of work was to be done according to a carefully co-ordinated series of tasks divided between different parts of the printing house, was the basis of dispute under Legate. Both in approach and in detail, it shared many of the features of similar pronouncements about the management of other printing houses elsewhere, large and small. In this, not surprisingly, Cambridge, London and continental houses, all engaged in the same processes, were remarkably similar.[31] But while such co-ordination, apparent efficiency and speed of production were both agreed between masters and men, and demonstrably achievable, there were inevitable interruptions.

When in 1626 the University Registrary James Tabor was attempting to understand the likely profits to be derived from the university press, he set down a memorandum

The ordenary worke of A press
is 3 Reames a day.
18 Remes ye weeke,
900 Remes ye yeare accomptinge 50 weeks to ye yeere.

From there he went on to calculate, on the basis of a cost of eight shillings a ream charged in turn at eight shillings a ream for ordinary work and fourteen for double, the sum to be expected of a year's work.[32] Like so many other outsiders attempting to understand manufacturing processes, he was obliged to accept what he was told, and to multiply towards annual output on the assumption that each week and each month proceeded at a regular pace.

This suggestion of regular uninterrupted production could only produce a maximum possible production. Another calculation was more valid for the reality of the printing house. Between 13 September 1625, when Legge's successors took over the printing house, and 21 February 1626/7, a total of seventy-five weeks, some 1,275 reams were printed, counting the red and the black printing of almanacs as double. The output, seventeen reams per week, was in fact so close to the optimum of eighteen as to suggest that the press during this time was working at very considerable pressure, even if it is suggested that double printing (red and black) did not take quite as much time as two separate formes. This work was costed at eight shillings a ream, a figure intended to include paper, presswork, correcting and carriage (much of it presumably to London, since almanacs formed a high proportion of the output). It was then sold at either eleven shillings a ream for single work, or fourteen shillings for double.[33] Such figures accord with Legge's agreement a few months earlier to supply Humphrey Atkins in London with six hundred reams of grammars and accidences at 11s.6d. a ream.[34]

That such regularity and productivity was by no means normal seems by now sufficiently obvious. In the 1590s, Benjamin Pryme, Simon Stafford and Thomas Parker had disputed over the usual speed at which sheets might be printed, asserting that it depended partly on the size of type. Varying edition sizes (requiring different proportions of the day to be spent in making ready), quite apart from weather, time of year, plague, or journeymen's anxiety to earn a full week's pay, all contributed to an erratic and irregular pattern of production. Although it seems probable (but it is no more) that the figures of 1,250 perfected sheets for a working day quoted when Legate's editions of Thomas's dictionary and Ramus's *Logic* were going through the press were equal to the edition sizes, it is clear that in many instances editions were considerably larger, and certain that others were much smaller. Indeed, as Stafford (an experienced London printer) himself admitted of the work in Legate's shop, 'they had diverse numbers upon Severall bookes and the numbers did alter'.[35]

Thomas's estate offers only one clue to the size of his editions. He had completed a single book in 1588, before he died in August of that year: William Whitaker's *Disputatio* against Bellarmine, its title-page dated 2 May. Three months later, 1,381 copies were still in stock, suggesting an edition of perhaps 1,500. Whitaker, Regius Professor of Divinity, was well known in Cambridge, and widely read both in London and on the continent, and it may be presumed that Thomas had printed as many as possible within his means.[36]

In other words, though Stationers' Company regulations, productivity agreements and paper trade conventions conspired to effect a norm, the varying daily requirements of a printing house engaged in the concurrent production of several books resulted in a routine marked, though not necessarily dominated, by irregularity.[37] Such was equally true of establishments in London, as elsewhere; and the larger the establishment, the greater the opportunities for variation. So it is important to distinguish between the small shop of Thomas and Legate, and the much larger establishment of Buck and Daniel in the 1630s, while recalling also that they differed in less than they shared in common.

As we have seen, the usual requirement of a day's work at press in the 1590s was 2,500 impressions, or 1,250 perfected sheets.[38] Essentially this remained the same throughout the seventeenth century, though in extremes this might be increased to 3,000, as seems to have happened with the edition of 1,500 copies printed by the Bucks of Gerhard's *Meditations* in 1631.[39] But this limit, imposed by the hours of the working day, enshrined in Stationers' Company orders, and confirmed to the University in 1593, was only a maximum for as long as an agreed trade equilibrium seemed desirable. Though in 1587 the Stationers' Company was obliged to forbid the keeping of standing formes of type (from which repeated series of impressions might be pulled), and to take cognizance of the much larger quantities recently printed of such assured regular sellers as the Psalms in metre and the ABC, this was not an easy rule to enforce.[40] Indeed, it seems to have been widely ignored, and with especial vigour by just those monopolists who were closest to the centre of power in the Company. By the early 1630s, editions of some of the most constantly demanded educational texts were being printed at Cambridge, on paper supplied by the Stationers, in editions of three thousand copies and upwards. The annual editions of Aesop and of Culmann's *Sententiae pueriles*, of four thousand and six thousand respectively, were the largest for the texts licensed to Cambridge by the Stationers; but most of the books that aimed at similar markets were also printed in editions that ignored ordinary, and outdated, regulations.[41] This variation of edition size (not only of books, but of occasional printing for the University as well) meant, of course, a much more complicated working day than is at first suggested by regulations agreed either in Antwerp by Plantin, or in London by the Stationers' Company. Editions could not be compartmentalized by the day, while the fact that journeymen were paid by the day or week, rather than by piecework, made concurrent printing essential if financial disaster was not to arrive with undue speed.

Edition limits based on a day's work and designed to preserve an approximate balance between composition time and presswork were eroded further by the practice of continuous reprinting of sheets for popular works, at Cambridge principally (but by no means uniquely) the Bible from the late 1620s, and at London exemplified by Kingston's printing of Speed's accompanying *Genealogies*.[42] The number of usable sheets in a ream of paper varied, as did spoilage at press: inconsistent quantities were inevitable, and made such practices irresistible in the face of consistently high demand for particular books. In London, the Stationers' Company sought to regulate printing for the English Stock by calling in superfluous sheets, but it was a regulation that was impossible to enforce.[43] In Cambridge, not only Bible editions became mixed. The first edition of Davenant's *Determinationes* (1634) made a reappearance in the second of 1639,[44] and the early editions of Herbert's *Temple*, for which there was a rapid demand, became similarly muddled.[45] Henry Ferne's rather more controversial *Resolving of conscience* (1642) achieved rapid notoriety, and the variations and mixtures of type-settings in surviving copies attest to the press's efforts to reprint, using as much of the existing formes as possible.[46]

More conventionally, Cicero, Corderius, Erasmus, Ovid, Mantuanus and

Vives were each printed in discrete editions of three thousand. So, too, were editions of the metrical Psalms, while almanacs took on an even greater momentum all of their own.[47]

Though such figures demonstrate that it no longer seemed necessary to link edition sizes to a day's work, the equivalent of up to three reams of paper, printed on both sides, they bear no relation to the remainder of the Cambridge press's output, that part which was not directed by London monopolies. There is no reason to suppose, for example, that rapidly repeated editions of other popular works were printed in similar edition sizes. Herbert's *Temple*, first printed by Buck and Daniel in 1633, was followed by a second edition the same year, a third in 1634 and a fourth in 1635. In terms of editions, it thus at least equalled the annual appearances of Aesop and of the *Sententiae pueriles*. But that the edition sizes equalled, or even challenged, such books is unlikely. For the London school-books, paper was supplied by the Stationers, in an arrangement that simultaneously saved Buck and Daniel's investment and ensured the Company's control over quantities. For *The Temple*, the cost of paper had to be met by the printers and, at some point, by the local bookseller Francis Greene who took so large a part in its publication. This cost, roughly fifty per cent of production costs to a printer, meant not only considerable investment. It also, in effect, controlled the usual size of editions, leading to unduly high unit costs for numbers in excess of 1,500–2,000 copies.[48]

It is clear from these very high figures of the early 1630s that whereas in the 1590s the difference between one work and another was relatively minor, forty years later the Cambridge press was dominated by work for the Stationers' Company. Edition sizes might be increased, but the rate of printing at each press could not. In 1633 some 994 reams of almanacs, metrical Psalms and Stationers' texts were printed, the equivalent of about 331 days' work. In 1634 the respective figures were 970 and about 323. In a year of about 300 working days, this meant that the equivalent of at least one press was occupied with Stationers' work for the whole of the year. In practice the seasonal nature of almanac printing, and the fact that it accounted for more than half of all the Stationers' paper (some 520 reams annually) meant that in the autumn up to three presses might have been occupied with this work alone, in a printing house that possessed but six in all, of which one may have been a rolling press.

Legge's equipment and stock in trade was bought from his widow by Thomas Buck and Leonard Greene, for a mere £155. At first, as Elizabeth Legge continued to live on Market Hill, new premises were found in Regent Walk, where printing began again on 13 September following Legge's death.[49] These premises were, however, too small; and after Greene had committed the partnership to extending next door, into unoccupied buildings, at considerable expense, Buck became dissatisfied and the press was moved again, to the Angel Inn on Market Hill. It was at this new address that the press now began to expand. Shortly after John Buck had joined his brother, there were four presses, managed by a staff of whom many were apprentices.[50] So large an establishment offended the 1586 regulations on several counts, as the Stationers' Company did not fail to point out. In London, the purpose of the 1586 decree had been to restrict the number of master printers, so as to ensure that none was without work, and to guard against there being too many contenders in the future for a restricted trade, by limiting the number of apprentices. In practice, only part of these intentions had been met, and the increasing output of the London publishers during the first decades of the seventeenth century had indeed required more press capacity than had been envisaged as adequate in the 1580s. Between the early 1580s and the 1630s the number of books published in England more than doubled. For many subjects, the buoyant import trade was a reflection of London's manufacturing inadequacy, as those who looked at the Bible trade in particular in the 1630s were quick to point out.

Not only did Buck and his partners now possess four times the number of presses permitted under the 1586 regulations. They also employed five apprentices, three or four workmen who were not (as they should have been) freemen of the City of London, and an unspecified number of 'other Iournemen'.[51] Who were these people, and where did they come from? Unlike the highly organized London trades, few records have survived for apprentices indentured to Cambridge craftsmen. But several names are known, and much of the rest of the establishment can be reconstructed. Although Greene complained vigorously of Buck's inexperience, his own acquaintance with the book trades had more to do with bookselling than with printing. In 1625, realizing this, Greene sought to persuade a printer to come from London, though this seems to have been vetoed by Buck: it is not clear whether the man Greene had in mind was Roger Daniel, who is not heard of at Cambridge until some years later. Greene expected then to have become warehouse keeper, while Buck acted as press corrector. However, this proposal was unacceptable to Buck, who not only removed the stock-in-trade while Greene was absent but, once again seeking as profitable a course as possible for himself, went on to claim a salary of £40 per annum as press corrector, a figure said by Greene to be at least four times what was paid in London for such work.[52] This argument had still not been settled in 1632, when Daniel agreed with Thomas Buck to provide correctors (more than one was envisaged), who were to be given 'sufficient help and convenient time': they were not, in other words, to have such other duties round the shop as would cause this aspect of the work to be skimped.

The most experienced journeyman among the press's staff was Robert Leet, who had been apprenticed to Cantrell Legge in 1614 and who was to remain with successive University Printers until his death in 1663.[53] He presided over a motley crew. When in August 1632 Daniel entered into a formal agreement to lease the printing business from Buck for £190 per annum, he took over five apprentices from Buck himself: Martin Hall, William Batty, William Flower,

Charles Flower and Edward Johnson. Thomas Dunster, John Buck's former apprentice, was also made over at the same time. Apart from these, there were three apprentices whose origins were unspecified: John Sill, John Folkes and Edward Christopher.[54] Eighteen months later, still further apprentices had been indentured: Edward Plumer, George Linsey and Thomas Jones.[55] Among the other staff of the printing house was William Bentley, warehouse keeper and accountant, duties for which he was paid £32 per annum.[56] In 1630 there was also at least one other person whose name is still known and who was described as a printer. Thomas Milborne caused offence during plague time by removing his family from the town to his family's home at Great Chesterford, just over the Essex border, and then commuting to work each week. Milborne's status is however unclear, in that he had been apprenticed to a London printer, Felix Kingston, in 1627 and was not to be freed until July 1634: it seems unlikely that he worked at the Cambridge press for more than a short time.[57]

The number of journeymen working with these apprentices is not known; but an informed guess is possible, based partly on the number of presses in the shop, and partly on the nature of most of its work. In the mid-1560s, and for about a decade from 1576, the Plantin press at Antwerp was not engaged (as it so often was) on a heavy programme of liturgical printing, requiring a disproportionate amount of time at press to allow for the separate red workings. During these years, it pursued, rather, a programme not unlike Daniel's, at least from a technical point of view. With five presses in 1565, it employed nine pressmen and eleven compositors. In 1578–9, when there were again five or six presses at work (the number had reached sixteen in 1574, and dropped to three in 1577), eighteen or nineteen pressmen and compositors were employed, the division of tasks being roughly equal. In 1584, again with six presses, twenty-four men were needed in all – enough to run eight presses in 1582 and a figure that suggests unusual circumstances. In Cambridge, Buck handed over an establishment of six presses, requiring, in a staff that included nine apprentices (and assuming that every press was fully manned and occupied with work, which was not necessarily the case) about ten further journeymen. It is possible that the agreement to work only three presses reflected the number of staff available, though the number of prentice hands would then have been disproportionately high; and as Daniel realized new journeymen could only be recruited from London.[58]

The premises that Daniel now took over from Buck were in the old Austin Friars, buildings dating back in part to the late thirteenth century and standing in an area bounded by the modern Free School Lane, Downing Street, Corn Exchange Street and Peas Hill. The watercolour sketch of the building executed by a member of Corpus Christi College in the mid-eighteenth century (see fig. 25) shows the old refectory, remains of what had once been a court.[59] In 1632 Thomas Buck rented it from Perse Beck (a member of the same family as Stephen Perse, founder of the local schools named after him), and he was to

The Refectory of St Augustins Monastery Cambridge — 1780.

Fig. 25 The old Augustinian friary, Free School Lane, home of the press in the mid-seventeenth century. From a drawing made in 1780.

rent it until his death in 1670.[60] Here he had the press installed, moving it from the Angel Inn, and here in turn Daniel was installed by agreement reached on 22 August 1632. In the mid-sixteenth century, the building had been easily the grandest private house in Cambridge, the dimensions of its rooms (including a parlour far beyond ordinary needs) almost princely. Since very little is known about the disposition of the buildings, or the state of their dilapidation by the early 1630s, it is not clear how much space Daniel had at his disposal, but he was granted virtually the whole apart from two rooms and a coal hole, which Buck reserved for his own use. The agreements between Buck and Daniel of 1632 and 1633/4 listed the rooms and, despite the dimensions being unclear, these documents provide an unusually detailed account of the disposition of a printing house and its related premises. The press room was separate from the composing room, which was in turn separated off from a room which did duty both as a 'letterhouse' (presumably type store) and as counting house. This counting house seems to have been quite spacious, for it was divided up into studies, of which Buck kept two and one was for Daniel's private corner. A further study was available to Daniel, at the head of the stairs and looking out over the garden. Paper was stored in two small rooms under the corn chamber, next to a privy, and once printed was to be dried in a gallery. Two warehouses, middle and upper, with a closet adjoining the latter and a chamber over the 'little hall' were available for storage. The accommodation was completed by a lye-house,[61] a coal cellar for the printing house, and use of the old kitchen for making ink.[62]

By this date, the equipment was considerable. Among the most notable items, which determined the organization and output of the press, were six presses, thirteen composing frames, $56\frac{1}{2}$ pairs of cases of metal type, twenty-five chases, twenty galleys, and seven 'great stones', presumably correcting stones – preferably but not essentially of marble – for compositors to use when imposing formes of type. A further indication of the scale envisaged by Buck is in the fifty paper and letter boards, the latter used when storing tied-up type.[63] The full list, apart from these principals, was as follows:

five copper plates, six banks, one mullet, poles for drying books, twelve candlesticks. two frames to put cases in, one case for wood letter, two trestle tables, four tables with drawers, two lead troughs [for damping paper, etc.]

Daniel also obtained further shelving in the woolhouse, an otherwise unspecified part of the building.

The floor area required for such equipment was substantial. In 1683, Moxon calculated that each press required a space seven feet square, and each composing frame one measuring $4\frac{1}{2}$ by $5\frac{1}{2}$ feet, these figures allowing space for circulation. The seven correction stones would have had to be at least $4\frac{1}{2}$ by 2 feet in order to accommodate the inner and outer formes of a sheet.[64] Thus, these parts of the equipment alone would have required about 670 square feet in all; besides this, space had to be found for trestle tables, banks of paper, four other tables, troughs of water and cases for storing type not kept in the composing frames, and finally, as well as all these things, somewhere for a paper store and a finished stock room.

There is no reason to suppose that the great increase in the size of the premises under Buck and Daniel, in the presses, type and other equipment available, or in the staff employed, made any difference to what was expected of a day's work, for which the principal evidence at Cambridge dates from the 1590s. By the 1630s, the Cambridge press was no longer in the crowded central part of the town, but working conditions still remained much the same, based on a twelve-hour day for pressman and compositor alike.[65]

Although in 1594 the University authorities had had described to them a week made up regularly of six days of twelve hours' work each, this pattern was liable to interruption. At the end of the seventeenth century, the working week was determined by piece-work, not by the hour; the linking in the 1590s of output to time, for both compositors and pressmen, suggests that this became customary only later, as agricultural and other services' assumptions about a daily or weekly rate gave way to the requirements of the irregularities of industrial production.[66] Beside his ordinary pay, a pressman or compositor might also hope for, or expect, further rewards. By custom, he was entitled to one or more copies of each book he worked on, though this was so liable to abuse that in 1635 the Stationers' Company forbade it, replacing such 'copy-books' by an extra wage of threepence a week. Whether or not the mid-century Cambridge printing house followed rule rather than custom in this respect is not clear.[67] Apart from this regular practice, workmen might also sometimes receive *ex gratia* payments for various reasons. Few records survive of this, but a few notes among the University's records of payments for official verses cast a little light on what must always have been a sensitive topic. Much later in the century, in 1685 and in 1688, the compositors received an extra 8s.6d. and 8s. for their work on the poems marking respectively the accession of James II and the birth of a successor to the throne, and in 1689 the printers (it was not specified whether compositors or pressmen: perhaps both) shared an extra five shillings between them. In the winter of 1694–5 the compositors at work on the verses on the death of the Queen received 7s.6d. between them 'to hasten them in their work'.[68]

Seasonal variations in the hours of daylight meant shorter working days in the winter. With the windows papered (rather than glazed) against the cold, conditions for close work became more difficult still during the winter months. Darkness, or poor light, was a hindrance for everyone, though for the pressmen the early part of the day would have been occupied with making ready, and perhaps proofing: an even light was essential if each impression throughout a run was to be of a consistent colour – to the extent that Moxon was to suggest that ideally presses should be set in a northern light.[69] Work could be slowed or interrupted by the weather, a feature that seems to have been so much taken for granted that it only rarely caused comment.[70]

Plague, however, the terror of almost everyone, was the chief threat to production. Outbreaks occurred frequently, in Cambridge in 1593, 1603, 1605, 1608, 1610, 1625, 1630–1, 1636, 1638, 1641, 1643, 1644–5 and 1646. It brought first dread, and then terror. An outbreak in London was perceived, with justice, as a threat to the provinces as well, while the annual Stourbridge Fair, bringing together people from all over the country, was a hazard of potentially disastrous proportions. 'We are yet at Cambridge well, God be ever blessed for it', wrote Joseph Mede in May 1625, as he kept a tally of mortalities in London. Communications were cut, and Hobson's and other carriers' trips to London forbidden. By September, with the plague spread to Norwich and labour for the harvest scarce in the fields round Royston and Barkway, south of Cambridge, the University was almost under siege. Members were confined to their colleges, and food was running short. 'They will suffer nothing to come from Ely. Eeles are absolutely forbidden to be brought to our market; so are rootes. You see what tis to have a physitian among the Heads.' The beginning of the Michaelmas term was adjourned, sermons in Great St Mary's temporarily abandoned. The 1630 outbreak at Cambridge, recorded in bills of mortality printed at the University press, lasted from April to the following winter, and carried off Leonard Greene in October.[71] The few members of the University who dared remain kept shut in their colleges even at the end of November, numbering the illness and deaths of townsmen on whom they depended. 'We have not had this week company enough to be in commons in the hall, but on Sunday we hope we shall. It is not to be beleeued how slowly the Universitie returneth, none almost but a few sophisters to keep their Acts. We are now [at Christ's] 8 fellowes; Bennet Colledg but 4, schollers not so many. The most in Trinity & St. John's &c. The reassembling of the Universitie for Acts and Sermons is therefore againe deferred to the .16. of December.'[72]

So serious had been the plague's effects even the following year that they were alluded to by way of apology for the delayed appearance of the University's verses *Genethliacum*, belatedly marking the birth of Prince Charles in May 1630 and of his sister Mary in November 1631.

In 1603, 1630, 1636 and 1637 plague caused the cancellation of Stourbridge Fair, and so removed the principal occasion in the year for Cambridge printers, stationers and customers to trade or consort with booksellers from elsewhere. Connections with London, the source of paper and books alike, were disrupted. It caused the wholesale cancellation of teaching and, sometimes, the disbanding of the University. People watched it make its inexorable progress, anxious lest it threaten to approach their own houses or college. 'It is much in Bridge Street, and so up towards Sidney College', wrote one observer to John Worthington in October 1665: 'Cambridge is almost disuniversitied, and either there will be no winter term, or nothing to do in it.'[73] By the following January, the press having been virtually silent for the whole of the autumn,[74] trade in books was almost at a standstill. And on 17 July 1666 Francis Wilford, the Vice-Chancellor, wrote to John Cosin, 'The removall of the University, and the greatest part of the able men of the Towne, have left us no good store of poore, in whome only we are rich, they amounting to above 4000 by the lest computation we can make, and they are the more by reason of last yeare's sicknesse.'[75] Plague ceased to be endemic only after 1666.

15

Type, paper and other necessities

The officially specified rates of production discussed in the last chapter were based on the output of the pressmen, not of compositors, though the dependence of one on the other will be self-evident. The last few pages have been concerned with presses, with pressmen and with personnel. It remains to examine the materials with which books were printed: type, decorative matter (whether ornamental initials or illustrations), ink and paper.

Until well into the seventeenth century, printers at Cambridge rarely considered it necessary to buy much fresh type once they had made an initial outlay. The parlous state of Thomas's numerous, though much worn, cases became a matter for dispute after his death. Legate himself, who inherited them, faced shortages within a very few years: his complaints at the cost of replacement were by no means mere bluster. Wrong-fount letters became frequent even on his title-pages in his later years as University Printer, and it was left to Legge in 1608 to introduce new display founts: among them were Granjon's double pica, and a new two-line great primer to supplement Guyot's rather lighter version of the same size on which Legate had relied for his larger books. The range of types that resulted during Legge's early years was to remain the mainstay of the larger displays at the press until the 1640s.

Inevitably, there was much that was ordinary in the design of the books printed at the press, even under otherwise innovative figures such as Buck and Daniel. For many of their books, constraints of size and format made experiment impossible, even had it been necessary or thought desirable, given the limited range of types available to them, and a tendency to economize on paper sizes. The costing of grammars, almanacs, Latin texts and Bibles alike relied on as close a similarity as possible to the penny-pinching of established London or foreign-printed models. All too often, this cramped effect, of small sizes of type occupying as much of the page as possible, was reproduced in works that had no direct London (or indeed continental) competitors. Nor were all purchases of fresh types necessarily improvements. A pica roman, used in (amongst others) Francis Quarles' *Judgement and mercy for afflicted souls* (1646) and William Harvey's *Exercitatio anatomica de circulatione sanguinis* (1649) was cast on so wide a set that the composition of these books looks disjointed. But among the ordinary, some books were typographically distinguished in that their design successfully met the challenges of their unusual or innovative texts. By far the most celebrated of these books, Herbert's *Temple* (1633, etc.), with its pictorial reproductions for 'Easter wings' and 'The altar' was however no innovation, falling in an early Greek tradition led by Simmias of Rhodes and by Theocritus, and beautifully demonstrated typographically in Henri Estienne's 1566 edition of the Greek poets.[1] More recent English parallels were to be found in the typographical contrivances of Richard Willes' *Poemata* (1573) and in Andrew Willet's *Sacrorum emblematum centuria*, printed by Legate in probably 1592. Prose texts could be set, where necessary, with the same aplomb. Gabriel Dugrès' French grammar, printed in 1636 'impensis authoris amicorum gratia', repeated London (and continental) conventions in printing English in black letter, French in italic, and the principal Latin text in roman. Davenant's *Praelectiones*, published only two years before *The Temple*, interspersed both italic and small capitals in the ordinary English roman, though the effect was spoiled by foul case and an inadequate italic fount. By the time that Edward Kellet's *Miscellanies of divinitie*, another folio, came to be printed in 1633, new founts were in use, bringing considerable improvement to a similarly complex text. Whelock's edition of Bede was an especial challenge. The new fount of great primer Anglo-Saxon set the pace typographically, but although the slightly fuller Latin text was set in English-size type, the two did not always run exactly parallel: both had frequently to depart from the double-column arrangement, and take up the full measure across the page. The different sizes of type, moreover, caused particular difficulties in the extended notes which punctuate the volume: the difficulties ended only with the later acquisition of a smaller size Anglo-Saxon, used in the notes to the edition of Ἀρχαιονομία designed in 1644 to accompany Whelock's work.

In a few books, such as the Bede, some lavishness was justifiable, though even here the later arrival of a smaller-size fount of Anglo-Saxon suggests unease. For the folio Bibles produced in 1629 and 1638, an appearance of generosity had to be balanced by economy in the face of entrenched and powerful London competition. Although paper was expensive, and labour comparatively cheap, the circumstances of the production of the 1629 Bible, in the immediate aftermath of Charles I's confirmation of the University's privilege in February 1627/8, made speed essential. That could only be achieved by reducing the number of sheets to be worked. A lower price (governed by the paper consumed) would follow. These considerations help to explain the unusual diversity of paper quality among the different issues of this book, which gained an appearance of generosity simply by offering larger page size and thus left it open for costs to be contained in the smaller paper copies. The 1629 Cambridge Bible, with its accompanying Book of Common Prayer and metrical Psalms, embodied a series of typographical decisions whose principal intention was therefore to economize within a framework established by convention. The only other folio edition of the Authorized Version set in roman type was that printed at the King's Printing House in 1616: it offered a model against which to set an alternative. Both the King's Printers and the Bucks printed folio editions in 1629, each prompted – though for different reasons – by the decisions of the previous year, which effectively licensed competition for the first time. Although the King's Printers were able to command a better stock of decorative material than the Cambridge press, whose investment in an engraved title-page was made thereby all the more noticeable, the two editions had sufficient in common to suggest that one imitated the other. The horizontal lines bounding the running heads in 1616 were abandoned; both editions were set in long primer, rather than the 1616 pica; and both had the same page depth. Cambridge, however, gained further by setting the italic summaries at the head of each chapter in a size smaller still, brevier, and by extending the column width by two ems. So, even though the London edition of 1629 consumed approximately ten per cent less paper than that of 1616 for each copy, the Cambridge edition used still less, reducing the figure by about twenty per cent. The Book of Common Prayer, set principally in long primer in both the London edition of 1616 and the Cambridge of 1629, offered less room for manoeuvre, as a generally more complex text; but the lavish lay-out of the metrical Psalms in 1616 provided ample space, and was likewise compacted into fewer sheets by the simple device of using smaller type both for the music and for the text.

For the much more genuinely lavish 1638 Bible, in which the text was so carefully corrected, the press could afford to take a more relaxed attitude, setting the text in a larger size and allowing the volume to take up much the same number of sheets as the previous London folio, of 1632/3. Scholarship was harnessed to the service of commerce; but in the choice of decorative initials employed for chapter or book openings, there were also signs of fresh investment and application to detail. So the opening 'I' in Genesis, 'In the beginning', featured Adam and Eve (fig. 18), the 'B' at the beginning of the Psalms, 'Blessed is the man', depicted King David, and the 'A' in the preliminaries to Morning Prayer in the prayer book showed a figure indeed at prayer. The introduction of such traditional features, with histories going back several centuries, may be viewed as an expression of the religious conservatism at Cambridge at this time; but such figures had to be paid for, and their introduction was not less an affirmation of the Press's seriousness of purpose in its investments.

There was a direct precedent for the 1642 New Testament, with its triple-column arrangement of the three texts (Vulgate, Beza's text and Greek) coupled with a double-column commentary and a fourth, narrower, column that usually existed only marginally but had on occasion to spread across the page. The edition's principal copy-text, printed by Vignon at Geneva in 1598, made little change necessary. The whole was accomplished, however, with more economy than in 1598, when pica had been used for Latin, and English for Greek: Daniel used the very noticeably smaller long primer for both.

The most noticeable feature of all in Buck and Daniel's press was however not typographical, but illustrative. Despite the fact that no rolling press is specifically mentioned among any equipment inventory, the press embarked under the two men on a programme that transformed the presentation of both quite ordinary and more ambitious books. By 1634 the Cambridge printing house contained five copper plates.[2] The cost of engraving was high, as was its printing, with the consequence that it was usually commercially practicable only to embark on illustration of this kind if either reprints of a book could be expected within a short time, or a book was deemed sufficiently important to meet the cost anyway, or if an author or patron was prepared to meet the cost. Gerhard's *Meditations* (1633, etc.), Terence (1633), Winterton's Greek poets (1635) and Drexelius on eternity (1632, etc.) all fell within the first category. In the second, the series of folio and quarto Bibles and New Testaments were the most prominent. John Payne's engraved title to the 1629 Bible was matched in 1638 by another, the work of William Marshall, which included both a rebus for Buck and Daniel's motto *Assurgo pressa* with its accompanying palm tree. The 1642 New Testament brought a further development, prompted probably by the London trade. On this occasion the engraved title was abandoned, and a freshly etched version by Hollar of the 'Hinc lucem' device graced the title-page instead.[3]

The decision to use these plates was a commercial one in that they matched, or challenged, those in other similar books with which they had to compete. The plates by Cornelis van Dalen for John Cruso's *Militarie instructions for the cavall'rie* (1632 and 1644) were probably paid for by Cruso himself: the existence of an early state omitting the University Printers' imprint altogether suggests that the plates were cut before any decision as to printer had been made.[4] So, too, the other great illustrated book to come from Buck and Daniel's press, Fuller's *Holy state* (1642), with its series of engraved portraits by Marshall, may well have been partially financed by its author, if Fuller's remarks of 1662 do indeed relate to this book: 'Cuts are cuts, as I have found by dear Experience. Besides, when they are done, they are not done, the working them off at the Rowling Presse being as expensive as the Graving them.'[5] He may likewise have been responsible for paying for the pictorial title-page to the *Holy warre* in 1639, an essential part of the book but one of an unaccustomed kind for the Cambridge press.

> Before you travel to the Holy land,
> Behold a Page that in the front doth stand
> To give you aym and guidance i'the way.[6]

More ambiguously, the three plates included in some copies of Phineas Fletcher's *Purple island* (1633) were paid for by Edward Benlowes, 'Benevolus'. Whether they were printed at Cambridge, or on a press under Benlowes' private control, is not clear; but Buck and Daniel did not meet their cost, and they can be confidently excluded from the census of plates conducted at Cambridge in 1634.[7]

Of the cost of new type, little record has so far been found respecting the Cambridge press. In the mid-1650s it was supplied by Alexander Fifield, who was paid either by the Stationers' Company or by the printers, according to the intended purpose.[8] In the eventual use of both type and ink there must have been regular overlaps, though scandal did not touch the printing house in this respect until the 1660s. In 1668, Field owed as much as £225.14s.6d. to Alexander and Thomas Fifield, a sum comparable with the expenditure authorized by the Delegates at Oxford to be spent on type in 1668–9, as they sought from London typefounders to equip the new printing office in the Sheldonian Theatre, before Fell determined to approach Dutch typefounders instead.[9]

Finally, type required ink. Ink required oil and ground pigment: the Stationers supplied both in at least the 1650s for almanac and other printing, paying £2.10s. for oil and carriage in 1655. Black ink came by the barrel, apparently ready made; vermilion (supplied as pigment only, much superior to red lead, and, notwithstanding Moxon, apparently used even in almanacs) cost ten shillings for 2 lbs. in 1654 and 7s.6d. a lb. in the year following, both prices including carriage.[10]

For all the approximations and assumptions consequent on the tension between the theoretical achievements and the everyday experience of the printing shop,[11] one point is manifest. The press was economically dependent on the Stationers. There also remains unanswered the question of how far production costs of assured work such as that offered by the Stationers were allowed to influence the pricing of other books. Many details are known of retail prices, through booksellers' bills and private accounts; something is known of retail stock valuations through booksellers' daybooks, post-mortem inventories of stock, and surveys taken in connection with actions for debt, and the standard (but not necessarily usual) charges for straightforward binding are also known; but the overall manufacturing costs of books in England in the early seventeenth century remain elusive.[12] It seems however that while retail costs were often calculated by the sheet, the natural measure in a single copy of a book, manufacturing costs were calculated by the ream. In 1598 the Stationers' Company set the retail charge of books in pica or English letter at not more than a halfpenny a sheet, and that for books in smaller sizes, of brevier or long primer, at not more than a penny for $1\frac{1}{2}$ sheets. The distinction, based on type sizes, was thus related to composition charges, though it will be recalled that in 1593–4 part of the argument over rates of pay for work on

Thomas's dictionary had hinged on its type size, nonpareil.[13] These figures proved no more than a guide, were in any case not intended for books carrying illustrations, and took no account of binding costs. Nor, in seeking to fix retail charges, did they take into account a trade structure where middlemen and distance from the ultimate market might play havoc with an ideal. Most seriously of all, in a product so much of whose cost was in materials, they ignored paper quality and size.

Of all the costs involved in manufacturing a book, by far the largest was for paper. It accounted for well over half the total even at foreign presses with easier access to supplies than English presses could claim. For Plantin's press in the late sixteenth century, paper accounted for 60 per cent of the production cost, and up to 75 per cent for longer runs.[14] In the virtually complete absence of white paper manufactured by English mills, all printing paper for London and Cambridge had to be imported, some from Germany but most from France or Italy, and was subject to a duty of five per cent.[15] For printers, though paper was sold by the ream, only part of each ream was usable. Outside quires, known as the cording quires, were commonly made up of inferior paper, to serve as protection to the better sheets within. A printer was expected to cull from this such sheets as he thought were also usable for his purposes. Second, some allowances had to be made for proofing or spoilage at the press: Moxon set this at a little more than five per cent.[16] The University Printers, like most others, accordingly counted a ream as 480 sheets.[17] This figure was of considerable importance, since all trade calculations as to cost were on the basis of reams, or paper consumption.[18]

Between 1583, the date of Thomas's appointment, and 1652, just after Daniel's return to London, the decennial average for paper prices rose by approximately one-third; but most of this change occurred at the beginning and end of the period. From 1593 to 1642 it rose only by about fourpence a ream, or less than seven per cent. For roughly fifty years, the price thus remained remarkably consistent, until duties imposed under Richelieu helped bring to an end a period of extraordinary stability.[19] This consistency in much the largest component of the press's costs makes it possible to adduce evidence that might otherwise seem unrelated. It also adds a gloss to the discomfiture claimed by the Cambridge stationers at Buck's hands, since his activities helped to exacerbate an already difficult situation. For this general trend was not repeated in all its details. The papers offered by the retail trade for writing differed from those available from other dealers to printers. The printing trade had available to it a range varying considerably in price and in quality. Thomas Thomas left stocks of four different sizes and qualities – described as pot, hand, small Rochelle and demy.[20] In 1593 John Legate, beset by plague in London and Cambridge, asked a London colleague that he would 'send me word what paper is in London of pot hand rochell smale and great or any other sorte', before going on to request '6 reame of your best writing pot paper 4 reames of the buckes head 2 reame of damuske paper 1 reame of 6 lines ruled paper and 1 reame of V lines ruled paper'. His distinction between the paper for printing and various writing, damasked, or music papers gives a glimpse of a trade divided in two according to use and, to a great extent, manufacture.[21] In 1612 the Stationers' Company ordered that ballads were not to be printed on paper costing less than 2s.8d. a ream.[22] One of the complaints which the 1625 proclamation against foreign reprints of books printed originally at the two university presses sought to redress was that overseas editions were printed on inferior paper.[23] In 1622 the price of printing paper was reported to range between 3s.4d. and 5s.6d. a ream, while in 1640 paper for schoolbooks cost 3s.6d. a ream.[24] Though post-mortem valuations often bear only a loose relation to current prices, it is worth remark that in 1588 Thomas Thomas's four different stocks were valued for probate at between 2s.8d. and 6s. a ream. Nearly forty years later, in 1625, Cantrell Legge's effects included forty-six reams of white paper valued, rather conservatively, at £9.4s., or four shillings a ream, and thirty of 'course' paper at £4.10s., or three shillings a ream.[25] The difference in quality even in a single book could be dramatic. Although printers usually endeavoured to ensure reasonable continuity of quality and colour throughout a volume, there were exceptions: in 1648 Roger Daniel's edition of Wendelin's *Admiranda Nili* was printed on stocks varying in colour between shades of brown and white. As has already been mentioned, Michael Sparke wrote in 1641 of the 1638 Bible being printed on three different papers, corresponding to three separate issues. The folio Greek New Testament of 1642 was likewise printed on several sizes. No less than seven different stocks, divided between discrete issues, have been identified in the Bible of 1629, though this was unique in Cambridge, and possibly for its time.[26]

Most of the surviving evidence of Buck and Daniel's costing relates to schoolbooks, rather than to editions with shorter press-runs. Here, the differences between London and Cambridge prices were critical; and so, too, was the need to use paper stocks as economically as possible. Prices could be reduced only by reducing the quantity of paper or its size, or the number of sheets needed to print a book. Popular books, requiring constant new editions, owe much of their success to their readers' conservative expectations. When these were met by a typographical conservatism whose first priority was economy, the result was a series of conventions that made editions of the same text look very similar – whether printed at Cambridge or elsewhere. Thus there developed around classical texts for the use of schools, elementary grammars and Bibles, all books of lasting demand, a consistency in design assumed by manufacturer, bookseller and reader alike. Format, paper size, page lay-out and type design each contributed to a longevity in such works that depended originally on the cost of paper.

Because of the stability of paper prices, it was not wholly unreasonable to legislate on the price of books *in vacuo*, although such exercises were obliged to make assumptions about paper quality. In 1598, the Stationers' Company regulations on the subject took as a base a book set from manuscript, rather than a reprint, and directed charges according to the size of type used: books set in pica or English were not to be sold retail at more than a halfpenny a sheet, and those set in smaller sizes (brevier and long primer) at not more than two-thirds of a penny.[27] In practice, there were inevitably many exceptions to this, but these rules were not often breached dramatically. At Cambridge, where the rules governing the press obliged the Vice-Chancellor to set the price, a rule of thumb was set out in a memorandum, clearly by somebody who was professionally competent, prepared as an aid to the University's officers in its dealings with the Stationers over the printing of schoolbooks, Bibles, etc. It summarized the consequent costing. On the one hand, it was explained, there were octavo Bibles and Psalters '& such like bookes in that Letter', by which was meant nonpareil, the smallest usually available, printed on fine paper and costing probably 13s.4d. a ream to print. At the other extreme were grammars and schoolbooks, estimated at 8s. a ream 'though ye Londiner geiveth but vj^s 8^d at the most'. Thus an average book, costing ten shillings a ream in paper and printing, might cost a farthing a sheet, while a book costing a penny a sheet was equal to no less than £2.0.0. a ream.

Anxious to demonstrate the profits being taken by the Stationers' Company for their privileges, the memorialist then continued:

Yf vpon the first sight of any booke printed in England you desire to knowe the Chardge of the Printer for paper, & printinge

Looke in the Alphabett what Letter the last sheete beareth, then reckon to that, for yf it be course paper such as the Grammer, & all schoole bookes are; you must reckon thus; for example take Leggs Grammer, the Letter is O so ther are 14 sheetes in that booke, I reckon their chardge of printinge, & paper is but vj^s-8^d., wch is not above ij^d qr the Grammer in Quiers, but yf you will allowe them x^s a Reame, that is qr the sheete, it is 3^d. ob for the Grammer in Quiers, & now ye Stationers sell them for 8^d. in Quiers, & so they get 4^d. ob in every eight pence after x^s. the reame.

The Psalmes are printed for the Stationers at } 0—12^s—0
London in 7 sheetes for xij^s. the reame   } the reame
They sell these 7 sheetes for vj^d. that is   } 1—17—0
neere a j^d the sheete, & it is at least   } the ream
So they gayne cleerly for euery 12^s layed out   1—5—0
The like proporcon you may make of all oth^r. english, and forraine bookes.[28]

It was calculations of this kind that gave Legge the fortitude to agree with Humphrey Atkins, the London grocer, on a price of 11s.6d. a ream.[29] And as with the grammars, so with the metrical Psalms, printed for the London stationers at 12s. a ream. The price for these in quires was sixpence, roughly a penny a sheet, or 37s. a ream. At such a rate of profit it was little wonder that the Cambridge printers felt confident of breaching the market with success. In general, the Cambridge price for manufacturing standard school texts might be as little as 65–75 per cent of that obtaining in London. Testaments and grammars, it was suggested, could be printed for half, and metrical Psalms for 43 per cent or less.[30]

The books with which these calculations were principally concerned were not necessarily a fair reflection of the pricing of other, less popular, work. Furthermore, the ordinary cost of printing in Cambridge was considered by Leonard Greene to be higher than in London,[31] though it is not clear what sort of work he had in mind: subject to paper costs, large editions of schoolbooks or almanacs or Psalters offered more opportunity to spread costs (and at the same time reap a rapid return) than, for example, sermons or ordinary theological controversy.[32] Impressions of such books were always much larger than those of the sermons, biblical commentaries, more specialist university texts and occasional poetry that made up the bulk of the press's output. But further evidence can be adduced, for books which were not in direct competition with London printers and London rates, and where the only ways of ensuring a profit lay in reducing paper costs by cutting quality or contriving to fit the whole of a text into a smaller number of sheets.

In other words, and to repeat: while labour costs of composition and of presswork remained constant, the ratio between the two varying with the size of edition (and hence length of press-runs), the principal controlling factor in the cost of presswork, regardless of the size of the edition, was the cost of paper. Printers thought in terms of reams not only because paper represented so high a percentage of production investment, but also because each ream represented so many hours' work. It is thus the most reliable base on which to cost work, and to judge movements in prices over the century. Retail prices inevitably bore varying relationships to manufacturing or wholesale costs. In London, the Stationers' Company had sought to control them in 1598, with provisos that books set in pica or English type, with no illustrations, should be charged at a halfpenny a sheet, unbound, and books set in brevier or long primer at $\frac{2}{3}$d.[33] With some exceptions for particular genres, of which the most notable was the customary sixpence for a play of ordinary length,[34] these figures were complied with to a remarkable extent. In Cambridge, even in the 1630s, the University paid only $\frac{1}{2}$d. to $\frac{2}{3}$d. per sheet for volumes of verses printed by Buck and Daniel.

From the beginning of Thomas Thomas's work, the retail price of books in Cambridge was to be regulated not by the printers or booksellers, but by the Vice-Chancellor, who might, however, either take specialist scholarly advice or consult with those stationers having an interest in the book in question.[35] The same was intended when in 1590 the University gave permission to the bookseller Manasses Vautrollier to settle in the town: the conditions imposed on this occasion are of extra interest in that they restricted Vautrollier to selling foreign-printed books, only unbound books (which meant, in effect, only new ones), and to price them 'as good cheape as they are or shalbe bought or solde in London'.[36] It was intended, in other words, that there should be no differential between London and a provincial university town. How far this was achieved in Vautrollier's case is not recorded; but the clear implication of such a requirement is that, for many members of the trade at least, such a differential was inescapable and justified.

While the prices of a few books in sheets are known, most of those recorded are of bound copies – figures usually for retail, and usually including an unknown amount for the cost of binding. A copy of Legate's quarto edition of Thomas's *Dictionary* (1596), bound in plain calf with a blind-stamped ornament, cost seven shillings, for example, the equivalent of 0·6 pence per sheet. Thomas Taylor's commentary on the Epistle to Titus, printed by Legge in 1619, and also in plain calf, likewise cost seven shillings, or 0·86 pence per sheet. Both were on a small crown paper, but it is possible that the lower retail price set on the dictionary was part of a deliberate policy to keep the book as competitive as possible.[37]

But movement of stock from one bookseller to another, such as that between Atkinson and Allot and Francis Greene, implied also a progression of increasing prices. Thus, for example, the University bought from the printers copies of the collection of verses on the King's recovery from illness, *Anthologia in Regis exanthemata* (1632), at sixpence a copy in sheets, whereas Troylus Atkinson, selling within the trade, charged the London bookseller Robert Allot eightpence a copy – a margin of $33\frac{1}{3}$ per cent.[38] Again within the trade, but as a re-importation of stock (since the book had been printed in Cambridge), Allot charged Atkinson £1.0.10 for twenty-five copies of Herbert's *Temple* (i.e. 10d. a copy, also unbound), whereas the retail price of this much printed book was probably about 1s.6d., bound.[39]

The prices charged by successive University Printers remained below a penny a sheet for ordinary books until about 1670. The schoolbooks printed in the 1630s, on paper supplied from London and produced in such immense quantities, were cheapest of all. Aesop was available wholesale in London at 13s.4d. a ream (just under 4d. a copy) even after profits had already been taken by Buck and the London wholesalers; the *Sententiae pueriles* cost 16s.8d. a ream, or about $1\frac{1}{4}$d. apiece.[40] When Roger Suckerman, the local Cambridge bookseller, bought six copies of an octavo Virgil from Buck and Daniel in June 1638, he was charged tenpence apiece, or just over a penny less than the wholesale price (33s. a ream) in London, and Mantuanus' *Adolescentia* cost him fourpence apiece. On the basis of these, London wholesale prices for schoolbooks were between seven and eleven per cent higher than locally in Cambridge.[41] Of books printed in more modest editions than those intended for the general education market, few wholesale prices – either from printer or stationer – are known, and the evidence seems sometimes conflicting. The price of Duport's Θρηνοθρίαμβος (1637, a parallel Latin and Greek text) was set by the Vice-Chancellor, in a rare instance of his exercising his ordained authority. At a shilling in quires, it cost about four-fifths of a penny in sheets, or about 35s. a ream.[42] Once books were away from Buck and Daniel, or other printers, market forces created their own price structure. The translation of Lessius' *Hygiasticon*, a duodecimo printed in minute type on the smallest sheets of paper, cost Robert Allot but 1s.9d. each when he bought several hundred copies from Atkinson in 1633–4 – a price of less than a halfpenny a sheet, or about 18s.10d. a ream, and only two or three shillings more per ream than the London wholesale price for schoolbooks. Robert Shelford's *Five pious and learned discourses* (1635), a quarto of $42\frac{1}{2}$ sheets charged to Allot by Atkinson at 1s.9d. each, cost a halfpenny a sheet, or £1.0s.10d. a ream.[43]

All these prices, however, date from the mid-1630s, a period that has been identified with a sharp rise in the price of printed books.[44] Until that time, the usual charge to the University when it bought copies of University verses from the printer of the day was about two-thirds of a penny a sheet.[45] These volumes, all the same quarto format until a belated change to folio in 1697 when the type size was changed to double pica, were set in either pica or (from 1632) English type according to lay-outs that rapidly established their own broad conventions. Despite changes in paper size and quality, they are the best available general guidance to the overall rise in printing prices at Cambridge in the seventeenth century. Such a sampling carries many dangers. No account can be taken of real paper costs (none of which was invoiced separately to the University); correction charges presumably varied, but though the University often met the cost of an official corrector, his payment was quite different to that for the printing house; some volumes were more straightforward to set than others, according to the proportion of Latin to Greek, Hebrew or Anglo-Saxon; some required cancel leaves; for some (as in 1612, 1633, 1637, 1640, 1658 and 1660) the text seems to have been supplied piecemeal, resulting in differing issues longer or shorter than the next; for others, type was awaited, most dramatically in 1697, when the new Greek type from Holland was expected, and the sheets containing contributions requiring it were kept until the end.[46] Any of these factors might mean production complications or delays, and any might lead to variant costings. These books were produced in the minimum possible time, since verses had to be written, the sheets composed and printed off, presentation copies bound, and presentations made while excitement was still alive. It was this, no doubt, that led the University occasionally to pay small extra sums of the kind alluded to earlier.[47] If incentive payments of this kind were common, they were not usually recorded as separate items in the accounts.

Apart from such production complications, from 1669 onwards verses were produced on two qualities or sizes of paper, the printers' vouchers or audit book usually distinguishing between the two. Copies were supplied to the University in quires, to be bound up in a variety of styles as the University chose. There was of course no obligation for the University to take up the whole edition of any volume, and it is unlikely that it ever did so. The number of copies taken in this way varied, like a thermometer of public opinion on the events being commemorated, between the rather tepid figures of 130 to mark the birth of James Duke of York in 1633, 180 on the death of Oliver Cromwell in 1658, 170 on the death of Anne Duchess of York in 1671, 163 on the marriage of Princess Mary to William of Orange in 1677, to a much warmer 731 for the Restoration, 526 for the accession of William and Mary in 1689 and 530 on the death of the Queen in 1694.

The price of these books rose steadily, from two-thirds of a penny per sheet in the 1630s to 0.87d. in 1658, before dropping abruptly in 1660, when Field charged the University what may well have been a rate intended to court favour. Within two years, the price per sheet had risen to just under three farthings, and by 1670 it was a penny. Though it rose as high as 1.37d. in 1683 (the University paying £27 for three hundred copies, including sixty on royal paper, on the marriage of Princess Anne and Prince George of Denmark, the same sum it had paid in 1662 for seven hundred copies of the somewhat shorter volume on the marriage of Charles II), by the end of the 1680s the price had settled back to about a penny a sheet. Large or fine paper copies were charged generally at about fifteen per cent extra.[48]

Outside the better documented 1630s, figures can only be presented piecemeal once one sets aside this periodic expenditure on a somewhat specialist genre. Evidence from Cambridge is lacking, but that from Oxford in the 1670s suggests, not surprisingly, that composition (and imposition) costs depended partly on the size of type, partly on the complexity or otherwise of the page design, and partly on difficult languages (Greek being the principle). Presswork was charged according to the size of the sheet as well as the size of the type. For most work, composition costs were between two and four times those of presswork for editions of 500 to 1,500 copies. Engravings and their printing incurred further expense, the prices for printing again varying greatly depending on the size and complexity of the plate.[49] At Cambridge, Whelock's edition of Lambard's Ἀρχαιονομία (1644), with its engraved map, large and good quality paper, and recently acquired new type, was one of Daniel's more expensive productions. But a copy in sheets cost Sir Simonds D'Ewes only seven shillings, or three farthings a sheet (the equivalent of £1.11s.3d. a ream) in 1646. Bought probably from the London publisher Cornelius Bee,[50] it was in line with the trends suggested by the verse anthologies: the collection marking the King's return from Scotland, in 1641, had cost £1.11s.4d. a ream. Other available figures of which I am aware are less useful when set beside the verses, since they are all for books that had few pretensions as to their physical appearance. For one book printed much later, by Hayes, more detailed costs survive. John Armstrong, Fellow of St John's, became Vicar of Cartmel in Lancashire in 1665, where he was eventually buried in 1698. In 1677 he turned to the printer of his University, John Hayes, for a small volume of *Secret and family prayers* 'fitted for the use and benefit of the inhabitants of Cartmel in Lancashire' and an accompanying sermon. The two together, printed on an ordinary foolscap and in English type, ran to twelve sheets octavo. For this, Armstrong paid six shillings a ream for the paper, and sixteen shillings a sheet for printing, a total for 656 copies (the odd figure the result of waste) of £14.17s. To this he had then to add carriage to his parish, and binding – the last paid for apparently as successive stocks became low.[51] Other examples of costs date from the 1690s when, for reasons no longer clear, the University bought multiple copies of various books printed by Hayes: copies of Cicero's *Orationes selectae* in 1692 and 1699, a dozen of John Edwards' *Enquiry into four remarkable texts of the New Testament* in 1691–2, a dozen of a defence of the Thirty-nine Articles by John Ellis, Rector of Dolgellau, and fifteen each of the Book of Common Prayer and Barnes' Euripides in 1694–5, and (apart from Cicero) sixteen copies of Edward Leedes' Greek grammar in 1699. None of these books, mostly with cramped typography and parsimonious in their use of paper (even Barnes' Euripides was not a generously designed book) could compare with the display typography of the books of University verses. It is not clear that they were bought in sheets, rather than bound. Hayes had no bindery, and no binding costs were specified either in his accounts to the University or elsewhere in the audit book. The prices paid for these books (equivalent to about $1\frac{1}{4}$d. to just under twopence a sheet if the books were unbound, or just under a penny to just under $1\frac{3}{4}$d. if they had simple calf bindings) depended partly on the size of type, but at least equally on the size of paper. Such a range, and such relationships, were universal, nor is there any evidence to be found here of how far prices were affected by edition sizes. Though Barnes' Euripides, a small, if substantial, folio, at 24s. a copy, was by far the most expensive individual book in these transactions, its cost per sheet was in fact among the lowest of all, about three-fifths that of the crown octavo Cicero of 1692 and (in slightly expanded form) of 1699.[52]

These prices were those charged by the printer to the University. Neither Buck nor Daniel, Field nor Hayes, were obliged to charge a wholesale price, and there is no reason why their assumptions should have changed over the years, or according to the nature of their transactions: the substantially higher charges for those books in the 1690s may reflect simply the University's slightly more distant position as customer for books that it had in no sense commissioned. Equally, the very low charge made by Field for the verses on the Restoration did not signify massively lower costs, but merely a decision not to apply so great a multiplier to the actual cost of paper, labour and plant.

There remains one group of evidence that supplements all these various approaches to the cost of production in Cambridge. Although different in its purpose from many of the examples cited above, since its figures are for valuation purposes rather than for present or imminent trade, it presents an exceptionally detailed view of an aspect of the press for which concurrent information has proved otherwise so far elusive.

The inventory of Field's stock taken on 7 October 1668, shortly after his death, is a document of interest as much for what it omits as for what it includes.[53] For years, Field's work had come principally from two customers: the local booksellers and, more importantly, the English Stock under the control of George Sawbridge. As a printer, rather than a publishing stationer, Field owned, for the most part, only such stock as had been recently completed, and not yet delivered. The exceptions to this general rule consisted either of stock ready to be drawn on by particular parties (usually the English Stock) or of the few books whose costs he had underwritten himself. Of the recent octavo Aesop, he had only 111 copies left, the rest presumably having been sent to London. Of Winterton's *Poetae minores Graeci*, also recently finished, he had but half a dozen. But of other schoolbooks he had thirty-three reams of Lucius Florus (1667), and 132 reams of Lily's grammar. Of the 1667 octavo Cicero *De officiis* there was no trace; nor was there of Schrevelius' *Lexicon manuale* (1668), nor of Bullokar's *English expositor* (1667). Apart from a substantial stock of Corderius' *Colloquia*, of which the only known surviving edition from Field's press dates from 1657, but of which he had printed a more recent one for the English Stock, now lost, the oldest stocks were of Sophocles, an attack by Joseph Beaumont against Henry More, and Duport's duodecimo prayer book and Psalms in Greek, all of 1665.

The valuations set on this stock – principally but not entirely of cheap editions of classical texts, Bibles, concordances and prayer books – were set partly in terms of copies, but principally by ream. To a very great extent, it seems to have been a valuation by manufacturing cost, not by potential sale.

Valuations were established by the size and quality of the paper employed, and by the size of type – the latter implying a labour cost expressed in ens, or the amount of text set. For such a valuation, the number of copies of completed books was immaterial: the critical factor lay in how many sheets remained. Leaving aside those books valued by the number of volumes, rather than by the ream, most valuations ranged from 3s.4d. per ream (for the Psalter in Greek) to perhaps as much as 13s.4d. per ream for Corderius. The small type (nonparcil) Bibles were valued at 18s. per ream, and their accompanying concordances at 20s.; but with the sole exception of Gouldman's dictionary, at 6s., and two reams of University oaths, at 4s., other ream valuations all fell between eight and ten shillings. Two hundred and ninety-one reams of almanacs (presumably for the following year, as the valuation was taken in October) were valued at ten shillings a ream.

If the Corderius is set aside (as it must be, since there is no evidence that Field's 1667 edition followed that of 1657 in its typography or pagination), the most expensive stocks were of the Bible and its concordance, both on crown paper rather than the smaller pot used to print most of the rest, and both set in the smallest type available. But Gouldman's dictionary was also on crown paper, and even though set in brevier (like the Lucius Florus, valued at ten shillings per ream, or Burgersdijck's logic textbook, at eight shillings), it was valued at a mere six shillings per ream – a third of the figure set on the Bible sheets. If the appraisers found something inadequate or imperfect about the sheets for the dictionary, they did not record it. It seems possible that this part of the stock was deliberately undervalued for the sake of Sawbridge, publisher of the dictionary and one of Field's executors. The edition in question was not published until 1669, and since the printing bill must have remained unpaid at the time of the stocktaking, a low valuation would allow a low invoice figure subsequently.

The appraisers' valuation of the quality of the paper stocks was undiscriminating beyond the simplest terms, 'fine' and 'coarse' with respect both to the prayer books and the Testaments and to the white paper stock. Of a total of 223 reams of white paper, thirty-five of foolscap (its quality unspecified) were valued at 4s.6d. a ream; and crown (the only other size apparently in stock) was divided between a hundred reams of 'coarse' at four shillings a ream, and 88 reams of 'fine' at eight shillings. In sum, the relationship between valuations for white paper and those for most of the finished sheets suggests yet again that the materials cost accounted for up to half the total, even for the large editions entailed in most of these publications.[54]

Thus, while considerable details are known, if only piecemeal, about the statistics and calculations that underlay the daily working of the Cambridge printing houses in the seventeenth century, there are still very large areas of ignorance even with respect to general questions as to costs. Edition sizes in the new printing house, established after the reorganization of the University Press in 1698, were usually in multiples of parts of a ream, from five hundred to a thousand or, exceptionally, two thousand. For earlier periods they were, with the exception of schoolbooks, almanacs and Bibles, probably much the same: but we cannot be certain. Nor do the surviving prices provide an answer to the actual cost of printing, since the printers's profit is never known, nor indeed are the cost centres which it was deemed necessary to take into account. The explanation of costings quoted earlier in this chapter unfortunately did not specify any particular book, but took a general principle. As a guide, the note is a valuable one, but it has been so simplified for the benefit of a non-specialist that it is difficult to apply to the ordinary output of a printing house in the expectation of thereby coming to overall assessments of the cost of publishing. Much of the later part of this chapter has had to be tentative in its conclusions, because so many of the figures quoted exist in but imperfect contexts. But their rehearsal provides a series of glimpses of a subject of which all too little is known. The view is incomplete, and often unfocused; but it still reveals an unexpected amount about the working of the Cambridge printers, many of whose practices were the same as those of the equally inadequately understood London trade.[55]

It was not simply that the staff employed by Legge, Buck, Daniel, Field and Hayes were trained in London, and therefore tended to follow London insofar as the isolation of the Cambridge press allowed. No less importantly, and particularly in the case of books printed for the English Stock, prices from the Cambridge press had to be compatible with those from London presses. Sawbridge's presence for many years as both customer (Treasurer of the English Stock) and as supplier (owner of the Cambridge press) was some protection from competition. But Hayes was to continue to print successfully for the Stock long after his unmasking and departure. It remained, that since wholesale prices from Cambridge had to include the cost of carriage of paper in both directions, the local manufacturing cost had actually to be lower than that obtaining in London.

16

Civil war and inter-regnum

Depressa resurgo. Daniel's chosen emblem, the palm tree able, even when weighed down, to spring back to its original shape with extra vigour, was one familiar to his contemporaries. With the deer chosen by Buck as his own rebus (alluding also to Psalm 42: 'Like as the hart desireth the water-brooks'), it had appeared on the elaborate engraved title-page to the 1638 Bible (fig. 17 on p. 198 above). In 1640 Daniel introduced it, as his motto, on his title-pages in its own right, using it on one of his most substantial achievements, Heinsius' *Sacrarum exercitationum ad Novum Testamentum libri XX.* Inspired perhaps partly by the engraving in George Wither's *Collection of emblemes* (1634–5), it aptly summarized his position, and his continuing ability to rebound to new achievement in the face of adversity or malice.[1] In Wither's words,

> Truth, oft oppressed, wee may see,
> But, quite supprest it cannot be.

Daniel's successful printing of Whelock's Bede was the more remarkable in that it was done when many of the University's affairs were slipping into turmoil, his own among them. The book of verses prepared for Charles I's lacklustre return from Scotland in November 1641, *Irenodia Cantabrigiensis*, had been the dutiful manifestation of habit; and for all the entertainment offered when the young Prince Charles visited the University in the following March (cheered by a performance at Trinity of Abraham Cowley's comedy *The Guardian*),[2] the King's own visit two days later was marred by the failure of the townspeople to share in the celebrations. For the colleges, Charles I's call first for money and then for their plate in June and July 1642[3] was to prove but the beginning of a sequence of events that led eventually to the unseating of ten heads of houses, the expulsion of fellows and the imposition of new ones and, for many, several years of acute poverty.[4] Expenditure on new liturgical arrangements in college chapels was reversed with a new need for conformity, exemplified in the winter of 1643–4 by William Dowsing's eagerness to destroy images and traces of Laudianism. In August 1642 Cromwell, Member of Parliament for the town, was put in charge of the defence of Cambridge, a position which helped give credibility to his authority in sending the Heads of

St John's, Queens' and Jesus Colleges as prisoners to London for their part in attempting to send plate to the King.[5] In December, the formation of the Eastern Association closed a year in which Charles I had retreated to Oxford following the battle of Edgehill. Cambridge was fortified, with the help of materials from the new buildings at Clare and from the colleges' bridges, in March 1643.[6] The royalist inclinations of the University were targets for attack not only in these arrests and assaults, but also in the overturning of the University statute requiring subscription,[7] and in the Act of Sequestration of 1643. In March 1642/3 the House of Lords found it expedient to promulgate orders designed to guard against the plundering or despoiling of chapels, libraries and university buildings, and to protect the personal property of members of the University.

For Daniel, the collapse of university authority brought demands which he could not easily escape, and re-examination of the auspices under which he worked. A fresh phase of the King's propaganda war, begun with his removal to York in the spring of 1642, brought with it the need to disperse royal declarations and other public communications as speedily as possible from a centre that, unlike London, did not offer regular communications with the whole of the country (see fig. 26). Packets of printed papers were sent to Oxford with instructions that they should be published in the University;[8] and though no evidence survives, it may be assumed that, notwithstanding the sympathies of the town, as distinct from the University, similar packets were sent also to Cambridge. On this authority, which he was careful to state on his title-pages, Daniel printed more than a dozen quarto and broadside communications from York, between May and August 1642, some more than once, and he continued to do so after the King had moved back south. If there was any intent to embarrass Parliament by this action, it was effective. Daniel was summoned before the Commons on 23 August for printing the King's answer to Parliament concerning the Commission of Array; but having expressed its disapproval the Commons discharged him on 3 September after enjoining him not to print matters concerning either House without the consent of both.[9] No further action seems to have been taken against Daniel for the rest of the year, as he continued to print papers which openly flouted this injunction.

Henry Ferne's *The resolving of conscience*, an outspoken and explicit attack on the constitutional failings of Parliament, was printed by Daniel later in the year. It provided an opportunity for further assault on his press at a moment when the Parliamentary forces, having fenced the King into Oxford and being strengthened by the formation of the Eastern Association, could be more confident. Ferne had been elected to a Fellowship at Trinity in 1624, and while Archdeacon of Leicester he composed his pamphlet, designed to demonstrate that resistance to royal authority was not only unwarrantable, but even (according to St Paul) damnable.[10] Ferne expected resistance, and met it. 'He

HIS
MAJESTIES
DECLARATION
to all His loving Subjects.

Of *August* 12 1642.

Printed by his Majesties speciall command,

At *CAMBRIDGE*,

By ROGER DANIEL, Printer to the
famous Universitie. 1642.

Fig. 26 Charles I, *His Majesties declaration to all his loving subjects*,
12 August 1642. Height of original, 189 mm.

that in these times will speak any thing to the people in behalf of the King, is likely to do it upon disadvantage', he wrote as his opening words. For doing so, he was sent for by the Commons on Christmas Eve 1642, and Daniel was taken into the custody of the Serjeant-at-Arms. By producing the warrant to print the book, signed by Richard Holdsworth as Vice-Chancellor, Daniel was however able to prove that he was no more than an agent, and so was ordered to be given bail on 2 February.[11] Instead Holdsworth was sent for, and imprisoned, first at Ely House and then in the Tower, for having (according to the author of the *Querela Cantabrigiensis*) licensed the reprinting of Charles I's declarations.[12] Ferne's work had meanwhile thrived, and become a *succès de scandale*. Apart from copies sold in Cambridge by Daniel, others were despatched to London for the booksellers E. Freeman and Thomas Dunster, and the differing settings of type in surviving copies suggest that Daniel increased the edition size part of the way through the print run. It was reprinted at London and York almost immediately, and a 'second edition' appeared at Oxford in 1643. The Commons' displeasure is understandable.

Ferne was not the only commoner author from Cambridge to incur parliamentary disapproval. He had the advantage that his book was finished, and so was available to be reprinted. Lionel Gatford, Rector of Dennington in Suffolk and formerly Fellow of Jesus, was less fortunate. In his *Harmonie of the doctrine of the reformed churches* he planned an examination, based on the teaching of both the Anglican and other reformed churches, of royal authority and the loyalty due from subjects – 'together with a discovery of who and what sort of men have been the prime disturbers of Peace, and raysers of Rebellion'. But (in his own words)

This my intention was frustrated; for on Jan. 26. [1642/3] in the night, Master Crumwell, a Member of the House of Commons, seized upon the Coppy of that Tractat composed by me for that purpose, as it was then in the presse at *Cambridge*, and fifteen or sixteen sheets thereof printed, and the same *night with his Troopes he apprehended my person* quietly reposed in Jesus-Colledge, which with the Coppy he transmitted hither to *London, on the next Lords day* following.[13]

The Commons speedily committed him to Ely House, where he was still imprisoned in February, with no charges brought against him. With the departure of both author and copy, printing of the book had to be abandoned: the single recorded surviving example lacks one sheet in the middle of the text and ends in mid-flight at sheet N.[14]

Though, at the time of Gatford's arrest, Daniel was (as we have seen) also under restraint, he was to be given bail within a few days. Neither of the two Cambridge booksellers whose names were printed on the title-page of Gatford's book, Richard Ireland and John Milleson, is known to have been imprisoned. In other words, the thrust of the parliamentary attack was not – at least in Cambridge – directed at the executive parts of the book trade, but at authors and at those responsible for the good conduct of the trade. In

Cambridge, this was the Vice-Chancellor. Gatford's case came before the Commons again in July, when the Committee for Cambridge (acting under Francis Rous, who had taken a leading part in the proceedings against John Cosin) was instructed to consider a sermon in which he had given an account of his earlier work and of his arrest.[15]

Holdsworth remained imprisoned, from the spring of 1643 until 1645, the object of the Commons' displeasure for 'licensing books to be reprinted, in Prejudice, and to the Scandal, of the Parliament'.[16] Ralph Brownrigg, Master of St Catharine's and Bishop of Exeter, who had already served two terms in the position in 1637–9, succeeded him as Vice-Chancellor in autumn 1643, but the University took the opportunity of the death of Samuel Ward, Master of Sidney and Lady Margaret's Professor, on 7 September, to elect Holdsworth to the chair. Its challenge was one made in desperation, and it was unsuccessful in that Holdsworth remained a prisoner: he was never to return to Cambridge before his death in 1649.

Having survived at the expense of the Vice-Chancellor, in 1644 Daniel was able to consolidate his position by printing for the Earl of Manchester, and by 1647 he was printing the official papers for Thomas Fairfax. The possession of the only press in a small town garrisoned and defended by a rebel authority virtually obliged him to sail with the political wind if he was not to risk losing his livelihood.[17] Although 1643 saw the appearance from his press of the first of three volumes of a substantial biblical commentary by Arthur Jackson, 'preacher of Gods word in Woodstreet, London', his usual work was displaced by political and military – some printed anonymously. 'Arms are in farre more request then books', wrote Jackson in his dedication to his London charges, echoing a feeling common in literary circles. Some of Daniel's most distinguished books, including Lambard's Ἀρχαιονομία (1644), Cruso's *Military instructions for the cavall'rie* (1644), Francis Quarles' *Judgment and mercy* (1646), Henry More's *Democritus Platonissans* (1646), William Harvey's *Exercitatio anatomica de circulatione sanguinis* (1649), and Joseph Mede's *Clavis Apocalyptica* (1649) had still to appear. But they did so amidst political uncertainty and the abandonment of many previously held assumptions respecting the structure of the book trade in both Cambridge and London.

Thomas and John Buck, and especially Thomas as the elder, made considerable play of their responsibilities as University Printers. But it is clear from Thomas's willingness to make over printing equipment to Daniel in 1632 that they held different opinions from Daniel as to the value of the press. For Daniel it was a livelihood; for the Bucks it was an office that could be made to produce a modest profit. For the University, on the other hand, the Bucks' presence provided a continuity of academic legitimacy assumed by Thomas Thomas in 1583, and, where necessary, a voice that could be distinct among the jealousies of the printing trade more generally. Although by the end of 1632 Daniel was installed as the single active University Printer, he enjoyed his position thanks to the forebearance of two men, Thomas and John Buck, more interested in the University's general affairs than only in its printing house, and more interested in their own financial well-being than either. The imprints on books printed at the Austin Friars between 1632 and 1650 are a poor guide to the consortium's real inter-relationship, or to how the books were either financed or sold.[18] Even when they seemed clear and explicit, imprints did not necessarily reveal where responsibility lay. Daniel, not Buck, printed the first edition of Fuller's *Holy warre* in 1639, (fig. 15 on p. 181 above), even though his name was entirely absent from the book. The second edition (1640) reflected the position more fully: 'Printed by R. Daniel for Thomas Buck, and are to be sold by John Williams...in Pauls Church-yard'. The book (it was later claimed) was Buck's copy, and Daniel was therefore infringing his property when in 1647 he printed an unauthorized third edition and, to compound matters, omitted Buck's name from the title-page.[19]

Over the previous two decades, from about 1627 onwards, Thomas Buck and Daniel had collaborated in a spirit of mutual suspicion, reflected on the one hand in the tortuous and overbearing manner by which Buck had manoeuvred himself into a position where he could dispense university offices on payment to him of a suitable fee, and on the other by the long series of detailed legal documents that ordained his own and his brother's relations with Daniel. In 1639 John Buck assigned his own interest in the press to Daniel in return for £50 per annum, and Thomas entered into a yet further covenant.[20] Such agreements gave to Daniel a large measure of freedom; but they also placed him in a position where it was not easy to act to the best advantage. The impressive achievements of 1639–42 were cut short by the arrival of civil war; but for Daniel the 1640s were overshadowed also by a steady deterioration in his relations with Buck, who was able to claim, however, that Daniel's own behaviour was sometimes contrary either to their agreements or to the regulations of the University. Certainly Daniel could be high-handed. His preface to Heinsius' study in comparative religion *Crepundia Siliana* (1646) apologized for printing the book without permission, but explained that its scarcity seemed to justify such an action. The copyright in Fuller's *Holy warre*, already mentioned, was one source of discord. When in 1648 Buck brought a devastating series of charges against Daniel, it figured first on the list; but others were hardly less damaging. He claimed to have bought from Daniel, for £10, the copy of Ralph Winterton's translation of Johann Gerhard's *Meditations and prayers*, the latter part first published at London in 1625 and the former by Thomas and John Buck at Cambridge in 1627. Daniel's own title to sell is obscure, but his subsequent actions were not, in that he countered Buck's editions with one more compact and cheaper – even, claimed his accuser, when he knew that Buck still had five hundred copies in stock.

These accusations over copy need to be seen in the context of arguments at other times over the extent of University Printers' ownership of the copy of books printed at Cambridge. In principle, copies were often assumed to be shared, and to be passed from printer to printer. As so often, however, Thomas Buck introduced a different opinion. His own share in the ownership of copy was a complicated one, which he traded or exploited when necessary. Though his position as University Printer gave him, in principle at least, a one-third share in all titles printed and published by him and his two partners, there were many exceptions. His brother John's subservient position gave Thomas Buck one immediate advantage. Accidentally or no, Edmund Gurnay's *Toward the vindication of the second commandment* (1639) was licensed to Buck alone. The strife over Fuller's works also suggests a more complex ownership structure than a simple tripartite arrangement.[21] But while he naturally regarded his shares in other books as a commercial property, he also thought that like other such property they could be passed on. This was not a view that would have been approved by Legge, as he had sought to establish himself, or by those who had thought that University Printers' property in copies remained corporate. But Buck, as part of his policy of introducing George Sawbridge to the Cambridge press, and so improving its resources for investment, found it eventually prudent to assign to him his own parts of copies held by the Printers jointly. Thus on 18 December 1656 he passed on, amongst others, shares in Fuller's *Holy warre*, in Gerhard's *Meditations*, in Davenant's commentary on Colossians and his *Praelectiones*, in Golius' *Ethicks*, in Burgersdijck's *Institutiones logicae*, in Duport's *Job* and in 'the copies of ye small poets in Greek & Lattin'. By no means all, in 1656, could be considered exhausted or worthless.[22] The ownership of the press's books was made no clearer a decade or so later, by an enigmatic judgement in the Vice-Chancellor's Court that 'Mr Iohn Field whensoever he prints any of Mr Thomas Buck's or Mr Iohn Bucks Copies, he shall give them full satisfaction'.[23]

In 1648, Buck's further accusations against Daniel covered a range of misdemeanours: failing to have books properly licensed by the Vice-Chancellor, printing books that were the copyright of London stationers, printing an edition of Thomas Farnaby's *Index rhetoricus et oratoricus* (a standard schoolbook) with a false Lyon imprint, 'apud G. F.', printing other books without setting his name on them as required by parliamentary authority of 14 June 1643,[24] and attempting (though seemingly unsuccessfully) to print editions of Sir Kenelm Digby on the immortality of the soul (first published at Paris in 1644 and at London the following year) and of *Janua linguarum* which (Buck claimed) he might have finished 'had he not been restrayned by the stationers of London & such others as had just title & interest in the aforsayd Coppies'.

So Buck astutely accused Daniel of crossing every possible authority: the University, the Crown and Parliament, and the Stationers. In his willingness to introduce the Stationers' Company into the argument, he also by implication dismissed any claim the University had made to independence of the London copyrights under the 1534 charter. Daniel's position, already thus dangerously challenged, was made the more difficult when John Buck took his turn to attack a few months later. Daniel, he alleged, had agreed to deliver to him £45 worth of books, but he had failed to make good imperfect copies, and had failed also to provide, as fellow University Printer, one copy of every book that he printed. Like another small suit against Daniel in the Vice-Chancellor's Court at about the same time, the matter was a simple one of debt; but it served further to undermine Daniel's position. In April 1648 Thomas Buck had concluded his attack by emphasizing equally the damage sustained both by the claimant and by the University: 'And by these & many other wayes & meanes He hath dishonered the universitie, deceived the trust reposed in him, & ever since He had the managinge of the whole printinge buisiness in his owne handes He hath acted for sinister respects & profitt to himself, & to the great loss, dammage & preiudice of the sayd T. B.'[25]

The sum for which he now sued Daniel, £260, was designed as much to reflect the value he set on his own reputation in this respect as any commercial loss. Daniel had already lost one tussle with him in court, in 1644;[26] but this case four years later was to prove the two men's final public conflict. The new Printing Act of September 1649, with its requirement that printers should enter into sureties of £300 apiece, brought in its wake in October an opportunity for the University to reconsider Daniel's position, as the Vice-Chancellor gathered in the necessary affirmations. Thomas and John Buck entered their sureties (as did Leonard Lichfield and Henry Hall at Oxford); Daniel did not.[27] Whether he did not wish to, or was disallowed, is not clear. The imprints on Cambridge books in the 1640s had recorded little of the Bucks, as Daniel reaped not only title-page credit, but also isolation. In 1649–50 both a translation of Aesop and a commentary on the Epistle to the Hebrews by David Dickson, the energetic Professor of Divinity at Glasgow (and in ordinary times an unlikely figure for Daniel's attention), were printed by Daniel for the London bookseller Francis Eglesfield. It was perhaps becoming clear that Daniel's future could no longer be considered secure at Cambridge. Eglesfield shared with him many elements of a common tradition, reflected in the list of books appended to the end as an advertisement in Dickson's commentary and including notices of Quarles, Gerhard, Bedell, Lisle's edition of Ælfric, and Phineas Fletcher's *The purple island*.

Daniel's position had been made untenable. The agreements with John and Thomas Buck in 1639 should have given him freedom to pursue the printing patent unhindered by the difficulties which must always be expected in so loose a consortium as the triumvirate elected by the University. Instead they were turned into staves wherewith to beat Daniel on points of copyright, and in the end formed the weapons by which to eject him. The Grace for his dismissal was passed on 1 June 1650. It spoke of his having betrayed the honour of the University, of *supina*, *neglicentia* and *infamia*.[28] The wording might have been drafted by the Bucks. By then Tabor, Thomas Buck's old enemy as Registrary, had been dead five years, and could no longer therefore offer a diversion. But Buck, unlike Daniel, had never printed for the King, and had never angered the House of Commons. Despite Cromwell's proximity, much of Cambridge remained persistently loyalist. In the year in which Fellows and heads of houses lost their places for refusing to subscribe to the new authority, there may have been about Daniel's case something of the sacrificial lamb.

Formally, if not wholly (as it proved), rejected by Cambridge, Daniel removed some of his equipment and rapidly re-established himself in London as bookseller, printer and printseller.[29] He shared in the printing of Edward Leigh's *Critica sacra*, published in the year of his dismissal, and in the following year issued over his own name alone a major edition and translation of the letters of the ninth-century Patriarch of Constantinople, Photius, edited by Richard Montagu, Bishop of Norwich, who had died ten years previously. The edition was based on the late ninth-century Barocci manuscript in the Bodleian Library; and if, as is possible, it was a casualty from Laud's intentions, it may perhaps have given Daniel some wry satisfaction.[30] Save that it was quickly overshadowed by Walton's much more ambitious, and more authoritative, polyglot Bible, Daniel's most enduring achievement of these years might have been the first edition of the Septuagint to be published in England, completed in 1653 and published by John Martyn and James Allestry of St Paul's Churchyard. Such an edition had been called for, and even expected, for several years, following the acquisition in 1628 by Charles I of the Codex Alexandrinus. Parts of the manuscript were published by Patrick Young in 1633 and 1637, but the idea that he then conceived, of publishing the whole manuscript using a fount designed as a facsimile of the Greek majuscules, proved ill-considered in that it distracted from the production of a less ambitious edition.[31] In January 1644/5 the House of Commons received a petition from a group of booksellers seeking to hasten Young in his work, and several sums of money were voted to him; but when he died in 1652, with the Codex Alexandrinus in his house, no edition had so far appeared.[32] His annotations were incorporated by Walton in 1657 into his own prolegomena. By then Daniel's less ambitious edition had appeared, based ostensibly on the Sixtine text published at Rome in 1586 but in fact, as Walton soon made clear, a somewhat idiosyncratic text. The dedication, to Westminster School, was initialled by Daniel, who printed the book in two forms, adjusting the type slightly for the larger pages, and retained a part of the edition for himself.

A noticeably compact edition, printed in bourgeois type, of the collected works of Ovid, paid for by the Stationers' Company,[33] was prefixed with verses written by Ralph Winterton of King's, who had died in 1636. And a Hebrew grammar, designed for the use of Westminster School by its undergraduate author William James, who was a member of Christ Church, Oxford, was soon taken up at Cambridge as well.[34]

Not surprisingly, much of Daniel's output derived in one way or another from his years at Cambridge, including works by Henry More and by Drexel, and cheap editions of classical texts. Several editions of works by Adrian Heereboord, of Leiden, appeared in the 1650s, small manuals of logic and moral philosophy drawn partly from the work of his predecessor, already familiar in the Cambridge press, Fr. Burgersdijck: the work of both men became standard texts at Oxford as well as Cambridge.[35] To some extent, the Cambridge booksellers also followed Daniel's press, most notably in the case of Barrow's new, and full, edition of Euclid. The first edition, in Latin, was printed in Cambridge for the local bookseller William Nealand, and published in 1655/6, a little after Legate's dismissal. Plans for the book had been laid several months previously, Nealand having had the manuscript in his hands since June 1654: the delay in publication was due not so much to Legate's impending departure, as to Nealand's need to assemble sufficient subscriptions.[36] But when in 1659 a second edition was required, Nealand found it most convenient to turn to Daniel, now in London; and it was Daniel, again (possessing the appropriate woodcut diagrams) who printed the English translation in 1660. Thus, for a few years, rival booksellers in Cambridge (Edward Story and William Nealand) offered rival editions (Story's being only the first six books) in rival formats (duodecimo and octavo) with different explanatory figures and, since Story remained with Field, printed by different printers.

In Cambridge, Daniel had set his own stamp on his books by his habit of writing, or at least signing, prefaces.[37] This practice continued in London, and these fragments reveal a little of his private world. An edition of selections from Aristotle made by Theophilus Golius, and published by the Cambridge bookseller Edward Story in 1662, prompted him to address the younger members of both universities when he could no longer work beside either. The occasion brought back memories not only of his time as University Printer, but also, in particular, of Ralph Winterton, Hellenist, Regius Professor of Physic and Fellow of King's, who had been a mainstay in the 1630s. Another book brought a dedication to Francis Finch, second son of Sir Heneage Finch and a Bencher of the Inner Temple.[38] Daniel continued to print until 1666, among his last books being a third edition of Walter Charleton's *Oeconomia animalis*, of which he had printed part of the first edition in 1659. Like so many others, Daniel hoped with the restoration of the monarchy for a restoration to his former position. His appeal on the subject claimed that he had been dismissed as a result of having printed for the royalist cause in 1642, and it was a claim that was at least partially true. But despite the support of, among others, his old Cambridge acquaintance John Pearson, whose *Exposition of the Creed* Daniel had printed in 1659, its title-page boldly bearing a crown at its centre, the attempt failed.[39] Daniel lived on for a few months, but what remained of his business, latterly in Paternoster Row, was a casualty of the Great Fire. Among his last acts in the trade, in July 1667, he gave a recognizance to free the London printer Thomas Milbourne for printing unlicensed books.[40] He died in London on 5 October.[41]

There were some who did not remember him favourably. John Beale, writing to Henry Oldenburg, Secretary of the Royal Society, in 1671, recalled his annoyance partly at a poorly printed text and partly at Daniel's having either ignored or misunderstood his wish that his work on Herefordshire orchards should be published anonymously: 'The print was very fair, but very false, & much to my prejudice, and with J. B. in the front, contrary to my convention with Mr. H[artlib].'[42] But for another member of the circle, whose activities foreshadowed the beginning of the Royal Society, J. A. Comenius, Daniel was a man to be addressed as 'viro solerti ac strenuo' – apt words from one who himself took so alert an interest in the international fortunes of his publications.[43]

For yet others, Daniel's time as University Printer remained a period which had seen an extraordinary succession of publishing triumphs. William Dillingham graduated BD from Emmanuel in the same year that Daniel's patent as University Printer was cancelled, and contrived to accommodate himself so well to the new regime that he was appointed Master of his college three years later, in 1653. When he came to write the preface to a new edition of Ferrari's *Lexicon geographicum* in 1657/8, printed by Daniel in London, he was fresh from seeing through the Cambridge press (run now by Field) an ambitiously produced edition of Sir Francis Vere's military commentaries. To Dillingham, Daniel's printing house seemed like the Trojan horse, from which issued such heroes as the Greek New Testament, Heinsius on the New Testament, Bede in Anglo-Saxon and in Latin, Photius, Hierocles, Eustachius, and Wendelin: whether they were printed at Cambridge or London made no difference. All this was done thanks partly to his extraordinary editorial gifts, his passion for accuracy of which his dealing with the mistakes in Ferrari's *Lexicon* was but the latest example ('At quis Augiae stabulam expurgabit'). Here, indeed, was 'vir musis plaudentibus natus, atque in gratiam studiosorum semper ad audendum paratissimus'. Even William Moore, Whelock's distinguished successor as University Librarian and a close friend of Dillingham ('virum doctissimum amicissimumque') had to wait his turn after these encomia.[44]

The Grace that terminated Daniel's appointment on 1 June 1650 was followed by another approving the sealing of his successor on 5 July.[45] The authorities had considered the matter, but had not looked far. John Legate, University Printer at the beginning of the century, had died in 1620, leaving his business and printing equipment in the hands of his son, also called John.[46] For years after he had left Cambridge, Legate had continued to use the University Printer's device, and his son inherited the habit: it had appeared as recently as 1648 on an edition of Farnaby's Juvenal and Pesius.[47]

The younger Legate had much to gain from his appointment to Cambridge. The 1639 agreement restricting Bible and schoolbook printing, to which he had been a signatory,[48] had expired in September 1649, and had not been replaced. At Cambridge, he would be in a position to ensure both the English Stock's interest and, with the press's capacity, to profit further personally, especially in almanac printing.[49] It is not clear how much influence Thomas Buck had in the appointment: he is unlikely to have remained silent. Not surprisingly, the Heads thought it necessary to draw up in August a fresh series of orders governing the press. In doing so they seem to have had especial regard for the fact that Legate now controlled presses in both London and Cambridge. As University Printer, he was to live 'constantly' in Cambridge, while any work he undertook as Printer was to be done only in Cambridge, not in London. Other clauses were the result of arguments between Daniel and the Bucks over copyright, which had helped to precipitate Daniel's departure. Now, for the first time, a register was to be established by the University Registrary, in which all books licensed by the Vice-Chancellor were to be listed, together with the names of those who had licensed them. The entry fee, of one shilling, was just twice that charged by the Stationers' Company. Copies of new books were to be lodged in the University Library.[50]

The last regulation, repeating an agreement to which Thomas Thomas and Legate's own father had both been subject, and which had been by them but intermittently observed, remained honoured generally in the breach. However, it is notable that neither on this occasion nor on any other in the century, when the University legislated in this manner, was the press expected to return any profit for the University. At Harvard, so closely modelled on Cambridge in other ways, the income from the equivalent source was insignificant, amounting to only £20 in 1654–63; but its payment betokened a relationship quite different from the commercial (as distinct from the legislative) independence enjoyed by Legate, Field, their predecessors and successors.[51] At this time, the University neither invested in, nor expected profits of, its printers. But its influence on the economic well-being of its Printer could be decisive, as Legate quickly discovered.

In expecting Legate to remain in Cambridge and to devote himself to the University's printing, the Heads were asking the impossible. His London business, much contracted in the previous two years or so, still remained, as did his London apprentices. From July 1651 to July 1653 he was also to be one of the Wardens of the Stationers' Company. In 1653, exasperated at Legate's refusal to work in Cambridge, Buck threatened to resign from his office. His threat was considered sufficiently serious for the Stationer's Company to send a special delegation to discuss the matter;[52] but Legate's continuing absenteeism had become a running sore which, at last, was sapping Buck's determination. Ever venal, he found accommodation easy once the matter could be arranged. For ten years from 1639 he had received £75 per annum from the Stationers'

Company. This had been reduced in 1650 (following Legate's appointment) to £25, with a like sum for his brother John.[53] Now, in October 1653, he agreed to £25, John Buck receiving only one-fifth of that. The figures smack more of expediency than of relative value. Once again the London stationers promised to market Cambridge-printed stock, some of which Buck himself had been responsible for printing 'whilst he freed M[r]. Legate from takeing the Care of the Presse in Cambridge whereunto he had otherwise been obliged', and for which, indeed, he had been paid.[54] So, having reduced his price, Buck (still an Esquire Bedell, and therefore having some responsibilities in the University) had proceeded to connive at Legate's ignoring the Vice-Chancellor's and Heads' regulations respecting attendance at the press.

Having raised what he could from his office, Thomas Buck now also parted with his equipment, type and presses, including even the new long primer only recently received from the London typefounder Alexander Fifield, and not yet paid for. Legate obtained the older type at two-thirds its new price, and the other equipment at a price set by himself and Robert Leet, one of Buck's journeymen.[55] So Buck's press came to an end, and with it payments to him by the Stationers' Company. Born out of disputes with Leonard Greene in the mid-1620s, leased to Daniel and thus the means to what was to prove the most distinguished period seen by any University Printer until the very last years of the century, it was now sold back into the hands of those who had the greatest interest in its dismemberment. Even by the standards of the 1650s this was discreditable.

What, if any, advantage Legate hoped to gain from his appointment at Cambridge was rapidly dissipated by his conspicuous failure to make any mark beside the Bucks. Even the Stationers found themselves powerless to intervene when in April their agent (and now Legate's employee) Robert Leet alerted them to the potential danger.[56] On 10 October 1655 Legate's patent, too, was cancelled on grounds of neglect, and he returned to London where in the following March he took on two fresh apprentices.[57] The brief remainder of his life suggests that in doing so he was either incautiously optimistic or approaching senility; but perhaps there was as yet no sign of his end, which came on 4 November 1658: 'Mr. Legat in Little Wood Street, printer, once printer at Cambridge, since distempered in his senses, died.'[58] It was not quite seventy years almost to the day since his father had been appointed to succeed Thomas Thomas.

During Legate's unsatisfactory incumbency, Thomas Buck had overseen the printing of a dozen or so books that bore his own name. Daniel's departure made easier a fresh edition of Fuller's *Holy warre*. It was marketed in London by Philemon Stephens, rather than by that other bookseller in St Paul's Churchyard, John Williams, who had dealt with most of Fuller's earlier works. Buck's other major books had a rather more parochial air about their imprints, if not always about their contents. Joseph Mede's *Opuscula* (1652) was one of the first books to bear the imprint of a Cambridge bookseller whose influence was to become considerable, William Morden.[59] But it was to another bookseller, Anthony Nicholson, that those responsible turned for the sale of the single major scholarly achievement of the press during this difficult period. Thomas Gataker's edition of Marcus Aurelius Antoninus' *De rebus suis*, the work of many years, and finally published (according to one story) only after the importunities of William Dillingham, presented the Greek text with a parallel Latin translation and a long commentary. It was dedicated to three of the most powerful men in the University, all recent Vice-Chancellors, the Masters of Emmanuel, St John's and Trinity; but in its format, the unusual expense of an engraved portrait frontispiece by William Faithorne, and the tone of Gataker's own 'praeloquium', it looked to a more ambitious market – not merely British, but European. Among the throng of almanacs, sermons, and workaday editions for the ordinary curriculum, it was one of the few occasions in these years on which the press was enabled, or persuaded, to have wider issues in mind.[60]

It was partly because of the press's growing debilities that the names of local booksellers appeared with increasing frequency on title-pages. In the 1620s and the 1630s this had been a rare event. By the 1650s it had become commonplace, the booksellers either taking shares in or commissioning books printed not at Cambridge but in London. The reasons for this development were complex. Apart from the fact that the press itself was less active in producing books, Buck too was less anxious to invest in stock for which his restricted business had no need: like Daniel and most of his predecessors he had no retail outlet of his own. John Field, who became University Printer in 1655, was likewise noticeably cautious. In a university community where writing and publishing were habits, the onus therefore fell on booksellers, who were obliged to turn publishers. The change was to have profound consequences, in that, from the mid-seventeenth century, printers and booksellers, after sharing the responsibilities of publishing, each drifted towards a separate function where previously printers at least had been able to act in either capacity, as a normal practice. This separation, moreover, affected the relationship of the Cambridge bookselling and printing trades to those in London. Many of the old animosities were perceived as before, especially (as we shall see) in the Bible and almanac trades; but the Cambridge booksellers Richard Ireland, Anthony Nicholson, William Nealand, William Morden, Edmund Beeching, John Creed, Robert Nicholson and Henry Dickinson had all had stock printed in London by 1670.[61] Cambridge booksellers looked increasingly southwards; and having looked to London, were obliged to look also at their own corporate identity as expressed in the books they published. The results were to be seen in the lists of books included in many of the publications of booksellers such as Morden. In Cambridge, the local populace had no need of such information, which would have been well known and therefore superfluous. The lists were aimed at a London, and even a national, market.

They all looked, or were obliged to look, overseas, though it seems that they sometimes did so with others' eyes rather than their own. It was Samuel Hartlib, not the booksellers Anthony Nicholson or William Morden, who saw that it would have been valuable had details been sent to Frankfurt of Thomas Gataker's edition of Marcus Aurelius Antoninus (1652), and of the 1655 editions of Epictetus and Porphyry. It was Hartlib, too, who saw that Barrow's Euclid did receive such attention.[62] For all Cambridge's dependence on books from overseas, there was little awareness, among the book trade, of how much might be offered in return. The stimulus to a larger view came from those who had no professional experience of printing and publishing.

Legate, whose interests fell both in Cambridge and London, could not hope to meet the stipulations of the agreement governing his position that had been drawn up in 1650. As the somewhat prolix Grace which ended his career in Cambridge made explicit, his behaviour was a disappointment.[63] After so inglorious an episode, the election of his successor was carried through with a wilfulness on the part of the Heads that fully matched the tarnished career of the man of their choice. In some respects, however, his credentials were impeccable for an inter-regnum appointment.

John Field, University Printer until 1668 (and therefore one of the University officials to survive the Restoration) was elected only two days after Legate's departure, on 12 October 1655,[64] and twenty-four hours after the Heads had re-examined and confirmed the regulations which had been Legate's downfall.[65] He came with a career behind him that had been frequently controversial, for much of it his name linked with Henry Hills.[66] Thus far, it had been principally in parliamentary printing, in 1642 briefly in partnership with Luke Norton. For most of the 1640s, however, his name did not appear on parliamentary books, which had by the end of the decade fallen principally to the responsibility of Edward Husbands. Field finally managed to regain a foothold in parliamentary work in September 1649; and then on 25 January following he was appointed, with Husbands, to an equal share in a regular (and therefore potentially profitable) source of orders.[67] It was this early introduction to parliamentary printing that was to enable him to become at once one of the most influential members of the book trade, and one of the least respected. His printing of parliamentary proceedings in 1646 took him briefly to imprisonment in Newgate,[68] but by 1652 his printing for the Long Parliament had run up the considerable debt of £1,274.3s.5d.[69]

Field's position as official printer was only lucrative (potentially, at least) and unassailable so long as there was no change in government. But on 20 April 1653 Cromwell dissolved Parliament, and after a few months' turmoil the Little Parliament dispersed. Cromwell became Protector on 16 December. As printer of parliamentary statutes and other papers, Field could no longer look forward to that regular flow of work that he had hitherto enjoyed. The printing of Cromwell's ordinances during the next nine months became the responsibility of Henry Hills and of William Du-Gard, a member of Cromwell's own college, Sidney Sussex, now turned reprobate owner of a private press in London. But Du-Gard himself disappeared from Cromwellian imprints the following autumn, and in February 1654/5 Hills was rejoined in turn by Field, who thus brought to an end a year's disappearance. His absence, far from being politically motivated, was almost certainly due to financial difficulties, bringing him close to ruin. By December 1653 he was owed £1,665.15s.9d. for parliamentary printing, a sum swelled by no less than £1,000 in interest payments. With no Parliament, he was no longer credit-worthy, and the money remained unpaid even after the debt was once again acknowledged in February 1655/6.[70]

His partnership with Hills as printer to the Protector may therefore have been one born of necessity, rather than simply a combination of political and financial acumen. Under the second Protectorate Parliament, from 17 September 1656, Field and Hills were named together as printers to Cromwell. The connection between the two men survived, albeit intermittently, into the restored Rump of 1659, but neither took any part in parliamentary printing for the brief few weeks of the inter-regnum after the autumn of that year.[71]

As Field's several enemies were to remember, his official work had entailed his printing the Act prohibiting the proclamation of a new monarch following the execution of Charles I. He had shared with Hills most Cromwellian or parliamentary work for the next decade. It was not a background that suggests that the University authorities, or even perhaps Buck, had much influence over the appointment to Cambridge. Only three days before his election, an order in Council had been approved giving commissioners power not only to enforce existing laws concerning unlicensed printing, but also to compile a detailed survey of the whole of the London printing trade, with notes on its members' attitudes to the government.[72] Field, a person who by then could be relied on by the government not to produce seditious or scandalous books, was a timely appointment, and in 1658 he was to be charged, with Hills and with the Stationers' Company more generally, with searching out unlicensed, seditious or popish books.[73]

The Cambridge press, when it became clear that it was to become vacant in 1655, offered the chance to regain both some independence and, eventually, financial success. Provided accommodation could be made with the Stationers' Company, little investment was required, since the Company owned the equipment. For its part, the Company could exact terms that would ensure the press's continued co-operation, and dependency.

Notwithstanding the Heads' determination in 1655 that a University Printer should reside in Cambridge, and devote himself to the University press there, Field kept establishments both in London and in Cambridge. Indeed, his responsibilities in London increased. He continued as parliamentary printer, overstepping the Restoration and so causing offence in August 1660. But while Field was a creature of the government, he was not one of the Stationers' Company. By 1648 he had become a well-established printer, yet he was not of the livery, and preferred indeed to remain an outsider to the Company. A prolonged dispute with the Stationers in 1653–4, involving also the Haberdashers, confirmed his determined independence and, by this time, obstreperousness: the affair was eased by the intervention of no less a person than the Recorder of the City of London, William Steele, whose proximity to Cromwell may have helped matters,[74] but it was still not settled when in the spring of 1655 it became clear that Legate's days as University Printer were numbered.[75]

Field's appointment in succession to Legate was therefore not of the Stationers' making. Even Buck, kingmaker for more than a quarter of a century, seems to have had little influence in the matter, which was probably decided by Cromwell and his circle. All that the Stationers could do thus far was to resolve that neither the printing house, presses, nor type at Cambridge should be disposed of without the Court's agreement.[76] With Field still, in October 1655, at odds with the Company, their conclusion seemed only dogged in defeat. Then on 18 December the Court heard that Field was offering an agreement 'for quiet composing of all differences', and that he was inclined to buy the the presses and type belonging to the English Stock and now, following Legate's departure from Cambridge, lying idle. His application prompted long debate, raising issues both of Field's appropriateness and of the possibility of comprinting with the University: after a series of meetings between Field and the English Stock-keepers, it was resolved on 20 May 1656 that the existing arrangements for comprinting with the Cambridge press were to be renewed.[77]

Both sides had more to gain from collaboration than confrontation, and during the following months they mended their differences. On 17 October, Field, with his associate Hills, was admitted to the livery of the Company, with a promise of a share in the English Stock when one should next fall vacant.[78] So, once again, the Stationers had obtained a foothold in the Cambridge press, which continued to provide almanacs and schoolbooks for the Stock, Field now being paid a fixed quarterly fee.[79] Relations with Field, who proved perhaps predictably to be a rather wayward convert, were never easy, but he was to show himself able to serve two masters simultaneously, as Legate had never seriously attempted and as his successor, John Hayes, had no need.

Thus the University, having rid itself of Legate, whose interests in his London obligations threatened both the independence and the productive capacity of the Cambridge press, was encumbered by a situation certainly no better, and perhaps worse. Thomas Buck's own reaction was straightforward and, characteristically, was designed to exclude his fellow University Printer. In December 1656, following Field's agreement with the Stationers' Company,

Buck assigned his copies to George Sawbridge, Treasurer of the English Stock. There may have been an element of spite in his action; but in Sawbridge Buck was dealing with a shrewd, calculating and powerful man who was later to become landlord of the Cambridge press. From Buck he now acquired either interests in or outright ownership of copyrights that included some of the press's most successful books, most of them dating from Daniel's time though the octavo Statius, edited by Thomas Stephens, schoolmaster at Bury St Edmunds, had appeared over Buck's name alone in 1651, the first year of Legate's tenure.[80] It would have been out of Buck's nature to withdraw entirely from the press, and he was later to take an active part in appointing Field's successor; but with this sale he relinquished the last of his interests in the press's everyday affairs.

With Legate's departure, Buck was no longer prepared to subvent the press's premises. By 1656, therefore, Field obtained fresh accommodation on the corner of Silver Street and Queens' Lane, directly opposite the gateway to Queens' College (see fig. 27).[81] This substantial house belonged to the college, and was to remain a part of the Press's premises until the occupation of the Pitt Building, on the other side of Silver Street, in the nineteenth century. In the late sixteenth century it had been the house of Matthew Stokys, University Registrary, and one of the wealthiest resident members of the University, until his death in 1591. As had been the case with the premises occupied by Daniel in the old Augustinian Friary, it is noticeable that the printing house was located in one of the most extensive buildings available outside the colleges themselves. The new premises, though ample as domestic accommodation, nevertheless lacked the spaciousness of the old ones, and were in fact insufficient for a printing house of any size. If Field was to expand, let alone attain the scale of operations of Buck and Daniel in their heyday, further building was essential. For the first few years, until 1663, he seems to have held his lease from Queens' at a remove; the first surviving lease between him and the College was sealed on 20 October that year. But the rate of increase in volume of work from the Cambridge press suggests that he had completed a new printing house in the adjoining garden several years before then, perhaps in 1660 or 1661.

The new printing house, the first of its kind to be built in Cambridge, was a long open room running east-west, of which the earliest known surviving visitor's impression dates from June 1689, when Samuel Sewall of Massachusetts visited the premises:

By it [St Catharine's College], the Printing Room, which is about 60 foot long and 20 foot broad. Six Presses. Had my Cousin Hull and my name printed there. Paper windows, and a pleasant Garden along one side between Katherine Hall and that. Had there a Print of the Combinations.[82]

This 'pretty, large & lightsome room', as another visitor described it in 1708,[83] housed not only the presses, but also the type-cases and imposing

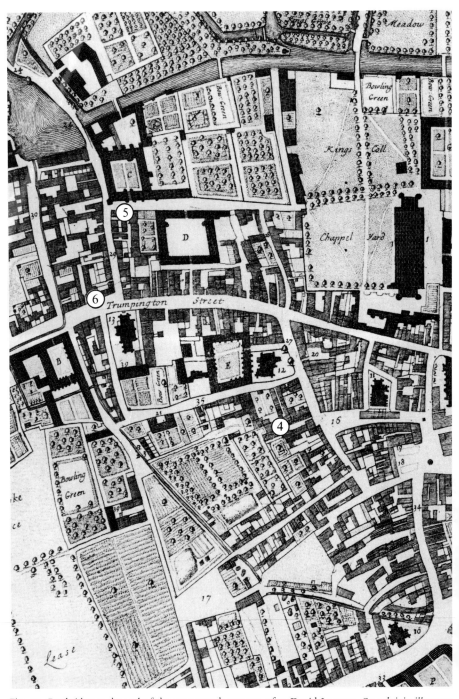

Fig. 27 Cambridge at the end of the seventeenth century, after David Loggan, *Cantabrigia illustrata* [1690]. The principal buildings are marked as follows:

B Pembroke College
C Queens' College
D St Catharine's College
E Corpus Christi College
F King's College (Old Court, now part of the Old Schools)
G Clare College
H Trinity Hall
I Gonville and Caius College

K Trinity College
L St John's College
O Sidney Sussex College
P Christ's College
R The Schools and Library

1 King's College chapel
2 Great St Mary's Church
3 St Michael's Church, Trinity Street

4 All Saints' Church, St John's Street
11 St Edward's Church
12 St Bene't's Church
13 St Botolph's Church
15 Market Hill
16 Peas Market
18 Town Hall
26 Regent Walk

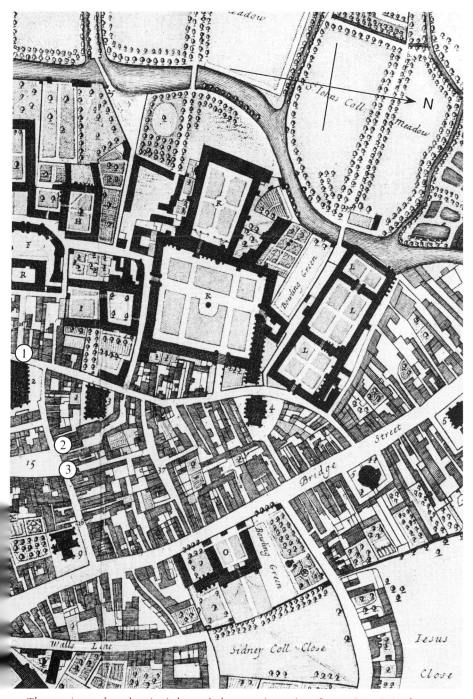

The superimposed numbers in circles mark the approximate sites of successive printing houses:

1 University Street, or Regent Walk (Thomas Thomas, John Legate the elder)

2 Next to the Rose Inn, Market Hill (Cantrell Legge)

3 The Angel Inn, near the market (Leonard Greene, Thomas and John Buck)

4 The Austin Friary (Thomas and John Buck, Roger Daniel, John Legate the younger)

5 Queens' Lane and Silver Street (John Field, John Hayes)

6 Site of the new Pitt Press, built 1831–3

stones. Upstairs there was a paper store and provision for hanging sheets to dry. Sewall seems to have under-estimated the length of the room a good deal, since a plan dating from 1828 records it as measuring 79′ by 22′;[84] but it was ample for its purpose.

Field's precarious financial position when he became University Printer was reflected in his first few months' output. Books from the press in the mid-fifties bore (as they had for some years) either the printer's own name or some general allusion to 'Printers to the University' or the even less personal 'ex Academiae typographeo'. But this was to change in 1656 to a more generally personal appellation, following Thomas Buck's withdrawal. Meanwhile, for Field, there were few opportunities at first for him to assume in the colophon sole authority by name: none in 1655, while most of the general imprints for almanacs disappeared only with those for 1658, printed in the latter part of 1657. Until 1660, the Cambridge press provided a modest living consisting predominantly of almanac printing: it was easily outweighed for Field by his London interest, where Cromwellian and parliamentary printing each offered employment until one was brought to an end by death, and resignation, and the other by the Restoration. By April 1659 Field and Hills were entitled to receive no less than £2,783, a sum which was added to the convenient head of naval expenditure, and so added its mite to the Navy's financial embarrassments in the months after Oliver Cromwell's death.[85]

Although, therefore, Field served uninterruptedly as University Printer through 1660 and beyond, this year forms a natural point at which to end a survey of his first years specifically as a Cambridge, rather than as a London, printer.

By the Restoration, the University found itself countenancing the career of a Printer whom many were only too anxious to denigrate. As the number of printing houses in the capital swelled, so the search for scapegoats took a commercial, as well as a political, aspect. Moreover, the booksellers' increasing domination of the Stationers' Company meant that the proportion of old copies available to printers – the chance of profit not dependent on being employed by booksellers – was declining.[86] Field and Hills, both of whom had found a moment of glory in walking in Cromwell's funeral cortège,[87] were obvious targets, men to be excluded from the London trade on political grounds, but for commercial reasons. Thus, in September 1660, Field became a pariah to parts at least of the London trade, denigrated, as Hills was to be repeatedly, as turncoat, opportunist and, with the Restoration, effectively an enemy of the state. Whether as printers to Parliament or to Cromwell, or as Bible printers or as pirates, Field and Hills became the epitome of what, with the Restoration, might be ended.

As the Stationers' Company disputed within itself about the dominating influence of the booksellers, and printers made attempts to secede to form a new company, Field and Hills' record seemed all the more blameworthy. The fiercest attack came, however, from a disaffected printer, for whom the disorderly state of printing, and the growth in the number of printing houses, seemed reason enough for reform.[88]

Who Printed the pretended Act of the Commons of England for the setting up an High Court of Justice, for the tryall of his Martyred Majesty in 1648? Or, The Acts for abolishing King-ship, and renouncing the Royall Line and Title of the Stuarts? Or, for the Declaring what offences should be adjudged Treason? For taking the Engagement? for sale of Dean and Chapters Lands? for sale of the Kings, Queens, and Princes Goods and Lands; and the Fee-farme Rents? for sale of Delinquents Lands; or, the Proclamation of 13. of September 1652. After the fight at WORCESTER, offering, One Thousand pound to any person, to bring in his Majesties person? but only John Feild, Printer to the Parliament of England (and since by Cromwell was and is continued Printer to the University of Cambridge!) Omitting many other Treasonable Offences, and egregious Indignities done by him and H. Hills to the Royal Family, and good old Cause of the King and Kingdome, in all the late Tyrannicall Usurpations...

But we cannot as yet pass over his Majesties good friends, Hills and Feild (take them coniunctim or divisim;) What Zealots and Factors, (or blood-hounds and Tarriers rather) they have been for that abstract of Traitors, Tyrants and Usurpers, Oliver Cromwell, his sonne Richard, and the pretended Committee of Safety, in searching for, seazing and suppressing (as far as they could) all Books, Treatises, and Papers, asserting the Kings Right and Title to the Crown, or tending to the Promotion of his Interest and Vindication of his Authority, the worst of his Majesties enemies must necessarily, with shame and Detestation confesse! And is this all that hath been done by Hills and Feild to his Majesty onely, and his Royall Relations and Interests? No! Their Impieties and Insolences have mounted as high, as to become actuall and professed Traitors against the glorious Crown and Dignity of the King of Kings, blessed for ever: Have they not invaded and still do intrude upon his Majesties Royall Priviledge, Prerogative and Præeminence; And by the pusillanimous Cowardize and insignificant Compact of Mr. Christopher Barker, and another of his name, and (not without probable suspicion,) by the consent and connivence of Mr. John Bill (though he was artificially defeated in his expectations of profit;) Have they not obtained (and now keep in their actual possession) the Manuscript Copy of the last Translation of the holy Bible in English, (attested with the hands of the Venerable and learned Translators in King James his time) ever since 6 March 1655. And thereupon by colour of an unlawfull and enforced entrance in the Stationers Registry, printed and published ever since for the most part in severall Editions of Bibles (consisting of great numbers) such egregious Blasphemies and damnable Errata's, as have corrupted the pure Fountain, and rendred Gods holy Word contemptible to multitudes of the people at home, and a Ludibricum to all the Adversaries of our Religion? Have they not suffocated and suppressed all Books containing Pious and Religious Prayers and Devotions to be presented and offered to the blessed Trinity for the blessing of Heaven upon his Majesties Royall Person and Family, and the Church and State, by preventing and obstructing the Printing of the Common Prayer, Primars, and Psalters, contrary to the Statute of 1. Q.Elizabeth c.2. and other good Laws and

Ordinances, and the Ecclesiasticall Canons of the Church of England; unlesse that they contained Prayers for their late Protector! And are these small Offences to be past and pardoned, or such as shall deserve the favour of Indempnity and Oblivion? God forbid![89]

As the University gathered itself together in the wake of the Restoration, its members returned from exile, old appointments were once again taken up, and new appointments made, the position of University Printer was hardly to be compared with headships of colleges, or with professorships. It was a time for readjustment, as well as for rejoicing; and readjustment was easier lower down the hierarchy of university office. Field's reward for an early career which showed to so little advantage, was a much reduced place in London, but security and title at Cambridge.

17

John Field and the opportunities of office

Though many of the books printed in Cambridge followed a course to their readers that involved printer, publishing stationer, bookshop and binder, others, and particularly the almanacs and Bibles, were handled by entirely different parts of a trade whose complexities were all too clear in 1663 to Sir Roger L'Estrange as he sought to control the circulation of printed matter. Late sixteenth-century assumptions about the books that Thomas Thomas had printed, though they also involved sales at fairs, were by the 1660s entirely inadequate in the much more disparate market now necessary to the well-being of Field's and Hayes' business. Like street ballads, almanacs were a principal part of an energetic and ingenious mass-market. L'Estrange, from his own particular viewpoint, wrote of 'delinquents'; but he also conveniently summarized the structure of an extended trade:

Advisers, Authors, Compilers, Writers, Printers, Correctors, Stitchers, and Binders... together with all Publishers, Dispersers...and all Stationers, Posts, Hackny-Coachmen, Carryers, Boat-men, Mariners, Hawkers, Mercury-Women, Pedlers, and Ballad-Singers.[1]

However his earlier career may have beeen viewed, as recollected in the 1660s, Field's books were in no sense delinquent in the last few years of his life. But it is well to recall how manifold and varied was the book trade, and how far removed were some of its members from any concept of a learned press in the sense assumed by some of Field's and Hayes' authors at Cambridge.

For Field, as for many of his contemporaries, the theological disputes of Cambridge dons were of rather less interest than his editions of the Bible. With the collapse of royal authority in the mid 1640s, and the dispersal of the King's Printing House staff in 1642,[2] the exclusive rights of the King's Printers and of the University lapsed. The market was rapidly flooded with Dutch-printed imports,[3] and for a few years the Stationers' Company itself issued editions. More traditionally, a printer in Finsbury, William Bentley, took up the challenge to print the most consistently saleable book in the whole of the trade, at a price that comfortably undercut that charged by the Stationers.

This loosening of the trade was, however, full of dangers. An offensive monopoly was seen to have been removed; but on the other hand a multiplicity

Fig. 28 *The Holy Bible*, f°, 1659–60. The frontispiece of the
royal arms is by Wenceslaus Hollar, and the title-page is
engraved by Pierre Lombart after a design by Abraham van
Diepenbeeck. Height of original platemarks, 298 mm and
418 mm.

THE HOLY
BIBLE
Containing the Bookes
of the Old & New
TESTAMENT
CAMBRIDGE.
Printed by John Field
Printer to the Universitie
And illustrated w.th Chorographical Sculps by J Ogilby.
1660

Fig 28 continued.

of editions could breed an equal multiplicity of errors. No book required such textual conformity for its authority; yet none, for a few years, was more common property. Daniel's edition of the Septuagint, biblical criticism by scholars such as Henry Hammond and John Lightfoot and, above all, Walton's six-volume polyglot of 1655–7, were each in their way manifestations of a new importance accorded to the scriptures, for which, it rapidly became clear, some central distributive and textual authority was essential. This in turn could be viewed in two different ways. On the one hand, while it was recognized that the 1638 Cambridge text was unequalled ('The *Bible* was never better printed than by Mr *Buck* and Mr *Daniel* at Cambridg'[4]), there seemed, in the minds of some, to be cause for revision. On the other, the need for an approved controlling text suggested a unitary authority that over-rode the received multi-partite character of the printed word produced at the hands of different compositors, readers and pressmen working in their various establishments. Or, as one reformer proposed,

That there may bee a fair Copie of the last Translation of the BIBLE, ingrossed either in Parchment or Vellom, in a full Character, which may bee compared with the Original, by four or five Ministers, and so kept in Sion-College, as an Authentick Record: for Orthography so truely and critically written, that hereafter a Letter shall not bee altered: That so all people, upon any doubt, may have recours to the Original, to prove whether their Printed Copies varie, or not.[5]

Such a copy, though admittedly no longer 'fair', existed of the 1611 Authorized Version. By the mid-1650s, interlineations and obliterations had defaced what once had been fair,[6] and added fuel to the demands for a fresh start. In January 1652/3 the Commons resolved that a Bill should be introduced to authorize a new translation, at the hands of translators to be named. Such a project would of course also have provided the opportunity to remove any taint of episcopacy.[7] It would also have ended, at a stroke, the row that broke out among London printers consequent on the end of the King's Printers' monopoly. When in 1646 the Authorized text was first printed by Bentley, it was claimed that no other London printer would agree to produce a new and cheap edition proposed by the Westminster Assembly. Bentley's new and lucrative trade, bolstered by contracts to supply the army,[8] was rewarded with ostracization by the Stationers' Company; but both in 1649 and in 1652 his special status was confirmed in legislation. By 1648 a confused situation threatened to become chaotic, with editions either of the Bible or of the New Testament not only from Bentley, but also from the Company, a consortium of two other booksellers, Robert White and Thomas Brudenell and, for the first time, a quarto edition from Field:[9] the false edition of '1648' dates from about two decades later. In 1652, Field produced another, duodecimo edition that vaunted on its title-page his appointment as 'Printer to the Parliament of England'. From then until 1664 there was hardly a year when he was not responsible for one or more editions; his last appeared in 1668. As a Bible printer he was to prove an innovator, and he made important contributions to the well-known forms of presentation. But though in the end he attained respectability, and even respect, his earliest efforts were irresponsible and damaging to those on whose trust he preyed.

His principal critic, William Kilburne, was both partial and accurate in his accusations. With pharisaical zeal, Kilburne defended the interests of Bentley's Finsbury press in 1659, in an outspoken attack on the inaccuracy of Field's texts. By then there was ample evidence of neglect on a scale that was nothing short of scandalous. Kilburne's pamphlet was, however, only one further broadside in a battle that had involved Parliament, the Council of State, and the Cambridge authorities. By April 1656, when the Council of State heard Bentley's case, Henry Hills had been implicated as well, as the second of the two printers to the Protector: their copyright in the English Bible had been entered in the Stationers' Register the month before on Cromwell's own authority – the unique instance of his wielding his position in this manner.[10] Though much was made of inaccuracies, an argument that was wielded almost traditionally in disputes concerning copy (and one not unfamiliar in Cambridge earlier in the century), the issue was commercial as much as textual, as John Streater and others concerned in Bible printing pointed out. Cromwell's entry had only served to heighten a crisis in the trade. By legislation of 1649, anyone engaged in printing or selling the Bible might now be sued by Field and Hills; and yet this seemed to implicate not only the Finsbury press, but also the Stationers' Company, who had likewise invested in Bibles. Cromwell's act had left printers with books half complete and with stock on their hands.[11] By the end of July, Field and Hills had consolidated their position, heading off a challenge from another London stationer, Andrew Crooke, and entering into an agreement with Oxford, the sole other possible challenge. In return for a payment of £80 per annum, the University agreed to farm out its Bible privilege for three years.[12] In this manner, Field and Hills had gained an absolute monopoly in domestic production: experience had shown that very little could be done about imports.

The trade's quarrel was with both Field and Hills; but the responsibility for a series of abominably erroneous texts was Field's, his appointment at Cambridge making at first no difference save that it provided a refuge from too pressing embarrassments in London.[13] Kilburne's attack, published in 1659 but its preliminary findings already available in Cambridge only a few months after the University had elected his victim, concentrated on half a dozen editions: a 24° of 1653 ('very small to carry in pockets'), two duodecimos of 1655, another duodecimo of 1656, an octavo of 1657 (the first Bible Field printed at Cambridge) and a duodecimo printed by Field and Hills together in 1656. The lamentable quality of Field's texts was no secret. In November 1656 it had been the subject of enquiry by the House of Commons Committee for religion, especial attention being paid then to the defective 24° 1653 edition – of which Field admitted to having printed about 2,000 copies.[14] Field's own stock of Bibles, some 7,900 copies, was secured pending the Committee's further consideration. By the following January the investigation had become more particular, as a Bible Committee turned its attention to particular faults, not only in the texts printed by Field, but also in a recent edition from Hills' press. Though it was possible to claim that most faults were 'but slight' – in commas, full stops, italics, or odd letters – it remained that the text had become neglected, and consequently corrupt. The Committee considered a list of two thousand errata alleged by the Stationers' Company against one of Hills' Bibles, while 'one Robinson, a Scotchman, corrector of his Highness's press, a very busy person, and something in his own opinion, and skill in the tongues' arraigned not only the recent Cambridge editions, but all other recent ones as well.[15] Field's stock was impounded by the whole House the following June, and Field was called to present himself in November – a confrontation he escaped thanks to an adjournment of business between the end of June and late January following. The dissolution of Parliament in June 1657 not only saved Field, it also brought to an untimely end efforts under way for a new translation, one which promised fresh linguistic accuracy (it was to have involved at least Brian Walton, Edmund Castell, Samuel Clarke and Ralph Cudworth) and the cessation of an embarrassment of error-ridden reprints of the Authorized Version.[16] But it could not resolve the continuing problem set by inaccurate books, for which the trade had in the end to find its own solution.

As one step, in October 1658 the Court of the Stationers' Company, noting that the Psalter recently printed by Field and Hills for the English Stock was 'printed in an vnhandsome manner', had ordered the entire edition to be withdrawn from sale.[17] The scale of Field's business, and the extent of the mistakes, made control impossible. In 1657 the Commons had considered it realistic to seize no less than 7,900 surviving copies of the offending edition of 1653, though it had to acknowledge that many more had already gone into circulation. Kilburne claimed to have been told that 20,000 copies had been printed of Hills and Field's 1656 octavo. Altogether, he told the Vice-Chancellor, some 80,000 copies had been printed of four faulty editions.[18] Parliament might seize copies, and London stationers might decline to deal in them; but this could not prevent their dispersal through channels other than the ordinary shops: country fairs and markets, book-binders and petty-chapmen, all offered alternative means of sale to customers unused to bookshops or to spending much on a book.[19] Such quantities in the hands of a monopoly seemed, moreover, an offence to the well-being of the trade at large. Hills and Field, it was alleged, employed no more than ten or a dozen men. It was not clear, from a petition addressed by journeymen-printers to Parliament in spring

1659, how a loosening of the privilege might result in dramatically more jobs; but the two men became a convenient target at a time when the printing trade was feeling itself under threat. The government, in other words, and however illogically, was placed in a position of seeming to condone or even encourage unemployment.[20]

Kilburne did not restrict his campaign to pointing out textual errors and omissions. He also took exception to the fact that marginal references had been discarded as a means of cost-cutting, and that Field and Hills had employed no English corrector, but 'one Mr Robinson (a Scotch Rabbi)': in his intemperate excitement at this foreign spectre, who had sought so assiduously to justify himself before Parliament, he muddled his victim's name, William Robertson, who qualified for Kilburne's description only as an Edinburgh MA now settled in London and teaching Hebrew: he was to become a familiar name on the title-pages of books printed at Cambridge by Field and his successor.[21]

Field was thus upbraided by Parliament, criticized by the Stationers' Company, attacked by Kilburne in Cambridge and the object of public denunciation in London. Yet he retained his patent to print the Bible in London until after the Restoration, and he did so without being disciplined as had been those responsible for the 'wicked' Bible in 1631.[22] Such an achievement, in London, lends some credibility to Kilburne's allegations of bribery:

For (as it is credibly reported,) Mr. *Hills* and Mr. *Field* have several times affirmed, that they are engaged to pay 500*l per Annum*. to some, whose names out of respect to them I forbear to mention, over and above 100*l per Annum* to Mr. Marchamont Needham, and his wife, out of the profits of the sale of their Bibles, deriding, insulting, & triumphing over others of the Printing Mysterie, out of their confidence in their great Friends and purse, as it is said, as if they were lawlesse, and free (notwithstanding the truth of the premisses and other grand Enormities often committed by them) both from offence and punishment, to the great dishonour of the Commonwealth in general, and dammage of many private persons in particular.[23]

The rewards were high, and thanks to their rights of search and seizure Field and Hills had the power to impose by force their own monopoly. Under Field, the price of Bibles and singing Psalms was said to have been forced up; he brought to an end the work of William Bentley, his principal rival, by the simple but effective expedient of proceeding with some soldiers to Bentley's shop on 28 August 1656 and 'did carry away…the Form and Materials for printing a part of the *New Testament*, and seized the Sheets to his *Highnesse* use, as if the same were scandalous'. Further harassment threatened Bentley and his family with ruin.[24]

Within a few weeks there appeared in *Mercurius politicus*, among notices for missing persons, stolen horses, lozenges and new books, an advertisement of a disingenuousness that few can have failed to recognize:

Whereas for the space of about Twelve years past, the Printing of the Bible lay in Common; so that every man presumed to Print it at pleasure (which was never permitted before in any Country, the Magistrate in all States and Kingdoms, ever committing it to the care of persons of his own appointment) it so fell out through the Arbitrary and Licencious custom of Printing, that many Hundreds of very gross Errors are escaped in the Common Impressions now abroad, to the great scandal of *Religion* and *Government*, and abuse of the people.

For remedy whereof, due care hath been had to settle the Printing of the *Holy Scriptures*, in an orderly way for time to come; and there is now a Bible finished, *By his Highnesses special Command*, free from those *Errors* which are crept into many of the other Impressions, it being examined, corrected, and amended according to the Original Manuscript Copy of the *Translators*.

And to the end, that a Book of so sacred concernment, may be exactly and truly Printed for the future, there are two Correctors kept to correct all Bibles that shall be printed hereafter; and over and above, there is a very learned person appointed by his Highness, carefully to Revise every Sheet before it be wrought off at the Press.

Such regard hath been had likewise to the Publick, and ease of the people, in the price of Bibles, that his Highness printers (notwithstanding they have purchased the translated Copy in the Manuscript, which cost them Twelve hundred pounds; and by entring it in the *Stationers* Register-Book, have a Legal Title to the sole Printing of it, and are at the great Charge aforesaid of Correcting it) are obliged to sell Bibles in the Common Volumes without Notes (called *Twelves*) at no more but Two shillings a Book in quires. At which price, the Corrected Impression aforesaid, is now to be sold at the House of *Henry Hills* in *Aldersgate street*, next door to the sign of the *Peacock*.[25]

Thus a University Printer advertised his reform, concealed safely in anonymous seclusion behind his partner. The Bentleys were still an annoyance two years later, when the Stationers heard a complaint that Field and Hills had seized a forme of type as well as the bar and spindle of their press following the discovery on their premises of a New Testament in preparation.[26]

Though, with the restoration of the monarchy, Hills and Field were obliged eventually to countenance the restoration of Bill and Barker as royal printers,[27] they retained their own position as London Bible printers sufficiently long to extract from Oxford yet further agreement to the University of Cambridge's right to print Bibles on a continued payment of £80 per annum.[28] This agreement (coming less than six weeks after the Restoration in May) was perhaps meant as an insurance against restitution, but it resulted in little printing in London. Much more importantly, it ensured for Field's Cambridge press continuing dominance in the Bible trade, and in particular it protected him from the danger of competition for the most ambitious of all his projects, the folio Bible of 1659 (see fig. 28).

His poor reputation for accuracy has lived on, even to Isaac D'Israeli's undocumented allegation in the nineteenth century that he was said to have received from the Independents a bribe of £1,500 to corrupt the crucial text at Acts vi.3 on the making of deacons, changing 'we' to 'ye' in the phrase 'whom we may appoint'.[29] But Field, and others both in London and in Scotland, had simply followed their Cambridge 1638 copy, itself a mistake that would have been countenanced neither by Buck, Daniel nor Laud had it been seen in time. So error led to embarrassment and to false accusation. Field's Bibles, especially his early ones, were grossly inaccurate; but there is no evidence that he deliberately tampered with the text in such a manner.

He attained his position in London by bullying. It was one of power rather than of respect. He used his power not only to bring Bentley's press to an end, but also to attempt in 1658 to end Roger Daniel's now controversial career for good.[30] Within the Stationers' Company he commanded only limited respect. His Bible printing, notoriously poor, became an encumbrance on the English Stock, whose members, sympathetic to profit, could not easily countenance inaccuracy and poor standards in the face of cheap Dutch imports. There was even some doubt as to Field and Hills' honesty in their returns to the Stock, for whom during a short period they printed as many as 24,000 copies of Sternhold and Hopkins' metrical Psalms each year.[31]

But by the time that Kilburne's strictures on the smaller format Bibles were published in 1659, Field was well advanced at Cambridge on the project that was to recover his reputation among his contemporaries, and provide an honourable foundation for it among generations to come. In 1658, work on the folio Bible was authorized by John Worthington, as Vice-Chancellor, 'several months' before he stepped down in November. Its production meant the delay of other projects in the press, and may have been the reason why the local booksellers William Morden and William Nealand had to seek out alternative printers in London. But for Worthington, this hardly mattered. 'For a fair large letter, large paper, with fair margin, &c., there was never such a Bible in being', he enthused.[32] Certainly it was large, with its double pica type even for the text. It was also the first folio edition of the Authorized Version, of a size suitable for the lectern or for the amplest libraries, since the black letter edition issued by the King's Printer in 1640. It still perpetuated the mistake at Acts vi.3 made in 1638, however, and to that extent did not vindicate Field's reputation: the error was made good only in his later, and less ostentatious, editions.

Though Worthington had sanctioned it, the 1659 Bible became, in the end, associated most with John Ogilby, an entrepreneur whose lavish editions of Virgil (1654 and 1658) and of Aesop, unprecedented in England, were made possible not by the ordinary book trade, but by subscription. The *Iliad* followed in 1660, 'adorned with sculpture', and the *Odyssey* in 1665: all of these were printed in London. Field finished his Bible in 1659, but much of the edition was taken up by Ogilby, who decked it with an elaborate new title-page (issues survive with and without his own name) and, more particularly, imported from Holland a series of magnificent double-page engraved illustrations cast on a scale commensurate with the awesome magnitude of Field's printing. These 'chorographical Sculps', after paintings by Rubens, Tintoretto, Maerten de Vos, Abraham Bloemaert, Jacob Jordaens, Nicolaes de Bruyn and others, helped eventually to make this Bible one of the most sought after of all, though for some it was too large. 'It is like to be so big, that I shall not use it', noted Pepys on being shown it in 1667.[33] In return for a very considerable investment, Ogilby had acquired a book whose sales could not be monitored from the start by subscription. Despite his ingenuity in advertising his new book, by ostentatiously presenting a copy to the King and extracting £50 from the House of Commons for a copy it had not requested, his petition to the King in 1661, seeking to prevent the printing of any other illustrated folio Bible for ten years, indicates the scale of his concern, and incidentally of his investment.[34]

Ogilby's innovations in publishing, involving (for the Bible) the purchase and importation of engraved plates from overseas, and no less expense from the London engraving, etching and rolling-press trade for his other projects such as Aesop (1651), Virgil (1658), Homer (1660–5) and *Coronation* of Charles II (1662) proved over-ambitious. Left with stock on his hands, he found himself obliged by 'very good advice' to 'propound an expeditious means to dispose of this his whole stock within a few months, which else would not drop off Book by Book, in many years'. To this end, in 1665 he proposed a lottery, offering as first prize seven of his publications, valued in all at £49, of which the Bible on imperial paper, with a hundred 'Historical Sculps' was by far the most expensive, at £25. More ordinary, and lesser, prizes included ninety Bibles on royal paper, valued at £5 apiece. A further lottery proved necessary the following year, again featuring the grandest of the Bibles among the books offered in first prize, as Ogilby sought also to repair losses and disruption occasioned first by plague and then by fire.[35]

Field's unfettered access to the Bible trade, enabling him to print editions in whatever format he pleased, was at odds with the 1629 ruling limiting the University to quartos and folios only. With the Restoration, he lost what government protection he might have claimed. There was therefore a familiar ring to the royal petitions and consequent correspondence with the Vice-Chancellor, that was triggered by the continuing appearance of octavo editions and, especially, by Field's preparations for an octavo edition of the New Testament alone. To the accompaniment of appeals to the wording of the 1534 charter, and avowals that to stop production either of this New Testament or of the equally new Book of Common Prayer (to which the King's Printers laid sole claim) would mean the ruin of families, the case was heard this time by the Lord Chancellor, Clarendon, Field meanwhile having given a written undertaking not to publish any Book of Common Prayer until further instructed.[36] Similar questions faced Oxford, where, it was reported, some difficulty was feared in recruiting a Vice-Chancellor lest his duties should lead to legal proceedings at Westminster.[37] The spectre of Cambridge farming out its privileges, as had Oxford, loomed large, and, to some, malevolently, in the autumn of 1662.[38] There seems to have been some confusion in Cambridge (and especially in Field's mind) between the argument over privileged printing and the provisions of the new Licensing Act, which came into force on 19 May that year. It was a muddle succinctly corrected by William Thursby, the University Counsel, on his return from presenting the University's case in London:

Y^e fault or occasion is not upon ye penning of this new Act or of any clause or saving therein the same being as full & as beneficiall for ye university & as generall & comprehensive in words & meaning as could possibly have been penned or devised But the doubt & controversy is upon ye exposicion of y^r university charter these words therein whereby ye claime *privilegium imprimendi omnes & omnimodos libros* wch by reason of ye generallity of y^m seems unreasonable & to comprehend to much & if they should be construed soe generall as they import would distroy, all other ye kings charters of privilege wch cannot be suffered ... But as touching ye new Act it confirmes y^r privilege be it what it will & saves y^r rights all be they what they will, so noe neglect can be charged upon y^{ou} or me.[39]

Field's fears as to the University's privileges may have been unjustified; but his farming of the Oxford privilege came to an end with the King's Printers' reassertion of their position. In its place, in October 1661, Oxford had agreed with the Stationers' Company to accept an annual payment of £200 for three years, in return for forbearing to print Bibles, prayer books, grammars or almanacs, and thus reverted to similar arrangements which had obtained before 1643. Inevitably, the question arose of Cambridge following, especially when in the winter of 1662–3 it was rumoured that the King's Printers were waiting to farm out privileged printing to Cambridge itself. Field, who would thereby have been able to gain doubly, was in favour of imitating Oxford;[41] but such a procedure would have nullified any further claims by the University to print *omnimodos libros*, and there were other arguments also suggesting that it was 'neither safe nor honourable'. In the eyes of William Dillingham, former Vice-Chancellor, and Master of Emmanuel, it was a matter of trusteeship:

The Vniversity'es privilege is looked upon as a trust for the publick good, & theire printing of these bookes will force the Londoners to printe something tolerably true (else they shall not be able to sell while better may be had from Camb) who otherwise looking meerly at gaine will not care how corruptly they print, witnes the 200 blasphemy's which Mr B. found in their bibles; & the millions of faults in theire schoolbookes, increasing in every edition, so long as M^r B's composition with the stationers held; (So that the bookes were rather to be new made then mended). whence it was that often errors were drunk in in grammer schooles scarcely after to be corrected at the Vniversity, unlesse schoolmasters were so carefull as to correct bookes by hand before they lett theire boys have them.

   It being therfore the Vniversityes interest to have youths well & truly grounded in school bookes & the interest of the whole nation to have true bibles, I cannot but think the Vniversity trustees in both respects, & feare they would afterwards rew the betraying of so great a trust if they should sell it by farming; if they do not forfeit theire charter by it.[42]

Field's own position in all this was complicated, in that his reputation for inaccuracy and his status as University Printer were incompatible with the kinds of arguments for textual responsibility and authority put forward by Dillingham. The University's solution was however a simple one, in presenting to the King a petition on behalf not of a man who would at best have prompted unease, but of Thomas Buck, by now the respected elder statesman of the Cambridge press, senior by far to Field, and still one of the three Printers to the University.[43]

By this time, the first Cambridge edition of the new Book of Common Prayer had been printed (see fig. 29), as well as octavo editions of the Bible and of the New Testament: the University's petition to the King claimed that some ten thousand had been prepared.[44] The renewed argument delayed, but did not prevent, their appearance. But within a year, the range of books issued by Field suggested that the relationship of the Cambridge to the London printers had reverted approximately to the mutual forbearance and accommodation of before the Civil War. With Field's death, and with Thomas Buck's steadying hand no longer present, the position was to become very different.

Field's reputation as a Bible printer foundered in his own lifetime on the disparity between his claim to the Authorized text, and the manifest inaccuracy of many of the editions to which his name was attached. The fact that these complaints receded after the Restoration did not affect this view. Yet as the publisher of a text available also in many editions printed overseas, imported and made available at prices that undercut those printed in England, he was innovative in the face of difficult, aggressive and surreptitious competition. His own imprint was pirated.[45] He succeeded, moreover, in a notably conservative market. Whatever the quality of their texts, the small 24° edition of 1653 and, at the opposite extreme, the magnificent lectern folio of 1659–60, many copies of the latter embellished thanks to John Ogilby, were both responses to their time in that they each identified fresh niches in the market. Though many of the copies of the Ogilby folio found their way into the larger private and institutional libraries, the edition also had the advantage of being the first folio edition of the Authorized Version of the Bible in roman letter to have been printed in England since 1639. So, too, his 1668 quarto, the so-called 'preaching' Bible thanks to its slim yet visible form, marked a new departure. It was achieved not simply by using noticeably thinner paper, but also by reducing the type size from the pica used in his previous quarto of 1663 to nonpareil. The number of sheets required was cut by one-third, a valuable achievement at a time when the British paper trade was disrupted by the Great Fire.[46]

In the end, Field's earlier reputation had been so much forgotten that his name was acclaimed even where his work was forgotten. His 1665 duodecimo Greek Bible, the work of John Pearson, was reissued by Hayes without acknowledgement in 1684, the title-page still showing Field's name. Further

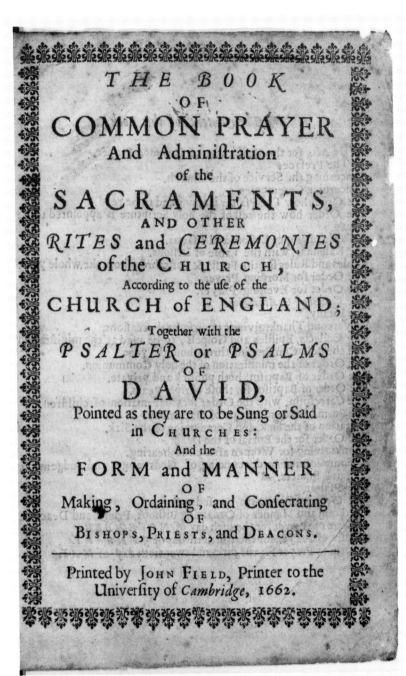

THE BOOK
OF
COMMON PRAYER
And Administration
of the
SACRAMENTS,
AND OTHER
RITES and CEREMONIES
of the CHURCH,
According to the use of the
CHURCH of ENGLAND;
Together with the
PSALTER or PSALMS
OF
DAVID,
Pointed as they are to be Sung or Said
in CHURCHES:
And the
FORM and MANNER
OF
Making, Ordaining, and Consecrating
OF
BISHOPS, PRIESTS, and DEACONS.

Printed by JOHN FIELD, Printer to the
University of *Cambridge*, 1662.

Fig. 29 The Book of Common Prayer, 8°, 1662. Height of original, 169 mm.

sheets from the same edition appeared overseas. By 1743, opinion had swung so far towards Field that a casual observer convinced himself that Hayes' reissue was a fraud, and a poor one at that:

But as he took care to print it Page for Page, and, I suppose, Line for Line with Field's, so he put Field's Name to it, and dated it as Field's was, 1665. By which he put a Cheat upon the World: his Letter being not so clear, nor his Book so correct as Field's is.[47]

After Cromwell's death, Field proved himself a competent, rather than inspired, printer, content to concentrate on the regular work of Bibles, school texts and almanacs, rather than launch unnecessarily often into ventures of the kind which Buck and Daniel had faced. Under the eye of its Treasurer, George Sawbridge, he exercised a modest, but lucrative, part as shareholder in the English Stock, a part valued at his death at £140 but in fact worth in his lifetime far more in terms of regular and assured business.[48] He had possessed a half share since 1656, shortly after his election at Cambridge.[49] The periodic dividends were of less significance to a printer than the cartel created for the printing of books such as elementary grammars, school texts, metrical Psalters, and above all almanacs, for which there was a dependable and heavy demand. In effect, the English Stock acted as a publisher – but a publisher that was also a printer, able to rely entirely (with the exception of the annual almanacs) on an established backlist, so long as interlopers and unauthorized editions were excluded. It regularly spent money to protect itself, and to suppress such intrusions into its own market. But for the university presses – first Cambridge and then Oxford – no such legal action was possible. Instead, their activities were both curtailed and encouraged by arrangements that brought rewards with the vindictiveness and animosity that had so frequently characterized dealings between Cambridge and the Company in the past. The English Stock's repeated calls for edition quantities far in excess of those for most new publications brought assured profit at a controlled price, and required little imagination, though little evidence now survives of the extent to which the Stock's activities permeated the experience of the literate population. Some fourteen editions printed at Cambridge of Lily's *Short introduction of grammar* are recorded for the period 1660–99, printed by either Field or Hayes. It was, as it had been in one form or another since the sixteenth century, the first textbook of all for those seeking to learn Latin. Other editions were printed at Oxford and in London. Most were issued with Lily's longer *Brevissima institutio*. But the repeated demand evidenced in the survival of these editions (many existing now only in a single copy) was much greater than Wing suggests. In 1681, for example, two editions were printed at Cambridge alone.[50] The stock book of the English Stock records purchases of many more, from both London and Cambridge printers, than seem now to have survived. Aesop, the metrical Psalms, Lily, Cicero, Terence, Culman's *Sententiae*,

Corderius and Lucius Florus, as well as almanacs, all fell within the interests of the English Stock; and all were at one time or another printed by Field or Hayes. In 1669, no less than ten thousand Latin primers were supplied, at a cost of as little as £50.

However, not all copies in an edition were supplied at once to the London warehouse of the English Stock. At his death in 1668, Field still had sixty reams of Corderius' *Colloquia* remaining over and above the three thousand copies he had supplied to London in the summer of the previous year.[51] So, too, he had thirty-three reams of Lucius Florus (another English Stock title), and 132 reams of Lily's grammar. The 227 copies of the metrical Psalms were presumably the balance of the main stock in London; and the 111 copies of Acsop were likewise presumably the residue of the 3,000 copies supplied to the English Stock a few weeks before Field died. It may be that these stocks were intended for local consumption – in the same way that a number of copies of almanacs were held back annually for sale in and about Cambridge. But, as they were listed among the rest of the property in his estate, it seems more probable that Field was both bearing the cost of warehousing and, having printed these various books, being paid only as the English Stock required them to be delivered.

There was still no University commitment to the development, or even encouragement, of a press that would be more than ordinary. The Cambridge press depended on individual, not on corporate, enterprise, and was to remain so until almost the end of the century. Privately published works continued to appear, among them George Atwell's *Faithfull surveyor*, published in 1658 with the help of friends made at Cambridge;[52] Field and the booksellers proving at first cautious at such a book. 'And what,' demanded Atwell of his dedicatee William Dillingham, Master of Emmanuel College, 'can be more beneficial than quenching an house on fire?' More flamboyantly, Field also printed, again privately, an illustrated edition of Sir Francis Vere's autobiographical *Commentaries* on his military experience in the Low Countries, edited by William Dillingham. Field had already printed two of Dillingham's sermons for the local bookseller William Morden, and he gave Vere's work an air of distinction (if a slightly old-fashioned one typographically) that was not always to be found in his other work.[53] A few books were printed directly for London booksellers, among them a folio edition of the sermons of John Frost, former Fellow of St John's and now in a city parish, and works by the Master of Trinity, John Arrowsmith.

Local booksellers proved to be more enterprising, principal among them William Morden, William Nealand and William Graves. The first volume of John Lightfoot's *Horae Hebraicae et Talmudicae*, printed for another Cambridge bookseller, Edward Story, in 1658, marked the beginning of an intended series, a further sign of renewed interest in Hebraic studies in the University.[54] Amidst much that was of the everyday, Origen's *Contra Celsum*, copiously annotated by William Spencer, Fellow of Trinity, was all the more unusual. Spencer based his parallel text edition on David Hoeschel's edition of the Greek, published at Augsburg in 1605,[55] and on the Czech humanist Sigismund Gelenius' Latin translation prepared originally for Froben the previous century. Textually, Spencer's edition therefore offered nothing that was new: its occasion lay in the long commentary hitched onto the end, and the book met with success sufficient to call for a page-for-page reprint from John Hayes in 1677. Of the other booksellers, it was Morden who was responsible for books by Henry More, and Nealand who published John Ray's *Catalogus plantarum circa Cantabrigiam nascentium* (1660), the first such local flora ever to be published in England (see fig. 30).[56] It was also Morden of whom Worthington thought when in 1668 there was talk of Christopher Wase editing Maximus.[57] These two men, Morden and Nealand, invested in more books than the title-page imprints suggest. Among Morden's other interests were Francis Glisson's controversial *Tractatus de natura substantiae energetica* (1672), a book of obvious local interest as the work of an eminent, if usually absentee, Regius Professor of Physic,[58] a Greek grammar by Matthaeus Devarius, and the first English edition (1668) of Descartes' *Epistolae*, originally published at Amsterdam in the same year.[59] By no means all of Morden's and Nealand's books were printed at Cambridge. Morden enjoyed particularly close connections with the London printer James Flesher. Although there is some evidence that earlier Cambridge booksellers had had an interest in the publication of London-printed books, even those that did not bear their names,[60] the scale of at least Morden's and Nealand's operations suggest a trend towards a greater geographical distribution of capitalization. Nealand sold most of the impression of Ray's catalogue to a group of London booksellers, and thus recouped his production costs.[61] Morden, on his death in March 1678/9, left the principal part of his extensive property to his son Charles, including stock held in both London and Cambridge: his London estate was sufficiently large for it to be necessary to prove his will there as well as in Cambridge.[62] The Stationers' Company's readiness to see first Field, and then Hayes, installed as University Printers was not only because in them it saw the means to control potential rivals: the wealth of some parts of the provinces also made such collaboration seem natural.[63]

Field established his press in Cambridge gradually. In 1656 he issued only four books there, rather than in London, including workaday editions of Aesop and Terence. In the following three years, during the last part of which the Cambridge press was taken up with his folio Bible, his output came overwhelmingly from London, as he concentrated on Cromwellian and parliamentary needs. But this meant that in 1660 he was responsible for a stock that was both irrelevant and potentially damaging. He met the new regime by virtually closing down his London premises (one of the few books printed there was a volume of royalist verses by William Fairebrother, a Fellow of

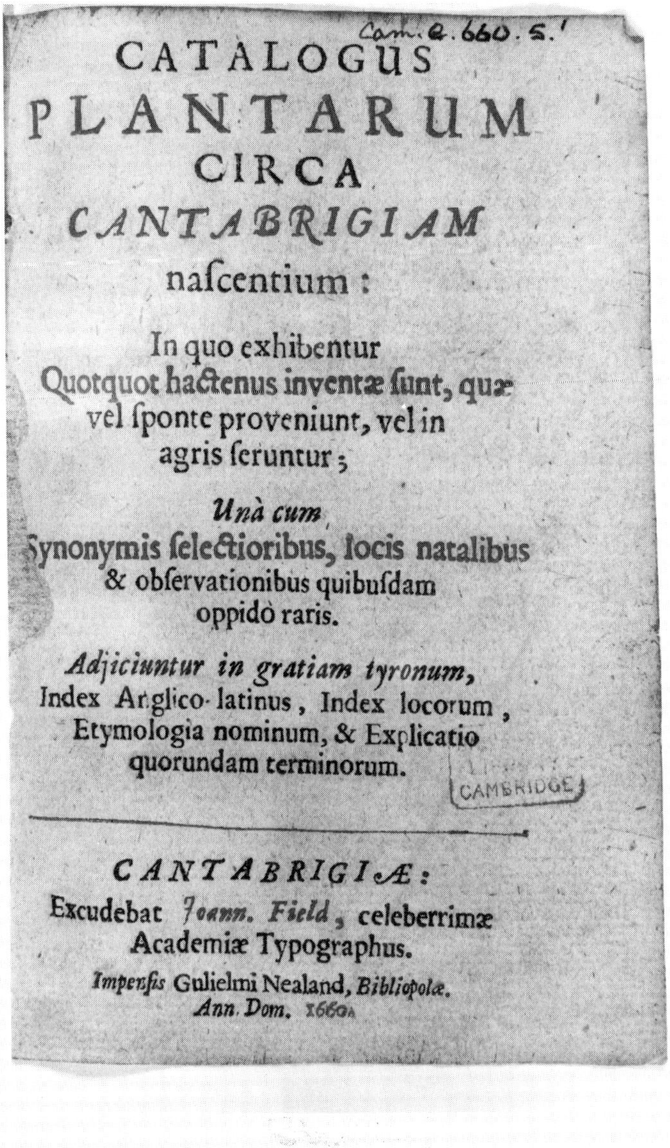

CATALOGUS
PLANTARUM
CIRCA
CANTABRIGIAM
nascentium :

In quo exhibentur
Quotquot hactenus inventæ sunt, quæ
vel sponte proveniunt, vel in
agris seruntur ;

Unà cum
Synonymis selectioribus, locis natalibus
& observationibus quibusdam
oppidò raris.

Adjiciuntur in gratiam tyronum,
Index Anglico-latinus , Index locorum ,
Etymologia nominum, & Explicatio
quorundam terminorum.

CANTABRIGIÆ:

Excudebat *Joann. Field ,* celeberrimæ
Academiæ Typographus.

Impensis Gulielmi Nealand, *Bibliopolæ.*
Ann. Dom. 1660.

Fig. 30 John Ray (1627–1705), *Catalogus plantarum circa Cantabrigiam
nascentium*, 8°, 1660. Height of original, 143 mm.

King's), and by attending to Cambridge. Thenceforth, although he was partly responsible for Sir George Croke's *Reports* (in which he had a share),[64] few books bore his London imprint; and though he still retained his printing house there,[65] most Bible printing was transferred to Cambridge. However, he did keep warehouse space in London, for the storing of imported white paper stock.[66]

It is not clear how rapidly he accommodated himself to the needs, or possibilities, of post-Restoration England. Daniel's challenge for his old position was seen off, as has already been described. There may be some significance in the circumstances of the publication of the University sermon that marked the Restoration, preached by William Godman, Fellow of King's, on Thursday 24 May, before Charles had even landed at Dover: it was published by Morden, but printed in London by James Flesher, rather than by Field. For many, its appearance was the more urgent since it was the first available vehicle for members of the University to assure the world of their delight at the King's return. Not all the preliminary verses were especially well turned:

> Doth not his Hair like *Sampson*'s guard his head
> And gather up in links and chains? Let dread
> Fear then seize those that stand his opposite,
> Lest they be fetter'd in't and feel its weight.[67]

Goodman dated his preface 6 June, and it may be assumed that the book was published a few days later.

The official University verses, printed by Field, took a little longer to assemble. Those who had mourned Cromwell's passing and extolled the virtues of his successor now produced encomia on the Restoration: among the heads of houses, those of St John's, Queens', King's, Christ's, Clare, Jesus, Emmanuel and Pembroke all found the necessary skill. The volume was assembled and seen through the press by James Duport, by now Vice-Master of Trinity, whose close interest in the printing house was no less now than it had been when, in 1637, Buck and Daniel had printed his rendering of *Job* in Greek verse. Field was to die still owing Duport £65 in 1668.[68] Duport's concluding poem, with appropriate Homeric allusions to mark a return, contrived also to introduce the legend from the press's device, 'Hinc lucem et pocula sacra'; but it was to be the last of his marks set on the press's publications. In the same year, 1660, Field also printed Duport's *Homeri Gnomologia*,[69] dedicated in suitably hortatory terms to a group of the author's distinguished former pupils. Adulation continued still in 1666/7, with the publication of Duport's version of the Psalms, again turned into Greek verse. The frontispiece portrait of Charles II, facing the image of King David, was reinforced by the accompanying verses drawing the link between the two.[70] Under Duport, the press issued a series of central Greek texts during the first years following the Restoration: the *Iliad* and *Odyssey* in 1664, followed by

Sophocles, the Septuagint and Duport's own translation of the Book of Common Prayer in 1665. These were intended as working texts, not for show, and with the exception of John Pearson's edition of the Septuagint laid few claims to originality. The Septuagint, Sophocles, and both the volumes of Homer observed Duport's own precept, printing Latin and Greek in parallel and so helping to promote an understanding of each language simultaneously.[71] The *Iliad* rapidly established itself as the ordinary English edition, in tandem with an Oxford Greek text from 1676: new editions were called for every few years, while the Sophocles enjoyed a spurious appearance of success created by a series of rejuvenating title-pages, sheets of the original edition being passed on Field's death to the local bookseller John Hare, who reissued them with a fresh title-page dated 1669, before in 1673 a further residue passed to the London bookseller Robert Scott. Extra sheets were printed for both the Septuagint and the prayer book, in order to make up inadequacies in the stock.[72]

Duport's penchant for imitation did not find favour with later generations. J. H. Monk, the biographer of Bentley, wrote of classical learning in England being then 'by no means well directed', and was frank in his opinion of his abilities. 'His lines exhibit all metrical licences for which authority could be drawn from ancient poets, without due consideration of the laws of the particular compositions which he was imitating.'[73] But such strictures, strengthened by comparisons with Milton, could not deny Duport's enthusiasm, or his support for the press at a critical juncture. His close interest in the concerns of printing manifested itself not only in the work he undertook directly for the Cambridge press, but also in his occasional verse, including compositions on the new Oxford press in the Sheldonian, and the rival claims for the place of printing's invention.[74] Away from the printed page, his priorities in the early 1660s were made equally clear by the list of books he selected to give to Trinity College library, gifts that in many instances clearly related to his work for the press, among them not only the works of Charles I and a group of his own works, but also a late manuscript of Sophocles.[75]

Parts of Duport's programme (it was little less) were eccentric, and much of it was too disorganized to be effective. But it had about it a vitality usually missing from Field's own work. How much more Duport might have accomplished can only be guessed. His enthusiasm and energy were unquestionable, and he carried the necessary weight of seniority. But he found few disciples, and some of his plans were therefore much reduced in their development. It was almost certainly he who was behind a scheme in 1662 to print the scholiasts with the Greek poets, one which, had it been completed, would have set the Cambridge press next to the Estiennes themselves and would have offered the learned world a very considerable saving. He found an ally in William Dillingham at Emmanuel, but the scheme seems to have been short-lived. Editions of Homer and Sophocles appeared, but not the single-volume annotated edition of all the poets that Duport and Dillingham envisaged.[76]

After 1661, when Field's share in Croke's reports was entered in the Stationers' register, only one further book was entered in it to him, Descartes' *Principia philosophiae*, entered in December 1663 and printed for the London bookseller Jonas Hart in the following year. Like other Cambridge printers before him, Field had no need to use the Stationers' Register. In 1660, fifty titles had been assigned to him by John Legate's widow, but he took little advantage of them: the entry seems to have been occasioned more by prudence and tidiness than by any serious expectation on Field's part that he would ever exploit most of them.[77] When in 1663 he had entered Descartes' *Principia philosophiae*, he had taken what was for him an unusual step, on this occasion perhaps to protect Hart more than himself. Though he remained committed to recompensing Buck when printing his copies,[78] he found, like others, that Cambridge gave him independence. In 1662, he himself published the first edition of a new Biblical concordance by Samuel Newman of Massachusetts. It was a direct challenge to London, replacing more cheaply and more compactly Newman's earlier one originally published in 1643 and in its third edition by 1658.[79] Newman, 'a very Lively Preacher, and a very Preaching Liver',[80] died in 1663, the first American author to have his book printed at Cambridge; and Cambridge found itself with an assured success. First in Field's hands, and then in Hayes', the revised version had appeared five times in Cambridge by the end of the century as 'the most excellent concordance that ever was printed'.[81] It lasted as the usual resort for ordinary purposes until Alexander Cruden's concordance gained credence in the 1760s.[82] Newman's folio had its quarto counterpart in John Jackson's more concise guide published in 1668 and printed with a typographical compactness comparable with one of the most ingenious of all Field's books, the thin quarto Bible of the same year.[83] Of all Field's other books, apart from traditionally established titles, only Francis Gouldman's Latin dictionary, first printed in London in 1664 and then repeatedly reprinted at Cambridge by both Field and Hayes, commanded for a few years the consistent success, in both Britain and North America, comparable to Newman's work and its derivatives.

The conjunction of Newman's ability as author to build on others' experience, and Field's ingenuity as printer, ensured a continuing success that depended essentially on economy. So the preface spoke of the fullness and completeness of Newman's work, and of the skilful way in which he had been served by Field.

As this Book containeth more, so is the volume less then formerly, it being 1. printed in a more small and close letter, and 2. of a method as *Newmans*, the Scriptures transcribed in full sentences; yet also in part as *Wickens* and *Bennets*, the figures onely of chapter and verse set down, which hath abbreviated the work by thousands of lines, yet fully as compleat and usefull.

The volume is indeed not only noticeably sleeker than earlier editions of Newman, but is of a size more akin to Richard Bernard's briefer, and confessedly inaccurate, *Thesaurus biblicum*, printed at London in 1661. Under Hayes, Newman's concordance kept its reputation. 'How much the *Cambridge* Concordance excels all others, and in what Particulars, you may satisfie your self from the Preface', wrote Awnsham and John Churchill in their edition of 1698, before explaining some of the typographical advantages:

There is one thing more peculiar (though no great advantage) to this Edition, which is that every Page is Twenty Lines longer (Ten in each Column) then in the former Editions; Which is the Reason that This will not so much exceed the Former Editions in Outward bulk, as it doth the Inward and Real Improvements.

All books are governed not only by their authors, but also by decisions of the printer or publisher – decisions as to format, paper size, type size and page lay-out. On these depend manufacturing costs, of materials (especially paper) and time. For titles in competitive genres such as dictionaries, concordances, Bibles or educational texts, the successful printers and publishers were those who best trimmed these design considerations to the market. Field was spectacularly successful with his preachers' Bible, and Hayes hardly less so with the Cambridge concordance.

Ever since 1584, the Cambridge press had found its identity in comparisons with London: in classical texts for children and undergraduates, in almanacs, in Bibles and, to some extent, in prayer books. Commercial alertness defined these mainstays of the press's output, and provided the only continuous thread through almost a century of printing and publication. The farrago of sermons, university divinity, occasional private printing and smattering of poetry, which formed a mainstay of the seventeenth-century press, cannot be said to have constituted together any policy other than one of survival, while the major works of erudition such as Whelock's Bede, Fuller's *Holy war*, Lightfoot's commentaries, or Ray's catalogue of Cambridgeshire flora, shone therefore all the more brightly. But Oxford could not be ignored. Laud's efforts to establish a learned press there in the 1630s, and a revival of learned printing in London at roughly the same time, each contributed to the mood of educational expansion which enabled Buck and Daniel to invest heavily in spectacular publication.

With the establishment of the Royal Society, and the accompanying encouragement of specialist publication,[84] and with Fell's plans in Oxford for a new press, Cambridge once again faced a challenge. Although the Sheldonian Theatre was not finished until 1669, printers were installed there some months earlier. This development, the beginning of the modern Oxford Press, had been several years under discussion until in June 1668 Samuel Clarke, the Oxford Architypographus, was offered a printing press and turned his thoughts also to new type.[85] Rumour had, however, reached Cambridge some weeks earlier, as

Worthington explained to Henry More on 17 April: 'By a friend from London I hear that Oxford university is about setting up a famous Press, for the printing of good Authors, and that for this purpose, they have £2000 in Stock.' But his next sentence passed from gossip to a devastating indictment, by one thoroughly knowledgeable, of the Cambridge press:

Cambridge Press should be busied about something better than Almanacks, and books for children.[86]

The charge came with all the more determination from a man noted for his fairness and generosity, in the aftermath of two serious outbreaks of plague in Cambridge in the summers of 1665 and 1666, and as the book trade nationally faced the consequences of the Fire of London, which was considered to have affected the Latin trade especially.[87] Field's business, already heavily dependent on his contractual obligations to the London trade, did not recover, and Worthington's challenge was one to which he was unable to respond. He died on 12 August,[88] and his successor, too, was to prove unequal to the task.

Field recorded in his will some of his principal obligations and friends in the London trade. George Sawbridge, one of his executors, was the effective controller of the English Stock, while the appearance of James Flesher, the London printer, among those for whom mourning rings were to be provided, may have commemorated past co-operation: it will be recalled that Flesher had been regularly employed by William Morden. With the other beneficiaries under this head, the London stationers James Crump, and Edmund Paxton, Field's connections are more obscure.

Among those owing him money at his death were six London booksellers: Francis Tyton, long familiar to Field as supplier of government printing; Robert Boulter, one of those involved in the publication only a few months previously of the first edition of *Paradise lost*; John Martin, one of the largest of the London booksellers; and Richard Chiswell, still only recently established. Two other debts were written off, as both Joseph Cranford and Christopher Eccleston had lost their premises in the Great Fire a few months before. All the sums involved were modest, the largest being Cranford's debt of £150, presumably still outstanding from 1663, when Field had printed for him Edward Reyner's *Treatise of the necessity of humane learning*.[89] His printing equipment was valued at £358.3s.8d., and his stock of books and paper at £1,129.3s.9d.[90]

To his fellow University Printers his death brought only renewed ill-feeling. Thomas and John Buck, already jealous for their share of profits, and not averse to interfering (particularly with respect to the London trade), had taken no active part in the running of the press. They were nevertheless entitled to annual payments. Field had paid only irregularly and incompletely, despite prosecution in the Vice-Chancellor's Court.[91] Moreover, it seemed to the two brothers that the profits from schoolbooks, almanacs, Bibles and prayer books had been such that they, too, should have had a share: profits of £2,400 over thirteen years were suggested for schoolbooks and almanacs, though no source was given for this calculation. As always, the Bucks' venality was supported by more public-spirited appeals; and in Sawbridge, one of Field's executors, they saw another opportunity: 'divers things have beene printed & sold by the said Executors tending much to the dishonour of the University'. Thomas Buck claimed to have lost £2,000; but he also claimed to be much more concerned at the University's dishonour.[92] Had the Bucks' suggestion been pursued, that an enquiry should be initiated, headed by Duport or some other senior member of the University, the history of the Press might have taken a different turn. Instead, Thomas Buck himself died in March 1669/70. The University, timorous, ill-informed, and misled, preferred to entrench itself in a form of established custom that did it little credit.

✥ 18 ✥

John Hayes and the limits of independence

At his death on 12 August 1668, Field left a printing house in full production, and both the University and the Stationers' Company unprepared. His son John, no doubt with the connivance of the other executor, the wealthy and powerful London stationer George Sawbridge, immediately petitioned the King that the University should forbear to appoint another printer until the work in hand could be completed.[1] This bought time not only for Field's widow and son, but also for Sawbridge and the Stationers' Company, to ensure that no investment was lost,[2] and that the latter in particular were in control of the transition.

The succession, of personal as well as corporate concern to Sawbridge, was to be a matter in which the Company ostensibly consulted with the University, but in which Sawbridge was ultimately able to impose his will. It was also complicated by the wish in Cambridge for a change. Field's name had brought little credit, his printing was often slovenly, and he had no university training. The appointment of Hayes would merely extend this course. And so, having supported Hayes' candidature, Buck found himself obliged to support a Fellow of King's.

The Vice-Chancellor in 1668–9 was Edmund Boldero, Master of Jesus, to whose generosity his college's library owes its present appearance.[3] He found much to dislike in Buck, as Buck did in him. By September 1669 the Heads also had agreed with Sawbridge that the new printer should be John Hayes, a London printer with an unpromising future in the city. However, Buck now considered that Ezechiel Foxcroft of King's, who wanted the place, should be given it. He lobbied vigorously on Foxcroft's behalf (so irritating Boldero), and he carried his case to the Vice-Chancellor's Court with an argument that made much play with Boldero's alleged disposal of duplicates from the University Library. To Buck, Foxcroft seemed both just and had the advantage of learning, sufficient guarantee against 'such vile & erroneous printing as was done by Mr Field, or such unconscionable sale as was made by Mr Hayes 'both tending exceeding much to the dishonour of the University, and to the great injury of his Majesties subjects'.[4] Buck, however, lost his campaign, and thus found himself obliged to exist invidiously as University Printer with a man whose course he had first promoted, and then abandoned. Earlier in life, this might have mattered to him more. But now he allowed it to pass. His interest in the press had declined, as other concerns had taken its place. As one of the executors of Henry Lucas, who died in 1663, he found himself responsible both for seeing Lucas's fine collection of books into the University Library, and also for the establishment of the Lucasian chair in mathematics: the first holder of the chair, Isaac Barrow, dedicated his *Lectiones XVIII* (including his inaugural lecture) to Buck and his fellow executor, Robert Raworth of Gray's Inn.[5]

John Hayes, who was said as early as March 1669 to have caught Buck's eye,[6] had grown up at Ashford in Kent, before being apprenticed to George Miller, printer in Blackfriars, in 1646. On Miller's death five months later, he had been turned over to his son Abraham, and he was freed in October 1653. By 1662 (and probably even by 1658) he was independent, one of the master printers identified in London that year; but his business was brought to a halt by the Great Fire, when he was among eight who were said to have been 'disabled' from printing further.[7] Unlike Field, who had rapidly seized opportunity at this stage of his career, and attached to himself the privilege of printing for Parliament, Hayes had become embroiled in illicit presbyterian printing. He came to L'Estrange's attention as a result of printing two pamphlets for Edward Bagshaw, attacking the Bishop of Worcester. Though Hayes had not put his name to them, his part was discovered, and it was his confession to having printed five hundred copies of each that led L'Estrange to Bagshaw: the episode seems to have been a critical one in strengthening L'Estrange's resolve to bring the press and the book trade generally to heel.[8] In 1662 his house in Wood Street was searched on L'Estrange's orders: among the sixteen titles seized were several dozen copies of pamphlets by Richard Baxter and by George Wither, as well as accounts of the life and death of John James, a seventh-day Baptist whose millenarian preaching helped bring him to Tyburn in 1661.[9] Hayes made his position in the commercial hierarchy of the London printers clearer in the following year, in a petition from eleven printers (out of total of nearly sixty) that sought to establish a company of printers separate from the Stationers. The petition, the work of an uninfluential minority, disaffected with the dominating establishment, had little chance of success: it came too soon after the events of 1662 to make acceptable any claim that printers would be especially adept at unearthing illegal printers. Many of the other ten signatories had also offended authority, and the protest was less against the over-riding powers of the booksellers, than against the more entrenched, and powerful, printers.[10]

Such was the unlikely background of the man elected on 14 October 1669 as the new University Printer.[11] A sympathizer with nonconformity, a man already familiar to, but having little influence in, the Stationers' Company,[12] and impoverished by the Great Fire, Hayes was an unconventional candidate for an establishment post. Though in 1664 he had made the acquaintance of William Croone, one of the early promoters of the Royal Society, in printing his book *De ratione motus musculorum*, he had in no sense become an establishment figure. But the weakness of his previous position explains his being chosen. The University may have been appeased by Buck's at least initial approval; but Hayes' true patron was Sawbridge, Treasurer of the English Stock and therefore in large measure responsible for ensuring the University's continuing compliance with the Company's interests. As one of Field's executors, Sawbridge was in a doubly influential position to see through the appointment of a man whose circumstances, in the words of one observer, 'were such as rendered him obsequious' to the Stationers.[13] In Cambridge, moreover, patience ran thin. There was disagreement among the Heads as to how to proceed with the Stationers, and on 7 July 1669 (almost a year after Field's death) a majority, including James Fleetwood, James Duport, Peter Gunning, Ralph Cudworth, Theophilus Dillingham and John Spencer forced through a resolution that negotiations should be ended, and Hayes was to have the privilege for £100 per annum. Pragmatism, rather than principle, won the day.[14]

Two months after Hayes' election, Sawbridge secured for himself the lease on Field's old premises opposite Queens' College (see Fig. 27 on pp. 314–15 above), which Field had been forced to assign to Isaac Honeywood of Hampstead after the Fire.[15] Thus, by the time that the University, Hayes and the Stationers' Company agreed new terms for regulating the work of the new University Printer, Sawbridge was in effect negotiating as owner with himself as agent of the Company. This swindle, enabling him to take profits from Hayes' work twice over, seems not to have been discovered in London for a decade; and meanwhile Hayes put his name to a series of agreements which in some measure paralleled those of Field before him. In return for £200 per annum from the Stationers' Company, in consideration of the University's printing privilege, the University had modestly requested that the Company should assign 'some competent worke' to the Cambridge printer, such as the University might choose itself. Hayes at first hoped for a salary of £150 per annum, but the Company agreed to £100. For this, the man who thus became the Company's salaried employee was to print for the English Stock five hundred reams at twenty shillings a ream, priority to be given to almanacs before schoolbooks. For any printing over and above this, Hayes was to be paid for paper and printing only. Any books thus printed, which he sold at Cambridge, were to be sold at the London rates. Hayes was to be responsible for meeting the cost of carriage to and from London.[16]

Suspicion about Sawbridge's part in the Cambridge printing house began to take shape in April 1678; but even then he was able to delay matters for ten months, before he was explicitly asked by the Court of the Company whether he was, or was not, Hayes' 'partner'. The table did not believe his denial, and 'being desirous to have matters amicably composed' appointed an investigating committee – of which Sawbridge was a member. The Court's mood was made clear in a series of strict rules laid down a month later for the conduct of the English Stock, and in particular of its treasurer. It was only at that point that Sawbridge found it prudent to plead illness as cause for absence. His influence, and talent for prevarication, put final confrontation off until the end of May 1679; but the account was not settled until May 1683, three months after his death.[17] The same unsatisfactory situation persisted for several years more, however. Sawbridge's business, run at first by his widow, then passed in turn to Edward Brewster, who refused to treat with the Company when in 1686 he was called on to do so as administrator of the interests of George Sawbridge's son Thomas.[18]

Hayes' own position at the outset, as Sawbridge's servant, is not recorded. But it is unlikely to have been different from that agreed in 1686, on the death of Sawbridge's widow, when all profits were to belong to Sawbridge. His salary was now set at £60, presumably in addition to the £100 already agreed by the Company; he was also to continue to have use of as much of the house as was necessary for his family. It was not a generous portion, and it offered no incentive whatever to more than modest effort on Hayes' part.

Brewster himself became first Upper Warden, and then in 1689 Master of the Stationers' Company. Thus he became a member of the committee empowered to deal with Hayes' affairs in March 1689/90, when the 1686 agreement still had three and a half years to run. The price set by Brewster on the Cambridge press now dropped rapidly, and in April 1690 the Court agreed to buy it as a going concern for a hundred guineas, plus the value of the stock of schoolbooks and printing materials. The Company continued to pay the University £100 per annum for the printing privilege, a sum increased in 1703 to £150;[19] but from midsummer 1690 the Company became owners of the press which, little more than a century before, it had first sought to suppress.[20] Between 1690 and his death in 1705, Hayes was thus an employee of the Company, in premises leased by the Company, using the Company's equipment to print, on paper supplied by the Company, what the Company chose to have printed at prices the Company set.[21] That apart, he was obliged to rely on the ordinary investments of the booksellers, whether in London, Cambridge or Norwich, and on those who were willing to finance their own work. The result was that Hayes' press became a learned one on account of its location, not because of conviction or direction.

The potential of the Cambridge press depended not least on the size of the English printing trade generally. As the number of printers and presses expanded rapidly during the later part of the seventeenth century, so the assurance of a reliable and profitable monopoly was an insurance against any unexpected contraction in a trade whose demands and overall output fluctuated widely from year to year. In 1662 the Licensing Act sought to reduce the number of London printers to twenty-four, apart from the King's Printers. By 1668 there were thirty-three. Twenty years later, the Licensing Act having lapsed in 1679, there were about fifty-five printing houses in London alone. The sizes of their establishments grew as well. In 1688 these printers shared about 145 presses, and of them at least seven possessed four or more.[22] In 1668 there had been just over eighty. While the immediate consequences for the Cambridge press of this expansion were never recorded explicitly, and any possible causal connection is complicated, it remains that though monopolies such as almanac and schoolbook printing flourished at Cambridge, most of the rest of the press's production seemed increasingly marginal.

Hayes' menial position, while it ensured him employment, also ensured the University of a press in which it could take little pride. Meanwhile, the tradition continued that one of the Printers should be a senior member of the University. Following Thomas Buck's death on 4 March 1669/70, a succession of such figures held appointments, more or less briefly, with Hayes, as University Printer: Matthew Whinn of St John's, University Registrary, from March 1669/70; John Peck, also of St John's, Esquire Bedell, from 1680; Hugh Martin, of Pembroke, another Esquire Bedell, from 1682; James Jackson, Fellow of Clare, from 1683; and Henry Jenks, Fellow of Caius, from 1693.[23] Such a series of elections from amongst the University's own might have continued; but in 1686 the mould was broken, or at least spoiled. The post of Printer was one conferred by election, a process customarily followed with amity and with little ado. But in 1686 two candidates were put forward who were each, in their different ways, unusual. Neither held a Cambridge degree; and one, moreover, was a person who had no pretensions to academic positions or distinction. Although he was described on some of the voting papers as an MA, and indeed had (perfectly properly) appeared thus on the title-page of his *Manipulus linguae sanctae* printed by Hayes in 1683, William Robertson's degree was from elsewhere. His opponent was Jonathan Pindar, a local stationer. The course which brought these two to the hustings is now obscure, but each commanded a substantial body of support. Pindar, with many acquaintances, faced a man who had taught Hebrew in the University for six years but whose connections with George Sawbridge (and thus the Stationers' Company) may have prompted fears as to his independence. Sawbridge had published Robertson's well-known Hebrew concordance, and both the *Manipulus* and his previous *Phraseologia generalis* (also printed by Hayes) were handled in London by the man who, in practice if not openly, controlled the Cambridge press. Only the previous year, yet another of Robertson's books, a Hebrew Psalter, had been printed and marketed under the same arrangement. A substantial minority voted for Robertson, the candidate with the claims to scholarship; but most, including the heads of houses, preferred Pindar.[24] In 1697 he was succeeded by another Pindar. But all these sinecurist Printers, mostly senior members of the University unfamiliar with publishing save as authors, seem to have had a negligible effect on the conduct of the press, or on its output.

Instead, this was controlled by five factors: the requirements of Sawbridge, of the English Stock, of the local Cambridge booksellers, of University printing and, occasionally but by no means insignificantly, of private individuals. Although Hayes continued to print Bibles until 1683, the re-establishment of the King's Printers, the strength of the Dutch trade in printing English Bibles, the rapid development of the Oxford Bible press after 1679, even in the face of the King's Printers, and the consequent slump in prices, made continuance at Cambridge unrealistic. Overseas-printed Bibles were seized at the Midsummer Fair in 1669 from two London traders, as well as from a cloth merchant from Potton in Bedfordshire.[25] Nor was the market uniformly strong. It was a measure of the hold taken on what was inevitably rather a slow market (since churches did not re-equip frequently, and the number of private buyers was severely limited) that Field's lectern folio of 1659–60 remained sufficient until the early 1670s.[26] Apart from two Amsterdam editions, the only English lectern Bible printed between 1660 and the first Oxford edition of 1680 was one by Hayes, in 1674, a production that offered much of the ostentation but little of the splendour of Field's. It, too, was made the vehicle for interleaved engravings, though Jean Drapentière's crude reworking of the engraved title-page made it but a poor relative.

For other books, Sawbridge, as owner, must be presumed to have had a powerful voice until his death and the subsequent take-over by the Stationers' Company. His name, however, appeared on only a handful of publications printed at Cambridge, those where it would either have seemed innocuous or where a publisher's absence might have aroused suspicion. His acknowledged books included, therefore, Newman's concordance (1672), Francis Gouldman's Latin dictionary (1674), Robertson's Greek thesaurus (1676),[27] and a new expanded edition of North's Plutarch (1676), for which Hayes used many of the old woodcuts employed in the previous editions printed at London. Each represented a major investment, and a major property. He took a similar interest in John Bullokar's *English expositour*, a long-established aid for those who wished to elevate 'ordinary English words into the more Scholastick, or those derived from other Languages', but had not had the benefit of a Latin education. Hannah Sawbridge, and then Edward Brewster, continued in similar vein, the publications of Sawbridge's widow including a folio Eusebius in 1683. Almanac printing, though strictly limited, was a regular component of the press's annual output (see fig. 31), while schoolbooks and elementary Latin texts continued to make their appearance. The manufacture of each was almost wholly controlled by the English Stock, who exploited both price structures and shortages in the paper trade during the Dutch wars to maintain their control.[28] Thanks to the interest of the English Stock, and in particular of George Sawbridge, whose lack of candour with the shareholders remained

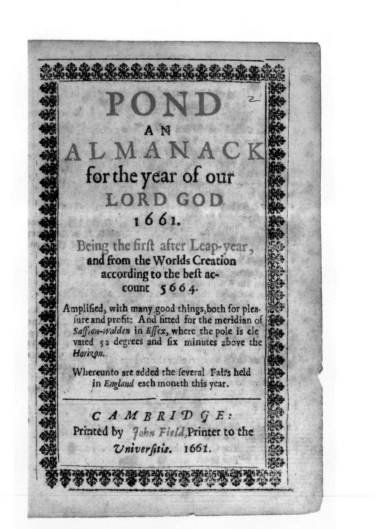

POND
AN
ALMANACK
for the year of our
LORD GOD
1661.

Being the first after Leap-year,
and from the Worlds Creation
according to the best ac-
count 5664.

Amplified, with many good things, both for pleasure and profit: And fitted for the meridian of
Saffron-walden in *Essex*, where the pole is ele
vated 52 degrees and six minutes above the
Horizon.

Whereunto are added the several Fairs held
in *England* each moneth this year.

CAMBRIDGE:
Printed by *John Field,* Printer to the
Universitie. 1661.

Fig. 31 Pond's almanac for 1661, 8°, '1661' [1660].
Height of original, 145 mm.

May hath xxxi days.

Full moon the 4 day, 48 min paſt 5 in the morn.
Laſt quarter the 11 day, 31 min. paſt 8 in the morning.
New moon the 18 day, 38 min. paſt 4 in the morning.
Firſt quarter the 25 day, 39 min. paſt 9 at night.

1	b	Term begins	4	22	7	38	Libra	19	Phil.& James
2	c	Athanaſius	4	21	7	39	Scorp.	1	SS ♂ ☾
3	d	Invent. Cruc.	4	19	7	41		14	☌ ♀ ☿
4	e	Florianus	4	17	7	43		27	☍ ☉ ☾
5	F	3 after Eaſter	4	16	7	44	Sag.	10	⚹ ♃ ☾
6	g	Tres Paſch.	4	14	7	46		23	
7	a	Juvenal	4	13	7	47	Capr.	7	□ ♃ ☾
8	b	Stanſlaus	4	11	7	49		20	⚹ ♄ ☾
9	c	Nicholaus	4	9	7	51	Aquar.	4	□ ☿ ☾
10	d	Pancrace	4	7	7	53		18	□ ♀ ☾
11	e	Sun in Gem.	4	6	7	54	Piſces	2	⚹ ☿ ☾
12	F	4 after Eaſter	4	5	7	55		16	☍ ♄ ☿
13	g	Menſ. Paſch.	4	4	7	56	Aries	0	☍ ♃ ☾
14	a	Fortunatus	4	2	7	58		15	△ ☉ ♃
15	b	Sophia	4	1	7	59		29	
16	c	Adelgune	3	0	8	0	Taur.	13	Venus with
17	d	Jodocus	3	59	8	1		27	the Pleiades.
18	e	Potentia	3	58	8	2	Gem.	11	☌ ☉ ☾
19	F	Rogation ſund.	3	57	8	3		24	⚹ ♂ ☾
20	g	Quinq; Paſch.	3	56	8	4	Canc.	8	□ ♃ ☾
21	a	Prudentius	3	55	8	5		21	△ ♄ ☾
22	b	Juliana	3	54	8	6	Leo	3	⚹ ♃ ☾
23	c	Aſcention day	3	53	8	7		15	☍ ♄ ☿
24	d	Craſt. Aſcen.	3	52	8	8		27	△ ♂ ☾
25	e	Urbanus	3	51	8	9	Virgo	9	□ ♀ ☾
26	F	6 after Eaſter	3	52	8	10		21	△ ☿ ☾
27	g	Term ends.	3	49	8	11	Libra	3	☌ ♃ ☾
28	a	Wilhelmus	3	48	8	12		15	△ ☉ ☾
29	b	Coronis M.	3	47	8	13		27	☍ ♂ ☾
30	c	Wigand	3	46	8	14	Scorp.	9	
31	d	Petronclla	3	46	8	14	Gem.	22	☌ ♄ ☾

A cold beginning with wind and ſhowers, and ſcarce better till ſunday : but from thence we have hopes of far better weather. the 10 ſome rain or thunder. the 12 cool and moiſt. the 13 fair. the 14 thunder-like. the 15 and 16 a moiſt cloudy air. thence moſt part fair and good to the 23 day : then wind and ſome wet. the 25 thunder or rain. the 26, 27, 28 very good. the reſt more various.

May.

1	*Cal.*
2	6
3	5
4	4
5	3
6	*Prid.*
7	*Non.*
8	8
9	7
10	6
11	5
12	4
13	3
14	*Prid.*
15	*Idus.*
16	17
17	16
18	15
19	14
20	13
21	12
22	11
23	10
24	9
25	8
26	7
27	6
28	5
29	4
30	3
31	*Prid.*

Fig. 31 continued.

Fig. 32 Samuel Newman (1600?–63), *A concordance to the Holy Scriptures*, 2nd edition, f°, 1672. The vertical title printed opposite the title-page served to identify the book when it was still in sheets, before it was bound up. Height of original, 296 mm.

A

CONCORDANCE

To the

HOLY

SCRIPTURES;

With the various Readings both of Text and Margin.

IN

A more exact METHOD then hath hitherto
been Extant.

By *S. N.*

The second Edition Corrected and Enlarged.

CAMBRIDGE,

Printed by JOHN HAYES, Printer to the University: for *George Sawbridge.*

And are also to be sold by *John Martin*, *Robert Horne*, *Henry Brome* , *Richard Chiswell*,
Robert Boulter, *John Wright*, and *William Jacob*, Booksellers in *London*. 1672.

Fig. 32 continued.

undetected for ten years, as he meanwhile printed at Cambridge on his own account, the Cambridge press became the country's single most important provider of almanacs. The market reached more of, and more strata of, the population than any other kind of printed text. The accounts of the English Stock record that over 400,000 of the various kinds – sort, blank and sheet – were printed for 1665, and that nearby years did not fall far short. Of these, Field printed 22 per cent of the sorts and blanks, and just over 50 per cent of all sheet almanacs. Though the proportion of the former printed at Cambridge fell in 1668 to 16 per cent, it recovered by the 1680s to between 18 per cent and 19 per cent. For sheet almanacs, Hayes shared in a demand that by the 1680s had more than doubled in twenty years, as sheets took a larger and larger proportion of the market. In the mid-1660s Field had printed usually about 15,000 a year. By 1685–7 Hayes watched production rise from 34,000 to 40,000. In 1687 the Cambridge press printed over 100,000 almanacs of various kinds, almost 25 per cent of all those produced under the Company's auspices. Some of the titles – Pond, Dove and Swallow – were of long standing, though Culpeper had appeared for the first time in 1680, as had John Wing (successor to the long-running Vincent Wing, once by far the most popular of all). In the 1680s the printing of 24,000 copies annually of Fly was divided between London and Cambridge in a proportion of 3:8.[29] These were the official figures only, and represented London receipts. They do not, therefore, include the numbers kept back by Field and Hayes for sale locally; nor do they take account of other almanacs whose printing was shared between Cambridge and London; nor do they reflect in any way the substantial contributions of pirates to this immense trade, or other almanac printing (albeit on a lesser scale) in Scotland or Ireland, Oxford or even London.[30] The edition sizes of each of these, not issued under the immediate auspices of the Stationers' Company English Stock, are not recorded, and it is impossible to estimate accurately the proportion of the almanac trade that Cambridge in fact contributed. But even without these details, it is clear that no other press played so important a part. To many people, the Cambridge press can only have been known from the title-pages of their annual purchases of almanacs.[31]

However, not all of Hayes' books were for the Stationers' Company. In 1672 he printed John Pearson's *Vindiciae Epistolarum S. Ignatii* for William Wells and his brother-in-law Robert Scott, two booksellers in Little Britain who could expect to export much of the edition. So, too, Gouldman's dictionary brought Hayes further contact with London interests.

The Cambridge tradition of Latin dictionaries, established by Thomas himself, saw a remarkable revival in the later part of the century, the 'Cambridge dictionary' eventually becoming, like Newman's 'Cambridge concordance' (see fig. 32) and Robertson's 'Cambridge phrases', a term of common reference. Though he inherited a position already established by Field, Hayes seems to have taken no lead in it. Field had printed the first edition of a new Latin dictionary at London in 1664: one, in the words of Worthington, that was expected to replace Thomas's, so that 'a book of general use amongst young scholars may be made more advantageous to them'.[32] The work of Francis Gouldman of Christ's, Rector of South Ockenden in Essex save for an intermission after his ejection in 1644, and part editor of Pearson's *Critici sacri*, it was one of several such efforts that marked a new post-Restoration generation: another was by Christopher Wase, of King's, Gouldman's junior by several years. Gouldman's own *Copious dictionary* made full use of its predecessors – Thomas, Rider, Holland, Holyoke – on its title-page, but was said to contain about ten thousand more words than any previous work.[33] It passed into a second edition in 1669, by then taken up by Sawbridge and printed, again by Field, in Cambridge. The third edition of 1674, revised by Robertson, was more complicated, printed partly by Hayes in Cambridge and partly by William Rawlins in London, Rawlins' part (dated 1673) having apparently been printed first. Hayes took some of the edition, and gave it his own title-page, while the rest was taken by a consortium of London stationers: John and William Place, Thomas Bassett, Thomas Dring and John Leigh, all headed by Sawbridge himself. In this group, and their successors, lay the beginning of a consortium that was to control much of the trade in Latin dictionaries for several decades, employing Hayes for a while but where Rawlins took an increasingly prominent part. Hayes' name appeared solitarily on the edition of Gouldman in 1678, revised now also (if moderately) by Anthony Scattergood of Trinity College, who had worked with Gouldman at the *Critici sacri*.[34]

In 1678, the same year that Hayes printed what was to prove the last edition of Gouldman, there appeared in London a new dictionary by Adam Littleton, once of Christ Church, former Second Master at Westminster School, since 1670 Rector of Chelsea and chaplain to Charles II, and a man widely respected for his learning. Littleton's was to remain the standard work in its field, capacious yet reasonably compact, the everyday *vade-mecum* for the more knowledgeable schoolboy and for undergraduates, until it was displaced in the 1730s by Ainsworth's *Lexicon*. Unlike his predecessors, who had emphasized their dependence on similar earlier authorities, Littleton professed to claim originality.[35] But though it was difficult to sustain his claim for long, he won the support of the booksellers. Littleton thrived; Gouldman was seen no more, and the last edition of Holyoke appeared in 1677. The first edition of Littleton, of 1678, was printed in London for three booksellers, and a second, over the same names, in 1684. Its rapid establishment in the market owed more to the booksellers than to the authors, editors or revisers. Of the four booksellers who entered Holyoke in the Stationers' Register in 1671, Thomas Bassett was among the three to promote Littleton seven years later. Three of the four – Thomas Dring, John Place and the successors of John Leigh – maintained a continuing, and expanding, interest in Latin dictionaries.[36] All these men were booksellers who dealt particularly in law, while both Place and Bassett had been named in Dring's father's will.[37] In 1692 they brought in further capital, which seems to have funded the somewhat revised edition printed at Cambridge in 1693. It was the last edition to appear in Littleton's lifetime, for he died in 1694. By the time that edition appeared, there were seven shareholders owning one-sixth or one-twelfth part each, a division of ownership reflected in the varying imprints on the title-page. For some reason perhaps connected with a complicated series of transactions recorded in the Stationers' Register respecting Littleton's dictionary proper, and the work which appeared in 1693 as *Linguae Romanae dictionarium luculentum novum*, Littleton was not acknowledged in 1693 as author of a text which nonetheless was essentially his. No further edition of his dictionary was required until 1703, when his authorship was restored to the title-page. But whereas in the 1660s and 1670s editions of Gouldman had appeared every four or five years, there had since 1678 been only three editions of Littleton – the others in 1684 and 1693. In the absence of competitors (no edition of the nearest rival, by Coles, appeared between 1679 and 1711), and on the assumption that demand remained reasonably consistent, it seems probable that the edition sizes of Littleton were substantially larger than those of their predecessors, and especially so for Hayes' edition of 1693. The different settings of the title-page (quite apart from the differing imprints) and of some sheets within the volume lend support to the supposition that the edition of '1693' was a large one.[38]

Such major demands apart, among the sermons, commendatory verses and other miscellaneous printing expected by the University, most of it bearing Hayes' name alone, there was a flow of work instigated by the local booksellers, whose position was complicated by trading with London and with London importers, and not all of whose manufacturing requirements were met by Hayes.

William Morden, for example, turned repeatedly to the London printer James Flesher and then to his widow, rather than to the Cambridge press: it was a habit begun in Field's time, and continued after Hayes' arrival. For an author in London it offered easier access to the press for proof-reading; but the little known of most authors' movements does not suggest that this was a dictating factor. Henry More, who was normally resident in Christ's, took a close interest in the printing and publication of his several works. In 1664 he went to London so as to be available while Flesher printed his *Modest enquiry into the mystery of iniquity*, published by Morden in Cambridge.[39] Again in 1671, he was at Flesher's shop seeing his *Enchiridion metaphysicum* to press, using the same visit also to see it in person safely past the licenser, the chaplain to the Archbishop of Canterbury. His personal address was rewarded on this occasion: it may perhaps have been prompted by the same licenser's requirement that he rewrite part of his *Divine dialogues* back in 1668 – when he had dealt with the matter by correspondence.[40] Such personal concern was perhaps unusual, and certainly More was capable also of working from Cambridge with his printers. In spring 1660, for example, he had sent about one-third of his *Explanation of the grand mystery of godliness to* Flesher. By 6 May that year he had received back six sheets, with further sheets promised at a rate of six a week.[41] These sheets, sent piecemeal to their author, may have been proofs in the sense that Flesher expected to receive corrections before the sheets were machined. More probably, they were sent after machining – a timetable that was reflected in the closing list of errata which (unusually) distinguishes between author's mistakes in his copy, and printer's mistakes in composition.

Authors', and editors', long standing abilities to deal with London printers, enabled Cambridge booksellers to extend their investments unhampered by Field's and Hayes' inability to print all that was required. Given the cheaper manufacturing costs in London, and the wider opportunities for sales, it was actually advantageous to print there if a book was expected to have more than a merely local appeal. In a system that depended so much on credit and exchange, the size, turnover and profitability of all but the smallest bookselling firm presumed an active role either in publishing over the firm's own imprint, or substantial shared investment, overt or no, in manufacture. It might even be in a country bookseller's interest to invest in a larger share than he would require for his own local retail or wholesale trade, if thereby he gained additional credit in the London trade.[42] In such a situation, the University press could expect only a very limited future. It could offer no unusual skills or equipment, had no established international channels for trade, and its management was circumvented by the Stationers' Company.[43] The late seventeenth-century Cambridge press, seen (as it must be) in the light of an increasingly active local bookselling community and a changing trade in London itself, was one threatened with starvation, relying on rations from London and on unpredictable crumbs discovered locally.

In the series of Greek and Latin parallel texts published at Cambridge in 1670–3, for example, a group clearly influenced by the earlier editions of Homer and Sophocles, no organizing unity is to be found in the book trade, though the volumes themselves have a family resemblance. Epictetus was printed by James Flesher in London, and published by William Morden; Plato's dialogues and Thomas Gale's *Opuscula mythologica*, printed by Hayes, were published by another Cambridge bookseller, John Creed; and Hesiod *in usum scholarum omnium* bore Hayes' name only.

The disabilities of Hayes' press were sufficiently obvious to his con-temporaries, both in the trade and in the colleges. It was perhaps for this reason that after his death in 1697 Henry Jenks, even though he was a University Printer, was found to be contracted to a London bookseller, Richard Chiswell, for the publication of his *Rationale biblicum*: Chiswell could certainly offer international status and connections.[44] Hayes' commitment to the London stationers left too little capacity for other, Cambridge, work; he could offer few specialist skills for tasks such as mathematics printing; apart from Sawbridge and his successors he had few links with the London trade. Both the University and the Stationers regarded him merely as their servant, and his duties impinged so little on the University's consciousness that work done in January 1687/8 was not paid for until October 1689, the invoice apparently having been mislaid for a year.[45] It was no wonder that Barrow had looked back, however misguidedly, to the press under Buck, a press directed by an innovator which had managed to balance the demands of London quotas with a publishing programme of originality and scholarship.

Yet, Hayes' premises were substantial, his equipment equally so, and his staff commensurate with it. The nature of much of his printing, in almanacs and school texts, means that much has now disappeared; but despite the long press-runs entailed in such work his reputation was not one of outstanding efficiency. Although many of the details of his business are tantalizingly vague, it is possible to arrive at a reasonably informed estimate of his staff, to set beside the much more detailed records of his equipment. The schedule to the 1690 agreement[46] between the Stationers' Company and Hayes specified six presses. This is the least fallible of all figures for equipment in judging the capacity of a seventeenth-century printing house, as the Stationers and, through them, the government, had long realized. Type, galleys, racks, chases and drying poles, though each had a commercial value which meant that they were listed in inventories and legal schedules, could all accumulate without necessarily reflecting the amount of work expected of the printing house in question. The finite capacity of presses, and their requirements for operation, in effect signify the maximum possible production – assuming that all presses listed were in working order and all were being fully operated.

At Oxford, at about the same time, there were eight presses besides two rolling presses.[47] But set within the context of the London printing houses in 1668, twenty-odd years before, the year in which a uniquely detailed survey was conducted in connection with L'Estrange's measures to control the London press,[48] Hayes' workshop was a large one. Of twenty-six premises surveyed in 1668, only one, the King's Printing House, possessed six presses. Two, belonging to James Flesher and John Streater, had five, and one, that of Thomas Roycroft, had four. These printing houses, the largest in London, employed eighteen, fifteen, eight and twelve men respectively, both Flesher's and Roycroft's staff including a couple of apprentices.[49] The division of labour, between compositors and pressmen, was not usually specified, and in at least some houses some of the workforce must have been expected to be capable of both skills. But in those of the larger houses where a distinction was made, each press required approximately three people – not necessarily in a proportion of one compositor to two pressmen. At the King's Printing House, eight compositors and ten pressmen ran the six presses; at Thomas Newcombe's shop, seven compositors, five pressmen and an apprentice ran three presses (he also kept a proofing press, an unusual distinction in the list); at John Redmayne's shop, with two presses, there were four compositors, two pressmen and an apprentice; John Streater, with five presses, employed six compositors and only two pressmen, a staff so unbalanced in its proportions as to suggest a pause in business. Four years later, in 1672, the Oxford press employed over twenty men, a figure that seems to have included staff for the rolling press, and a newly arrived typefounder, besides the usual compositors and pressmen.[50]

If Hayes were in 1690 to run his shop at full capacity, it is therefore probable that he would have required eighteen men, of whom not more than two could be apprentices if he were to abide by the rules of the Stationers' Company. This was however a maximum, and it is at least possible that his equipment was not, in fact, fully employed: the nature of much of his work, in cheap, disposable and heavily used texts, makes it impossible to be certain on this point, while large editions required proportionately less composition time to each forme. In 1690 he had just completed Launoi's substantial *Epistolae*; but a very large part of his business, then as in previous years, came from almanac printing: no further folio came from his press until an English Eusebius, in 1692. Compared with that at Oxford, Hayes' equipment was under-used. Leaving aside its two rolling presses, the Oxford house possessed two more presses than Cambridge, supported by '117 Upper and lower Cases' to eighty-seven at Cambridge, while Cambridge could produce slightly more Greek type than the sister university. For once, comparison between the two universities is useful, in that the appearance in 1693 of the *Specimen* of printing types given to Oxford by Fell also made public the principal equipment (presses, type, chases) available there.[51]

Although the size of Hayes' staff was governed to a great extent by the number of presses in his shop, the vicissitudes of production, and the fluctuations of seasonal and annual demand, meant that while the presses governed a maximum capacity, in practice activity varied considerably, and could be noticeably slack. This slackness, unrelieved by other work, was cause for concern to the court of the Stationers' Company in 1691;[52] but it was virtually inevitable in a printing house that had no near neighbour from whom to take in extra work.[53] For long periods in the seventeenth century, agreements with the Stationers' Company ensured an adequate flow of production: of almanacs, elementary Latin texts and grammars. The Bible trade provided a further surety. But as the Company limited the manufacture of its Cambridge outpost and also apportioned work to Oxford, and as the Bible trade too slipped away, so Hayes had to compromise with a much less evenly founded demand.

No list survives of his staff. But in any case (as a result of fluctuating activity) they cannot all have been regarded as permanent in the sense that they had regular weekly employment: this was still not the norm even in the new printing house in the early years of the eighteenth century.[54] The idea of a weekly wage, prevalent in Cambridge and in London printing in the earlier part of the seventeenth century, had by Moxon's and Hayes' time been abandoned in favour of piece-work.[55] Irregular wages, endemic in the printing (and many other) trades for years afterwards, seem to have been supported by other means of income. When one of Hayes' compositors, John Johnson, died in 1679, he left a modestly equipped shop, and so did Thomas Isburne, also of the press, in 1686.[56] Such arrangements made more tolerable, both for masters and men, the fluctuations in an industry large parts of which were obliged to respond to the whims and vagaries of authors, readers and national events, and (in Hayes' case, as for Field before him) to the late autumn publication of several thousand almanacs.[57]

Among the staff Hayes inherited from Field in 1669 was Thomas Peckett, to be freed from his apprenticeship only in 1676. He took on as another apprentice, in December 1668, James Bechinoe, a member of the family of a local stationer, and during the next twenty years was to take on six further apprentices, nearly all of them from Cambridge or nearby.[58] Three were indentured in 1676 alone, the same year in which two new journeymen, Clement Knell and Thomas Isburne, were registered by the University: a further journeyman, John Johnson, was registered in 1677. By the late 1670s, therefore, Hayes could call on, or was responsible for, at least nine workmen. In 1680 they were either joined or replaced by at least two further journeymen, William Bartram and Matthew Duckett.[59] Of the journeymen recruited during this period, at least two came with several years' experience of London, Clement Knell in Evan Taylor's shop, and Duckett as a compositor in that of Thomas Newcomb.[60] How many further came from London, how many more survived from Field's shop into Hayes' first years, and how many other assistants contributed to the shop, are all, however, far from clear. The University kept no regular complete record of those whom it had licensed to work in Cambridge, the principal surviving list being demonstrably insufficient. It seems, however, not unreasonable to suppose that even if Hayes did not employ regularly the putative maximum of eighteen suggested above, he did call on several more than these surviving names suggest.

Henry Dickinson, whose first publication had been among the last books printed by Field, died in the winter of 1694/5[61]. His business, at the corner of Trinity Street, was taken over by Edmund Jeffery, who began his own career as a publisher with a modest edition of Plato's *Menexenus* and *Lysis*, the work of an undergraduate at Trinity, Michael Busteed. It appeared in 1696, a few months after some members of the University had begun to formulate plans for a new University Press under the guidance not of the Stationers' Company, but of curators drawn from the University itself. On 29 June the Duke of Somerset,

Chancellor of the University, proposed formally 'to have a Presse once more erected at Cambridge', a phrase which suggests that he misunderstood those who advised him but which accurately reflected responsible opinion. Moving with unexpected celerity, the University gave permission on 10 July to Richard Bentley to buy fresh types. Henry Jenks, University Printer since 1693, seems to have taken no part in these developments, and died in August 1697.[62] The whole of the initiative was almost certainly Bentley's, whose energy made it possible, despite delays caused by those over whom he had no control, for there to be a new press, overseen by a new body of curators and housed in a new printing house, to begin work on its first substantial book in November 1698.[63]

The new building, converted from the stage house belonging to Queens' College, stood next to Hayes' premises in Queens' Lane; and it was Hayes who, for a few months in 1697–8, printed with the types acquired by Bentley. But in the winter of 1697–8 this type was removed from Hayes' premises to the new printing house, under the supervision of a new printer, Cornelius Crownfield.[64] The establishment of this new Press removed virtually all of Hayes' business other than that generated by the Stationers' Company or by a few London booksellers. Initial negotiations with the Company, in the autumn of 1696, had concluded that Hayes' printing house should be abandoned for the new one next door. But it was in the interests of neither Hayes, nor Queens', as landlords, to do so, and in April 1698 Hayes secured the College's agreement that he should remain tenant in his old premises.

The University and the Stationers' Company reached an agreement with almost practised ease, helped on the one hand by the Company's wish to ensure a continuing profit, and on the other by the fact that it possessed in Cambridge an ailing press. The University's reassurances suggest by the tone in which they were recorded in the Company's Court Book, as well as by their content, that the Company feared little:

they had no intencon to print anything in prejudice to the Company in any wise but only to print some Classick Authors, and such Bookes of Learning as they shall find to be wanted, and that their desire was to Rent the Companyes Printing-house to carry on this their designe, or to give such a summe of money as the University and the Company shall agree on.[65]

Hayes' printing house was over-equipped and under-used. Besides the six presses already alluded to, it contained eighty-seven pairs of cases of type and forty chases. Of the roman and italic type, he had over 3,000 lbs. apiece of pica, long primer and brevier, of which the last had been only recently cast. The importance to him of the smaller types was reflected in the almanacs, in particular, which formed so large a proportion of his output whether expressed as printed sheets or as titles. The founts of Greek, Hebrew and

Arabic (the last recorded mistakenly as 'Syriack', and bought expressly for the use of John Luke, Professor of Arabic), were necessary to a printing house with a learned side, and had been used to excellent effect by Robertson, Spencer and Barnes. But even the Greek was not stocked in full range.[66] New display types had been added in 1671, but their paucity is to be seen in Hayes' larger title-pages.

With six presses at Cambridge, the Company had easily realized that its newly acquired premises were under-used; and in September 1691 the Court had decided to print English Stock books there, including grammars.[67] A cheap duodecimo Terence (1692), Lily's grammar (1695) and an Ovid, *Metamorphoses* (1698),[68] were among the results; but they were hardly adequate to exploit the premises, and the interests of the London trade no doubt helped to ensure that Hayes kept to the edition quantities set sixty years previously.[69] In other words, the Company's most valuable asset at Cambridge, other than the plant, remained the University's agreement to print neither almanacs, Bibles nor schoolbooks without authorization. Following the creation in 1693 of a new Stock (its membership restricted to existing shareholders in the English Stock), the Stationers' Company invested heavily in the Cambridge press, paying £300 for new type for schoolbooks and almanacs as well as rent for the printing house and the annual £100 due to the University. The new venture proved to be commercially unsound, and most of the printing for it was done at Oxford, but the investment was a measure of the Company's determination and assumptions.[70]

Hayes died on 28 November 1705.[71] In his remaining years he had become increasingly obstinate, in control of a business from which neither the University nor the Stationers managed to extricate themselves, and in premises of whose value Queens' was well aware.[72] Work for Cambridge booksellers went almost invariably to the new University Press, and Edmund Jeffery, in particular, began to build for himself a position as publisher of classical texts. At Hayes' shop, fresh editions of Newman's concordance (1698), and of the Greek minor poets (1700), both for the London booksellers A. and J. Churchill, consorted with other work for the Stationers' Company such as an octavo Ovid, *Tristia*, in 1703 and an octavo *Metamorphoses* in 1706. In a mood that looked more to the future, copies of John Patrick's version of Tate and Brady's new Psalms in metre appeared over his name in 1698, followed by a further edition in 1702.[73] At a time before Tate and Brady had become established as a popular alternative to the old and familiar Sternhold and Hopkins, there was about such an enterprise an element of challenge unexpected in Hayes. It seems unlikely that the challenge was his in any sense. In more familiar vein again, in 1700 he printed, for publication in Cambridge, a second edition of the *Tables for renewing leases* he had originally printed in 1686, and he proved a conveniently placed printer for the works of Edward Leedes, Headmaster of the grammar school at Bury St Edmunds (see fig. 33). But

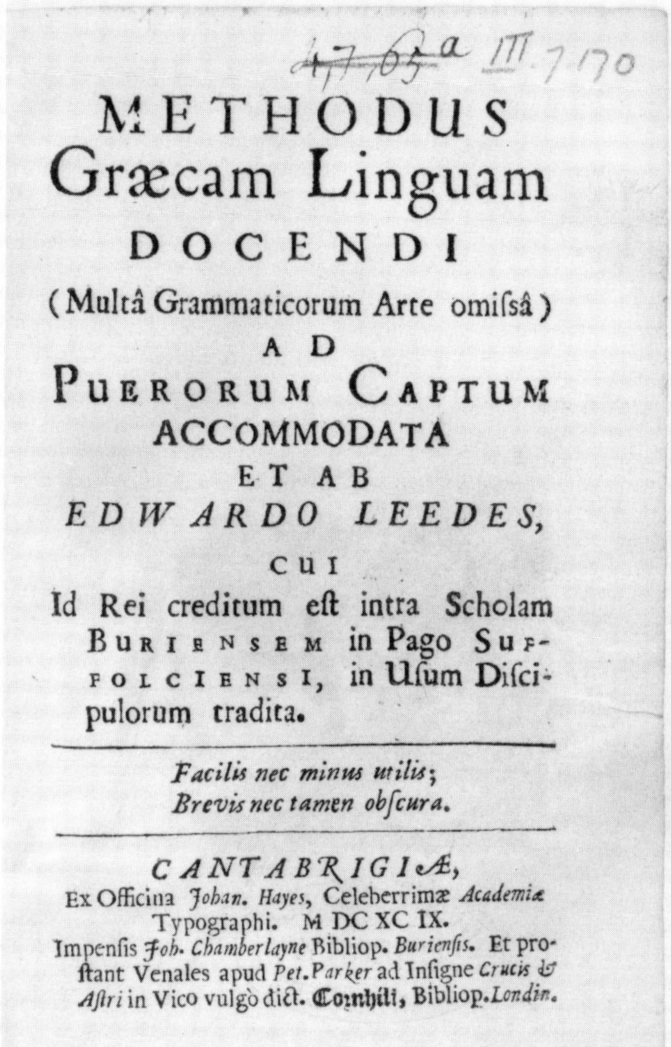

47,765ᵃ III. 7 170

METHODUS
Græcam Linguam
DOCENDI
(Multâ Grammaticorum Arte omiſsâ)
A D
PUERORUM CAPTUM
ACCOMMODATA
ET AB
EDWARDO LEEDES,
CUI
Id Rei creditum eſt intra Scholam
BURIENSEM in Pago SUF-
FOLCIENSI, in Uſum Diſci-
pulorum tradita.

Facilis nec minus utilis;
Brevis nec tamen obſcura.

CANTABRIGIÆ,
Ex Officina *Johan. Hayes,* Celeberrimæ *Academiæ*
Typographi. M DC XC IX.
Impenſis *Joh. Chamberlayne* Bibliop. *Burienſis.* Et pro-
ſtant Venales apud *Pet.Parker* ad Inſigne *Crucis &*
Aſtri in Vico vulgò dict. **Cornhill,** Bibliop.*Londin.*

Fig. 33 Edward Leedes (1627–1707), *Methodus Graecam linguam docendi*, 8°,
1699. One of several manuals prepared by Leedes for the use of the grammar
school at Bury St Edmunds, where he was Master from 1663 to 1707. This
was published by a local bookseller; like Leedes' other works, it was also
available in London from Peter Parker in Cornhill. Height of original,
146 mm.

however convenient or useful, the press was clearly in decline. It was an inglorious end to a career which, notwithstanding so many financial and commercial limitations, had in its earlier years sustained respectability, met many of the University's needs and lived up to its admittedly not very high expectations.

☙ 19 ❧

Looking at a wider world

Although a few of the local publishing booksellers had direct contact with the
international trade, it does not seem that these were sufficient to be called on
regularly for other than the most ordinary books. Family connections helped
the young John North, at Jesus College, to begin the assembling of a
substantial private library with the aid of the London bookseller Robert Scott,
who not only had a much larger stock than any in Cambridge, but could also
call on further supplies kept in Frankfurt, Cologne and other centres.[1] College
libraries, to whom reliable continental connections were equally essential,
tended also towards London. At Trinity, Scott found it worthwhile to present
the new Bodleian Library catalogue in 1676, together with a copy of Isaac
Vossius' edition of Ignatius, *Epistolae* (Amsterdam 1646).[2] Scott, too, supplied
books in 1673–4.[3] The University Library, able at last to buy thanks to the
bequest of Tobias Rustat, turned principally to Scott and to Samuel Smith, and
only occasionally to local men – William Graves, Henry Dickinson, Thomas
Dawson.[4] Purchases were erratic and irregular (libraries depended much more
on donations in kind); but the preference for London rather than Cambridge
booksellers is a further reminder of the differences in both trading connections
and wealth between the two. Local booksellers on the whole continued to
concentrate, probably wisely, on the more everyday and cheaper parts of the
market.

The changes to the undergraduate curriculum in the second half of the
seventeenth century were not sanctioned by statute. By regulation, Cambridge
remained Aristotelian. But by interpretation and custom it took account,
gradually and thanks more to individuals or small informal groups, of modern
natural philosophy embodied especially in the work of Descartes and Boyle.[5]
In the 1690s, Abraham de la Pryme was examined by his college (St John's) in
logic, rhetoric, ethics, physics and astronomy. But he had also found time as an
undergraduate to study chemistry, botany, magic and ancient history.[6] Change
came about principally as a result of the increasing influence of individual
tutors. Like Mede before him, Samuel Blythe at Clare College[7] continued to
recommend Johann Alsted (whose work was all but unobtainable from English
presses, let alone Cambridge), Bartholin for medicine, Burgersdijck on logic,

Thomas Jack of Edinburgh on Latin prosody, and Bartholomaeus Keckerman on mathematics. Ramus's *Dialectica* was printed in London for the Cambridge trade in 1669, and then, by Hayes, for the last time in seventeenth-century Cambridge, in 1672. 'Follow not Ramus in Logick nor Lipsius in Latin, but Aristotle in one and Tully in the other', advised Duport in 1660, in terms that seemed simultaneously to dismiss Ramus's adaptation of Aristotelianism and to sound more reactionary than Duport perhaps meant.[8]

The Jansenist, or Port Royal, *Logica*, by Antoine Arnauld and Pierre Nicole, was published in England for the first time in 1674, its cost shared between John Martyn in London and Edward Story in Cambridge. The same partnership was responsible for another edition, in 1677. However, the following edition, in 1682, was shared between J. Green in Cambridge and a quartet of London booksellers; and another, in 1687, was divided between Richard Green of Cambridge and the London trade, copies being provided with different title-pages as necessary. The book's importance to the Cambridge curriculum was further exemplified in the first edition in English, printed in London in 1685 for George Sawbridge's widow Hannah. Increasingly, Burgersdijck was either accompanied or expounded by the cognate work of Adrian Heereboord.[9]

But Blythe also introduced students to Gassendi's *Institutio astronomica*, published by the Cambridge bookseller William Morden (though printed in London), and also to Galileo, William Harvey, Willis and Glanvill. John Wallis, who graduated from Emmanuel in 1632, claimed to have been the first, unwittingly, to defend Harvey's theory of the circulation of the blood in a public disputation. Under Francis Glisson (Regius Professor of Physic from 1636 to 1677), a member of Caius, Harveian medicine became established.[10] At Trinity, Isaac Newton read Magirus' *Physiologia peripatetica*, originally published at Frankfurt in 1597 and printed at Cambridge in 1642: there were several continental editions available, and the book was widespread in Cambridge, recommended alike by Mede, Blythe and, at Emmanuel, Joshua Barnes.[11] In the light of such demand, it is noticeable that Magirus was never republished at Cambridge after 1642: henceforth students had to use second-hand editions. It was but one example of a book much recommended and read, but not much printed. The irregular appearance of new editions of many of these and other such texts widely used by undergraduates is not of itself a guide to their popularity or otherwise, or indeed necessarily an indication of the commercial or educational alertness of the University Printers. In a community that depended, like all universities, on a strong second-hand market, and where large editions might remain in print for many years, there was no necessary correlation between publication frequency and demand.

Furthermore, like Mede's, Blythe's students also bought – both new and second-hand – beyond the formal subjects, whether in poetry (Cowley; Milton; Katherine Philips), geography (Mercator; Varenius on Japan, printed by Hayes in 1673; Richard Blome's folio maps of Britain), history (Gage on the West Indies; Ogilby on China; Rycaut on Turkey; Goodwin on Jewish, Greek and Roman antiquities) or theology (Cave and Hammond, as well as more popular books). Some students were in a position to indulge more expensive tastes, such as the Mercator which cost one of Blythe's students the sum of £3.10s. But for most students at Cambridge the principal investments were in dictionaries. For Latin, Gouldman's or Adam Littleton's cost about 14s.–16s.; for Greek, Schrevelius' octavo lexicon (printed at Cambridge in 1663, 1668 and 1685) could be had for about 5s.–6s., and Robertson's quarto lexicon, printed by Hayes in 1676, for about 15s.[12]

Apart from the more general needs of those not reading for a degree, or who wished to explore more widely, the traditional curriculum was challenged principally by mathematics, by the natural sciences and by medicine. Like Duport, Roger North, who came up to Jesus College as a Fellow-Commoner in 1667, found the traditional logic unappealing – 'a very dull science, especially that which relates to disputation, and must be driven by a tutor well versed in it, as a smith hammers iron out of a lump into a bar'. And like so many others, he tackled Euclid in Fournier's edition, recently printed at the Cambridge press, but found Isaac Barrow's edition preferable.[13] Not surprisingly, it was Barrow's, printed generally not in Cambridge but in London, that became established as the Cambridge text.

So, too, the diffusion of Cartesian thought in Cambridge caught the young North's imagination. 'But I found such a stir about Descartes, some railing at him and forbidding the reading him as if he had impugned the very Gospel. And yet there was a general inclination, especially of the brisk part of the University, to use him, which made me conclude there was somewhat extraordinary in him, which I was resolved to find out, and at length did so.'[14] Again it was left principally to London and the Low Countries printers to meet a vigorous market. In 1663 Field had responded to the tide of opinion by entering Descartes' *Principia philosophiae* in the Stationers' Register.[15] But only one edition followed, printed for the Cambridge bookseller Jonas Hart in 1664. Even when Henry More's *Apologia* for Descartes was published by William Morden, also in 1664, it was printed in London. The pusillanimous approach adopted by the University Printers unable or unwilling to meet such change was broken for a few years only in the 1680s in a brief flurry of publication of the work of the Dutchman Jan Schuler, whose *Exercitationes ad principiorum philosophiae Renati Des-Cartes* (1682) had been originally published at Amsterdam in 1667.

Of those in Cambridge who were most forward in pursuing and persuading the local book trades, Henry Jenks, of Caius,[16] was responsible for introducing editions of Stephanus Curcellaeus' *Synopsis ethices*, published by Henry Dickinson in Cambridge (though printed in London) in 1684 before it was taken up by Hayes in 1702. But though in 1683 Jenks recommended (not surprisingly) Varenius' *Geographia* in his *Christian tutor*, few of the books he singled out in mathematics or philosophy were available in editions printed or published at Cambridge. The work given pride of place, Le Grand's *Institutio philosophiae* ('grounded', in Jenks' words, 'upon the Great Des-Cartes his Principles') had been printed four times in London, most recently in 1680, but never in Cambridge. Gassendi's *Philosophiae Epicuri syntagma* had been last printed in London in 1668. So, too, Pierre Charron's *Of wisdome* had been repeatedly printed in London since the beginning of the century, but never in Cambridge. Jacques Rohault's *Tractatus physicus Gallice* had appeared in London in 1682, and was not published at Cambridge until 1692; Tacquet's *Opera mathematica* had been published at Antwerp in 1669 and C. F. Millet de Chales' *Cursus mathematicus* ('the most complete System of Mathematical Learning that I know') at Lyons in 1674. Among the shorter books, Grotius' *De iure belli ac pace* had been published at London in translation, but Hermann Conring's *Propolitica* had never been printed or published in England. In Cambridge itself, apart from William Morden's edition of Henry More's *Enchyridion ethicum*, recommended by Jenks, the Cambridge press had printed of his other recommendations only Gautruche's *Mathematicae institutio* (the 1683 edition came out in London, however), and a cheap edition of Pufendorf, *De officiis hominis & civis*, printed by Hayes for John Creed in 1682.[17] Jenks' list, encompassing if not necessarily typifying Cartesian inclinations of late seventeenth-century Cambridge, revealed the commercial structure of the trade in relation to the aspirations of those in the University willing or anxious to explore such fresh approaches. The dabblings of the London trade, and its circumspection displayed in repeated editions of a few titles, were matched on the one hand by imports of continental editions of the more expensive or less popular works, for which there was insufficient investment capital or interest in England, and on the other by timidity in Cambridge. Not until the 1680s could a distinctive trend be discerned among Cambridge booksellers, let alone in the press; and even then the experiment seems to have been short-lived, as copies were dispersed only gradually.

There was no reason why the University Printers should of their own volition, or at their own risk, supply the teaching needs of the University. Texts from London, from Oxford, and from overseas (especially Holland) were usually plentiful and easily obtained. The anxieties and aspirations that had fired Thomas Thomas were no longer appropriate a century later. Nonetheless, it is noticeable that only one textbook, and that by far the most widely used among tutors, was printed repeatedly at Cambridge in the later seventeenth century, Burgersdijck's *Institutiones logicarum*, 'ad juventutem Cantabrigiensem'. Such concentration suggests, at least so far as the University's immediate teaching needs were concerned, either a failure of nerve or active uninterest, and probably both. When in 1675 the books of Henry Gostling, a twenty-eight year old Fellow of Corpus but lately deceased, were listed, only four out of 120 had been printed at Cambridge, including Barrow's Euclid, Lambard's Ἀρχαιονομία and, as an accompaniment to a considerable library of French light literature, Dugrès' French grammar of 1636.[18] Several of Gostling's more elementary books, also intended for his college's library, were no doubt quietly set aside, and among them there may have been one or two more printed at Cambridge. But his collection was not atypical. Cambridge-printed books, with their emphasis on widespread steady sellers such as elementary Latin texts, Bibles and, above all, almanacs, were directed more at readers outside the University than those within it.

The University continued to depend for many of its texts on the London or import trade not least because of lower printing costs overseas. Books were both cheaper in Holland and, in at least one witness's eyes, better printed on better paper as well.[19] In 1695 the Cambridge bookseller William Graves even turned to Hendrik Wetstein in Amsterdam for a new edition of the latest best-seller on the curriculum, J. H. Schweitzer's *Compendium physicae Aristotelico-Cartesianae*, a work first printed there in 1685 and by 1695 already published in Cambridge twice over by Edward Hall, in 1687 and 1694.[20] But quite apart from this unusual step, the contributions of local booksellers became of increasing importance in the last decades of the century. Gradually they became more confident in publishing to meet specific local demands, turning either to Hayes or to the London press for manufacture. Financially, the Cambridge booksellers were considerably wealthier than Hayes. William Morden, probably the wealthiest, was able to leave £500 to his son Charles alone, besides a freehold in St Michael's parish and land at Exning in Suffolk.[21] William Graves, much less wealthy, nevertheless left an estate valued at £667, over 60 per cent of it as stock.[22] Edward Story, Alderman and Justice of the Peace, left at his death in 1692/3 money sufficient to build ten almshouses.[23] Henry Dickinson, who died in 1694/5, left an estate valued at £2,243, including debts due to him of £1,575.[24] These men were able to invest in publication, not simply in stock-holding. In 1683 John Creed listed seventeen different works 'printed for, and to be sold by' him.[25] Some of this was stock taken over from others; but it was by no means a negligible catalogue. In 1678 William Morden was in a position to attach a list of thirty-three titles to his second edition of Ray's *Collection of English proverbs*, printed by Hayes in that year; and in 1686 Richard Green advertised no less than forty-five, including not only books which he had instigated and financed, but also stock taken over from others, including most of that of Edward Story, perhaps on the latter's retirement. By 1693 Graves' list was headed by a folio set of chronological tables, but it also included educational texts in more modest formats (Terence, Burgersdijck and Heereboord) and a trio of established religious works uniform in duodecimo, besides Fleetwood's sermons and paraphrases of the *Te Deum* and *Benedicite* by a Fellow of Sidney Sussex College.[26] Many of those chosen by the local trade were intended, naturally, for a predictable and convenient local market. Creed's 1686 catalogue included not only Thomas Gale's edition of several short classical texts, but also a sermon by Humfrey Gower (Master of St John's), Pufendorf, William Groot, *De principiis iuris naturalis*, Barclay's *Argenis*, Du Moulin's and Crashaw's Latin poetry, and Terence. By no means all the books in these lists were either recent or published originally by the bookseller in question. Part of Morden's list was twenty and more years old. Green's 1686 catalogue,[27] containing stock dating partly from the 1650s, gives a profile of his business very different from that shown by his own imprints alone, one that in its ties with London as well as with other Cambridge booksellers records stock transfers as well as new works: exchange, inheritance and retirements as well as innovation. Only about one-quarter of Green's list represented his own original publications.

The increasing capitalization by local booksellers of Cambridge printing and publishing contributed by the end of the 1670s to sharing of the kind long established in London. In 1679 Creed and Henry Dickinson shared in the publication of Livy; and whereas in 1684 the Oxford University Press was able to publish an edition of Lactantius unsponsored by booksellers, the Cambridge edition of the following year, printed by Hayes, was shared by Dickinson and Richard Green. Their edition, introducing readings from two fifteenth-century Cambridge manuscripts, one in the University Library and the other in Emmanuel, had also an element of novelty, if not of importance.[28] Shared investment amongst the Cambridge trade was not so much to ensure equitable distribution of assumed profits, as to raise sufficient capital without impoverishing individuals. It followed that any profits were shared *pro rata*.

The booksellers, though richer than Hayes, were thus possessed of only modest wealth. Their presence, and their demands, supplemented Hayes' work, but usually in circumstances that were much circumscribed despite Creed's and Dickinson's contacts with the continental trade.[29] The support provided for the press by Sawbridge and the Stationers' Company in effect subsidized local publishing, by sustaining a press of a size unwarranted by local capital.

Nonetheless, the publications for which they were responsible were not confined entirely to the established demands of the University. In 1670 Edward Story had printed by Hayes Robert Sheringham's *De Anglorum gentis origine desceptatio*; though dismissed since by David Douglas as 'a mass of laboriously collected and misapplied learning', it was welcomed for that learning by others nearer to Sheringham's own day, and it proved a critical link in the development of Anglo-Saxon studies at Cambridge.[30] Innovation, where it occurred, was sometimes a declaration of independence from the Latin trade's stranglehold over ordinary degree courses, and interest. The octavo Livy printed by Hayes for Creed and Dickinson in 1679 was the first in Latin to have been either printed or published in England since 1589. Richard Green's edition of Anacreon, printed by Hayes in 1684, was the first edition of the Greek text printed in England. These were conceived very differently from

Joshua Barnes' folio Euripides, printed by Hayes and published by Green with its editor's considerable help in 1694: Barnes' ambitions were, justifiably, international, whereas Green was able to exploit it also as the first collected edition of the original text printed in England.[31] Though Barnes himself was criticised, and his ambitions made him an easy butt for ridicule, his edition proved one of the most enduring of all the books published at Cambridge in the late seventeenth century.

Born of a need perceived in the University and the rest of the scholarly world, it was inspired by a new attention to the editing of major classical texts, prepared to ambitious standards, in which English classical scholarship of this kind challenged what had been overwhelmingly a continental tradition. Thomas Stanley's Aeschylus (1664) had set the scene.[32] Thomas Gale, owner of a remarkable collection of Greek manuscripts, and briefly Regius Professor of Greek at Cambridge in 1672, followed with Herodotus in 1679, in an edition that also announced editions of Epiphanius and Dionysius Halicarnassus in preparation, and that suggested further (Philo Judaeus, Clemens Alexandrinus, Philostratus, Diodorus Siculus, Thucydides and others) would follow. In the end, despite these hopes, Thucydides had to await John Hudson's edition printed at Oxford in 1696.[33]

The same mingling in Cambridge of established texts and original work is to be seen in the Hebrew books contained in the local booksellers' lists, themselves part of a vigorous and widespread interest in the University in Hebrew studies in general. This tendency owed much to Ralph Cudworth of Christ's, Regius Professor of Hebrew since 1645, as well as to John Worthington of Jesus, Edmund Castell of Emmanuel and St John's, and John Lightfoot of St Catharine's: it was manifested at college level in specially appointed teachers such as Robertson (paid, at least in some years, by the University), or Isaac Abendana at Trinity, and more generally by a sequence of books of more or less importance. If nothing came finally of ambitious plans, laid in the early 1660s, for Abendana to translate the Mishnah (he was still receiving payments from the University in 1692), there were various other projects that met with more rapid success.[34] Again, the local booksellers, rather than Hayes, usually took the lead. Though William Robertson had to finance the production of his guide to the language in 1683, Sawbridge only taking copies for sale, the work of the immigrant Polish Hebraist Victorinus Bythner, which had first appeared from the Cambridge press in 1648, continued in the 1660s and 1670s to be handled by Edmund Beeching and William Morden, Bythner himself having by then returned from Oxford to Cambridge. John Lightfoot's commentary on St Luke was printed by Hayes at Story's behest in 1674. But in this field too the limitations of the Cambridge trade were discovered. John Spencer's pioneering work in comparative religion *Dissertatio de Urim et Thummin*, printed in Cambridge, was published in 1669 (two years after Spencer had been elected Master of Corpus) by a London bookseller,

Timothy Garthwait – not by a Cambridge one. So too, in 1685, his developed and enlarged work on the subject, *De legibus Hebraeorum ritualibus*, was again printed at Cambridge, but was published in London, by Richard Chiswell. In this manner it was also possible to protect copyright by entering it in the Stationers' Register, a course barred in practice to the local booksellers. The market, again, was foreign as well as domestic. Both Barnes and Spencer made their way successfully into the international trade, and achieved with it international reputations, but the decision to print in Cambridge was not one that was to be made lightly. It was in many respects forced on Barnes, who claimed to have found difficulty in finding a bookseller (whether he tried beyond Cambridge is not clear), and whose parsimoniousness or want of means is to be seen both in the cramped typography of his edition and the diversity of paper stocks on which it is printed. But for Ralph Cudworth, John Ray (after his earliest work), Newton, and for others ambitious for or already enjoying international reputations, the Cambridge press presented only handicaps.[35]

Other titles, printed in Cambridge for the local booksellers, bear witness also to the University's developing interests in opinion and research elsewhere. Jonas Hart's editions of Descartes' *Meditationes* and *Principia philosophiae* (1664), John Creed's of Walter Charleton's *Oeconomia animalis* (1669) and Samuel Simpson's of Bernhard Varenius' *Descriptio regni Iaponiae* (1673), spoke of enterprise as well as its necessary accompanying market demand. William Briggs, whose career as an oculist took him from a Cambridge MD in 1677 to the Royal College of Physicians, a place in Hooke's *Philosophical collections* and a position at St Thomas's Hospital in 1682, saw most of his work published at Cambridge either by Simpson or by Hart. But Briggs' experience was exceptional, and few others could boast such consistent attention by the local book trades.

In oriental studies other than Hebrew, the foundation of Sir Thomas Adams' professorship in Arabic, and the efforts of its first holder, Abraham Whelock, had brought no oriental press, despite the efforts and hopes of a devoted clique. Whelock's posthumous edition of the Gospels in Persian (1657) was printed and published in London, and the whole of the work of his successor Edmund Castell was likewise issued there. Of Castell's successor, John Luke, little survives in print after his appointment to the chair in 1685 save for a contribution, in Turkish, to the University's unfortunately timed verses on the birth of a son to James II in 1688. The modest fount of new Arabic type, acquired perhaps especially for the occasion, remained little used. Cambridge was not only under-equipped. It was also unable to offer the resources to publicize and circulate major undertakings.

It might have been otherwise in mathematics and the natural sciences. The uneven and irregular progress of these subjects in Cambridge in the later seventeenth century, dominated by Barrow and Newton, was reflected only palely in either Hayes' printing or local booksellers' investments. While in London the Royal Society began to set a publishing programme in train, the University saw published a mixture of original research and of established but otherwise scarce titles. From 1672, with the publication of Varenius' *Geographia generalis* (see fig. 34), Newton's influence furthered a course in publishing already taken by the local booksellers some years before. Though Hayes printed both the 1672 and 1681 editions of Varenius, for Henry Dickinson, this course depended very little on the Cambridge printers, who were frequently passed over in favour of those in London. Barrow's Euclid in English (1660), printed by Daniel in London at a time when the Cambridge press was disorganized, had been printed for the Cambridge bookseller William Nealand, whose responsibility for Ray's *Catalogus plantarum* (1660) and George Atwell's *Faithfull surveyour* has already been noticed. After Nealand's death, Edward Story took up his position, albeit briefly, as one especially willing to publish in the sciences: Duhamel's *Elementa astronomica* and Fournier's Euclid (both 1665) were followed in 1668 by Gautruche's *Mathematicae totius institutio*. Thereafter, however, even this limited special-ization ceased. It was Creed who took copies of Walter Charleton in 1669; Morden the 1675 edition and Dickinson the 1683 edition of Gassendi's *Institutio astronomica*; Jonas Hart who published Briggs' *Ophthalmographia* (1676); Samuel Simpson who issued Nicolaus Mercator's *Institutionum astronomicarum libri duo* (1676), a second edition of Briggs' book (1685), and his second treatise *Nova visionis theoria* (1685); and Richard Green who in 1683 again issued Gautruche. Of the books in this series published after Hayes became University Printer, only one, by Briggs, was printed at Cambridge. Although Newton might arrange for Varenius to be reprinted as an aid to his pupils, lend a benevolent hand to Nicolaus Mercator in his efforts to obtain a post at Cambridge[36] and in 1685 encourage Briggs with a commendatory essay for his *Nova visionis theoria*,[37] Cambridge was no place either to print or to publish *de novo* in the sciences. Gassendi, first published at Paris in 1647 and already scarce in Cambridge by December 1652, was printed in response to local needs, just as was Fournier's Euclid.[38] In 1667, hopes that the London bookseller John Martyn, who had also published the Euclid, might be further prevailed on to publish other suitable brief mathematical textbooks for the University, came to nothing.[39] Martyn did, however, handle Varenius' *Geographia generalis* for Dickinson in London in 1672, even though his name does not appear in the imprint.[40]

For most, London dominated. The pioneering medical work of Francis Glisson, Regius Professor of Physic from 1636 to 1677, was published not in Cambridge, but in London, where he preferred to work. His monograph on rickets, *De rachitide* (1650), printed three times over by 1660, as well as once in translation, achieved a rapid success that could never have been matched by Field. Disorganized, ill-led, and inadequately connected amongst London or

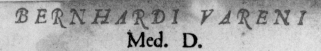

BERNHARDI VARENI
Med. D.

GEOGRAPHIA
GENERALIS,

In qua affectiones generales Telluris
explicantur,

Summâ curâ quam plurimis in locis emendata, &
XXXIII Schematibus novis, ære incifis, unâ
cum Tabb. aliquot quæ defiderabantur aucta
& illuftrata.

Ab ISAACO NEWTON
Math. Prof. Lucafiano
Apud CANTABRIGIENSES.

CANTABRIGIÆ,
Ex Officina Joann. Hayes, Celeberrimæ Academiæ Typographi.
Sumptibus Henrici Dickinfon Bibliopolæ. MDCLXXII.

Fig. 34 Bernhard Varenius (c. 1620–80), *Geographia generalis*, 8°, 1672. This was Newton's first
work to be printed at Cambridge. Height of original, 173 mm.

1. *Hyp.* Si fieri poteſt , ſit D ipſarum AC,
AB communis menſura. ª ergò D metitur
FD. ᵇ ergò AB ⊓ BC, contra
Hypoth.
2. *Hyp.* Dic AB ⊐ BC, ᶜ ergò AC ⊓
AB, contra Hypoth.

a 3. *ax.* 10.
b 1. *def.* 10.
c 16. 10.

Coroll.

Hinc etiam , ſi tota magnitudo ex duabus
compoſita, incommenſurabilis ſit alteri ipſarum, eadem & reliquæ incommenſurabilis erit.

PROP. XVIII.

Si fuerint
duæ rectæ li-
neæ inæquales
AB , GK;
quartæ autem
parti quadra-
ti, quod ſit à
minori GK,
æquale paral-
lelogrammum
ADB ad majorem AB applicetur, deficiens figurâ
quadratâ, & in partes AD, DB longitudine commenſurabiles ipſam dividat, major AB tanto plus
poterit quàm minor GK, quantum eſt quadratum
rectæ lineæ FD ſibi longitudine commenſurabilis :
Quòd ſi major AB tanto plus poſſit, quàm minor
GK, quantum eſt quadratum rectæ lineæ FD ſibi
longitudine commenſurabilis; quartæ autem parti
quadrati, quod ſit à minori GK, æquale parallelogrammum ADB ad majorem AB applicetur,
deficiens figurâ quadratâ, in partes AD, DB longitudine commenſurabiles ipſam dividet.

ª Biſeca GK in H; & ᵇ fac rectang. ADB =
GHq: abſcinde AF = DB. Eſtque AB] ᶜ =
4 ADB ᵈ (4 GHq, vel ▦Kq) + FDq. Jam
primò,

a 10. 1.
b 28. 6.
c 8. 2.
d *conſtr.* &
4. 2.

primò, Si AD ⊓ DB, erit AB ᵉ ⊓ DB ᵉ ⊓
2 DB ᶠ (AF + DB, vel AB — FD) ᵍ ergò
AB ⊓ FD. Q. E. D. Sin ſecundò, AB ⊓
FD, ʰ erit ideò AB ⊓ AB — FD (2 DB)
ᵏ ergò AB ⊓ DB. ˡ quare AD ⊓ DB.
Q. E. D.

e 16. 10.
f *conſtr.*
g cor. 16 10.
h cor. 16.40.
k 12 10.
l 16. 10.

PROP. XIX.

Si fuerint
duæ rectæ
lineæ inæ-
quales, AB,
GK, quartæ
autem per-
ti quadrati,
quod ſit à
minore GK,
æquale pa-
rallelogram-
mum ADB ad majorem AB applicetur deficiens figurâ quadratâ; & in partes incommenſurabiles
longitudine AD, DB, ipſam AB dividat; maxor
AB tanto plus poterit, quàm minor GK, quantum
eſt quadratum rectæ lineæ FD, ſibi longitudine in-
commenſurabile : Quòd ſi major AB tanto plus
poſſit, quàm minor GK, quantum eſt quadratum rectæ lineæ FD ſibi longitudine incommenſurabilis;
quartæ autem parti quadrati, quod ſit à minore
GK, æquale parallelogrammum ADB ad majorem
AB applicetur, deficiens figurâ quadratâ, in partes
longitudine incommenſurabiles AD, DB ipſam AB
dividet.

Facta puta, & dicta eadem, quæ in præce-
denti. Itáꝗ primò, Si AD ⊓ DB, ª erit pro-
pterea AB ⊓ DB; ᵇ quare AB ⊐ DB
(AB — FD) ᶜ ergò AB ⊓ FD. Q. E. D.
Secundò, Si AB ⊓ FD; ᶜ ergò AB ⊓
AB — FD (2 DB); ᵈ quare AB ⊓ DB, &
ſ proinde AD ⊓ DB. Q. E. D.   PROP.

a 17. 10.
b 13. 10.

c cor. 17.10.
...10.

...10.

overseas booksellers, the Cambridge press offered but a poor prospect. Hopes raised with the Restoration proved short-lived. Even had the circumstances of its composition and preparation for printing suggested it, there was never any question of Newton's *Principia* (1687) being published at Cambridge. It was written with a London, and overseas, readership in mind; its publication, in which the London bookseller Samuel Smith took stocks for the foreign market, depended on financial and distributory resources greater than those available in the nearest printing house to Trinity College.[41] The *Principia* was by no means unique in this respect. Apart from his edition of Euclid (see figs. 35, 36), none of Barrow's work was printed or published at Cambridge. John Ray was an exception – for a little while. But his first book, a flora of Cambridgeshire (1660) (see fig. 30 on p. 335 above), had a special local interest, and he considered his own *Collection of English proverbs* (1670) 'a toy and trifle not worth the owning'. Otherwise, from his second book (the *Catalogus plantarum Angliae*, 1670) onwards, his work was issued in London, of whose printers he was at first nevertheless suspicious: 'The Letter and paper I like well, and the correcting is tolerable, much better than I expected at London', he wrote to Martin Lister in 1670.[42] Among lesser figures, Giovanni Francesco Vigani, the Italian who taught chemistry at Cambridge from about 1683 and who in 1703 was appointed the University's first Professor of the subject, had written his sole book *Medulla chymiae* before his arrival: published originally in 1682 at Danzig, editions also appeared in Leiden (1693) and Nuremberg (1718–19). Only one edition was published in England, by Henry Faithorne and John Kersey at London in 1683: none was printed at Cambridge. Mathematical and scientific activity was established in the University. Its publication was not.[43]

The difficulties, and limitations, facing the Cambridge trade were not unique to the provinces. Mathematics printing required special skills, as well as special sorts and diagrams.[44] 'There is not any Printer now in London accustomed to Mathematicall worke, or indeed fitted with all convenient Characters, and those handsome fractions but Mr Godbid where your *Exercitationes* were printed, and at present he is full of this kind of worke', wrote John Collins to James Gregory in 1670.[45] Publishing, even in London, was no easier, the foreign trade offering very little to help speed return on investment. As Collins, again, explained to Newton seventeen months later,

Our Latin Booksellers here are averse to ye Printing of Mathematicall Bookes there being scarce any of them that have a forreigne Correspondence for Vent, and so when such a Coppy is offered, in stead of rewarding the Author they rather expect a Dowry with ye Treatise.[46]

With his background in the book trade (he had begun his career as an Oxford bookseller's apprentice), Collins was in a peculiarly authoritative position, both on this occasion and about five years later when he explained to John Wallis that 'we have very few Latin booksellers that trade beyond Sea and such

Fig. 36 Barrow's Euclid; the volume in the subject's hands is the Cambridge edition of 1655. It is thought that the portrait is of Barrow himself.

as doe make a more quick and profitable return of their Stock than to adventure it in printing of Latin Mathematiques'.[47] Under ordinary circumstances, uninfluenced by University requirements, Robert Scott, the principal importer of French books, expected to sell no more than twenty to thirty copies of a new mathematics book from abroad.[48] Over-ambitious edition sizes led only to a slump in wholesale and retail prices: even Barrow's Euclid was to be found at a shilling in quires.[49] All these issues affected the London trade. In Cambridge the risk was all the greater.

In some respects, and especially in printing, scientific publishing presented difficulties not found in the ordinary book. But in other respects, all learned publishing faced the same difficulties, from initial finance to final distribution.

Barnes published his first major book, the life of Edward III, himself. But its considerable size (it is a folio of 911 pages), and the fact that Barnes, though proud to a fault, was not obviously wealthy, raise questions as to the exact meaning of the time-honoured phrase of the title-page, 'for the author', or 'impensis auctoris'. The whole of the cost did not necessarily fall on an author who chose to publish in this way, as printers were in practice often willing to share in an edition. Circumstances of course varied. The *Select and family prayers* printed by Hayes and published by their author John Armstrong, Vicar of Cartmel in Lancashire, in 1677, were not intended for a Cambridge audience.[50] How far Thomas Heyrick, curate of Market Harborough and member of Peterhouse, had to finance his undistinguished poems in 1691 is not clear: besides himself, he named no less than three booksellers on his title-page, including one in Cambridge, one in Fleet Street, and his namesake Samuel Heyrick at Gray's Inn Gate. Mace's *Musick's monument* was published by Mace himself in Cambridge and by the specialist music dealer John Carr in London, where it was also printed.[51] Private publication of this kind led to arrangements between bookseller, author and printer on which it is difficult to generalize very much, and where, again, title-pages do not reveal the nature of agreements.

In 1658 the aged Cambridge mathematics teacher George Atwell had complained vigorously of a trade unwilling either to pay him in cash for his copy (this was not unusual), or to risk production costs in his work. Only the private enterprise of his son-in-law, Nathanael Rowls, made print possible:

For amongst all our Book-sellers none would ever bid me a penny for my copy; so that I have lost all mine own labour, and a great deal of charge in transcribing; so that had not Doctor *Rowls* beg'd a pardon for it, it had gone to the pot.[52]

Atwell died the same year; four years later the residue of stock was reissued by William Nealand, who having refused Atwell's work originally nevertheless thought it worthwhile to print the first, preliminary, sheet anew with his own name. In 1683 William Robertson published his own *Manipulus linguae sanctae* 'pro authore', with an additional statement that copies were also for sale at Sawbridge's shop in Ludgate Hill. A few years later the book was noticed briefly in the Leipzig *Acta Eruditorum*, and in the Amsterdam *Bibliothèque Universelle et Historique*, in both cases next to Sawbridge's edition of his *Thesaurus linguae sanctae*; the conjunction and the timing imply that it was booksellers', rather than private, stock under review.[53] Little is known of the details of publication arrangements for such books.

In practice, and despite Barnes' claims, private publication of this kind could sometimes mean relatively little investment, depending on the subject. Writing presumably of mathematical or other scientific books in 1671, John Collins reported that one London bookseller would print any book, provided he was assured of the sale of eighty or a hundred copies for ready money.[54] (The corollary, linking long-term credit to larger, more nearly normal-sized editions, offers a fruitful topic for investigation.) Six years' further experience did not cause Collins to change his mind:

If an author, or any person in his behalf, will pay a stationer for one hundred books, ready money, at a rate he sells them in his shop, there are stationers, [who] will undertake any book proposed, and even the books so bought may, within a few years, be bartered away with some money for other books, that little loss may ensue.[55]

Ready money (and particularly at retail rather than trade prices), rather than several years' credit, enabled not only private individuals such as Barnes or Heyrick to publish their own work. It may also have lain, in no doubt a more complicated form, behind the proliferation of publications by so many of the Cambridge booksellers in the last four decades or so of the century. It meant, in effect, that perhaps only one-tenth of an edition had to be paid for by the initiating publisher.

As Henry More explained in 1673 of his *Opera theologica* – a book neither printed nor published by Hayes, but as the work of a Cambridge author one offering useful comparative evidence:

I have 25 copies that cost me nothing, and buy but 100 copies of the 500, and not at such a rate as they usually sell such small Impressions at the booksellers, that is twice the value of what they cost at the printing house, but onely half as much againe, in that proportion that 3 is to 2, so that if a book for example, stand them at the printing house, papyr and printing 10s, I shall pay fifting shillinges, and I thought this was a better way then to pay one fifth part less then the booksellers would sell it for.[56]

Costs of production could be shared between printer and bookseller, as well as between various booksellers. Private publication often meant that the author, rather than a bookseller, simply shared printing costs with a printer. Publication by subscription offered a further alternative, that circumvented the requirements of the ordinary trade, and considerably (though by no means entirely) reduced the element of risk. Known in England at least since 1617,[57] it offered a means of issuing books seemingly far larger than the ordinary work of a modest bookseller might seem to justify. Its increasing popularity after the 1680s, supported by the existence and development of a specialist bib-

Fig. 37 Euripides, edited by Joshua Barnes (1654–1712), f⁰, 1694. Height of original, 321 mm.

ΕΥΡΙΠΙΔΟΥ

Σωζόμενα ἅπαντα·

Δηλονότι Τραγῳδίαι Εἴκοσι, πλὴν ὑφάτῃ, πᾶσαι τέλειαι· Ἔτι δὴ κ̀ Ἀποσπασμάτια τῶν ἄλλων
ὑπέρ τας Ἑξήκοντα· Καὶ Ἐπιστολαὶ Πέντε, κ̀ αὐταὶ νῦν πρῶτον τι περισπερεαγεαφᾶσαι.

ΣΧΟΛΙΑ ΤΩΝ ΠΑΝΥ ΔΟΚΙΜΩΝ
ΕΙΣ

Ἑπτά τὰς πρότερας Τραγῳδίας, συλλεγέντα ἐκ Διαφόρων παλαιῶν Βιβλίων, κ̀ συναγ-
μολογηθέντα παρὰ ΑΡΣΕΝΙΟΥ Ἀρχιεπισκόπου ΜΟΝΕΜΒΑΣΙΑΣ.

EURIPIDIS

Quæ Extant Omnia:

TRAGOEDIÆ nempe XX,

Præter ultimam, Omnes Completæ: Item

FRAGMENTA

Aliarum plusquam LX Tragœdiarum; Et

EPISTOLÆ V.

Nunc primùm & ipsæ hùc adjectæ:

SCHOLIA demùm DOCTORUM VIRORUM
IN

Septem Priores Tragœdias, *ex Diversis Antiquis Exemplaribus undiquaque
Collecta & Concinnata ab* ARSENIO Monembasiæ *Archiepiscopo.*

Præmittitur *Euripidis* Vita ex Variis Authoribus accuratiùs descripta.

Etiam Tractatus de *Tragœdiâ* Veterum Græcorum.

Adduntur suis locis *Scholia* aliquot MSS. item Selectiores Doctorum Virorum Notæ &
Conjecturæ cum Perpetuis ad Posteriores Fabulas Commentariis.

Genuinæ Lectiones afferuntur, Carminum ratione diligentèr observatâ.

Scholia Vetera & *Latina* Versio, omniáque adeò multò quàm antehàc Emendatiora.

Accedit *Index* Triplex, 1. In Authorem. 2. In Scholia. 3. Authorum in Scholiis &
Notis laudatorum.

Operâ & Studio JOSUÆ BARNES *S.T.B.* Emmanuelis
Collegii apud Cantabrigienses *Socii maximè Senioris.*

CANTABRIGIÆ,
Ex Officinâ *Johan. Hayes,* Celeberrimæ *Academiæ* Typographi. Impensis *Richardi
Green* Bibliopolæ *Cantab.* An. Dom. MDCXCIV.

Fig. 37 continued.

liographical press that presented regular opportunities to advertise, reflected the advantages to author, publisher, bookseller and customer alike. Thomas Mace, lutenist and clerk in Trinity College chapel, had collected over three hundred subscriptions to help finance his *Musick's monument* in 1676, though the fact that he still had stock in hand fourteen years later suggests that he paid for a substantial part of the edition himself. By the time that Joshua Barnes of Emmanuel came to publish his own history of Edward III in 1688, subscription publication had become familiar, and its pitfalls therefore known. Like Mace, Barnes arranged for an agent in London, in his case not a bookseller, but John Harborough, former Fellow-Commoner of his own college and now practising medicine in the capital. No Cambridge bookseller appeared on the title-page, and the investment seems to have been wholly Barnes': he later claimed that it had cost him over £600, a substantial sum for a Fellow of a Cambridge college and of modest background. It may be unjustifiable to assume too much, but it is worth remark that Barnes indulged in this conspicuous expenditure only a few months after defeat in the election to the chair of Greek, and was perhaps seeking justification for his work.[58] The dedication to James II, wishing him a flourishing family, quiet and secure government, obedient subjects and a wise and loyal Parliament, could have scarcely been more ineptly timed.[59] The trade found itself amply supplied, even as Barnes gradually sought out new attractions for his work: a commendatory poem by Thomas Heyrick in 1690, and an engraving of himself by Robert White in 1694.[60] Such enterprise speaks more of seeking after satisfaction in self-aggrandisement than of expectation of any serious financial reward. It proved very different from his edition of Euripides (1694) (see fig. 37), dedicated more circumspectly to the Chancellor and other members of the University and a work of obvious importance and assured interest well beyond any private circle of acquaintance. In 1694, not only was Barnes rewarded with £50 from the University Chest. His Euripides was taken up by the Cambridge bookseller Richard Green, who paid him for his work and helped him to obtain texts.[61] In the case both of this and of Jean de Launoi's folio *Epistolae* (1689, published by another Cambridge bookseller, Edward Hall),[62] subscription publication was designed to raise capital from an international market (via London booksellers) as well as from the interested scholarly community locally: neither Green nor Hall had the resources to meet the costs of production of such books by themselves, but both had influential London connections.

The prospectus for Barnes' Euripides, issued by the 'undertaker' Richard Green, offered what had by February 1690/1, when it was issued, a contract that had in its essentials become familiar:[63]

I.   That the Book shall be Printed on the same Paper and Character with the *Specimen* here exhibited; and will contain about 200 Sheets.

II.   That every *Subscriber* shall pay the *Undertaker* Eight Shillings down in hand, and Eight Shillings more upon delivery of a perfect Book in Sheets.

III. That whoever shall Subscribe, or procure Subscriptions for *Six Books*, shall have a *Seventh gratis*; so that he who takes this Advantage, will have each Book for Thirteen Shillings and Four Pence.

IV. That the Price to any other than a Subscriber, shall be not less than *Twenty Two Shillings* and *Six Pence* in Sheets.

V. That in order to a full and exact Compliance with the above-written Proposals, every single Sheet, over and above the usual Methods of Correction, will be carefully revised by *Joshua Barnes*, B.D. Fellow of Emmanuel-College, Cambridge.

Barnes followed Gale in thus seeking to publish a major Greek author (Gale's proposals had appeared in 1678), and, at another extreme, John Dunton (among others) in offering seven copies for the price of six. Of the fifteen booksellers named as agents other than Green, seven were in London, including two, Matthew Gilliflower and William Hensman, in Westminster Hall. If success depended on the reputation or customers of those booksellers willing to accept orders, then Barnes' project, involving some of the largest and most respected, must have seemed set fair. The other London agents were Thomas Dring and Christopher Wilkinson in Fleet Street, Richard Chiswell, Robert Clavell (publisher of the *Term Catalogues*) and Walter Kettilby in St Paul's Churchyard, and Joseph Hindmarsh and Thomas Horne in Cornhill. Oxford was placed in the hands of John Crosley and Henry Clements; Eton in those of John Slater; York, of Francis Hildyard; Norwich, of George Rose; and Worcester, of John Jones, who also had a business in St Paul's Churchyard. Copies were promised 'by Easter-term come Twelve-Month at farthest'. But although Barnes' expectations of the length of his edition proved remarkably accurate – and necessarily so, since the price had been settled – it took much longer to print the sheets than expected: the title-page is dated 1694.

The international market was dominated, not surprisingly so far as English exports were concerned, by theological, classical, scientific, historical and mathematical scholarship. Protestant interest in the Low Countries, and the establishment of national and local academies of *savants*, were two major factors in the development of the international book trade in the second half of the century, a trade still hampered by war (much of the trade with France had to be conducted via Holland) but made at least temporarily easier by the Treaty of Nijmegen in 1678.[64] Editors such as Otto Mencke of the Leipzig *Acta Eruditorum*, Pierre Bayle of the *Nouvelles de la République des Lettres* and Jean Leclerc of the *Bibliothèque Universelle et Historique*, took particular pride in their familiarity with scholarly activity in England, while booksellers followed their interest by stocking books they chose to notice. The gradual blurring of linguistic barriers, and the adoption of French and English (especially as a consequence of the royalist exodus in mid-century) as means of international discourse in place of Latin, contributed further to a market in which England took an increasing part as supplier.[65] So, in France, the *Journal des Sçavans* noticed Pearson's *Vindiciae epistolarum Ignatii* at some length in 1674/5, Briggs' *Ophthalmographia* in 1677, and Joseph Hill's much enlarged edition of Schrevelius' well-established Greek–Latin lexicon in 1685. Copies of Pearson were available from the Parisian bookseller Fréderic Léonard, and of Schrevelius from Sebastien Mabre-Cramoisy.[66] In Holland, the *Histoire des Ouvrages des Sçavans* first announced that Barnes was at work on his Euripides in February 1693/4, then reported in November that it had been published, and finally ran a review in March 1695/6, describing it as 'la plus parfaite qui ait paru jusqu'à présent': the effect was spoiled only by some carefree remarks about the spurious letters that Barnes had added at the end: 'L'espace en est si court, & elles sont si peu importantes, qu'elles ne valent pas la peine d'en disputer.'[67] His edition, by then already reviewed in the *Acta Eruditorum*, was available in Amsterdam from Reinier Leers, as well as in Paris from Jean Anisson.[68]

But this was not a market in which either booksellers or authors felt always comfortable. William Saywell, editor of Jean de Launoi's *Epistolae* (1689), and a Fellow of Jesus College, opened his preface with an *apologia* lest the reader should wonder at the publication of such a book in Cambridge. Abroad, his edition was taken up, like Robertson's *Manipulus linguae sanctae* of three years earlier, by the Amsterdam booksellers, and so given further exposure in the *Bibliothèque Universelle et Historique*. Leclerc took fifty pages to summarize and welcome the book; and in Saywell's arguments for an historically based, specifically Anglican, church, he found also the excuse for an attack on French censorship more generally. The Cambridge press was put to a rare use:

Mais on ne l'auroit peutêtre jamais rimprimé en France, parce que depuis qu'on a établi des Censeurs des livres, ces Messieurs ont pris tant d'autorité, & se soucient si peu de l'avancement des Sciences, qu'ils font supprimer tout ce qui n'est pas à leur goût, lequel n'est pas ordinairement des meilleurs. Ainsi l'on a de l'obligation à ceux qui ont pris soin de publier ces Lettres à Cambridge, sans quoi elles seroient devenuës trop rares avec le temps.[69]

The success of Launoi, which was taken up instantly in Rotterdam as well,[70] and likewise caught the attention of the *Acta Eruditorum* on account of Saywell's outspoken introduction,[71] had political and religious overtones that did not however affect most of the press's books abroad.

Nor was the interest taken in its books there always to the press's best advantage. While some were treated quickly, there was a pause of three years before Pearson's work was noticed in Paris; and Spencer's *De legibus Hebraeorum* was noticed in Holland and France not in its folio Cambridge edition of 1685, but in the revised quarto edition published at The Hague in 1686.[72] For religious, family and commercial reasons, the Dutch trade had a particular interest in England, not only in its scholarly market but also, for some, as a political and religious adversary.[73] The share of the Cambridge press in the resulting trade was modest enough; but it provided an international context for some of its activities unmatched since Thomas and Legate had printed the work of William Whitaker and Perkins.[74] Newton's edition of Varenius' *Geographia generalis*, printed by Hayes, was taken up and printed, albeit in a slightly less generous form, by Heinrich Groker at Jena in 1693, *iuxta exemplar Cantabrigia*. It was a compliment of a sort, one that had had no parallels since the beginning of the century. And for those who wished it, England's two learned presses could be seen side by side, as the *Acta Eruditorum* reviewed first Thomas Spark's edition of Lactantius from Oxford in 1684, and then the Cambridge edition in 1685; the *Histoire des Ouvrages des Sçavans* followed its review of Barnes' Euripides in March 1695/6 with one of John Hudson's Oxford Thucydides the following June. Such juxtapositions, inevitable in a reviewing journal, helped to form a climate in which the true achievement of Hayes' press could be evaluated, criticized, and eventually found wanting by those who, like Bentley, also conceived their work and counted their acquaintance in international terms.

Conclusion

The link perceived between Thomas Thomas and his Estienne predecessors, and Barnes' allusion to the old standard editions of Euripides, notably that printed by Paul Estienne in 1602, expressed claims for the Cambridge press that were more usually simply assumed.[1] The Press was in a learned tradition, even if those for the time being responsible for its prosecution frequently resorted to a more populist role in order to further their well-being. If Thomas, Legate and Legge were slow to take up the international trade consistently (and there is little evidence, so far, of their involvement, direct or otherwise, in the Frankfurt book fairs), much of the theological controversy which they printed was inescapably international in its audience. The advent of reviewing journals in the latter part of the seventeenth century made the position of the Cambridge press seem even more prominent on the continent than it had been; but in practice its work had been long familiar. In 1633 it was claimed from The Hague that Mede's *Clavis apocalyptica*, published by Buck, was 'very much sought' − 'and certainly these parts would have taken off above two hundred, if sent at first'.[2] Even if the estimate was over-sanguine, it is of significance that the claim was made at a time when the University had ambitions of acquiring the means to print oriental languages in considerable quantity and variety − ambitions that were to be frustrated, as Hebrew type was perforce used until the eighteenth century to print Arabic texts. But despite Dutch interest in Mede's Hebrew scholarship in the 1630s, printers at Cambridge could in the seventeenth century pretend to few achievements as an international oriental learned press.

Yet the major books of these years − Fuller's *Holy warre* (1639) and *Holy and profane state* (1642), the folio Greek New Testament (1642), Whelock's Bede (1643) and, in another vein, Cruso's *Military instructions* (1644) were achievements of unquestionable magnitude. So, too, the Bible of 1638 became the touchstone for textual authority for more than a century. Beside these might be placed smaller quartos, octavos and duodecimos of equal significance. In all of them, Buck and Daniel pursued a course of exceptional scholarly and technical distinction, even if it did not have such obvious trappings of an international learned press as a consistent achievement in oriental languages.

As has been repeatedly stressed, the University's requirements for its teaching, and printers' responses to them, were in their turn inseparable from the commercial constraints of an international market, organized through London and in practice for most of the sixteenth and seventeenth centuries dominated by only a few individuals. But just as Cambridge booksellers and customers depended for their supplies on London and overseas, so London and overseas came to depend on Cambridge. A learned world partly defined by its internationalism was also the vehicle for a trade that is but inadequately accounted as that existing between the capital and its nearby countryside. Although on the one hand it may be argued that Cambridge supplied printed books to London just as Cambridgeshire or Hertfordshire supplied food, on the other hand the Letters Patent of 1534, and the successive confirmations of Henry VIII's initial legislation, created an environment of equality, not of dependence. It was on such terms of equality that the agreements between Buck and the English Stock, and between Field and Hayes and George Sawbridge, were predicated.

For so long as national legislation restricted the places in which presses might be established; for so long as the Stationers' Company, its emissaries, or (however changing their array) the licensing authorities, retained an authority, albeit sometimes more manifest than real; and for so long as more powerful or wealthy members of the Stationers' Company consequently remained able both to limit the number of presses in the country and also apportion some of the most profitable work; so the University Printers, at Oxford and Cambridge, held the balance between the entrenched conservatism of legally protected interests and a market thirsty for ever more printed matter as the population expanded. In this context, the sequence of entries into different parts of what may be termed the national popular market are of interest beyond the commonplace of disputes between the University and the Stationers' Company, and between each side's various apologists in London, Lambeth or West-minster. The University Printers never attempted to enter the separate markets served by specialist printers and sales outlets, for broadside ballads or for chap-books.[3] But they did successfully tackle three other major segments: of Bibles, of school texts and of almanacs. While for each of these there was a measure of investment at risk, in every case the Cambridge printers were in practice hazarding very little initially: the markets for all were well established, and either under-supplied or inadequately supplied (with insufficient variation, or with excessive charges) by goods already available. The Stationers' Company notwithstanding, printers in Cambridge after 1583 always had, in the sixteenth and seventeenth centuries, the benefit of working in the face of expanding demand. Setbacks such as those experienced by Legge in the 1620s, or by Buck and Daniel after the mid-1630s, could only be temporary (however disabling in Legge's case, or requiring alternative policies, in Buck and Daniel's), as the literate population grew. Bible ownership became so widespread as to be all but everywhere, and popular taste for almanacs blossomed into a fashion affecting most levels of society. Demand for such books exceeded the ability of London printers to meet it, that for Bibles in particular being met only by means of countless imports, legal and surreptitious, from the Low Countries. The place of the Cambridge press was thus established as of national, not merely peripheral, significance.

The press envisaged by Thomas Thomas, defined essentially by its University commitment, dependent on the forbearance of the London stationers, gradually lost both its original character and, for many observers, its purpose in a university environment. The price of success was too high.

Field died affluent,[4] but not thanks to the University or to its members. Rather, it was thanks to his place as essentially an undistinguished London printer, partner in the English Stock, surreptitious collaborator with the Stationers' Company Treasurer, and enjoying also a part in the Bible trade into which he threw himself with more energy than any of his contemporaries. Under Hayes, Field's successor, the effect on the Cambridge press of the Company's collaboration was little changed. In a policy that became ever more restricted, the dominating authors of the earlier part of the century, authors drawn from the University, were not replaced by later equivalents of such overwhelming presence. Preferences among the more prolific Cambridge authors shifted to London, with good reason; for not only were the printers there demonstrably better accustomed to scholarly printing: the London trade also offered easier access to an international readership.

Perkins, Davenant and Fuller, mainstays of the University Printers earlier in the century, were moreover not only Cambridge authors. The appearance of their words on the page, and therefore the manner in which they were read, were created by Cambridge compositors. To read Perkins' collected works was to read them in a style established at Cambridge, and manifested in their many editions for long after Legate had left to continue printing them not in Cambridge, but in London. So too, and in much more than typographical arrangement of one or two well-known poems, was the case with Herbert's *Temple*, a book whose format, bulk and appearance was established for generations by the decision in 1633 to print the poems not (as Donne's in the same year) in quarto, nor (as Quarles') in octavo, but in duodecimo – a size which for all its allusions to the meditative and religious content of the poems, was nonetheless markedly at variance with the small folio of the licensed manuscript. The typographical influence of Cambridge later in the century lay in different spheres, no less remarkable. But it is noticeable that the commercial implications were paramount, whether in the small type, double columns and thin paper of some of Field's and Hayes' quarto Bibles, or the proud boast prefixing the Cambridge concordances.[5] Both were to triumph in fiercely competitive markets, while the school and other basic Latin texts printed at Cambridge in the last decades of the seventeenth century demonstrated similar skills in achieving economies. But they met expectations also to be found with respect to other, less frequently published books: for smaller volumes, for economic typography, and, largely beyond the printer's control but inevitably affecting the result, for cheaper bindings.

Typography apart, the Cambridge press became identified for the great majority of its readers in the late seventeenth century with a small range of crucial texts. Thomas's dictionary, last printed in 1644, had its several successors. By the 1690s it had been displaced, for students elsewhere as well as in Cambridge, by the compilations of Francis Gouldman and Adam Littleton. William Robertson's *Phraseologia generalis*, first published at Cambridge and soon exported to America, was still available in a revised version for the renascent interest in schools in Latin composition in the 1820s.[6] For undergraduates at late seventeenth-century Oxford and Cambridge, such aids were joined by Gautruche's *Mathematica*, Burgersdijck's *Institutiones logicae*, Gassendi on philosophy, Vigerus on Greek and Fournier's Euclid.[7]

Much more generally, the Cambridge press became identified, far beyond university and other educational or scholarly circles, with almanacs. Of the thirty or so different titles offered for sale in the 1680s, Hayes printed about one-fifth, including fifty-five per cent of all sheet almanacs.[8] Such sales made the name of the Cambridge press everywhere familiar in England, and no doubt established its popular identity just as the many different almanacs achieved much of their success thanks to a bibliopolic equivalent of brand loyalty. This popular image, as principal supplier of by far the widest selling printed matter in the late seventeenth century, was balanced by the vision seen by Thomas, appealed to by Buck, and frequently alluded to by members of the University: a vision of a learned, or at any rate academic, press. But the balance was uneven. Certainly many individuals found in the Cambridge press of the late seventeenth century much that had the trappings of learning. The various works of Joshua Barnes, the Epistles of Jean de Launoi, the Jewish studies of John Spencer, William Robertson and Bythner, and the 1685 edition of Lactantius, all bore the stamp of a learned press. But such isolated examples offered neither a programme nor a claim to a reputation that could be convincingly sustained. It was such a programme that Bentley and his allies sought, as they repudiated – albeit temporarily – general printing, equipped themselves with new type from Holland (the only source capable of providing what was needed) and forged a policy based partly on links with new parts of the London trade and partly on claims of meeting the needs of the scholarly world. Typographically, organizationally, personally and ideologically, the Press founded in 1698 was intended to replace a disjointed and ill-conceived business with a clearly identifiable vision, a logically conceived partnership between Press and University. How far that renewed vision became a reality, and what happened to it subsequently, will form the subject of the next volume.

APPENDIX 1

(*see page 322*)

Humble proposals concerning the printing of the Bible

I.   That there may bee a fair Copie of the last Translation of the BIBLE, ingrossed either in Parchment or Vellom, in a full Character, which may bee compared with the Original, by four or five Ministers, and so kept in *Sion*-College, as an Authentick Record: for Orthography so truely and critically written, that hereafter a Letter shall not bee altered: That so all people, upon any doubt, may have recours to the Original, to prove whether their Printed Copies varie, or not.

The Jews were so accurate, that they knew the number of words, syllables, nay letters in every book: whose diligence and industry in that kinde God's Providence hath used as a means to keep the Scriptures from corruption.

And in the Primitive times one ἰῶτα (*the least letter in the Alphabet*) *made a mighty controversie in the Church of God: For in the doctrine of the Trinitie, the Orthodox partie held that Christ was* ὁμοουσιος: *the Heterodox* ὁμοιουσιος: *which two words differ but in one onely letter.*

And wee read Judg. 12.6. *that it cost* 42000 *men their lives for missing one letter in* Shibboleth.

II. That the Bible hereafter may bee Printed truly, according to the Translator's Copie, with the Divers Readings, and Paralel-places in the Margin, as formerly hath been don: which are helps for the comparing of som, and illustration of other places.

Reas. For this endeavor to bring it into a narrow Compass, hath been the cause of leaving out letters, words, lines, and the crouding together, and so corrupting many words.

III. That som able Scholars may bee appointed to mannage the Correction, who have skill in the Original, and not left to Mercenary Correctors. The *Bible* was never better printed than by Mr *Buck* and Mr *Daniel* at Cambridg: And the most famous Printers of *Europe* have been both great Scholars, and Master-Printers: as *Robert, Henrie*, and *Paul* STEPHEN, *Plantine, Erpenius, Manutius, Frobenius, Thomas Thomasius*, Mr *Buck*, and the *Elzivirs* now living.

IV. That (notwithstanding many faults were amended in the *Cambridg*-Edition, partly by som of the Translators themselves, partly by others, yet) the whole Translation may bee revised by Learned men, and publick notice given, that so others from all parts may suggest to the Reviewers, their Opinions concerning amendments.

Source: Cambridge University Archives, CUR 33.6 (25).

APPENDIX 2

(see page 322)

Proposals humbly presented to publick consideration, but more particularly, to the Right-honourable the Sub-Committee of the Parliament for Religion, concerning the Future printing of BIBLES *in* ENGLISH.

I.   That all *Bibles* in *English*, heretofore false printed (considering the multitude of *Errata's* notoriously escaped in many late Impressions (to the great scandal of *Religion*, and corruption of sound Doctrine) may be speedily called in, suppressed, and none permitted to be sold hereafter, under a severe penalty: That it may be an example for time to come, to cause all men to be more carefull in undertaking such a weighty work.

II.   That a stricter Law be made, than formerly (under the penalty of a *Praemunire*) against the importation of any *Bibles* in *English*, printed beyond the Seas, into *England*, *Scotland*, or *Ireland*, or the Dominions thereunto belonging; That thereby the *Bible* may not be falsified, or corrupted, by Jesuites, or others, beyond the Seas: And no *Translation* be printed in *England*, but what is considerately approved, and established by the *State*.

III.   That the said *Translation* may be forthwith exactly compared, and revised by, and with the *Original*, by *Divines*, and other learned men, appointed by the *State*: And a *Copy* thereof so seeled by the *Parliament*, That nothing may be printed, disagreeing thereunto in the least *iota*; And the same to be fairly ingrossed, and transcribed in Velom (as well as the Evidences, and Records of temporal estates,) And safely kept as a Publick Record in the *Tower*, and other Treasuries of Records, as the common Evidence of the 3. Nations.

IV.   That the said *Copy* may not be appropriated (as a peculiar *Copy*) for any mans particular profit whatsoever, to any private person, or more: For if it should be permitted to such by colur of any title in Law; Then they may alter the *Copy* as they please, or sell it to any Priest, or Jesuite, or other *Heterodoxe* person: Or if they print the *Copy* justly, and truely, Yet they may print as many, and as few as they please, And set their own prices upon their books; to the great oppression of the Common-wealth: Insomuch as that they may gain by printing Bibles in all Volumes 10000.*l. per annum de claro.*

V.   That neither the Company of Stationers, nor any particular Society of Booksellers, may have any Interest, or Title in the Copy of the Bible, or any propriety in the printing thereof: For if they, or any of them, have liberty to manage any *Printery*, they will expose to sale no books, but of their own printing: And thereby (having the advantage of a powerful purse) will debilitate, and discourage all others, that print never so well. And in truth (if a book will but sell well (as Bibles are the most certain) let the printing be never so bad) they look no further. So that in time (by beating out all other men) they will print what they please, and get the whole trade into their own hands, and then set their prices at pleasure: And therby in fine it will be as prejudicial to the Common-weath upon that accompt, as if the *Copy* of the Bible were Monopolized in the hands of one, or two particular persons.

VI. That (for the encouragement of such an Ingenious Mystery) the printing of the Bible (reserving alwayes the Interest, and propriety thereof in the *State*) may be committed to the care of so many able Master-Printers (as the State shall think fit) but to such especially, as have already printed Bibles best, and sold them cheapest. And that Order be taken, that the books shall alwayes be fairly printed in good paper, and in convenient Volumes, with the Marginal References, and so carefully revised, and corrected, by able men of the *English Nation*, and not of any other, (out of honour and respect to the propriety of our speech, according to the custome of all victorious Nations) before they be exposed to sale, and certified, that they are well, and truely printed. And that such persons, (and none others) be admitted (so long as they do well) to print the Bible: That it may be exactly done, and the Printers publickly known, to avoid the selling of forreign Bibles, or any other sort, that shall be basely, or irregularly printed.

VII. That no Printer be admitted to put any Title upon any Bible but his own, with his name, and Licence: That the Book, and Printer may be known by the goodnesse, or badnesse of the work; and one man may not use another mans name, or Title, whereby to vend, and put off his Books (under a penalty:) that so all people may know, what, and how they buy, and of them that print the best, and truest Bibles, and will sell them cheapest.

VIII. That if any of those Printers (so appointed to print) shall have printed an Impression: And upon examination it shall be found to be false printed: in such case no Certificate, or Licence to be given, that his Book hath been examined, and approved to be well, and rightly printed: And this *Order* being duely observed, will make Printers more vigilant to print true Bibles, in respect of the discredit, and losse that will fall upon them thereby.

IX. That he, or they, that shall (by Authority of the *State*) examine, and approve of the Impressions of any Bibles) may sign one of the said Books to be safely kept in some Treasury of Records: Which signature to be printed with the rest, as a Licence: And that if they prove faulty, the blame may be laid upon him, or them, and not on the Printers. For which care, approbation, and Licence, the particular Printers shall be at the charge of allowing to the said persons such yearly considerable sallary, as the *State* shall think fit.

X. That for as much, as the Bible (the word of GOD) is to be prized and esteemed above all wordly respects, (as well in Honour, of our dear and precious LORD, and Saviour *Jesus Christ*, as also in opposition to the Papists, Jews, Turks, Atheists, Infidels, Miscreants, and all other Sects of *Heterogeneous* principles,) That for the better regulation of the matters before proposed, the care thereof be delegated (in the Intervals of Parliament) to the principal Officers of *State*, and the *Courts* of Justice (*pro tempore*) as shall be held requisite by his *Highnesse*, and the *Parliament*: And not to be trusted with any Inferior Orders, or Degrees of men; Whereby an Intrinsecal value may be justly set upon the sacred Scriptures by the Authority of their Promulgation, as becometh the Holy, and innocent profession of *Christians*.

By Wm Kilburne

Source: Cambridge University Archives, CUR 33.6 (24); the subscription is in manuscript.

NOTES

Preface

1 *Grace Book* Θ, p. 428; McKenzie, *Cambridge University Press*, 1, pp. 94–5, 2, p. 1.

2 University Archives, Pr.v.1, Min.vi.1.

3 McKenzie, *Cambridge University Press*, 1, pp. 6–15; and 'Richard Bentley's design for the Cambridge University Press, c. 1696', *TCBS*, 6 (1976) pp. 322–7.

4 For a general, if idiosyncratic, view, see Stanley Morison, 'The learned press as an institution', in *Bibliotheca docet; Festgaber für Carl Wehmer* (Amsterdam 1963), repr. in his *Selected essays*, ed. D. McKitterick, 2 vols. (Cambridge 1980), pp. 361–82. His remarks on Thomas Thomas should be treated with caution. For Oxford in this respect, see Stanley Morison, *John Fell* (Oxford 1967), and Nicolas Barker, *Oxford University Press and the spread of learning* (Oxford 1978). For a recent discussion of the historic position at Cambridge, see Black, *Cambridge University Press*, pp. 265–83.

5 See below, p. 33.

6 Raymond Astbury, 'The renewal of the Licensing Act in 1693 and its lapse in 1695', *The Library*, 5th ser. 33 (1978), pp. 296–322.

7 Cf. J. Twigg, *The University of Cambridge and the English revolution, 1625–1688* (Woodbridge 1990), p. 84: [Roger Daniel] 'was only a functionary who published books on the orders of the Vice-chancellor of the day'. For licence (a very different concept from orders) see pp. 254–64 below.

1 Perspectives

1 E. A. Wrigley and R. S. Schofield, *The population history of England, 1541–1871* (Cambridge 1989), pp. 208–9, 528–9.

2 For terminology, and much of the technical background in the following pages, see Gaskell, *New introduction*, and Bernard Middleton, *A history of English craft bookbinding technique*, 2nd supplemented edn (1978).

3 D. F. McKenzie, 'Typography and meaning: the case of William Congreve', in G. Barber and B. Fabian, eds., *Buch und Buchhandel in Europa im achtzehnten Jahrhundert* (Hamburg 1981), pp. 81–125; and McKenzie, *Bibliography and the sociology of texts* (Panizzi Lectures, 1985) (1986); J. J. McGann, *A critique of modern textual criticism* (Chicago 1983); and McGann, *The beauty of inflections; literary investigations in historical method and theory* (Oxford 1988), especially chapter II, 'Textual studies and practical criticism' (see also McGann's review of McKenzie's Panizzi Lectures in the *London Review of Books*, 18 February 1988, pp. 20–1); G. Thomas Tanselle, *The history of books as a field of study* (Chapel Hill 1981: first published in the *Times Literary Supplement*, 5 June 1981); and Tanselle, 'Historicism and critical editing', *SB*, 39 (1986), pp. 1–46. Tanselle summarized

the position, as he saw it, in 1981: 'There has been a strange reluctance to recognize that what written or printed works say is affected by the physical means through which they are transmitted. Once one does understand this point, one perceives not only that every edition of a work may differ, but that every copy of every edition is a separate piece of historical evidence.' These points have been more readily appreciated by some medieval historians: see for example M. T. Clanchy, *From memory to written record 1066–1307* (1979) and R. McKitterick, *The Carolingians and the written word* (Cambridge 1989).

4 Graham Pollard, 'The Company of Stationers before 1557', *The Library*, 4th ser. 18 (1937), pp. 1–38; Blagden, *Stationers' Company*.

5 Sir C. Sibthorp, *A reply to an answere, made by a Popish adversarie, to ... A friendly advertisement* (Dublin 1625), fo. C1r; Harold Love, 'Scribal publication in seventeenth-century England', *TCBS*, 9 (1987), pp. 130–54; see further below, p. 242. In this context it may be remarked that Alan H. Nelson's *Cambridge* volumes for the *Records of early English drama* (Toronto 1989) record that of some sixty-five college plays known to survive from the period *c.* 1539–1642, thirty-eight survive in manuscript alone, and ten in print alone. Fifty-five plays survive in a total of 127 manuscripts. For other examples, cf. Sir Thomas Smith, *De republica Anglorum*, ed. Mary Dewar (Cambridge 1982); Peter Beal, *Index of English literary manuscripts*, 1 (1450–1625) (1980–), 2 (1625–1700), (1987–); and G. K. Fortescue, *Catalogue of the pamphlets ... collected by George Thomason, 1640–1661*, 2 vols. (1908), 1, pp. xxi–xxiii, 2, pp. 739–40. More generally, the vigorous arguments put forward by E. Eisenstein, *The printing press as an agent of change*, 2 vols. (Cambridge 1979), have been challenged by, among others, Anthony Grafton, 'The importance of being printed', *Journal of Interdisciplinary History*, 11 (1980), pp. 265–86. (For an extensive list of reviews of Eisenstein's work see Peter F. McNally, *The advent of printing: historians of science respond to Elizabeth Eisenstein's The printing press as an agent of change* (Graduate School of Library and Information Studies, McGill University, Occasional paper 10; Montreal 1987).)

6 Neil McKendrick, John Brewer and J. H. Plumb, *The birth of a consumer society; the commercialization of eighteenth-century England* (1982); E. Jones, 'The fashion manipulators: consumer tastes and British industries, 1660–1800', in *Business enterprise and economic change; essays in honor of Harold F. Williamson*, ed. L. P. Cain and Paul J. Uselding (Kent, Ohio 1973), pp. 198–226.

7 [Edward Polhill], *The Samaritan* (1682), p. 1. Cf. also J.-F. Gilmont, 'Introduction', to *La réforme et le livre; l'Europe de l'imprimé (1517–v. 1570)*, ed. J. F. Gilmont, (Paris 1990), pp. 10–11.

8 Ecclesiastes xii.12; Juvenal, *Satires* VII.52; H. S. Bennett, *English books & readers 1558 to 1603* (Cambridge 1965), pp. 3–4, 267–8.

9 D. Cressy, *Literacy and the social order; reading and writing in Tudor and Stuart England* (Cambridge 1980), p. 47. Cressy's summary of the principal statistics of the number of editions published each year in the sixteenth and seventeenth centuries can now be supplemented by P. Rider's chronological index in *STC*, vol. 3. There are however still no comprehensive estimates for the period as a whole, while Rider's figures are at once over-comprehensive for this purpose (being based on *STC*'s bibliographical distinctions, which often allocate several numbers to the same edition, and record even the most minute piece of print with as much care as the fattest book) and inadequate in that they cannot include the many books now entirely lost: on this see Franklin B. Williams, 'Lost books of Tudor England', *The Library*, 5th ser. 33 (1978), pp. 1–14.

10 [William London], *Catalogue; the most vendible books in England* (1657), fo. B2v.

11 Margaret Spufford, *Small books and pleasant histories* (1981), pp. 91–101.

12 See below, pp. 205–6, 332–3. In 1587 the Stationers' Company agreed measures that restricted edition sizes to not more than 1,500 copies, save for some specified works, including

393

grammars, accidences, Bibles in octavo, Psalters in 32°, proclamations, statutes, almanacs and works printed by Her Majesty's Printers requiring larger editions for government purposes (Arber, II.43; Greg, *Companion*, pp. 43–4; Greg and Boswell, pp. lvi, 25).

13 Wilmer G. Mason, 'The annual output of Wing-listed titles, 1649–1684', *The Library*, 5th ser. 29 (1974), pp. 219–20; John M. Wallace, 'The Engagement Controversy 1649–1652; an annotated list of pamphlets', *BNYPL*, 68 (1984), pp. 384–405; Mark Goldie, 'The revolution of 1689 and the structure of political argument', *Bulletin of Research in the Humanities*, 83 (1980), pp. 473–564. I am grateful to Maureen Bell for her provisional analysis (presented at a conference at Kenilworth in December 1990) of the chronological index by Philip Rider contained in *STC*, vol. 3. I have deliberately rounded the figures for the 1580s up slightly, to take account of books now lost.

14 Wing, C5630, G496; cf. *Narcissus Luttrell's Popish Plot catalogues*, introd. F. C. Francis (Luttrell Soc. 1956), a facsimile of Luttrell's interleaved and annotated copies (now in the British Library) of the *Continuation* and *Second Continuation*. One of the largest of such collections, offered at Sotheby's 23–4 July 1987, Lot 262, is now in Cambridge University Library.

15 Cressy, *Literacy and the social order*, esp. chs. 3 and 7; Spufford, *Small books and pleasant histories*, esp. chs. 2 and 3.

16 Sears Jayne, *Library catalogues of the English renaissance*, 2nd edn (Winchester 1983); Ian Philip, *The Bodleian Library in the seventeenth and eighteenth centuries* (Oxford 1983), pp. 44–7; Oates, *Cambridge University Library*, pp. 258–64.

17 J. W. Clark, *The care of books* (Cambridge 1909), pp. 165–88; N. Pevsner, *A history of building types* (1976), pp. 101–2; N. R. Ker, 'Oxford college libraries in the sixteenth century', *Bodleian Library Record*, 6 (1957–61), pp. 459–515, repr. in his *Books, collectors and libraries; studies in the medieval heritage* (1985), pp. 379–436.

18 J. W. Clark, *The care of books*, pp. 277, 280–2, with illustration; Wren's designs are reproduced in the Wren Society, vol. 5 (1928), plates xv–xxvi, and in M. Whinney, *Wren* (1971), p. 138. For a general survey of this subject, albeit one with a German bias, see E. Hanebutt-Benz, *Die Kunst des Lesens; Lesemöbel und Leseverhalten vom Mittelalter bis zur Gegenwart* (Frankfurt am Main 1985).

19 Cf. R. Clavell, *General catalogue of books printed in England … to the end of Trinity Term MDCLXXX* (1680), 'To the reader'. For auctions, see J. Lawler, *Book auctions in England in the seventeenth century* (1898), and Pollard and Ehrman, pp. 216–48. Auctions had been long established in the Low Countries: see B. van Selm, *Een menighte treffelijcke Boecken; Nederlandse boekhandelscatalogi in het begin van de zeventiende eeuw* (Utrecht 1987). For booksellers' anxiety at the effect of auction sales on existing practices at Leiden in 1608, see J. G. C. Briels, *Zuidnederlandse boekdrukkers en boekverkopers in de Republiek der Verenigde Nederlanden omstreeks 1570–1630* (Nieuwkoop 1974), pp. 562–4, and van Selm, pp. 33–5, 65.

20 Andrew Maunsell, *Catalogue* (1595), fo. π4r. For the allied question of bibliographical handbooks in the sixteenth and seventeenth centuries, see Archer Taylor, *Renaissance guides to books* (Berkeley 1945); and *Book catalogues; their varieties and uses*, 2nd edn, rev. William P. Barlow, Jr (Winchester 1986); Theodore Besterman, *Les débuts de la bibliographie méthodique*, 3e edn (Paris 1950).

21 William London, *Catalogue*, fo. B2v.

22 Marian Eames, 'John Ogilby and his Aesop; the fortunes and foibles of a seventeenth-century virtuoso', *BNYPL*, 65 (1961), pp. 73–88, reproducing the notice for Ogilby's first lottery [1665]; for his second lottery, a few months later, see *The Gentleman's Magazine*, 84, pt 1 (1814), pp. 646–8. For earlier lotteries, see also S. L. C. Clapp, 'The subscription enterprises of John Ogilby and Richard Blome', *Modern Philology*, 30 (1933), pp. 365–79.

23 F. Dahl, *A bibliography of English corantos and periodical newsbooks, 1620–1642* (Bibliographical Soc. 1952), pp. 31–41; *The first newspapers of England printed in Holland, 1620–1621* (The Hague 1914; facsimiles); and 'Amsterdam, cradle of English newspapers', *The Library*, 5th ser. 4 (1949), pp. 166–78; M. A. Shaaber, *Some fore-runners of the newspaper in England, 1476–1622* (Philadelphia 1929); S. Morison, *The English newspaper* (Cambridge 1932) and 'The origins of the newspaper', *Selected essays*, ed. D. McKitterick, 2 vols. (Cambridge 1980), 2, pp. 325–57; D. C. Collins, *Handlist of news pamphlets, 1590–1610* (1943); J. C. T. Oates, 'The trewe encountre: a pamphlet on Flodden Field', *TCBS*, 1 (1950), pp. 126–9; Joseph Frank, *The beginnings of the English newspaper, 1620–1660* (Cambridge, Mass. 1961).

24 C. Nelson and M. Seccombe, *British newspapers and periodicals, 1641–1700* (New York 1987).

25 R. M. Wiles, *Serial publication in England before 1750* (Cambridge 1957); M. Treadwell, 'London trade publishers, 1675–1750', *The Library*, 6th ser. 4 (1982), pp. 99–134; S. L. C. Clapp, 'The subscription enterprises of John Ogilby'; and 'Subscription publishers prior to Jacob Tonson', *The Library*, 4th ser. 13 (1933), pp. 158–83; J. Barnard, 'Dryden, Tonson and subscriptions for the 1697 Virgil', *PBSA*, 57 (1963), pp. 129–51; Pollard and Ehrman, pp. 178–95. Wiles suggests that the first English 'number book' was Moxon's *Mechanick exercises* (1677–83); but cf. Richard Yonge, *The poores advocate* (1654), described as being of eight parts: 'If any shall ask, why this Treatise is cast into so many several Divisions, and sold single? I answer, even for her sake that sells them, and others that buy them; it faring with *Books* offered, as with *Briefs*: for let the charge be great or small; mans bounty shall be still the same, and many peny-Books, will sell for one of two pence or three pence price' (D. F. McKenzie, *Bibliography Newsletter*, 1, no. 8 (1973), p. 11). For early examples in Amsterdam and Hamburg, see Peter T. van Rooden and Jan Wim Wesselius, 'Two early cases of publication by subscription in Holland and Germany: Jacob Abendana's *Mikhlal Yophi* (1661) and David Cohen de Lara's *Keter Kehunna* (1668)', *Quaerendo*, 16 (1986), pp. 110–30. For France, see Wallace Kirsop, 'Pour une histoire bibliographique de la souscription en France au XVIIIe siècle', in *Trasmissione dei testi a stampa nel periodo moderno*, ed. G. Crapulli, 2 vols. (Rome 1985–7), 2, pp. 255–82, with further references.

26 Helen M. Wallis, 'Geographie is better than divinitie: maps, globes and geography in the days of Samuel Pepys', in *The compleat plattmaker; essays on chart, map and globe making in England in the seventeenth and eighteenth centuries*, ed. Norman J. W. Thrower (Berkeley 1978), pp. 1–43; David A. Woodward, 'English cartography, 1650–1750; a summary', *ibid.*, pp. 159–93; Sarah Tyacke, *London map-sellers, 1660–1720* (Tring 1978); Sir H. G. Fordham, 'John Ogilby (1600–1676); his *Britannia* and the British itineraries of the eighteenth century', *The Library*, 4th ser. 6 (1925), pp. 157–78; R. A. Skelton, *County atlases of the British Isles, 1579–1850* (1970). For the first printed pilot guide (Waghenaer's *Spieghel der zeevaerdt*, 1584), see C. Koeman, 'Lucas Janszoon Waghenaer: a sixteenth century marine cartographer', *Geographical Jnl*, 131 (1965), pp. 202–17, repr. in his *Miscellanea cartographica* (Utrecht 1988), pp. 49–66; Koeman, 'The lead by the Dutch in world charting in the seventeenth and first half of the eighteenth century', *Procs. Royal Society of Edinburgh*, ser. 3, 73 (1971–2), pp. 47–53, repr. in *Miscellanea cartographica*, pp. 213–20; and Koeman, *Atlantes Neerlandici; bibliography of terrestrial, maritime and celestial atlases and pilot books, published in the Netherlands up to 1880*, 6 vols. (Amsterdam 1967–85). For the business press, see especially John J. McCusker, 'The business press in England before 1775', *The Library*, 6th ser. 8 (1986), pp. 205–31. For music, see Charles C. Humphries and William C. Smith, *Music publishing in the British Isles*, 2nd edn (Oxford 1970), pp. 6–20, and D. W. Krummel, *English music printing 1553–1700* (Bibliographical Soc. 1975).

27 The following remarks are generally confined to books in Britain. For a continental perspective, albeit one to be viewed cautiously, see the summary in L. Febvre and H.-J. Martin, *L'apparition du livre* (Paris 1958), ch. 3, translated as *The coming of the book; the impact of printing 1450–1800* (1976), pp. 77–108. For France, see especially H.-J. Martin, *Livre, pouvoirs et société à Paris au XVIIe siècle (1598–1701)*, 2 vols. (Geneva 1969), and H.-J. Martin, Roger Chartier and Jean-Pierre Vivet, eds., *Histoire de l'édition française. 1. Le livre conquérant, du moyen âge au milieu du XVIIe siècle* (Paris 1982).

28 Peter Thornton, *Seventeenth-century interior decoration in England, France & Holland* (New Haven 1978), pp. 303–15; J. W. Clark, *The care of books*, 2nd edn (Cambridge 1902). The first of Pepys' celebrated glazed bookcases was supplied to him in 1666, and is now in Magdalene College, Cambridge. For an example of a late sixteenth-century wall bookcase, or *bufet*, see the *Premier volume de la bibliothèque du Sieur de la Croix-Du Maine* (Paris 1584), fo. Vv4r. See also, for France more generally, Claude Jolly, 'Bâtiments, mobilier, décors', in *Histoire des bibliothèques françaises. 2. Les bibliothèques sous l'Ancien Régime*, ed. C. Jolly (Paris 1988), pp. 361–71.

29 Graham Pollard, 'Changes in the style of bookbindings, 1550–1830', *The Library*, 5th ser. 11 (1956), pp. 71–94; H. M. Nixon, *Broxbourne Library; styles and designs of bookbindings from the twelfth to the twentieth century* (1956), pp. 114–16; and *Five centuries of English bookbindings* (1978), pp. 79–81 (Foxe's *Book of martyrs*, bound in 1660). For examples of the many books bound in the following decades without spine titles, see for example *ibid.*, nos. 37, 38, 41, 42, and Maggs Brothers, *Catalogue*, no. 1075 (1987), nos. 67, 71, etc. By no means all these bindings were on books intended to lie flat, as a prayer book or anthem book might in a chapel. But the gradual change in practice proved overwhelming. For Dennis, see Gray and Palmer, p. 57. The 'alphabet of Roman letters' owned by Dennis (Gray and Palmer, p. 56) cannot have been intended for lettering spines; it was more probably used for lettering the boards of books, either with owners' initials (such as Andrew Perne's books at Peterhouse) or perhaps for music part books. In 1604, Manasses Vautrollier (see below, pp. 122–3) was said to own 'xxj smale letters', valued at 2s.6d. (University Archives, VC Ct III.11 (29)). For Williamson, see Nixon, *Broxbourne Library*, pp. 115–16.

30 G. Naudé, *Instructions concerning erecting of a library*, translated by John Evelyn (1661), p. 84.

31 Roll tools appear however on Oxford bindings as late as 1620: see N. R. Ker, *Pastedowns in Oxford bindings* (Oxford Bibliographical Soc. 1954), p. 214; Maggs, *Catalogue*, 1075 (1987), no. 27; J. B. Oldham, *Blind panels of English binders* (Cambridge 1958), p. 2.

32 Gray, *Earlier Cambridge stationers*.

33 H. M. Nixon, *Broxbourne Library*, p. 119, describing a gold-blocked binding. For gold tooling in England in the early sixteenth century more generally, see Nixon, 'Early English gold-tooled bookbindings', *Studi di bibliografia e di storia, in onore di Tammaro de Marinis*, 3 (Verona 1964), pp. 283–306; A. R. A. Hobson, *Humanists and bookbinders* (Cambridge 1989); H. M. Nixon, *Sixteenth-century gold-tooled bookbindings in the Pierpont Morgan Library* (New York 1971), pp. 2–5; but cf. also the exceptional gilded Romanesque binding on Pierpont Morgan Library, MS M338, a Psalter from northern France, *c.* 1190–5, described in Paul Needham, *Twelve centuries of bookbindings, 400–1600* (New York 1979), pp. 61–4.

34 Middleton, *English craft bookbinding technique*, pp. 65–6.

35 Douglas Cockerell, *Some notes on bookbinding* (Oxford 1929), p. 47: 'The old calf used in the fifteenth century was the skin of a beast somewhere about a year old, and has some of the qualities of hide.' English skins were oak tanned; the younger (and thinner) the skin the less time was required in the bath, so resulting in lighter colours at the end.

36 H. M. Nixon, 'Elizabethan gold-tooled bindings', in *Essays in honour of Victor Scholderer*,

ed. D. E. Rhodes (Mainz 1970), pp. 219–70, at 233–43. 'At this date it is correct to talk of turkey leather rather than morocco, since it is doubtful if leather from Morocco was used in England at all extensively before 1721' (p. 237).

37 Middleton, *English craft bookbinding technique*, p. 160.

38 Pepys, *Diary*, 8 July 1664 (ed. Latham and Matthews, 5, p. 199); H. M. Nixon, *Catalogue of the Pepys Library*. 6. *Bindings* (Woodbridge 1984), p. xiii, plate 2 (SP 2365). Pepys owned two copies of Chaucer. The other (SP 2053, Westminster (Caxton) [1483]: Duff 88) is in one of his standard bindings of sprinkled calf (Nixon, *Bindings*, p. 30, plate 13).

39 C. E. Wright, 'The dispersal of the libraries in the sixteenth century', in *The English library before 1700*, ed. F. Wormald and C. E. Wright (1958), pp. 148–75.

40 Ker, *Pastedowns*, pp. vii–viii. It will be gathered from these dates that the dissolution of monastic libraries did not necessarily make as great a contribution to the history of the morphology of the book as did the casting aside of unwanted manuscripts by secular bodies and private individuals. For the use of manuscripts as binding materials at Canterbury in the second half of the sixteenth century, see N. R. Ker, *Medieval manuscripts in British libraries*, 2 (Oxford 1977), pp. 312–30.

41 Mirjam M. Foot, 'Some bookbinders' price lists of the seventeenth and eighteenth centuries', *De libris compactis miscellanea*, ed. G. Colin (Aubel 1984), pp. 273–319.

42 Cf., for example, the Peterborough Cathedral copy of William Lambard, *Eirenarcha* (1581) with one in Cambridge University Library (Q*.12.38(E)): both are in limp vellum, with yapp edges and decorated with the same ornaments, gilt. Two copies of George Ruggle, *Ignoramus* (1630) in Cambridge University Library (Syn.8.63.385, 386) and one in Trinity College (Grylls 32.40) are in identical calf bindings, decorated in gilt in the same manner.

43 J. C. T. Oates, 'Cambridge books of congratulatory verses, 1603–1640, and their binders', *TCBS*, 1 (1953), pp. 395–421.

44 For priced books where the cost of binding is included, see *Term Catalogues*. For examples of other catalogues in this period listing specifically *bound* and *priced* books, cf. those of John Starkey (appended to Nicolas Perrault, *The Jesuits morals*, 1670), T. Sowle (appended to George Fox, *A collection of epistles*, 1698), and Joseph Marshal (appended to Edmund Hickeringill, *Works*, vols. 2–3, 1716): examples of all three are in Trinity College Library. By these dates, the practice of selling bound books at fixed prices seems to have been established: cf., for example, Pietro Paravicino, *The true idioma of the Italian tongue* (8°, Printed by E. C., sold by H. Seile *et al.*, 1660), which had printed on its title-page 'At 1s.6d. Bound.' Some aspects of the identification of decorative binding tools with particular publishers are discussed in H. de la Fontaine Verwey, 'Amsterdam publishers' bindings from about 1600', *Quaerendo*, 5 (1975), pp. 283–302.

45 Graham Pollard, 'Notes on the size of the sheet', *The Library*, 4th ser. 22 (1941), pp. 105–37; Roger Stoddard, 'Morphology and the book', *Printing History*, 9 (1987), pp. 2–14; Gaskell, *New introduction*, pp. 66–8 (derived from conversations with A. H. Stevenson).

46 H. Hornschuch (*Orthotypographia*, ed. and translated by Philip Gaskell and Patricia Bradford (Cambridge 1972)) wrote in 1608 of printing on 'almost crumbling, dust-coloured paper'.

47 The celebrated engraving of Caxton presenting his *Recuyell of the historyes of Troye* [Bruges? 1474] to Margaret of York (reproduced in A. M. Hind, *Engraving in England in the sixteenth & seventeenth centuries*, 1 (Cambridge 1952), plate 1; Lotte Hellinga, *Caxton in focus* (1982), fig. 6) is Flemish, and need not date from 1474. On Geminus, see Hind, pp. 39–58, and plates 17–28. But cf. also *STC*, 21153 (Eucharius Roesslin, *The byrth of mankynde*, 1540), a few copies of which were provided with engraved plates. For

comparison, see Michel Pastoureau, 'L'illustration du livre: comprendre ou rêver?', *Histoire de l'édition française*, 1, pp. 501–29, and bibliography, pp. 608–9.

48 Ludovico Ariosto, *Orlando Furioso in English heroical verse*, translated by John Harington (1591), fo. A1r. The book by Broughton to which he refers is *A concent of scripture* (1590? *STC*, 3850ff.). See also Hind, *Engraving in England*, 1, pp. 251–2, 295–6, and plate 132, and (for the Venice original) Ruth Mortimer, *Harvard College Library*, *Dept of Printing and Graphic Arts. Catalogue of books and manuscripts*. Pt II. *Italian 16th century books*, 2 vols. (Cambridge, Mass. 1974), 1, pp. 37–43.

49 *Anvers, ville de Plantin et de Rubens* (Bibliothèque Nationale 1954); *P. P. Rubens als boekillustrator* (Plantin-Moretus Museum 1977); J. Richard Judson and Carl van de Velde, *Book illustrations and title-pages* (Corpus Rubenianum Ludwig Burchard 21), 2 vols. (1978). For Paris, see H.-J. Martin, *Livre, pouvoirs et société à Paris au XVIIe siècle (1598–1701)*, 2 vols. (Geneva 1969), 1, pp. 346–56, 381–6. There is as yet no survey as wide-ranging for England as Marianne Grivel, *Le commerce de l'estampe à Paris au xviie siècle* (Geneva 1986): see however Hind, *Engraving in England*; R. Pennington, *A descriptive catalogue of the etched work of Wenceslaus Hollar 1607–1677* (Cambridge 1982); Alexander Globe, *Peter Stent, London printseller circa 1642–1665* (Vancouver 1985); Leona Rostenberg, *English publishers in the graphic arts 1599–1700* (New York 1963).

50 A. F. Johnson, *A catalogue of engraved and etched English title-pages down to the death of William Faithorne, 1691* (Bibliographical Soc. 1934); M. Corbett and R. Lightbown, *The comely frontispiece; the emblematic title-page in England, 1550–1660* (1979); Philip Hofer, *Baroque book illustration*, 2nd printing, with new introductory material (Cambridge, Mass. 1951).

51 John Evelyn, *Sculptura: or the history, and art of chalcography ... to which is annexed a new manner of engraving, or mezzo tinto* (1662). William Faithorne, *The art of graveing and etching* (1662), a partial translation of Abraham Bosse's *Traicté des manières de graver en taille douce sur l'airin* (1645). See also Howard C. Levis, *Extracts from the diaries and correspondence of John Evelyn and Samuel Pepys relating to engraving* (1915); Antony Griffiths, 'Early mezzotint publishing in England. I. John Smith, 1652–1743', *Print Quarterly*, 6 (1989), pp. 243–57.

52 E.g. George Henderson, 'Bible illustration in the age of Laud', *TCBS*, 8 (1982), pp. 173–216. See also below, pp. 327–8.

53 Harry Carter, *A view of early typography* (Oxford 1969); F. Isaac, *English & Scottish printing types 1501–35 * 1508–41* (Bibliographical Soc. 1930).

54 Giovanni Mardersteig, 'Aldo Manuzio e i caratteri di Franceso Griffo da Bologna', *Studi di bibliografia e di storia in onore di Tammaro de Marinis* (Verona 1964), 3, pp. 105–47, at pp. 132–3; Nicolas Barker, 'The Aldine Roman in Paris, 1530–1534', *The Library*, 5th ser. 29 (1974), pp. 5–20; W. Craig Ferguson, *Pica Roman type in Elizabethan England* (Aldershot 1989); J. G. Dreyfus et al., eds., *Type specimen facsimiles 1–18*, 2 vols. (1963–72); H. D. L. Vervliet, *Sixteenth-century printing types of the Low Countries* (Amsterdam 1968). For Haultin, see below, p. 83; for Guyot, see also J. G. C. A. Briels *Zuidnederlandse boekdrukkers en boekverkopers in de Republiek der Verenigde Nederlanden omstreeks 1570–1630* (Nieuwkoop 1974), pp. 292–303, etc. For the design of French books, and more general remarks on sixteenth- and seventeenth-century lay-out, see, for example, Roger Laufer, 'L'espace visuel du livre ancien', *Histoire de l'édition française*, 1, pp. 479–97.

55 T. B. Reed, *A history of the Old English letter foundries*, revised by A. F. Johnson (1952).

56 Voet, *Golden compasses*, 2, pp. 80, 108, etc; Dreyfus et al., *Type specimen facsimiles*, 2, pp. 6–11, with reproductions.

57 Charles Enschedé, *Typefoundries in the Netherlands from the fifteenth to the nineteenth*

century, translated and ed. H. Carter, N. Hoeflake, Lotte Hellinga (Haarlem 1978); Stanley Morison, *John Fell* (Oxford 1967); David McKitterick, 'A type specimen of Christoffel van Dijck?', *Quaerendo*, 7 (1977), pp. 66–75.

58 György Haiman, *Nicholas Kis, a Hungarian punch-cutter and printer, 1650–1702* (San Francisco 1983), especially pp. 33–65, with a useful selection of illustrations.

59 Moxon, *Mechanick exercises*, pp. 22–3; his own type specimen of 1669 is reproduced at the end of Davis and Carter's edition.

60 P. S. Fournier, *Manuel typographique* (Paris 1764–6 [8]), 2, pp. vii–viii.

61 For a general, and partisan, summary, see H. de la Fontaine Verwey, 'The seventeenth century', in *Copy and print in the Netherlands; an atlas of historical bibliography*, ed. W. Gs. Hellinga (Amsterdam 1962), pp. 29–42.

62 Morison, *John Fell*, pp. 70–2, 134–49; McKenzie, *Cambridge University Press*, 1, pp. 36–7, 52, 370–411.

63 H. C. Darby, *The draining of the fens*, 2nd edn (Cambridge 1956); and *The changing fenland* (Cambridge 1983), pp. 92–102; C. Taylor, *The Cambridgeshire landscape: Cambridge and the southern fens* (1973), pp. 188–202; N. J. Williams, *The maritime trade of the East Anglian ports 1550–1590* (Oxford 1988), pp. 55–7. Unfortunately the King's Lynn Water Bailiff's accounts provide little detail of the shipping trade between Cambridge and the sea. For the local countryside more generally see M. Spufford, *Contrasting communities: English villages in the sixteenth and seventeenth centuries* (Cambridge 1974) and J. R. Ravensdale, *Liable to floods; village landscape on the edge of the fens, A.D. 450–1850* (Cambridge 1974).

64 R. Thoresby, *Diary*, ed. J. Hunter (1830), 1, pp. 68, 295. See also S. Pepys, *Diary*, ed. R. Latham and William Matthews (1970–83), 1, p. 66; 2, p. 180; 9, p. 210; 10 (*Companion*), pp. 448–56; Joan Parkes, *Travel in England in the seventeenth century* (Oxford 1925); John Ogilby, *Britannia*, 1 (all published, 1675). Instead of the route via Ware and Barkway, travellers could also choose one via Hadham and Saffron Walden: this was described in the late sixteenth century as 'better' by William Harrison (*The description of England*, ed. G. Edelen (Ithaca, N.Y. 1968), p. 403), but Harrison had personal reasons for preferring Essex.

65 E. A. Wrigley, 'A simple model of London's importance in changing English society and economy, 1650–1750', *Past and Present*, 37 (1967), pp. 44–70, with further references; K. Fairclough, 'A Tudor canal scheme for the River Lea', *London Journal*, 5 (1979), pp. 218–27. The principal heavy commodities carried from south Cambridgeshire to London were grain and hops, and the wagons caused considerable wear to the roads. See Nigel R. Goose, 'Economic and social aspects of provincial towns; a comparative study of Cambridge, Colchester and Reading, c. 1500–1700' (PhD, Cambridge 1984), pp. 39–41, 142. For details of Cambridge's land and water links more generally, see Mary C. Siraut, 'Some aspects of the economic and social history of Cambridge under Elizabeth' (MLitt Cambridge, 1978).

66 Robert Jahn, 'Letters and booklists of Thomas Chard (or Chare) of London, 1583–4', *The Library*, 4th ser. 4 (1924), pp. 219–37: Chard sent his books and other goods by the much celebrated Thomas Hobson. Stationers' Company, 'Journal book of money disbursed, 1650–98', at 2 January 1650/1 (£10 paid to the carrier, on Legate's instructions), 29 August 1651 (120 reams of an almanac brought from Cambridge), etc. In 1654–5 the carrier is named as Ashpole. In 1625, books brought by carrier (again including Hobson) for the Cambridge stationers Leonard Greene and William Williams were to be aired as a precaution against plague (University Archives, T.X.19, fo. 7). In 1591 Hobson charged the Cambridge bookseller Reginald Bridges sums between a penny and fourpence for carrying parcels of books, but unfortunately neither their origins, destinations nor contents are recorded. He also charged sixpence for the carriage of two

reams of small-size paper, presumably from London (University Archives, VC Ct III.2 (89)).

67 T. De-Laune, *The present state of London* (1681), pp. 394–5; F. Clifford, *A history of private bill legislation* (1887), 2, pp. 12–13, 55; W. Albert, *The turnpike road system in England 1663–1840* (Cambridge 1972), pp. 17–20; J. A. Chartres, 'Road carrying in England in the seventeenth century; myth and reality', *Economic History Review*, 2nd ser. 30 (1977), pp. 73–94, but see also his subsequent exchanges with C. H. Wilson, *ibid.*, 2nd ser. 33 (1980), pp. 92–9. In 1585 the Norwich carrier could be met at Babraham, en route from the south (University Archives, Comm. Ct III.3, concerning the delivery of a parcel of books including Cooper's Latin dictionary, a Greek grammar, and a volume of Cicero). For the early book trade in King's Lynn, see David Stoker, 'The early printers and booksellers of King's Lynn', in *Studies in the provincial book trade of England, Scotland and Wales before 1900*, ed. D. Stoker (Aberystwyth 1990), pp. 76–105.

68 Philip Gaskell, 'Notes on eighteenth-century British paper', *The Library*, 5th ser. 12 (1957), pp. 34–42. Writing paper was heavier.

69 Despite the Stationers' Company guidelines, this was not unusual: Thomas Thomas still had 1,381 copies left of Whitaker's *Disputatio* (1588: 67½ sheets per copy) when he died later that year (Gray and Palmer, p. 68).

70 Cf. the appeal from the University to its Chancellor, the Earl of Holland, in 1629/30, that Hobson the carrier be allowed to continue to use four-wheeled vehicles, so that he could continue to carry not only fish, but also books (Cooper, *Annals*, 5, p. 373).

71 F. W. Maitland and M. Bateson, eds., *The charters of the borough of Cambridge* (Cambridge 1901), pp. 96–8.

72 William Camden, *Britain*, translated by P. Holland (1610).

73 Cooper, *Annals*, 2, pp. 18–21. Maitland and Bateson, *Charters*, pp. 109–11. See also T. S. Willan, *The inland trade* (Manchester 1976), pp. 52–3.

74 VCH, *Cambs.*, 3, p. 93; Cooper, *Annals*, 3, p. 103 (the cost of the passes was ten shillings: they were printed by Legge).

75 Cooper, *Annals*, 3, p. 445; see also Darby, *The draining of the fens*, pp. 18–19, 103. It was claimed in 1725 that before the Denver Sluice was built in the mid-seventeenth century, the river above Ely had been at least five feet deeper (T. Badeslade, *The history of the … navigation of the port of King's Lynn* (1725), p. 62).

76 [Ned Ward], *A step to Stir-bitch fair* (1700), pp. 13, 15–16. Many of the known facts concerning the fair at this period are assembled in J. E. B. Mayor, ed., *Cambridge under Queen Anne* (Cambridge 1911), pp. 239–51. The fullest account of the fair is assembled in Mary Siraut, 'Some aspects', pp. 73–110.

77 Lawler, *Book auctions in England*, pp. 70–3.

78 Legate to an unidentified London bookseller, 29 August 1593, in M. S. G. Hands, 'The cathedral libraries catalogue', *The Library*, 5th ser. 2 (1947), pp. 1–13, at pp. 9–10. For controls, see Cooper, *Annals*, 2, p. 396.

79 University Archives, Comm. Ct v.7, p. 338, 9 September 1602; on Bankworth, see McKerrow, *Dictionary*, pp. 17–18.

80 University Archives, Comm. Ct v.9, fo. 88r; McKerrow, *Dictionary*, p. 291. Comm. Ct v.9, fo. 87v; McKerrow, *Dictionary*, p. 126.

81 See below, p. 347.

82 John Dunton, *Life and errors* (1818), p. 222; Stationers' Company 'Journal book for money disbursed, 1650–1698', September 1696. For the English Stock see below, p. 412, n. 27.

83 *A step to Stir-bitch fair* (1700), p. 15. For a mid-seventeenth-century survey of the booths, row by row, in the fair, see Downing College MS Bowtell 37 (a later copy); for a sketch-map of the fair, see *Bibliotheca topographica Britannica*, 5 (1790), opposite p. 73. The

modern Garlic Row, Mercers' Row and Oyster Road still approximately reflect the fair's topography.

84 Wrigley and Schofield, pp. 208–9, 531–3, 571. The change was very unequally distributed in Cambridgeshire: see M. Spufford, *Contrasting communities* (n. 63 above), pp. 18–28.

85 Wrigley and Schofield, p. 472; R. Finlay and B. Shearer, 'Population growth and social expansion', in *London 1500–1700; the making of the metropolis* ed. A. L. Beier and R. Finlay (1986), pp. 37–59, especially p. 39; A. L. Beier, 'Engines of manufacture: the trades of London', *ibid.*, pp. 141–67.

86 L. Stone, 'The size and composition of the Oxford student body, 1580–1910', in *The university in society*, ed. L. Stone, 2 vols. (Princeton 1974–5), 1, pp. 3–110, table 1B (p. 92); J. D. Twigg, *The University of Cambridge and the English revolution, 1625–1688* (Woodbridge 1990), p. i; J. Gascoigne, *Cambridge in the age of the Enlightenment* (Cambridge 1989), p. 17; W. R. Prest, *The Inns of Court under Elizabeth I and the early Stuarts, 1590–1640* (1972), pp. 6, 16, 19–20; J. Morgan, *Godly learning* (Cambridge 1986), pp. 229, 263–8; Joan Simon, *Education and society in Tudor England* (Cambridge 1967), pp. 353–7.

87 J. Caius, *Historiae Cantabrigiensis Academiae* (1574), in *Works*, ed. J. Venn and E. S. Roberts (Cambridge 1912), pp. 43–64; British Library MS Lansdowne 33, no. 43; John Ivory, *The foundation of the University of Cambridge* (Cambridge 1672); Cooper, *Annals*, 2, pp. 269, 315–16 (correcting Caius' arithmetic), 3, p. 148; Christopher Wordsworth, *Social life at the English universities in the eighteenth century* (Cambridge 1874), pp. 641–3; W. W. Rouse Ball, *Trinity College, Cambridge* (1906), p. 51.

88 Willis and Clark, 1, pp. 142, 260, 298, 625; 2, pp. 246–8; Oates, *Cambridge University Library*, pp. 89–118, 123–6; David Cressy, *Literacy and the social order* (Cambridge 1980), pp. 168, 171; Frank Stubbings, ed., *The statutes of Sir Walter Mildmay Kt…for the government of Emmanuel College* (Cambridge 1983); Victor Morgan, 'Approaches to the history of the English universities in the sixteenth and seventeenth centuries', in *Bildung, Politik und Gesellschaft*, ed. G. Klingenstein, H. Lutz and G. Stourzh (Wiener Beiträge zur Geschichte der Neuzeit 5, Vienna 1978), pp. 138–64. See also Mark H. Curtis, *Oxford and Cambridge in transition, 1558–1642* (Oxford 1959), p. 3. Two returns of members made to Cecil survive, for 1575 and 1589. Invaluably, they provide individual names, but that for 1575 lists about 450 people fewer than the figures given by Caius two years earlier. In 1589 the number of those attending lectures was given as 1,671, but it is not clear on what basis this was calculated (British Library, MSS Lansdowne 20, fos. 200–15, and Lansdowne 57, fos. 213–19). On these lists, see also M. Feingold, *The mathematicians' apprenticeship; science, universities and society in England, 1560–1640* (Cambridge 1984), pp. 46–7.

89 C. W. Scott-Giles, *Sidney Sussex College; a short history* (Cambridge 1975).

90 Historical MSS Commn, *Salisbury*, 12, pp. 187–8 (Harington to Sir Robert Cecil, 7 June 1602).

91 Willis and Clark, 1, pp. 93–102; 2, pp. 98–106, 201–5, 474–95, 517–19.

92 Willis and Clark, 2, pp. 19–20; Thomas Fuller, *Church-history of Britain* (1655), *History of the University of Cambridge*, p. 167. Fuller went on to explain that particular attention was paid to chapels, and to the installation of organs: 'yet some took great distaste thereat as attendancie to superstition' (*ibid.*).

93 Baker–Mayor, 1, pp. 208–10; Willis and Clark, 2, pp. 263–71; R. F. Scott, 'Notes from the College records', *The Eagle*, 17 (1891–2), pp. 1–15, etc.; Willis and Clark, 2, pp. 531–47; Philip Gaskell and Robert Robson, *The library of Trinity College, Cambridge* (Cambridge 1971); Philip Gaskell, *Trinity College library; the first 150 years* (Cambridge 1980).

94 Oates, *Cambridge University Library*, pp. 159–71, 247–53.

95 J. W. Clark, *The care of books*, pp. 248–9; Willis and Clark, 1, pp. 33, 136, 149, 200; 2, pp. 165, 531–51, 710; 3, pp. 451–68.

96 *Historical register*, pp. 81–4; Clark, *Endowments*, pp. 165–80.

97 H. F. Howard, *An account of the finances of the College of St John the Evangelist* (Cambridge 1935), pp. 63–70; V. Morgan, 'Approaches to the history of the English universities', pp. 148–56; J. Gascoigne, *Cambridge in the age of the Enlightenment*, pp. 15–16.

98 For general remarks on the ownership of books in a non-university context, see P. Clark, 'The ownership of books in England, 1560–1640: the example of some Kentish townsfolk', in *Schooling and society; studies in the history of education* ed. L. Stone (Baltimore 1976), pp. 95–111. Clark's examples were taken from Canterbury, Faversham and Maidstone – three towns much more prosperous than Cambridge – and his evidence is based on post-mortem inventories, where much minor reading was usually ignored: cf. the remarks in David Cressy, *Literacy and the social order*, pp. 48–9. For another general stock, cf. that of John Foster in York, d. 1616 (see Robert Davies, *A memoir of the York press* (1868), pp. 342–71), including several books printed at Cambridge – notably three copies of Heydon's *Defence of judiciall astrologie* (1603), valued at six shillings.

99 VCH, *Cambs.*, 3, pp. 97–8; F. W. Maitland, *Township and borough* (Cambridge 1898), pp. 102–5; Nigel R. Goose, 'Household size and structure in early Stuart Cambridge', *Social History*, 5 (1980), repr. in *The Tudor and Stuart town; a reader in English urban history, 1530–1688*, ed. Jonathan Barry (1990), pp. 74–120, especially pp. 81–2; Goose, 'Economic and social aspects of provincial towns', pp. 241–5.

100 University Archives, VC Ct Inventories, John Bell (grocer, 1578). For the chapbook and other popular trades, see M. Spufford, *Small books and pleasant histories* (1981), especially pp. 83–128, and *The great reclothing of rural England; petty chapmen and their wares in the seventeenth century* (1984). For shops stocking ranges of goods including books and stationery, see T. S. Willan, *The inland trade* (Manchester 1976), pp. 60–2, 78, 80.

101 For Penrith, see Peter Isaac, *An inventory of books sold by a seventeenth-century Penrith grocer* (*History of the Book Trade in the North*, PH 53, 1989).

2 *The charter of 1534*

1 For late thirteenth-century legislation concerning Cambridge University stationers, see M. B. Hackett, *The original statutes of Cambridge University; the text and its history* (Cambridge 1970), pp. 228–9. For subsequent privileges respecting stationers see *Grace Book A*, pp. xliii–xliv; Dyer, *Privileges*, 1, pp. 86–8, 97–9; H. E. Peek and C. P. Hall, *The archives of the University of Cambridge* (Cambridge 1962), pp. 57–9; Alan B. Cobban, *The medieval English universities: Oxford and Cambridge to c. 1500* (Berkeley 1988), pp. 94–5.

2 Margaret Deanesly, *The Lollard Bible* (Cambridge 1920), pp. 294–7, 351–70; Anne Hudson, *The premature Reformation; Wycliffite texts and Lollard history* (Oxford 1986), pp. 15, 82–5, 231–4. Arundel's legislation was aimed at Oxford: Cambridge seems to have been very little influenced by Wycliffite opinion (D. R. Leader, *A history of the University of Cambridge. The University to 1546* (Cambridge 1988), p. 223). But cf. Cobban, *Medieval English universities*, pp. 236–7.

3 Hudson, *The premature Reformation*, p. 489.

4 For Tunstall and the book trade, see most recently Susan Brigden, *London and the Reformation* (Oxford 1989), pp. 157–60, with further references.

5 *Grace Book B*, pt ii, pp. 411, 416 (ed. Bateson, pp. 90, 93).

6 On official opposition to Luther see most recently Richard Rex, 'The English campaign against Luther in the 1520s', *Trans. Royal Historical Soc.*, 5th ser. 39 (1989), pp. 85–106;

see also Rex, 'The polemical theologian', in *Humanism, reform and the Reformation; the career of Bishop John Fisher*, ed. B. Bradshaw and E. Duffy (Cambridge 1989), pp. 109–30, and Brigden, *London and the Reformation*, pp. 151–2.

7 A. W. Reed, 'The regulation of the book trade before the proclamation of 1538', *TCBS*, 15 (1917–19), pp. 157–84: the quotation is from Reed's summary of Tunstall's admonition, at p. 170; *Tudor royal proclamations*, 1, p. 133; Margaret Bowker, *The Henrician reformation; the diocese of Lincoln under John Longland, 1521–1547* (Cambridge 1981), pp. 58–9.

8 *L. and P. Henry VIII*, 4 ii, no. 4030; A. W. Pollard, *Records of the English Bible* (Oxford 1911), pp. 79–196; Herbert, *Historical catalogue*, pp. 1–2.

9 *STC*, 11394: the book consisted of translations from Luther and Melanchthon. *L. and P. Henry VIII*, 4 ii, no. 2607.

10 Bowker, *Henrician reformation*, pp. 60–1; Hudson, *Premature Reformation*, pp. 464–72, 505–7.

11 Sir Thomas More, *Apologye* (1533), fos. 192v–193r.

12 *L. and P. Henry VIII*, 4 ii, no. 2903.

13 Pollard, *Records*, pp. 135–49.

14 For the early years of the Reformation in Essex, see VCH, *Essex* 2 (1907), pp. 20–1, and James E. Oxley, *The Reformation in Essex to the death of Queen Mary* (Manchester 1965), especially, for Tunstall and Tyndale's New Testament, pp. 41–2. For neighbouring Suffolk see Diarmaid MacCulloch, *Suffolk and the Tudors; politics and religion in an English county, 1500–1600* (Oxford 1986), and R. Houlbrooke, 'Persecution of heresey and Protestantism in the diocese of Norwich under Henry VIII', *Norfolk Archaeology*, 35 (1970), pp. 308–26.

15 *L. and P. Henry VIII*, 4 ii, no. 4004 (John Longland to Wolsey, 3 March 1528). For a summary of Garrett's career see Emden, *BRUO 1501–1540* pp. 228–9. A. G. Dickens (*Lollards and Protestants in the diocese of York 1509–1558* (Oxford 1959), p. 58) follows the *DNB* in confusing Garrett (or Gerard) with Garrett Godfrey the Cambridge stationer.

16 *L. and P. Henry VIII*, 4 ii, no. 3968 (25 February 1528).

17 *Ibid.*, no. 4073 (Tunstall to Wolsey, 15 March 1528). For Clarke and Goodale see Emden, *BRUO 1501–1540*. See also Pollard, *Records*, pp. 155–61; Hudson, *Premature Reformation*, pp. 481–3, 486–8, 492; Brigden, *London and the Reformation*, pp. 113–18.

18 Cooper, *Annals*, 1, pp. 311–23.

19 Mullinger 1, p. 584.

20 Cooper, *Annals*, 1, p. 325; for Bilney, see Hudson, *Premature Reformation*, pp. 496–8.

21 J. Strype, *The life and acts of Matthew Parker* (1711), pp. 6–7; V. J. K. Brook, *A life of Archbishop Parker* (Oxford 1962), pp. 10–12; H. C. Porter, *Reformation and reaction in Tudor Cambridge* (Cambridge 1958), pp. 41–9.

22 Strype, *Parker*, p. 6.

23 John Twigg, *A history of Queens' College, Cambridge 1448–1986* (Woodbridge 1987), p. 17.

24 Cooper, *Annals*, 1, pp. 260–70, esp. p. 269.

25 *Grace Book B*, pt ii, p. 116.

26 Cooper, *Annals*, 1, pp. 323–4.

27 Mullinger 1, p. 546; Cooper, *Annals*, 1, p. 303.

28 Mullinger 1, p. 575.

29 *Ibid.*, pp. 550–1; Cooper, *Annals*, 1, pp. 307–9.

30 R. Fiddes, *The life of Cardinal Wolsey*, 2nd edn (1726), *Collections*, pp. 38–9; Lamb, *Collection*, pp. 12–14. These early years of the Reformation in the diocese of Ely are

discussed in Felicity Heal, 'The bishops of Ely and their diocese during the Reformation period: ca. 1515–1600' (PhD, Cambridge 1972).

31 Hastings Rashdall, *The universities of Europe in the middle ages*, new edn, 3 vols. (Oxford 1936), 3, pp. 279–82; A. B. Cobban, 'Episcopal control in the mediaeval universities', *Studies in Church History*, 5 (1969), pp. 1–22 (Cobban takes issue with Rashdall's opinion that Cambridge was lethargic in establishing its independence); Cobban, *Medieval English universities*, pp. 274–99; and Cobban, *The King's Hall* (Cambridge 1969), pp. 86–111. See also Pearl Kibre, *Scholarly privileges in the middle ages* (1961), ch. ix.

32 Wilkins, *Concilia*, 3, pp. 712–13.

33 *L. and P. Henry VIII*, 4 iii, no. 5639 (Wolsey to Sir Gregory Casale and Peter Vannes: draft).

34 Fiddes, *Collections* (see n. 30 above), p. 40; a copy is preserved in *Grace Book B*.

35 1 Richard III *c.* 9; 14–15 Henry VIII *c.* 2. Cf. Graham Pollard, 'The Company of Stationers before 1557', *The Library*, 4th ser. 18 (1937), pp. 1–38.

36 J. Thirsk, *Economic policy and projects: the development of a consumer society in early modern England* (Oxford 1978), p. 179.

37 Outside Oxford and Cambridge, and the London sanctuary of St Martin le Grand, no alien who was not a householder by 15 February 1528/9 was allowed to keep a shop in which to exercise any craft. Early legislation against aliens is summarized in the preface to William Page, ed., *Letters of denization and acts of naturalization for aliens in England 1509–1603* (Huguenot Society 1893).

38 Fiddes, *Collections*, p. 49. For the tensions between strangers and native interests, see S. Rappaport, *Worlds within worlds; structures of life in sixteenth-century London* (Cambridge 1989), pp. 42–7.

39 W. H. J. Weale, *Bookbindings and rubbings of bindings in the National Art Library, South Kensington Museum* (1896–8), 1, p. xxxviii.

40 A. de Schrijver, 'Nicolas Spierinc, calligraphe et enlumineur des Ordonnances des états de l'hôtel de Charles le Téméraire', *Scriptorium*, 23 (1969), pp. 434–58; Klaas van der Hoek, 'De Noordhollandse verluchter Spierinck, Haarlem en/of Beverwijk circa 1485–1519', in *Middeleeuwse handschriftenkunde in de Nederlanden 1988; veslag van de Groningse Codicologendagen 28–29 april 1988*, ed. Jos M. M. Hermans (Grave 1989), pp. 163–82.

41 H. R. Plomer, 'The importation of books into England in the fifteenth and sixteenth centuries; an examination of some customs rolls', *The Library*, 4th ser. 4 (1924), pp. 146–50, at p. 50. For more general background, see Nicolas Barker, 'The importation of books into England, 1460–1526', in *Beiträge zur Geschichte des Buchwesens im konfessionellen Zeitalter*, ed. H. G. Göpfert, P. Vodosek, E. Weyrauch and R. Wittmann (Wiesbaden 1985), pp. 251–66; Anne Rouzet, *Dictionnaire des imprimeurs, libraires, et éditeurs des XVe et XVIe siècles dans les limites géographiques de la Belgique actuelle* (Nieuwkoop 1975), pp. 16–20; J. Cools, 'Arnold Birckman', *De Gulden Passer*, new ser. 2 (1924), pp. 71–82.

42 *Grace Book B*, pt i, ed. M. Bateson (Cambridge 1903), p. 211.

43 Gray, *Earlier Cambridge stationers*, p. 28. I am grateful for help on this point to Louise H. Maas of the P. J. Meertens-Instituut of the Koninklijke Nederlandse Akademie van Wetenschappen. On Godfrey see C. Coppens, 'Een Nederlander in Cambridge: Garrett Godfrey', *Ex Officina; Bulletin van de Vrienden van de Leuvense Universiteitsbibliotheek*, 7 (1990), pp. 161–71 and p. 407 n. 19 below.

44 Cooper, *Annals*, 1, p. 270; University Archives, Luard 143b, 145.

45 Gray, *Earlier Cambridge stationers*, pp. 30–1; Foster, *Church-wardens' accounts*, pp. 39–40.

46 *Grace Book B*, pt ii, p. 44. For Lenton see Emden, *BRUC*, p. 363.

47 Gray and Palmer, p. 10.

48 Gray, *Earlier Cambridge stationers*, pp. 64–5; Gray and Palmer, pp. 5–10; Baker–Mayor 1, p. 347.

49 Gray and Palmer, pp. 4–5.

50 Gray, *Earlier Cambridge stationers*, p. 65.

51 Queens' College muniments, *Journale*, II (1518–35), fo. 131v.

52 The matriculation lists for the University of Louvain in 1523 include 'Nicolaus Segart de Cameraco', but there seems to be no reason to unite the two men: cf. A. Schillings, ed., *Matricule de l'Université de Louvain*, 3 (Brussels 1958), p. 714.

53 Quoted in Venn, *Gonville and Caius*, 1, p. xviii, n. 2. See also C. Brooke, *A history of Gonville and Caius College* (Woodbridge 1985), pp. 48–52.

54 Venn, *Gonville and Caius*, 1, pp. 17–24 and (for Skipp) 3, pp. 25–7; for Harman see Emden, *BRUO 1501–1540*, p. 267.

55 In 1523–4 Haynes was paid two shillings for writing two letters, and in 1533–4 a shilling for a transcript of an agreement between the town and the University (*Grace Book B*, pt ii, pp. 118, 182).

56 *Grace Book B*, pt ii, p. 163.

57 Sir Thomas More, *Apologye* (1533), fos. 199v–200r; ed. J. B. Trapp, *Complete works* (New Haven 1979), pp. 119–20, 356, 363, 368.

58 J. Strype, *Ecclesiastical memorials*, 1 ii (Oxford 1822), p. 179, quoting Foxe's papers (British Library, MS Harley 422).

59 Quoted in Gray, *Earlier Cambridge stationers*, p. 62.

60 *Tudor royal proclamations*, 1, pp. 193–7.

61 Strype, *Ecclesiastical memorials*, 1 i, pp. 255–6; for Constantine, see A. W. Pollard, *Records of the English Bible*, pp. 152–3, 155–6.

62 Porter, *Reformation and reaction*, p. 49; J. A. Guy, *The public career of Sir Thomas More* (Brighton 1980), pp. 167–71; other arrests following the proclamations (both dated 1530 by Guy: see p. 172, n. 164) are described *ibid.*, pp. 173–4.

63 Claire Cross, 'Oxford and the Tudor state', in *The collegiate university* (*History of the University of Oxford*, 3), ed. J. K. McConica (Oxford 1986), pp. 117–49; Gerald B. Skelly, 'Henry VIII consults the Universities of Oxford and Cambridge', in *Le 'divorce' du Roi Henry VIII* ed. G. Bedouelle and P. Le Gal (Geneva 1987), pp. 59–75.

64 Guy, *Public career of Sir Thomas More*, p. 173.

65 Brigden, *London and the Reformation*, pp. 179–98, again with further references.

66 For much of what follows I am indebted to G. R. Elton, *Policy and police; the enforcement of the Reformation in the age of Thomas Cromwell* (Cambridge 1972), esp. ch. 4, and also his *Reform and renewal; Thomas Cromwell and the common weal* (Cambridge 1973).

67 *Tudor royal proclamations*, 1, p. 195.

68 *STC*, 14286–7; 11918–19; 11919·5; 9177–8.

69 *STC*, 21561, etc.; ed. T. F. Plucknett and J. L. Barton (Selden Soc. 1974). Guy (pp. 151–6) assigns a much more prominent place in policy to St Germain than does Elton (*Policy and police*, pp. 173–4).

70 J. K. McConica, *English humanists and Reformation politics under Henry VIII and Edward VI* (Oxford 1965), pp. 114–49. Elton (*Reform and renewal*, pp. 3–5, 16–17, 61–2) argues that 'it is not possible to go all the way with McConica who sees Cromwell officially promoting every piece of reformist literature from about 1532 or 1534 onwards' (p. 16).

71 McConica, *English humanists*, pp. 145–6; E. J. Devereux, *Renaissance English translations of Erasmus; a bibliography to 1700* (Toronto 1983), pp. 104–14, with further references.

72 Ed. Louis A. Schuster *et al.*, *Complete works*, 8 (New Haven 1973). See also Anthea Hume, 'English Protestant books printed abroad, 1525–1535: an annotated bibliography',

Complete works, 8, pt II, pp. 1063–91, and Louis A. Schuster, 'Thomas More's polemical career, 1523–1533', *Complete works*, 8, pt III, pp. 1135–1268.

73 25 Henry VIII cap. XV; Blagden, *Stationers' Company*, p. 27; H. G. Pollard, 'The Company of Stationers before 1557', *The Library* 4 ser. 18 (1937) pp. 1–38, at p. 27.

74 H. Gee and W. J. Hardy, *Documents illustrative of English church history* (1896), pp. 232–43, 247–51; Elton, *Policy and police*, pp. 222–9, 282–92; Brigden, *London and the Reformation*, pp. 222–7; Jasper Ridley, *Thomas Cranmer* (Oxford 1962), pp. 125–6.

75 *L. and P. Henry VIII*, 7, no. 1003.

76 Mere's diary: *Grace Book A*, p. 230. The mayor's affirmation that Cambridge had 'as good a corporatyon as london', and his exposition of the choice, to become either freemen or scholars, is a yet further example of sixteenth-century jealousy between town and University – in this instance one with far-reaching consequences.

77 University Archives, Luard 162; copy in Hare A. II (307). See also Dyer, *Privileges*, I, pp. 107–8, and Clark, *Endowments*, p. 31. The translation is reprinted from Black, *Cambridge University Press*, pp. 24–5.

78 *Grace Book* Γ, fo. 148a (ed. Searle, p. 289).

3 *University stationers, 1534–1583*

1 *Grace Book* Γ, fo. 105r (ed. Searle, p. 196).

2 Otto Treptow, *John Siberch*; *Johann Lair von Siegburg* (Cambridge Bibliographical Soc. 1970); and 'Johann Lair von Siegburg – John Siberch – der erste Buchdrucker der Universität Cambridge', in *Heimatbuch der Stadt Siegburg*, 2, ed. J. Roggendorf (Siegburg 1967), pp. 654–761; S. Corsten, 'Primus utriusque linguae in Anglia impressor – Johann Lair von Siegburg und seine Typen', *ibid.*, pp. 762–75; *Johann Lair von Siegburg – John Siberch – der erstdrucker von Cambridge und seine Welt* (Austellung aus Anlass der 900-Jahrfeier Siegburgs, Siegburg 1964).

3 E. P. Goldschmidt, *The first Cambridge press in its European setting* (Cambridge 1955), pp. 5–9.

4 *Ibid.*, p. 16.

5 For the following, see E. Gordon Duff, *The English provincial printers, stationers and bookbinders to 1557* (Cambridge 1912).

6 Michael L. Zell, 'An early press in Canterbury', *The Library*, 5th ser. 32 (1977), pp. 155–6.

7 Printing in continental university towns is discussed in Goldschmidt, *The first Cambridge press*; see also R. Hirsch, *Printing, selling and reading, 1450–1550* (Wiesbaden 1967), pp. 50–2. For aspects of the Paris trade see A. Renaudet, *Préréforme et humanisme à Paris 1494–1517* (Paris 1916); A. Tilley, *The dawn of the French renaissance* (Cambridge 1918); P. Bietenholz, *Basle and France in the sixteenth century* (Geneva 1971), pp. 175–80. For fifteenth-century Paris, see Jeanne Veyrin-Forrer, 'Aux origines de l'imprimerie française; l'atelier de la Sorbonne et ses mécènes (1470–1473)', in *L'art du livre à l'Imprimerie Nationale* (Paris 1973), pp. 32–53, repr. in her *La lettre et le texte* (Paris 1987), pp. 161–87. For Bologna, see Curt F. Bühler, *The University and the press in fifteenth-century Bologna* (Notre Dame, Ind. 1958). Goldschmidt considered Thierry Martens 'the humanist printer *par excellence*' (p. 53): for his relations with the University of Louvain, combined with a successful and widespread business, see *Tentoonstelling Dirk Martens, 1473–1973* (Aalst 1973). For fifteenth-century Cologne, see Severin Corsten, 'Universität und Buchdruck in Köln. Versuch eines Überblicks für das 15. Jahrhundert', in *Buch und Text im 15. Jahrhundert*, ed. L. Hellinga and H. Härtel (Hamburg 1981), pp. 189–201. The whole subject is surveyed more generally in Severin Corsten,

'Universities and early printing', in *Bibliography and the study of 15th-century civilisation*, ed. L. Hellinga and J. Goldfinch (1987), pp. 83–123.

8 *Grace Book B*, pt ii, pp. vi–vii. The degree in Canon Law was abolished in 1535.

9 Roger Ascham, *Whole works*, ed. J. A. Giles (1865), 1, pt i, p. 143.

10 David Knowles and R. Neville Hadcock, *Medieval religious houses in England and Wales* (London 1953), pp. 348–9.

11 See pp. 15–17.

12 R. Whittinton, *De nominum generibus* (1521), at Shrewsbury School (J. B. Oldham, *Shrewsbury School library bindings* (Oxford 1943), p. 165 and plate VIIb; W. Horman, or W. Lily, *Antibossicon*, in the Huntingdon Library.

13 Cambridge University Library, Rel. b.52.1.

14 Recorded by the late Neil Ker at Charlecote House.

15 Now in the library of St John's College Cambridge.

16 Yale University Library, Ocp 78.531e.

17 J. C. T. Oates and H. L. Pink, 'Three sixteenth-century catalogues of the University Library', *TCBS*, 1 (1952), pp. 310–40; Emden, *BRUC*, pp. 597–8; Oates, *Cambridge University Library*, pp. 60–7. Apart from the evidence of catalogues and surviving books in contemporary bindings, much remains to be discovered from the discarded leaves used in covers. Cf., for example, the pieces of Nonius Marcellus, *De proprietate sermonum* (Venice, Jenson, 1476) in the volume of tracts by Erasmus and Hadrianus Barlandus (Basel, Antwerp and Louvain, 1524) now in Leuven Universiteitsbibliotheek: see C. Coppens, 'Een Nederlander in Cambridge: Garrett Godfrey', *Ex Officina; Bulletin van de Vrienden van de Leuvense Universiteitsbibliotheek*, 7 (1990), pp. 161–71, at p. 169.

18 R. Breugelmans, 'Barker's *Scutum inexpugnabile* defeated; an addition to Nijhoff-Kronenberg', *Quaerendo*, 6 (1976), pp. 360–4.

19 Only four editions are listed in *STC*, and others must be presumed lost. For examples of Oxford textbooks printed in London, see Carter, *Oxford University Press*, p. 17. See also, for the book trade, F. Madan, ed., 'Day-book of John Dorne, bookseller in Oxford, A.D. 1520', Oxford Historical Soc. *Collectanea*, 1st ser. (Oxford 1885), pp. 71–177, and Henry Bradshaw, *A half-century of notes on the day-book of John Dorne* (Cambridge 1886), repr. in his *Collected papers* (Cambridge 1889), pp. 421–50. For Cambridge, see Elisabeth Leedham-Green, *Garrett Godfrey's accounts, c. 1527–1533* (Cambridge Bibliographical Soc. 1992) which supplements the above at many points.

20 Translated in Mullinger 1, p. 630. The encouragement to new studies in and after 1535 is discussed in Paul Needham, 'Sir John Cheke at Cambridge and court' (PhD, Harvard 1971).

21 Roger Ascham, *English works*, ed. W. Aldis Wright (Cambridge 1904), p. 277.

22 T. Wright, ed., *Three chapters of letters relating to the suppression of the monasteries* (Camden Soc. 1843), pp. 70–2; Claire Cross, 'Oxford and the Tudor state', in *The history of the University of Oxford. 3. The collegiate university*, ed. J. McConica (Oxford 1988), pp. 117–49, at pp. 178–9.

23 Cooper, *Annals*, 1, pp. 398–9.

24 Roger Ascham, *Whole works*, 1, pt i, p. 26. John Cheke, *De pronuntiatione Graecae potissimum linguae disputationes cum Stephano Wintoniensi Episcopo, septem contrariis epistolis comprehensae...* (Basel 1555).

25 For Greek studies more generally, see Anthony Grafton and Lisa Jardine, *From humanism to the humanities; education and the liberal arts in fifteenth- and sixteenth-century Europe* (1986), pp. 110–27.

26 Julian Roberts and Andrew Watson, eds., *John Dee's library catalogue* (Bibliographical Soc. 1990), nos. 525, 823–4 (both Spierinck, acquired 1544), 16, 246, 718 (all acquired 1545), 402, 715–17 (all acquired 1546).

27 J. E. B. Mayor, ed., *Early statutes of the College of St. John the Evangelist* (Cambridge 1859).

28 R. G. Lewis, 'The Linacre lectureships subsequent to their foundation', in *Linacre studies; essays on the life and work of Thomas Linacre, c. 1460–1524*, ed. F. Maddison, M. Pelling and C. Webster (Oxford 1977), pp. 223–64; Giles Barber, 'Thomas Linacre; a bibliographical survey of his work', *ibid.*, pp. 290–336.

29 The course of publication of these various books in England may be followed in *STC*. For overseas editions, on which England relied, see (for Galen) Richard J. Durling, 'A chronological census of renaissance editions and translations of Galen', *Journal of the Warburg and Courtauld Institutes*, 24 (1961), pp. 230–305; (for Aristotle) F. E. Cranz, *A bibliography of Aristotle editions, 1501–1600*, 2nd edn, rev. C. B. Schmitt (Baden Baden 1984), and C. H. Lohr, *Latin Aristotle commentaries. II. Renaissance authors* (Florence 1988); (for Euclid) Max Steck, *Bibliographia Euclideana*, ed. Menso Folkerts (Hildesheim 1981) and Diana M. Simpkins, 'Early editions of Euclid in England', *Annals of Science*, 22 (1966), pp. 225–49. These supersede in most respects Henrietta R. Palmer, *List of English editions and translations of Greek and Latin classics printed before 1641* (Bibliographical Soc. 1911).

30 The list of books prescribed by the Elizabethan statutes of 1570 is printed in *Documents relating to the University and colleges of Cambridge* (1852), I, p. 457.

31 Philip Gaskell, 'Books bought by Whitgift's pupils in the 1570s', *TCBS*, 7 (1979), pp. 284–93.

32 Gray and Palmer, pp. 39, 43, 47. The earliest surviving copy of Carter's edition is of 1563, printed by Thomas Marsh in London. Marsh held the book until his death, and it passed ultimately to the Stationers' Company, entered to the English Stock in 1620. Only one copy survives of the earlier version of 1545 (*STC*, 22250), and that imperfect: it is possible that there was an earlier edition still.

33 W. S. Howell, *Logic and rhetoric in England, 1500–1700* (Princeton 1956); Lisa Jardine, 'The place of dialectic teaching in sixteenth-century Cambridge', *Studies in the Renaissance*, 21 (1974), pp. 31–62. See also below, pp. 91–2.

34 Arber, II.746, 886.

35 For Vautrollier as an importer, cf. his alliance with Jean Dessarans in 1567–8 and their links through Plantin with the European trade: C. Plantin, *Correspondance*, 6 vols. (Antwerp 1883–1918), I, pp. 144–7, 163–76, 262–4.

36 W. J. Ong, *Ramus and Talon inventory* (Cambridge, Mass. 1958). For Gabriel Harvey and Ramist texts, see Grafton and Jardine, *From humanism to the humanities*, pp. 184–96, and V. F. Stern, *Gabriel Harvey; his life, marginalia and library* (Oxford 1979).

37 *STC*, 15244·3 and 23659·3. Talon's *Rhetorica* had been entered to W. Norton and J. Harrison I in London on 11 November 1577, and to J. Harrison alone on 6 December 1588. The 1592 edition, a 24°, survives in a unique copy, and earlier editions, again, cannot be discounted.

38 Lisa Jardine, 'Humanism and the sixteenth century Cambridge arts course', *History of Education*, 4 (1975), pp. 16–31; Leedham-Green, *Books in Cambridge inventories*.

39 See below, pp. 65–6.

40 David Shaw, 'The first English editions of Horace, Juvenal and Persius', *The Library*, 5th ser. 25 (1970), pp. 219–25. For Aristotle, see n. 29 above.

41 Gray and Palmer, p. 2.

42 *Grace Book* Γ, fo. 167r (ed. Searle, p. 340).

43 Gray, *Earlier Cambridge stationers*, p. 66. For the use of some of Godfrey's binding tools in London, see Oldham, *Shrewsbury School library bindings*, pp. 50–1. It is probable that Godfrey, like Spierinck, had disposed of at least part of his equipment some years before his death.

44 Gray and Palmer, p. 31.

45 *Grace Book* Δ, fo. 13r; ed. Venn, p. 29. Besides those who became established at Cambridge, there were others who are less satisfactorily documented. The presence in the early 1540s of Elisabeth Birckman, widow, may be explained by her family connection with Nicholas Spierinck: Arnold Birckman died at Cologne in April 1541 or 1542 (Corpus Christi College MS 106, fo. 167v).

46 *Grace Book* Δ, fo. 121v; ed. Venn, p. 303.

47 C. P. Hall, 'Two licences granted to Cambridge stationers', *TCBS*, 1 (1953), pp. 443–4; *Grace Book* Γ, fo. 167v; ed. Searle, p. 341. His patent as University Appraiser, dated 10 May 1540, is in the University Archives, VC Ct III.1(10).

48 32 Henry VIII *c.* 16, s. 2; Cooper, *Annals*, 1, p. 396; A. Pettegree, *Foreign protestant communities in sixteenth-century London* (Oxford 1986), p. 15.

49 R. E. G. Kirk and E. F. Kirk, eds., *Returns of aliens dwelling in the city and suburbs of London* (Huguenot Soc. 1900–8), 1, pp. 411, etc.; E. J. Worman, *Alien members of the book-trade during the Tudor period* (Bibliographical Soc. 1906), p. 61; Arber, 1.48.

50 Gray, *Earlier Cambridge stationers*, p. 63; some details of Nicholson's business as a brewer, next to the bridge, between 1555 and 1568–9 may be followed in the Jesus College Audit Book. In a tax assessment of 1540, Nicholson was noted as having in his household two Scotsmen, Robert Ryklet and Robert Lekprevik: Lekprevik subsequently made a notable career for himself as an Edinburgh printer (Corpus Christi College MS 106, fo. 167v).

51 R. Ascham, *Whole Works*, 4 vols. (1864–5), 1, pt i, p. 140; Baker–Mayor, 1, pp. 368–9; VCH, *Cambs.*, 3, pp. 177–80, 344, 462; Charles Crawley, *Trinity Hall; the history of a Cambridge college, 1350–1975* (Cambridge 1976), pp. 52–3; Clark, *Endowments*, pp. 153–6; Lawrence V. Ryan, *Roger Ascham* (Stanford 1963), pp. 82–101.

52 Mullinger 2, pp. 88–9; W. K. Jordan, *Philanthropy in England, 1480–1660* (1959), pp. 291–5, 373.

53 Ascham, *English works*, pp. 280–1.

54 M. H. Curtis, *Oxford and Cambridge in transition, 1558–1642* (Oxford 1959), pp. 54–82.

55 *Tudor royal proclamations*, 1, p. 375.

56 Graham Pollard, 'The Company of Stationers before 1557', *The Library*, 4th ser. 18 (1937), pp. 1–38; Blagden, *Stationers' Company*, pp. 28–31. Neither alludes to the University at this point.

57 Arber, 1.xxxviii–xxxix.

58 See below, pp. 54–5. Not everyone depended on the stationers for their supply. For numerous examples of gifts, exchanges and requests concerning the import and export of books in the mid-century, by private individuals, see Hastings Robinson, ed., *The Zurich letters* (1558–1602), 2 vols. (Parker Soc. 1842–5), and *Original letters relating to the English Reformation*, 2 vols. (Parker Soc. 1846–7).

59 Gray and Palmer, pp. 32–3.

60 University Archives, VC Ct 1.1, fo. 7r.

61 J. E. Foster, ed., *Great St Mary's*, pp. 130ff.

62 University Archives, Comm. Ct II.1, fo. 19v.

63 Gray, *Earlier Cambridge stationers*, p. 67.

64 *Grace Book* Δ, fo. 102v; ed. Venn, p. 240; Hall, 'Two licences'.

65 University Archives, Collect. Admin. 13, fo. 133v.

66 *Ibid.*, fo. 137v.

67 Gray and Palmer, p. 63.

68 University Archives, Comm. Ct II.1, fo. 19v.

69 University Archives, Comm. Ct III.4, fo. 18r; Cambridge University Library, W. M. Palmer papers, bundle 9, box 41, list of privileged persons, 1591–2.

70 University Archives, Collect. Admin. 13, fo. 80. There is no real evidence to connect him with the John Dennis from the dominion of the King of Spain (i.e. the Low Countries) whose name appears among the denizations and naturalizations of aliens on 4 February 1561/2 (W. Page, ed., *Letters of denization and acts of naturalization for aliens in England 1509–1603* (Huguenot Soc. 1893), p. 73).

71 University Archives, Collect. Admin. 13, fo. 194v.

72 Gray and Palmer, p. 59.

73 University Archives, VC Ct I.2 (1), fo. 5; Bartholomew was still in Cambridge in March 1593/4, when he was accused of assaulting a bookbinder named John Jones (University Archives, VC Ct III.4(130).

74 McKerrow, *Dictionary*, p. 272; see also pp. 122–3.

75 University Archives, VC Ct I.24, fos. 67r–68v.

76 Gray and Palmer, pp. 33–5.

77 Gray, *Earlier Cambridge stationers*, p. 70.

78 Foster, *Great St Mary's*, p. 140; R. F. Scott, 'Notes from College records', *The Eagle*, 28, no. 142 (1907), p. 25. For some of his wine trade interests, see Foster, pp. 185, 187, and *Grace Book* Δ, fo. 78r (ed. Venn, p. 181).

79 H. P. Stokes, *The Esquire Bedells of the University of Cambridge* (Cambridge Antiquarian Soc. 1911), pp. 84–5.

80 University Archives, VC Ct III.1(62).

81 Duff, *Century*, suggests 'he may very probably have been one of the London family of printers named Waterson', but he offers no evidence for this assertion (p. 167).

82 Graham Pollard, 'The Company of Stationers before 1557', *The Library*, 4th ser. 18 (1937), pp. 1–38; and 'The early constitution of the Stationers' Company', *The Library*, 4th ser. 18 (1937), pp. 235–60; C. Paul Christianson, *A directory of London stationers and book artisans, 1300–1500* (New York 1990), Introduction.

83 Arber, v.lii.

84 McKerrow, *Dictionary*, p. 83; Gray, *Earlier Cambridge stationers*, p. 71; University Archives, Collect. Admin. 13, fos. 220r and 229r.

85 Arber, I.374, 375.

86 University Archives, Comm. Ct II.3, fo. 204v.

87 *Ibid.*, fo. 203v.

88 University Archives, Comm. Ct I.1, fo. 74r.

89 *Ibid.*, fo. 77v.

90 University Archives, Comm. Ct III.2, fo. 120r.

91 Gray and Palmer, p. 64; University Archives, VC Ct III.2(40, 41).

92 Gray and Palmer, p. 36.

93 Foster, *Great St Mary's*, pp. 213–14.

94 University Archives, Collect. Admin. 13, fo. 232r.

95 University Archives, Comm. Ct II.2, fo. 52v.

96 Gray and Palmer, pp. 72–6.

97 University Archives, VC Ct I.27 fo. 83v, I.72.5.

98 Gray and Palmer, pp. 10–30, 35–59.

99 *Ibid*, p. 34.

100 Arber, I.318, 446; II.84, 120, 685. See also Robert Jahn, 'Letters and booklists of Thomas Chard (or Chare) of London, 1583–4', *The Library*, 4th ser. 4 (1923–4), pp. 219–37, at pp. 219–20.

101 For du Puys, see Worman, *Alien members*, p. 52; for Seres, see Duff, *Century*, pp. 145–6; for Laughton, McKerrow, *Dictionary*, p. 168; for the Birckmans, see note 105, and pp. 29, 51. One of Seres' lettes, dated 5 December 1571 and alluding *inter alia* to books bought by Edward de Vere, Earl of Oxford, is preserved in University Archives, CUR 6.2, no. 4.

102 University Archives, Collect. Admin. 13, fo. 133v. For drapers and the book trade, see Plomer, *Wills*; A. H. Johnson, *The history of the Worshipful Company of the Drapers of London* (Oxford 1915), 2, pp. 169–71; Gerald D. Johnson, 'The Stationers versus the Drapers: control of the press in the late sixteenth century', *The Library*, 6th ser. 10 (1988), pp. 1–17.

103 University Archives, Collect. Admin. 13, fo. 142v.

104 For details of the following, see Gray and Palmer, pp. 59–60.

105 Colin Clair, 'Christopher Plantin's trade-connexions with England and Scotland', *The Library*, 5th ser. 14 (1959), pp. 28–45; Voet, *Golden compasses*, 2, pp. 440–53. In 1566 Plantin dealt with four members of the London book trade: Jean Desserans, Nicholas England, Toye and du Puys. For the Birckman family, who for years dominated the London overseas trade thanks to their family connections with the southern Netherlands and the lower Rhine, see Anne Rouzet, *Dictionnaire des imprimeurs, libraires, et éditeurs des XVe et XVIe siècles dans les limites géographiques de la Belgique actuelle* (Nieuwkoop 1975), pp. 16–20, with further references. For François, see Ph. Renouard, *Documents sur les imprimeurs, libraires...à Paris de 1450 à 1600* (Paris 1901), pp. 102–3. In 1556 Arnold Birckman was among the wealthiest members of the London trade (Arber, 1.48). For François' dealings with Edinburgh, see F. S. Ferguson, 'Relations between London and Edinburgh printers and stationers (–1640)', *The Library*, 4th ser. 8 (1927), pp. 145–98, at pp. 178–9.

106 Duff, *Century*, p. 67.

107 University Archives, Comm. Ct III.2(76).

108 University Archives, Comm. Ct III.2 (55, 59).

109 University Archives, Comm. Ct III.2 (20, 21).

110 University Archives, VC Ct III.1(119); VC Ct I.2 fos. 6r–6v.

111 See above, p. 54.

112 Jahn, 'Letters and booklists of Thomas Chard'. The papers on which Jahn based his article were found in the binding of an edition of Justinus (Heidelberg 1593), but he unfortunately failed to record who owned them in 1923.

113 *STC*, 19491·5.

4 *Prejudice and the printing privilege*

1 For details of this episode, see University Archives, VC Ct I.1, fos. 7r–8v, 9v–10r.

2 *Tudor royal proclamations*, 1, pp. 523–4.

3 Gray and Palmer, p. 34.

4 For John Hatcher, Thomas's father and a man of very considerable wealth, see especially Leedham-Green, *Books in Cambridge inventories*, 1, pp. 367–82, and W. M. Palmer, 'Cambridgeshire doctors in the olden time', *Procs. Cambridge Antiquarian Soc.*, 15 (1911), pp. 200–79, at pp. 238–45, 261–2.

5 Nicholas Carr, *De scriptorum Britannicorum paucitate* (1576), π 2v–3r. Brief portions are quoted in J. W. Binns, *Intellectual culture in Elizabethan and Jacobean England; the Latin writings of the age* (Leeds 1990), pp. 402–3. Wilson's English translation from Demosthenes was published in 1570, and Carr's Latin selection in 1571: none of the Greek text appears to have been printed in England until 1586. See also C. B. Schmitt, *John Case and Aristotelianism in renaissance England* (Kingston, Ont. 1983), pp. 33–4, n. 67, and J. W. Binns, 'Latin translations from the Greek in the English renaissance', *Humanistica Lovaniensia*, 27 (1978), pp. 128–59, at pp. 148–52.

6 For Lever, see Baker–Mayor, 1, pp. 130–6 (where Baker describes him as 'one of the best masters as well as one of the best men the college ever bred'), *DNB*, and Garrett, *Marian exiles*, pp. 219–21.

7 Greg and Boswell, p. 9.

8 Arber, I.111; British Library, MS Lansdowne 48, art. 78 (fos. 180–1); C. Blagden, 'The English Stock of the Stationers' Company', *The Library*, 5th ser. 10 (1955), pp. 163–85.

9 M. Parker, *Correspondence*, ed. T. T. Perowne (Parker Soc. 1853), p. 352; Arber, I.418.

10 Calendar of Patent Rolls; *Elizabeth I*, 5, no. 2445.

11 For Vautrollier's Letters Patent, see Arber, II.746–7 and Calendar of Patent Rolls; *Elizabeth I*, 6, no. 1445.

12 Georg Willer, *Catalogus*, autumn 1576, fo. A3r v. For the Frankfurt fair at this period see especially James Westfall Thompson, *The Frankfurt Book Fair* (Chicago 1911, repr. New York 1968); A. Ruppel, 'Die Bücherwelt des 16. Jahrhunderts und die Frankfurter Büchermessen', *Gedenkboek der Plantin-Dagen, 1555–1955* (Antwerp 1956), pp. 146–65; Pollard and Ehrman, pp. 70–84.

13 *Grace Book* Δ, fo. 121v; ed. Venn, p. 303.

14 Arber, I.111. British Library, MS Lansdowne 48, art. 78 (fos. 180–1).

15 Arber, II.15; W. W. Greg, *Some aspects and problems of London publishing* (Oxford 1956), p. 97; Calendar of Patent Rolls, *Elizabeth I*, 6, no. 1556.

16 Arber, II.795.

17 University Archives, Lett. 9 B12a, 10 July 1577.

18 University Archives, Lett. 9 B12b, 18 July 1577.

19 Greg, *Companion*, p. 4; *Calendar of Patent Rolls; Elizabeth I*, 5, no. 2126.

20 Blagden, 'English Stock', p. 179.

21 Calendar of Patent Rolls; *Elizabeth I*, 4, no. 675 (cf. 6, no. 1181).

22 A. N. L. Munby, 'The gifts of Elizabethan printers to the library of King's College, Cambridge', *The Library*, 5th ser. 2 (1948), pp. 224–32. A list of books presented by Jugge is printed on p. 230.

23 Arber, I.111; Greg, *Companion*, p. 18. For details of some of these privileges, see Calendar of Patent Rolls, *Elizabeth I*, 4, no. 675 (John Day: Psalms in English; ABC. 2 June 1557); 5, no. 1952 (Richard Watkins and James Roberts: almanacs and prognostications. 12 May 1571); no. 2126 (William Seres and his son: private prayers. 23 August 1571); no. 2445 (Thomas Marsh: elementary Latin texts, etc. 29 September 1572); Arber, II.746–7 and Greg, *Companion*, p. 16 (Thomas Vautrollier: Beza's New Testament, Ovid, Cicero, etc. 19 June 1574).

24 Arber, I.116; Greg, *Companion*, p. 44.

25 For a summary of some of this, see Blagden, 'English Stock', especially pp. 167–70.

26 Arber, I.505, II.144, 776–7; Greg, *Companion*, pp. 24, 26.

27 Blagden, *Stationers' Company*, pp. 75–6. The English Stock in its mature form was authoritatively described by Blagden as 'a book-producing and book-wholesaling organization run from Stationers' Hall by a paid Treasurer under the immediate control of six Stock-keepers, elected annually, and under the general control of the Master, Wardens, and Assistants; it dealt very profitably in cheap and popular publications – mainly school-books, psalm-books, and almanacks; the shareholders were limited to fifteen Assistants, thirty members of the Livery, and sixty of the Yeomanry, the value of whose shares quickly settled down respectively at £320, £160, and £80 each; the turn-over was often well over £5,000 a year and the dividend often as much as $12\frac{1}{2}$ per cent' ('English Stock', p. 163n.).

28 Greg, *Companion*, pp. 11, 16, 18. For measures taken in connection with strangers in 1574–83, see I. Scouloudi, ed., *Returns of strangers in the metropolis 1593, 1627, 1635, 1639* (Huguenot Soc. 1985), pp. 46–7, 60–1, and 'The Stranger community in the metropolis, 1558–1640' in *Huguenots in Britain and their French background, 1550–1800*, ed. I. Scouloudi (1987), pp. 42–55, at pp. 49–50. In January–February 1580/1 Parliament considered a Bill proposing that children of Strangers born in England

should not be accepted as English: the Bill was not passed (Scouloudi, *Returns*, p. 2). See also Andrew Pettegree, *Foreign Protestant communities in sixteenth-century London* (Oxford 1986), pp. 271–2, 289–91; Joan Thirsk, *Economic policy and projects; the development of a consumer society in early modern England* (Oxford 1978), pp. 43–4, etc.; and S. Rappaport, *Worlds within worlds; structures of life in sixteenth-century London* (Cambridge 1989), pp. 104–5.

29 For a while Arnold Birckman employed Rumold Mercator, Gerard Mercator's youngest son, who was thus in a position to be influential in the international map trade. See *Returns of aliens*, 10, pt iii, p. 343 and Walter Ghim's *Life* of Mercator: an English translation is included in A. S. Osley, *Mercator* (1969), at pp. 185–94.

30 CLRO *Remembrancia*, I.14 (Council to Lord Mayor, 29 May 1579).

31 *Ibid.*, I.15 (Lord Mayor to Council, 31 May 1579).

32 University Archives, Lett. 9 D3a. For Norton, see also M. A. R. Graves, 'Thomas Norton the Parliament man: an Elizabethan M.P., 1559–1581', *Historical Journal*, 23 (1980), pp. 17–35; P. W. Hasler, *The House of Commons 1558–1603* (1981), 3, pp. 145–9; J. Morgan, *Godly learning; puritan attitudes towards reason, learning and education, 1560–1640* (Cambridge 1986), pp. 193–5, 239–40. 'Thomas Norton was to London what Cecil was to all England, its principal secretary and the guarantor of administrative continuity' (P. Collinson, 'Puritans, men of business and Elizabethan parliaments', *Parliamentary History*, 7 (1988), pp. 187–211, at p. 197).

33 University Archives, Lett. 9 D3c.

34 *Ibid.* See also CLRO, *Remembrancia*, I.125. For Sheres, see David Pearson, 'A Cambridge bookseller's accounts of 1572', *TCBS*, 9 (1988), pp. 230–47; Gray and Palmer, pp. 61–3, with remarks on his family circle. His stock of books was valued in 1581 at three times that of John Dennis (d. 1578).

35 For details, see Greg, *Companion*, pp. 117–33, 136–7.

36 *Ibid.*, pp. 139–44.

37 See above, p. 62 and n. 23.

38 Greg, *Companion*, p. 129.

39 University Archives, CUR 33.2(67). It is undated, and filed among later papers; but Norton died on 10 March 1583/4, and an early terminus is set by its allusion to Bynneman's edition of Cooper's *Thesaurus*, of which he published a single edition in 1584. Cooper is referred to as Bishop of Lincoln, a see he left for Winchester in March 1583/4. There is a transcript by Thomas Baker in Cambridge University Library, MS Mm.1.40, p. 402.

40 University Archives, Lett. 9 D3b.

41 Lawrence Stone, 'The size and composition of the Oxford student body, 1580–1910', in *The university in society*, ed. L. Stone (Princeton 1974–5), 1, pp. 3–110, at p. 92.

42 University Archives, CUR 33.2(66).

43 The 1570 Statutes are printed in *Documents relating to the University and colleges of Cambridge* (1852), 1: see especially caps IV and VI. Those of Edward VI are included in J. Lamb, ed., *A collection of letters, statutes, and other documents...illustrative of the history of the University of Cambridge* (1838): see especially pp. 124–5. See also, more generally, Lisa Jardine, 'The place of dialectic teaching in sixteenth-century Cambridge', *Studies in the Renaissance*, 21 (1974), pp. 31–62. Though attributed generally to Whitgift, the 1570 statutes have also been linked with Andrew Perne: see British Library, MS Add. 4223, fo. 135, and P. Collinson, 'Andrew Perne and his times', in *Andrew Perne; quatercentenary studies*, ed. D. McKitterick (Cambridge Bibliographical Soc. 1991), pp. 1–34, at p. 11.

44 *Statuta Collegii Sanctae et Individuae Trinitatis* (Cambridge 1773), pp. 14–16. For

Clenardus, see L. Bakelants and R. Hoven, *Bibliographie des oeuvres de Nicolas Clénard 1529–1700*, 2 vols. (Verviers 1981).

45 Although I have used the terms 'curriculum', 'standard textbook' and 'textbook' frequently in the following pages in a university context, they need to be interpreted with caution. In a university where, apart from those entering holy orders, perhaps as little as twenty per cent took a degree, it was normal for students to read a great variety of courses, directed by their tutors towards their expected place in life: a 'curriculum' in the modern sense of a shared course of study, imposed by some corporate authority, had therefore only very limited application. Similarly, 'textbooks', servicing such curricula or used as components of a course of reading not requiring examination, had a different status from that assumed nowadays. For remarks on the proportions of those taking degrees, see T. G. Barnes, *Somerset, 1625–1640* (Cambridge, Mass. 1961), p. 31. See also, more generally, the analysis of assigned reading as recorded in Joseph Mede's notebooks, in J. Looney, 'Undergraduate education at early Stuart Cambridge', *History of Education*, 10 (1981), pp. 9–19.

46 Philip Gaskell, 'Books bought by Whitgift's pupils in the 1570s', *TCBS*, 7 (1979), pp. 284–93.

47 At Queens' College, for example, a succession of the younger Fellows was paid to lecture on Seton, while others lectured on Greek grammar (Queens' College, *Journale, 1560–87*, throughout). The earliest surviving printed edition of Seton's *Dialectica* is of 1545 (*STC*, 22250: unique, imperfect and not necessarily the first, in view of the absolute rarity of the early editions).

48 British Library, MS Lansdowne 25, art. 50; printed in Cooper, *Annals*, 2, p. 354. See also Leedham-Green, *Books in Cambridge inventories*, 1, p. 325.

49 Cf., for comparison, René Hoven, 'Enseignement du Grec et livres scolaires dans les anciens Pays-Bas et la Principauté de Liège de 1483 à 1600. 2me partie: 1551–1600', *GJ*, 55 (1980), pp. 118–26.

50 For Dennis's inventory, see now Leedham-Green, *Books in Cambridge inventories*, 1, pp. 326–40, correcting Gray and Palmer's transcription. The index of works listed in these inventories (Leedham-Green, 2) reveals something of comparative popularity. However, at the lower end of the financial scale many books have been forgotten in jaded generalization: cf. the inventory of the young William Mydson (1579: Leedham-Green, 1, pp. 342–3) listing seventeen titles and 'certayne other old bookes', a term which on this occasion almost certainly encompassed his ordinary undergraduate texts.

51 For these, and for Hebrew studies more generally, see G. Lloyd Jones, *The discovery of Hebrew in Tudor England; a third language* (Manchester 1983).

52 See also R. Jahn, 'Letters and booklists of Thomas Chard (or Chare) of London, 1583–4', *The Library*, 4th ser. 4 (1924), pp. 219–37.

53 Cf. the preface to Paulus Manutius, *In Epistolas familiares Ciceronis commentarii* (Frankfurt: Wechel, 1580): 'posse igitur volumen, in gratiam iuventutis, excudi forma et charactere minore, sic que fore portatile, et ad usus quotidianos magis aptum' (quoted in Ian Maclean, 'André Wechel at Frankfurt, 1572–1581', *GJ*, 63 (1988), p. 153 n. 41).

54 Virginia F. Stern, *Gabriel Harvey; his life, marginalia and library* (Oxford 1979), p. 225. Harvey's octavo Quintilian (Paris 1542), bought for 3s.6d. in March 1567, is now in the British Library (*ibid.*, pp. 231–2).

55 Jahn, 'Letters and booklists of Thomas Chard'.

56 Editions of Clenardus' *Institutiones* were published in the late 1570s and early 1580s at, among other cities, Frankfurt, Paris, Lyons, Cologne, Antwerp, La Rochelle and London. Compared with those of many other books, edition quantities were large: 2,500 copies were printed of Plantin's edition of 1562–4 (Bakelants and Hoven, *Bibliographie*, p. viii and nos. 170–1; Leon Voet, *The Plantin Press (1555–1589)* (Amsterdam 1980–3), 2,

pp. 660–2). In a world-wide search, only four copies have been located, less than 0·2 per cent of the edition. Such destruction rates, implying also the complete disappearance of many editions, suggest that the educational market was very much larger than surviving copies, or editions, themselves indicate.

57 University Archives, Pr.P.4(3); Cooper, *Annals*, 2, pp. 395–7; Gray, *Earlier Cambridge stationers*, pp. 72–3.

5 *Thomas Thomas, 'that puritan printer'*

1 Ian Maclean, 'André Wechel at Frankfurt, 1572–1581', *GJ*, 63 (1988), pp. 146–76. C. B. Schmitt, *John Case and Aristotelianism in Renaissance England* (Kingston, Ont. 1983), pp. 7, 50–1. For an examination of several of the more general questions respecting scholarly printing in the sixteenth century, see Maclean, 'L'économie du livre érudit: le cas Wechel (1527–1627)', in *Le livre dans l'Europe de la renaissance: actes du XXVIIIe colloque international d'études humanistes de Tours*, ed. P. Aquilon, H.-J. Martin and F. Dupuigrenet Desrousilles (Paris 1988), pp. 230–9.

2 Shaaber, *Check-list*, throughout; Josef Benzing, *Die Buchdrucker des 16. und 17. Jahrhunderts im Deutschen Sprachgebiet* (Wiesbaden 1982), p. 203; H. Gerber, 'Christoph Corvin', *Nassausche Lebensbilder* (Wiesbaden 1948), pp. 117–26.

3 Voet, *Golden compasses*, 1, pp. 105–13. E. van Gulik, 'Drukkers en geleerden; de Leidse Officina Plantiniana (1583–1619), in *Leiden University in the seventeenth century*, ed. Th. H. Lunsingh Scheurleer *et al.* (Leiden 1975), pp. 366–93. It is perhaps also appropriate to record here that in Mallorca the Guasp family began its long career in printing in 1579, and that its doors were closed only in 1958: see Isabel Quigly, 'The house of Guasp', *The Book Collector*, 2 (1953), pp. 265–9 and Gaspar Sabater, *La imprenta y las xylografias de los Guasp* (Palma de Mallorca 1985).

4 P. Collinson, 'England and international Calvinism, 1558–1640', in *International Calvinism 1541–1715*, ed. M. Prestwich (Oxford 1985), pp. 197–223, at pp. 205–7. For examples of generosity to the French community in London see Collinson, 'The Elizabethan puritans and the foreign reformed churches', *Proc. of the Huguenot Soc.*, 20 (1964), pp. 528–55, repr. in his *Godly people* (1983), pp. 245–72.

5 M. Prestwich, 'Calvinism in France, 1555–1629', in *International Calvinism*, pp. 71–107, at p. 98; Collinson, 'England and international Calvinism', p. 204. For England's trade with La Rochelle see E. Trocmé and M. Delafosse, *Le commerce rochelais de la fin du XVe siècle au début du XVIIe* (Paris 1952); for the paper trade see *ibid.* p. 140.

6 Arber, 1.502; *STC*, 8141; *Tudor royal proclamations*, 2, *pp.* 501–2.

7 British Library, MS Lansdowne 42, art. 78; Greg, *Companion*, p. 36; Arber, 1.492. The date, 1584, is not entirely certain.

8 *STC*, 8146; *Tudor royal proclamations*, 2, pp. 506–8.

9 H. R. Plomer, 'The Eliot's Court printing house, 1584–1674', *The Library*, 2nd ser. 2 (1922), pp. 175–84.

10 The annual output of publications in the early 1580s, measured by title, was between about 150 and 200, a figure that was more than to double by the late 1630s.

11 *STC*, 22857. See also Sir Thomas Smith, *De republica Anglorum*, ed. Mary Dewar (Cambridge 1982); C. L. Oastler, *John Day, the Elizabethan Printer* (Oxford Bibliographical Soc. 1975), pp. 67, 69.

12 These activities can be followed in Denis B. Woodfield, *Surreptitious printing in England 1550–1640* (New York 1973), pp. 19–21, 62–8.

13 Arber, 11.787.

14 *STC*, 22465. No copy is now known.

15 Keith Thomas, *Religion and the decline of magic* (Harmondsworth 1973), p. 685.

16 Frank Stubbings, ed., *The statutes of Sir Walter Mildmay ... for the government of Emmanuel College* (Cambridge 1983); J. Morgan, *Godly learning* (Cambridge 1986), pp. 247–55.

17 British Library, MS Lansdowne 48, fos. 189–94; Arber, 1.114–16, 144; Greg, *Companion*, pp. 25–6.

18 British Library, MS Lansdowne 48, fo. 195; Greg, *Companion*, pp. 26–7, 116–17.

19 Greg, *Companion*, pp. 27, 117–33.

20 *CSPD; Elizabeth I*, vol. 15, no. 38; Greg, *Companion*, pp. 27–8.

21 University Archives, Lett. 9.B.19a; John Morris, 'Restrictive practices', at p. 277; H. E. Peek and C. P. Hall, *The archives of the University of Cambridge* (Cambridge 1962), plate 15.

22 John Saltmarsh, *King's College; a short history* (Cambridge 1958), p. 56; VCH, *Cambs.*, 3, p. 396.

23 Gray and Palmer, pp. 61–2.

24 No record of their marriage has been discovered, but their daughter Joan was baptized at Great St Mary's on 1 December 1583.

25 The text of the 1583 regulations respecting bookselling and bookbinding in Cambridge is in University Archives, Pr.P.4(3), repr. in Cooper, *Annals*, 2, pp. 395–7; the 1585/6 articles respecting printing are discussed below, pp. 99–100. For Thomas's few possessions relating to bookbinding, see Gray and Palmer, pp. 70–1, which should be compared with the substantial and detailed list of equipment left by John Dennis in 1578 (Gray and Palmer, pp. 56–8). On Thomas and bookbinding see John Morris, 'Thomas Thomas, Printer to the University of Cambridge, 1583–8. Part II', *TCBS*, 4 (1968), pp. 339–62, at pp. 350–62, and the corrections offered by H. M. Nixon, 'Elizabethan gold-tooled bindings', in *Essays in honour of Victor Scholderer*, ed. D. E. Rhodes (Mainz 1970), pp. 219–70, at pp. 221–3. One of the University shield centrepieces (Morris, no. 3) was still in use as a binding ornament in 1604 or later (Trinity College, VI.8.89: Thomas Wright, *The passions of the minde in generall* (1604)).

26 *Grace Book* Δ, fo. 142a (ed. Venn, p. 370). The wording of the conditions was careful: 'Conceditur 3º Maii vt magister Thomas sit vnus ex tribus vestris librorum impressoribus cum omnibus privilegiis eiisdem impressoribus assignatis et super hac vestra concessione literas vestras habeat sigillatas sigillo vestro communi ea tamen conditione vt antequam hoc vestro privilegio gaudeat obligetur ad illas conditiones articulos et leges que prenobilis noster Cancellarius vicecancellarius et maior pars prefectorum collegiorum in scriptis indentatis assignabunt.'

27 *CSPD; Elizabeth I*, vol. 16, no. 1; Morris, 'Restrictive practices', pp. 279–80.

28 *Ibid.*

29 University Archives, Lett. 9. B19b; Morris, 'Restrictive practices', p. 281.

30 British Library, MS Lansdowne 40, fo. 36; Morris, 'Restrictive practices', pp. 281–2.

31 Arber, 1.505.

32 Arber, 1.248; Harry R. Hoppe, 'John Wolfe, printer and publisher, 1579–1601', *The Library*, 4th ser. 14 (1933), pp. 241–88.

33 D. F. McKenzie, 'Notes on printing at Cambridge c. 1590', *TCBS*, 3 (1959), pp. 96–103, at p. 97. Blayney (*Nicholas Okes*, pp. 40–1) argues that 'for a one-press printer whose livelihood depended on keeping his press in use, a spare press would have been an economic necessity': this may well have been true in London, but there is no evidence that Thomas owned more than one.

34 R. E. G. Kirk and E. F. Kirk, eds., *Returns of aliens*, 4 vols. (Huguenot Soc. 1900–8), 3, p. 338 ('Jerome Holten'; 'Hubart Dovylley, a caster of pryntinge lettres').

35 Louis Desgraves, *Les Haultin, 1571–1623* (*L'imprimerie à La Rochelle* 2) (Geneva 1960), pp. xvii–xviii; M. G. Musset, 'Vente de matrices d'imprimerie par Pierre Haultin', *Bull.*

Archéologique du Comité des Travaux Historiques et Scientifiques (1889), pp. 202–4. Books printed at La Rochelle in the sixteenth century are listed in Louis Desgraves, *Répertoire bibliographique des livres imprimés en France au seizième siècle. 127. La Rochelle* (Bibliotheca Bibliographica Aureliana 51, Baden Baden 1973).

36 W. Craig Ferguson, *Pica Roman type in Elizabethan England* (Aldershot 1989); C. L. Oastler, *John Day, the Elizabethan printer* (Oxford Bibliographical Soc. 1975), pp. 33–8.

37 *OED*, s.v. 'Geneva', quoting Massinger, *The Duke of Milan*: 'If you meet An officer preaching of sobriety, Vnlesse he read it in *Geneva* print, Lay him by the heeles.' Cf. also *The pilgrimage to Parnassus* (in *Three Parnassus plays*, ed. J. B. Leishman (1949)), l. 350: 'two or three hundreth of chatechismes of Ieneuas printe'. See below, p. 115.

38 Morris, 'Thomas Thomas', p. 341: to the copies or versions listed as belonging to nine printers by Morris may be added those of Vautrollier, Bollifant, Windet and Bynneman.

39 Not surprisingly, Morris's survey of other uses of these designs is far from complete, even for English printing. The circular ornament (Morris tailpiece 7) can also be found in the work of John Wolfe; see also, for Morris tailpieces 6 and 7, Desgraves, *Haultin*, pp. 48, 77. Most of Thomas's decorative stock, and with it therefore many of the ornamental designs in use in London, may be usefully compared with the Haultin press, particularly after Jérome Haultin took it over on his uncle's death in 1588.

40 Cf. Harry Carter, 'Huguenot typography', *Procs. of the Huguenot Soc.*, 21 (1970), pp. 532–44. For connections between continental centres, see, for example, L. Desgraves, 'Les relations entre les imprimeurs de Genève et de La Rochelle à la fin du XVIe siècle et au début du XVIIe siècle', in J.-D. Candaux and B. Lescaze, eds., *Cinq siècles d'imprimerie genevoise; actes du colloque international sur l'histoire de l'imprimerie et du livre à Genève, 1978*, 2 vols. (Geneva 1980), I, pp. 199–207, and Eugénie Droz, 'Pierre Haultin à Genève, ou la lutte pour la liberté', in her *Chemins de l'hérésie*, 4 vols. (Geneva 1970–6), 4, pp. 373–8.

41 Geoffrey Keynes, *Dr Timothie Bright 1550–1615; a survey of his life with a bibliography of his writings* (1962), p. 30 and plate 10; David McKitterick, *Four hundred years of University printing and publishing at Cambridge* (Cambridge 1984), p. 27. See also n. 25, above.

42 Morris, 'Thomas Thomas', pp. 346–7. Morris thought that it seemed 'not unlikely that the four allegorical sidepieces came to Thomas by way of Waldegrave'. But the figure of Humility is clearly a cast, of only part of the block used by Day. Day's blocks, still complete, can be seen in Waldegrave's printing in Edinburgh in the early 1590s.

43 Gray and Palmer, pp. 70–1. Paper was imported through London and overwhelmingly from France, only a little coming from Italy. (A. M. Millard, 'The import trade of London, 1600–1640 (PhD, University of London, 1956), opposite p. 150; D. C. Coleman, *The British paper industry 1495–1860* (Oxford 1958), pp. 17–18).

44 C. B. Schmitt, *John Case and Aristotelianism*, pp. 45–6, 48–52, 68–73.

45 G. Schwetschke, *Codex nundinarius Germaniae literatae bisecularis* (Halle 1850–77, repr. Nieuwkoop 1963); the seasonal catalogues have been repr. as *Die Messkataloge Georg Willers* (1564–92), ed. Bernhard Fabian, 4 vols. (Hildesheim 1972–8). Although most entries are straightforward, the reasons for the inclusion of a quantity of old stock in spring 1579 are unclear. In that catalogue there appeared Bullinger's *Bullae papisticae* (John Day 1571), Laurence Humphrey's life of Jewell (John Day 1573), Richard Stanyhurst's *Harmonia in Porphyrianas institutiones* (R. Wolf 1570) and John Dee's *Propaedeumata aphoristica* (R. Wolf 1568: '1579' in Willer's catalogue is probably a misprint). These aberrations may perhaps offer a clue to more complex and extensive trading than the normal entries suggest. For John Wolfe's activities at the fair, see Woodfield, *Surreptitious printing in England 1550–1640*, pp. 187–8.

46 While private correspondence reveals much about individual tastes and private

arrangements for international book-buying, systematic exports are more sparsely documented. For example, in 1571 those copies intended for circulation in France and French-influenced parts of the continent of Pierre Pena and M. de l'Obel's *Stirpium adversaria nova*, printed by Thomas Purfoot, contained the privilege obtained by de l'Obel from Charles IX: Plantin bought 800 copies. (Blanche Henrey, *British botanical and horticultural literature before 1800* (Oxford 1975), 1, pp. 30, 263–5; Max Rooses, *Christophe Plantin* (Antwerp 1882), p. 333). The route to European sales, even on an appreciable scale, was not always by conventional trade. For the diplomatic channels employed to advertise and market the Eton Chrysostom (1610–13), see S. van der Woude, 'Sir Henry Savile's Chrysostom edition in the Netherlands', *Studia bibliographica in honorem Herman de la Fontaine Verwey* (Amsterdam 1966), pp. 437–47.

47 British Library, MS Lansdowne 57, fos. 213–19.

48 *STC* 3368·5; A. N. L. Munby, *Donors' labels printed for King's College library, Cambridge* (Cambridge 1950); B. N. Lee, *Early printed book labels* (1976), pp. 2–3.

49 The unique sheet (*STC*, 20028·9) survives in the binding of Queens' College I.12.5 (John Christopherson, ed., *Historiae ecclesiasticae scriptores* (Cologne 1581)). The same binding also contains fragments of two other books printed by Thomas: T. Bright, *In Physicam G. A. Scribonii…animadversiones* (1584) and P. Ramus, *Dialecticae libri duo* (1584). The conjunction of these books lends further support to the likelihood, suggested by their pairing in University Library, Syn. 8.58.128, that they were published at about the same time in 1584, and were possibly Thomas's first completed books.

50 *Statutes*, cap. IV, 'De temporibus lectionum et libris praelegendis'.

51 This was one of five books to be advertised by Vautrollier in the Frankfurt catalogue for autumn 1578.

52 For Vautrollier, see below, pp. 91–2; for Chard, see pp. 97, 98.

53 British Library, MS Lansdowne 40, fo. 36; Morris, 'Restrictive practices', pp. 281–2.

54 Peter Milward, *Religious controversies of the Elizabethan age; a survey of printed sources* (1977), pp. 14, 47–8, 57–8.

55 *STC*, 25362; Morris, 'Restrictive practices', p. 282, n. 1, suggests the other, *STC*, 25357, but gives no reason for doing so.

56 For Plantin, see Voet, *Golden compasses* and *The Plantin press (1555–1589)*, 6 vols. (Amsterdam 1980–3); for Wechel, see H. Elie, 'Chrétien Wechel, imprimeur à Paris', *GJ* (1954), pp. 181–97; W. R. Lefanu, 'André Wechel', *Proc. Huguenot Soc. of London*, 21 (1966), pp. 58–81; A. Labarre, 'Editions et privilèges des héritiers d'André Wechel à Francfort et à Hanau 1582–1627', *GJ* (1970), pp. 238–50, and 'Les éditions des héritiers Wechel à Francfort et à Hanau 1582–1627', *GJ* (1971), pp. 209–23; see also Colin Clair, 'Thomas Vautrollier', *GJ* (1960), pp. 223–8; W. R. Lefanu, 'Thomas Vautrollier', *Proc. Huguenot Soc. of London*, 20 (1959), pp. 12–25, and Harry Carter, 'Huguenot typography'.

57 *STC*, 3745 (Bright); *STC*, 22109·5–22110·5 (Scribonius); see also W. S. Howell, *Logic and rhetoric in England, 1500–1700* (Princeton 1956), pp. 203–4 and, for Bright, W. J. Carlton, *Timothie Bright, Doctor of Physicke* (1911) and Geoffrey Keynes, *Dr Timothie Bright 1550–1615*.

58 Frank Stubbings, ed., *The statutes of Sir Walter Mildmay*, p. 90.

59 Garrett, *Marian exiles*, p. 303. After leaving Cambridge, Temple briefly became Master of Lincoln grammar school before joining the household of Sir Philip Sidney. He became Provost of Trinity College Dublin in 1609 (Venn; VCH, *Lincs.*, 2, pp. 441–2; J. W. F. Hill, *Tudor & Stuart Lincoln* (Cambridge 1956), pp. 103–4; R. B. McDowell and D. A. Webb, *Trinity College Dublin, 1592–1952* (Cambridge 1982).)

60 For background on the place of Ramus in sixteenth and seventeenth-century Cambridge, see Howell, *Logic and rhetoric*, and W. J. Ong, *Ramus; method, and the decay of dialogue*

(Cambridge, Mass. 1958), pp. 302–4: but cf. Ong's remarks (p. 303): 'to complement this ebullient youthful Ramism there is practically no serious and mature scholarship oriented by Ramism in the British Isles'. For more recent work, see, in particular, Lisa Jardine, 'The place of dialectic teaching in sixteenth-century Cambridge', *Studies in the Renaissance*, 21 (1974), pp. 31–62; John Morgan, *Godly learning*, especially ch. 11; and A. Grafton and L. Jardine, *From humanism to the humanities; education and the liberal arts in fifteenth- and sixteenth-century Europe* (1986), especially pp. 184–96. For Ramus and Protestantism, see Donald R. Kelley, *The beginning of ideology; consciousness and society in the French Reformation* (Cambridge 1981), pp. 131–50.

61 Arber, ii.746, 886.

62 Sir Philip Sidney, *The defence of poesie*, etc., ed. A. Feuillerat (Cambridge 1912), p. 145; Howell, *Logic and rhetoric*, p. 205.

63 The Cambridge University Library copy of the Wittenberg, 1559 edition (Adams S 29) belonged in 1578 to Thomas Ravys, a pupil at Christ Church, Oxford.

64 For the fortunes of Ovid in sixteenth-century France, see, for example, Ann Moss, *Ovid in Renaissance France; a survey of the Latin editions of Ovid and commentaries printed in France before 1600* (1982), and Ann M. Blair, 'Lectures on Ovid's *Metamorphoses*; the class notes of a 16th-century Paris schoolboy', *Princeton University Library Chronicle* (1989), pp. 117–44. For Ovid's fortunes as an English textbook, see T. W. Baldwin, *William Shakspere's small Latine & lesse Greeke*, 2 vols. (Urbana 1944), pp. 417–55. London rights to Latin schoolbooks are summarized in *STC*, vol. 3, Appendix D. A copy of Thomas's Ovid bearing the University shield on each cover survives in the Houghton Library, Harvard University.

65 A. F. Johnson, 'Books printed at Heidelberg for Thomas Cartwright', *The Library*, 5th ser. 2 (1948), pp. 284–6; P. Collinson, *The Elizabethan Puritan movement* (1967), pp. 243–88.

66 [Richard Bancroft], *Dangerous positions and proceedings* (1593), pp. 88–9.

67 British Library, MS Lansdowne 42, fo. 109; Morris, 'Restrictive practices', p. 284 (dating the letter 24 June).

68 British Library, MS Harley 7030, p. 430; Morris, 'Restrictive practices', p. 284 (the original seems not to have survived).

69 For the careers of these two men, see E. and E. Haag, *La France protestante*, 7 (Paris 1857), pp. 37–40 and 9 (Paris 1859), pp. 22–3.

70 Haag, *La France protestante*, 2nd edn, 3 (Paris 1881), cols. 1049–58. See also the introduction to Chandieu's *Octonaires sur la vanité et inconstance du monde*, ed. F. Bonali-Fiquet (Geneva 1979), and Kelley, *Beginning of ideology*, pp. 119–21.

71 The quotations from Psalms 140 and 145 on the title-page are from Vatable's revised versions of Pagnini's Latin text, printed at Basel by Guarinus in 1564.

72 For example, Plantin's edition of 1584 and, indeed, Wechel's Paris edition of 1560, of which Thomas Byng (MA 1559; Master of Clare Hall 1571) possessed a copy, now Cambridge University Library, Aa*.6.22(F).

73 On Willet, see *DNB*. In 1592 his most influential book, *Synopsis papismi*, was however printed and published in London, not Cambridge; see also Milward, *Religious controversies of the Elizabethan age*, pp. 130–1.

74 Pilkington, *Works*, ed. James Scholefield (Parker Soc. 1842); for his earlier career see Garrett, *Marian exiles*, pp. 250–1.

75 *STC*, 22910; entered in the Stationers' Register to Bishop, 12 November 1582.

76 On Ursinus, see Franciscus Junius' funeral oration in *STC*, 24527; on Goulart, see Haag, *La France protestante*, 5 (Paris 1855), pp. 329–37. For Oxford, see C. M. Dent, *Protestant reformers in Elizabethan Oxford* (Oxford 1983), pp. 80–1, 91.

77 Note to *STC*, 25364; Morris, 'Thomas Thomas', pp. 346–7 (headpiece 3 belonged

formerly to John Day, and was used for example in Foxe's *Book of martyrs*, 1583); P. W. M. Blayney, *The bookshops in Paul's Cross churchyard* (Bibliographical Soc. 1990), pp. 12–14.

78 McKerrow, *Dictionary*, p. 278.

79 Morris, 'Thomas Thomas', pp. 346–8, believed that the ornaments in question (his headpieces 3 and 5, tailpiece 5) were lent to Thomas, perhaps as part of a 'deliberate attempt at mystification in the printing of this book'. It should also be noted that the large initial I, depicting a saint, which likewise appears in the preliminaries to Whitaker's book, was part of a set of similar letters owned by Waldegrave. For shared printing in London, see P. W. M. Blayney 'The prevalence of shared printing in the early seventeenth century', *PBSA*, 67 (1973), pp. 437–42, and *The texts of King Lear and their origins. 1. Nicholas Okes and the first quarto* (Cambridge 1982).

80 Donald Paige, 'An additional letter and booklist of Thomas Chard, stationer of London', *The Library*, 4th ser. 21 (1940), pp. 26–43.

81 For remarks on some of the complicated trade relationships, and their bearing on the form of late sixteenth and early seventeenth-century imprints, cf. M. A. Shaaber, 'The meaning of the imprint in early printed books', *The Library*, 4th ser. 24 (1943–4), pp. 120–41; and W. W. Greg, *Some aspects and problems of London publishing between 1550 and 1650* (Oxford 1956), pp. 85–9: 'At the root of the trouble lies the assumption that it was the owner of the copy who financed the printing of a book' (p. 87). In practice colophons and imprints provide only an incomplete record of the ownership of copy and the dispersal of stock.

82 Arber, I.501.

83 Gray and Palmer, p. 69.

84 W. J. Ong, *Ramus and Talon inventory* (Cambridge, Mass. 1958) pp. 310–23.

85 *Grace Book* Δ, fo. 150v (ed. Venn, p. 404). Once again he was referred to as 'unus ex tribus vestris librorum impressoribus'; but there were no other Printers.

86 Oates, *Cambridge University Library*, pp. 89–141.

87 University Archives, Pr. B.2.2; CUR 33.1(4); Morris, 'Restrictive practices', pp. 285–6.

88 Carter, *Oxford University Press*, pp. 19–21.

89 *Grace Book* Δ, fo. 150v (ed. Venn, p. 404).

90 Arber, II.806–12; Carter, *Oxford University Press*, pp. 21–2.

91 *STC*, 5009; Milward, *Religious controversies of the Elizabethan age*, p. 56.

92 University Archives, Lett. 9.c.12; Morris, 'Restrictive practices', pp. 286–7; Strype, *Annals*, 3 ii (Oxford 1824), p. 444.

93 On the principal editor, Jean-François Salvart, see Haag, *La France protestante*, 9 (Paris 1859), p. 133. Genevan publications during this period are listed in P. Chaix, A. Dufour and G. Moeckli, *Les livres imprimés à Genève de 1550 à 1600*, 2nd edn (Travaux d'Humanisme et Renaissance 86) (Geneva 1966) and H. J. Bremme, 'Genfer Drucke aus dem 16. Jahrhundert', *Bibliothèque d'Humanisme et Renaissance*, 38 (1976), pp. 113–44. See also Olivier Labarthe, 'Une liste genevoise de livres imprimés 1567–1586', in *Cinq siècles d'imprimerie genevoise*, 2 vols. (Geneva 1980), 1, pp. 171–97, and H. J. Bremme, *Buchdrucker und Buchhändler zur Zeit der Glaubenskämpfe; Studien zur Genfer Druckgeschichte 1565–1580* (Travaux d'Humanisme et Renaissance 104) (Geneva 1969).

94 Arber, I.543. Nonetheless, the book has survived in considerable numbers. See also 'M. Marprelate' *Oh read ouer D. Iohn Bridges, for it is a worthy worke* [1588] (*STC*, 17454), p. 6: 'And trust me, but his grace will owe that puritan printer as good a tune, as hee paide vnto Robert Walde-graue for his sawcines, in printing my frend and deare brother Diotrephes his Dialogue. Well frend Thomas I warne you before hand / looke to your selfe.'

95 These were probably shipped via King's Lynn. In December 1586 the Mary Fortune of Lynn carried a maund of unspecified books to Edinburgh (Customs accounts 101/32). For this, and for traffic between East Anglia and Scotland, see N. J. Williams, *The maritime trade of the East Anglian ports 1550–1590* (Oxford 1988), pp. 80–5.

96 James Melvill, *Autobiography and diary*, ed. R. Pitcairn (Wodrow Soc. 1842), p. 219; Gordon Donaldson, 'Scottish presbyterian exiles in England, 1584–8', *Records of the Scottish Church History Soc.*, 14 (1960), pp. 66–80; P. Collinson, 'The Elizabethan puritans and the foreign reformed churches in London', *Proc. of the Huguenot Soc.*, 20 (1964), pp. 528–55, repr. in his *Godly people* (1983), pp. 245–72. For Carmichael's educational work, see I. D. McFarlane, *Buchanan* (1981), pp. 442–3.

97 Allan Stevenson, 'Thomas Thomas makes a dictionary', *The Library*, 5th ser. 3 (1958), pp. 234–46. See also Starnes, *Renaissance dictionaries*, pp. 114–38.

98 Arber, II.438, 788.

99 For Bynneman, who had also sought to control various Latin and Greek texts, see Mark Eccles, 'Bynneman's books', *The Library*, 5th ser. 12 (1957), pp. 81–92.

100 British Library, MS Lansdowne 57, fo. 192; Morris, 'Restrictive practices', p. 288.

101 For an English translation, see *A disputation on holy scripture, against the Papists*, ed. William Fitzgerald (Parker Soc. 1849).

102 Gray and Palmer, p. 69.

103 For Walsingham, see above, n. 48; for Wickham, see Lee, *Early printed book labels*, pp. 3–4.

104 For a list of printed verses, see *STC*, 4474, where they are concisely described as 'briefly propounded theses... circulated by those taking part in public disputations as Acts for degrees'. See also A. Wall, *The ceremonies observed in the Senate House of the University of Cambridge*, ed. Henry Gunning (Cambridge 1828), pp. 84, 89.

105 Gray and Palmer, pp. 68–71.

106 Arber, II.43; Greg, *Companion*, pp. 43–4.

107 It is probably over-hasty to assume, however, that their value (£48.4s.2d.) reflected their production cost very exactly. See also below, p. 271.

108 Starnes, *Renaissance dictionaries*, pp. 249–55.

109 Dedication to Thomas, *Dictionarium*, 11th edn (1619). The dictionary continued to be printed in Thomas's own name until 1644, and was still prescribed as one of the standard authorities for school use in the 1650s, along with Stephanus and, Thomas's closest rival, John Rider's *Bibliotheca scholastica* (cf. M. Claire Cross, *The Free Grammar School at Leicester* (Leicester 1953), p. 34). Some of the principal changes to editions of Thomas's dictionary are summarized in Starnes, *Renaissance dictionaries*, pp. 119–33. For the subsequent career of Rider's dictionary, see Starnes, pp. 270–1; see also below, p. 231.

110 *Oh read ouer D. Iohn Bridges, for it is a worthy worke* [1588], p. 6.

111 This document is printed in the original Latin in S. Gibson and D. M. Rogers, 'The Earl of Leicester and printing at Oxford', *Bodleian Library Record*, 2 (1949), pp. 240–5, and in translation in Carter, *Oxford University Press*, pp. 19–20.

112 Cf. the Bishop of Lincoln's letter to Burghley, 27 July 1588 (British Library, MS Lansdowne 57, art. 74; Heywood and Wright, 1, p. 534).

113 Gray and Palmer, p. 69; H. Zanchius, *Epistolarum libri duo* (Hanau 1609).

114 This copy is now in Cambridge University Library, Cam.c.588.1; on Gerrard, see Venn, *Gonville and Caius*, 1, p. 61.

115 Summarized in Gray and Palmer, p. 65; transcript in University Archives, Wills II.108.

116 This was to be held in trust by John Rogers and by Thomas Browne, school-master of St Antholin's, in London: Thomas's choice of trustees offers a clue to his background, as St Antholin's was well known for its puritan stance, having founded a lectureship (the first

of its kind in London) in 1559. Cf. Paul S. Seaver, *The puritan lectureships; the politics of religious dissent, 1560–1662* (Stanford, Ca. 1970).

6 *John Legate, printer by profession*

1 The most convenient summary of these relationships is in the family tree included in Morris, 'Thomas Thomas', at p. 355.

2 Details are printed in Gray and Palmer, pp. 64–71.

3 *STC*, 3599. By Stephen Bredwell. Arber, II.491. Peter Milward, *Religious controversies of the Elizabethan age* (1977), no. 145. S. C. Roberts is mistaken in stating (*History*, p. 33) that Legate became Master of the Stationers' Company in 1604.

4 University Archives, VC Ct I.26, fo. 165v (Deposition of Michael Woolf, Anne Thomas's brother); VC Ct III.2(85) (Legate's answer).

5 University Archives, VC Ct I.26, fo. 165v. For much of the evidence presented in 1593/4 see also D. F. McKenzie, 'Notes on printing at Cambridge c. 1590', *TCBS*, 3 (1959), pp. 96–103.

6 This change is tabulated in C. B. Schmitt, *John Case and Aristotelianism*, pp. 225–9.

7 University Archives, VC Ct I.26, fo. 165r.

8 *Ibid.*, fo. 165v.

9 University Archives, CUR 6.2, identifying Thomas's widow as Agnes.

10 University Archives, VC Ct III.2(41); Almond's inventory is printed (with several inaccuracies) in Gray and Palmer, p. 64. Anne Thomas's claim was for £36, whereas Almond's entire estate amounted to only £19: he was said also to owe Thomas Bradshaw £12 (VC Ct III.2(40)).

11 *Grace Book* Δ, fo. 159v. Previous authorities have dated this event wrongly in 1588. Apart from the premises he shared with his mother-in-law, Legate also leased the shops formerly occupied successively by John Scarlet and Thomas Bradshaw at the west end of Great St Mary's. However, I have found no evidence that he used these premises for his press. See G. J. Gray, 'The shops at the west end of Great St Mary's Church, Cambridge', *Proc. Cambridge Antiquarian Soc.*, 13, no. 54 (1909), pp. 235–49. A copy of the lease of 6 October 1589 (i.e. before his election as University Printer), bearing Legate's signature, is in Trinity College muniments, Box 25, no. 26.

12 These and the following details are drawn from University Archives, VC Ct III.2(85).

13 University Archives, VC Ct III.2(116); VC Ct III.2(85).

14 University Archives, VC Ct III.2(116).

15 Smith (or Smythe), described in the Cambridge records as 'typographus', was translated into the Stationers' Company from the Drapers on 30 March 1585 (Arber, II.694). In 1586 he was accused (with Robert Bourn and Henry Jefferson) of printing grammars that were the privilege of Francis Flower (Arber, II.800–4; Greg, *Companion*, pp. 39–40).

16 The depositions of these men are in the University Archives, VC Ct III.2(141).

17 Gray and Palmer, pp. 70–1.

18 University Archives, VC Ct III.2(116).

19 University Archives, VC Ct III.2(141).

20 Arber, II.807–12.

21 Sheila Lambert, 'The printers and the government, 1604–1637', in *Aspects of printing from 1600*, ed. R. Myers and M. Harris (Oxford 1987), pp. 1–29.

22 C. Blagden, 'The English Stock of the Stationers' Company; an account of its origins', *The Library*, 5th ser. 10 (1955), pp. 163–85; Gerald D. Johnson, 'The Stationers versus the Drapers: control of the press in the late sixteenth century', *The Library*, 6th ser. 10 (1988), pp. 1–17; S. Rappaport, *Worlds within worlds; structures of life in sixteenth-century London* (Cambridge 1989), pp. 110–17, 164–5. But see also Rappaport's emphasis

on the power of the livery companies to regulate trade, control careers and determine everyday life (pp. 184–201).

23 For the dominance of the Stationers' Company by the English Stock, see C. Blagden, 'The Stationers' Company in the Civil War period', *The Library*, 5th ser. 13 (1958), pp. 1–17.

24 The most convenient summary of Elizabethan patents to stationers is in Arber, II.15–16. See also *ibid.*, pp. 775–6.

25 British Library, MS Lansdowne 62, fo. 86; Cooper, *Annals*, 2, pp. 477–8; Heywood and Wright, 2, pp. 1–3.

26 Herbert, *Historical catalogue*, p. 70. In 1587 Whitgift found it necessary to remind the Bishop of Lincoln (no doubt among others) of the need to place the Bible in places of worship: see Herbert, p. 98.

27 Stanley Morison, *The Geneva Bible* (1955); see above, p. 83.

28 Herbert, *Historical catalogue*, p. 102, stumbles in saying 1558.

29 M. H. Black touches on some aspects of standardization in his 'The evolution of a book-form: the octavo Bible from manuscript to the Geneva version', *The Library*, 5th ser. 16 (1961), pp. 15–28.

30 *STC*, 2889; Herbert, *Historical catalogue*, no. 207. British Library, MS Lansdowne 68, no. 31; Cooper, *Annals*, 2, p. 491; Heywood and Wright, 2, pp. 25–7; Greg, *Companion*, pp. 46, 148–51 (with translation).

31 See n. 29.

32 University Archives, VC Ct II.2(124).

33 *STC*, 2477·5. This did not include the music, for which Legate was then unequipped. The chance survival of one copy of this edition, and the extreme rarity of 32° editions generally, make it difficult to place Legate's work here in a proper publishing context. For further details of the Stationers' Company response, and for the gradual organization of what became known as the English Stock (to distinguish it from the Latin Stock and the Irish Stock), see C. Blagden, 'The English Stock of the Stationers' Company; an account of its origins', *The Library*, 5th ser. 10 (1955), pp. 163–85.

34 Arber, II.819–20; J. Strype, *Annals of the Reformation*, new edn (Oxford 1824), 4, pp. 103–5.

35 British Library, MS Lansdowne 68, no. 32. Heywood and Wright, 2, pp. 27–9; Cooper, *Annals*, 2, pp. 491–2; Arber, II.819–20; Greg, *Companion*, pp. 46–7. Cf. also the similar arguments summarized in University Archives, CUR 33.2(2b).

36 British Library, MS Lansdowne 48, no. 74; Arber, II.805; Greg, *Companion*, p. 40.

37 Greg and Boswell, p. 39. From 1585 until 1591 John Wolf was the customary printer of the metrical Psalms for Day's assigns.

38 Greg and Boswell, p. 41.

39 *Ibid.*, pp. 39–40.

40 *Ibid.*, p. liv, n. 1.

41 For Frankfurt fairs, see below, p. 144. For the terms 'entry', 'copy', 'assign', 'licence', etc., see W. W. Greg, *Some aspects and problems of London publishing between 1550 and 1650* (Oxford 1956), ch. 3 ('Licensing for the press') and ch. 4 ('Entrance and copyright').

42 Legate's edition does not include the dedication to Horatio Palavicino, dated Neustadt, Cal. August. 1590.

43 *STC*, 15516: the note of entry to Bishop on 9 December 1588 (Arber, II.510) obscures the true position. Cf. also Georg Willer, *Catalogus novus nundinarum vernalium Francofurti ad Moenum* (Frankfurt am Main 1591), fo. G2r. For Zanchius (*STC*, 26119·5), cf. Willer, *Catalogus*, fo. A3r; C. M. Dent, *Protestant reformers in Elizabethan Oxford* (Oxford 1983), pp. 96–102; and Leedham-Green, *Books in Cambridge inventories*.

44 *STC*, 15702, 15703. Cf. Lipsius to Jan Moretus, 14 June 1592, in *La correspondance de Juste Lipse conservée au Musée Plantin-Moretus*, ed. A. Gerlo and H. D. L. Vervliet (Antwerp 1967), pp. 39–40.

45 Quoted in. M. S. G. Hands, 'The cathedral libraries catalogue', *The Library*, 5th ser. 2 (1947), pp. 1–13, at pp. 9–10. (The original is in Lincoln Cathedral Library.)

46 Starnes, *Renaissance dictionaries*, p. 242, provides a summary of these entries.

47 Thomas Fuller, *The history of the worthies of England* (1662), p. 128, quoted in Starnes, *Renaissance dictionaries*, p. 240. Starnes unravels the mistakes made by Fuller in his account of this episode. See also pp. 440–1, below.

48 Jackson, *Records*, p. 18.

49 Greg, *Companion*, pp. 60, 178; Jackson, *Records*, p. 175. Greg is mistaken in suggesting that the copy of Thomas's Latin dictionary 'presumably belonged to the University'. For further details in the dispute, see C. J. Sisson, 'The laws of Elizabethan copyright: the Stationers' view', *The Library*, 5th ser. 15 (1960), pp. 8–20.

50 University Archives, Misc. Collect. 7, pp. 20–2.

51 Plomer *Wills*, p. 25.

52 Arber, II.779.

53 O*.13.2b(G) and P*.14.54(G) respectively. A copy of Downes' *Eratosthenes* in Cambridge University Library (W.4.43) is copiously annotated, perhaps by one of his auditors.

54 Downes (see also above, p. 103) was originally a Fellow of St John's, but he migrated to Trinity. Legate's deposit copy of Lysias now stands in the University Library at M*.14.13(F). The text was taken from the Stephanus edition of the Greek orators (1575).

55 For Legate's will, see below, p. 429, n. 44.

56 Bowes, 'University printers', p. 296.

57 H. R. Plomer, 'The Edinburgh edition of Sidney's "Arcadia"', *The Library*, 2nd ser. 1 (1900), pp. 195–205.

58 For Thomas and Manasses Vautrollier, both of whom worked in Edinburgh, see F. S. Ferguson, 'Relations between London and Edinburgh printers and stationers (–1640)', *The Library*, 4th ser. 8 (1927), pp. 145–98.

59 See above, p. 71. Cooper, *Annals*, 2, pp. 395–7.

60 Whitgift to the Vice-Chancellor (Some), 4 November 1590 (University Archives, Collect. Admin. 5, fo. 206r). For Thomas Vautrollier's will (proved 22 July 1587), see Plomer, *Wills*, pp. 27–8.

61 University Archives, CUR 33.6(3,4), 10 December 1590. For the contemporary anxiety at Strangers' effects on native trades, see A. Pettegree, *Foreign protestant communities in sixteenth-century London* (Oxford 1986), pp. 290–5. In 1593 a bill was prompted in Parliament to limit Strangers' rights to sell by retail, but it failed – thanks probably once again to Cecil (*ibid.*, pp. 291–2).

62 University Archives, Comm. Ct III.7(110–11). Bovier, or Bouvier, had been Thomas Vautrollier's executor in 1587 (Plomer, *Wills*, pp. 27, 35–6). Cf. also W. R. Lefanu, 'Thomas Vautrollier, printer and bookseller', *Proc. Huguenot Society of London*, 20 (1959), pp. 12–25. The licensed stationers in Cambridge in 1591–2 were (in descending order of the sums for which they were liable for taxation) Watson, Legate, John Porter, John Cuthbert, Thomas Bradshaw, Hugh Burwell, Vautrollier, John Jones, Benjamin Pryme and William Scarlet. The sums set against them ranged from twopence to two shillings, and some idea of their financial standing may be gained from comparing them with apothecaries (fourpence to 1s.8d.), surgeons (sixpence), and barbers (twopence to a shilling) (University Library, W. M. Palmer papers, bundle 9, box 41).

63 University Archives, VC Ct II.8(63); Arber, II.737; University Archives, VC Ct III.9(96) (bond); VC Ct III.11(29) (inventory).

64 University Archives, CUR 33.2(1). Barley specialized in ballads, cheap literature and music (McKerrow, *Dictionary*, pp. 20–1).

65 Harold Forster, 'The rise and fall of the Cambridge muses (1603–1763)', *TCBS*, 8 (1982), pp. 141–72. The practice of presenting specially commissioned books of verses to mark royal occasions was already established in manuscript. When in 1564 Elizabeth I visited Cambridge, the Provost of King's presented to her 'a fair book, covered with red velvet, containing all such verses as his company had made of her Grace's coming'. This volume was the work of one college. But order had also been given previously that there should be a more general volume containing verses, 'written, in the Roman hand, all the verses both of Greek and Latin, Hebrew, Caldee, and English, which were made of her coming, and otherwise set up in divers places of the town'. In this gathering together of verses, both official and unofficial, may be seen the beginning of a tradition by which the University set increasing store, as the opportunity for lobbying and statements of loyalty. Increasingly lavish sums were spent on the production and presentation of these volumes, until their demise in the mid-eighteenth century. For the proceedings in 1564, see J. Nichols, ed., *The progresses and public processions of Queen Elizabeth* (1788), p. 18. See also J. W. Binns, *Intellectual culture in Elizabethan and Jacobean England; the Latin writings of the age* (Leeds 1990), pp. 34–45.

66 *STC*, 10235 (1598), 10235·5 (1601), 10236 (1604), 10236·5 (1607). It is most unlikely that copies of all contemporary visitation articles have survived.

67 *STC*, 15516 (entered to G. Bishop 9 December 1588; sold in London by Kitson); *STC* 26120 (entered to S. Waterson 26 June 1598).

68 For details of other livings, see *DNB*, s.v. Willet.

69 Peter Smith's 'Life' of Willet, prefixed to *Synopsis Papismi* (1634), fo. a4v. For similar remarks, see Thomas Fuller, *Abel redevivus: or, the dead yet speaking* (1651), p. 567. For Willet in the Netherlands, see C. W. Schoneveld, *Intertraffic of the mind; studies in seventeenth-century Anglo-Dutch translation with a checklist of books translated from English into Dutch, 1600–1700* (Leiden 1983), p. 244.

70 A. Willet, *Hexapla in Genesin* (Cambridge 1605), fo. Ttlr.

71 *STC*, 25675.

72 *STC*, 25695, dated [1592?]. The book is perhaps more likely to have been published in 1591, as it includes verses to John Bull, Dean of Ely, who died on 31 October that year. See also Rosemary Freeman, *English emblem books* (1948), pp. 64–5.

73 The 1634 edition was published 'by ... royall letters patens': the patent, granted by James I, was the property of Willet's son Paul (Arber, V.lviii).

74 *STC*, 25682; Arber, III.290.

75 *STC*, 25698·7.

76 *STC*, 25677.

77 For his career, see *DNB*; Peile, *Christ's*, pp. 141–2; and, for a summary of his theology, H. C. Porter, *Reformation and reaction in Tudor Cambridge* (Cambridge 1958), especially pp. 288–313.

78 *STC*, 19724·5. The book was entered to Jackson (Arber, III.80), and Burwell may be presumed simply to have taken a modest number of copies for the Cambridge trade.

79 Perkins' popularity in Dutch is, again, most clearly set out in C. W. Schoneveld, *Intertraffic of the mind*, pp. 124–5, 220–6; see also Shaaber, *Check-list*, pp. 105–110. For the Cloppenburch press, see E. W. Moes and C. P. Burger, *De Amsterdamsche boekdrukkers en uitgevers in de zestiende eeuw*, 4 vols. (Amsterdam 1900–15), 3, pp. 322–35, and M. M. Kleerkooper and W. P. van Stockum, *De boekhandel te Amsterdam voornamelijk in de 17e eeuw*, 2 vols. ('s-Gravenhage 1914–16), 1, pp. 129–33.

80 Greg and Boswell, p. 45.

81 *STC*, 19752ff.

82 See the headnote under 'Perkins, William [*Works*]' in *STC*.

83 Thomas Pierson, 'An advertisement to the Christian reader', *STC*, 19649, vol. 3 (1609).

84 Jackson, *Records*, p. 439. The case is referred to under *STC*, 19724·7, but this may pertain to another edition, now lost.

85 *STC*, 13479. Hill's other books were printed in London.

86 *STC*, 17257. This was Manning's only book.

87 *STC*, 13429.

88 *STC*, 18209.

89 *STC*, 12100. The dedication of Gostwicke's earlier book, a translation of an anti-Bellarmine work by Polanus (*STC*, 20086) was dated from Cambridge, 28 January 1598.

90 STC 14369.

91 For details, see Peile, *Christ's*, 1, p. 205.

92 *STC*, 23820.

93 S. E. Morison, *The intellectual life of colonial New England*, 2nd edn (Ithaca, N.Y. 1956), p. 134; Perry Miller, *The New England mind; the seventeenth century* (New York 1939), pp. 335 ff.

94 W. T. Mitchell, ed., *Epistolae Academicae, 1508–1596* (Oxford Historical Soc. 1980), pp. 361–2.

95 *STC*, 25363.

96 The fragments survive as flyleaves in Cambridge University Library, Hhh.956, and comprise printers' copy for parts of fos. F1r-v, F3r-v. The presentation copy from Whitaker to John Duport, Vice-Chancellor in 1593–5, is now in Peterborough Cathedral Library, R.4.6.

97 *STC*, 19749, 19647, 19648, 19649, 25682.

98 Both this (*STC*, 13429) and his first (*STC*, 13419, *The preachers plea*, 1604) were printed for Simon Waterson.

99 *STC*, 1830. The title-page is notable for including a quotation in Hebrew from the book of Exodus: no extended work in Hebrew was printed at Cambridge until 1632 (see below, p. 183).

100 *Catalogue of the fifty manuscripts and printed books bequeathed to the British Museum by Alfred H. Huth* (1912), pp. 69–71; Lloyd E. Berry, 'Giles Fletcher the Elder's *Licia*', *The Library*, 5th ser. 15 (1960), pp. 133–4; and 'Giles Fletcher the Elder; a bibliography', *TCBS*, 3 (1961), pp. 200–15.

101 Arber, II.15–16. For a list of books affected by Tottel's monopoly see *ibid.*, II.419. Yetsweirt died in 1595, and his widow held the patent until 1597 (McKerrow, *Dictionary*, p. 305).

102 *STC*, 6443. This did not, apparently, sell well; remainder copies were issued with a cancel title-page in 1634 (*STC*, 6443·5).

103 J. Cowell, *The interpreter* (1701), Preface; R. Coke, *A detection of the court and state of England*, 3rd edn (1697), p. 60; S. B. Chrimes, 'The constitutional ideas of Dr John Cowell', *EHR*, 64 (1949), pp. 461–87; Sir William Holdsworth, *A history of English law*, 5 (3rd edn 1945), pp. 20–2; Sir Jocelyn Simon, 'Dr Cowell', *Cambridge Law Jnl*, 26 (1968), pp. 260–72; *Stuart royal proclamations*, 1, pp. 243–4. The copy of the 1607 edition in the University Library (Adv.d.28.4) is said to contain a transcript of Cowell's own notes.

104 Letters from Sir Thomas Edmondes to William Trumbull, March 1609–10: Historical MSS Commn, *Downshire*, 2, pp. 257–8, 262, 267.

105 Arber, II.724.

106 See above, p. 101.

107 *STC*, 25678, 25678a, 25693.

108 *STC*, 19722.

109 R. B. McKerrow and F. S. Ferguson, *Title-page borders used in England & Scotland 1485–1640* (Bibliographical Soc. 1932), no. 46.

110 *Grace Book E*, p. 209; on Brooke generally see H. P. Stokes, *The Esquire Bedells of the University of Cambridge* (Cambridge Antiquarian Soc. 1911), pp. 92–3 and Oates, *Cambridge University Library*, p. 154.

111 R. B. McKerrow, *Printers' & publishers' devices in England & Scotland 1485–1640* (Bibliographical Soc. 1913), nos. 325–7, 329, 416; H. P. Stokes, *The emblem, the arms & the motto of the University of Cambridge* (Cambridge [1928]); Suzanne M. Eward, 'Alma mater Cantabrigia: a device in print and plaster', *Proc. Cambridge Antiquarian Soc.*, 77 (1988), pp. 137–43.

112 In 1644 John Legate the younger had not yet been appointed University Printer.

113 F. Madan, *The early Oxford press* (Oxford Historical Soc. 1895), pp. 296, etc.

114 *STC*, 19726, 19730, 19746.

115 A second edition was published at Cambridge in 1607 (*STC*, 23891): no copy of the third edition is recorded.

116 For the complicated course of this book, see *STC*, 13378ff. A second, posthumous, volume, assembled in 1620, was printed not by Legate but by Stansby.

7 Cantrell Legge and the University's common cause

1 University Archives, CUR 11.20(1).

2 *STC*, 10683 (*A supplication*). For one exception, in 1613, cf. *STC*, 25434.

3 B. E. Supple, *Commercial crisis and change in England, 1600–1642* (Cambridge 1959), pp. 52–72.

4 Arber, III.321.

5 *STC*, 24996·5; 24996a.

6 *STC*, 19755: Perkins, *A treatise tending vnto a declaration whether a man be in the estate of damnation or in the estate of grace*, first published probably in 1590. Greene's was at least the ninth edition. Porter had had an interest in the book since its publication, and it is not impossible (given the fragile surviving evidence) that Legate shared the cost of the 1608 edition with Greene.

7 *Grace Book Z*, p. 121.

8 Foster, *Great St Mary's*, pp. 330, 332, 335, 341, 344. For his later career, after Legge's death, see pp. 161–3.

9 Arber, III.386–7, 397.

10 Arber, II.226; *STC*, 20270. The book proved a success. Two editions appeared in 1630, and after Greene's death Boler continued to publish it with his widow Joan.

11 The evolution of Cambridge theological opinion in these years may be followed in N. Tyacke, *Anti-Calvinists; the rise of English Arminianism c. 1590–1640* (Oxford 1987), especially pp. 29–57.

12 See above, pp. 131–2.

13 *STC*, 3368·5; Brian North Lee, *Early printed book labels; a catalogue of dated personal labels and gift labels printed in Britain to the year 1760* (London 1976).

14 Harold Forster, 'The rise and fall of the Cambridge muses', *TCBS*, 8 (1962), pp. 141–72. Not for the last time, the press could not always cope with the demands of contributors to these volumes. One copy of the *Lacrymae* marking the death of Queen Anne in 1619 (Edinburgh University Library, De.3.42) includes an extra leaf bearing verses partly in Hebrew, by Nathanael Flick of Corpus Christi College. The Hebrew has been added in manuscript. See Robert H. MacDonald, *The library of Drummond of Hawthornden* (Edinburgh 1971), p. 163.

15 Cooper, *Annals*, 3, pp. 56–7; Vatican, MS Pal. Lat. 1736; Leicester Bradner, 'New poems

by George Herbert; the Cambridge gratulatory anthology of 1613', *Renaissance News*, 15 (1962), pp. 208–11; Ilse Schunke, *Die Einbände der Palatina in der Vatikanischen Bibliothek*, 2 vols. in 3 (Vatican 1962), 1, p. 250, and plate cxxxi; Elmar Mittler, ed., *Bibliotheca Palatina*, 2 vols. (Heidelberg 1986), pp. 265–6 and plate 186; P. C. Dust, ed., *The carmen gratulans adventu Serenissimi Principis Frederici Comitis Palatini ad Academiam Cantabrigiensem*, 2 vols. (Salzburg 1975).

16 See, for example, *STC* 4471·5 (order for vagrants: one copy only), 7686·4 (notice about fen drainage: six copies only), 8851·3, 8851·5 (notices about farthing tokens: three copies only). It may be assumed that many printed visitation articles for this period have also disappeared completely.

17 These were also produced in various manuscript versions. Scot originally drew up his list by 1617 (Mullinger 2, p. 468), though he had been preceded not only by Thomas, but also by Matthew Parker, whose *Catalogus cancellariorum* was added to his *De antiquitate Britannicae ecclesiae* (1572–4: *STC*, 19292, of which the ornate Burghley copy is now in Cambridge University Library, Sel.3.229). Examples of Scot's ornate manuscripts survive *inter alia* as British Library, MS Harley 4017 and Cambridge University Library, MS Gg.5.21.

18 See below, pp. 149–53. For plans for editions of the Fathers, cf. Thomas Goad to Samuel Ward, 26 January 1620/1, Bodleian Library, MS Tanner 290, fo. 49.

19 University Archives, VC Ct III.28(19).

20 University Archives, VC Ct III.26(62).

21 University Archives, VC Ct III.28(19), VC Ct Accounts 2 (1622–47), nos. 46–7; Gray and Palmer, pp. 85–6. For Twells, see J. M. Gray, *Biographical notes on the mayors of Cambridge* (Cambridge 1922).

22 For the beginning of the English Stock, a business within the Stationers' Company run ostensibly for the benefit of the Company's poorer members, and controlling some of the most lucrative monopolies in publishing, see Blagden, *Stationers' Company*, pp. 75–6. For its books, see *STC*, vol. 3, appendices. Cf. also C. Blagden, 'The English Stock of the Stationers' Company in the time of the Stuarts', *The Library*, 5th ser. 12 (1957), pp. 167–86.

23 University Archives, CUR 33.2(15). I have not attempted to identify Legge's work, which was presumably absorbed into Barker's own.

24 Blagden, *Stationers' Company*, pp. 105–7; Jackson, *Records*, p. 95n; Pollard and Ehrman, pp. 87–9.

25 University Archives, CUR 33.2(86, 88), undated papers in which Fetherstone alluded to having served Norton for nine years (i.e. the term of his apprenticeship) and having traded independently in foreign books for six. Since Fetherstone was freed in 1607, this suggests a date of *c.* 1613 (McKenzie, *Apprentices 1605–40*, no. 380).

26 Fetherstone's father, a wealthy man, had died in 1615: see Lois Spencer, 'The professional and literary connexions of George Thomason', *The Library*, 5th ser. 13 (1958), pp. 102–18, at p. 105.

27 University Archives, CUR 33.2(88). For the Frankfurt fair in the seventeenth century, see F. Kapp and J. Goldfriedrich, *Geschichte des deutschen Buchhandels* (Leipzig 1886–1923); W. Born, *Catalogi nundinales, 1571–1852; die Frankfurter und Leipziger Messkataloge der Herzog August Bibliothek Wolfenbüttel* (Wolfenbüttel 1982); and H. J. Koppitz, 'The two bookmarkets in Germany in the XVII and XVIII centuries', in *Le livre dans les sociétés pré-industrielles* (Athens 1982), pp. 77–93. For English books, see M. Spirgatis, 'Englische Literatur auf der Frankfurter Messe von 1561–1620', in *Beiträge zur Kennt des Schrift-, Buch-, und Bibliothekswesen*, 7 (Leipzig 1902), pp. 37–89. But although the 1625 edition of Draud's *Bibliotheca exotica* included a section of 'Libri Britannici' (probably in response to English interests in Heidelberg), the books listed there (including a copy of

the St Albans Chronicle (Wynkyn de Worde, 1502) and a manuscript verse account of the Kings of England) appear to relate to a private library rather than the recent international trade in new books. For the English part in this trade, see Pollard and Ehrman, pp. 85–102, though Pollard's reliance on Schwetschke is misleading.

28 University Archives, CUR 33.2(87, 88).

29 Jackson, *Records*, p. 94.

30 Public Record Office, C.3/334/73. It is not clear from this, despite Robert G. Long, 'London's aldermen in business, 1600–1625', *Guildhall Miscellany*, 3 (1971), pp. 242–64, that these assets included a printing works as well.

31 Possibly an allusion to the ten-volume edition of St Augustine published at Cologne by Antonius Hierat in 1616.

32 University Archives, CUR 33.2(87); Sheila Lambert, 'The printers and the government, 1604–1637', in *Aspects of printing from 1600*, ed. R. Myers and Michael Harris (Oxford 1987), pp. 1–29, at p. 6; Graham Pollard and Albert Ehrman, *The distribution of books by catalogue from the invention of printing to A.D. 1800* (Roxburghe Club 1965), pp. 87–92.

33 *STC*, 20567·3, printed at Frankfurt at the expense of H[umphrey] Robinson (of London) and William Fitzer (of Frankfurt). The sole copy recorded in *STC*, at Cambridge University Library, is in an Oxford binding, and was bought there in 1631 by Henry Kent, a student at St John's College. Many other copies were presumably imported as well. On Fitzer, see also E. Weil, 'William Fitzer, the publisher of Harvey's *De motu cordis*, 1628', *The Library*, 4th ser. 24 (1943–4), pp. 142–64.

34 And so he continued to supply books to the University and as middleman to the local booksellers (University Archives, CUR 33.6(13); Comm. Ct III.18(103–7, etc.). For profits, see CUR 33.2 (87).

35 University Archives, CUR 33.2(88).

36 Cooper, *Annals*, 3, pp. 144–5; *Grace Book* Z, pp. 39–41.

37 The Latin Stock, floated in January 1616, paid a single dividend (in November 1619 – and that out of capital which had to be raised by a loan almost immediately afterwards), and collapsed in 1627: its failure was finally accepted in 1636. See H. R. Plomer, 'Some notes on the Latin and Irish Stocks of the Company of Stationers', *The Library*, 2nd ser. 8 (1907), pp. 286–97; Blagden, *Stationers' Company*, pp. 105–7; Jackson, *Records*, pp. 278–9. For Bill and Norton, see McKerrow, *Dictionary*, pp. 31–3, 201–3.

38 Bodleian Library, MS Tanner 290, fos. 46, 47.

39 Gwen Hampshire, ed., *The Bodleian Library account book, 1613–1646* (Oxford Bibliographical Soc. 1983), p. 41. From 1621–2 the Bodleian employed Fetherstone (*ibid.*, pp. 45 ff.).

40 Bodleian Library, MS Tanner 290, fo. 49.

41 University Archives, CUR 33.2(95), fo. 15r.

42 University Archives, CUR 33.2(65), fo. 53r; J. W. Thompson, *The Frankfurt book fair* (Chicago 1911; repr. New York 1968), pp. 63–4. On the European effects of the Thirty Years War on the book trade, see also H.-J. Martin, *Livre, pouvoirs et société à Paris au XVIIe siècle (1598–1701)*, 2 vols. (Geneva 1969), pp. 303–6.

43 See below, pp. 210–11.

44 Arber, IV.45–6; Jackson, *Records*, p. 130 (4 September 1620). Legate's will is in the Guildhall Library, Commissary Court of London: original Will, and Register 24, fo. 5v (copy). Under its terms, all his printing equipment passed to his son; the list of his copies, contained in a codicil, does not survive, but he singled out Thomas's dictionary for particular mention in the will itself: 'all my right, tittle, interest Estate, terme, & terme of yeares, wch I have in Thomas Thomasius his dictionarie by his M^ties Graunte made vnto me, vnder the Great Seale of England'.

45 Greg, *Companion*, pp. 60, 178.

46 *Grace Book* Z, pp. 39–41; Heywood and Wright, 2, pp. 306–8; translated in Cooper, *Annals*, 3, pp. 144–5. For the Latin Stock see below, p. 210.

47 University Archives, U.Ac.2(1), University audit book, 1545–1659: 1613–14.

48 University Archives, CUR 33.2(5), fo. 5r; CUR 33.2(15).

49 The English Stock was summarized in a highly critical manner by George Wood in 1621: University Archives, CUR 33.2(93). This document is misdated by Blagden and others, and is discussed briefly in S. Lambert, 'The printers and the government 1604–1637', p. 5 and n. 13.

50 Jackson, *Records*, pp. 74, 117. A list of titles in the Stock is provided *ibid.*, p. 165.

51 Stationers' Company Letter Book, fo. 90r; Jackson, *Records*, p. 371.

52 *Ibid.*, fo. 98ᵛ; pp. 372–3.

53 University Archives, CUR 33.2(25). These figures should be compared with the quantities of stock listed in March 1624 in the control of the London partners, including 3,000 Lily, 3,625 Camden, 3,000 (unidentified) Accidences, and 2,578 Clenardus (Jackson, *Records*, p. 165).

54 Greg, *Companion*, p. 179. See also Stationers' Company Letter Book, fo. 98ᵛ; Jackson, *Records* pp. 373–4.

55 Jackson, *Records*, pp. 117–18, 147.

56 University Archives, CUR 33.2(31); CUR 33.2(35).

57 Greg, *Companion*, p. 181. See also Stationers' Company Letter Book, fo. 103r; Jackson, *Records*, p. 382.

58 University Archives, CUR 33.2(41). See also Pr.P.4(4, 6).

59 *STC*, 2584 (other copies survive also), 2584·5.

60 University Archives, VC Ct III.27(192).

61 University Archives, CUR 33.2(43).

62 Greg, *Companion*, p. 183.

63 *Ibid.*, p. 185. See also Stationers' Company Letter Book, fo. 104r–v, Jackson, *Records*, pp. 382–4.

64 Arber, IV.527. For the almanac trade, see E. F. Bosanquet, *English printed almanacks and prognostications; a bibliographical history to the year 1600* (Bibliographical Soc. 1917) and Bernard F. Capp, *Astrology and the popular press; English almanacs 1500–1800* (1979).

65 Greg, *Companion*, p. 69; Arber, IV. 527.

66 For the background, cf. also University Archives, CUR 33.2(63), including a legal definition of Prognostication.

67 University Archives, CUR 36.3(6 and 7).

68 *STC*, 14345, first published in 1616 (*STC*, 14344).

69 University Archives, CUR 36.3(6 and 7).

70 Greg, *Companion*, pp. 190–2.

71 See below, pp. 196–7.

72 University Archives, CUR 33.2(56 and 57).

73 University Archives, CUR 33.2(62).

74 Greg, *Companion*, pp. 233–4. *A proclamation to inhibit the sale of Latine bookes reprinted beyond the seas, hauing been first printed in Oxford or Cambridge* (1625).

75 University Archives, CUR 33.2(9).

76 University Archives, CUR 33.1(5).

77 University Archives, U.Ac.2(1), p. 541. Legge had entered into a bond of £500 with the University on 28 January 1628 not to enter into any agreement with the Stationers' Company save with the University's agreement, and to contribute to legal costs (University Archives, Pr.B.2.11).

78 University Archives, CUR 33.2(9).

79 See above, pp. 148–9.

80 See below, chapter 13.

81 British Library, MS Harley 7040. Heywood and Wright, 2, pp. 303–5; *Acts P.C.*, 1621–3, p. 237; University Archives, VC Ct III.26 (37–48); MS Harley 389, fo. 206 (Joseph Mede to Sir Martin Stutevile, 22 June 1629); *DNB*, s.v. Owen, David.

82 University Archives, VC Ct III.26(49).

83 As his name suggests, Owen was a Welshman, 'Monensi'. The first words of Welsh to be printed in a Cambridge book, so far as I know, appear at the end of his treatise, quoting 1 Peter ii.17.

84 See above, p. 148.

85 *Grace Book* Z, pp. 39–41.

86 *STC*, 5973, 5129.

87 *Grace Book* Z, p. 62; see below, p. 161.

88 University Archives, VC Ct III.28(19).

89 Arber, IV.212; McKenzie, *Apprentices 1605–40*, p. 46.

8 *A new beginning: Thomas Buck and Roger Daniel*

1 University Archives, CUR 33.6(10); CUR 33.6(5).

2 See above, pp. 132–3. On Brooke as University Librarian (a post which he held from 1623), see also Oates, *Cambridge University Library*; for the office of Esquire Bedell, see *Historical Register*, pp. 58–62 and, especially for further biographical details, H. P. Stokes, *The Esquire Bedells of the University of Cambridge from the 13th century to the 20th century* (Cambridge Antiquarian Soc. 1911).

3 W. H. S. Jones, *A history of St Catharine's College* (Cambridge 1936), pp. 10–11, 14; Willis and Clark, 2, pp. 74–8, 92–6; Stokes, *Esquire Bedells*, pp. 96–9. For the Buck family, see the wills of Thomas Buck, yeoman, of Ugley, Essex (d. 1612), PCC 50 Fenner, and of Mary Buck his widow (d. 1619), PCC 98 Parker. Cole's notes on the family, after the Cambridgeshire visitation, 1684, are in British Library, MS Add. 5822, fos. 22v–23r.

4 *Grace Book* Z, p. 121.

5 For his will, see Gray and Palmer, pp. 110–11.

6 McKenzie, *Apprentices 1605–40*, p. 109.

7 Gray and Palmer, p. 78; Arber, III.321. No edition of Hall's *Meditations* is known bearing Porter's and Greene's joint imprint, though several appeared in 1606 with Porter's name alone – all printed in London by Lownes (*STC*, 12680).

8 Arber, IV.86; III.566.

9 Arber, IV.201, 223, 226.

10 *STC*, 20270, 20270·5 (1630).

11 University Archives, CUR 33.1(11).

12 University Archives, CUR 33.1(8); CUR 33.2(76), fo. 1r; Grace Book Z, pp. 106, 121. Stokes, *Esquire Bedells*, p. 99.

13 For example, University Archives, VC Ct III.33(135).

14 VC Ct III.28(19).

15 For details, see University Archives, CUR 33.1(11).

16 *Ibid.*

17 *STC*, 20270, 20270·5.

18 Greg, *Companion*, pp. 73, 193.

19 For the election, see Mullinger 3, (Cambridge 1911), pp. 56–64 and Oates, *Cambridge University Library*, pp. 162–3.

20 Greg, *Companion*, pp. 71, 191.

21 Arber, II.807–12; Greg, *Companion*, pp. 41–2.

22 Arber, v.lii.

23 *STC*, 16786·3 (Lemon 312, misdated 1641?).

24 See above, pp. 143–4.

25 *Commons Journal*, I, pp. 470, 490.

26 Jackson, *Records*, p. 75.

27 Jackson, *Records*, p. 158.

28 Jackson, *Records*, p. 146.

29 Jackson, *Records*, pp. 158–9, 161, 168, 169, 174, 187, 190, 201.

30 Jackson, *Records*, pp. xiv–xvi, 142; Letter Book, fos. 99a, etc. (ed. Jackson, pp. 375–80).

31 Jackson, *Records*, pp. 169, 194.

32 Jackson, *Records*, p. 186.

33 Greg, *Companion*, p. 197.

34 Greg, *Companion*, pp. 76–7, 203–5; *Acts P.C.*, 1628–9, pp. 403–7.

35 *Life of James Usher*, ed. R. Parr (1686), p. 394.

36 Greg, *Companion*, pp. 65, 183; see above, pp. 153–4.

37 University Archives, CUR 33.2(9).

38 Greg, *Companion*, pp. 206–7 (letter from the University to Viscount Dorchester, Secretary to Charles I, 20 January 1629). The University also addressed a letter of quite exceptional effusiveness to Thomas Howard, Earl of Arundel, thanking him for his assistance in this *causa typographica*: the need for such a tone was presumably because his uncle, the Earl of Suffolk, had been succeeded as Chancellor on his death in 1626 by Buckingham, no friend to the family (Greg, *Companion*, pp. 186–90).

39 See below, p. 274.

40 On 6 February 1634/5 he was said to be about forty-two (University Archives, CUR 33.1(21).

41 *STC*, 794, 794·5, 653, 4955·5, 17467, 22527a·5. Alexander Globe *Peter Stent, London printseller c. 1642–1665* (Vancouver 1985), nos. 145, 184, 419, 496, 525. Hind, *Engraving in England*, 2, nos. 365, etc.

42 See below, pp. 177, 182.

43 *STC*, 794·5, assigned to Shefford on 4 July 1626 'ex consensu magistri Daniel'.

44 See above, pp. 145–6.

45 *STC*, 2609ff. At least one of the several editions dated 1628, and bearing a Cambridge/Daniel imprint, is false.

46 Greg, *Companion*, p. 205. *STC* records only a single copy of a 1629 Cambridge edition of Lily, though the agreement of 16 April 1629 alludes to 304 grammars, 900 *Accidences*, and 7,000 unfinished grammars.

47 Greg, *Companion*, p. 271.

48 Jackson, *Records*, p. 223; University Archives, CUR 33.2(7).

49 Joseph Mede to Sir Martin Stuteville, 27 October 1630 (British Library, MS Harley 390, fo. 521).

50 University Archives, CUR 33.1(21).

51 See below, pp. 202–3. For the King's Printing House at this period, see P. M. Handover, *The 'wicked' Bible and the King's Printing House, Blackfriars* (1958) and H. R. Plomer, 'The King's Printing House under the Stuarts', *The Library*, new ser. 2 (1901), 353–75.

52 University Archives, CUR 33.1(21).

53 University Archives, CUR 33.1(15). By the same agreement Thomas Buck arranged for John to take on most of his duties as Esquire Bedell.

54 *Grace Book* Z, p. 197; CUR 33.1(16).

55 University Archives, CUR 33.1(22), undated.

56 University Archives, CUR 33.1(21).

57 *Grace Book* Z, p. 233 (24 July 1632).

58 University Archives, CUR 33.1(19).

59 University Archives, CUR 33.1(18); CUR 33.1(13) (copy).

60 University Archives, CUR 33.1(20).

61 See pp. 205–14.

62 Greg, *Companion*, pp. 76–7, 203–5.

63 For one complaint that it had been kept secret even from the University, see University Archives, CUR 33.2(75).

64 University Archives, CUR 33.1(13).

65 University Archives, CUR 33.1(22).

9 *An uneasy partnership*

1 'One of the most distinguished Cambridge printers of the seventeenth century. He had many partners, with most of whom he quarrelled, and he produced many fine books' (Roberts, *History*, pp. 44–5).

2 Cf. Minucius Felix (1643); Ames (1646); Heinsius (1646); Burgersdijck (1650).

3 'Oratio praefatoria' to Isaac Barrow, *Lectiones mathematicae* (1683), in his *Mathematical works*, ed. W. Whewell (Cambridge 1860), pp. 12–13. In 1669 Barrow dedicated his *Lectiones opticae* to Lucas's two executors, Buck and Robert Raworth. P. Osmond (*Isaac Barrow; his life and times* (1944), pp. 110–11) slightly muddles Barrow's remarks on Buck as Esquire Bedell and as University Printer. For the Lucasian chair see Clark, *Endowments*, pp. 165–6. See also M. Feingold, 'Isaac Barrow: divine, scholar, mathematician', in *Before Newton; the life and times of Isaac Barrow*, ed. Feingold (Cambridge 1990), pp. 1–104, at p. 65.

4 University Archives, CUR 33.2(17, 48).

5 Winterton's own copy, bound by one of two local bookbinders, Henry Moody or John Houlden, in purple stained deerskin, gilt, is now in the Pierpont Morgan Library, PML 77688.

6 University Archives, CUR 33.1(22).

7 *Ibid.*

8 University Archives, CUR 33.1(23).

9 H. Jenkins, *Edward Benlowes* (1952), pp. 68–75. See also p. 284 below.

10 T. A. Birrell, 'The influence of seventeenth-century publishers on the presentation of English literature', in *Historical & editorial studies in medieval & early modern English for Johan Gerritsen*, ed. M.-J. Arn, H. Wirtjes and H. Jansen (Groningen 1985), pp. 163–73.

11 For Crashaw, see P. Beal, *Index of English literary manuscripts. 2. 1625–1700*, pt 1 (1987), pp. 268–9; for Herrick, *ibid.*, pp. 529–34; for Randolph, Thomas Randolph, *Poems*, ed. G. Thorn-Drury (1929); for Phineas Fletcher, Beal, *Index*, 1, pt 2 (1980), pp. 83–4, and Giles Fletcher and Phineas Fletcher, *Poetical works*, ed. F. S. Boas, 2 vols. (Cambridge 1908–9). Cf. also T.-L. Pebworth and C. J. Summers, 'Recovering an important seventeenth-century poetical miscellany: Cambridge Add. MS 4138', *TCBS* 7 (1978), pp. 156–69.

12 Brian Morris, *John Cleveland (1613–1658); a bibliography of his poems* (Bibliographical Soc. 1967), pp. 5–6, 26–7; J. C[leveland], *Poems* (1653); Alan H. Nelson, ed., *Records of early English drama. Cambridge*, 2 vols. (Toronto 1989), pp. 902–3, 908–9, 974, 975. Manuscripts of several of these plays are currently being published in facsimile in the series *Renaissance Latin drama in England*, 2nd ser., ed. M. Spevack, J. W. Binns and H.-J. Weckermann (Hildesheim 1987–).

13 For one example of skills in Italian a generation earlier that did not get into print, cf. Trinity College, MS R.10.6, a manuscript by Guglielmo Valerio, *Di varie maniere di*

parlare della Italica lingua, dated 'In Cantabrigia A xxix d'Agusto MDCXIII'. English versions have been added to parts of the text in another hand, and on fo. 142 is a note that the volume had been prepared with the help of William Woodford (Fellow of King's from 1602, and chaplain to Viscount Dorchester). The manuscript may have been intended for the circle of Prince Henry. Peripatetic, or semi-settled, teachers of modern languages remained common in Cambridge throughout the century, their presence attested often in college (rather than University) payments: see, for example, payments by Trinity in 1658 of five shillings each to 'Jacobus a Fraxino' and J. Martyn (Steward's accounts, 1639–60).

14 Geoffrey Keynes, *The life of William Harvey* (Oxford 1966); and *A bibliography of the writings of Dr William Harvey, 1578–1657*, 3rd edn, rev. G. Whitteridge and C. English (Winchester 1989), pp. 72–7.

15 One of the Cambridge University Library copies (M.8.24) is on large paper, and was presented by Cruso to Jonas Proast, son of the pastor of the Dutch church at Colchester and his senior by a few years (cf. Venn): 'The worke I acknowledge to be but weakely performed, my more serious imployments permitting me (ut Caius ad Nilam) onely to do it by snatches.' The copy in Gonville and Caius College (L.18.14) is inscribed 'Ex dono Johis Cruso Gener: & Mercatoris Norwicensis'. Cf. also Venn, *Gonville and Caius*, 1, p. 304.

16 Newton's and Duport's books are now in Trinity College. These treatises are described in M. Cockle, *A bibliography of English military books up to 1642* (1900) and in Max Jähns, *Geschichte der Kriegswissenschaften, vornehmlich in Deutschland*, 3 vols. (Munich 1889–91).

17 Arber, IV.267. Blount died in October 1632 (Plomer, p. 39).

18 See pp. 240–2.

19 For Winterton, see *DNB*.

20 *Irenodia Cantabrigiensis*, celebrating the King's return from Scotland in November 1641. But cf. above, p. 428 n.14.

21 Like his contemporaries, Mede sought a greater impact for his book by giving elaborately bound copies to influential friends or acquaintances. The copy given to John Williams, Bishop of Lincoln, is now in St John's College (Qq.11.5), and that given to Nathaniel Rich is now in the British Library (C.66.c.14). Both were bound in Cambridge. See H. M. Nixon, *Broxbourne Library; styles and designs of bookbindings from the twelfth to the twentieth century* (1956), p. 130 and M. M. Foot, *The Henry Davis gift; a collection of bookbindings*, 2 vols. (1978–83), 1, pp. 65–6, 70.

22 Clark, *Endowments*, pp. 172–7: Oates, *Cambridge University Library*, pp. 178–9, 184–5, 188. For Metcalfe, see A. F. Torry, *Founders and benefactors of St John's College, Cambridge* (Cambridge 1888), pp. 28–9, 106, and Cambridge University Library, MS Dd.11.61.

23 H. D. L. Vervliet, 'Robert Granjon à Rome, 1578–1589', *Bull. de l'Institute Historique Belge à Rome*, 38 (1967), pp. 177–231; *The type specimen of the Vatican Press, 1628*, facsimile with an introduction and notes by H. D. L. Vervliet (Amsterdam 1967); L. Fuks and R. G. Fuks-Mansfeld, *Hebrew typography in the northern Netherlands, 1585–1815*, 2 vols. (Leiden 1984–7).

24 James Usher, *Works*, 17 vols. (Dublin 1847–64), 15, pp. 253–4 (letter from Usher to Sir Robert Cotton, 12 July 1625).

25 Oates, *Cambridge University Library*, pp. 164–7, 217–31.

26 Stanley Morison, *John Fell* (Oxford 1967), p. 16, with further references to Erpenius' type; H. J. Todd, *Memoirs of the life and writings of the Right Rev Brian Walton* (1821), 1, pp. 193–4; Sir Henry Ellis, ed., *Original letters of eminent literary men* (1843), pp. 133–4.

27 A. Willems, *Les Elzevier* (Brussels 1880), p. cxiii.

28 Greaves to Usher, 30 November 1627, quoted in Todd, *Walton*, 1, p. 195. Greaves revealed his inadequate knowledge of the matter in writing of the sorts required for his proposal that 'matrices may be easily cast for them all': matrices are struck, not cast. For his later use of oriental type, see Morison, *John Fell*, pp. 25, 161, 241–2.

29 University Archives, CUR 33.6(16).

30 Now Cambridge University Library, MSS Hh.6.1–2; Hh.5.1–7.

31 Clarke to Oley, 29 June 1632, Cambridge University Library, MS Dd.3.12, III(2), i and ii.

32 Adams to Whelock, 8 November 1632, Cambridge University Library, MS Dd.3.12, IV(15).

33 On this episode, see Oates, *Cambridge University Library*, pp. 213–16, and *Grace Book* H, pp. 22–3; see also Alastair Hamilton, *William Bedwell the Arabist, 1563–1632* (Leiden 1985), pp. 85–94.

34 On Adams, see *DNB*. Cf. also a copy of an undated letter from the University to Adams, announcing the setting up of an Arabic press, University Archives, CUR.33.6(16).

35 Arber, III.634; IV.255.

36 Darlow and Moule, no. 4678, count eleven variants. For Daniel's folio Greek New Testament, see below, p. 192.

37 Madan, *Oxford books*, 1, p. 121 (*Camdeni insignia*). The matrices are still in the possession of the Oxford University Press: see Morison, *John Fell*, pp. 102–3 (notes by Harry Carter). Carter points out that Savile's set of matrices had been contaminated by 1629, and that the Cambridge Greek Testament contains capitals and many ligatures different from the Eton Chrysostom.

38 The relevant correspondence is printed in Madan, *Oxford books*, 2, pp. 517–20.

39 Syn.5.63.14.

40 Madan, *Oxford books*, 1, p. 166; Morison, *John Fell*, pp. 13–15, 20–2.

41 Ælfric, *A Saxon treatise* (1632), fo. e3r. See also Lisle's more general hopes of publishing 'more of the same kind', on fo. b1r.

42 Bodleian Library, MS Laud Misc. 201, fo. 1r; see also below, pp. 258–9.

43 His edition of Ælfric was remaindered in 1638 (see Bruce Dickins, 'William L'isle the Saxonist and three XVIIth century remainder-issues', *English and Germanic Studies*, 1 (1948), pp. 53–5), but this need not have affected the decision not to publish in 1630–1. Lisle's last years seem to have been spent in straitened circumstances: in 1654 Trinity College gave him five shillings out of charity (Trinity College Steward's accounts, 1654).

44 McKitterick, *Cambridge University Library*, p. 137.

45 M. Murphy, 'Abraham Wheloc's edition of Bede's *History* in OE', *Studia Neophilologica* 39 (1967), pp. 46–59; Murphy and E. Barrett, 'Abraham Wheelock, Arabist and Saxonist', *Biography*, 8 (1985), pp. 163–85; Oates, *Cambridge University Library*, chs. 7–9; and Oates, 'Abraham Whelock', Sandars Lectures (1966); typescript copies in Cambridge University Library, Cam.b.966.2, and in the British Library, Ac.2660.m(20). Whelock's omnivorous reading, and his contributions to the University's *Irenodia Cantabrigiensis* (1641) in Hebrew and Anglo-Saxon, provided inspiration for John Cleveland's 'Smectymnuus', written probably early in the following year: cf. John Cleveland, *Poems*, ed. B. Morris and E. Withington (Oxford 1967), pp. 23, 102–3.

46 Oates, *Cambridge University Library*, pp. 198–9.

47 Whelock to Henry Spelman, 13 June 1638, British Library, MS Add. 25384, art. 8.

48 Simonds D'Ewes to Whelock, 26 August 1639, Cambridge University Library, MS Dd.3.12 V (10a); Oates, *Cambridge University Library*, p. 204.

49 N. R. Ker, *Catalogue of manuscripts containing Anglo-Saxon* (Oxford 1957), nos. 23, 39, 180. (For William Lisle's interest in Cotton's manuscripts in this respect, see Ker, p. 234, citing MS Harley 6018.)

50 British Library, MS Add. 34600, fo. 195; Oates, *Cambridge University Library*, pp. 202–3;

D. McKitterick, 'The Eadwine Psalter rediscovered', in *The Eadwine Psalter*, ed. M. Gibson, T. A. Heslop and R. W. Pfaff (1992).

51 Both the *Concilia* and Bede provide (incomplete) specimens as part of their prefatory instruction in the Saxon alphabet. See also E. R. Mores, *A dissertation upon English typographical founders and founderies* (1778), ed. H. Carter and C. Ricks (Oxford Bibliographical Soc. 1961), pp. lxxii, 10; [Bruce Dickins], *Printing with Anglo-Saxon types 1566–1715* [Cambridge 1947].

52 Whelock to D'Ewes, 30 March 1640, British Library, MS Harley 374, no. 85, repr. in *Bibliotheca topographica Britannica*, 6, pt ii (1790), pp. 78–9.

53 See also Whelock to D'Ewes, 23 September 1642, British Library, MS Harley 374, fo. 209.

54 Corpus Christi College, MS 139. Whelock to D'Ewes, 30 March 1640 (see n. 52 above).

55 Greg, *Companion*, pp. 106, 310–18.

56 W. Somner, *Dictionarium Saxonico-Latino-Anglicum* (Oxford 1659), fo. a4b, translated by White Kennet as 'a man who had deserv'd very well of the republic of letters, by publishing, at his own care and cost, many books of better note, wherein he was so industrious, as literally to answer his own name' (Life of Somner, in William Somner, *A treatise of Gavelkind*, 2nd edn (1726), p. 79).

57 David Douglas, *English scholars* (1939), p. 211.

58 White Kennet, Life of William Somner, p. 74. 'Bennet' refers to Corpus Christi College.

59 George Hickes' copy of the 1644 edition is in Cambridge University Library, Cam.a.644.2; for his work, Whelock borrowed the copy of the 1568 edition from Peterhouse, and annotated it copiously: see D. McKitterick, 'Andrew Perne and his books', in *Andrew Perne; quatercentenary studies* ed. McKitterick (Cambridge Bibliographical Soc. 1991), pp. 35–61, at pp. 55–6.

60 Whelock explained his views concerning his post in the Library in 1652/3, in a letter to W. Minshull, the Vice-Chancellor: 'I am tied by my places as Librarie-Keeper, and Amanuensis to the Librarie, to promote and assist what I can the publishing of the Saxon and Oriental antiquities' (Todd, *Life of Walton*, 1, p. 232).

61 For details, see Oates, *Cambridge University Library*, pp. 208–9. Further details of contemporary interest in Lambard may be followed in *Correspondence of John Morris with Johannes de Laet (1634–1649)*, ed. J. A. F. Bekkers (Nijmegen 1970).

62 British Library, MS Harley 7660, fo. 79v; A. G. Watson, *The library of Sir Simonds D'Ewes* (1966), p. 266.

63 Plomer, *Dictionary*, pp. 1–2; Darlow and Moule, no. 4686.

64 *STC*, 6903: cf. *STC*, 794 and 794·5. It is extremely unlikely that examples of all issues of all these plates have survived.

65 The plates are conveniently described in Hind, *Engraving in England*, 3, pp. 135–40. See also J. E. Bailey, *The life of Thomas Fuller, D.D.* (Manchester 1874) and Strickland Gibson, *A bibliography of Thomas Fuller D.D.* (Oxford Bibliographical Soc., *Proceedings and Papers*, 4 (1936)).

66 Greg, *Companion*, pp. 203–5.

10 Privileged books

1 William Laud, *The second volume of the Remains* (1700), p. 58.

2 *Ibid.*, p. 59.

3 *Ibid.*, p. 126.

4 Legge's abortive edition, *c.* 1614, was bought by Barker (University Archives, CUR 33.2(15)). See also p. 143 above.

5 University Archives, CUR 33.2(71); S. Lambert, 'The printers and the government, 1604–1637', in *Aspects of printing from 1600*, ed. R. Myers and M. Harris (Oxford 1987),

pp. 1–29, at pp. 4, 19, 25. Excluding the King's Printing House, this resulted in thirty-eight presses in London.

6 B. J. McMullin, 'The Bible and continuous reprinting in the early seventeenth century', *The Library*, 6th ser. 5 (1983), pp. 256–63, a discussion of the 1628 octavo.

7 Historical MSS Commn, *Hatfield*, pt XIV, pp. 179–80.

8 Greg, *Companion*, pp. 261–5; Sotheby's, 14 December 1989 (Trumbull papers), lot 24. For Sparke, see L. Rostenberg, *Literary, political, scientific, religious & legal publishing, printing & bookselling in England, 1551–1700; twelve studies*, 2 vols. (New York 1965), 1, pp. 161–202.

9 S. R. Gardiner, ed. *Reports of cases in the Courts of Star Chamber and High Commission* (1886), p. 274.

10 W. Prynne, *Canterburies doom* (1646), p. 513. Laud's complaint was at Geneva Bibles, not at invasive Authorized Versions.

11 Greg, *Companion*, pp. 92, 305–9.

12 *Acts P.C.*, 1630–31, pp. 189–90.

13 See pp. 211–13.

14 Christianus Ravius, *Prima tredecim partium Alcorani Arabico-Latini* [Amsterdam 1646], fo. B2r: 'Quod si forte non videatur credibile, sciendum, nullam nationem, ne ipsam quidem Germaniam, ut typographia longe anteriorem, tot editiones Bibliorum annumerare posse, quot sola Anglia: cum unus vir Anglus, hic Amstelodami intra 4. vel 5. annos ad 40000 exemplarium impresserit, ubi ultima editio erat 12500 exemplarium; & hic Amstelodami ultra centum quinquaginta millia exemplarium Bibliorum Anglicanorum sint impressa, praeterquam quae in Anglia ipsa ad duas myriadas exemplarium impressa sunt.'

15 A. F. Johnson, 'J. F. Stam, Amsterdam and English Bibles', *The Library*, 5th ser. 9 (1954), pp. 185–93; Herbert, *Historical catalogue*, pp. 115–16, 167, 191–2; *STC*, 2174–80. See also p. 319 below.

16 M. M. Kleerkooper and W. P. van Stockum, *De boekhandel te Amsterdam* ('s Gravenhage 1914–16), p. 1453. For Amsterdam Bibles seized in January 1639/40, cf. Bodleian Library, MS Tanner 67, fo. 164.

17 Herbert, *Historical catalogue*, pp. 193, 195. For Tomas Loof and Stam in the 1640s see also Kleerkooper and van Stockum, p. 1371; for Daniel, see Herbert, *Historical catalogue*, nos. 586 and 587, two different issues (one Joachim Nosche, Amsterdam, the other Daniel) of an eighteenmo edition (not a duodecimo) printed at Amsterdam: B. J. McMullin, 'An eighteenmo gathered in twelves', *Bulletin of the Bibliographical Society of Australia and New Zealand*, 10 (1986), pp. 139–40.

18 Greg, *Companion*, pp. 77, 203.

19 [P. Handover], *The "Wicked" Bible and the King's Printing House*, Blackfriars (1958).

20 Gardiner, *Reports of cases*; High Commission cases, pp. 297, 305.

21 William Kilburne, *Dangerous errors in several late printed Bibles* (Finsbury 1659), p. 6. For the two editions, see F. H. A. Scrivener, *The Authorized edition of the English Bible* (Cambridge 1884), pp. 20–3.

22 Kilburne, *Dangerous errors*, p. 6. Cf. the title-page of Herbert, *Historical catalogue*, no. 584: 'according to the copie, printed by Roger Daniel, printer to the Universitie of Cambridge'. In other Dutch editions, claims were sometimes made of the Geneva text printed at Edinburgh in 1610 (cf. Herbert, *Historical catalogue*, nos. 545, 579).

23 Thomas Fuller, *Church-history of Britain* (1655), 'History of the University of Cambridge', p. 59. It was this text that the University put forward in its defence against the Basketts in the 1740s: see the inscription in Cambridge University Library, Rel.bb.63.1; Black, *Cambridge University Press 1584–1984*, pp. 108–10.

24 B. J. McMullin, 'The 1629 Cambridge Bible', *TCBS* 8 (1984), pp. 381–97.

25 Cf. Mede to Sir Martin Stuteville, 20 February 1629/30 (British Library, MS Harley 390, fo. 496r): 'I will (as soon as I can) go out to giue directions for your Bible. But I doubt I shall not gett it in quires without taking the Service & Psalmes with it, because they haue printed a like number of both; but if I can, I will; if not, I will bind the Psalmes & Common prayer together by themselues.'

26 British Library, MS Harley 390, fo. 499v. The Venice paper issue was apparently slightly more expensive: in 1632–3 the University was charged 13s.4d. 'for a folio Bible of Venice paper' (University Archives, Original vouchers, 1632–3).

27 Compared with a trade price of ten shillings for the quarto long primer edition of 1635, and 7s.4d. for the quarto brevier edition of 1637 (University Archives, VC Ct III.35(4)). For a summary of retail prices, see M. Sparke, *Scintilla, or a light broken into dark warehouses* (1641), reprinted in Herbert, *Historical catalogue*, pp. 182–7. McMullin, 'The 1629 Cambridge Bible', assumes that Sparke's remarks refer to the edition of 1629.

28 Sparke, *Scintilla* (Herbert, *Historical catalogue*, p. 183). 'Roman' and 'English' refer here to roman and black letter type.

29 Sheets were however reissued in c. 1635, using the altered state of the engraved title-page first employed in a quarto edition of that year (*STC*, 2285·5).

30 Sparke, *Scintilla*, p. 184.

31 University Archives, CUR 33.2(95); J. D. Gould, 'The trade depression of the early 1620s', *Econ. Hist. Rev.*, 2nd ser. 7 (1954), pp. 81–8; B. E. Supple, *Commercial crisis and change in England, 1600–1642* (Cambridge 1959), p. 139. For some comparisons of retail book prices between England and France, see Robert H. MacDonald, *The library of Drummond of Hawthornden* (Edinburgh 1971), pp. 38–40.

32 University Archives, CUR 33.2(95), fo. 15r.

33 *STC*, 8764; Greg, *Companion*, pp. 233–4; see above, pp. 155–6.

34 It had been first published at Leiden in 1639.

35 University Archives, CUR 33.2(46); CUR 33.2(65), fo. 20v.

36 University Archives, CUR 33.2(48); CUR 33.2(95), fos. 15v–16r.

37 University Archives, CUR 33.2(65).

38 University Archives, CUR 33.6(15+); CUR 33.6(14); CUR 33.6(10).

39 University Archives, CUR 33.2(82).

40 Jackson, *Records*, p. 224.

41 University Archives, CUR 33.6(15); CUR 33.2(76).

42 For the general background, see E. F. Bosanquet, 'English seventeenth-century almanacks', *The Library*, 4th ser. 10 (1930), pp. 361–97; Keith Thomas, *Religion and the decline of magic* (1971), ch. 10; Bernard Capp, *Astrology and the popular press* (1979); and (especially with regard to William Lily) J. K. Moore, 'Copy and print in English books of the sixteenth and seventeenth centuries' (D. Phil., Oxford 1989), ch. 5. For one aspect of their contents, see M. Nicolson, 'English almanacs and the "New astronomy"', *Annals of Science*, 4 (1939), pp. 1–33.

43 *STC*, 441·9.

44 University Archives, CUR 33.6(15); Comm. Ct III.18(97), November 1631.

45 Greg, *Companion*, p. 69; Arber, IV.527.

46 Of Waters, only a single copy survives for a single year, 1627 (*STC*, 524).

47 Capp, *Astrology and the popular press*, p. 44.

48 The payment was raised to £250 in 1747, and £500 in 1767: see Blagden, *Stationers' Company*, pp. 203–4.

49 'Blanks' were so named because they provided a whole opening, rather than a single page, for each month, with blank spaces for private entries. They were half a sheet (eight pages) longer than 'sorts', and their first two sheets were printed in two colours, compared with only the first in sorts. 'Blanks' seem to have taken an increasing

proportion of the market in the 1660s (C. Blagden, 'The distribution of almanacks in the second half of the seventeenth century', *SB*, 11 (1958), pp. 107–16, at p. 110).

50 University Archives, CUR 33.6(15). It is not clear whether this alludes to printing for outside Cambridge only: Buck and Daniel were licensed to print 590 reams.

51 Blagden, 'Distribution'.

52 VCH, *Cambs.*, 2, pp. 321–9, 331. See also the circumspect remarks on schooling in Cambridgeshire more generally in M. Spufford, *Contrasting communities* (Cambridge 1974), pp. 183–91, and her 'The schooling of the peasantry in Cambridgeshire, 1575–1700', in *Land, church and people; essays presented to H. P. R. Finberg*, ed. Joan Thirsk (Reading 1970), pp. 112–47.

53 For a survey of endowed grammar and other secondary schools founded 1547–1701, see *Parliamentary Papers*, 1867–8, XXVIII, pt I, Appendix, pp. 44–78. See also W. K. Jordan, *Philanthropy in England 1480–1660* (1959), especially pp. 283, 291; D. Cressy, 'Educational opportunity in Tudor and Stuart England', *History of Education Quarterly*, 16 (1976), pp. 301–20; and Cressy, *Literacy and the social order* (Cambridge 1980), especially pp. 164, 169–71; C. Wase, *Considerations concerning free-schools as settled in England* (Oxford 1678).

54 Many of these are discussed in exhaustive detail in T. W. Baldwin, *William Shakspere's small Latine & lesse Greeke*, 2 vols. (Urbana 1944).

55 Greg, *Companion*, p. 69; Arber, IV.527.

56 University Archives, CUR 33.2(73); Greg, *Companion*, pp. 203–5.

57 University Archives, CUR 33.2(37).

58 Foster Watson, *The English grammar schools to 1660: their curriculum and practice* (Cambridge 1908), pp. 358–9.

59 Cambridge edition sizes are taken from University Archives, CUR 33.6(15). For Gallus, see Watson, *The English grammar schools*, pp. 347–8.

60 On Brinsley, see Joan Simon, *Education and society in Tudor England* (Cambridge 1967), pp. 375, 379–80, 381, 403. For several of these books, all long established, see Baldwin, *William Shakspere's small Latine & lesse Greeke*, 1, pp. 591–5 (*Sententiae pueriles*, 'so elementary as to belong with the very first things studied in grammar school'), 607–40 (Aesop), 641–2 (Terence), 642–52 (Mantuanus). For a convenient summary of the patents controlling these publications, and the contribution of the Stationers' Company, see *STC*, vol. 3, Appendix D.

61 Note in the Trinity College Cambridge copy of Withals' *Dictionary* (1634), VI.11.73.

62 University Archives, VC Ct III.33(138).

63 University Archives, VC Ct III.33(138, 139). See also William M. Baillie, 'The printing of privileged books at Cambridge 1631–1634', *TCBS*, 5 (1971) pp. 155–66.

64 The Stationers' Company school-book privilege expired in 1634, and in 1631 had been granted to Georg Rudolph Weckherlin, diplomat and statesman. Within six weeks of his patent, however, 'the Company had come to such satisfactory terms with him that the Court voted him a piece of plate "for his extraordinary paynes"' (Blagden, *Stationers' Company*, p. 193). For Weckherlin see most recently the long account of his papers (*ex* Downshire Collection) in Sotheby's catalogue of the Trumbull papers, 14 December 1989, now in the British Library. The Stationers regained the school-book privilege only in 1665 (Blagden, p. 194).

65 University Archives, CUR 33.2(37); see also Blagden, *Stationers' Company*, pp. 105–7. Tabor's summary of the position is now CUR 33.2(17). For efforts to control the price of schoolbooks elsewhere in the early seventeenth century, see for example V. A. de la Montagne, 'Schoolboken te Antwerpen in de 17e eeuw', *Tijdschrift voor Boek- en Bibliotheekwezen*, 5 (1907), pp. 1–35, reprinting the detailed *Taxatie oft priisen vande*

ghemeyne school-boecken (Antwerp 1642); a copy of the original is in the Plantin-Moretus Museum.

66 Madan, *Oxford books*, 2, pp. 520–4; Greg, *Companion*, pp. 81, 82–4, 268–73. On 10 May 1631 Sparke confessed to having a great store of Cambridge books, as well as to being one of six partners (the others are unspecified) in a Cambridge warehouse 'abroade' (*CSPD*, 1631–3, p. 39; Greg, *Companion*, pp. 272–3).

67 University Archives, CUR 33.2(80), 13 February 1634/5.

68 University Archives, CUR 33.2(81), Sparke to Ireland, 19 March 1634/5.

69 University Archives, CUR 33.2(83), draft letter to Sparke, 23 March 1634/5.

70 University Archives, CUR 33.2(84), draft letter to Sparke, 12 May 1635.

71 See above, pp. 143–6. He had brought the Barocci manuscripts to England, bought in 1629 by the Earl of Pembroke and presented to the Bodleian. For his later attempts at reform in the Stationers' Company, see Blagden, *Stationers' Company*.

72 University Archives, CUR 33.2(90).

73 University Archives, CUR 33.2(86, 87).

74 Universtiy Archives, CUR 33.2(90), Fetherstone to Tabor 8 May 1635.

75 University Archives, CUR 33.2(91), Fetherstone to Tabor 15 May 1635.

76 University Archives, CUR 33.2(96).

77 University Archives, CUR 33.1(24).

78 Greg, *Companion*, pp. 100, 340–1.

79 No Bible or New Testament was printed at Oxford until 1675.

80 The agreement is printed in F. Madan, *The early Oxford press* (Oxford 1895), pp. 285–7.

81 University Archives, CUR 33.1(24), transcript; Blagden, *Stationers' Company*, p. 104.

11 *Books for university teaching*

1 Calendar of Patent Rolls, *Elizabeth I*, 5, no. 2445. See also p. 60 above.

2 For the University curriculum in the first half of the seventeenth century, see S. E. Morison, *The founding of Harvard College* (Cambridge, Mass. 1935), esp. pp. 60–78; and 'President Dunster's Quadriennium memoir, 1654', *Publs. of the Colonial Soc. of Massachusetts*, 31 (1935), pp. 279–300; W. Costello, *The scholastic curriculum at early seventeenth century Cambridge* (Cambridge, Mass. 1958); VCH *Cambs.*, 3, pp. 204–6; H. F. Fletcher, *The intellectual development of John Milton*, 2 (Urbana 1961), reprinting Holdsworth's 'Directions for a student in the universitie', pp. 623–64, and summarizing the books listed in Joseph Mede's accounts, pp. 553–622; Mark Curtis, *Oxford and Cambridge in transition, 1558–1642* (Oxford 1959); Patricia Reif, 'The textbook tradition in natural philosophy, 1600–1650', *Journal of the History of Ideas*, 30 (1969), pp. 17–32; Hugh Kearney, *Scholars and gentlemen; universities and society in pre-industrial Britain, 1500–1700* (1970); John A. Trentman, 'The authorship of *Directions for a student in the universitie*', *TCBS*, 7 (1978), pp. 170–83; Charles Webster, *The great instauration; science, medicine and reform, 1626–1660* (1975), esp. pp. 115–44. For a balancing recent view, see J. Looney, 'Undergraduate education at early Stuart Cambridge', *History of Education*, 10 (1981), pp. 9–19, and, for mathematics and natural philosophy, M. Feingold, *The mathematicians' apprenticeship; science, universities and society in England, 1560–1640* (Cambridge 1984), esp. pp. 86–121.

3 This did not, however, prevent an attack by Fuller on the manner in which Thomas's dictionary was hijacked:

This *Rider* did Borrow (to say no worse) both his *Saddle* and *Bridle* from *Thomas Thomatius*, who being bred *Fellow* of *Kings-colledge* in *Cambridge*, set forth that *Dictionary* known by his *Name*, then which, Men, have not a *Better* nor *Truer*; Children, no *Plainer* and *Briefer*. But *Rider* after *Thomas* his death, set forth his *Dictionary*, the same in effect, under his own Name, the property thereof, being but little disguised with any Additions.

Such *Plageary-ship* ill becometh *Authors* or *Printers*, and the *Dove* being the Crest of the *Stationers Armes*, should mind them, not like *Rooks*, to filch copies one from an other. The Executors of *Thomas Thomatius* entring an Action against *Rider*, occasioned him in his own defence to make those Numerous Additions, to his *Dictionary*, that it seems to differ rather in *Kind* then *Degree*, from his *first Edition*.

(Thomas Fuller, *The history of the worthies of England* (1662), fo. Qqq 4v, p. 128).

For Rider in the curriculum, cf. Fletcher, *Intellectual development of John Milton*, p. 618, quoting Mede's accounts.

4 For Burgersdijck (b. 1590), see P. Dibon, *La philosophie néerlandaise au siècle d'or* (Paris 1954), 1, pp. 90–119, and C. de Pater, 'Experimental physics', in *Leiden University in the seventeenth century; an exchange of learning*, ed. Th. H. Lusingh Scheurleer, *et al.* (Leiden 1975), pp. 309–27, at pp. 311–12.

5 Eyre and Rivington, 1, p. 157.

6 Eyre and Rivington, 1, pp. 128, 157, 238, 415, 422; 2, pp. 232, 238, 331, 470.

7 University Archives, VC Ct III.15(42). Venn records nothing of the owner, Henry Metham, save that he matriculated as pensioner at Magdalene in 1608. His tutor was William Burton.

8 Curtis, *Oxford and Cambridge in transition*, pp. 78–81, 102–9; Morgan, 'Approaches', pp. 156–7; Feingold, *Mathematicians' apprenticeship*, pp. 61–8.

9 Morgan, 'Approaches', pp. 156–60. Mede's accounts for books are abstracted, with copious notes, in Fletcher, *Intellectual development of John Milton*; see also Feingold, *Mathematicians' apprenticeship*, pp. 96–8.

10 Joseph Mede, *Works* (1672), p. iv.

11 *STC*, 14895. Only four copies survive, and it might be argued that other editions have disappeared entirely.

12 John Peile, 'On four MS. books of accounts kept by Joseph Mead, BD, Fellow of Christ's College, with his pupils between 1614 and 1633', *Proc. Cambridge Antiquarian Soc.*, 13 (1909), no. 54, pp. 250–61, at p. 256.

13 Mede, *Works*, pp. ii–iii.

14 Christopher J. Scriba, 'The autobiography of John Wallis, FRS', *Notes and Records of the Royal Society of London*, 25 (1970), pp. 17–46, at p. 27; Feingold, *Mathematicians' apprenticeship*, pp. 86–90.

15 Scriba, 'John Wallis', p. 29.

16 John Milton, *The reason of church government* (1641), p. 62.

17 Walter Pope, *The life of Seth, Lord Bishop of Salisbury* (1697), pp. 9–10; Fletcher, *Intellectual development of John Milton*, 2, pp. 312–21.

18 Fletcher, *Intellectual development of John Milton*, 2, pp. 147–8.

19 Cf. Trinity College statutes, as quoted to the House of Commons Select Committee on Education, 1818 (*Documents*, p. 369), following British Library, MS Sloane 659 (a Fellow's copy of the statutes): 'Quartus et infimus interpretetur Dialecticae introductionem Johannis Setoni, sic ut classis infima commoda introductione veniat ad Porphyrium paratior.' The words 'Johannis Setoni' do not appear in the Elizabethan statutes (printed 1773), or in various early transcripts in Trinity College Library, including the official copy, MS O.17.10). See also Lisa Jardine, 'The place of dialectic teaching in sixteenth-century Cambridge', *Studies in the Renaissance*, 21 (1974), pp. 31–62, and particularly her puzzled remarks on pp. 44–5.

20 I. Thomas, 'Medieval aftermath: Oxford logic and logicians of the seventeenth century', *Oxford studies presented to Daniel Callus* (Oxford Historical Soc. 1964), pp. 297–311. Cf.

Holdsworth's comments: 'I shall chiefly commend Burgerdicius; it is commonly approv'd & received; and contains a more perfect, & usefull Logic than most doe: it aquaints you with Aristotles termes. The Comments of it well understood, serves to decide most controversies in Logic. It hath whatever is deficient in Molinus, Kekerman, Rhamus, &c.' (Fletcher, *Intellectual development of John Milton*, p. 634).

21 Thomas Randolph, *Aristippus* (1635), p. 21. See also Curtis, *Oxford and Cambridge in transition*, p. 129, and Morgan, 'Approaches', pp. 156–63.

22 Fletcher, *Intellectual development of John Milton*, 2, pp. 647 8. Holdsworth's best documented pupil at St John's was Simonds D'Ewes, admitted Fellow-Commoner in 1618, whose reading seems to have been both studious and often conservative: Sir Simonds D'Ewes, *Autobiography and correspondence*, ed. J. O. Halliwell, 2 vols. (1845), and Curtis, *Oxford and Cambridge in transition*, pp. 98–9.

23 University Archives, VC Ct III.36(40).

24 A few of the books belonging to Henry Dunster (later President of Harvard) during his time as a student at Magdalene College from 1627 are discussed in Morison, *The founding of Harvard College*, pp. 111–13, with an illustration showing his three bookplates printed in Cambridge.

25 For Ames' influence in England see K. L. Sprunger, *The learned Doctor William Ames: Dutch backgrounds of English and American puritanism* (Urbana 1972), and 'John Yates of Norfolk: the radical puritan preacher as Ramist philosopher', *Journal of the History of Ideas*, 37 (1976), pp. 697–706.

26 University Archives, VC Ct III.35(45). Suckerman had served his apprenticeship with the bookseller Philip Scarlet. By 1634 he was established as bookseller and bookbinder, but the evil reputation he gained as an apprentice remained with him. After trading for a few years he was sued for a series of debts in 1638, whereupon he fled Cambridge, pursued by a warrant for his arrest. Among his creditors was Michael Sparke, who had presumably supplied him with books from London (VC Ct III.33(33); III.35(49, 52)).

27 University Archives, Comm. Ct III.18, nos. 97, 103.

28 The following is based on University Archives, VC Ct III.36(78), listing books supplied by Allot and his widow Mary between September 1633 and December 1635. Atkinson paid church rates to Great St Mary's from 1626 until at least 1635 (Foster, *Great St Mary's*, pp. 403, 410, 416, 424, 435, 443, 450, 459, 468).

29 University Archives, VC Ct III.37(12).

30 University Archives, VC Ct III.36(80).

31 University Archives, VC Ct III.36(81, 82).

32 University Archives, VC Ct III.35(45). The inventory, taken as a result of a debt suit by Buck and Daniel and other parties, is damaged and incomplete.

33 Cf. S. E. Morison, *The intellectual life of colonial New England*, 2nd edn (Ithaca 1956), p. 149. The question is explored by Hugh Amory in 'Historians and cataloguers: enumerating the libraries of early New England', a paper delivered at the American Antiquarian Society, summer 1990: I am grateful to him for allowing me to read it in advance of publication. For Ramism, see Perry Miller, *The New England mind; the seventeenth century* (New York 1939), pp. 116–53; for Keckerman and Alsted, see S. E. Morison, *Harvard College in the seventeenth century* (Cambridge, Mass. 1936), p. 158 and Miller, *The New England mind*, pp. 102–3, 510, with further references.

34 G. E. Littlefield, *Early Boston booksellers 1642–1711* (1910; repr. New York 1969).

35 Lawrence C. Wroth, *The colonial printer* (Charlottesville 1938; repr. 1964), pp. 19–20; Hugh Amory, *First impressions; printing at Cambridge 1639–1989* (Cambridge, Mass. 1989).

36 For Brewster (1567–1644), cf. T. A. Walker, *A Peterhouse bibliography* (Cambridge 1924), p. 19, and *Dictionary of American Biography*.

37 S. E. Morison, *The founding of Harvard College*; J. Morgan, *Godly learning* (Cambridge 1966), pp. 258–63.

38 T. G. Wright, *Literary culture in early New England, 1620–1730* (New Haven 1920), pp. 254–65; see also *Proc. Massachusetts Historical Soc.*, 2nd ser. 3, pp. 261–74, and 5, pp. 37ff.

39 For Harvard's career see Morison, *The founding of Harvard College*, esp. pp. 103–7, 210–27. His library is listed in Alfred C. Potter, 'Catalogue of John Harvard's library', *Pubns. of the Colonial Soc. of Massachusetts*, 21 (1920), pp. 190–230, and (with various caveats) in H. J. Cadbury, 'John Harvard's library', *Pubns. of the Colonial Soc. of Massachusetts*, 34 (1943), pp. 353–77.

40 Morison, *The founding of Harvard College*, p. 265.

41 C. F. and R. Robinson, 'Three early Massachusetts libraries', *Pubns. of the Colonial Soc. of Massachusetts*, 28 (1935), pp. 107–75; Peile, *Christ's*, 1, p. 356.

42 S. E. Morison, *The intellectual life of colonial New England*, p. 139, quoting Middlesex Court files, docket 15, 284 (post-mortem inventory, 30 September 1668). I am grateful to Mary Rhinelander and Hugh Amory for providing me with a copy of this list, and so allowing me to extend Morison's observations. I have refrained from pursuing these questions in other colonies: cf. for example the remarks on libraries (with a bias towards English-language and non-theological interests) in P. A. Bruce, *Institutional history of Virginia in the seventeenth century* (New York 1910), 1, pp. 402–41.

43 *Catalogus variorum & insignium librorum clariss. viri D. G. Amesii* (Amsterdam 1634; facsimile ed. introd. by K. L. Sprunger, Utrecht 1988); for Ames more generally, see K. L. Sprunger, *The learned Doctor William Ames*. There is little to support the theory that Ames' books were taken to North America (cf. Morison, *The founding of Harvard College*, p. 267; Sprunger, *The learned Doctor*, pp. 255–6).

44 W. M. Whitehill, 'The King's Chapel library', *Pubns. of the Colonial Soc. of Massachusetts*, 38 (Transactions 1947–51), pp. 274–89.

45 C. F. and R. Robinson, 'Three early Massachusetts libraries', *Pubns. of the Colonial Soc. of Massachusetts*, 28 (1935), pp. 107–75. For Newman's *Concordance*, on sale in Boston, Mass. in 1700, see John Dunton, *Letters from New England* (Boston 1867), pp. 314–19. Inventory of the stock of the Boston bookseller Michael Perry. For further remarks on the North American trade, see below, p. 466 n. 79.

46 Dunton, *Letters from New England*, p. 75; J. H. Tuttle, 'The libraries of the Mathers', *Proc. American Antiquarian Soc.*, ns 20 (1909–10), pp. 269–356.

47 Prince's books, mostly now in Boston Public Library, bear dated notes of provenance on the versos of many title-pages. For his library, cf. *A Catalogue of the collection of books and manuscripts which formerly belonged to the Reverend Thomas Prince and was by him bequeathed to the Old South Church, and is now deposited in the Public Library* (Boston 1870).

48 Harvard College records: College Book, 1, pp. 250, 263, printed in *Pubns. of the Colonial Soc. of Massachusetts*, 15 (1925).

49 S. E. Morison, *Harvard College in the seventeenth century* (Cambridge, Mass. 1936), pp. 191, 198–9, 218–19, 261, 263; Arthur O. Norton, 'Harvard text-books and reference books of the seventeenth century', *Pubns. of the Colonial Soc. of Massachusetts*, 28 (1935), pp. 361–438. David Cressy, *Coming over; migration and communication between England and New England in the seventeenth century* (Cambridge 1987), has little to say about the export of books either in passengers' luggage or as a commercial commodity. But for a convenient summary of the pertinent and long-running debate on the extent to which migration to New England was specifically a puritan one, rather than one encouraged by social or economic motivation, see his ch. 3. This debate can be usefully examined in the context of surviving books and book-lists – sources tending of course to reflect a

distinctively literate body of opinion. For one example of the treatment of a single author, see Mel Gorman, 'Gassendi in America', *Isis* 55 (1964), pp. 409–17. Many aspects of the North American trade, albeit principally for later periods, are usefully surveyed in James Gilreath, 'American book distribution', *Proc. American Antiquarian Soc.*, 95 (1985), pp. 501–83, repr. in David D. Hall and John B. Hench, eds., *Needs and opportunities in the history of the book: America, 1639–1876* (Worcester, Mass. 1987), pp. 103–85.

50 See below, pp. 381–3.

12 *Authors and printers*

1 Sheila Lambert, 'The printers and the Government, 1604–1637', in *Aspects of printing from 1600*, ed. R. Myers and M. Harris (Oxford 1987), pp. 1–29. London printers limited themselves to two presses each in 1628, the King's Printing House being exempt.

2 Some of Farnaby's work is listed in Shaaber, *Check-list.*

3 E. Weil, 'William Fitzer, the publisher of Harvey's *Du motu cordis*, 1628', *The Library*, 4th ser. 24 (1943–4), pp. 142–64, and Shaaber, *Check-list.*

4 University Archives, CUR 33.1(23).

5 See above, pp. 58–9. For a comparative view of these and cognate questions, see L. Voet, 'Plantin et ses auteurs; quelques considérations sur les relations entre imprimeurs et auteurs sur le plan typographique-littéraire au XVIe siècle', in *Trasmissione dei testi a stampa nel periodo moderno*, ed. G. Crapulli (Rome 1985–7), 1, pp. 61–76.

6 Richard Montagu, *Analecta ecclesiasticarum exercitationum* (1662), dedication. Quoted in J. W. Binns, *Intellectual culture in Elizabethan and Jacobean England* (Leeds 1990), p. 403.

7 See, for example, the remarks by John Barkham, editor of Richard Crakanthorp's posthumously published *Defensio ecclesiae anglicanae* (1625), fo. 4N3v, quoted in Binns, *Intellectual culture*, pp. 404–5. Crakanthorp's *De providentia dei* had been printed at Cambridge in 1623.

8 Cf. J. C. Reed, 'Humphrey Moseley, publisher', *Proc. Oxford Bibl. Soc.*, 2 (1928), pp. 57–142, and L. Rostenberg, *Literary, political, scientific and legal publishing, printing and bookselling in England, 1551–1700*, 2 vols. (New York 1965): the latter is of varying reliability.

9 John Cosin, *Correspondence*, Surtees Soc., vols. 52, 55 (Durham 1869–72), 1, p. 21. The sermon was not published.

10 Montagu to Cosin, 11 January 1624/5 (Cosin, *Correspondence*, 1, p. 45). 'Niggling' remained unaltered, and is not listed in the errata contained in some copies. This was not the first time he had complained: 'Theise βάναυσοι *typographi* are telluris inutile pondus, lucripetae mali, Lownes *inter primos*', he wrote to Cosin on 28 November previously (*ibid.*, 1, p. 29). See also Sheila Lambert, 'Richard Montagu, Arminianism and censorship', *Past and Present*, 124 (1989), pp. 36–68.

11 See the latter part of D. F. McKenzie, 'Printers of the mind: some notes on bibliographical theories and printing-house practices', *SB*, 22 (1969), pp. 1–75. 'All printing houses were alike in being different ... I have tried to suggest that all printing houses were more alike over the years than many bibliographers are prepared to allow' (p. 60).

12 For London and Oxford, see especially Simpson, *Proof-reading.*

13 Cf. the treatment of Nathaniel Butter in *The staple of news* and of Nicholas Okes in *News from the new world discovered in the moon*, and D. F. McKenzie, *The London book trade in the later seventeenth century*, Sandars Lectures (Cambridge 1976), pp. 1–10 (copies of the typescript of these lectures are in the British Library, Cambridge University Library and elsewhere).

14 Ingenioso has been identified with Thomas Nashe. Danter was named after John Danter, who enjoyed a dubious reputation as a printer. See J. B. Leishman, ed., *The three*

Parnassus plays, 1598–1601 (London 1949). For correctors of the press, cf. J. C. Zeltner, *C.D. Correctorum in typographiis eruditorum centuria* (Nuremberg 1716), whose vigorous language emphasizes how, in general, he considered seventeenth-century printers inferior to those of the sixteenth in this respect. See also, more particularly, H. Hornschuch, Ὀρθοτυπογραφία (Leipzig 1608), ed. P. Gaskell and transl. P. Bradford (Cambridge 1972); Moxon, *Mechanick exercises*, pp. 246–50, 282–3; Simpson, *Proof-reading*, chs. 3–4; H. D. L. Vervliet, 'Une instruction Plantinienne à l'intention des correcteurs', *GJ* (1959), pp. 99–103 (no date is given, but the text of the Instruction appears in Plantin archives vol. 13 (a volume covering 1597–1617), fo. 164, and vol. 118 (1600–25), fo. 1); L. Voet, *Golden compasses*, 2, pp. 176–7; M. Boghardt, 'Instruktionen für Korrektoren der Officina Plantiniana', in Crapulli, *Trasmissione dei testi a stampa*, 2, pp. 1–15; and Alastair Hamilton and Chris. Heesakker, 'Bernardus Sellius Noviomagus (c. 1551–93), proof-reader and poet', *Quaerendo*, 19 (1989), pp. 163–224.

15 The second part of *The return from Parnassus*, Act I, scene ii.
16 *Ibid.*, Act I, scene iii.
17 Thomas Rogers, *The faith, doctrine, and religion*, fo. Hh1^r.
18 Andrew Willet, *Hexapla in Genesin* (J. Legate 1605), fo. Tt1^r.
19 Andrew Willet, *Hexapla: that is, a six-fold commentarie vpon...Romanes* (C. Legge 1611), 'The printer to the reader'.
20 E. J. Kenney, *The classical text* (Berkely 1974), p. 19; E. Eisenstein, *The printing press as an agent of change* (Cambridge 1979), 1, pp. 80–1. Both under-estimate the implications of these procedures as well as their bibliographical consequences. For the Bible, see M. H. Black, 'The printed Bible', in *The Cambridge history of the Bible; the west from the Reformation to the present day*, ed. S. L. Greenslade (Cambridge 1963), pp. 408–75, esp. pp. 451 (Clementine text) and 458–9 (Authorized Version).
21 See below, pp. 322–5.
22 *An historical collection, of the most memorable accidents, and tragicall massacres of France* (London: Thomas Creede, 1598), fo. A4^r.
23 *STC*, 113479, fo. ¶¶1v.
24 Fletcher received his copy *ex dono authoris* on 1 February 1602/3 (Dawsons of Pall Mall, catalogue 162 (1966), no. 52, improbably confusing Fletcher with his namesake the dramatist). For Fletcher, see Venn, *Gonville and Caius*, 1, p. 95; J. Venn, 'An astrological Fellow', *The Caian*, 6 (1897), pp. 28–36; M. Feingold, *The mathematicians' apprenticeship* (Cambridge 1984), p. 79.
25 Gonville and Caius College, MS James 73, fo. 370.
26 Gonville and Caius College, MS James 73, fo. 381.
27 Bodleian Library, MS Tanner 70, fo. 41.
28 Bodleian Library, MS Tanner 65, fo. 80.
29 Bodleian Library, MS Tanner 72, fo. 52.
30 Bodleian Library, MS Tanner 72, fo. 174.
31 Bodleian Library, MS Tanner 71, fos. 105–6.
32 *STC*, 21768 and 21767; see E. S. Schuckburgh, *Two biographies of William Bedell...with a selection of his letters* (Cambridge 1902), pp. 291–2.
33 Bodleian Library, MS Tanner 72, fo. 61.
34 Harold Love, 'Scribal publication in seventeenth-century England', *TCBS*, 9 (1987), pp. 130–54; P. Beal, *Index of English literary manuscripts*, vols. 1–2 (1980–7). See above, p. 175.
35 Bodleian Library, MS Tanner 72, fo. 52.
36 Bodleian Library, MS Tanner 73, fo. 273.
37 John Donne, *Sermons*, ed. George R. Potter and Evelyn M. Simpson (Berkeley, 1953–62), 1, pp. 23–6.

38 A. Willet, *An harmonie vpon the First Booke of Samuel* (C. Legge 1614), 'The preface to the reader'.

39 J. E. Bailey, *The life of Fuller* (1874), pp. 220–1.

40 Ralph Cudworth no doubt had this in mind when in 1647 he had his *Sermon* preached before the House of Commons earlier that year, and ordered by the House to be printed, printed not in London but by Daniel in Cambridge.

41 Heydon to Fletcher, 2 February 1602/3, Gonville and Caius College, MS James 73, fo. 381.

42 *Ibid.*, fos. 379, 384. Sixteen pages – the whole of D^4 and E^4 – were cancelled and replaced by twenty-two, D^4, DD^4, E_1–3.

43 Fo. Yyy 4r; Gonville and Caius, MS James 73, fo. 381. For Blackbourne, see Venn, *Gonville and Caius*, I, p. 167.

44 Cf. Simpson, *Proof-reading*, p. 11.

45 Samuel Collins, *Increpatio Andreae Eudaemono Iohannis* (C. Legge 1612), fo. ¶4v, Kkk 1v.

46 (William Perkins), *De praedestinationis modo et ordine* (J. Legate 1598), fo. ¶4v. For comparable examples from other presses, in London and Oxford, see two articles by James Binns, 'STC Latin books: evidence for printing-house practice', *The Library*, 5th ser. 32 (1977), pp. 1–27, and 'STC Latin books: further evidence for printing-house practice', *The Library*, 6th ser. 1 (1979), pp. 347–54.

47 Apart from Simpson, *Proof-reading*, see also Blayney, *Nicholas Okes*, chs. 6 and 7, with further references. Blayney restricts himself to London, but since Cambridge looked to London for most of its journeymen there is no reason to suppose that practices varied very seriously. The size of the printing establishment, and attitudes to texts, were more relevant, and the latter are especially difficult to judge. Proof-correction in the second half of the seventeenth century, particularly in parts of the London trade, is discussed in McKenzie, *The London book trade*, pp. 29–34.

48 Moxon, *Mechanick exercises*, p. 247.

49 Simpson, *Proof-reading*, p. 137. They included Robert Futter, formerly Fellow of Jesus College, and Thomas Pakeman, formerly of Clare. All four are described as MAs, so the document cannot date from before Pakeman took his in 1637: Greg, *Companion*, p. 92, misdates it [1634?].

50 The proofs survive in Cambridge University Library, Syn.2.59.2. See D. F. McKenzie, 'Eight quarto proof sheets of 1594 set by formes: *A fruitfull commentarie*', *The Library*, 5th ser. 28 (1973), pp. 1–13. See also James P. Hammersmith, 'Early proofing: the evidence of extant proof sheets', *Analytical and Enumerative Bibliography*, 7 (1983), pp. 188–215. Hammersmith is perhaps too respectful of assumptions and subsequent claims that either Legate at Cambridge or Turner at Oxford was a learned printer simply by virtue of his location, and thus, that they were to be distinguished from ordinary London printers (pp. 196–7). The fragment of proof of *STC*, 18983 (David Owen, *Herod and Pilate reconciled* (Cantrell Legge, 1610), bound into Cambridge University Library, D*.10.35(C), Andrew Willet, *Hexapla on the Epistle of St Paul to the Romans* (Cambridge: Leonard Greene, 1611), *STC*, 25690), is printed on one side of the paper only, and bears several marks correcting spelling. It is possible that it is author's proof, but only the upper parts of pages 44–5 survive, and the evidence is too slight for serious extrapolation.

51 For background details, see John Milton, *Works*, ed. F. A. Patterson *et al.*, I, ii (New York 1931), pp. 459–74. The proof is in Cambridge University Library, Adv. d.38.6.

52 Apart from Simpson, *Proof-reading*, see in particular D. F. Foxon's account of the press at Oxford in the 1630s: 'The varieties of early proof: Cartwright's *Royal slave*, 1639, 1640', *The Library*, 5th ser. 25 (1970), pp. 151–4. The Eustachius proof (in the binding of Trinity College, VI.11.58) supports the conclusion of John T. Shawcross that many

alterations to capitalization, spelling, etc., emanated from the printing house: see his 'Establishment of a text of Milton's poems through a study of *Lycidas*', *PBSA*, 56 (1962), pp. 317–31.

53 Herbert, *Works*, ed. F. E. Hutchinson (Oxford 1941), reiterated by M. C. Bradbrook in her introduction to the Scolar Press facsimile (Menston 1973).

54 One Trinity College copy has the title-page ornament upside down.

55 See above, p. 243.

56 See A4r in Cambridge University Library, Dd.*.4.24[10](E) and Cam.d.619.3, for example.

57 W. R. Parker, *Milton: a biography* (Oxford 1968), 2, p. 814. For some other examples of systematic correction, outside Cambridge, cf. *The mirrour for magistrates* (1587), Chapman's Homer, and Davenant's *Gondibert* (1651), all described in *The Carl H. Pforzheimer library; English literature 1475–1700* (New York 1940), nos. 737, 165 and 252 respectively.

58 *STC*, 10299, 10300.

59 J. Gerhard, *Meditations* (1631), dedication to the second part. The brother of the new dedicatees, William Bonham (d. *c.* 1629) had been a contemporary of Winterton's at Eton and King's before he was admitted at Grays Inn.

60 See below, pp. 257–8.

61 Voet, *Golden compasses*, 2, p. 284; Abraham Ortelius, *Epistulae*, ed. J. H. Hessels (Cambridge 1887), pp. 341–5. For Plantin's payments to authors, see *Golden compasses*, 2, pp. 286–97. Payments to authors in England – both in books and cash – are discussed in H. S. Bennett, *English books & readers 1603–1640* (Cambridge 1970), pp. 228–30. Prynne received about thirty-five copies for *Histrio-Mastix* (1633) rather than money (Greg, *Companion*, p. 278): the custom of paying in copies was not restricted to the 'learned' presses.

62 George Wither, *The schollers purgatory* [1624].

63 See above, p. 174.

64 British Library, MS Add. 18648, quoted in Allan Pritchard, 'George Wither's quarrel with the stationers: an anonymous reply to *The schollers purgatory*', *SB*, 16 (1963), pp. 27–42, at p. 37.

65 For Simmons, Tonson and *Paradise Lost*, see W. R. Parker, *Milton; a biography*, 2 vols. (Oxford 1968), 1, pp. 601, 651–2; 2, pp. 1108, 1162; for Tonson and Dryden's translation of Virgil, see H. B. Wheatley, 'Dryden's publishers', *Trans. Bibliographical Soc.*, 11 (1909–11), pp. 17–38; J. Barnard, 'Dryden, Tonson and subscriptions for the 1697 Virgil', *PBSA*, 57 (1963), pp. 129–51; J. A. Winn, *John Dryden and his world* (New Haven 1987), pp. 475–83. For comparative French examples, cf. H.-J. Martin, *Livre, pouvoirs et société à Paris au XVIIe siècle (1598–1701)*, 2 vols. (Geneva 1969), 1, pp. 425–9; 2, pp. 907–21.

66 Quoted in T. E. Scrutton, *The law of copyright* (1903), pp. 19–20, and in L. Kirschbaum, 'Authors' copyright in England before 1640', *PBSA*, 40 (1946), pp. 43–80, at p. 79. Authors of almanacs were usually paid £2 for their copyright, though some commanded more: see C. Blagden, 'The distribution of almanacks in the second half of the seventeenth century', *SB*, 11 (1958), pp. 107–16, at p. 111, and *Stationers' Company*, pp. 191–2; and B. Capp, *Astrology and the popular press* (1979), pp. 45, 51–2.

67 Bodleian Library, MS Tanner 72, fo. 61.

68 Bodleian Library, MS Tanner 71, fos. 105–6.

69 Bodleian Library, MS Tanner 65, fo. 80.

70 *Ibid.*, fo. 118.

71 Bodleian Library, MS Tanner 70, fo. 48.

72 Bodleian Library, MS Tanner 72, fo. 61.

73 L. Voet, *The Plantin press (1555–1589); a bibliography* (Amsterdam 1980–3), 4, p. 1711, and *Golden compasses*, 2, pp. 285, 288.

74 Gonville and Caius College, MS James 73, fo. 381.

75 E. S. Shuckburgh, *Two biographies of William Bedell* (Cambridge 1902), p. 295.

76 For London examples, see again Bennett, *English books & readers 1603 to 1640*, pp. 228–30.

77 I. G. Philip, 'A seventeenth-century agreement between author and printer', *Bodleian Library Record*, 10 (1978–82), pp. 68–73.

78 Hall to Samuel Hartlib, April 1647 (Sheffield University Library, Hartlib papers 60/14/32).

79 John Horden, *Francis Quarles; a bibliography of his works to the year 1800* (Oxford Bibliographical Soc. 1953), p. 47. See also below, pp. 283–4.

80 Moxon, *Mechanick exercises*, pp. 192, 250–1, 381.

81 Fragments of Barnes' manuscript, marked up in the printing house, are in Emmanuel College Library, MS III.1.1 (James 169).

82 Andrew Willet, *An harmonie upon the First Booke of Samuel* (Cambridge 1614), 'Preface to the reader'.

13 By due authority: licence and the title to print

1 Arber, I.xxxviii–xxxix; *STC*, 10095; Greg, *Companion*, p. 5 (no. 20).

2 Greg, *Companion*, pp. 60, 65, 179, 184, 194. Amidst a burgeoning literature on seventeenth-century licensing and its relationship to censorship, the following remain the standard accounts for the first half of the period: W. W. Greg, *Some aspects and problems of London publishing between 1550 and 1650* (Oxford 1956), esp. ch. III and *Licensers for the press &c. to 1640* (Oxford Bibliographical Soc., 1962), and *Companion*; F. B. Williams, 'The Laudian imprimatur', *The Library*, 5th ser. 15 (1960), pp. 96–104. Much recent influential work draws heavily on F. S. Siebert's misleading *Freedom of the press in England, 1476–1776* (Urbana 1952): see especially C. Hill, 'Censorship and English literature', in his *Collected essays*, 3 vols. (Brighton 1985), 1, and Annabel Patterson, *Censorship and interpretation; the conditions of writing and reading in early modern England* (Madison, Wisc. 1985). For more recent investigations into the evidence, see S. Lambert, 'The printers and the government, 1604–1637', in *Aspects of printing from 1600*, ed. Myers and Harris, pp. 1–29, 'Richard Montagu, Arminianism and censorship', *Past and Present*, 124 (1989), pp. 36–68, and 'Committees, religion, and parliamentary encroachment on royal authority in early Stuart England', *English Historical Review*, 105 (1990), pp. 60–95. The following account draws principally on Cambridge, rather than metropolitan, experiences, but likewise offers little to support theories of monolithic central authority.

3 W. W. Greg, 'Entrance in the Stationers' Register: some statistics', in his *Collected essays*, ed. J. C. Maxwell (Oxford 1966), pp. 341–8; C. J. Sisson, 'The laws of Elizabethan copyright: the Stationers' view', *The Library*, 5th ser. 15 (1960), pp. 8–20.

4 Arber, III.88; Greg, *Licensers*, pp. 16–17; *STC*, 19735·8.

5 Arber, III.124; Greg, *Licensers*, p. 52; *STC*, 22882. The other licenser was Samuel Harsnett, of Pembroke College: see Greg, *Licensers*, p. 42.

6 Arber, IV.318; Greg, *Licensers*, p. 64; *STC*, 20540. See John Horden, *Francis Quarles (1592–1644); a bibliography of his works to the year 1800* (Oxford Bibliographical Soc. 1953), pp. 344–5. Daniel's edition of this book was published in 1643.

7 The 1637 decree is printed in Arber, IV.529–36.

8 Eyre and Rivington, 1, p. 22 (28 April 1641: William Fenner, *The souls looking-glasse*); 1, p. 35 (9 October 1641: *Warme beere*). Daniel possessed only a share in each.

9 The same was repeated in the 1630 edition, printed in London. The 1617 edition (*STC*, 14954·7) survives as a title-page only.

10 *A brief treatise concerning the regulating of printing* (1651); 14 Car. II c. 33.

11 British Library, MS Harley 6996, fo. 25. One of those who had begun, but abandoned, the task was the Oxford theologian John Reynolds (brother of the Catholic William Reynolds). See Peter Milward, *Religious controversies of the Elizabethan age; a survey of printed sources* (1977), pp. 47–8, 72.

12 George Downame to Samuel Ward, 5 April 1635 or 1636, Bodleian Library, MS Tanner 67, fo. 3. For George and John Downame, see Peile, *Christ's*, and *DNB*. See also Greg, *Licensers*, pp. 30–1. George Downame presumably had in mind the attempted suppression of his brother's anti-Arminian *Covenant of grace* (Dublin 1631: *STC*, 7114). See William Prynne, *Canterburies doome* (1646), p. 271 and J. H. Dredge, *Dr. George Downame, Bishop of Derry* (Manchester 1881).

13 Prynne, *Canterburies doome*, p. 255.

14 *STC*, 1313; Arber, IV.504. Brownrigg's imprimatur, printed at the end of the book, is dated 9 October 1639, but the book was not entered until 2 April 1640.

15 Bodleian Library, MS Laud Misc. 201: the imprimatur is dated 3 December 1630.

16 Gonville and Caius College, MS 442/637. Cf. also W. M. Palmer, *John Layer (1586–1640) of Shepreth, Cambridgeshire; a seventeenth-century local historian* (Cambridge Antiquarian Soc. 1935), esp. pp. 22–6. Palmer's statement that licence was obtained in 1633 is incorrect: Holdsworth became Vice-Chancellor for the first time in 1640.

17 Baker–Mayor, I, pp. 216–18, 630–1; N. Tyacke, *Anti-Calvinists; the rise of English Arminianism c. 1590–1640* (Oxford 1987), p. 194.

18 James Usher, *Life*, ed. R. Parr (1686), p. 477.

19 So it was listed as one of the books wherewith to berate Laud, who 'with his Chaplaines Agents, by his instigation or command, compiled Authorized, imprinted, published divers Bookes... in defence of Popish Errors, Superstitious [sic], Ceremonies, practises, almost to the totall corruption and subversion of our Religion' (Prynne, *Canterburies doome*, p. 186).

20 Jackson, *Records*, p. 234. Yet only 35 per cent of the London trade output in 1640 contained imprimaturs (F. B. Williams, 'The Laudian imprimatur', p. 97). For Oxford, see J. Johnson and S. Gibson, *Print and privilege at Oxford to the year 1700* (Oxford Bibliographical Soc. 1946), pp. 8–9.

21 Davenant's *Declamationes* had been first printed, at Cambridge, in 1634. The Star Chamber decree of 11 July 1637 required new editions to be newly licensed (Greg, *Companion*, p. 347; Arber, IV.533). Caesar's *Complete captain* (1640) was also licensed by John Cosin alone, on 24 April 1640.

22 F. B. Williams' statement that 'the University imprimatur is normal in Cambridge books during the period 1633–1640' ('The Laudian imprimatur', p. 104) is not correct.

23 Bodleian Library, MS Tanner 307. Cf. P. Simpson, *Proof-reading*, pp. 37–8.

24 Trinity College, Cambridge, MS B.14.22(1).

25 Trinity College, E.14.5. R. B. McKerrow's assumption (*Introduction to bibliography* (Oxford 1927), p. 186, n. 1) that licensed copy and compositors' copy were identical is over-general, and inaccurate. Cf. J. Moore, 'Copy and print in English books of the sixteenth and seventeenth centuries' (D.Phil., Oxford 1989), p. 120.

26 Bodleian Library, MSS Laud Misc. 201 (*Summary catalogue* 852), Laud Misc. 381, Laud Misc. 509 (N. R. Ker, *Catalogue of manuscripts containing Anglo-Saxon* (Oxford 1957), no. 344), Laud Misc. 636 (Ker, *Anglo-Saxon*, no. 346).

27 *Commons Journal*, 2 February 1642/3: the licence was Holdsworth's for Ferne's *Resolves*.

28 University Archives, Pr. P.4(8).

29 University Archives, Pr. P.4(8) (formerly CUR 33.6.22).

30 Cf. T. Browne, *Concio ad clerum* (1688: imprimatur signed by John Balderston, etc.); Thomas Walker, *Sermon... at the assizes* (1693: imprimatur signed by George Oxenden, etc.). Neither is entered in the University's register.

31 Thus George Atwell, whose *Faithfull surveyor* was finally published in 1658, after years in which he had unsuccessfully sought to put his various works into print, addressed his dedicatee, William Dillingham, Master of Emanuel, and wrote of '*My direction, and method of teaching school*: (which yourself, Sir, have both read and examined; together with another piece of *Common arithmetick*, and *The Doctrine of Triangles*, and a fourth piece of *Dialling*.) wherof both the Reverend Vice-chancellour, and others the Heads of the Universitie, have so willingly and freely long since granted me their hands for licence of impression.'

32 14 Car. II, cap. XXXIII. The parts relating to Oxford and Cambridge are printed in L. L. Shadwell, ed., *Enactments in Parliament specially concerning the Universities of Oxford and Cambridge*, 4 vols. (Oxford Historical Soc. 1912), 1, pp. 282–5.

33 Sir R. L'Estrange, *Considerations and proposals in order to the regulation of the press* (1663).

34 G. Kitchin, *Sir Roger L'Estrange; a contribution to the history of the press in the seventeenth century* (1913); T. J. Crist, 'Francis Smith and the opposition press in England, 1660–1688' (PhD, Cambridge 1977); Leona Rostenberg, 'Subversion and repression: Robert Stephens, messenger of the press', in her *Literary, political, scientific, religious & legal publishing in England, 1551–1700*, 2 vols. (New York 1965), 2, pp. 344–67; J. S. T. Hetet, 'A literary underground in Restoration England; printers and dissenters in the context of constraint, 1660–1689' (PhD, Cambridge 1987), ch. 3.

35 Various states of copies of Archimedes may be compared in the University Library: M.5.45, T.30.29, and U*.5.103. Presentation copies of the *Lectiones XVIII* are in the University Library (Adv.d.27.4) and Trinity College (Q.15.73).

36 See p. 344; C. Blagden, 'Early Cambridge printers and the Stationers' Company', *TCBS*, 2 (1957), pp. 275–89.

14 *Running the Printing House*

1 See above, p. 15.

2 Gray and Palmer, pp. 70–1; see above, p. 85.

3 Blayney, *Nicholas Okes*, p. 95.

4 Gray and Palmer, pp. 82–3.

5 Arber, II.807.12; Greg, *Companion*, p. 41.

6 Arber, I.248; Greg, *Companion*, pp. 29–30.

7 Arber, v.lii.

8 Greg, *Companion*, p. 54; Arber, III.699; Jackson, *Records*, p. 75.

9 Carter, *Oxford University Press*, pp. 23–4; Jackson, *Records*, pp. 104–5, 245.

10 Greg, *Companion*, pp. 94–8, 324–6.

11 University Archives, CUR 6.2(53) (Pryme); Arber, II.157 (Legge). The record of his apprenticeship describes Legge as the son of Edward Legge of Burcham [Bircham], yeoman. For further particulars about the Legge family in Norfolk, see Venn, *Gonville and Caius*, 3, p. 64 (discussing Thomas Legge, Master of the College from 1573 to 1607).

12 University Archives, CUR 6.2(53).

13 Arber, II.723; McKerrow, *Dictionary*, pp. 254–5.

14 University Archives, Comm. Ct III.8.

15 Arber, III.58. For Stafford's subsequent career, see Gerald D. Johnson, 'The Stationers versus the Drapers: control of the press in the late sixteenth century', *The Library*, 6th ser. 10 (1988), pp. 1–17. No copy of *The black dog of Newgate* is known to have survived from his press. Hutton was executed for robbery in 1598 (*DNB*).

16 For Smith, see, again, Johnson, 'Stationers versus the Drapers.'

17 Arber, II.694, 800–2; Greg, *Companion*, pp. 39–40. See also above, p. 422, n. 15.

18 University Archives, VC Ct III.2(124).

19 Details from University Archives, Comm. Ct II.4, II.6, VC Ct III.2(251, 252); Legate claimed that Pryme's slackness affected the work of three compositors and a pressman. See also D. F. McKenzie, 'Notes on printing at Cambridge, *c.* 1590', *TCBS*, 3 (1959), pp. 96–103: for 'Prince' read 'Pryme' throughout.

20 University Archives, Comm. Ct II.6(1).

21 University Archives, VC Ct III.8(63).

22 University Archives, Comm. Ct II.6, fo. 17v.

23 In 1593/4, for example, Thomas Parker explained in the Commissary's Court that he and Legge had printed 1,250 sheets per day for about ten weeks, then 1,800 a day for the next Quarter, then about 2,500 a day for six months while they worked at the second edition of Thomas's dictionary (University Archives, Comm. Ct II.6, fo. 3r).

24 Voet, *Golden compasses*, 2, pp. 325–6. Moxon's figures (pp. 292, 320–1) suggest that three thousand impressions were possible in a twelve-hour day; but in fact work was much less regular: cf. Charlton Hinman, *The printing and proof-reading of the First Folio of Shakespeare*, 2 vols. (Oxford 1963), I, p. 42. See also Gaskell, *New introduction*, pp. 140–1. Although later on in the century rates varied according to the size of type, in Cambridge in the 1590s the rate was specifically said to be the same (Comm. Ct III.8(14)).

25 Arber, II.43; Greg and Boswell, p. 25; Greg, *Companion*, pp. 43–4.

26 So Legate: University Archives, Comm. Ct III.8(14). Parker, however, claimed that smaller type took longer to machine than larger (Comm. Ct II.6(1)).

27 University Archives, Comm. Ct III.8(14). No equivalent word seems to exist in England for *l'embauche*, or *embauché*, meaning that 'printers were contracted to work on such and such a book, and to do so many pages of it a day', contracts running by the month. This system was described as that customary in a memoir from seventeenth-century Paris, piece-work being least common. See J.-F. Gilmont, 'Printers by the rules', *The Library*, 6th ser. 2 (1980), pp. 130–55, and P. Chauvet, *Les ouvriers du livre en France des origines à la Révolution de 1789* (Paris 1959), pp. 430–1. For payment by the day in sixteenth-century Geneva, see P. Chaix, *Recherches sur l'imprimerie à Genève de 1550 à 1564* (Geneva 1954), pp. 39–40.

28 University Archives, Comm. Ct II.6, fo. 17r; Comm. Ct III.8(15, 17). This was considerable pay, and may be compared with other Cambridge rates of 12d. a day (carpenters, 1591), or 16d. a day (plumbers, 1600): see Mary C. Siraut, 'Some aspects of the economic and social history of Cambridge under Elizabeth', (MLitt, Cambridge 1978), p. 242. None of the trades listed in the 1589 'Letter to the Lord Chancellor for regulating of servants' wages' approached ten shillings a week, though several in the metal-working trades fell between six and eight shillings. A common labourer in London might receive ninepence a day (*Tudor royal proclamations*, 3, pp. 40–2; Ann Jennalie Cook, *The privileged playgoers of Shakespeare's London, 1576–1642* (Princeton 1981), pp. 228–34, with further references). The cost of living in Cambridge was not necessarily the same. But see also John Chartres, 'Food consumption and internal trade', in *London 1500–1700; the making of the metropolis*, ed. A. L. Beier and R. Finlay (1986), pp. 168–96, table 16, suggesting that London craftsmen's wages in the 1590s were eighteenpence per day, and in southern England were a shilling per day: see also E. A. Wrigley and R. S. Schofield, *The population history of Enland 1541–1871* (1981, repr. Cambridge 1989), pp. 638–41. F. C. Avis, 'Miscellaneous costs in sixteenth century English printing', *GJ* (1976), pp. 306–10, assembles some more figures, but is unsatisfactory with respect to wages.

29 See above, n. 19.

30 University Archives, Comm. Ct III.8(17). It should be noted that in the case of other skilled crafts, London wages were higher than those in the country or at Oxford and Cambridge: see S. Rappaport, *Worlds within worlds; structures of life in sixteenth-century London* (Cambridge 1989), pp. 83–4, with further references. For wage inflation in the 1590s, see *ibid.*, pp. 149–50.

31 Gilmont, 'Printers by the rules'; L. and W. Hellinga, 'Regulations relating to the planning and organization of work by the Master Printer in the ordinances of Christopher Plantin', *The Library*, 5th ser. 29 (1974), pp. 52–60, with earlier references.

32 University Archives, Pr.P.4(7).

33 University Archives, CUR 33.2(95); Pr.P.4(7).

34 University Archives, CUR 33.2(55); see also above, p. 153.

35 University Archives, Comm. Ct II.6, fos. 1–6, 17v; McKenzie, 'Notes on printing at Cambridge'. For concurrent printing, cf. Blayney, *Nicholas Okes*, pp. 34–5, and throughout.

36 Gray and Palmer, p. 68 (*STC*, 25366).

37 See principally Hinman, *Printing and proof-reading*, esp. 1, pp. 334–65; D. F. McKenzie, 'Printers of the mind: some notes on bibliographical theories and printing-house practices', *SB*, 22 (1969), pp. 1–75; Blayney, *Nicholas Okes*, esp. pp. 31–59.

38 See above, pp. 268–9; Arber, II.43.

39 *STC*, 11773; Greg, *Companion*, p. 271.

40 Arber, II.43, 790–3; Greg, *Companion*, pp. 37, 43; University Archives, Comm. Ct III.8(17).

41 No protest, for example, seems to have been made at an edition of three thousand copies of Arthur Hopton's *Concordancy of yeares* ([Nicholas Okes] for the Company of Stationers, 1612: *STC*, 13778). The argument that brought the book to the attention of the Court of the Stationers' Company was over ownership, not the size of the impression: but this was not surprising in this context, given the Company's interest (Jackson, *Records*, p. 83).

42 For a summary, see the long note prefacing the entry in *STC* to 23039ff.

43 Jackson, *Records*, pp. x, 200.

44 See, for example, the Cambridge University Library copy Qq*.2.77(C), 1639, but including sheets G and Y from 1634: the volume is in a contemporary Cambridge binding.

45 Three copies of the 'third' edition in Cambridge University Library (Syn.8.63.413; Syn.8.63.240; Cam.e.634.2) offer convenient evidence of this. The last, in contemporary vellum, is made up from sheets drawn from all three of the first three editions.

46 Of the seven copies in Cambridge University Library, only four are identical apart from a variant imprint. The confusion between some modern bibliographical practice and contemporary custom is explored, with particular reference to the octavo Bible of '1628', in B. J. McMullin, 'The Bible and continuous reprinting in the early seventeenth century', *The Library*, 6th ser. 5 (1983), pp. 256–63. See also the remarks on Prynne's *Popish royall favourite* (1643) in David McKitterick, 'Changes for the better?', *The Book Collector*, 37 (1988), pp. 461–78, and the examples cited in *The Carl H. Pforzheimer Library. English literature 1475–1700* (New York 1940), under 'Resetting in part', p. 1304.

47 These figures are gathered most conveniently in William M. Baillie, 'The printing of privileged books at Cambridge 1631–1634', *TCBS*, 5 (1971), pp. 155–66, at p. 166. Edition sizes of 3,000 for English Stock books had been long established: in 1589 this had been the figure set for editions of Corderius printed by Robert Robinson. See Greg and Boswell, p. 32.

48 Gaskell, *New introduction*, pp. 161–2; cf. Carter, *Oxford University Press*, p. 213: 'The

[Oxford] Press Accounts of 1690–1713 show that the cost of paper was seldom less than half the expense of producing a book.'

49 University Archives, CUR 33.6(15).

50 University Archives, CUR 33.2(71).

51 *Ibid.*

52 University Achives, CUR 33.1(11), fos. 4r, 7r. Compare this with the sum of £3.0.0 paid for correcting Lambard's *Eirenarcha* printed by Adam Islip in 1606 (Jackson, *Records*, p. 22): as a law book this may have commanded a higher fee than usual. In 1625 the University paid £5.0.0 to the customary Corrector of the University's two collections of verses on the death of James I and the marriage of Charles I (University Archives, U.Ac.2(1), 1624–5).

53 McKenzie, *Apprentices 1605–40*, no. 349; for Leet's modest worldly goods in 1663, see Gray and Palmer, pp. 98–100.

54 University Archives, CUR.33.1(15, 19).

55 University Archives, CUR 33.1(20).

56 *Ibid.*; VC Ct. III.38(24) (1644); VC Ct III.36(80).

57 *CSPD*, 1629–31, p. 258.

58 For labour migration in Cambridge, see Nigel Goose, 'Household size and structure in early-Stuart Cambridge', *Social History*, 5 (1980), repr. in Jonathan Barry, ed., *The Tudor and Stuart town; a reader in English urban history, 1530–1688* (1990), pp. 74–120. There is substantial further evidence in depositions in the records of the Vice-Chancellor's Court and the Commissary's Court. For more general considerations, and comparative discussions of other areas, cf. Peter Clark and David Souden, eds., *Migration and society in early modern England* (1987); Peter Clark, 'The migrant in Kentish towns, 1580–1640', in *Crisis and order in English towns, 1500–1700*, ed. P. Clark and P. Slack (1972), pp. 117–63, and J. H. C. Patten 'The urban structure of East Anglia in the sixteenth and seventeenth centuries' (PhD, Cambridge 1972), pp. 264–362. For the book trade, see McKenzie, *Apprentices*.

59 Cambridge University Library, Views aa.53.91.2(70).

60 D. H. S. Cranage and H. P. Stokes, 'The Augustinian Friary in Cambridge, and the history of its site', *Proc. Cambridge Antiquarian Soc.*, 16 (1921), pp. 53–75; see also *The University Printing Houses at Cambridge from the sixteenth to the twentieth century* (Cambridge 1962).

61 The detergent properties of lye were essential for cleaning ink off formes of type: see Moxon, *Mechanick exercises*, pp. 80–1, 198, 310–11. Daniel was fortunate in being able to house the lye-trough outside his working premises. Cf. Moxon, p. 18: 'The *Lye-Trough* and *Rincing-Trough* he places towards some corner of the Room, yet so as they may have a good Light; and under these he causes a *Sink* to be made to convey the Water out of the Room: But if he have other conveniences for the placing these Troughs, he will rather set them out of the Room to avoid the slabbering they cause in.'

62 University Archives, CUR 33.1(19, 20). For details of the Austin Friars in 1587, contained in the post-mortem inventory of John Hatcher, see the inventory in the University Archives, VC Ct inventories; W. M. Palmer, 'Cambridgeshire doctors in the olden time', *Proc. Cambridge Antiquarian Soc.*, 15 (1911), pp. 200–79, at pp. 238–45; and Leedham-Green, *Books in Cambridge inventories*, 1, pp. 367–82.

63 Moxon, *Mechanick exercises*, pp. 35–6.

64 *Ibid.*, pp. 16, 35.

65 University Archives, Comm. Ct III.8(5); see above, pp. 271–2. A twelve-hour day was also observed at the Plantin house: see Voet, *Golden compasses*, 2, pp. 326, 343–4.

66 McKenzie, *Cambridge University Press*, 1, pp. 89–93; J. Rule, *The experience of labour in eighteenth-century industry* (1981), pp. 49–73.

67 Simpson, *Proof-reading*, pp. 150–3; Francis R. Johnson, 'Printers' "copy-books" and the black market in the Elizabethan book trade', *The Library*, 5th ser. 1 (1946), pp. 97–105; I. G. Philip, 'A seventeenth-century agreement between author and printer', *Bodleian Library Record*, 10 (1978–82), pp. 68–73.

68 University Archives, U.Ac.2(2), 1684–5, 1687–8, 1688–9, 1694–5; U.Ac.1(6), 31 May 1695.

69 Moxon, *Mechanick exercises*, p. 17: this also made the hard manual labour of running the presses easier during the summer heat.

70 'If the *Inck* be too *Hard*, as sometimes in very frosty Weather it will be, then, though his Work be curious, yet he must *Rub* in a little *Soft Inck* to soften it' (*Mechanick exercises*, pp. 288–9). The humidity of the weather also affected the printing, and drying, of paper which was itself printed damp. For a later example of unusual explicitness, cf. the warning prefaced to Conyers Middleton, *A free inquiry into the miraculous powers which are supposed to have subsisted in the Christian church* (1749): the note is dated 12 December 1748: 'Dr. *Middleton's* Free Inquiry &c. having been printed in such hast, and at such a season of the year, that the sheets have not had sufficient time to dry, it is thought proper to give this notice to Gentlemen, not to have their books bound in less than two months or they will run the hazard of having them spoiled.'

71 British Library, MS Harley 389, fos. 450r, 484r; Cooper, *Annals*, 3, pp. 222–8, 239–40, 243; University Archives, T.X.19.

72 British Library, MS Harley 390, fo. 523r.

73 George Evans to John Worthington, 8 October 1665 (Worthington, *Diary and correspondence* (Manchester 1847–86), 2, pt i, p. 179).

74 Worthington to Henry More, 24 January 1665/6; Worthington to Evans, 24 January 1665/6 (*ibid.*, pp. 200–1).

75 John Cosin, *Correspondence* (Durham 1869–72), 2, p. 151. See also Cooper, *Annals*, vols 1–3; J. F. D. Shrewsbury, *A history of Bubonic plague in the British Isles* (Cambridge 1971); Paul Slack, *The impact of plague in Tudor and Stuart England* (1985); Raymond Williamson, 'The plague in Cambridge', *Medical History*, 1 (1957) pp. 51–64. The letters of Mede are full of his fears, and of references to the effects of the plague.

15 *Type, paper and other necessities*

1 Henri Estienne, ed., *Poetae Graeci principes heroici carminis* (Geneva 1566), vol. 2. See also Dick Higgins, *George Herbert's pattern poems: in their tradition* (New York 1977), and *Pattern poetry; guide to an unknown literature* (Albany, N.Y. 1987); J. Adler and U. Ernst, *Text als Figur; visuelle Poesie von der Antike bis zur Moderne* (Weinheim 1987); J. W. Binns, *Intellectual culture in Elizabethan and Jacobean England; the Latin writings of the age* (Leeds 1990), pp. 50–1, 466 n.33.

2 University Archives, CUR 33.1(20).

3 These plates are most fully listed in A. F. Johnson, *A catalogue of engraved and etched English title-pages down to the death of William Faithorne, 1691* (Bibliographical Soc. 1934), and in Hind, *Engraving in England*; for Hollar's 'Hinc lucem' device, see Richard Pennington, *A descriptive catalogue of the etched work of Wenceslaus Hollar 1607–1677* (Cambridge 1982), no. 486.

4 Hind, *Engraving in England*, 3, pp. 256–7.

5 Thomas Fuller, *History of the worthies of England* (1662), p. 77; see also Strickland Gibson, *A bibliography of the works of Thomas Fuller* (Oxford Bibliographical Soc., *Proceedings and Papers*, 4 (1936)), p. 63, and Hind, *Engraving in England*, 3, pp. 135–40.

6 Thomas Fuller, *The historie of the holy warre* (Cambridge 1639), 'A declaration of the frontispice', by J. C. The topic is discussed more generally, without specific reference to

Fuller, in Margery Corbett and Ronald Lightbown, *The comely frontispiece; the emblematic title-page in England, 1550–1650* (1979). See fig. 15.

7 Harold Jenkins, *Edward Benlowes (1602–1676); biography of a minor poet* (1952), pp. 67–76, 102. Benlowes, described by Anthony à Wood as 'a weak and imprudent man as to the knowledge of men and things of the world', was said to have spent the better part of £700 a year 'on vertuositie and flattering poets' (Wood, *Life and times*, ed. A. Clark (Oxford Historical Soc. 1891–1900), 2, pp. 360–2, citing also Bodleian Library, MS Wood F. 4, p. 135). Benlowes died in poverty at Oxford.

8 Stationers' Company Journal Book for Money Disbursed, 1650–98, March 1654/5, December 1655. See also p. 308.

9 PRO, Prob 5/1054; *The first minute book of the Delegates of the Oxford University Press, 1668–1756* (Oxford 1943), pp. 3–6 (the typefounders involved were Nicholas Nicholls and Joseph Leigh; no mention was made of the Fifields).

10 Stationers' Company Journal Book for Money Disbursed, 1650–98, July, October 1654, January, March 1654/5, April 1655. The earliest reference to independent ink-makers is by Evelyn (1660): see C. H. Bloy, *A history of printing ink, balls and rollers 1440–1850* (1967), p. 66. '*Vermillion* is the deepest and purest Red, and always used to Books of Price. Red-Lead is much more faint and foul, and though more used than Vermillion, yet used only to Books of Vulgar Sale and Low price, as Almanacs, &c.' (Moxon, *Mechanick exercises*, p. 300). For ink-making, see Moxon, pp. 82–6. He complained that English master printers tended to avoid the unpleasant and noisome processes of ink-making, 'and instead of having good *Inck*, content themselves that they pay an *Inck-maker* for good *Inck*, which may yet be better or worse according to the Conscience of the *Inck-maker*' (p. 82).

11 Cf. the caveats of D. F. McKenzie, 'Printers of the mind', *SB*, 22 (1969), pp. 1–75: 'We should normally proceed in our inquiries by the hypothetico-deductive method which welcomes conjectures in the positive knowledge that productive conditions were extraordinarily complex and unpredictable, but which also insists that such conjectures be scrutinized with the greatest rigour and, if refuted, rejected' (p. 6).

12 These distinctions are insufficiently emphasized in the most extended survey of prices in sixteenth and seventeenth-century England: F. R. Johnson, 'Notes on English retail book prices, 1550–1640', *The Library*, 5th ser. 5 (1950), pp. 83–112. For binding charges (so far as they can be tabulated or said to be standard), see M. M. Foot, 'Some bookbinders' price lists of the seventeenth and eighteenth centuries', in *De libris compactis miscellanea*, ed. G. Colin (Brussels 1984), pp. 273–319, and reprinting, on pp. 286–91, *A generall note of the prises for binding of all sorts of bookes*, 1619. (This article is also included in R. Myers and M. Harris, eds., *Economics of the British book trade, 1605–1939* (Cambridge 1985), pp. 124–75.) The price for binding a quarto Bible ranged from 5s.6d. 'gilt over one way' down to 1s.10d. for a plain fillet binding, or 1s.2d. for one with only an oval centre-piece; ordinary quartos, in a plain binding with a centre-piece, cost 10d., and grammars, etc. in sheep 2$\frac{1}{2}$d.

13 Greg and Boswell, pp. 58–9; see above, p. 269.

14 The cost of paper as a proportion of the total cost of printing fell between the sixteenth and the eighteenth centuries. For the Plantin 16° Virgil (1564) it represented 73 per cent of the total for 2,500 copies, and for the 16° Horace (1564) the cost of paper was almost double that for printing 1,250 copies: as the edition run was increased, so did the proportion of paper costs. Cf. R. de Roover, 'The business organisation of the Plantin Press in the setting of sixteenth century Antwerp', *Gedenkboek der Plantin-Dagen, 1555–1955* (Antwerp 1956), pp. 230–46, at pp. 235–6; Gaskell, *New introduction*, p. 177. For more detail, see Leon Voet, *The Plantin Press, 1555–1589*, 6 vols. (Amsterdam 1980–83), and *Golden compasses*, 2, p. 19. For some notes on the paper of a later

University Printer, John Field, see D. McKitterick, 'John Field in 1668; the affairs of a University Printer', *TCBS*, 9 (1990), pp. 497–516.

15 D. C. Coleman, *The British paper industry, 1495–1860* (Oxford 1958), pp. 13–19, 123. For details of Subsidy and Impost charges, based on notional values set on the various sizes and qualities, see *The rates of marchandizes, as they are set down in the book of rates* [1608] (*STC*, 7691), fos. K1v–K2r. There is no evidence that the Cambridge printers ever used paper from the mill at Barnwell, near Cambridge, mentioned by Meres in 1557 (J. Lamb, *A collection of letters … in the … library of Corpus Christi College, illustrative of the history of the University of Cambridge* (1838), p. 231). In 1662 Thomas Fuller spoke of the manufacture there being 'disused'. See also Cooper, *Annals*, 2, pp. 132, 265 and A. H. Shorter, *Paper mills and paper makers in England 1495–1800* (Paper Publications Soc. 1957), p. 147.

16 Moxon, *Mechanick exercises*, pp. 320–2.

17 University Archives, CUR 33.6(8), describing practice in 1622. Apart from this, see also, more generally, M. Sparke, *Scintilla* (1641), repr. in Herbert, *Historical catalogue*, pp. 183–7.

18 James E. Thorold Rogers, *A history of agriculture and prices in England* (Oxford 1866–1902), 5, p. 607. Thorold Rogers' figures are drawn from sources in Oxford, Lancashire, London, Worksop, Wormleighton (Warwickshire) and, particularly usefully, Eton, where prices are recorded regularly over a long period. At Eton, the price of a ream remained constant at five shillings from 1584 to 1620, when it rose to 5s.4d., before advancing to seven shillings in 1646 (*ibid.*, 6, pp. 565–8).

19 H.-J. Martin, *Livre, pouvoirs et société à Paris au XVIIe siècle*, 2 vols. (Geneva 1969), 2, pp. 583–5.

20 Gray and Palmer, p. 70. Pot, hand and Rochelle were fairly small (*c*. 40 × 30 cm.); demy measured *c*. 50 × 35 cm. (Gaskell, *New introduction*, pp. 73–5). For a later example, cf. R. W. Chapman, 'An inventory of paper, 1674', *The Library*, 4th ser. 7 (1927), pp. 402–8: the prices, quoted from Bodleian Library, MS Rawl.D.398, fos. 156–7, ranged from 2s.8d. for a ream of pot, to £2.16s. for a ream of super royal; ordinary demy cost about 8s.6d.

21 Legate to an unidentified London stationer, 29 August 1593 (M. S. G. Hands, 'The Cathedral Libraries Catalogue', *The Library*, 5th ser. 2 (1947), pp. 1–13, at pp. 9–10).

22 Jackson, *Records*, p. 54.

23 Greg, *Companion*, pp. 233–4.

24 University Archives, CUR 33.2(95); Jackson, *Records*, p. 335.

25 'Hand' 2s.8d.; 'Small Rochelle' 3s.1d.; 'Pott' 4s.2d.; 'Demy' 6s.: Gray and Palmer, pp. 70, 83. (For Legge's forty reams of white paper should be read forty-six.)

26 See above, p. 197.

27 Greg and Boswell, p. 58; Johnson, 'Notes on English retail book prices', p. 84.

28 University Archives, CUR 33.6(8), CUR 33.2(95), fo. 25r; 'ob' = a halfpenny.

29 University Archives, CUR 33.2(62); see also above, p. 155.

30 University Archives, CUR 33.2(95), CUR 33.6(8) – two copies of the same calculations. Tabor also summarized the costs of the privileged books in Pr.P.4(1).

31 University Archives, CUR 33.1(11).

32 Cf. Thomas Brudnell's charges to John Partridge for various almanacs and other popular works in 1644–8, the prices ranging from 4s. to 6s.8d. a ream (H. R. Plomer, 'A printer's bill in the seventeenth century', *The Library*, new ser. 7 (1906), pp. 32–45).

33 See above, p. 284.

34 Cf. Thomas Randolph, *The iealous lovers* (Cambridge 1634): 'I beg thy pardon if I put thee to the expence of a sixpence, and the losse of an houre' ('To the reader').

35 Thomas Thomas articles, 1586 (University Archives, Pr.B.2.2); John Legate articles

(CUR 33.1(5)). The memorandum in CUR 33.2(65), fo. 69r, suggests that this had fallen into abeyance in Buck's hands.

36 University Archivess, CUR 33.6(3). See above, p. 123.

37 For Thomas's dictionary, see University Library, M*.10.14(D), described in Oates, *Cambridge University Library*, p. 363. The copy of Taylor is in my own possession. The price of five shillings for a bound copy of Thomas recorded by Johnson in 'Notes on English retail book prices', p. 111, is for a quarto printed at London in 1620. If a shilling is deducted for binding the two Cambridge books, the respective costs per sheet are about a halfpenny and about three farthings.

38 University Archives, U.Ac.2 (1), p. 622; U.Ac.1 (3), 1633–4; Oates 'Congratulatory verses', pp. 404–5.

39 University Archives, VC Ct III.36(78), fo. 2; M. E. Bohannon, 'A London bookseller's bill: 1635–1639', *The Library*, 4th ser. 18 (1937–8), pp. 417–46.

40 Baillie, 'Privileged books', p. 166.

41 *Ibid.*; University Archives, VC Ct III.35(43). The only known surviving Cambridge edition of the 1630s is *STC*, 24793 (1632), of which three copies remain out of an edition of three thousand.

42 Inscription in the Cambridge University Library copy, Cam.d.637.4. See also p. 183.

43 University Archives, VC Ct III.36(78, 80).

44 Johnson, 'Notes on English retail book prices', p. 90.

45 Oates, 'Congratulatory verses'; Harold Forster, 'The rise and fall of the Cambridge muses', *TCBS*, 8 (1982), pp. 141–72.

46 *Gratulatio Academiae Cantabrigiensis de reditu Gulielmi III post pacem* (1697), fo. Hh2v; McKenzie, *Cambridge University Press*, 1, p. 176.

47 University Archives, U.Ac.2(2), 1688–9, 1694–5.

48 Compare this with the prices quoted in *A compleat catalogue of all the stitch'd books* (1680) and its *Continuations*, the latter ed. F. C. Francis (Luttrell Soc. 1956), which conveniently provide both retail prices and the number of sheets in each publication listed: the price was, again, approximately a penny a sheet. Details of prices in Cambridge discussed in this paragraph are taken from the University Audit Books (U.Ac.2(1,2) and Vouchers (U.Ac.1(4,5,6)).

49 Bodleian Library, MS Rawl. D.397, fos. 409, etc. For example, the 1678 Oxford edition of Cornelius Nepos (Madan, *Oxford books*, no. 3185; Wing, N431), a duodecimo set mostly in pica, cost nine shillings a sheet for Latin setting, and ten shillings for Greek. Presswork was four shillings a sheet. For detailed comment on a similar range of charges to those sketched here, at Cambridge after 1698, see McKenzie, *Cambridge University Press*, 1 pp. 76–89.

50 Andrew G. Watson, *The library of Sir Simonds D'Ewes* (1966), p. 266.

51 F. Barnes and J. C. Dickinson, 'A seventeenth-century Cambridge book and its cost', *TCBS*, 2 (1958), pp. 376–81.

52 University Archives, U.Ac.1(6), 1691–2, 1694–5, 1698–9. I have assumed that the bill for Barnes' Euripides was for the ordinary paper issue. Standard binding charges (which can be no more than a general guide) are listed in *A general note of the prices of binding all sorts of books in calves-leather* (1695), repr. in M. M. Foot, 'Some bookbinders' price lists', at pp. 305–7.

53 PRO, Prob 5/1054. I have not attempted to estimate the inflation in the cost of paper in particular following the Great Fire. The valuers were all Cambridge men, experienced in the book trade but not in printing: John Aungier, Matthew Eusden, Robert Browne and Robert Nicholson. Gray and Palmer, working from a fragmentary original in the University Archives, name only the last two. The full valuation is printed in McKitterick, 'John Field in 1668'.

54 Cf. p. 285 above.

55 Full extrapolation of some of these questions was not even possible for the much better documented period after 1696: McKenzie, *Cambridge University Press*, 1, p. 145.

16 Civil war and inter-regnum

1 McKerrow, *Devices*, no. 428; Guy de Tervarent, *Attributs et symboles dans l'art profane, 1450–1600*, 2 vols. (Geneva 1958–9), 2, p. 296. For Wither, and his debt to Gabriel Rollenhagen and the two engravers named Crispyn van de Passe, see Hind, *Engraving in England*, 2, p. 245, and 3, pp. 186–8, and John Horden's introduction to the Scolar Press facsimile (Menston, 1968). For a literary parallel, cf. Vaughan, 'The palm-tree', discussed in R. Freeman, *English emblem books* (1948), pp. 150–1. In 1660, Daniel adopted another device, incorporating an eagle and serpent, on the title-page of the translation of Barrow's Euclid printed for the Cambridge bookseller William Nealand: for other examples of this, cf. R. Wittkower, 'Eagle and serpent; a study in the migration of symbols', *Journal of the Warburg Institute*, 2 (1938–9), pp. 293–5.

2 Alan H. Nelson, ed., *Records of early English drama. Cambridge* (Toronto 1989), 2, pp. 884–5, 899; Cooper, *Annals*, 3, pp. 321–3.

3 Cooper, *Annals*, 3, pp. 325–8.

4 See most recently, J. D. Twigg, *The University of Cambridge and the English revolution, 1625–1688* (Woodbridge, 1990), with further references.

5 Cooper, *Annals*, 3, pp. 328, 331. Versions of Dowsing's journal have been printed in Cooper, *Annals*, 3, pp. 364–7; Mullinger 3, pp. 267–72; and the *History Teachers' Miscellany*, 1926, ed. A. C. Moule. See also Margaret Aston, *England's iconoclasts. 1. Laws against images* (Oxford 1988), pp. 74–84.

6 Cooper, *Annals*, 3, pp. 340–1.

7 *Commons Journal*, 2, p. 922 (12 January 1642/3); *Lords Journal*, 5, p. 559 (16 January); Cooper, *Annals*, 3, p. 336.

8 Madan, *Oxford books*, 2, p. 159.

9 *Commons Journal*, 2, pp. 733, 751.

10 Ferne quoted Romans xiii on his title-page; he later became Master of Trinity (in 1660) and (in 1661/2) Bishop of Chester: see *DNB* and A. G. Matthews, *Walker revised* (Oxford 1948), p. 235.

11 *Commons Journal*, 2, pp. 900, 951.

12 *Querela Cantabrigiensis* (1646, reprinted in *Mercurius rusticus*, 1685), p. 185. Though the *Querela* has been attributed to John Barwick, Madan (*Oxford books*, no. 1889) considered it to have been compiled by Bruno Ryves. It is not clear whether Ryves was mistaken in his reason for Holdsworth's imprisonment; but he did record that Holdsworth denied having licensed the King's pieces, professing himself 'not to be so saucy as to offer to License any thing which His Majesty Commanded to be Printed'. See also Twigg, *University of Cambridge*, p. 71; for Cambridge and the Long Parliament, see *ibid.*, pp. 42–65.

13 Gatford, *An exhortation to peace...lately delivered in a sermon* (1643), fos. A1v–A2r. The remarks are dated from Ely House, February 1642/3. See also Matthews, *Walker revised*, p. 334.

14 Peterborough Cathedral Library, K.5.2[8] (on deposit in Cambridge University Library).

15 *Commons Journal*, 3, p. 153; Cooper, *Annals*, 3, p. 349, n. 5.

16 *Commons Journal*, 3, p. 124; Cooper, *Annals*, 3, pp. 348–9.

17 These difficulties, and printers' neutrality or otherwise in the face of political power, may be compared with cases discussed in Stephen Botein, '"Meer mechanics" and an open

press: the business and political strategies of colonial American printers', *Perspectives in American History*, 9 (1975), pp. 127–225.

18 Cf. M. A. Shaaber, 'The meaning of the imprint in early printed books', *The Library*, new ser. 24 (1943–4), pp. 120–41, and W. W. Greg, *Some aspects and problems of London publishing* (Oxford 1956), pp. 85–9.

19 University Archives, VC Ct III.39 (29).

20 University Archives, VC Ct III.38 (22), VC Ct III.39 (29, 30, 57).

21 See above, p. 193.

22 Eyre and Rivington, 2, p. 103. See also below, p. 316.

23 University Archives, VC Ct I (63), fo. 2, 24 January 1665/6; see also VC Ct III.42 (144), same date.

24 University Archives, VC Ct III.39 (29); C. H. Firth and R. S. Rait, eds., *Acts and ordinances of the inter-regnum, 1642–1660* (1911), I, pp. 184–7. Farnaby's work was originally printed by Felix Kyngston in 1625: for the privilege, see *STC*, 10704 and Greg, *Companion*, pp. 275–6.

25 University Archives, VC Ct III.39 (29).

26 University Archives, VC Ct III.39 (58A).

27 *CSPD*, 1649–50, pp. 344–5, 524. For the Printing Act of 20 September 1649 see Firth and Rait, *Acts and ordinances*, 2, pp. 245–54.

28 *Grace Book* H, p. 69.

29 Evelyn remembered him as one of the London printsellers, a trade led (in his estimation) by Peake: see Evelyn to Samuel Pepys, 26 September 1690 (S. Pepys, *Letters and second diary*, ed. R. G. Howarth (1932), p. 220).

30 Bodleian Library, MS Barocci 217; *Greek manuscripts in the Bodleian Library; an exhibition* (Bodleian Library 1966); R. W. Hunt *et al.*, *The survival of ancient literature* (Bodleian Library 1975), no. 57, with further references.

31 T. B. Reed, *A history of the old English letter foundries*, rev. A. F. Johnson (1952), pp. 192–4.

32 *Commons Journal*, 3 January 1644/5, 4 July 1645, 9 July 1645, 23 September 1645, 13 March 1645/6, 16 October 1646, 27 December 1647, 28 December 1647. British Library, MS Harley 374, fo. 265; Sir H. Ellis, ed., *Original letters* (1843), pp. 172–4; *CSPD*, Council of State, 1, pp. 47–50 (28 September 1652).

33 Stationers' Company Journal Book for Money Disbursed, 1650–98: 10 June 1656, and subsequently. The total paid to Daniel was £200. He also printed Dade's almanac for 1666 (*ibid.*, 13 October 1665, 13 April 1666).

34 See, for example, the copy in Trinity College Library (III.13.50), which in 1656 belonged to Wolfran Stubbe (admitted as a pensioner to the College 1657; Westminster Scholar 1658; Regius Professor of Hebrew 1688–99, and Vice-Master of the College). I have not attempted to explore Daniel's possible relations with Westminster School.

35 See below, p. 366. Trinity College, T.5.49 (*Collegium ethicum*, Roger Daniel, 1658), in a contemporary Cambridge binding, has a note that it was bought in Michaelmas term 1659 for two shillings.

36 M. Feingold, 'Isaac Barrow: divine, scholar, mathematician', in *Before Newton; the life and times of Isaac Barrow*, ed. Feingold (Cambridge 1990), pp. 1–104, at p. 42, with further references.

37 Anthony à Wood (*Fasti*, 2, cols. 193–4) claimed that the dedication in Johann Stier's *Praecepta doctrinae logicae* (Cambridge 1647), though attributed to Daniel, was in fact by James Windet.

38 Emmanuele Tesauro, *Patriarchae, sive Christi servatoris genealogia* (1651, 1657).

39 *CSPD*, 1660–1, p. 348; Cooper, *Annals*, 5, p. 435.

40 *CSPD*, 1667, p. 287, 11 July 1667.

41 Richard Smyth, *Obituary*, ed. Sir Henry Ellis (1849), p. 77.

42 Quoted in Blanche Henrey, *British botanical and horticultural literature before 1800*, 3 vols. (Oxford 1975), 1, p. 173. Beale had been a Fellow of King's in 1632–40, and subsequently held livings in Somerset; see also C. Webster, *The great instauration* (1975); M. Stubbs, 'John Beale, philosophical gardener of Herefordshire. 1. Prelude to the Royal Society (1608–1663)', *Annals of Science*, 39 (1982), pp. 463–89; M. Feingold, *The mathematicians' apprenticeship*, pp. 114–15.

43 J. A. Comenius, *Janua linguarum trilinguis* (1662). Comenius' commendatory note, prefixed to the volume, is dated 8 June 1659.

44 F. Ferrari, *Lexicon geographicum* (1657), fos. *3r–v. For Moore, and for Dillingham's contributions to the University Library, see Oates, *Cambridge University Library*, pp. 268–72, and esp. chs. 11 and 12.

45 *Grace Book* H, p. 67.

46 Arber, IV.45–6. Legate's will was proved in the Commissary Court of London (Register 24, fo. 5v: the original will also survives); the overseers were Simon Waterson and Thomas Mountford.

47 Versions of two of the Cambridge *Hinc lucem* blocks remained in the London trade much later in the century, and reappeared as incidental decoration to the street ballad *The loves of Jockey and Jenny: or, the Scotch wedding*, printed for P. Brooksby at the Golden Ball, West Smithfield, n.d. (copy in the Pepys Library, Magdalene College, reproduced in facsimile in W. G. Day, ed., *The Pepys ballads*, 5 vols. (Cambridge 1987), 4, p. 110.) One at least of these blocks, damaged by woodworm, was still in London and in use in 1700: see R. Russell, *A sermon of the unpardonable sin against the Holy Ghost* (printed for the author, and sold by J. Blare at the Looking Glass on London Bridge, 1700).

48 See above, p. 215.

49 Stationers' Company Journal Book for Money Disbursed, 1650–98, 1650–5, throughout.

50 University Archives, Pr.P.4 (8). For the register, see p. 261 above.

51 Harvard College Book, III, p. 47 (*Publs. of the Colonial Soc. of Massachusetts*, 15 (1925)) p. 213; S. Morison, *Harvard College in the seventeenth century* (Cambridge, Mass. 1936), pt I, p. 349; Margery Somers Foster, "*Oute of smalle beginnings*"; *an economic history of Harvard College in the puritan period (1636 to 1712)* (Cambridge, Mass. 1962), pp. 146–7, 153, 200.

52 Stationers' Company Court Book, C, fos. 283v, 284r, 285r.

53 *Ibid.*, fo. 263r.

54 Stationers' Company Journal Book for Money Disbursed, 1650–98.

55 University Archives, CUR 33.1 (27). For Leet, see above, p. 274, and Gray and Palmer, pp. 98–100; he had considerable managerial responsibility: several payments were made to him by the Stationers' Company in 1653/4–5 (Journal Book for Money Disbursed, 1650–98).

56 Stationers' Company Court Book, D, fo. 2r.

57 *Grace Book* H, p. 139; McKenzie, *Apprentices, 1641–1700*, nos. 2680, 2681. John Harding, bound apprentice to Legate on 3 March 1656, was freed after his master's death by John Hayes, later University Printer.

58 Smyth, *Obituary*, p. 49.

59 See below, p. 367.

60 For Thomas Dillingham's account of his father's part in the publication, and for the way in which it was sold (partly from the Porters' Lodge at Emmanuel), see Emmanuel College Archives, COL.9.10; 26. Thomas Dillingham claimed that four colleges (Emmanuel, St John's, Clare and Sidney) shared in the costs of publication; but in at least Emmanuel and St John's no records of such payments have been discovered: I am grateful to Dr F. H. Stubbings and Mr Malcolm Underwood for their help in this matter. The

printer's copy for the Praeloquium (only) survives in Emmanuel College, MS III.I.21 (James 189).

61 See below, p. 367. In light of what was to happen, the decision by Richard Ireland and Anthony Nicholson to join with the London printer William Bentley for the publication of William Sclater's *Concio ad clerum* delivered in Great St Mary's Church in June 1651, and printed in 1652, may have been unfortunate. Bentley's ambitions outran his skills, as his handling of the two-coloured title-page shows all too clearly. For Bentley, see also below, pp. 325–7.

62 John Worthington, *Diary and correspondence*, ed. J. Crossley, 3 vols. (Chetham's Soc. 1847–86), I, p. 83.

63 *Grace Book* H, p. 139.

64 *Grace Book* H, p. 147.

65 University Archives, Pr.P.4 (8).

66 Hills had no part in Field's activities as University Printer. For contemporary opinion of his career and its tergiversations, cf. *The London printers lamentation* (1660: see below, pp. 316–18), *A view of the many traiterous, disloyal, and turn-about actions of H. H. Senior* (1684), and *The life of H. H.* (1688). For Hills and the Oxford University Press, see J. Johnson and S. Gibson, *Print and privilege at Oxford to the year 1700* (Oxford Bibliographical Soc. 1946) and Carter, *Oxford University Press*, pp. 99, 101–3; see also A. F. Johnson, 'The King's Printers, 1660–1742', *The Library*, 5th ser. 3 (1949), pp. 33–8.

67 Cf. Sheila Lambert, *Printing for Parliament, 1641–1700*, Index Soc. Special Ser. 20 (1984), esp. pp. 25, 157, 171, 180.

68 *Commons Journal*, 14 October, 23 October 1646.

69 PRO, SP 18/71, fos. 94–8 (bill for printing Acts, Votes, etc., April 1652–November 1653); SP 18/71, fo. 91 (petition by Field to Cromwell).

70 *Ibid.*; *CSPD*, 1655–6, p. 181.

71 The imprints for these years may be followed most conveniently in Sheila Lambert, *Printing for Parliament, 1641–1700*, pp. 191–200.

72 *CSPD*, Council of State I 76A, pp. 134–6; I 76, p. 328.

73 *CSPD*, 1658–9, p. 71 i, Council of State I 78, pp. 709–11.

74 Stationers' Company Court Book C, fo. 250r (livery agreement); 277r, 287r (Haberdashers' Company). For Steele, see C. H. Firth in *DNB*.

75 Stationers' Company Court Book D, fos. 2r, 3r.

76 Stationers' Company Court Book D, fo. 7r.

77 Stationers' Company Court Book D, fos. 8r, 9v, 12r.

78 Stationers' Company Court Book D, fo. 15v.

79 Beginning with £125 on Christmas Eve 1656 (Journal Book for Money Disbursed, 1650–98).

80 Eyre and Rivington, 2, p. 103.

81 The following is drawn from McKenzie, *Cambridge University Press*, 1, pp. 25–33, PRO, Prob 5/1054, and from the Queens' College archives. (I am indebted to Professor Alan Nelson for guidance in the last.) See also D. McKitterick, 'John Field in 1668: the affairs of a University Printer', *TCBS*, 9 (1990), pp. 497–516.

82 'Diary of Samuel Sewall 1674–1729', Massachusetts Historical Soc. *Collections*, 5th ser. 5 (1878), p. 261; Sewall, *Diary*, ed. M. Halsey Thomas, 2 vols. (New York 1973), I, p. 221.

83 John Hudson to Thomas Hearne, 3 August 1708, in Hearne, *Remarks and collections*, 2, p. 123.

84 Reproduced in McKenzie, *Cambridge University Press*, 1, plate II; University Archives, CUR 33.5.19.

85 *CSPD*, 1658–9, p. 323; M. Ashley, *Financial and commercial policy under the Cromwellian*

Protectorate, 2nd edn (1962), ch. V, 'Government expenditure', pp. 46–8; Bernard Capp, *Cromwell's navy; the fleet and the English revolution, 1648–1660* (Oxford 1989), pp. 341–2.

86 Cyprian Blagden, 'The "Company" of printers', *SB*, 13 (1960), pp. 3–17, quoting (p. 9) *A brief discourse concerning printers and printing* (1663); *The London printers lamentation, or, the press opprest, and over prest* (1660), p. 4.

87 Thomas Burton, *Diary*, ed. J. Rutt (1828), 2, p. 521; Roy Sherwood, *The court of Oliver Cromwell* (1977), p. 115.

88 Blagden, 'The "Company" of printers', and *Stationers' Company*, pp. 147–52.

89 *The London printers lamentation*, pp. 5–6; compare the objections to the entry in the Stationers' Register by Oliver Cromwell allocating Bible printing to Field and Hills, made on 23 April 1656 by John Streater and others – that the Bible copy was not Barker's, but Bill's, and that it was only held in trust for Bill (*CSPD*, 1655–6, p. 289).

17 *John Field and the opportunities of office*

1 Sir Roger L'Estrange, *Considerations and proposals in order to the regulation of the press* (1663). For further comment on L'Estrange's remarks respecting the intense competition in the book trade outside the regular bookshops, see D. F. McKenzie, *The London book trade in the later seventeenth century* (Sandars Lectures, Cambridge 1976: copies of typescript in Cambridge University Library, the British Library, and Humanities Research Center, University of Texas at Austin; see also the review-summary by David Gerard, *The Library*, 5th ser. 33 (1978), pp. 242–6), pp. 26–8. For the emergence in the late seventeenth century of the trade publisher, see M. Treadwell, 'London trade publishers, 1675–1750', *The Library*, 6th ser. 4 (1982), pp. 99–134. The London retail book trade in the last years of the century is usefully surveyed in Michael Treadwell, 'The English book trade', in *The age of William III & Mary II; power, politics, and patronage, 1688–1702*, ed. Robert P. Maccubbin and Martha Hamilton-Phillips (Williamsburg, Va. 1988), pp. 358–65.

2 H. R. Plomer, 'The King's Printing House under the Stuarts', *The Library*, new ser. 2 (1901), pp. 353–75.

3 See, for example, M. M. Kleerkooper and W. P. van Stockum, *De boekhandel te Amsterdam voornamelijk in de 17e Eeuw* ('S-Gravenhage 1914–16), p. 1135.

4 *Humble proposals concerning the printing of the Bible*, n.d. (University Archives, CUR.33.6(25)): see Appendix 1, p. 388 below. See also William Kilburne's laudatory remarks in *Dangerous errors in several late printed bibles* (Finsbury 1659), p. 6.

5 *Humble proposals*; see also [William Kilburne] *Proposals humbly presented to public consideration, but more particularly, to ... Parliament*, n.d. (University Archives, CUR 33.6(24): see Appendix 2, pp. 389–91 below.

6 See Kilburne's remarks, CUR 33.6(26).

7 *Commons Journal*, 11 January 1652/3.

8 *The case of William Bentley* [1656]: copy in University Archives, CUR.33.2(110).

9 Herbert, *Historical catalogue*, nos. 604–17.

10 Eyre and Rivington, 2, p. 32. There was some doubt as to Hills' knowledge of printing: 'If his knowledge and experience in the Art of printing be duely inquired into, he may perhaps upon some good grounds, be adjudged no proper qualified person for so serious Employment' [as Bible printing] (*The case of William Bentley* [1656]).

11 *CSPD*, 1655–6, p. 289 (23 April 1656). Streater printed a black letter New Testament in 1656 (Herbert 652); Daniel's name was set to another similar edition in 1655 (Herbert 649). For Streater's tumultuous career, see Plomer, *Dictionary*, p. 173, Blagden,

Stationers' Company, pp. 154-5 and J. H. Hetet, 'A literary underground in Restoration England' (PhD, Cambridge 1987), pp. 19-21.

12 J. Johnson and S. Gibson, *Print and privilege at Oxford to the year 1700* (Oxford 1946), pp. 34-5.

13 University Archives, CUR 33.6(26).

14 *Commons Journal*, 20 November 1656, 11 June 1657.

15 Thomas Burton, *Diary*, ed. J. T. Rutt (1828), 1, p. 348, 2, pp. 221-3. In 1655 there was a corrector at the Cambridge press named Wray, though it is not clear whether, having worked for Legate, he continued to work for Field (Stationers' Company Journal Book for Money Disbursed, 1650-98: payment made in March 1661/2 for work done in 1655).

16 Burton, *Diary*, 1, pp. 351-2; H. J. Todd, *Memoirs of the life and writings of Brian Walton* (1821), 1, pp. 90-1.

17 Stationers' Company Court Book D, fo. 36v, 4 October 1658.

18 University Archives, CUR 33.6(27); Kilburne, *Dangerous errors*, p. 10.

19 Kilburne, *Dangerous errors*, p. 10.

20 *Humble petition of the workmen-printers, freemen of the City of London, addressed to Parliament*, dated in manuscript 14 April 1659 (copy in the British Library, 669.f.21(19)). Some of the subsequent developments are discussed in C. Blagden, 'The "Company" of printers', *SB*, 13 (1960), pp. 3-17.

21 *Ibid*. He gave the right name in his letter to the University on 20 January 1656/7 (University Archives, CUR 33.6(25)). Robertson published his own *Key to the Hebrew Bible* in 1656.

22 Herbert, *Historical catalogue*, no. 444. The (London) printers left the word 'not' out of the seventh commandment, 'Thou shalt not commit adultery'.

23 Kilburne, *Dangerous errors*, p. 14.

24 *The case of William Bentley* [1656].

25 *Mercurius politicus*, no. 334, 29 October-6 November 1656, p. 7366.

26 Stationers' Company Court Book D, fo. 35v (13 September 1658). Field and Hills wished also to be allowed to deface Bentley's type - a more serious matter than temporary confiscation (*ibid.*, fo. 36r (20 September 1658)).

27 *CSPD*, 1660-1, p. 272.

28 Herbert, *Historical catalogue*, no. 669. See also Madan, *Oxford books*, 3, p. xxx. The agreement, intended to last for four years, survived only two.

29 Isaac D'Israeli, *Curiosities of literature*, 2nd ser., 3 vols. (1823), 3, pp. 313-25, at p. 319; new edn (1859), 3, pp. 427-33, at p. 430. D'Israeli's essay, 'The pearl Bibles and six thousand errata', is dominated by a prolonged attack on Field and Hills. See also John Eadie, *The English Bible* (1876), pp. 295-6 and, for earlier remarks, Edward Wetenhall, *Scripture authentick* (1686): ''Tis not improbable it might be done at first with design, and particularly of those, who would establish the peoples power, not only in Electing, but even in Ordaining, their own Ministers' (pp. 18-19).

30 Stationers' Company Court Book D, fo. 38v (6 December 1658).

31 *Ibid.*, fo. 55v (4 June 1660); Journal Book for Money Disbursed, 1650-98. The regular charge in 1659-62 was £66 per six thousand, but in 1668 Field was paid fourpence per copy, octavo.

32 Worthington to Hartlib, 21 December 1658: J. Worthington, *Diary and correspondence*, ed. J. Crossley and R. C. Christie (Manchester 1847-86), 1, p. 119.

33 Pepys, *Diary*, ed. R. Latham and W. Matthews (1970-83), 8, pp. 237-8 (27 May 1667). But Evelyn did obtain a copy, now in Balliol College, Oxford (*Fine bindings in Oxford libraries* (Bodleian Library 1968) p. 121).

34 *CSPD*, Charles II, vol. 40, no. 66. On Ogilby, see especially M. Schuchard, *John Ogilby, 1600-1676: Lebensbild eines Gentleman mit vielen Karrieren* (Hamburg 1973);

Schuchard, *A descriptive bibliography of the works of John Ogilby and William Morgan* (Frankfurt a.M. 1975); and Katherine S. van Eerde, *John Ogilby and the taste of his times* (Folkestone 1976): neither author provides much detail on the printing of so large an enterprise. See also Worthington, *Diary and correspondence*, 1, pp. 191–2, 355.

35 For his first lottery notice, see Marian Eames, 'John Ogilby and his Aesop; the fortunes and fables of a seventeenth-century virtuoso', *BNYPL*, 65 (1961), pp. 73–88, at p. 82; for his second, see *The Gentleman's Magazine*, 84, pt 1 (1814), pp. 646–8.

36 *CSPD*, 1661–2, pp. 454, 468–9; University Archives, Lett. 13 (244 α, β, γ); CUR 33.2(100, 101, 102).

37 Letter from Anthony Sparrow, 5 September 1662, University Archives, CUR 33.2(103).

38 Madan, *Oxford books*, 3, p. xxx; letter from John Pearson, 10 September 1662 (University Archives, CUR 33.2(104). On the background more generally see Johnson and Gibson, *Print and privilege*, esp. chs. II and VI.

39 University Archives, CUR 33.2(105).

40 Madan, *Oxford books*, 3, p. xxxi; Johnson and Gibson, *Print and privilege*, p. 39.

41 Stationers' Company Court Book D, fo. 75v.

42 University Archives, CUR 33.2(106).

43 University Archives, VC Ct III.41(135); VC Ct III.42(52).

44 University Archives, VC Ct III.41(135). The large number of octavo prayer books required under the new Act of Uniformity is reflected in the several different settings of type, even of parts of the same formes. The introduction of further signs, such as ◆,)(, and ¶, to distinguish sheets in ways other than the ordinary alphabetic, provided another focus for printing house practice that remains, in this context, to be further investigated. But cf. B. J. McMullin, 'Paper quality marks and the Oxford Bible Press, 1682–1717', *The Library*, 6th ser. 6 (1984), pp. 39–49, and McMullin, 'The origins of press figures in English printing, 1629–1671', *The Library*, 6th ser. 1 (1979), pp. 307–35.

45 Thomas Hearne, *Remarks and collections*, ed. C. E. Salter *et al.* (Oxford 1885–1921), 3, p. 130.

46 For increases in the cost of paper consequent on the Fire, see *The life and times of Anthony Wood*, ed. A. Clark (Oxford 1891–1900), 2, pp. 87, 97.

47 T. Brett, *A letter shewing why our English Bibles differ so much from the Septuagint* (1743), p. 48. See also E. Nestle, 'The Cambridge Septuagint of 1665 and 1684. A bibliographical query', with a reply by J. F. Bethune-Baker, *Journal of Theological Studies*, 6 (1905), pp. 611–14, and Darlow and Moule, nos. 4701–2.

48 PRO, Prob 5/1054.

49 Details from Stationers' Company Dividend Book, 1644–1672. In 1667 *full* shares were held by Humphrey Robinson (Master), Evan Tyler, Samuel Man, William Lee, Philemon Stephens, Richard Thrale, Andrew Crooke, Octavian Pulleyn, Sir Thomas Davies, Margaret Pakeman, Susan Latham, Agatha Legate, Susan Norton, Ann Seile and William Leake: it will be noticed, crucially, that the great majority were either booksellers or widows of booksellers. A summary of the share division at a slightly earlier period is given in C. Blagden, 'The Stationers' Company in the Civil War period', *The Library*, 5th ser. 13 (1958), pp. 1–17, at p. 6.

50 But the *Short introduction* was printed (in two editions) alone in 1681 at Cambridge. See also Madan, *Oxford books*, no. 2982. Wing does not distinguish between editions with and without the *Brevissima institutio*, and the details provided, for example, by the *National Union Catalog* are often bibliographically contradictory.

51 This edition apparently no longer survives in any copy. But see, for this and the following information, Stationers' Company Books in the Treasurer's warehouse, 1663–1723. For Field's estate, see D. McKitterick, 'John Field in 1668; the affairs of a University Printer', *TCBS*, 9 (1990), pp. 497–516.

52 It was printed at the charge of Nathanael Rowls, Atwell's son-in-law, and was dedicated to Dillingham, his 'highly honoured friend'. On Atwell, whose connection with Trinity College was less close than he sought to suggest, see E. G. R. Taylor, *The mathematical practitioners of Tudor and Stuart England* (Cambridge 1954), p. 199, and p. 376 below.

53 The ornately bound copy of Vere's *Commentaries* (1657) now in the Broxbourne Collection, in the Bodleian Library, was evidently presented to Charles II by Dillingham shortly after the Restoration: see H. M. Nixon, *Broxbourne Library; styles and designs of bookbindings from the twelfth to the twentieth century* (1956), pp. 144–7.

54 Cf. Oates, *Cambridge University Library*, pp. 447–8. Although it was talked of even in 1692, the translation of the Mishnah commissioned by the University in the late 1660s from Isaac Abendana, a Jewish scholar first seen in Cambridge in 1663, was never printed: his manuscripts survive in the University Library, MSS Mm.1.4–9, with notes by Ralph Cudworth.

55 The licensed copy of the 1605 edition, approved by Dillingham, Benjamin Whichcote and Ralph Cudworth on 14 August 1657, is now in Trinity College Library, E.14.5. See also above, p. 260.

56 Geoffrey Keynes, *John Ray, 1627–1705; a bibliography*, augmented edn (Amsterdam 1976), pp. 1–11; Charles E. Raven, *John Ray, naturalist; his life and works* (Cambridge 1942), pp. 72–108.

57 John Worthington, *Diary and correspondence*, 2, pt ii, p. 273.

58 For Glisson, see Venn, *Gonville and Caius*; and R. Milnes Walker, 'Francis Glisson', in *Cambridge and its contribution to medicine*, ed. A. Rook (1971), pp. 35–47; John Henry, 'The matter of souls: medical theory and theology in seventeenth-century England', in *The medical revolution of the seventeenth century*, ed. R. French and A. Wear (Cambridge 1989), pp. 87–113, at pp. 109–12.

59 See Morden's advertisement at the end of J. Templer, *Idea theologiae Leviathanis* (1673).

60 See above, p. 227.

61 Keynes, *Ray*, pp. 6–7; John Worthington to Samuel Hartlib, 10 June 1661 (Worthington, *Diary and correspondence*, 1, p. 333).

62 Gray and Palmer, pp. 118–19; PCC, Wills 1679, fo. 35.

63 Lorna Weatherill, *Consumer behaviour and material culture in Britain, 1660–1760* (1988), pp. 43–69.

64 Eyre and Rivington, 2, pp. 197, 286, 294–5.

65 See above, pp. 334–6. Field is included both in the 1662 list of master printers (MS Lambeth 941/62) and in the list of printing houses made in July 1668 (PRO, SP29/243/126), both reprinted in Michael Treadwell, 'Lists of master printers: the size of the London printing trade, 1637–1723', in *Aspects of printing from 1600*, ed. R. Myers and M. Harris (Oxford 1987), pp. 141–70, at pp. 158–9.

66 And so suffered in the Fire of London: *CSPD*, 192, no. 68 (23 February 1666/7).

67 William Godman, *Filius Heröum* (1660), fo. b2v, verses by Theophilus Cleaver, Fellow of King's.

68 PRO, Prob 5/1054.

69 'A collection of all the sentences in the Iliad and Odyssey, containing any aphorism, sentiment, or remarkable opinion, illustrated by a two-fold series of quotations, first from the Scriptures, and next from the whole range of classical authors, wherever any parallel idea or expression can be found' (J. H. Monk, 'Memoir of Dr. James Duport', *Museum Criticum*, 2 (1826), pp. 672–98, at p. 684. The memoir is partly reprinted in Cooper, *Annals*, 3, pp. 581–2.

70 This version was issued both with and without a parallel text. The volume was further distinguished by being protected by royal patent.

71 Cf. Trinity College, MS O.10a.33.

72 For a partial description of the Septuagint's make-up, see Darlow and Moule, nos. 4701–2; see also above, n. 47.

73 Monk, 'Memoir of Duport'.

74 J. D[uport], *Musae subsecivae* (Cambridge 1676), pp. 124, 351–2.

75 Trinity College, MS Add.a.106, fo. 4r; the Sophocles is now MS R.3.31.

76 Dillingham to Sancroft, 1662 (British Library, MS Harley 3784, fo. 68r; transcript by Thomas Baker in Cambridge University Library, MS Mm.1.45, p. 48).

77 Eyre and Rivington, 2, pp. 284–5, 286, 294, 295, 335.

78 University Archives, VC Ct III.42(144).

79 For Newman (1600?–63) see Cotton Mather, *Magnalia Christi Americana* (1702), Bk III, pp. 113–16; W. K. Lowther Clarke, *Eighteenth century piety* (1944), pp. 31–2; Leonard W. Cowie, *Henry Newman, an American in London, 1708–43* (1956), pp. 1–3. For Newman's Concordance in the North American book trade, see for example Worthington Chauncey Ford, *The Boston book market 1679–1700* (Boston 1917). The books supplied by Richard Chiswell, the London bookseller, to John Usher in Boston in 1680 included one copy; those sent to John Ive in 1683/4 and 1684 five copies (valued at 11s.6d. each), and Michael Perry, in Boston, possessed two at the end of the century, valued at a pound each (pp. 62–4, 83–5, 121–7, 163–82). The presence of these copies among an inevitably highly selective view of the book trade preserved in the few documents described by Ford suggests a regular and continuing demand. As one of the standard necessities of theological study, the book was an essential part of the libraries sent to North America from the 1690s either by Thomas Bray or under his influence: see Charles T. Laugher, *Thomas Bray's grand design; libraries of the Church of England in America 1695–1785* (Chicago 1983), pp. 87–95.

80 Worthington to Hartlib, 26 October 1661 (Worthington, *Diary and correspondence*, 2, pt i, pp. 65–6).

81 The opinion was that of Thomas Baker, *socius ejectus* of St John's College (1656–1740), recorded in his copy of the 1682 edition, St John's College, Tt.2.15. (I am grateful to Professor Frans Korsten for this reference.)

82 Cruden's was first published in 1737, but did not find immediate favour; see Edith Olivier, *The eccentric life of Alexander Cruden* (1934).

83 'Here is printing at Cambridge an English Concordance, as full (it is said) as Newman, but so contrived that it will not be above 12s., which is half the price of Newman's' (Worthington to Hartlib, 26 October 1661 (Worthington, *Diary and correspondence*, 2, pt i, p. 65)). The book was, on this evidence, at least seven years in the press. On the 1668 Bible, see p. 330.

84 The first book to be printed by the order of the Royal Society was Evelyn's *Sylva* (1664), its imprimatur signed by the President, Viscount Brouncker, on 3 February 1663/4: see Geoffrey Keynes, *John Evelyn; a study in bibliophily with a bibliography of his writings*, 2nd edn (Oxford 1968), pp. 130–4.

85 Carter, *Oxford University Press*, p. 45.

86 Worthington to More, 17 April 1668 (Worthington, *Diary and correspondence*, 2, pt ii, p. 273).

87 Worthington to George Evans, 11 September 1666 (Worthington, *Diary and correspondence*, 2, pt i, p. 211). Cf. Pepys' remark, 'A great want thereof will be of books, especially Latin books and foreign books' (*Diary*, 7, p. 309). For the Cambridge plague, see the series of locally printed mortality bills (of which the unique copies survive in St John's College) for June to December 1666: C. Nelson and M. Seccombe, *British newspapers and periodicals 1641–1700* (New York 1987), no. 166.

88 University Archives, CUR 33.1(26).

89 PRO, Prob 5/1054. The London printer Richard Hodgkinson owed £12. For details, see, again, McKitterick, 'John Field in 1668'.

90 Gray and Palmer, pp. 107-8. The Cambridge copy of the inventory is very damaged: for details see PRO, Prob 5/1054, giving slightly different figures.

91 University Archives, VC Ct III.42(52, 117, 118).

92 University Archives, CUR 33.1(26).

18 John Hayes and the limits of independence

1 Charles II's ensuing letter to the University is in the University Archives, Lett. 13 (227), 17 August 1668.

2 The Court of the Stationers' Company appointed a committee to treat with the Vice-Chancellor on 31 August (Court Book D, fo. 144r).

3 Willis and Clark, 2, p. 165.

4 University Archives. VC Ct III.43, nos. 106, 107. Oates, *Cambridge University Library*, does not mention any sale of books under the aegis of Boldero, who was partly responsible (among many others) for the reception and organization of Richard Holdsworth's library (p. 327).

5 Clark, *Endowments*, pp. 165-71; Oates, *Cambridge University Library*, pp. 349-67. Lucas's copy of Statius (Cambridge 1651), now Cambridge University Library O*.6.7(E), was a present from Buck in 1660.

6 Stationers' Company Court Book D, 26 March 1669.

7 McKenzie, *Apprentices 1641-1700*, nos. 3038, 3044; Stationers' Company Journal Book for Money Disbursed, 1650-98, 8 June 1658; Lambeth Palace Library, MS 941/62; PRO, SP 29/243/126; M. Treadwell, 'Lists of master printers: the size of the London printing trade, 1637-1723', in Myers and Harris, *Aspects of printing from 1600* (Oxford 1987), pp. 141-70, at pp. 158, 159. For contemporary allusions to the fate of books and booksellers in the Fire cf. Samuel Rolle, שלהבתיה or, *the burning of London commemorated...in a CX. discourses, meditations, and contemplations* (1667), esp. part III, pp. 40-4; [Samuel Ford], *The conflagration of London: poetically delineated* (1667), lines 155-66; *Observations both historical and moral upon the burning of London* (1667), repr. in *Harleian Miscellany*, 3, pp. 282-94, at p. 287. The loss of books in St Faith's Church (underneath St Paul's) and in Stationers' Hall was estimated at £150,000: see further in Pepys, *Diary*, ed. Latham and Matthews, 7, pp. 297 and 209-10.

8 [Edward Bagshaw], *A letter unto a person of honour and quality, containing some animadversions upon the Bishop of Worcester's letter* (1662); *A second letter* (1662); Sir R. L'Estrange, *Truth and loyalty vindicated, from the reproaches and clamours of Mr. Edward Bagshaw* (1662), p. 2; and *Considerations and proposals in order to the regulation of the press* (1663), p. 16. George Kitchin, who dismisses Bagshaw as a 'distempered mortal', does not address himself to Hayes' part in this affair: see *Sir Roger L'Estrange; a contribution to the history of the press in the seventeenth century* (1913), pp. 81-2, 92. Cf. also A. G. Matthews, *Calamy revised* (Oxford 1934), pp. 21-2.

9 PRO, SP 29/51/8, 1662. Cf. J. S. T. Hetet, 'A literary underground in Restoration England; printers and dissenters in the context of constraints, 1660-1689' (PhD, Cambridge 1987), pp. 25-6.

10 Hetet, pp. 30-1. Hetet underestimates the jealousies among the printers: see also C. Blagden, 'The "Company" of Printers', *SB*, 13 (1960), pp. 1-15. In 1663 L'Estrange computed the number of printers at about sixty, having over a hundred apprentices and employing at least 150 journeymen. He thought the number of printers might be reduced to twenty or twenty-four. 'These Supernumary Printers were at first Introduced by the Book-sellers, as a sure way to bring them both to their Prices, and Purposes; for the

Number being greater then could honestly Live upon the Trade, the Printers were Enforc'd either to Print Treason, or Sedition, if the Stationer Offered it, or to want Lawful Work, by which Necessity on the one side, and Power on the other, the Combination became exceeding Dangerous, and so it still Continues; but how to Dissolve it, whether by barely Dis-incorporating the Company of Stationers, and subjecting the Printers to Rules apart, and by Themselves; or by Making them Two Distinct Companies, I do not Meddle' (*Considerations and proposals in order to the regulation of the press* (1663) p. 28).

11 *Grace Book* ϴ, p. 23.

12 Regular payments to Hayes for unspecified work are recorded from 1658 in the Stationers' Company Journal Book for Money Disbursed, 1650-98.

13 *The state of Bible printing*; cf. C. Blagden, 'Early Cambridge printers and the Stationers' Company', *TCBS*, 2 (1957), pp. 257-89.

14 University Archives, CUR 33.1(28, 29).

15 Stationers' Company Documents, nos. 165, 166.

16 Stationers' Company Court Book D, 26 March 1669, 21 April 1670.

17 Stationers' Company Court Book D, 26 April 1678, 6 October 1678, 3 February 1678/9, 1 March 1678/9, 3 March 1678/9, 7 April 1679, 19 May 1679; Blagden, 'Early Cambridge printers', p. 284.

18 Stationers' Company Court Book F, 8 November 1686, 19 November 1686.

19 University Archives, CUR 33.1(32).

20 Stationers' Company Court Book F, 1 March 1689/90, 11 April 1690, 5 May 1690. The Articles of Agreement between Hayes and the Company are dated 10 April 1690 (Stationers' Company Documents, no. 170).

21 On 24 October 1693 a committee was appointed to oversee the Company's printing at both Oxford and Cambridge (Stationers' Company Court Book F, 24 October 1693).

22 Treadwell, 'Lists of master printers', (n. 7 above).

23 For Whinn's licence, see University Archives, Pr.P.4(18); for the original votes at Jackson's election, see Pr.P.2(4); see also *Grace Book* ϴ, pp. 192, 193, 230, 246, 276, 365 and 366. John Buck died on 22 October 1680. (Samuel Newton, *Diary, 1662-1717*, ed. J. E. Foster (Cambridge Antiquarian Soc. 1890), p. 56). For Thomas Buck, see *ibid.*, p. 15: his monument is in the chancel of St Edward's Church and is reproduced in Royal Commission on Historical Monuments, *Cambridge* (1959), 1, plate 18.

24 The votes are preserved in University Archives, Pr.P.2(4).

25 Bibles, like Roman Catholic and Jewish service books, were printed in vast numbers in Holland for the overseas market, and were often funded from outside the book trade: see I. H. van Eeghen, *De Amsterdamse boekhandel 1680-1725*, 5(1) (Amsterdam 1978), pp. 60, etc. For the late seventeenth-century Dutch trade in English Bibles, and particularly the part of the Schipper printing house in Amsterdam, see M. M. Kleerkooper and W. P. van Stockum, *De boekhandel te Amsterdam voornamelijk in de 17e eeuw* ('s-Gravenhage 1914-16), pp. 687-91, 1137-8, and P. G. Hoftijzer, *Engelse boekverkopers bij de beurs* (Amsterdam 1987), pp. 11-13. The Schipper-Athias privilege was confirmed as late as 1703 (Kleerkooper and van Stockum, p. 18). William Nicholson visited the Schipper printing house in 1678, in the course of travelling with Sir Joseph Williamson, and left the following account: 'There were 18 hard at work printing, and 6 or 7 setting letters. They print many English Bibles of all sizes; upon the titlepages of which they sett – *London printed by R. Barker and the Assigns of John Bill* etc. And they were (whilst I lookt on) printeing a small English Bible in Octavo, which they sett printed by the aforesaid, A.D.1669. They showed me also severall books printed here with the titlepages as if at Collen, Leipsick, Mentz etc. whence it comes to pass that you may buy books cheaper at Amsterdam, in all languages, than at the places where they are first printed: for here the Copy costs them nothing' (Queen's College, Oxford, MS 68, fo. 27, quoted in Hoftijzer,

Engelse boekverkopers, p. 110). For comments from Oxford on prices, see Bodleian Library, MS Tanner 338, fos. 182–3, 198, repr. in John Gutch, *Miscellanea curiosa* (Oxford 1781), I, pp. 269–77. For struggles between Oxford and its competitors see also J. Johnson and S. Gibson, *Print and privilege*, pp. 77–9; S. Gibson and J. Johnson, eds., *The first minute book of the Delegates of the Oxford University Press, 1668–1756* (Oxford 1943), pp. xviii–xxv; Carter, *Oxford University Press*, pp. 93–105.

26 The neglected state of some church Bibles, and the uneven introduction of the 1662 Book of Common Prayer, are recorded, for example, in the archidiaconal visitation of Thomas Wren (son of Matthew Wren, the Bishop) in the diocese of Ely in 1665: see W. M. Palmer, *Episcopal visitation returns for Cambridgeshire; Matthew Wren, Bishop of Ely, 1638–1665* (Cambridge 1930), pp. 130–1.

27 Gouldman and Robertson were entered to Sawbridge on 3 October 1671 and 20 March 1675/6 respectively. As at Cambridge at various times, the Bible trade at Oxford was crucial to the financial success of the printing house: see, for example, correspondence on the matter between Sir Leoline Jenkins, Thomas Yate and John Fell, in Madan, *Oxford books*, 3, p. xxxvii. On the whole subject, see also Herbert, *Bibles*, nos. 744–6, with remarks on the contemporary trade. For the episode at Midsummer Fair, see University Archives, Comm. Court V.4, fos. 39v, 40r. One of the Londoners was a leather dealer, the other was Robert Duncomb.

28 Bodleian Library, MS Rawl.D.397, fo. 380r (list of wholesale prices of English Stock books in London); fos. 393, 397 (letters from Alexander Merreatt about a disaffected London stationer, Thomas Blashfield). The volume includes several letters from Merreatt, Thomas Carbonnel, Charles Mounteney and Thomas Papillon concerning paper shortages: Oxford was on several occasions unable to obtain what it wished because the Stationers' Company held the only stocks.

29 Details from C. Blagden, 'The distribution of almanacks in the second half of the seventeenth century', *SB*, 11 (1958), pp. 107–16; B. Capp, *Astrology and the popular press; English almanacs 1500–1800* (1979).

30 Capp, *Astrology*, pp. 37, 39–41.

31 In estimating (p. 23) that 'roughly one family in three bought an almanac each year', Capp forgets that rather than buy single almanacs, many customers, particularly among the more prosperous, preferred to buy several, and bind them up together: see, for example, the series in Cambridge University Library, Hhh.453, etc. and, for some of those in the Rawlinson collection in the Bodleian, *Fine bindings 1500–1700 in Oxford libraries* (Bodleian Library 1968), pp. 121–2. This means that it is difficult to gauge how many households were likely to have possessed almanacs, though the difficulty does not of course apply in the same way to sheet almanacs.

32 John Worthington, *Diary and correspondence*, 2, pt i, ed. J. Crossley (Chetham Society 1855), pp. 96–7 (Worthington to Hartlib, 9 January 1661/2). For Newman see above, p. 466, n. 79.

33 Peile, *Christ's*, I, p. 350; A. G. Matthews, *Walker revised* (Oxford 1948), p. 153. His dictionary is discussed by Starnes, *Renaissance dictionaries*, pp. 278–90 and, with others mentioned here, in J. Nichols, *Literary anecdotes of the eighteenth century*, 5 (1812), pp. 208–11.

34 Scattergood's busy literary career is summarized in *DNB*, though not all of his activities can be adequately documented.

35 *DNB*; G. F. Russell Barker and Alan H. Stenning, *The record of Old Westminsters*, II (1928), p. 581; Starnes, *Renaissance dictionaries*, pp. 309–24. For Gouldman's and Littleton's dictionaries in the North American market, see John Dunton, *Letters from New England* (Boston 1867), pp. 314–19, and Worthington Chauncey Ford, *The Boston book market, 1679–1700* (Boston 1917). In *c*. 1682 a speculative collection of books sent by

Robert Boulter included four copies of Gouldman, charged at £2.8s., among an assortment of popular theology, a dozen copies of Terence, thirty-eight of Bond's Horace, a half-dozen each of *Guy of Warwick*, *Reynard the fox* and *Fortunatus*, and a hundred-odd New Testaments. In view of the fact that Gouldman had been superseded by Littleton, it is tempting to suspect an example of colonial dumping.

36 Eyre and Rivington, 2, p. 428; 3, pp. 55, 411–12, 427–8. Wing, L2565 should be compared with the reproduction of the title-page of another issue on the part of the major shareholders, in Starnes, *Renaissance dictionaries*, p. 318. See also Bennet and Clements, *Notebooks*, p. 205.

37 PCC, 154 Hene. Plomer, *Dictionary*, p. 66.

38 Cambridge University Library has three copies, each with the long imprint as given in Wing; but one has a cancel title-leaf in a different setting from the other two, and two have different settings in sheets B-E: examination of further copies would no doubt be productive.

39 M. H. Nicolson, ed., *The Conway letters* (New Haven 1930), p. 223.

40 *Ibid.*, pp. 192, 303, 305–6.

41 *Ibid.*, pp. 162–3.

42 Cf. H.-J. Martin, *Livre, pouvoirs et société à Paris au XVIIe siècle*, 2 vols. (Geneva 1969), 1, p. 331.

43 The question of whether or not the press owned a rolling press remains unresolved: the nature of some of the books suggests that it did, but none is listed in any inventory.

44 Jenks left the manuscript 'which upon covenants drawne betwixt Mr Chiswell and my selfe, is now ready for the Presse' to James Halman, another Fellow of Caius, to see through the press or destroy (University Archives, Wills IV, p. 374).

45 University Archives, U.Ac.1(6): the bill, for printing University verses, was paid on 24 October 1689.

46 This seems to have been reached only after prolonged negotiation with the English Stock, to judge by the various payments for refreshment and travel recorded at this period in the Stationers' Company Journal Book for Money Disbursed, 1650–98.

47 Stanley Morison, *John Fell* (Oxford 1967), opposite p. 73 (reproduction of the so-called 'Christ Church specimen', *c.* 1687).

48 PRO, SP 29/243/181. Cf. D. F. McKenzie, 'The London book trade in 1668', *Words; Wai-te-ata Studies in Literature*, 4 (1974), pp. 75–92.

49 But cf., again, Oxford, where in November 1672 Fell claimed that there were 'above 20 hands at work', and where in the late 1660s there were at least five presses (Carter, *Oxford University Press*, p. 66).

50 Madan, *Oxford books*, 3, p. 412 (All Souls, MS 239, fo. 666).

51 *A specimen of the several sorts of letter given to the University by Dr. John Fell* (Oxford 1693), the specimen now listing seven presses, two rolling presses, 133 'Upper and lower Cases', ten pairs of Greek cases, and fifty chases.

52 Stationers' Company Court Book F, 7 September 1691.

53 In this lay the principal difference between the Cambridge press and the London presses: shared printing was most unusual. For London, cf. Blayney, *Nicholas Okes*, and, more generally, Blayney, 'The prevalence of shared printing in the early seventeenth century', *PBSA*, 67 (1973), pp. 437–42.

54 McKenzie, *Cambridge University Press*, 1, pp. 138–40.

55 See above, p. 269. Moxon, *Mechanick exercises*, pp. 203, 337; Carter, *Oxford University Press*, pp. 188–9.

56 Gray and Palmer, pp. 120–1, 126.

57 Almanac printing dominated the later part of each year. The earliest licence date to appear on William Lily's almanacs (not printed at Cambridge, but comparable for this purpose)

is 16 September (for the 1672 predictions), and the latest 29 October (for 1667), the latter retarded by the Great Fire (Bodleian Library, MS Ashmole 241). See J. K. Moore, 'Copy and print in English books of the sixteenth and seventeenth centuries' (DPhil, Oxford 1989), 1, pp. 155–6. Almanacs for the following year seem to have been available in the trade from mid-October: see R. Stewart-Brown, 'A Chester bookseller's lawsuit of 1653', *The Library*, 4th ser. 9 (1928), pp. 53–8, at p. 57. Some copies indeed appear to have been printed much earlier. Field died on 12 August 1668, yet his stock-in-trade (valued a few weeks later, but as part of his estate) included 291 reams of almanacs 'of all sorts', valued at ten shillings a ream. It is not clear whether 'of all sorts' here is meant in the technical sense (thus excluding blanks and sheet almanacs); but it is plain that this was a full valuation for stock that could be sold, i.e. of 1669 stock. By August, almanacs for the current year would have been worth no more than waste paper. See D. McKitterick, 'John Field in 1668; the affairs of a University Printer', *TCBS*, 9 (1990), pp. 497–516. On fluctuations more generally, see Wilmer G. Mason, 'The annual output of Wing-listed titles, 1649–1684', *The Library*, 5th ser. 29 (1974), pp. 219–20; Mark Goldie, 'The revolution of 1689 and the structure of political argument' *Bull. of Research in the Humanities*, 83 (1980), pp. 473–564, esp. pp. 478–82; D. F. McKenzie, 'The London book trade in 1668' (n. 48 above).

58 For Oxford, where six are known to have been bound to John Hall in the late seventeenth century, see Carter, *Oxford University Press*, pp. 195–6.

59 University Archives, VC Ct 1.2, fos. 154v, 155v, 158r, 159r; McKenzie, *Apprentices 1641–1700*, nos. 1507 (Peckett), 2024 (Bechinoe: see also Gray and Palmer, pp. 127–8), 2029 (Brampton Lowry), 2030 (John Petit), 2027 (James Haddy), 2032 (John Woodfield), 2031 (William Smith), 2026 (John Grumball). At least Lowry and Grumball (or Grumbold) were later employed at the new University Press. John Corbett, apprenticed to Legate in 1655/6 and registered as *typographus* by the University in 1665, may be the man of that name working as a compositor in the King's Printing House in 1668 (McKenzie, *Apprentices 1641–1700*, no. 2680; VC Ct 1.2, fo. 146v; PRO, SP 29/243).

60 PRO, SP 29/243.

61 The inventory of his goods (in the University Archives, but not included in Gray and Palmer) was taken on 5 February 1694/5: his estate totalled £2,243.19s.4d. See also PRO, Prob 4/405.

62 Venn, *Gonville and Caius*, 1, p. 387.

63 McKenzie, *Cambridge University Press*, 1, pp. 6–15; 2, p. 79; and 'Richard Bentley's design for the Cambridge University Press c. 1696', *TCBS*, 6 (1976), pp. 322–7.

64 McKenzie, *Cambridge University Press*, 1, pp. 176–7; 2, pp. 79, 83. It has been disputed whether the term 'stage house' refers to a modest theatre, or merely to the store in which the timbers, etc. required for such a theatre were stored. See McKenzie, *Cambridge University Press*, 1, pp. 16–29; McKenzie, 'A Cambridge playhouse of 1638', *Renaissance Drama*, 3 (1970), pp. 263–72; Alan Nelson, ed., *Records of early English drama. Cambridge*, 2 vols. (Toronto 1989), p. 994.

65 Stationers' Company Court Book F, 7 September 1696. See also McKenzie, *Cambridge University Press*, 1, p. 12.

66 An inventory of Hayes' equipment is attached to the 1690 Articles of agreement between him and the Stationers' Company (Stationers' Company documents, nos. 171, 172), and is printed in Blagden, 'Early Cambridge printers', at p. 289.

67 Stationers' Company Court Book F, 7 September 1691.

68 English Stock payments for Cambridge work in 1690/1 include £30.13s.4d. for paper for Terence, and no less than £9.2s.0d. for ink. The size of the edition of Terence is not recorded. For Ovid, 145 reams of paper were sent to Cambridge (Stationers' Company Journal Book for Money Disbursed, 13 April 1698).

69 Stationers' Company Court Book F, 18 September 1693.

70 Blagden, *Stationers' Company*, pp. 201–2. The increasing dependence on Oxford as a supplier can be followed in the last pages of the Journal Book for Money Disbursed, 1650–98. Blagden (p. 187) reproduces a convenient broadside advertisement listing 'Books printed for the Company of Stationers, and sold at their Ware-House in Stationers-Hall'.

71 Registers of St Botolph's parish; McKenzie, *Cambridge University Press*, 1, p. 27, n. 2. A memorial slab is in the floor of the chancel of St Botolph's Church.

72 McKenzie, *Cambridge University Press*, 1, pp. 26–7 summarizes the disputes over the printing privilege, for which payment was raised in 1703 to £150 per annum, and over Hayes' lease of the house.

73 Both copies I have seen of the 1698 edition have a cancel title-leaf with Hayes' name. Despite the mixed reception accorded to Tate and Brady, the 1702 edition was popular enough to be taken up at Great St Mary's, the University Church. (Cf. the copies in the University Library, Cam.e.702.5,6, uniformly bound.) For Tate and Brady, see Maurice Frost, ed., *Historical companion to Hymns ancient & modern* (1962), p. 84.

19 *Looking at a wider world*

1 R. North, *Lives of Francis North*, ed. A. Jessopp, 3 vols (1890) 2, pp. 279–80. For Scott, see Leona Rostenberg, *Literary, political, scientific, religious & legal publishing, printing & bookselling in England, 1551–1700*, 2 vols. (New York 1965), 2, pp. 281–313, and Pollard and Ehrman.

2 Trinity College, MS Add.a.106, fo. 21r.

3 At least the following in Peterhouse Library bear Scott's warranty: I.3.17,33–34; I.9.1; I.10.7; K.14.3; N.6.30–32, 34–36, 38–40. For booksellers' warranties, see F. C. Francis, 'Booksellers' warranties', *The Library*, 5th ser. 1 (1946–7), pp. 244–5 (including two mid-seventeenth century examples from Cambridge), and the series of notes by D. F. McKenzie, Paul Morgan *et al.*, in *Bibliography Newsletter*, 1–2 (1973–4).

4 Oates, *Cambridge University Library*, p. 390.

5 For further details, see most recently J. Gascoigne, 'The universities and the scientific revolution: the case of Newton and Restoration Cambridge', *History of Science*, 33 (1985), pp. 391–434; and his *Cambridge in the age of the Enlightenment* (Cambridge 1989); and M. Feingold, ed., *Before Newton; the life and times of Isaac Barrow* (Cambridge 1990).

6 Abraham de la Pryme, *Diary* (Surtees Soc. 1870), pp. 20–34.

7 W. J. Harrison, ed., *Life in Clare Hall, Cambridge, 1658–1713* (Cambridge 1958).

8 Trinity College, MS O.10a.33, p. 14. For religious reading, apart from the Bible, Duport recommended Sibbes, Preston, Boulton, Thomas Shepard, Baxter and George Herbert. See also M. Feingold, 'Isaac Barrow: divine, scholar, mathematician', in *Before Newton*, ed. Feingold, pp. 1–104, at pp. 13–14. But his remarks should be read in conjunction with the debate on Ramism and Aristotelianism in Cambridge in the 1590s: see C. B. Schmitt, *John Case and Aristotelianism in Renaissance England* (Kingston, Ont. 1983), pp. 35, 50–1.

9 For Adrian Heereboord, appointed to the chair of logic at Leiden in 1640, see F. Sassen, 'Adriaan Heereboord (1614–1661). De opkomst van het Cartesianisme te Leiden', *Algemeen Nederlands Tijdschrift voor Wijsbegeerte en Psychologie*, 36 (1942–3), pp. 12–22.

10 Christopher J. Scriba, 'The autobiography of John Wallis, F.R.S.', *Notes and Records of the Royal Society*, 25 (1970), pp. 17–46; *DSB*, s.v. 'Glisson'; R. Milnes Walker, 'Francis Glisson', in *Cambridge and its contribution to medicine*, ed. A. Rook (1971), pp. 35–47.

11 J. Gascoigne, 'The holy alliance: the rise and diffusion of Newtonian natural philosophy

and latitudinarian theology within Cambridge from the Restoration to the accession of George II' (PhD, Cambridge 1980), pp. 154–6; Harrison, *Life in Clare Hall*, pp. 50–1; Gascoigne, 'Universities', p. 411. On the popularity of Burgersdijck, see J. E. B. Mayor, ed., *Cambridge under Queen Anne* (Cambridge 1911), pp. 251–2. For Gassendi, see F. S. and E. Mitchell, 'A note on Gassendi in England', *Notes and Queries* (September 1990), pp. 297–9.

12 Harrison, *Life in Clare Hall*, p. 51; J. R. Magrath, ed., *The Flemings in Oxford*, 3 vols. (Oxford Historical Soc. 1903–24), 2, pp. 226–7, 273; *Term catalogues*, 1, p. 23.

13 Roger North, 'Autobiography', in his *Lives of the Right Hon. Francis North...*, ed. A. Jessopp, 3 vols. (1890), 3, p. 16.

14 *Ibid.*

15 Eyre and Rivington, 2, p. 335.

16 Venn, *Gonville and Caius*, 1, p. 387.

17 Henry Jenks, *The Christian tutor* (1683), pp. 33–5.

18 Bruce Dickins, 'Henry Gostling's library; a young don's books in 1674', *TCBS*, 3 (1961), pp. 216–24. Notwithstanding Elisabeth Leedham-Green's work on the Vice-Chancellor's Court inventories (*Books in Cambridge inventories*), a great deal remains to be discovered concerning book ownership in seventeenth-century Cambridge, and particularly in the second half of the century.

19 John Worthington, *Diary and correspondence*, ed. J. Crossley and R. C. Christie (Chetham Soc. 1847–86), 2, pt ii, pp. 316, 346.

20 On Wetstein, see I. H. van Eeghen, *De Amsterdamse boekhandel 1680–1725* (Amsterdam 1967), 4, pp. 169–73.

21 Gray and Palmer, pp. 118–19.

22 *Ibid.*, pp. 124–5.

23 Plomer, *Dictionary 1668–1725*, p. 282; Cooper, *Annals*, 4, pp. 21–2. Story died a self-styled gentleman, and seems to have retired from bookselling some years earlier. His family's armorial monument is in Great St Mary's.

24 University Archives, CUR 21, no. 83 (not in Gray and Palmer); Samuel Newton, *Diary, 1662–1717*, ed. J. E. Foster (Cambridge Antiquarian Soc. 1890), pp. 75, 76, 93, 107.

25 Printed in Jewell, *Apologia ecclesiae anglicanae* (Cambridge 1683). Another catalogue, of Creed imprints only, was included in Schuler's *Exercitationes* (1686).

26 Advertisement in Sir Norton Knatchbull, *Annotations upon some difficult texts in all the books of the New Testament* (1693). The religious works were Erasmus' *Enchiridion militis Christiani* and *De Christi imitando*, and Vincent of Lérins, *Adversus profanas omnium novitates haereticorum Commonitorium*.

27 Printed in Tertullian, *Apologeticus*, etc. (Cambridge 1686).

28 Cambridge University Library, MS Kk.4.17, copied from the edition printed at Subiaco, 1465, and therefore dated the same year; Emmanuel College, MS III.3.5 (James 238) (dated 1424). P. R. Robinson, *Catalogue of dated and datable manuscripts c. 737–1600 in Cambridge libraries*, 2 vols. (Woodbridge 1988), no. 191 (listing the Emmanuel manuscript).

29 For Creed and Dickinson's dealing with Elzevir, see van Eeghen, 3, p. 116.

30 William Nicholson, *English historical library* (1736), p. 50; D. Douglas, *English scholars* (1939), pp. 67–8.

31 In London, at least some copies of the Euripides passed into the international trade via Thomas Bennet, who offered it to the Leiden bookseller Pieter van der Aa on 6 January 1698/9 among other Latin and Greek texts (Bennet and Clements, *Notebooks*, pp. 47–8).

32 M. Flower, 'Thomas Stanley (1625–1678): a bibliography of his writings in prose and verse (1647–1743)', *TCBS*, 1 (1950), pp. 139–72.

33 For further examples, see J. E. Sandys, *A history of classical scholarship*, 2 (Cambridge

1908), pp. 349–58. For Gale's manuscripts, see M. R. James, *The western manuscripts in the Library of Trinity College, Cambridge*, 4 vols. (Cambridge 1900–4), vol. 3.

34 Oates, *Cambridge University Library*, pp. 447–8; I. Abrahams, 'Isaac Abendana's Cambridge Mishnah and Oxford calendars', *Trans. Jewish Historical Soc. of England*, 8 (1915–17), pp. 98–121; University Archives, U Ac.1(6), 8 August 1692.

35 Thus Cudworth published his *True intellectual system of the universe* (1678), in English rather than in Latin, with Richard Royston in London – and so had the benefit of sharing his stationer with Worthington's great edition of Joseph Mede. Cudworth's book was entered in the Stationers' Register on 13 September 1677.

36 For Mercator, also called Niklaus Kauffman (*c.* 1619–87), a Danish mathematician who spent the last thirty years or so of his life in London and became an FRS in 1666, see *DSB*. He dedicated his book to *Alma mater Cantabrigia*. See also Richard S. Westfall, *Never at rest* (Cambridge 1980), p. 258.

37 Westfall, *Never at rest*, pp. 397–8. See also Newton, *Correspondence*, 2, pp. 417–19.

38 Rob. Austin to William Oughtred, 3 December 1652; John Collins to John Pell, 9 April 1667; S. J. Rigaud, ed., *Correspondence of scientific men of the seventeenth century* (Oxford 1841), 1, pp. 74, 125.

39 Rigaud, *Correspondence*, 1, pp. 125–6. The works spoken of were Strauch's *Compendium arithmeticae*; Laurenberg, *Arithmetica principia* (originally published 1643); Frans van Schooten, *Principia matheseos* (originally published 1651). Van Schooten's *Exercitationum mathematicarum libri V* (1657) was among those studied with especial attention by Newton as an undergraduate (Westfall, *Never at rest*, pp. 98, 100, 106–9; his copy of the *Exercitationes* is in Trinity College Library, NQ. 16.184). Tacquet's *Arithmeticae theoria et praxis* (2nd edn Amsterdam 1665, 383 pp.) was considered too long for the purpose.

40 Newton to Collins 30 July 1672: *Correspondence*, 1, p. 222. Newton described his part in the new edition of Varenius with characteristic modesty: notwithstanding the title-page, 'Sr I. N. told Mr Jones all he did in the edition of Varenius before wch is put Curante Isaaco Newtono was to draw the schemes wch in the Elsever Edition were referred to, & were not there' (Isaac Newton, *Mathematical papers*, ed. D. T. Whiteside, 8 vols. (Cambridge 1967–81), 2, pp. 288–9, n. 43). For Newton's part in an unsuccessful attempt in the 1670s to get into print a Latin translation, from the Dutch, of Gerard Kinckhuysen's *Algebra*, see *ibid.*, pp. 279–91: it proved impossible to persuade either the University Printer or the local Cambridge booksellers to take an interest.

41 A. N. L. Munby, 'The distribution of the first edition of Newton's Principia', *Notes and Records of the Royal Society*, 10 (1952), pp. 28–39, repr. in his *Essays and papers* (1977), pp. 43–54. For Smith's activities in the overseas trade, see Bennet and Clements, *Notebook*, pp. 9–26, 114–15, Otto S. Lankhorst, *Reinier Leers (1654–1714) uitgever & boekverkoper te Rotterdam* (Amsterdam 1983), and P. G. Hoftijzer, *Engelse boekverkopers bij de beurs* (Amsterdam 1987), pp. 323–50, with further references.

42 G. Keynes, *John Ray, 1627–1705; a bibliography, 1660–1970* (Amsterdam 1976), pp. 14–15, 25.

43 On Vigani, see L. M. J. Coleby, 'John Francis Vigani, first Professor of Chemistry in the University of Cambridge', *Annals of Science*, 8 (1952), pp. 46–60. Abraham de la Pryme, who attended Vigani's course in chemistry in 1692, as an undergraduate, thought him 'a very learned chemist, and a great traveller, but a drunken fellow. Yet by reason of the abstruceness of the art, I got little or no good thereby' (*Diary* (Surtees Soc. 1870), p. 25). For Cambridge more generally, see n. 5 above (but Gascoigne's remarks on Gautruche in 'Universities', p. 413, should be treated circumspectly), and M. Hunter, *Science and society in Restoration England* (Cambridge 1981), pp. 53, 141–2, 190, with further references.

44 A comparison of the diagrams in successive editions of Gassendi's *Institutio astronomica* (1653) reveals a characteristic range of approximations to what was intended.

45 Newton, *Correspondence*, 1, pp. 55–6. For Collins, see most recently Feingold, *Before Newton*.

46 *Ibid.*, p. 147.

47 Collins to Wallis, ?1677/8: Newton, *Correspondence*, 2, p. 241.

48 Collins to John Beale, 20 August 1672: Rigaud, *Correspondence*, 1, p. 200.

49 Collins to Wallis, 2 February 1666/7: Rigaud, *Correspondence*, 2, p. 470.

50 See above, pp. 291–2.

51 For the lutenist (he also taught Worthington the viol) Thomas Mace, see Frida Knight, *Cambridge music from the middle ages to modern times* (Cambridge 1980), pp. 23, 32–3, 36–7.

52 George Atwell, alias Wells, *The faithfull surveyor* (For the author, at the charges of Nathanael Rowls, Doctor of Physick, 1658), fo. *2v. Rowls also held a living near King's Lynn.

53 *Acta Eruditorum* (1687), pp. 308–11; *Bibliothèque Universelle et Historique*, 2 (1686), pp. 55–6.

54 Collins to Vernon, 14 December 1671: Rigaud, *Correspondence*, 1, p. 178.

55 Collins to Thomas Baker, 24 April 1677: Rigaud, *Correspondence*, 2, p. 21.

56 M. H. Nicholson, ed., *Conway letters* (New Haven 1930), p. 371; R. B. McKerrow, 'A publishing agreement of the late seventeenth century', *The Library* 4th ser. 13 (1933), pp. 184–7.

57 *STC*, 17944–17944a. Cf. S. L. C. Clapp, 'Subscription publishers prior to Jacob Tonson', *The Library*, 4th ser. 13 (1932–3), pp. 158–83; Graham Pollard and Albert Ehrman, *The distribution of books by catalogue* (Roxburghe Club 1964), pp. 180–95; J. P. Feather, *Book prospectuses before 1801 in the John Johnson Collection, Bodleian Library* (with microfiche reproductions) (Oxford 1976).

58 Thomas Hearne, *Remarks and collections*, ed. C. E. Doble *et al.* (Oxford Historical Soc. 1885–1918), 1, pp. 269–70, 274.

59 'When Mr. Barnes presented his Edw. 3[d] ... to King James (to whom he dedicated it) his Majesty was pleas'd to talk very freely and kindly to him, & there is no doubt had given him preferment if the Troubles had not follow'd immediately, or if my L[d] Sunderland had acted fairly' (*Ibid.*, pp. 269–70). The context of Hearne's note suggests however that he had the story from the disappointed Barnes himself.

60 See, for example, the copy in Trinity College Library, and that described in Bowes, *Catalogue*, no. 179. Heyrick, curate of Market Harborough, Leics., had graduated from Peterhouse in 1670.

61 Hearne, *Remarks and collections*, 1, pp. 274–5; Bodleian Library, MS Ballard 33, fo. 33, quoted in Simpson, *Proof-reading*, p. 147. Barnes' autograph of much of his preliminary matter is in Emmanuel College Library. For University payments, see *Grace Book* Θ, p. 376 (23 March 1693/4), and Oates, *Cambridge University Library*, pp. 473–4.

62 Hall closed the subscription list for Launoi on 1 August 1688, having not only issued proposals, but also included an advertisement (dated 22 June) in Saywell's *Reformation of the Church of England*, which was distributed in London by Luke Meredith who had succeeded to the vast business of his father-in-law Richard Royston a few months previously. Green, too, married into the Royston family.

63 An incomplete copy of the prospectus survives, apparently unique, in British Library MS Harley 5929, no. 441. That for Dunton's *Young students library* (1691) is in the John Johnson collection, in the Bodleian Library; that for Gale's Herodotus is referred to in the *Term Catalogues*, 1, p. 307.

64 Cf. the remarks in the preface to the *Journal des Sçavans* (1680).

65 For increasing use of foreign vernaculars, rather than Latin, see H.-J. Martin, *Livre, pouvoirs et société à Paris au XVIIe siècle (1598–1701)*, 2 vols. (Geneva 1969), pp. 813–17. But for evidence of Dutch distrust of the English language, see C. W. Schoneveld, *Intertraffic of the mind* (Leiden 1983), pp. 119–21. The principal continental reviewing journals are described conveniently in the 'Notice abrégée des principaux journaux littéraires' attached to the 'Mémoire historique sur le Journal des Scavans', *Journal des Sçavans*, Table générale, vol. 10 (Paris 1764), pp. 649–730. See also J. Sgard, *Dictionnaire des journalistes* (1600–1789) (Grenoble 1976), and, more generally, H. J. Reesink, *L'Angleterre et la littérature anglaise dans les trois plus anciens périodiques français de Hollande de 1684 a 1709* (Zutphen 1931) and G. Ascoli, *La Grande-Bretagne devant l'opinion française au XVIIe siècle*, 2 vols. (Paris 1930). Apart from the major reviews (*Journal des Sçavans*, *Nouvelles de la République des Lettres*, *Bibliothèque Universelle et Historique*, etc.), cf. the various bibliographical compendia of Cornelius à Beughem, published from 1680 onwards. The trend should not however be over-estimated. England remained a net importer of books from Holland for most of the eighteenth century: cf. G. Barber, 'Books from the old world and for the new: the British international trade in books in the eighteenth century', *Studies on Voltaire and the Eighteenth Century*, 151 (1976), pp. 185–224, and 'Aspects of the booktrade between England and the Low Countries in the eighteenth century', *Werkgroep 18e Eeuw Dokumentieblad*, 34–5 (1977), pp. 47–63. On the *Acta Eruditorum*, see Joachim Kirchner, 'Zur Entstehungs- und Redaktionsgeschichte der *Acta Eruditorum*', in his *Ausgewählte Aufsätze* (Stuttgart 1970), pp. 153–72, and, with a useful but incomplete survey of English authors discussed in it, G. Waterhouse, *The literary relations of England and Germany in the seventeenth century* (Cambridge 1914), pp. 124–7. For Germany, see also in particular R. Prutz, *Geschichte des deutschen Journalismus* 1 (all published, Hannover 1845) pp. 260–333, and (in different vein) Hans Freydank, 'Christian Thomasius der Journalist', in *Christian Thomasius, Leben und Lebenswerk*, ed. M. Fleischman (Halle 1931), pp. 345–82, and Eric A. Blackall, *The emergence of German as a literary language 1700–1775* (Cambridge 1959), pp. 49–60. Reviews in the *Bibliothèque Universelle et Historique* are indexed in J.-P. Lobies, *La Bibliothèque Universelle et Historique 1686–1694* (Index Multiplex II, Osnabrück 1968–82).

66 *Journal des Sçavans*, 2, January 1674/5, 26 April 1677, 3 September 1685.

67 *Histoire des Ouvrages des Sçavans*, February 1693/4, pp. 277–8; November 1694, p. 129; March 1695/6, pp. 291–300.

68 *Acta Eruditorum*, August 1695, pp. 355–9; *Journal des Sçavans*, 25 April 1695.

69 *Bibliothèque Universelle et Historique*, 16 (March 1690), pp. 237–87, at p. 239. For some of the background, cf. H. Bots *et al.*, *De 'Bibliothèque Universelle et Historique' (1686–1693)* (Amsterdam 1981) and H.-J. Martin, *Livre, pouvoirs et société à Paris au XVII siècle*.

70 Reinier Leers to Samuel Smith, 1690: Bodleian Library, MS Rawl. Letters 114, fos. 88, 85, 91. Reprinted in Otto S. Lankhorst, *Reinier Leers (1654–1714), uitgever & boekverkoper te Rotterdam* (Amsterdam 1983), pp. 230–4.

71 *Acta Eruditorum*, April 1690, pp. 156–60.

72 *Journal des Sçavans*, 2 January 1674/5, 5 August 1686; *Nouvelles de la République des Lettres*, December 1685, p. 1383; April 1686, pp. 430–44.

73 Cf. P. G. Hoftijzer, *Engelse boekverkopers bij de beurs* (Amsterdam 1987), throughout.

74 See above, pp. 91, 127.

20 Conclusion

1 See above, p. 340; *Euripides*, ed. Barnes (Cambridge 1694), fo. a 3r.

2 Joseph Mede, *Diatribe and epistles* (1652), p. 571: letter from Sir William Boswell. Cf. the allusions to Mede's international reputation in his *Works* (1672), p. vii.

3 Margaret Spufford, *Small books and pleasant histories* (1981), pp. 83–128.

4 D. McKitterick, 'John Field in 1668: the affairs of a University Printer', *TCBS*, 9 (1990), pp. 497–516.

5 See above, pp. 330, 338–9.

6 William Robertson, *A dictionary of Latin phrases* (Baldwin and Craddock, 1829). The advertisement to this edition, which explained that the revision to it had been carried out with the particular needs of middle and upper classes of schools in mind, also remarked, 'The English is obsolete, the arrangement confused, the order of printing such as to render it difficult for consultation or reference, the redundancies so numerous as to increase most unnecessarily and seriously the bulk of the volume, and much of the Latin drawn from barbarous sources.'

7 *The Flemings at Oxford*, ed. J. R. Magrath (Oxford Historical Soc. 1903–24), 1, pp. 255, 295, 321–6; 2, pp. 28, 273, 274; 3, pp. 215–16, 319–23; D. G. Vaisey, 'Anthony Stephens; the rise and fall of an Oxford bookseller', *Studies in the book trade in honour of Graham Pollard* (Oxford Bibliographical Soc. 1975), pp. 91–117; P. R. Quarrie, 'The Christ Church collections books', in *The history of the University of Oxford*, ed. L. S. Sutherland and L. G. Mitchell, 5 (Oxford 1986), pp. 493–511.

8 C. Blagden, 'The distribution of almanacks in the second half of the seventeenth century', *SB*, 11 (1958), pp. 107–16, table I.

INDEX